XML Web Services for ASP.NET

XML Web Services for ASP.NET

Bill Evjen

Wiley Publishing, Inc.

Best-Selling Books • Digital Downloads • e-Books • Answer Networks • e-Newsletters • Branded Web Sites • e-Learning

New York, NY • Cleveland, OH • Indianapolis, IN

XML Web Services for ASP.NET

Published by
Wiley Publishing, Inc.
605 Third Avenue
New York, NY 10158
www.wiley.com

This book is printed on acid-free paper.

Copyright © 2002 by Wiley Publishing, Inc. All rights reserved.

Published by Wiley Publishing, Inc.

No part of this publication may be reproduced, stored in a retrieval system or transmitted in any form or by any means, electronic, mechanical, photocopying, recording, scanning or otherwise, except as permitted under Sections 107 or 108 of the 1976 United States Copyright Act, without either the prior written permission of the Publisher, or authorization through payment of the appropriate per-copy fee to the Copyright Clearance Center, 222 Rosewood Drive, Danvers, MA 01923, (978) 750-8400, fax (978) 750-4744. Requests to the Publisher for permission should be addressed to the Permissions Department, Wiley Publishing, Inc., 10475 Crosspoint Blvd., Indianapolis, IN 46256, (317) 572-3447, Fax: (317) 572-4447, E-Mail: permissions@wiley.com.

This publication is designed to provide accurate and authoritative information in regard to the subject matter covered. It is sold with the understanding that the publisher is not engaged in professional services. If professional advice or other expert assistance is required, the services of a competent professional person should be sought.

Library of Congress Cataloging-in-Publication Data: 2001093598

ISBN: 0-7645-4829-8

Printed in the United States of America.

10 9 8 7 6 5 4 3 2 1

1O/QV/QZ/QS/IN

About the Author

Bill Evjen is an active proponent of the .NET technologies and community-based learning initiatives for .NET. He has been actively involved with .NET since the first bits were released in 2000 and has since become the president of the St. Louis .NET User Group (www.stlnet.org) as well as the founder and executive director of the International .NET Association (www.ineta.org).

Bill, who co-authored the Visual Basic .NET Bible, is an active author and speaker on .NET technologies. He is presently a technical director for Reuters in St. Louis, Missouri. Bill graduated from Western Washington University in Bellingham, Washington, with a Russian language degree. When he isn't tinkering on the computer, he enjoys spending his free time in his summer place in Toivakka, Finland. You can reach Bill at evjen@yahoo.com.

About the Series Editor

Michael Lane Thomas is an active development community and computer industry analyst who spends a great deal of time spreading the gospel of Microsoft.NET in his current role as a .NET Technology Evangelist for Microsoft. In working with over a half-dozen publishing companies, Michael has written numerous technical articles and authored/contributed to almost 20 books on numerous technical topics including Visual Basic, Visual C++, and .NET technologies. He is a prolific supporter of the Microsoft certification programs, having earned his MCSD, MCSE+I, MCT, MCP+SB, and MCDBA.

In addition to technical writing, Michael can also be heard over the airwaves from time to time, including two weekly radio programs on Entercom stations, most often in Kansas City on News Radio 980KMBZ. He is also occasionally found on the Internet doing an MSDN Webcast discussing .NET, the next generation of Web application technologies. Michael can be reached via e-mail at mlthomas@microsoft.com.

Credits

Senior Acquisitions Editor
Sharon Cox

Project Editor
Sara Shlaer

Technical Editor
Richard Lassan

Copy Editor
Mary Lagu

Editorial Manager
Mary Beth Wakefield

Vice President and Executive Group Publisher
Richard Swadley

Vice President and Executive Publisher
Bob Ipsen

Vice President and Publisher
Joseph B. Wikert

Executive Editorial Director
Mary Bednarek

Project Coordinator
Nancee Reeves

Graphics Specialists
Kelly Hardesty
Rashell Smith

Proofreading
Mary Lagu

Indexing
Johnna VanHoose Dinse

Preface

Many people have been singing the praises of XML for a number of years now and, as it turns out, *they are right*! With the introduction of the .NET Framework in 2002, the capability to have your systems, servers, and applications communicate with a wide variety of disparate systems is built right in. How do these systems communicate with one another given the complexities of their differences? The answer is that they use XML, which is easily understood by most platforms today.

Not only has Microsoft and its .NET platform completely embraced the concept of Web services and the technologies that they are built upon, but all the other power hitters, including IBM, Sun Microsystems, and Oracle, have jumped on board and laid out their own Web services visions.

This book is written to show you what you need to know to start building XML Web services right away within the ASP.NET environment. This technology is a dramatic change from what you might be used to. Some describe it as an even bigger event in the technical world than the introduction of the client/server model.

This book shows you exactly how to build everything, from the most basic XML Web services to some of the more advanced elements. Besides covering various applications, this book deals with the issues of security, data access (ADO.NET), and the new Visual Studio .NET IDE. It introduces you to everything you need to know to fully understand the .NET Framework in how it relates to XML Web services.

If you are trying to learn not just how to build XML Web services, but how to consume them as well, this book will show you how to get the job done.

Who Should Read This Book?

This book is aimed at the developer who has already been introduced to .NET and ASP.NET. It focuses on both Visual Basic .NET and C#, although you can easily convert the examples from the book into other .NET-compliant languages.

If you are new to .NET developing, read this book to help you get started in the .NET Revolution! The first three chapters will get you ramped up fast in .NET development and help you select the language that you want to focus on for development.

What Hardware and Software Do You Need?

This book utilizes a great deal from the .NET Framework provided by Microsoft. You need to download the latest version of the .NET Framework, as well as the latest version of Visual Studio .NET. Visual Studio .NET is the development environment that you use to build all the sample applications that are provided in the book. Please note, however, that it is possible to use Notepad and compile your code on the command line with the compilers that are provided with the framework, thus avoiding the use of Visual Studio .NET.

Hardware Specifics

Here are the minimum requirements for running the .NET Framework and Visual Studio .NET:

- Intel Pentium processor; 450 MHz or equivalent processor
- Microsoft Windows 2000, Windows NT 4.0 or Windows XP
- 128MB of available RAM
- 3GB of available disk space
- Color monitor capable of 800 x 600 resolution
- CD-ROM drive

Microsoft recommends the following requirements for running the .NET Framework:

- Intel Pentium processor; 733 MHz or equivalent processor
- Microsoft Windows 2000, Windows NT 4.0 or Windows XP
- 256MB of available RAM
- 3GB of available disk space
- Color monitor capable of 1024 x 768 resolution
- CD-ROM drive

> **NOTE:** Please note that these are the minimum requirements. More capability is definitely better for using the .NET Framework and Visual Studio .NET, especially in terms of memory and processor speed. The author recommends running .NET with 512MB of available RAM.

How This Book Is Organized

This book is divided into ten parts. The following sections explain what you'll find.

Part I: The .NET Framework

Part I begins with an overview of the .NET Framework and what it's all about. Part I explains why Microsoft made this dramatic change in application development with the introduction of .NET. This part introduces you to the building blocks of the .NET Framework and everything you need to understand in order to get the overall picture. Also included is a discussion on the technologies of .NET, with a particular focus on the two languages that are used throughout the book for all the examples, Visual Basic .NET and C#.

Part II: The Basics of XML Web Services

Part II of the book covers an introduction to the XML Web services model and why it is so important. This section spends some serious time bringing to light this powerful new way of having remote objects communicate across boundaries to disparate systems. After an introduction, you learn how to build your own XML Web services with both Notepad and Visual Studio .NET, and you also are given everything that you need to know in order to consume XML Web services. Throughout this section, you will see concrete examples.

Part III: Building XML Web Services

Part III goes beyond the simple task of building and consuming XML Web services. It's here that you start to learn some of the finer points of this technology. In the first part of this section, you learn about some of the things that are happening behind the scenes with your XML Web services and how to modify your Web services to make them perform exactly as you want. You will also learn about state management and how that applies to XML Web services. Beyond that, you will learn how to build a meaningful XML Web service test page so that others can test what you have built. Finally, you will learn the importance of proxies on the client and how they work in dealing with remote objects.

Part IV: XML Web Services Description and Discovery

Part IV of the book covers some of the pillar technologies of XML Web services. Not only do you have to have the means of building and consuming XML Web services, but you must also be able to describe and discover them. If you aren't able to accomplish these steps, the XML Web services that you build will be for naught.

Part V: All About SOAP

Part V first provides an explanatory section on SOAP and brings you up to speed on how this XML-based protocol works. Beyond that, you learn how to manipulate the SOAP to suit your needs. Included are discussions on SOAP headers and SOAP extensions. You can strengthen your XML Web services when you expand upon the SOAP message that it is delivering. This section of the book will teach you all the tricks that you need to know in order to accomplish this.

Part VI: Security

Part VI provides a thorough overview of security in .NET and offers steps that you can take to ensure that your XML Web service is secure from unauthorized individuals. Included here are discussions on authorization and authentication models that you can use with your XML Web services. In the chapter on Advanced Security, you will learn how to use SOAP headers to pass in login credentials and how to encrypt your SOAP messages so that they can't be viewed by prying eyes.

Part VII: ADO.NET and XML Web Services

Part VII of the book covers data access, one of the most important features in all application development projects. Applications are built on data, and this section shows you what you need to know to access and manipulate your data using ADO.NET and XML. Here you will learn how to use ADO.NET to build truly robust and scalable XML Web services. Using SQL Server as the section's primary data source, you will learn everything that you need to know in order to build XML Web services that expose this data source.

Part VIII: Advanced XML Web Services

Part VIII is a collection of advanced issues that you are likely to face when dealing with the construction of XML Web services that go beyond some of the basic services built in the beginning of the book. This section of the book covers all the error handling and configuration steps you can take with your XML Web services. There are discussions on how to pass images with your XML Web services and how to program your XML Web services asynchronously. The final chapter of this section shows you the ease with which you can use the tools and technologies that are provided to screenscrape other sites for your own benefit.

Part IX: .NET My Services and .NET Remoting

Part IX of the book digs into some of the technologies out there that are related to XML Web services. .NET My Services is a new product line of XML Web services being offered by Microsoft. This section discusses this new set of products. It closes with a chapter on an alternative to XML Web services, .NET Remoting.

Appendixes

The appendixes of this book are meant purely for reference. They contain short descriptions of the classes and their associated properties that are available under the System.Web.Services namespace. In addition to this, you will find an XML and XSD primer for those who are encountering these technologies for the first time. Finally, there is a collection of links that you will find helpful in your pursuit of learning this outstanding technology.

Conventions Used in This Book

The following sections explain the conventions used in this book.

Menu commands

When you're instructed to select a command from a menu, you see the menu and the command separated by an arrow symbol. For example, when you're asked to choose the Open command from the File menu, you see the notation File ⇨ Open.

Typographical conventions

I use *italic* type to indicate new terms or to provide emphasis. I use **boldface** type to indicate text that you need to type directly on the keyboard.

Code

I use a special typeface to indicate code, as demonstrated in the following example of Visual Basic .NET code:

```
<WebMethod()> Public Function Add(ByVal a As Integer,
             ByVal b As Integer) As Integer
      Return a + b
End Function
```

This special code font is also used within paragraphs to make elements such as XML tags (`</name>`) stand out from the regular text.

Italic type is also used in code syntax definitions to indicate that you must substitute an actual parameter in place of the italicized word(s):

```
<asp:Label [attributes] >Hello World!</asp:Label>
```

Navigating This Book

This book is designed to be read from beginning to end, although if you have already been introduced to the basics of XML Web services, you can easily skip over the first set of chapters and return to them at some other time.

Tips, Notes, and Cross-References appear in the text to indicate important or especially helpful items. Here's a list of these items and their functions:

> **TIP:** Tips provide you with extra knowledge that separates the novice from the pro.
>
> **NOTE:** Notes provide additional or critical information and technical data on the current topic.
>
> **CROSS-REFERENCE:** Cross-Reference icons indicate places where you can find more information on a particular topic.

Companion Web Site

This book provides a companion Web site from which you can download the code from various chapters. All the code listings reside in a single WinZip file that you can download by going to `www.Wiley.com/extras` and selecting the XML Web services for ASP.NET link. After you download the file (XMLWS.zip), and if you have WinZip already on your system, you can open it and extract the contents by double-clicking. If you don't currently have WinZip, you can download an evaluation version from `www.WinZip.com`.

When extracting the files, use WinZip's default options (confirm that the Use Folder Names option is checked) and extract the XMLWS.zip file to a drive on your system that has at least 3MB of available space. The extraction process creates a folder called XMLWS. As long as the Use Folder Names option is checked in the Extract dialog box, an entire folder structure is created within the XMLWS folder. You'll see folders arranged by chapter number, and some of those chapter folders will contain subfolders.

If you'd rather download just the code you need from a particular chapter when you need it, simply click the separate chapter link on the Web site instead of downloading the entire WinZip file.

Further Information

You can find more help for specific problems and questions by investigating several Web sites. Microsoft's own .NET Web site is a good place to start:

`msdn.microsoft.com/net`

I also recommend visiting the following support sites:

`www.gotdotnet.com`

`msdn.microsoft.com/webservices`

`www.asp.net`

`www.aspng.com`

`www.123aspx.com`

`www.ibuyspy.com`

`www.stlnet.org`

`www.ineta.org`

Feel free to contact me with any questions or comments. I would really like to hear anything you have to say about the book (good or bad), so I can make sure you have the information you need to write the best applications you can.

Happy Coding!

Bill Evjen
evjen@yahoo.com
St. Charles, Missouri, USA
February 2002

This book is dedicated to my family (in alphabetical order):
Bill, Dean, George, Henri, Janet, Linda, Rauni, Sofia, Steve, and Tuija

Acknowledgments

As I have said before, writing books may seem like a great solo effort, but the author is just one of the contributors to what is really a team project. This book had a great team behind it and all of them worked really hard to bring you the best possible book on XML Web services.

From this group I would like to point out John Wiley Senior Acquisition Editor Sharon Cox for having the faith in me to put out such an important book. I want to personally thank the technical editor of this book, Rick Lassan, for doing such an excellent job. Also I would like to thank Jodi Jenson, Sara Shlaer, Mary Lagu and Michael Lane Thomas. Sara especially spent a great amount of time making sure everything came together so well.

Special thanks go to Kent Sharkey from Microsoft for providing such wonderful feedback at the beginning of this project and to Dave Wanta of 123aspx.com for his technical assistance with .NET Remoting.

Most importantly, I would not have the opportunity and time to write if it weren't for the commitment of my wife, Tuija. Not only did she provide me with the chance to write this book, but she also came up with a lot of the ideas for the examples throughout the chapters.

Finally, thanks go to my two kids, Sofia and Henri, for being so understanding when I had to spend my weekends and evenings typing on the computer when we should have been playing.

Contents

Preface vii
Acknowledgments xiv

Part I: The .NET Framework

Chapter 1: The .NET Foundation 3
What Is .NET? 3
    The .NET vision 5
    The .NET solution 7
        The .NET Framework 7
        The .NET IDE 8
        The .NET languages 8
        The .NET Enterprise Servers 8
.NET's Foundation 9
    The Common Language Runtime 9
        Compilation to managed code 9
        Jit compilation 10
        Assemblies 11
        The structure of an assembly 11
        Garbage collection 12
    Namespaces 13
    The Base Class Libraries 15
Summary 18

Chapter 2: The Technologies of .NET 19
The Languages of .NET 19
    What language should you choose? 20
    Visual Basic .NET 21
        Declaring variables 21
        Classes 21
        Methods 23
        Hello World in Visual Basic .NET 25
    C# 26
        Declaring variables 27
        Classes 27
        Methods 28
        Hello World! in C# 30
    Other languages 32
        JScript .NET 32
        Visual C++ .NET 33
        J# 33

Understanding Visual Studio .NET 33
    Start Page 34
    Server Explorer 35
    Solution Explorer 35
    Class View 36
    Toolbox 37
    Properties window 38
    Dynamic Help 38
    Code window 39
    Design vs. HTML 39
Introduction to ASP.NET 40
    Web Forms 40
        Introduction to Server controls 40
        HTML controls 41
        Web controls 42
    XML Web services 44
Windows Forms 44
Using ADO.NET 45
Summary 46

Part II: The Basics of XML Web Services

Chapter 3: Introduction to XML Web Services 49

What Is an XML Web Service? 49
Why Do You Need XML Web Services? 51
XML Web Services: Present and Future 52
    The microwave 52
    The refrigerator 53
    A calendar 53
    The multifunctional Web site 53
Composition of XML Web Services 54
    Data representation in XML Web services 55
        Introducing XML 55
        Advantages of using XML for data representation 56
        Understanding XML syntax 56
        XML Namespaces 58
        XML schemas 61
        Creating an XML file in Visual Studio .NET 63
    Communicating data from an XML Web service 66
        XML Web services via HTTP-GET and HTTP-POST 67
        XML Web services via SOAP 69
    Describing an XML Web service 71
    Providing a means of discovery for your XML Web service 74
    Discovering an XML Web service provider 75

The Business of XML Web Services 77
Summary 79

Chapter 4: Building a Simple XML Web Service 81
Requirements to Build XML Web Services 81
Setting Up Your Operating System with IIS 82
Your First XML Web Service 84
Looking at Your First XML Web Service 87
    XML Web services' Web interface: Testing your Web service 87
    Understanding the XML Web service interface 88
        The WSDL document 88
        Testing the WebMethod 89
XML Web Services and Visual Studio .NET 91
    Your first XML Web service in Visual Studio .NET 91
    Testing the CurrencyConverter XML Web service 97
Summary 99

Chapter 5: Consuming XML Web Services 101
Understanding the Consumption of XML Web Services 101
Accessing an XML Web Service from a Windows Form 103
Understanding the Code 111
Accessing an XML Web Service from a Web Form 112
    Browser-based applications have found the Web! 112
    Why use XML Web services with Web Forms? 113
    Building an ASP.NET Web application 114
From One XML Web Service to Another 121
    A simple example: The first XML Web service 121
    A simple example: The second XML Web service 122
Consuming an XML Web Service from a Visual Basic 6.0 Application 124
Consuming an XML Web Service from an Active Server Pages Application ... 129
    A more complicated example 131
    Examining the code 134
Summary 135

Part III: Building XML Web Services

Chapter 6: XML Web Services Architecture 139
The Architecture Basics of XML Web Services 139
    The process of working with an XML Web service 140
    Declaring an XML Web service 141
    Data types 143
    Defining methods 145

Transport Protocols 146
    HTTP-GET 147
        Understanding querystrings 147
        Using HTTP-GET with XML Web services 147
    HTTP-POST 149
    SOAP 150
XML Web Services in a Multitiered Development Environment 153
    Presentation layer 154
    Business layer 158
    Data layer 158
Summary 160

Chapter 7: The Visual Part of XML Web Services 161

Working with the WebService Attribute 161
    The WebService attribute and the Namespace property 162
    The Description property 163
    The Name property 165
Working with the WebMethod Attribute 166
    The Description property 167
    The MessageName property 168
Customizing the ASP.NET Test Page 168
Disabling the Test Page 169
Summary 169

Chapter 8: State Management 171

Understanding State in .NET 172
Understanding Sessions 173
    Running sessions in-process 175
    Running sessions out-of-process 175
    Maintaining sessions on SQL Server 178
    Deciding on the state of sessions 179
    Cookieless session state 179
Using the Application Object in XML Web Services 181
Using Cookies along with the Consumption of XML Web Services 185
    Advantages to using cookies 185
    Disadvantages to using cookies 185
Using ViewState along with the Consumption of XML Web Services 188
    Toggling ViewState on and off 189
    Extending ViewState 190
Summary 191

Chapter 9: Proxies 193

How XML Web Services Are Consumed 193
Creating Proxies 195

Using Visual Studio .NET to Create a Proxy Class	195
Results from making a reference in Visual Studio .NET	199
Updating a project's Web reference	204
wsdl.exe	205
Compiling the proxy class	210
Configuring wsdl.exe	213
Examining and Modifying the Proxy Class	214
The URL property	214
The Timeout property	215
Summary	216

Part IV: XML Web Services Description and Discovery

Chapter 10: WSDL 219
Introduction to the WSDL Document 219
Structure of WSDL Documents 225
    <definitions> 226
    <types> 228
    <message> 231
    <portType> 232
    <binding> 234
        <soap:binding> 234
        <soap:operation> 235
        <soap:body> 235
    <service> 235
    <imports> 236
    <documentation> 237
Summary 238

Chapter 11: UDDI 239
Why Do You Need UDDI? 239
What is UDDI? 240
    The Shared UDDI Business Registry 241
        An example 242
        Information replication 242
    Information types 243
Publishing Services with UDDI 244
    Registering 246
        Business Detail 247
        Contacts 247
        Services 248
        Identifiers 251
        Business Classifications 251
        Discovery URLs 251
    Registering capabilities 252
Finding Services with UDDI 252
UDDI API Specification 254
    UDDI data structure 254
        businessEntity 255

Contents

- businessService ... 256
- bindingTemplate ... 257
- tModel ... 259
- publisherAssertion ... 260
- The UDDI programming model ... 261
  - Publisher APIs ... 261
  - Inquiry APIs ... 263
- Using the Microsoft UDDI SDK ... 265
  - The UDDI sample application ... 266
  - Using the UDDI classes ... 267
  - Publishing to the UDDI registry using the UDDI SDK ... 269
    - Authenticating and authorizing yourself to register ... 269
    - Publishing a tModel ... 269
    - Publishing a businessEntity, businessService, and a bindingTemplate ... 271
- Windows .NET Servers ... 274
- Summary ... 275

Chapter 12: Disco ... 277

- The Discovery Step ... 277
- The Disco File ... 278
  - The Disco file structure ... 279
    - <discovery> ... 280
    - <contractRef> ... 280
    - <discoveryRef> ... 281
    - <schemaRef> ... 281
    - <soap> ... 281
  - Creating your own .disco file ... 282
- The .vsdisco File ... 285
- Using Disco.exe ... 288
- Summary ... 290

Part V: All About SOAP

Chapter 13: SOAP ... 293

- SOAP and XML Web Services ... 293
- Why SOAP? ... 294
- SOAP Basics ... 295
  - SOAP and XML ... 295
  - SOAP over HTTP ... 295
  - An example of a request/response SOAP message ... 296
- The SOAP Specification ... 300
- The SOAP Message ... 301
  - SOAP Envelope ... 302
  - SOAP Header ... 302
    - actor attribute ... 303
    - mustUnderstand attribute ... 304
  - SOAP Body ... 304
    - SOAP Body Request ... 304

        SOAP Body response 305
      SOAP Fault 305
        faultcode 306
        faultstring 306
        faultactor 306
        detail 307
      SOAP Encoding 307
      Watching SOAP Messages 309
        The Microsoft SOAP Toolkit 310
        Using the Trace Utility 310
      Summary 313

Chapter 14: Advanced SOAP 315
      Working with SOAP Headers 315
        Building XML Web services that accept SOAP Headers 316
        Building XML Web Service clients that pass SOAP Headers 319
        Requiring and not requiring SOAP Headers 321
        SOAP Header direction 322
        Validating SOAP Header information 325
          MustUnderstand 325
        SOAP Header exceptions 330
      SOAP Extensions 330
      The Formatting of SOAP 340
        Document encoding 341
        RPC encoding 341
        Using both RPC and document encoding 343
        Client-side RPC SOAP message generation 345
      Shaping the XML 345
      Summary 351

Chapter 15: Global XML Web Services Architecture 353
      Looking into the Crystal Ball 353
      GXA Specifications 354
      Is GXA Necessary? 355
      WS-Inspection 356
        WSIL documents 356
        The composition of a WSIL document 357
      WS-Routing 359
      WS-Referral 361

WS-Security 363
    Credential exchange 363
    Message integrity 363
    Message confidentiality 363
WS-License 364
The Future of XML Web Services 365
Summary 365

Part VI: Security

Chapter 16: General Security Issues 369
Using Security with XML Web Services 369
    Authentication 370
    Authorization 370
    web.config 371
        <authentication> node 371
        <authorization> node 372
Authentication for XML Web Services 373
IIS Authentication 373
    Integrated Windows authentication 373
    Basic authentication 374
    Digest authentication 375
    Working with users and groups 376
        Creating users 376
        Authenticating and authorizing a user 378
        Creating groups 380
        Authenticating and authorizing a group 381
    Consuming an XML Web service that requires Windows-based authentication 381
    Authentication on individual XML Web services 383
ASP.NET Authentication 384
Authorization for XML Web Services 384
    Context.User 385
        Context.User.Identity 385
        Context.User.IsInRole 387
    Using System.Security.Principal 389
        WindowsBuiltInRole enumeration 389
        Accessing additional user properties 390
Summary 392

Chapter 17: Advanced Security 393
Security via SOAP Headers 393
    Consuming an XML Web service with an authentication SOAP Header 397
    Verifying credentials against a data source 400
Using SOAP Extensions for Encryption 403

>   Partial Encryption Using DES 404
>   Creating the SOAP extension 404
>   Using the SOAP EncryptionEngine extension in an XML Web service 411
>   Building the rest of your XML Web service consumer 413
>   Consuming the XML Web service 414
>   Summary 416

Part VII: ADO.NET and XML Web Services

Chapter 18: Working with ADO.NET 419
>   ADO.NET and XML 419
>   ADO.NET Architecture 420
>   The DataSet 421
>   DataSet 422
>   DataTable 422
>   DataColumn 423
>   DataConstraint 423
>   DataRow 423
>   DataRelation 423
>   The Typed DataSet 423
>   The DataAdapter 424
>   Common ADO.NET Tasks 425
>   Connecting to a data source 426
>   Reading data 427
>   Inserting data 428
>   Updating data 429
>   Deleting data 430
>   Populating a DataSet 431
>   Summary 432

Chapter 19: XML Web Services and ADO.NET 433
>   Visual Studio .NET's Data Wizards 433
>   Visual Studio .NET's Component Designer 433
>   Creating a connection to the data source 435
>   The DataAdapter Wizard 437
>   Creating a typed DataSet 443
>   Building the XML Web Service 446
>   Summary 448

Part VIII: Advanced XML Web Services

Chapter 20: Error and Exception Handling 453
>   Types of Errors 453
>   Development errors 453
>   Runtime errors 454
>   Try ... Catch ... Finally 455
>   Exceptions 455
>   Using Try ... Catch 456

Try … Catch … and *Finally!* 458
Throwing Exceptions 459
Web.Config Settings 460
Using the Global.asax 461
Using ASP.NET Tracing with Your XML Web Services 462
    <trace> node 462
    Viewing tracing output 463
    Customizing the trace log 465
SOAP Exceptions 467
    Message 469
    Code 469
    Actor 469
    Detail 469
Summary 469

Chapter 21: Configuration and Optimization 471

Web.config 471
    <configuration> node 474
    <compilation> node 474
    <customErrors> node 475
    <authentication> node 475
    <authorization> node 476
    <sessionState> node 476
    <globalization> node 477
    <appSettings> node 478
    <httpRuntime> 479
Caching 479
    The benefits of caching 480
    Why not cache? 481
Application Center Test (ACT) 481
    Do you have ACT? 481
    What ACT does to your XML Web service 482
    Testing with ACT 483
    Changing the XML Web service and retesting 490
Summary 491

Chapter 22: Advanced Issues in XML Web Services 493

Passing Images in the SOAP Envelope 493
Overloading WebMethods 501
Asynchronous XML Web Services 502
Summary 506

Chapter 23: Screen Scraping 507
The Screen Scraping Process 507
Stock Quote Example 508
Find your data source 508
Building the WSDL document 509
Building the proxy class 513
The delicate nature of screen scraping 517
Building a consuming application 518
Summary 521

Part IX: .NET My Services and .NET Remoting

Chapter 24: .NET My Services 525
What Exactly Is .NET My Services? 525
Specific .NET My Services 526
Before .NET My Services 527
With .NET My Services 528
.NET Alerts 530
What's Next? 531
Now Wait a Minute 531
Summary 532

Chapter 25: .NET Remoting: An Alternative to XML Web Services 533
.NET Remoting Basics 533
XML Web Services versus .NET Remoting 533
.NET Remoting Architecture 534
Channels 534
Ports 535
Formatters 535
SoapFormatter 535
BinaryFormatter 535
.NET Remoting Example 536
Creating the remote object 537
Creating the host for the remote object 538
Creating the server configuration file 539
Creating the client application 540
Creating the client configuration file 542
Testing the remote call 543
Summary 545

Chapter 26: In Conclusion 547

Appendix A: XML Web Services Classes 549
System.Web.Services 549
System.Web.Services.Description 554
System.Web.Services.Discovery 563
System.Web.Services.Protocols 565

Appendix B: XML Primer 569
   What is XML? 569
   XML Structure 570
   Summary 575

Appendix C: XSD Primer 577
   The Purpose of an XSD Document 577
   Elements and Attributes 577
   Summary 581

Appendix D: Bill Evjen's .NET Resources 583

Index 585

Part I

The .NET Framework

Chapter 1: The .NET Foundation

Chapter 2: The Technologies of .NET

Chapter 1
The .NET Foundation

A rock pile ceases to be a rock pile the moment a single man contemplates it, bearing within him the image of a cathedral.
Saint Exupery, Flight to Arras (1942)

Welcome to XML Web services for ASP.NET. The Web services movement of today has been referred to as a technology that is heralding a new era of application design. You can think of Web services as a component or a method that can be called across the Web. Even though many companies are offering solutions to implement and consume Web services, this book focuses on Microsoft's solution. In this chapter, I will be reviewing the foundation of the .NET Framework and what you need to understand about this new platform in order to see how XML Web services fit into the whole picture. This chapter emphasizes the following topics:

- Grasping the idea of .NET
- Learning about the CLR
- Understanding the Base Class Libraries

What Is .NET?

This is a loaded question, but what it really comes down to is that .NET means different things to different people. Much of what Microsoft is now offering has the .NET name somewhere in its title, but what .NET means really depends on whom you ask. The official one-line answer is that .NET is Microsoft's platform for XML Web services.

Microsoft's .NET Framework is a new computing platform built with the Internet in mind, but without sacrificing the traditional desktop application platform. The Internet has been around for a number of years now, and Microsoft has been busy developing technologies and tools that are totally focused on it. These earlier technologies, however, were built on Windows DNA (Distributed interNet Applications Architecture), which was based on COM (Component Object Model). Microsoft's COM was in development many years before the Internet became the force that we know today. Consequently, the COM model has been built upon and added to in order to adapt it to the changes brought about by the Internet.

With the .NET Framework, Microsoft built everything from the ground up with Internet integration as the goal. Building a platform from the ground up also allowed the .NET Framework developers to look at the problems and limitations that inhibited application development in the past and to provide the solutions that were needed to quickly speed past these barriers.

.NET is a collection of tools, technologies, and languages that all work together in a framework to provide the solutions that are needed to easily build and deploy truly robust enterprise applications. These .NET applications are also able to easily communicate with one another and provide information and application logic, regardless of platforms and languages.

Sounds pretty outstanding, doesn't it?

Figure 1-1 shows an overview of the structure of the .NET Framework.

```
+------------------+  +----------+
| ASP.NET          |  | Windows  |
| XML Web Services |  | Forms    |
+------------------+  +----------+
+----------------------------------+
|       Base Class Libraries       |
+----------------------------------+
+----------------------------------+
|      Common Language Runtime     |
+----------------------------------+
+----------------------------------+
|         Operating System         |
+----------------------------------+
```

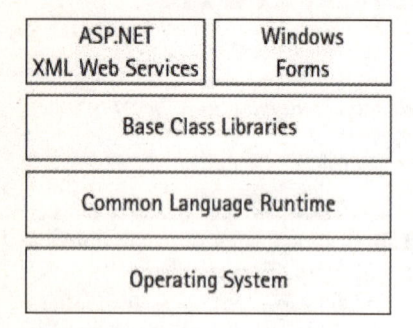

Figure 1-1: The .NET Framework.

The first thing that you should notice when looking at this diagram is that the .NET Framework sits on top of the operating system. Presently, the operating systems that can take the .NET Framework include Windows XP, Windows 2000, and Windows NT. There has also been a lot of talk about .NET being ported over by some third-party companies so that a majority of the .NET Framework could run on other platforms as well.

> **NOTE:** The support for the .NET Framework on Windows NT is limited to functioning only as a client. Windows NT will not support the Framework as a server.

At the base of the .NET Framework is the Common Language Runtime (CLR). The CLR is the engine that manages the execution of the code.

The next layer up is the .NET Framework Base Classes. This layer contains classes, value types, and interfaces that you will use often in your development process. Most notably within the .NET Framework Base Classes is ADO.NET, which provides access to and management of data.

The third layer of the framework is ASP.NET and Windows Forms. ASP.NET should not be viewed as the next version of Active Server Pages after ASP 3.0, but as a dramatically new shift in Web application development. Using ASP.NET, it's now possible to build robust Web applications that are even more functional than Win32 applications of the past. This was always quite difficult to do in the stateless nature of the Internet, but ASP.NET offers a number of different solutions to overcome the traditional limitations on the types of applications that were possible. The ASP.NET section of the .NET Framework is also where the XML Web services model resides.

The second part of the top layer of the .NET Framework is the Windows Forms section. This is where you can build the traditional executable applications that you built with Visual Basic 6.0 in the past. There are some new features here as well, such as a new drawing class and the capability to program these applications in any of the available .NET languages. You may view XML Web services as something you use within the ASP.NET applications that you build, but this isn't the only place where you can consume XML Web services. It's quite possible to consume XML Web services within a Windows Form application and a number of other application types, just as you can from any ASP.NET Web application.

> **CROSS REFERENCE:** ASP.NET and Windows Forms are covered in Chapter 2.

The .NET vision

There is a vision of the future at Microsoft, and this vision is strongly influencing the direction of its products. The vision is that in the future all devices will be connected in one way or another.

The view is that all business and household devices (telephones, microwaves, computers, televisions, and so forth) will be connected to the Internet one day and will, therefore, be able to communicate across this medium to perform the functionality needed to turn them into superior products. The thought is that these products and devices will use standardized languages such as XML and SOAP to communicate over standard protocols such as HTTP. That is where XML Web services come in! XML Web services are going to be the means for all these products and devices to communicate the information and requests that they will need to perform some type of functionality or registration.

Aside from that vision of the future, .NET today is able to solve similar problems in regard to connecting disparate applications and platforms that run on a wide variety of devices. Today there are walls between these differing systems, and .NET has been built to knock down these barriers by providing a common communication model using XML and SOAP.

Microsoft has truly taken hold of this idea and has developed the entire .NET Framework around it, and that is why you will find strong support for XML throughout the Framework. Also, you will notice that when you visit Microsoft's developer pages at MSDN, you cannot get away from stories and articles that are related in one way or another to Web services. This momentum will get stronger and stronger as .NET matures.

It isn't just Microsoft that has grabbed hold of this vision of the future. If you go to IBM's developer site you will notice that all the talk is also about XML Web services and how to use SOAP. Other companies, like Sun Microsystems, have joined in, promoting their own versions of Web services. So you don't need to worry and wonder if the Web services idea is simply a Microsoft fad — *it isn't*. Web services is a vision that comes from the computing industry and not just one company in particular. Almost every new platform version, database, and server application is being developed with Web services in mind. The companies and people developing these products realize that it is quite advantageous to expose platform or application functionality as Web services.

Imagine a world where all the commercial products and devices you can purchase off the shelf are connected via broadband connection to the Internet. They are thus enabled to trade information and report events with lightning-quick speed. The functionality that can be built upon this type of platform is limitless.

Devices and products of all kinds will be delivering or consuming Web services in this type of environment. In most cases, these Web services will not be developed with just one type of client in mind. Instead, Web services will offer their logic, information, registration service, or whatever they need to offer to a multitude of clients. Figure 1-2 gives you a better idea of what this world of Web services can mean to you.

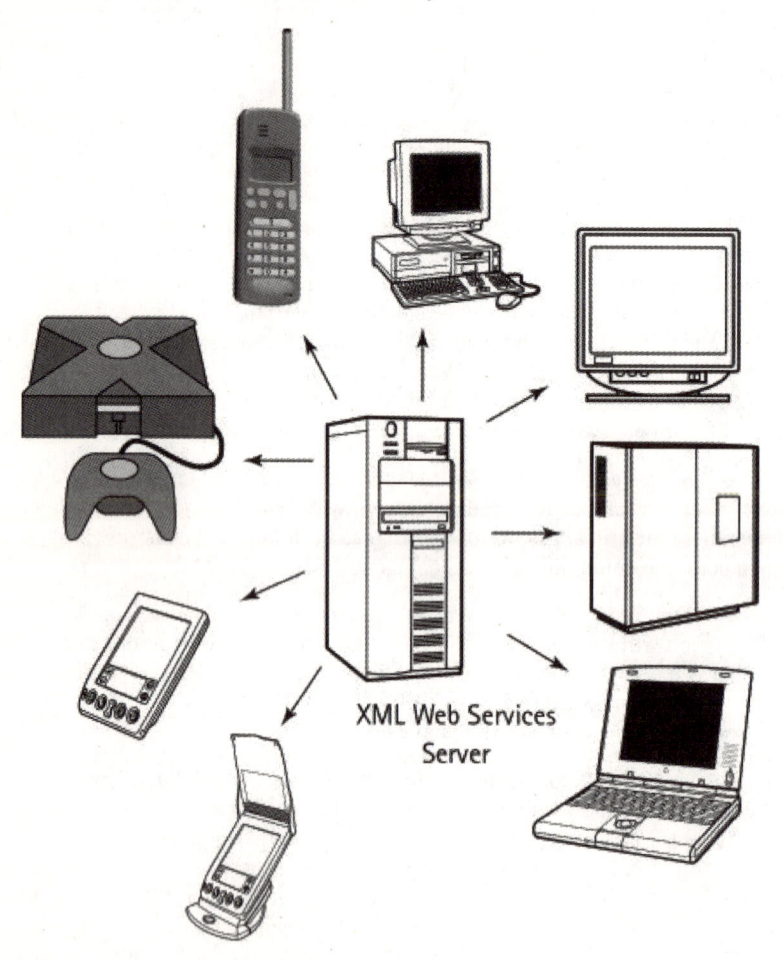

Figure 1-2: One Web service for multiple clients.

XML Web services will deliver these services over standard protocols such as HTTP and SOAP so that any device, regardless of platform, will be able to consume and utilize the information being sent. You, as a developer, will not have to build a new way to interact with each new device, but instead you can offer a single means for all devices or products to interact with the XML Web service that you will provide.

As a developer, you can see the benefit of an environment where you do not always need to reinvent the wheel but, instead, can procure the functionality and items that you need as you develop your applications or Web sites. You may now be wondering how hard it is to build and consume XML Web services.

Microsoft has realized that, in order for this type of platform to take hold, it has to be simple and easy to use. Development must be uncomplicated, and deployment needs to be a breeze – *and this is exactly what the .NET platform has delivered!*

The .NET solution

In anticipation of this future, Microsoft has developed the .NET Framework and the tools necessary to build in this new environment. Microsoft realized that it had many languages and tools that basically did the same thing. Admittedly, some languages and tools did certain things better than others, but all of them worked towards the same goal, and there was plenty of overlap.

Microsoft has taken the best of all these different worlds and has merged them into a single environment, as shown in Figure 1-3.

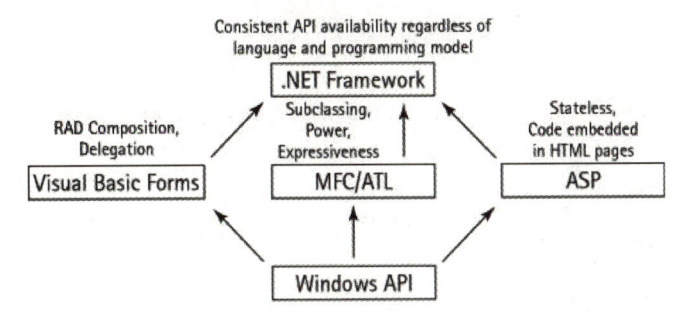

Figure 1-3: A unified model.

This new unified model will allow you, as a developer, to use one development environment and platform to build every application type that you need.

The .NET Framework

To get around the problem of having multiple development environments, Microsoft developed an environment that is a unified development environment. This framework is the platform for the entire .NET idea. The framework is language-neutral and built to provide you with the tools and solutions that you need to build rich applications in the stateless environment of the Internet.

The .NET Framework includes two main components — the Common Language Runtime and the Base Class Libraries. Each of these elements is explained later in this chapter.

One of the main objectives of the framework is to provide a simplified development model so that a lot of the plumbing that was required to develop in the past is eliminated. The .NET Framework is a simpler development environment and will give developers more power over their applications. This framework uses the latest in Internet standards such as XML, SOAP, and HTTP. You will also find the applications that you build on this platform are easy to deploy and maintain.

The .NET IDE

Instead of a multitude of tools for development, the .NET team created a single tool for developing Windows Forms, ASP.NET Web Applications, and XML Web services. This tool is Visual Studio .NET.

As a developer, you will find Visual Studio .NET an indispensable tool. It is finely interwoven within the .NET Framework and will give you full and complete access to everything that .NET has to offer. Visual Studio .NET is discussed further in the next chapter.

The .NET languages

In the past, you chose the development language for an application based upon the functionality that you were trying to perform. Some languages were more powerful than others, but at the same time they might have required a higher level of understanding and were, in most cases, more difficult to program in.

Now the .NET Framework provides you with a language-independent programming platform. You do not have to decide which language would provide a better solution. All languages are now on a level playing field.

In .NET, no one language is superior to any of the other languages. They all have equal access to everything that .NET offers.

To be part of the .NET Framework, a language only has to follow certain rules. The biggest and most important rule for inclusion is that the language needs to be an object-oriented language. Microsoft provides four languages with the .NET Framework: Visual Basic .NET, C#, C++.NET, and JScript .NET. Microsoft also provides J# (pronounced J-sharp), but in order to use this new language that is basically Java for .NET, you need to download the language to install it on your server. You can find this download at `http://msdn.microsoft.com`.

The .NET Enterprise Servers

The marketing folks at Microsoft made things a little more confusing when they started naming everything with a .NET suffix. Shortly after the introduction of .NET, all the forthcoming .NET Enterprise Servers rebranded themselves as part of the .NET platform.

The problem is that they *really* aren't part of the .NET platform at all. Yes, it is true that you can interact with some of these applications in an indirect way through the framework, but the first *true* .NET server will be the next version of Microsoft SQL Server following SQL Server 2000. There has been no indication of how this next version will be folded into the .NET platform. However, it has been stated that these servers will be deeply integrated and that, for instance, you will be able to write your stored procedures in any of the .NET languages.

This current set of .NET Enterprise Servers is considered part of the .NET platform mainly because they are tightly coupled with XML, a language the .NET platform understands very well, thus allowing them to communicate and work together with ease.

.NET's Foundation

The foundation of the .NET platform is the .NET Framework, which we have already introduced. The .NET Framework sits on top of the operating system and is made up of two parts, the Common Language Runtime and the Base Class Libraries. Each one of these parts plays an important role in the development of .NET applications and services.

The Common Language Runtime

Many different languages and platforms provide a runtime, and the .NET Framework is no exception. You will find, however, that this runtime is quite different from most.

The Common Language Runtime (CLR) in the .NET Framework manages the execution of the code and provides access to a variety of services that will make the development process easier.

The CLR has been developed to be far superior to previous runtimes, such as the VB runtime, by attaining the following:

- Cross-language integration
- Code access security
- Object lifetime management
- Debugging and profiling support

Code that is compiled and targeted to the CLR is known as *managed code*. Managed code provides *metadata* that is needed for the CLR to provide the services of multilanguage support, code security, object lifetime management, and memory management.

> **NOTE:** *Metadata* is basically "data about data" or a description of the contents of a .NET component. This metadata is stored within the assembly manifest. In the past, it was difficult for components written in competing languages to interact with one another. The .NET Framework uses metadata so that .NET components are self-describing, making them easy to interoperate with other components.

Compilation to managed code

The .NET Framework requires that you use a language compiler that is targeted at the CLR, such as the Visual Basic .NET, C#, C++ .NET, or JScript .NET compilers provided by Microsoft. Note that there are a lot of third-party compilers on the market (such as COBOL and Perl), and the number will continue to grow.

So how does the code that you typed into Visual Studio .NET become the code that the user receives when he is using your application? It is fairly simple and straightforward. Figure 1-4 shows a diagram of the compilation process.

After using one of the language compilers, your code is compiled down to *Microsoft Intermediate Language*. Microsoft Intermediate Language, known as MSIL or simply IL, is a CPU-independent set of instructions that can be easily converted to native code. The metadata is also contained within the IL.

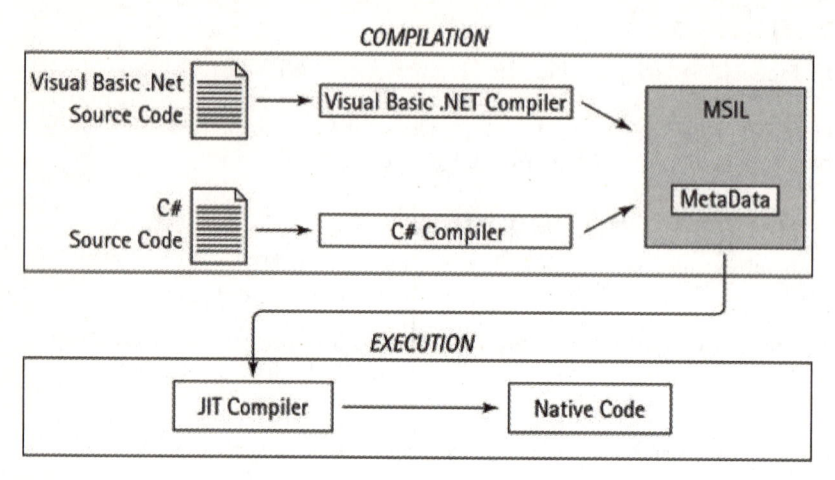

Figure 1-4: Managed code execution process.

The IL is CPU-independent. This means that IL code is not reliant on the specific computer that generated it. In other words, it can be moved from one computer to another (as long as the computer supports the .NET Framework) without any complications. This is what makes X-Copy, or just copying over the application, possible.

After IL, the code that you started with will be compiled down even further by the JIT compiler to *machine code* or *native code*. The IL contains everything that is needed to do this, such as the instructions to load and call methods and a number of other operations.

Jit compilation

The .NET Framework contains one or more JIT compilers that compile your IL code down to machine code, or code that is CPU-specific. This is done when the application is executed for the first time.

You will notice this process after you build your first ASP.NET page. After you build any ASP.NET page, you compile the page down to IL. When you go to the browser and call the page by typing its URL in the address bar, you notice a slight pause of a few seconds as the computer seems to think about what it is doing. It is actually calling this IL code and converting it with a JIT compiler to machine code. This happens only the first time that someone requests the page. After the first time, you can hit F5 to refresh the page, and the page is immediately executed. The page has already been converted to machine code and is now stored in memory. The CLR knows the JIT compiler has already compiled the page. Therefore, it gets the output of the page from memory. If you later make a change to your ASP.NET page, recompile, and then run the page again, CLR detects that there was a change to the original file. It uses the JIT compiler once again to compile the IL code down to machine code.

The JIT compiler, as it compiles to machine code, makes sure that the code is type safe. It does this to ensure that objects are separate, thereby making certain that objects won't unintentionally corrupt one another.

Assemblies

In the applications that you build within the .NET Framework, assemblies will always play an important role. Assemblies can be thought of as the building blocks of your applications. Without an associated assembly, code will not be able to compile from IL. When you are using the JIT compiler to compile your code from managed code to machine code, the JIT compiler will look for the IL code that is stored in a portable executable (PE) file along with the associated assembly manifest.

Every time you build a Web Form or Windows Form application in .NET, you are actually building an assembly. Every one of these applications will contain at least one assembly.

As in the Windows DNA world where DLLs and EXEs are the building blocks of applications, in the .NET world, it is the assembly that is the used as the foundation of applications.

In the world of Windows DNA and COM, there was a situation that was referred to as DLL Hell. COM components were generally designed so that there was only one version of that COM component on a machine at any given time. This was because the COM specification did not provide for the inclusion of dependency information in a component's type definition. When the developer had to make some changes to the COM component, this new component was introduced and, in many cases, broke applications.

With .NET, it is now possible to have multiple versions of components, or assemblies, running on the same server side by side. An application will always look for the assembly that built it.

When an application is started in .NET, the application will look for an assembly in the installation folder. Assemblies that are stored in a local installation folder are referred to as *private assemblies*. If the application cannot find the assembly within the installation folder, the application will turn to the *Global Assembly Cache (GAC)* for the assembly.

The GAC is a place where you can store assemblies that you want to share across applications. You can find the assemblies that are stored in the GAC in the `WINNT\ASSEMBLY` folder in your local disk drive.

The structure of an assembly

Assemblies contain code that is executed by the Common Language Runtime. The great thing about assemblies is that they are self-describing. All the details about the assembly are stored within the assembly itself. In the Windows DNA world, COM stored all its self-describing data within the server's registry, and so installing (as well as uninstalling) COM components meant shutting down IIS. Because .a NET assembly stores this information within itself, it makes XCOPY functionality possible. Installing an assembly is as simple as copying it, and there is no need to stop or start IIS while this is going on.

Figure 1-5 shows the structure of an assembly.

```
Assembly
┌─────────────────────────┐
│   Assembly Manifest     │
├─────────────────────────┤
│       Metadata          │
├─────────────────────────┤
│         MSIL            │
└─────────────────────────┘
```

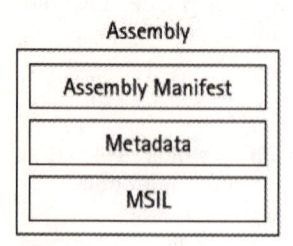

Figure 1-5: A diagram of an assembly.

Assemblies are made up of the following parts:

- The assembly manifest
- Type metadata
- Microsoft Intermediate Language (MSIL) code

The assembly manifest is where the details of the assembly are stored. The assembly is stored within the DLL or EXE itself. Assemblies can either be single or multifile assemblies and, therefore, assembly manifests can either be stored in the assembly or as a separate file. The assembly manifest also stores the version number of the assembly to ensure that the application always uses the correct version. When you are going to have multiple versions of an assembly on the same machine, it is important to label them carefully so that the CLR knows which one to use. Version numbers in assemblies are constructed in the following manner:

```
<major version>.<minor version>.<build number>.<revision>
```

Type metadata was explained earlier in this chapter as data about data. This metadata contains information on the types that are exposed by the assembly such as security permission information, class and interface information, and other assembly information.

Garbage collection

The .NET Framework is a garbage-collected environment. Garbage collection is the process of detecting when objects are no longer in use and automatically destroying those objects, thus freeing memory.

Garbage collection is not a new concept. It has been used in other languages for quite some time. In fact, Java has a garbage collection system in place. Other languages, such as C++, do not have a garbage collection. C++ developers themselves are required to take care of the destruction of objects and the freeing of memory. This results in a number of problems, such as memory leaks. If the developer forgets to free objects from the application, memory allocation of the application grows, sometimes substantially. Also, freeing objects too early causes application bugs to crop up; these kinds of errors are, in most cases, quite difficult to track down.

In .NET, this new garbage collector works so that you as a developer are no longer required to monitor your code for unneeded objects and destroy them. The garbage collector will take care of all this for you. Garbage collection does not happen immediately, but instead the garbage collector will occasionally make a sweep of the heap to determine which objects should be allocated for destruction. This new system completely absolves the developer from hunting down memory usage and deciding when to free memory.

With this new garbage collector, you can control certain aspects of its functions, as it works behind the scenes in your application. Within the SDK documentation, look under the `System.GC` class for more information.

Namespaces

The .NET Framework is made up of hundreds of classes. Many of the applications that you build in .NET are going to take advantage of these classes in one way or another. Because the number of classes is so large and you will need to get at them in a logical fashion, the .NET Framework organizes these classes into a class structure called a *namespace*. There are a number of namespaces, and they are organized in an understandable and straightforward way.

> **NOTE:** `System` is the base namespace in the .NET Framework. All namespaces that are provided in the framework start at this base namespace. For instance, the classes that deal with data access and manipulation are found in the `System.Data` namespace. Other examples include `System.IO`, `System.XML`, `System.Collections`, `System.Drawing`, and so forth. In the naming conventions of namespaces, `System.XML.XMLReader` represents the `XMLReader` type, which belongs to the `System.XML` namespace.

You can import a namespace into your application in the following manner:

VB

```
Imports System.Data
```

C#

```
using System.Data;
```

If you are going to import more than one namespace into your application, do so as shown in the following code:

VB

```
Imports System.Data
Imports System.Data.OleDb
```

C#

```
using System.Data;
using System.Data.OleDb;
```

By importing a namespace into your application, you no longer need to fully qualify the class. For example, if you do not import the namespace into your application, you must write out the full class name.

VB

```
myConnection = "Initial Catalog=Northwind;Data Source=localhost;
               Integrated Security=SSPI;"
Dim conn As New System.Data.SQLClient.SqlConnection(myConnection)
```

C#

```
myConnection = "Initial Catalog=Northwind;Data Source=localhost;
               Integrated Security=SSPI;";
SqlConnection conn = new
System.Data.SQLClient.SqlConnection(myConnection);
```

If you do import the `System.Data.SQLClient` namespace into your application or to the page where you need it, you can refer to the class quite simply, as shown in the following code:

VB

```
myConnection = "Initial Catalog=Northwind;Data Source=localhost;
               Integrated Security=SSPI;"
Dim conn As New SqlConnection(myConnection)
```

C#

```
myConnection = "Initial Catalog=Northwind;Data Source=localhost;
               Integrated Security=SSPI;";
SqlConnection conn = new SqlConnection(myConnection);
```

You can import a namespace directly to an `.aspx` page inline in the following manner for both Visual Basic .NET and C#:

VB and C#

```
<%@ Import Namespace="System.Data" %>
<%@ Import Namespace="System.Data.SqlClient" %>
```

Notice in the preceding code that because you imported two namespaces into the page inline, you had to put each of the namespaces within its own set of opening and closing brackets.

When building your .NET applications in the .NET Framework, a number of namespaces are already automatically imported into your application for use throughout. An ASP.NET Web application automatically imports the following namespaces:

```
System
System.Data
System.Drawing
System.Web
System.XML
```

You can find a list of all the imported namespaces in the References folder in the application root. A Windows Form application automatically imports the following namespaces:

```
System
System.Data
System.Drawing
System.Windows.Forms
System.XML
```

An ASP.NET Web Service automatically imports the following namespaces:

```
System
System.Data
System.Web
System.Web.Services
System.XML
```

It is possible to import additional namespaces for use application-wide by right-clicking on the References folder and selecting Add Reference. You will then be able to import any of the other namespaces that are available.

The Base Class Libraries

The Base Class Libraries (BCL) are a set of classes, value types, and interfaces that give you access to specific developer utilities and various system functions. The preceding section covered how these classes are organized by the system of namespaces that are in place in the .NET Framework. Now take a closer look at the classes that are provided in the .NET Framework.

All the languages that sit on top of the .NET Framework have equal access to all the classes that are contained within the BCL. This actually makes it quite easy to look at code from another .NET language and understand what is going on in the code. You use the `SQLConnection` class in Visual Basic .NET to connect to SQL Server exactly the way you do in C#, although the language semantics are different.

Table 1-1 gives a brief description of some of the classes available with the .NET Framework. This table is not a comprehensive list of available namespaces. You can find all the namespaces within the .NET SDK documentation. It is important to realize that you are not limited only to these namespaces. You can create your own namespaces to use within your applications, and there will be third-party namespaces on the market that are available to use as well. One example of a third-party namespace is the `System.Data.Oracle` namespace.

Table 1-1   Namespace Definitions

Namespace	Description
`System`	Provides base data types and almost 100 classes that deal with situations like exception handling, mathematical functions, and garbage collection.
`System.CodeDom`	Provides the classes needed to produce source files in all the .NET languages.

Namespace	Description
System.Collections	Provides access to collection classes such as lists, queues, bit arrays, hash tables, and dictionaries.
System.ComponentModel	Provides classes that are used to implement runtime and design-time behaviors of components and controls.
System.Configuration	Provides classes and interfaces that allow you to programmatically access the various configuration files that are on your system, such as the web.config and the machine.config files.
System.Data	Provides classes that allow data access and manipulation to SQL Server and OleDb data sources. These classes make up the ADO.NET architecture.
System.Diagnostics	Provides classes that allow you to debug and trace your application. There are classes to interact with event logs, performance counters, and system processes.
System.DirectoryServices	Provides classes that allow you to access Active Directory.
System.Drawing	Provides classes that allow you to access the basic and advanced features of the new GDI+ graphics functionality.
System.EnterpriseServices	Provides classes that allow you to access COM+ services.
System.Globalization	Provides classes that access the global system variables, such as calendar display, date and time settings, and currency display settings.
System.IO	Provides classes that allow access to file and stream control and manipulation.
System.Management	Provides access to a collection of management information and events about the system, devices, and applications designed for the Windows Management Instrumentation (WMI) infrastructure.
System.Messaging	Provides classes that allow you to access message queue controls and manipulators.
System.Net	Provides access to classes that control network services. These classes also allow control over the system's sockets.
System.Reflection	Provides classes that allow control to create and invoke loaded types, methods, and fields.
System.Resources	Provides classes that allow you to create and

Namespace	Description
	manage culture-specific resources.
`System.Runtime.Remoting`	Provides classes that allow the management of remote objects in a distributed environment.
`System.Security`	Provides classes that allow access to authentication, authorization, cryptography, permissions, and policies.
`System.ServiceProcess`	Provides classes that give control over Windows services.
`System.Text`	Provides classes for working with and manipulating text strings.
`System.Threading`	Provides classes for threading issues and allows you to create multithreaded applications.
`System.Timers`	Provides the capability to raise events on specified intervals.
`System.Web`	Provides numerous classes that are used in ASP.NET Web application development.
`System.Web.Services`	Provides classes that are used throughout this book to build, deploy, and consume Web services.
`System.Windows.Forms`	Provides classes to build and deploy Windows Forms applications.
`System.Xml`	Provides classes to work with and manipulate XML data.

As you can tell from the preceding table, many classes are at your disposal for building rich .NET applications. With these classes, much of the plumbing that you had to deal with in the past is now taken care of for you. This book will touch on a number of these classes as you build your XML Web services. With such a large number of classes at your disposal, you may find yourself searching high and low for a certain class. There are a few ways that you can look for the class that you are trying to find. The first is to try the .NET Framework SDK documentation. Another option is to use the Windows Forms Class Viewer, or the WinCV tool. This tool is provided with the .NET Framework. The WinCV tool enables you to quickly look up information on classes in the CLR based upon your custom search criteria. The WinCV tool displays information by reflecting on the type using the CLR reflection API.

To find the `WinCV.exe` tool, look in the `C:\Program Files\Microsoft Visual Studio .NET\FrameworkSDK\Bin` directory. The left-hand pane of the WinCV tool shows your search results, and the right-hand pane shows the type definition. The type definition is shown in a C#-like syntax (Figure 1-6).

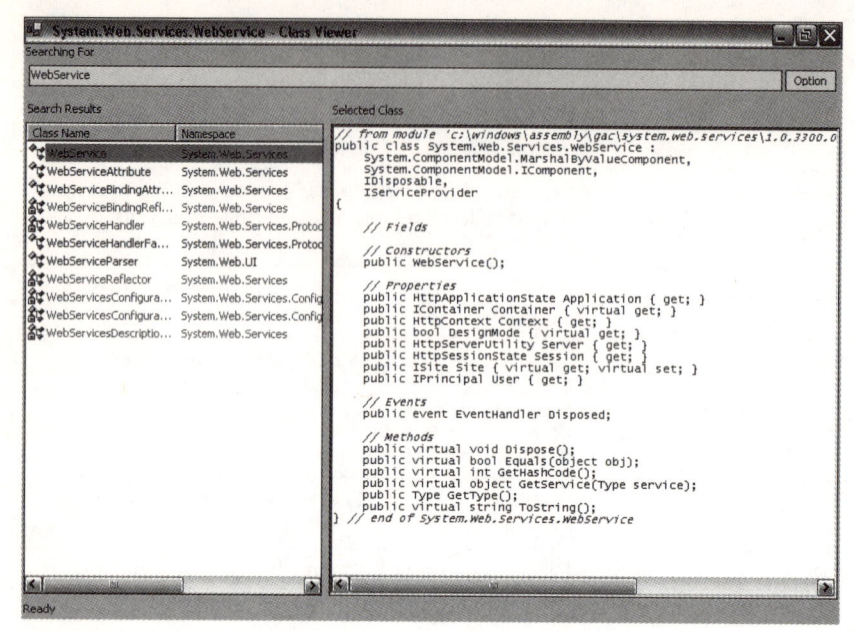

Figure 1-6: Looking at the WebService class with the Windows Forms Class Viewer.

To see the WinCV in action, type **WebService** into the search box. You are presented with a large list of classes in the left-hand pane. Clicking on the first choice, WebService, you are shown the type definition for the WebService class in the right-hand pane. The beginning of the definition tells you that the WebService class is part of the `System.Web.Services` namespace. This is a useful tool for search purposes and for a better understanding of classes within the .NET Framework.

Summary

This chapter provides a quick overview of the .NET Framework and gives you a better understanding of what you will use to build your XML Web services. This chapter was one of those 40,000-feet views of the framework, but it provides enough information for you to learn what you need to know to build XML Web services. If you are looking for more information, there are numerous books out there that focus primarily on the .NET Framework.

In the next chapter you look at some of the languages that you will use to build your XML Web services and how XML Web services interact with the .NET Framework. Now, take a closer look at the tools and technologies that you must understand to build XML Web services.

Chapter 2

The Technologies of .NET

> *Use what language you will, you can never say anything but what you are.*
> Emerson, "Worship," *The Conduct of Life* (1860).

In the first chapter, you took a quick look at the foundation of .NET, the .NET Framework. In addition to the .NET Framework, there are a number of tools and technologies that make it easy to build outstanding ASP.NET pages, Windows Forms, and XML Web services.

This chapter introduces the main technologies and tools that you will use when building your XML Web services on the .NET platform. You must understand each of these technologies if you are going to build XML Web services that provide you with new functionality for your applications, new ways for your customers to access data, and new revenue streams for your company.

In this chapter, I cover the following topics:

- The languages that you can use on the .NET platform
- The programming tool, Visual Studio .NET
- An overview of ASP.NET, Windows Forms, and ADO.NET

The Languages of .NET

Microsoft provides four languages that are targeted at the CLR to run on the .NET Framework: Visual Basic .NET, C#, Managed C++, and JScript .NET. An additional language, J#, can also be downloaded from Microsoft separately. This book focuses on using Visual Basic .NET and C# for building XML Web services. Although, it is quite possible to build XML Web services and ASP.NET Web applications using Managed C++ and JScript .NET, most of the development community is focusing its .NET efforts in the other two languages, so that is the model that I follow for this book as well.

Before .NET came along, Microsoft realized that it had a lot of products that were good at specific tasks or for a desired functionality; but making these technologies work together was complicated, if not downright impossible.

If you wanted to develop a rich Win32 application quickly, you used Visual Basic 6.0. If you wanted to develop a browser-independent and highly functional Web site, you used Active Server Pages 3.0 (written with VBScript or JScript). If you wanted to have complete control over an application, you used C++.

When it came time to build the .NET Framework, the developers at Microsoft realized that they needed to build a platform that was language independent, one where all the languages used in the platform could take advantage of everything that the framework had to offer.

And that is exactly what they did. The .NET platform is a language-independent platform in which the differences between the languages are merely syntactical. Instead of choosing or switching languages based upon performance or functionality, you choose a single language based purely upon the language style that you feel comfortable with.

The great advantage of this language-independent platform is that it allows the IDE, Visual Studio .NET, to be language independent as well. There isn't a separate IDE for each language in .NET because all the languages have equal and complete access to Visual Studio .NET.

Probably the greatest advantage to the language-independent .NET platform is that the languages can easily interact because they all abide by a Common Type System (CTS). Because the .NET languages abide by the CTS, you can easily inherit a C# class into your Visual Basic .NET application. This kind of model, where you are able to mix and match languages, allows you to work with a wider choice of reusable components for your applications.

> **NOTE:** The Common Type System is a set of rules for a language that is targeted to the CLR of the .NET Framework. The CTS defines how types are declared and used. It also forces a language to follow an object-oriented model, so that all the languages of the .NET platform can interact without any problems. Because the languages that are targeted at the .NET Framework abide by the CTS, a double in one language is always a double in another. Because these pieces are the same, the languages can share and pass information to a component or class that is written in another language.

What language should you choose?

If you are just starting out with .NET, you may be wondering what language you should choose. First of all, you will not gain an advantage by choosing one language over another. Within the .NET Framework, one language is not faster than another. You are not going to find a language that performs better, is better at scaling, or provides you with any more functionality than any of the other languages that are provided with the .NET platform.

It really all comes down to a matter of style. What style of computer language do you prefer? Are you more comfortable and familiar with a Visual Basic look to your code, or do you like the look and feel of a C-syntax language?

If you have been coding for years in Visual Basic 6 or ASP 3.0, I recommend that you chose Visual Basic .NET. You will learn how to program .NET applications more quickly if you do. If you were a C, C++, Java, JSP, or PHP programmer in your past, I suggest you use C#. You will find this style more to your liking.

Because the languages use the same class libraries (with the same class names), you will often look at a language in .NET that you don't know and yet be able understand the code and what the code is doing.

Visual Basic .NET

Visual Basic .NET is the next version of the Visual Basic language after VB6. Quite a bit has changed from VB6 to this latest version. Visual Basic developers will find that the changes are even greater than the changes that occurred when Visual Basic switched from VB3 to VB4. To abide by the Common Type System, Visual Basic .NET had to evolve and become a true object-oriented (OO) language.

> **NOTE:** A true object-oriented language is said to support the three pillars of PIE (polymorphism, inheritance, and encapsulation). All the languages of .NET are true OO languages.

Although not meant to be a complete reference to Visual Basic .NET, the following code samples will give you an idea of how to construct a Visual Basic .NET application. Because everything is class-based in the .NET Framework, I start by showing you how to declare variables and construct a class in Visual Basic.NET.

Declaring variables

In Visual Basic .Net, as in the other .NET languages, you have to declare your variables before you use them. By declaring variables, you are assigning a name to a type, sometimes along with the value, before you use this name elsewhere in your application. In Visual Basic .NET you declare your variables by using the Dim statement in the following manner:

```
Dim FirstName As String
Dim myNumber As Integer
```

It is also possible to assign a value to the variable at the same time that you make your declaration, as follows:

```
Dim FirstName As String = "William"
Dim myNumber As Integer = 31
```

You can declare multiple variables on the same line by using the following standard:

```
Dim FirstName, MiddleName, LastName As String
```

In this case, you just declared three variables, all of the type `String`. If you wish to declare multiple variables on the same line, but with different types, you do so in the following manner:

```
Dim FirstName As String, Age As Integer, Salary As Double
```

In this example, you just declared three variables, all of different types.

Classes

Everything in .NET is a class. Even the pages that you build in ASP.NET are now compiled into page classes. Therefore, you must understand how to construct a class in Visual Basic .NET. The following code shows how to do this.

```
[ Public | Private | Protected | Friend |
Protected Friend ] [ Shadows ] [ MustInherit | NotInheritable ] _
Class name
```

```
    [ Inherits classname ]
    [ Implements interfacenames ]
    [ statements ]
End Class
```

If you come from the VBScript or VB6 world, you will notice some new words in the preceding code block. Let's take a look at some of the options available in building your classes. Table 2-1 describes each of the modifiers that precede the class name. Note that all of the modifiers are optional.

TABLE 2-1   Modifier Definitions for a Class in Visual Basic .NET

Modifier	Description
Public	Makes the class publicly accessible. Public classes have no restrictions.
Private	Makes the class available only within the file where it was declared.
Protected	Makes the class available only to the containing class and any derived class.
Friend	Makes the class available only to the application where it was declared.
Protected Friend	This is a combination of the Protected and Friend modifiers. Protected Friend makes the class available only to the containing class and any derived class that is also contained within the same application.
Shadows	Makes the class shadow an identically named programming element in the base class.
MustInherit	Forces the class to inherit other classes.
NotInheritable	Makes the class not inheritable to other classes.

Looking at the code sample, note that you can now inherit other classes in Visual Basic .NET by using the Inherits keyword. Inherits is followed by the class name and must always precede the Implements keyword (if they are used together). Using the Implements keyword is optional and implements the members of an interface.

Here is an example of a class in Visual Basic .NET:

```
Private Class VacationNotification
    ' Coding statements go here
End Class
```

Methods

You must define all your executable code within a Sub or Function procedure. The difference between the two is that the Sub procedure does not return a value whereas the Function procedure can. The Sub procedure is written in the following syntax:

```
[ Overloads | Overrides | Overridable |
  NotOverridable | MustOverride | Shadows | Shared ]
[ Public | Protected | Friend | Protected Friend | Private ]
Sub name [(arglist)] [ Implements interface.definedname ]
    [ statements ]
    [ Exit Sub ]
    [ statements ]
End Sub
```

The Function procedure is written the following syntax:

```
[ Overloads | Overrides | Overridable |
  NotOverridable | MustOverride | Shadows | Shared ]
[ Public | Protected | Friend | Protected Friend | Private ]
Function name[(arglist)] [ As type ] [ Implements interface.definedname
]
    [ statements ]
    [ Exit Function ]
    [ statements ]
End Function
```

Looking over these code blocks, you will notice that there are a number of keywords that you can use to change how your procedures behave. Table 2-2 gives you a brief description of all the available keywords in both the Sub and Function procedures.

TABLE 2-2 Modifier Definitions for a Procedure

Modifier	Description
Overloads	Indicates that the procedure overloads one or more procedures that have a similar name. These procedures can have the same name, but must have either a different number of arguments, differing data types, or both. This is an optional keyword, even if you are overloading procedures.
Overrides	Indicates that the procedure will override a like-named procedure in the base class. Both procedures must have both the same number of arguments and data types.
Overridable	Indicates that the procedure can be overridden by a procedure in a derived class with the same name.
NotOverridable	Indicates that the procedure cannot be overridden under any circumstances.

Part I: The .NET Framework

Modifier	Description
`MustOverride`	Indicates that the procedure is not implemented in the class but instead must be implemented in the derived class.
`Shadows`	Indicates that the procedure shadows an identically named programming element in the base class.
`Shared`	Indicates that the procedure is not an associated class, but is shared.
`Public`	Makes the procedure publicly accessible. `Public` procedures have no restrictions.
`Protected`	Makes the procedure available only to the containing class and any derived class.
`Friend`	Makes the procedure available only to the application where it was declared.
`Protected Friend`	This is a combination of the `Protected` and `Friend` modifier. `Protected Friend` makes the procedure available only to the containing class and any derived class that is also contained within the same application.
`Private`	Makes the procedure available only within the file where it was declared.

To exit a Sub procedure, you can use `Exit Sub` or `Return` at any point in the procedure. There is no limit on the number of times you can place these points of exit in the procedure. Here is an example of how to use the Sub statement.

```
Sub RewardVacation(ByVal EmployeeName As String)
    If EmployeeName <> "Bill Evjen" Then
        Return
    Else
        ' Open database connection and add one week
        ' to vacation total.
    End If
End Sub
```

You construct the calling statement for this Sub procedure in the following manner:

```
RewardVacation(TextBox1.Text)
```

It is also possible to start this calling statement with the word `Call`, just as you did in VB6 and ASP 3.0, but you are no longer required to do so when programming in Visual Basic .NET.

A Function procedure works in a similar manner, except that you can return a value to your application from this procedure. The following is an example of using the Function procedure:

```
Function CalcAdd(ByVal a As Integer, ByVal b As Integer) As Integer
```

```
        Return a + b        ' Can also be written as CalcAdd = a + b
End Function
```

You construct the calling statement for this Function statement in the following manner:

```
MyNumber = CalcAdd(16, 15)
```

Note that you are passing back the value of the two numbers from the `CalcAdd` function as an integer because that is what is specified in the first line of the procedure.

Hello World in Visual Basic .NET

Listing 2-1 shows you a traditional *Hello World!* ASP.NET program that is written in Visual Basic .NET.

Listing 2-1: Hello World Program in Visual Basic .NET

```
<%@ Import Namespace="System.Data" %>
<%@ Import NameSpace="System.Data.SqlClient" %>

<html>
  <head>
    <title>Hello World in Visual Basic .NET</title>

    <script language=VB runat=server>
        Sub Page_Load(Sender As Object, E As EventArgs)
            If Not Page.IsPostBack Then
            Dim Conn As SqlConnection
            Dim Cmd As SqlCommand
            Dim SqlDR As SqlDataReader

            Conn = New SqlConnection("server=localhost;uid=sa;pwd=;
                                     database=HelloWorld")
            Conn.Open()
            Cmd = New SqlCommand("Select * from HelloWorldOutput", Conn
)
            SqlDR = Cmd.ExecuteReader()

            'Text from field says: "Hello From SQL!"
            While SqlDR.Read()
                Label1.Text = (SqlDR.Item("FirstColumn"))
            End While

            SqlDR.Close()
            Conn.Close()
          End If
        End Sub

        Sub Button1_Click(Sender As Object, E As EventArgs)
            Label1.Text = "Wrong Button!"
        End Sub
```

```
            Sub Button2_Click(Sender As Object, E As EventArgs)
                Label1.Text = "<b>Hello World!</b>"
            End Sub
        </script>

    </head>
    <body>

        <form id="Form1" method="post" runat="server">
          <p>
          <font face=Verdana size=2>
          <b>Press one of the buttons to get <i>Hello World</i>!</b>
          </font>
          </p><p>
          <asp:Button id=Button1 runat="server"
          Text="Button #1" onclick="Button1_Click" /> 
          <asp:Button id=Button2 runat="server" Text="Button #2"
          onclick="Button2_Click" />
          </p><p>
          <asp:Label id=Label1 runat="server"></asp:Label>
          </p>
        </form>

    </body>
</html>
```

This little Hello World! program first connects to SQL to pull out the string `Hello from SQL!` and puts that string of text into the Label1 Web control. Then based upon different button click events, it changes the text of the label control. If the user clicks Button #2, the label's text changes to `Hello World!`.

C#

The C# language (pronounced *c-sharp*) is a new language. The .NET. Framework is built on the C# language; there are literally millions of lines of C# code within the .NET Framework. If people were voting on the coolest .NET language, C# would probably be the winner. If there is one language making the biggest buzz, this is it.

What is all the hubbub about? C# is a new language in the C/C++ family, and it is quite simple to use compared to other programming languages. Many people, looking at the language for the first time, say that it looks a lot like Java; but all C-syntax languages look similar and are built using the same underlying principles. C# is no different.

C# is another true OO language that is simple, easy to use, modern, type safe, and not too verbose. Like the other languages of the .NET Framework that target the CLR, C# can take full advantage of everything that the framework has to offer. C# also has greatly improved upon the features of the other languages in the C family, such as versioning, events, type safety, and garbage collection.

Although not meant to be a complete reference to C#, the following code samples give you an idea of how C# works. As you look through the code, remember that unlike Visual Basic .NET, C# is a case-sensitive language. That means that `VariableName` is quite different than `variablename`.

Declaring variables

In C#, as in the other .NET languages, you have to declare your variables before you use them. By declaring variables, you are assigning a name to a type, sometimes along with the value, before you use this name elsewhere in your application. In C# you declare variables in the following manner:

```
string FirstName;
int myNumber;
```

It is also possible to assign a value to the variable at the same time that you make your declaration:

```
string FirstName = "William";
int myNumber = 31;
```

You can declare multiple variables on the same line by using the following standard:

```
string FirstName, MiddleName, LastName;
```

In this case, you just declared three variables all of the type String.

Classes

Everything in .NET is a class. Therefore, you must understand how to construct a class in C#. The following code shows you how to build a class in C#.

```
[ public | protected | internal | protected internal | private ]
[ abstract | sealed ] Class name[: classname | interfacename ]
{
    [ statements ]
}
```

To derive from another class in C#, you use the semicolon and then the class name of the class you wish to derive from. In Visual Basic .NET, you use the `Inherits` or `Implements` keywords. This is another example (C# programmers would glowingly point out) where C# is a less verbose language.

```
class FirstClass : SecondClass
{
    ... class details ...
}
```

Take a look at some of the options available for building your classes. Table 2-3 describes each of the modifiers that precede the class name. Note that all the modifiers are optional.

TABLE 2-3 Modifier Definitions for a Class in C#

Modifier	Description
public	Makes the class publicly accessible. `Public` classes have no restrictions.
Protected	Makes the class available only to the containing class and any derived class.
Internal	Makes the class available only to the application where it was declared. This is equivalent to the `Friend` modifier in Visual Basic .NET.
protected internal	This is a combination of the `protected` and `internal` modifiers. `Protected internal` makes the class available only to the containing class and any derived class that is also contained within the same application. This is equivalent to the `Protected Friend` modifier in Visual Basic .NET.
private	Makes the class available only within the file where it was declared.
Abstract	Forces the class to inherit other classes. This is equivalent to the `MustInherit` modifier in Visual Basic .NET.
sealed	Makes the class not inheritable to other classes. Equivalent to the `NotInheritable` in Visual Basic .NET.

Here's an example of a class in C#:

```
private class VacationNotification
{
     // Coding statements go here
}
```

Methods

In C#, you must define all your executable code within a procedure, also known as a function. Visual Basic .NET has two methods of writing out a procedure, by `Sub` or `Function`. In Visual Basic .NET, Sub procedures can perform some actions through code, but a Function can also return a value. In C#, there is only one way to perform a procedure, and it doesn't make any difference whether you return a value by the code contained within this procedure. In C#, you specify the type that is returned from the function. You use the keyword `void` to specify a case in which nothing is returned. A procedure in C# is written in the following syntax:

```
[ public | protected | internal | protected internal | private | static |
   virtual | override | abstract | extern ]
```

```
[ type | void ] name ([arglist])[: interfacename ]
{
   [ statements ]
}
```

Looking over these code blocks, you will notice a number of keywords that you can use to change how your procedures behave. Table 2-4 gives you a brief description of all the available keywords to use in your procedures.

TABLE 2-4 Modifier Definitions for a Procedure in C#

Modifier	Description
public	Makes the procedure publicly accessible. public procedures have no restrictions.
protected	Makes the procedure available only to the containing class and any derived class.
internal	Makes the procedure available only to the application where it was declared. This is equivalent to the Friend modifier in Visual Basic .NET.
protected internal	This is a combination of the protected and internal modifiers. protected internal makes the procedure available only to the containing class and any derived class that is also contained within the same application. This is equivalent to the Protected Friend modifier in Visual Basic .NET.
private	Makes the procedure available only within the file where it was declared.
static	Indicates that the procedure is not associated class, but is shared. This is equivalent to the Shared modifier in Visual Basic .NET.
virtual	Indicates that the procedure can be overridden by another procedure.
override	Indicates that the procedure will override a like-named procedure in the base class. Both procedures must have both the same number of arguments and data types.
abstract	Indicates that the procedure does not contain implementation and must be inherited in another procedure.
extern	Indicates that the method is implemented externally.

To exit a procedure, you can use `return` at any point in the procedure. There is also no limit on the number of times you can place these points of exit in the procedure. Here's an example of how to use a procedure in your C# application. In this example, you are not returning a value and, therefore, are using the `void` keyword.

```
public void RewardVacation(string EmployeeName)
{
    if (EmployeeName != "Bill Evjen")
    {
        return;
    }
    else
    {
        // Open database connection and add one week
        // to vacation total.
    }
}
```

You construct the calling statement for this type of procedure in the following manner:

```
RewardVacation(TextBox1.Text);
```

The other type of procedure is one that will return a value. The only difference between the two is the word `void`. The following is an example of this type of procedure:

```
public int CalcAdd(int a, int b)
{
    return a + b;      // Can also be written as CalcAdd = a + b;
}
```

You construct the calling statement for this statement in the following manner:

```
myNumber = CalcAdd(16, 15);
```

Note that you are passing back the value of the two numbers from the `CalcAdd` function as integers because that is what is specified in the first line of the procedure with the `int` that precedes the procedure name `CalcAdd`.

Hello World! in C#

Listing 2-2 shows you a traditional Hello World! ASP.NET program that is written in C#.

Listing 2-2: Hello World Program in C#

```
<%@ Import Namespace="System.Data" %>
<%@ Import NameSpace="System.Data.SqlClient" %>

<html>
  <head>
    <title>Hello World in C#</title>

    <script language=C# runat=server>
```

```
        void Page_Load(Object Source, EventArgs E) {
      if(Page.IsPostBack==false) {
      SqlDataReader sqldr;

      SqlConnection conn = new
SqlConnection("server=localhost;uid=sa;pwd=;database=HelloWorld");
      conn.Open();
      SqlCommand cmd = new SqlCommand("Select * from
HelloWorldOutput",
                                                  conn);
      sqldr = cmd.ExecuteReader();

      //Text from field says: "Hello From SQL!"
      while (sqldr.Read())
      {
              Label1.Text = (sqldr["FirstColumn"].ToString() );
      }
      sqldr.Close();
      conn.Close();
    }
   }

   void Button1_Click(Object Sender, EventArgs E) {
      Label1.Text = "Wrong Button!";
   }

   void Button2_Click(Object Sender, EventArgs E) {
      Label1.Text = "<b>Hello World!</b>";
   }
 </script>

</head>
<body>

   <form id="Form1" method="post" runat="server">
   <p>
   <font face=Verdana size=2>
   <b>Press one of the buttons to get <i>Hello World</i>!</b>
   </font>
   </p><p>
   <asp:Button id=Button1 runat="server"
   Text="Button #1" onclick="Button1_Click" /> 
   <asp:Button id=Button2 runat="server" Text="Button #2"
   onclick="Button2_Click" />
   </p><p>
   <asp:Label id=Label1 runat="server"></asp:Label>
   </p>
  </form>
```

```
</body>
</html>
```

Figure 2-1 shows you how the code from Listing 2-2 appears in your browser. Please note that all the examples in this book are using Windows XP and that what you see might be different if you are using a different operating system.

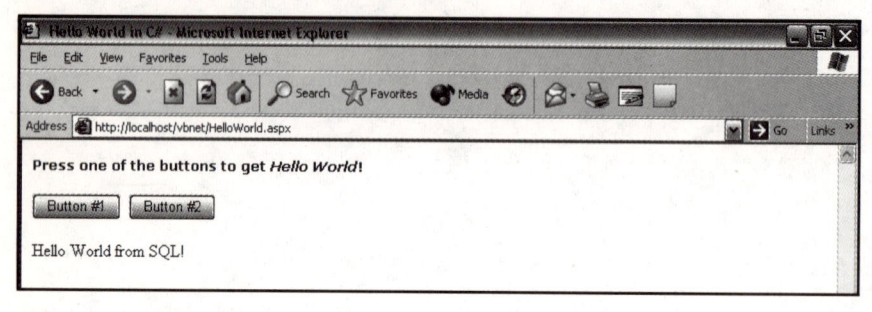

Figure 2-1: Showing the *Hello World* screen directly from SQL Server.

This Hello World! program is the same as the one that was done in Visual Basic .NET. It first connects to SQL Server to pull out the string `Hello from SQL!` and puts that string of text into the Label1 Web control. The user can change the text of the label control using different button click events. If the user clicks on Button #2, the label's text changes to `Hello World!`.

Other languages

In addition to Visual Basic .NET and C#, Microsoft includes some additional languages targeted at the .NET Framework: JScript .NET, Visual C++ .NET, and J#. You can use any of these languages to build ASP.NET applications and even XML Web services within the .NET Framework.

JScript .NET

The newer version of JScript has been changed to target the NET Framework's CLR. Although there may not be many JScript .NET programmers out there, all JScript programmers can program knowing that they have the same access to the resources of NET framework as programmers in all the other languages that are targeted to the framework.

In .NET, JScript .NET is a true object-oriented language. This newer version of JScript can have classes, types, and self-documenting code just like C#.

If you are a JScript programmer, you can adapt all the examples in this book to suit your needs and perform all the same operations. The best place to look for information on JScript .NET, as well as Visual C++ .NET or J#, is in the documentation that is provided with Visual Studio .NET.

Visual C++ .NET

C++ is still going strong, and now C++ programmers will now be able to extend their language with a Managed Extension version of the C++ language. Managed Extensions for C++ mainly encompass a set of keywords and attributes.

Unlike C++, Managed Extensions for C++ has a garbage collector. For more information on the C++ version for .NET, consult the .NET Framework SDK documentation.

J#

Officially titled Visual J# .NET, this new language is also .NET-compliant and was developed to make it easier for Java and Visual J++ developers to transition to .NET. Although, this language is not part of the initial installation package with Visual Studio .NET, you can easily install it from the Microsoft MSDN Web site at `http://msdn.microsoft.com/visualj/jsharp/beta.asp`. After it is installed, you can work with J# just as you do with any of the other .NET languages. The installation process also installs the documentation for working with this language. Also included in the installation are some tools and wizards that enable you to easily upgrade your Visual J++ projects to Visual J# .NET. As with other .NET languages, using J# allows you to work with ASP.NET, ADO.NET, and XML Web services.

Understanding Visual Studio .NET

The .NET Framework is not focused on any one particular language, but instead on the class functionality that is provided by the Base Class Libraries. These class libraries are not language specific by any means. Any language can take advantage of whatever the framework offers. Instead of having a different development environment for each of the languages, it makes more sense to have a single integrated development environment (IDE) that all the languages can share.

Visual Studio .NET is the .NET answer for a singular IDE that all the languages of .NET can use. Like NET Framework, Visual Studio .Net makes everything available to all the languages. So Visual Basic .NET uses the same coding window and debugger that is used in C#. When you build a C# ASP.NET Web Application, you use all the same tools as you do in any other language that is provided with the framework.

This also makes it easy to switch among languages.

Developers are usually smart people and, if given enough time and some resources to learn a new language, they can quickly type up a program that gives them "Hello World." What usually makes this difficult is not the syntactical difference between the languages that they know and the language that they are trying to learn. Computer languages are really quite similar in nature. What makes it difficult, in most cases, is that they must learn how to operate in a new development environment. It is difficult to learn how to save and compile code, switch views, and pull up the debugger (if one is available).

Now imagine that the same developers were given a new language (for example, Visual Basic .NET developers learning C#), but this time they could use the same IDE that they used to build their Visual Basic .NET applications. Think of how easy that would be.

Visual Studio .NET is a great multilanguage development environment and offers a complete set of tools to build Windows Forms, ASP.NET Web Applications, and XML Web services. Also Visual Studio .NET contains many technologies and wizards that will greatly simplify the development process for you. Let's take a quick tour of Visual Studio .NET.

Start Page

The Start Page displays when you start up Visual Studio .NET. The Start Page is really the launch pad for starting or continuing any of your projects. Figure 2-2 shows the Start Page.

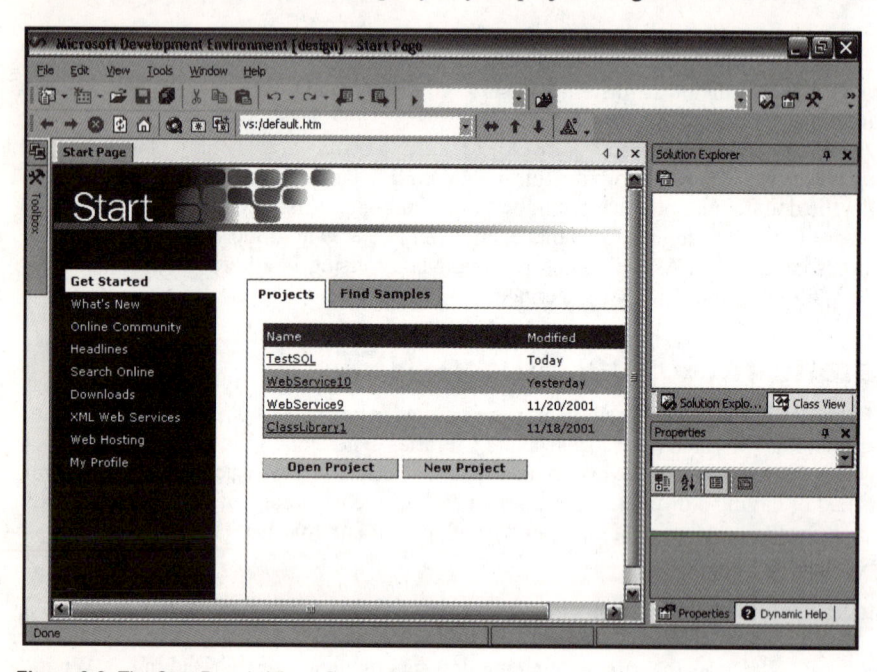

Figure 2-2: The Start Page in Visual Studio .NET.

The Start Page has a number of tabs on the left side of the window that will allow you to modify Visual Studio .NET as well as find important information. The tabs on the Start Page include: Get Started; What's New; Online Community; Headlines; Search Online; Downloads; XML Web Services; Web Hosting; and My Profile. Let's quickly go over each of these tabs in order to give you an idea of what is available.

Clicking the Get Started tab displays that page within the Start Page screen. The Get Started page has two tabs on the top. The first is Projects and the other is Find Samples. The Projects tab is where you start new projects and launch projects that you have worked on in the past. If the Projects tab is open, you see a list of the last four projects that you have worked on, as well as two buttons that enable you to either open a project or create a new project. The Find Samples tab allows you to customize a search of all the available samples from the help files. It also displays a list of online samples.

Besides the Get Started page, probably the most important page is the My Profile page. This page enables you to customize the Visual Studio .NET environment for the structured environment that you are familiar with. On this page, you can simply change the profile of the settings to Visual Basic Developer, Visual Studio Developer, or another one of the many options. It is also possible to modify the keyboard scheme, window layout, and help filter. Changing any of these settings does not block you from any of the functionality that the IDE provides. It does, however, move windows around in the IDE so that it is laid out in a more familiar manner. If you don't see a window that you need to work with for the examples in this book, click View within Visual Studio .NET. You will find a list of all the available windows that you can open or close.

> **NOTE:** Because you can change the way Visual Studio .NET presents your projects, you may find that your layout appears different from the Visual Studio .NET layouts that are shown in the illustrations in this book.

Server Explorer

One of the most valuable windows within Visual Studio .NET is the Server Explorer. This window enables you to perform a number of different functions, such as database connectivity, performance monitoring, and interacting with event logs. Figure 2-3 shows the Server Explorer.

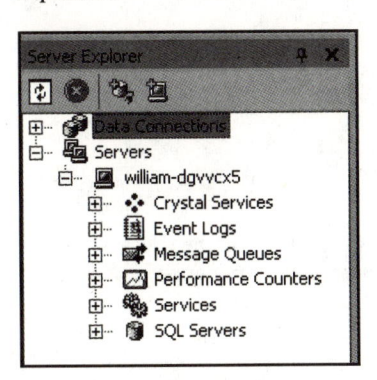

Figure 2-3: The Server Explorer.

The Server Explorer allows you to log onto remote servers and view database and system data about the server that you are viewing. With databases, a lot of the functionality that you performed with the Enterprise Manager in SQL Server is now here in the Server Explorer. Not only can you log into databases to view their data, but you can also view a server's event logs, message queues, performance counters, and the server services.

Solution Explorer

The Solution Explorer provides you with an organized view of the projects that are in your application. If you do not see the Solution Explorer open within Visual Studio .NET, click View ⇨ Solution Explorer. Figure 2-4 shows the Solution Explorer.

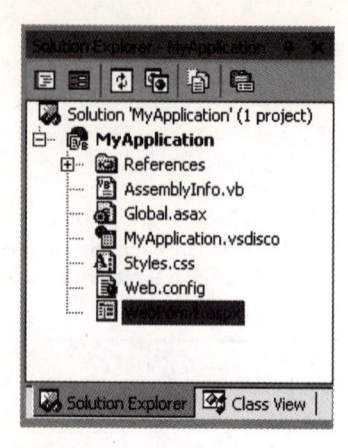

Figure 2-4: The Solution Explorer.

The toolbar within the Solution Explorer enables you to

- View code page of the selected item
- View design page of the selected item
- Refresh the state of the selected item
- Copy the Web project between Web servers
- Show all the files in the project, including the hidden files
- See Properties of the selected item

Class View

You can view the Class View window from the Start Page by clicking on the Class View tab. The Class View shows all the classes that are contained within your application. Figure 2-5 shows the Class View window.

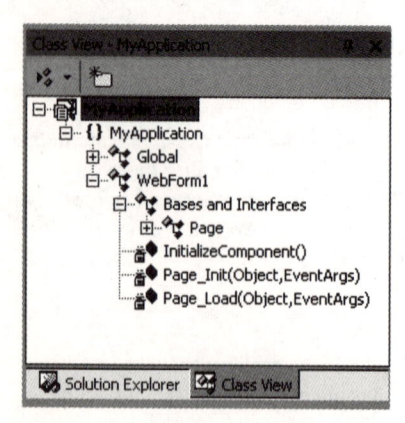

Figure 2-5: The Class View.

The Class View shows the hierarchical relationship between the classes that are in your project as well as a number of other items including *methods*, *enums*, *namespaces*, *unions*, *events*, and a number of other items. It is possible to organize the view of these items within the window.

Toolbox

The Toolbox is one of the more important windows within Visual Studio .NET when it comes time to actually build your applications. Figure 2-6 shows the Toolbox.

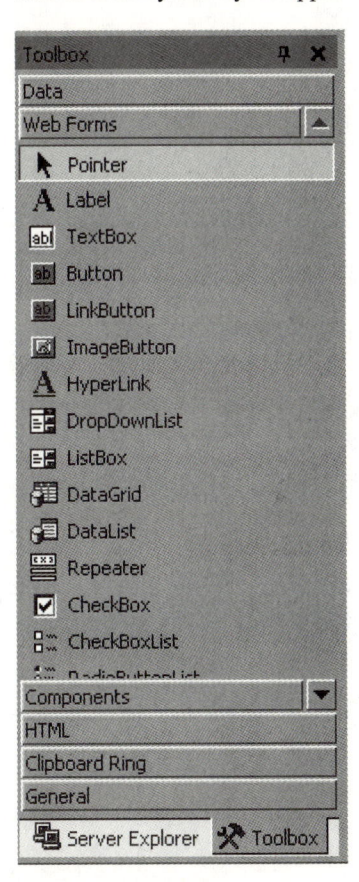

Figure 2-6: The Toolbox.

The Toolbox window enables you to specify elements that will be part of the Windows Forms or Web Forms that you are building. The Toolbox window provides a drag-and-drop means of adding elements and controls to your pages or forms. You are also able to store your code snippets within the Toolbox. In order to store code snippets, simply highlight any piece of code in the code window (discussed shortly) and drag and drop the selection onto the toolbar. This will allow you to store pieces of code that you can easily use later.

Properties window

When you wish to work with the properties of an item that is part of your application, you highlight the item and you will be presented with the highlighted item's properties within the Properties window. Figure 2-7 shows the Properties window.

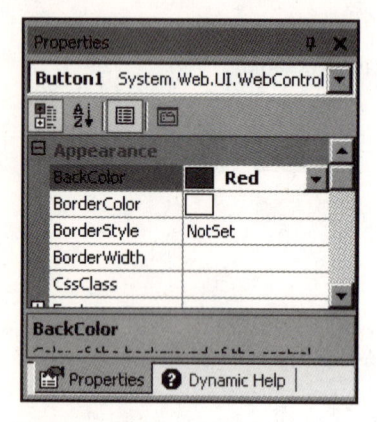

Figure 2-7: The Properties window.

The Properties window in Figure 2-7 shows the properties for a button that is on an `.aspx` page. By controlling the properties here, you are able to finely control the style and behavior of your button or any other item that you select to modify.

Dynamic Help

The Dynamic Help window shows a list of help topics. The help topics change based upon the item selected or the action being taken. Figure 2-8 shows the Dynamic Help window.

Figure 2-8: The Dynamic Help window.

The Dynamic Help window in Figure 2-8 shows the help that is displayed when you have a Button control on the page selected. After an item is selected, a list of targeted help topics displays. The topics are organized as a list of links. Clicking on one of the links in the Dynamic Help window will open the selected help topic in the Code window.

Code window

The Code window is the main window within Visual Studio .NET. This is where you build your applications. Figure 2-9 shows the Code window in the HTML mode.

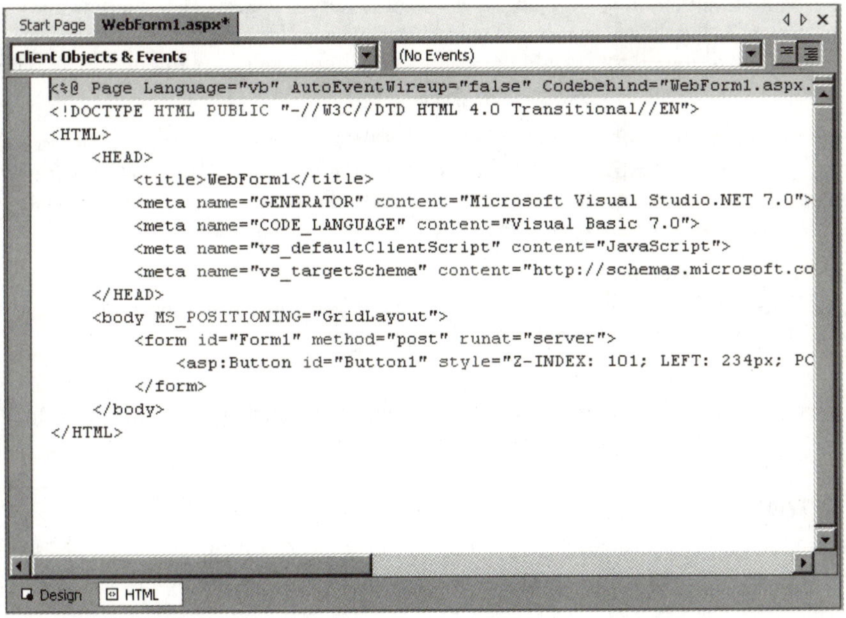

Figure 2-9: The Code window.

The Code window shows open files in either design or HTML (code) mode. Each file is represented with a tab at the top of the Code window. You can have any number of files open at the same time, and you switch between the open files by clicking on the appropriate tab.

> **TIP:** An asterisk next to the file's name means that the file is unsaved. Saving the file will cause the asterisk to disappear.

Design vs. HTML

There are two modes of viewing and building files within Visual Studio .NET. The first option is to build or view the file within the Design mode. By clicking on the Design tab at the bottom of the Code window you can see how the user views the page. You are also able to build the page by dragging-and-dropping elements directly onto the design page or form. As you do this, Visual Studio .NET automatically generates the appropriate code for you.

The other option is to view the page within the HTML mode. The HTML mode shows the code for the page. In this mode, you are able to directly modify the code to create the presentation of the page.

Introduction to ASP.NET

Among the multitude of new items included with the .NET Framework is ASP.NET, a powerful new way to build Web applications. ASP.NET is built upon the .NET Framework, which means that the entire framework is available for your ASP.NET application. Don't let the ASP.NET name fool you, however. This is *not* Active Server Pages 4.0, but a new and exciting way of populating data and controls onto Web pages on top of an outstanding new framework especially designed to work in the stateless environment of the Internet. ASP.NET is used to build Web Forms and XML Web services.

When Microsoft introduced ASP 3.0 with Windows 2000 and Internet Information Server 5.0, it was a small extension from ASP 2.0. With the introduction of ASP 3.0, there were some additional objects added (for example, `ASPError` Object). There were also some changes made to performance, as well as new commands such as `Server.Execute` and `Server.Transfer`.

ASP 3.0 used VBScript 5.0 or JScript 5.0, and this confined developers to the limited capabilities of these scripting languages.

With ASP.NET, Microsoft set aside VBScript and allowed developers to use richer languages to develop server-side code. Developers can now use any of the languages that are targeted at the .NET Framework, such as Visual Basic .NET and C#, to code their Web pages.

Web Forms

Web Forms consist of the traditional forms you can build in any HTML page. Web Forms are used whenever there is some interaction with the user on the page. Some examples include any of the form elements, such as text boxes, radio buttons, and check boxes. These elements demand interaction and, therefore, need to be encapsulated within a Web Form. With Web Forms, you can really get down to details and make each aspect of the form function as you see fit. In Chapter 6, you'll learn how to build some Web Forms that will interact with your XML Web services.

Developing Web Forms is fairly straightforward and can be done in a couple of different ways. The first is the method that most ASP programmers use: coding each of the elements straight into the code window of the page (HTML mode). The second way is more familiar to traditional Visual Basic 6.0 developers: using Visual Studio .NET to simply drag and drop the items onto the page, thereby building the form (Design mode).

Introduction to Server controls

The Server controls provided in the .NET Framework within ASP.NET are the building blocks that are required to build ASP.NET Web applications. In Chapter 6, you'll learn to build Web applications to consume your XML Web services.

There are two types of Server controls: HTML controls and Web controls. Each of these controls will be used frequently throughout any ASP.NET application.

HTML controls

By default, ASP.NET treats HTML elements as they have always been treated in the past – as literal text that is used as traditional HTML markup. But by adding a bit of code, programmers open the door to these elements and can easily manipulate them in a number of ways.

HTML Server controls map directly to their corresponding HTML elements. In order for traditional HTML elements to work as HTML Server controls, you have to add some common attributes to work against in order to change the element's functionality.

The first attribute that every HTML Server control must contain is a `runat=server` within the tag itself. The attribute `runat=server` tells the processing server that the tag will be processed on the server and is not to be considered a traditional HTML element. Also, the tag must contain an `ID` attribute in order for the server to identify it and for you to program it. The following example is an HTML control.

```
<a id="FirstLink" runat="server">Click Me!</a>
```

This `<a>` tag has been turned into an HTML control by its inclusion of the `ID` and the `runat=server` attributes.

Table 2-5 gives a brief description of each of the HTML controls at your disposal.

TABLE 2-5   HTML Controls

HTML control	Description
HTMLAnchor	Allows access to program against the `<a>` tag.
HTMLButton	Allows access to program against the `<button>` tag.
HTMLForm	Allows access to program against the `<form>` tag.
HTMLGeneric	This control allows access to HTML tags that are not represented by any HTML Server control specifically; for example, the `<span>`, `<div>`, and `<font>` tags.
HTMLImage	Allows access to program against the `<img>` tag.
HTMLInputButton	Allows access to program against the `<input type=button>`, `<input type=submit>`, and `<input type=reset>` tags.
HTMLInputCheckbox	Allows access to program against the `<input type=checkbox>` tag.
HTMLInputFile	Allows access to program against the `<input type=file>` tag.

HTML control	Description
HTMLInputHidden	Allows access to program against the `<input type=hidden>` tag.
HTMLInputRadioButton	Allows access to program against the `<input type=radio>` tag.
HTMLInputText	Allows access to program against the `<input type=text>` and `<input type=password>` tags.
HTMLSelect	Allows access to program against the `<select>` tag.
HTMLTable	Allows access to program against the `<table>` tag.
HTMLTableCell	Allows access to program against the `<td>` and `<th>` tags.
HTMLTableRow	Allows access to program against the `<tr>` tag.
HTMLTextArea	Allows access to program against the `<textarea>` tag.

The great thing about these controls is that all the normal attributes you would have in the tags are now dynamic and under your control. Very much like traditional Visual Basic controls, HTML Server controls can be programmed to dynamically change a number of attributes.

Web controls

Between Web controls and HTML Server controls, you will find Web controls to be the more sophisticated control type. They allow a higher level of functionality that is not found in HTML Server controls.

Unlike HTML Server controls, which map directly to their corresponding HTML elements, Web controls generate HTML code based upon functionality and the visiting client's browser type. With Web controls, you can decide that you want a dynamic table in your Web form. You can change the style of the table by just changing the properties of the Table control itself. By changing these properties, you can specify whether the control should output a regular table or a table with a lot of styles applied to it. For instance, the table can have an image in its background and can have a particular color for all the borders. When someone hits that particular page, ASP.NET sends the code that is appropriate for that client's browser. Each user may see different HTML code depending on what his browser supports. ASP.NET takes care of all the browser detection and the work that goes with doing this.

Not only are there Web controls for common Web form components, but also for other common (yet more advanced) Web page functionality — such as displaying data in tables, paging through information and data, and creating templates to display information. One example of a rich control that is now available in ASP.NET is the calendar control. In classic ASP, it would be a time-consuming task to develop a calendar that works in all the major browsers. ASP.NET provides you with a completely modifiable calendar that can be placed within your Web forms by just using one simple line of code.

Table 2-6 gives a brief description of each of the Web controls at your disposal.

TABLE 2-6   Web Controls

HTML Control	Description
`<asp:adrotator>`	Similar to the traditional ASP adrotator component. This control displays a specified order of images. It is also possible to set the sequence of images to be random.
`<asp:button>`	Used to perform a task or initiate an event. Used to submit forms to the server.
`<asp:calendar>`	A rich control that displays a graphical calendar and enables the user to select a date that can initiate an event on the page.
`<asp:checkbox>`	Displays a traditional HTML check box that allows users to click it on or off.
`<asp:checkboxlist>`	A group of check boxes that allow for multiple selections.
`<asp:datagrid>`	A list control that enables data-bound information to be displayed in tables. The tables can be constructed to allow for editing and sorting.
`<asp:datalist>`	A list control that allows data-bound information to be displayed. Construction of the display is done by using a customizable template.
`<asp:dropdownlist>`	Displays a traditional HTML select tag that enables users to select an item from a drop-down list of items.
`<asp:hyperlink>`	Displays a traditional HTML hyperlink that users click to perform an event (such as going to a new page).
`<asp:image>`	Displays an image.
`<asp:imagebutton>`	The same as a Button control, but allows an image to be used for the button.
`<asp:label>`	Displays text that the user cannot edit directly.
`<asp:linkbutton>`	The same as a Button control, but looks like a hyperlink.
`<asp:listbox>`	Similar to the drop-down list control, but instead of seeing just one list item, the user can see multiple list items. It also optionally allows for multiple selections.
`<asp:literal>`	Displays static text.

HTML Control	Description
`<asp:panel>`	Creates a borderless division on the form that serves as a container for other controls.
`<asp:placeholder>`	Reserves a location in the page control hierarchy for controls that are added programmatically.
`<asp:radiobutton>`	Displays a traditional HTML radio button.
`<asp:radiobuttonlist>`	Displays a group of traditional HTML radio buttons. The user can select only one choice from the group.
`<asp:repeater>`	A list control that allows for data-bound information to be displayed using any number of controls as a template.
`<asp:table>`	Displays a traditional HTML table.
`<asp:textbox>`	Displays a traditional HTML text box.
`<asp:xml>`	Displays XML documents, and allows XSL documents to transform them.

Web controls alleviate a lot of the problems that traditional ASP programmers of the past had to deal with. Now, with Web controls, you can build database-driven Internet applications with ease. You now know that even if you build for the highest common denominator (the highest level of browser available to the user), the user who is running around the Internet with Microsoft Internet Explorer 3.0 can still view the page because the controls will generate the appropriate code for the appropriate browser.

XML Web services

XML Web services can be built and consumed using the ASP.NET functionality that is provided with the .NET Framework. XML Web services are used to remotely call a specific functionality across the Internet using XML to transport the data. Chapter 3 gives an introduction to XML Web services and how your business needs to view this new application model and its uses.

Windows Forms

All the press and hype around .NET has been focused around XML Web services and ASP.NET. But there is another side of .NET that doesn't get much airplay but is still a vital part of the framework. Windows Forms is a part of the framework that enables you to develop what was traditionally a Win32 application. There are some great new features that the .NET version of a Win32 application, Windows Forms, has brought on the scene.

First of all, you can now develop Windows Forms in any of the .NET languages. Traditional Visual Basic developers now have the full object-oriented features of Visual Basic .NET at their disposal. It is also possible to fully develop these applications using C#.

In the past, if you needed to build a Web interface to an application alongside the traditional desktop application, you usually had to develop two separate applications.

Windows Forms is mentioned in this book because it is an important part of the .NET Framework. ASP.NET Web applications are not the only applications that are able to consume XML Web services. It is possible to consume XML Web services in a Windows Form as well.

Using ADO.NET

ADO.NET is not the next version of ADO 2.7, but a completely new way to access data. ADO.NET is the next evolutionary stage of ADO. ADO is a COM-based technology; ADO.NET is a brand new technology built with the stateless nature of the Internet in mind. It takes what is good from ADO.NET, and it eliminates the weaknesses that made ADO a limited technology.

An important feature of ADO.NET is that it fully supports XML data representation. XML is turning out to be the language of the Internet, and it plays an important role in the entire .NET Framework: ADO.NET is no exception. You will find XML support not only throughout the entire .NET Framework, but throughout ADO.NET as well.

ADO.NET is supported by several namespaces. Table 2-7 reviews each of the namespaces that are available in ADO.NET.

TABLE 2-7   System.Data Explained

Namespace	Description
System.Data	The root namespace that offers access to all the classes that deal with data representation. You will access the DataSet from this namespace.
System.Data.Common	This namespace contains classes shared by the .NET data providers.
System.Data.OleDb	This namespace offers all the classes that you can use to connect to any OLE-DB-compliant data source.
System.Data.SQLClient	This namespace offers access to classes that connect and manipulate SQL data. Using this class offers the fastest and best way to work with SQL 7.0 or higher.
System.Data.SQLTypes	This namespace offers classes that access native data types within SQL Server.

There will be other namespaces from third parties that will soon be available to better access a particular type of data source. For example, a System.Data.Oracle namespace is in the works for better access to Oracle databases.

In Part VII of this book, you use ADO.NET within your XML Web services.

Summary

In this chapter, you took a look at some of the important points of .NET Framework's technologies and tools. You learned about Web Forms, which is made up of XML Web services and ASP.NET. Also you took a quick look at Windows Forms and ADO.NET, giving you a well-rounded picture of the framework and everything it has to offer.

In the next chapter, you are introduced to XML Web services.

Part II

The Basics of XML Web Services

Chapter 3: Introduction to XML Web Services

Chapter 4: Building a Simple XML Web Service

Chapter 5: Consuming XML Web Services

Chapter 3
Introduction to XML Web Services

Nothing can be loved or hated unless it is first known.
Leonardo da Vinci, *Notebooks* (c. 1500)

Now that you have a general idea of the .NET platform and everything that it offers, it's time to concentrate on an important part of this platform, XML Web services. In this introductory chapter, you will gain an understanding of the basic concepts and the business of XML Web services. You will learn about some of the elements in the new version of Visual Studio .NET, and how they make it easy for you to build Web services. This introductory chapter covers the following:

- Understanding XML Web services
- The composition of XML Web services
- The business of Web services

What Is an XML Web Service?

XML Web services for ASP.NET is a new model of exposing application logic. The entire .NET Framework has been built around the Web services concept, and there are a number of tools and hidden functionality that make it quite simple to build and consume XML Web services in .NET.

One way to think of an XML Web service is that when you use a Web service, you are calling a function over *HyperText Transfer Protocol* (HTTP) or by a URL. This model of Web services is quite different from what was available in the past, but similar to some models that you are already familiar with. For example, the classic Active Server Pages model was based upon the client/server technologies. The client made a request over the Internet or HTTP; and the response, if there was one, was sent back by the same means. On the receiving end of the request, application logic or registration was applied and, in most cases, a response was sent back.

So, when the user opened his browser and typed in a URL, a request for the page was sent to a server. Then the server made note of the page being requested, and a stream of information (usually HTML) was sent back over the wire to the client. In some cases, before the server sent anything back over the wire, it went off to another location to check another server or database for some additional information. Figure 3-1 shows how this model looks visually.

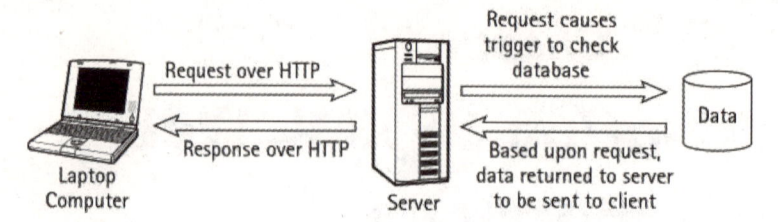

Figure 3-1: Requests/Responses over HTTP using classic ASP.

Working with XML Web services basically follows the same model, except that you are not using ASP or ASP.NET to build an interface to activate requests and receive responses over HTTP. There are many situations where you might want to expose the logic or information in a database, but you might not want to build a visual interface to that logic or information. Look at an example of this situation.

Say that you are a large wholesaler of a wide variety of widgets, and you have a number of customers that depend upon your current inventory status to allow their customers to place appropriate orders. The entire widget inventory is stored in a SQL Server database, and you want to give your customers access to this database. You could build a Web interface to this database in ASP.NET that would enable a client to log onto your system and gather the information that it needs. What if the customer doesn't want that, but instead wants to put this information in its own Web site or extranet for its own customers? This is where you can expose your database information by providing it as an XML Web service. Doing this enables the end user to utilize this information in whatever fashion it chooses. Now within its own Web page, the customer can make a call to your XML Web service and get the information in an XML format to use as it sees fit. So instead of building separate Web interfaces for different clients to access this data, you can just provide the application logic to the end users and let them deal with it in their own way.

The outstanding thing about this entire process is that it doesn't matter what system the end user employs to make this request. This is not a Microsoft-proprietary message format that is being sent to the end user. Instead, everything is being sent over standard protocols. What is happening is that this message is being sent over HTTP using SOAP, a flavor of XML. So any system that is able to consume XML over HTTP can use this model. Figure 3-2 shows an example of this.

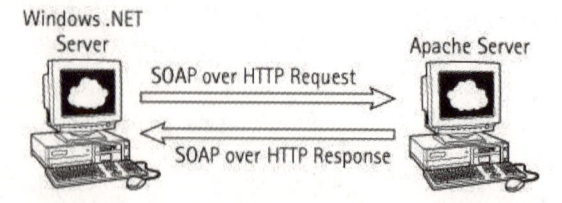

Figure 3-2: The XML Web services model: Request/Response over HTTP using SOAP.

It is true there are component technologies, already available for some time, that perform similar functions. However, these technologies, such as Distributed Component Object Model (DCOM), Remote Method Invocation (RMI), Common Object Request Broker Architecture (CORBA), and Internet Inter-ORB Protocol (IIOP) are accessed via object-model–specific protocols. The main difference between XML Web services and these component technologies is that XML Web services are accessed via standard Internet protocols such as HTTP and XML. This enables these services to be called across multiple platforms, regardless of the platform compatibility of the calling system.

Why Do You Need XML Web Services?

The Internet is constantly evolving and being used in new and exciting ways every day. In the past, the Internet was used primarily for static HTML brochure sites. Nowadays, as more people, organizations, and businesses are getting on the Internet, users realize that this medium is a great tool for collaborative and distributive applications.

Applications are moving to the Internet at an ever-increasing rate. Applications that were traditionally Win32 applications on the desktop are now being developed as applications that are browser-accessible. This new model brings many advantages to developers and the people who are in charge of implementing such software packages.

Formerly, in a large company when a new Win32 application came out, someone had to go to every desktop and install the application on every machine. Also during installation, each computer's hardware configuration had to be taken into account. Again, when it came time to upgrade the application or apply a patch, someone had to make rounds to each of the computers to make the necessary changes.

Browser-based applications are run on a server that users can interface with through their own browsers. Virtually every computer now has a browser, so the need for client-end software to run the application is never really an issue. Because the application is browser-based and is not residing on the client's computer, the client can be sure that he is accessing the latest and greatest version of the application. After the application is upgraded on the server, everyone instantaneously gains access to this upgraded version.

As more and more applications have become connected to the Internet, new means of accessing these applications have become available. For instance, salesmen who are consistently on the road find it beneficial to access a large database of contacts through either their cell phones or Pocket PCs. In this case, the end user (the salesman) has a device that is connected to the Internet. He is in an ideal situation to use application logic that was once available only to a Win32 desktop application or through a browser. Now new and exciting ways are being found to obtain that application logic.

Nowadays, as these applications are becoming more and more accessible by various means, people are requesting that the applications provide more logic and more access to data that can be spread across multiple machines as well as multiple platforms.

For instance, the traveling salesman may now need access not only to a contact's system, but also to the company's inventory system that is housed on a legacy machine. Next, the salesman may need to tie in the inventory system with the order entry system that is on a separate machine (as well as a separate platform). Has this been doable in the past? Yes it has, but with great difficulty and performance degradation, and it was usually done with proprietary formats.

An XML Web service is a new way of opening application logic and providing access to data using standard protocols that are available today. XML Web services are run across HTTP, employing the same means as general users do when they use their browsers to access Web sites. The communication vehicle is XML – the new *lingua franca* of the Internet. XML is not owned by anyone and is not proprietary to any one type of system. XML can be consumed and generated by almost any platform that is available on the market today.

So any platform that can consume XML over HTTP can now work with the XML Web services that you create on the .NET platform. XML Web services are not meant only for servers and Web sites that want to broaden their reach but also for the future line of products and devices that are going to be connected to the Internet. More and more devices and products are being developed with the Internet in mind.

XML Web Services: Present and Future

Here are some examples of what I mean when I say that various devices will be connected to the Internet to increase their functionality and, in turn, become better products.

The microwave

One example is the microwave in your kitchen. You may be wondering why a microwave might possibly need to be connected to the Internet. The microwave has pretty much remained unchanged since it was introduced, but there is always room for improvement.

The microwave of the future will be connected to the Internet. This microwave will be able to read barcodes on the packages of the items that you want to cook. Instead of reading through the instructions on the microwave dinner yourself, you hold up the bar code of the package to the microwave. The microwave scans the package and takes this bar code number to a small internal database. After finding the bar code of the frozen dinner, the microwave knows the exact time, power level, and rotation needed to cook the dinner.

But why does the microwave need to be connected to the Internet? Before long, there will certainly be new types of frozen dinners that the database of your bar-code–scanning microwave might be unable to identify because the bar codes of these new products are not in its database. If the microwave is connected to the Internet, it can send a request over the Internet using HTTP and XML to ask the manufacturer's database about an unknown bar code. The main database at the manufacturer's server would then send back the cooking instructions as an XML file to be consumed by the microwave. Upon receipt of this XML file, the microwave can cook the new product based upon the instructions contained within the file.

You can see how the microwave becomes a better product because it is connected to the Internet and, therefore, able to communicate with a remote server using XML. It could use XML Web services as the vehicle for the exchange of information between the appliance and the distant database.

Take a look at another appliance that uses XML Web services to turn itself into a better product.

The refrigerator

There was once a commercial that showed a housewife who answered the door for a refrigerator repairman. The housewife was surprised. *"I didn't call you,"* she said.

"No, your refrigerator did," the repairman replied.

The refrigerator, too, can be hooked up to the Internet, enabling it to make a monthly call to the manufacturer's Web service. The refrigerator sends along some information in the form of an XML file that reports on the status of the refrigerator. It can report on the status of the motor, indicating for example, whether it is running too hot. Then the Web service on the manufacturer's end receives and consumes the XML information coming over the HTTP wire and makes the necessary notifications based upon the information received.

Note that the refrigerator does not need to be running Windows XP or anything similar, but only needs to be able to send XML over HTTP to report on its status.

These are a couple of examples of what the future will hold, but let's take a look at an example of how you could use an XML Web service in today's world of ASP.NET applications.

A calendar

A digital calendar is important to keep track of appointments and day-to-day activities. To keep track of multiple individuals, often a group calendar makes the most sense and is the most convenient. How is this accomplished, however, if each of the individuals is in a different location?

Using XML Web services, you can have a group calendar that stays constantly updated. When an entry is added to the individual calendar of one group member, that addition is placed on each of the other calendars, thereby keeping a consistent group calendar for each of the participants despite their different locations.

The multifunctional Web site

Imagine that you are in charge of a new Web site that allows a client to check on the status of any used car by just entering the Vehicle Identification Number (VIN) number of the car. Not only will you provide the client with a car history of repairs and accidents, but you will also offer him loan proposals from three banks, as well as insurance proposals from three other companies.

This might seems like a daunting task after you start thinking about it. First of all, it seems quite impractical to house all that data from so many different companies. If you are hosting all that information on internal servers, not only would the data take up an enormous amount of space, but also it would be a huge task to constantly update the information.

This is actually a great opportunity to build your site around the concept of XML Web services. Instead of gathering all that data and working with it yourself, you can let others take care of all that data for you. Let the others work on the things that they are best at. Just have them provide you with the information that you need. In this situation, when the client clicks the Submit button (after he has entered the VIN number of the car that he is thinking of buying), you can send off requests to all the Web services that you need.

First, you send off requests (containing the VIN number within XML) to the Web services of a number of loan institutions, insurance companies, and any Web services that will give you the information on the car's history. When you get back this information, you can decipher the XML and use it to give a report to the client on the car he is thinking of buying.

The goal when using XML Web services within your Web applications is to concentrate solely on your core business and utilize third-party XML Web services to take care of content and functionality that is not part of your core business offerings. For instance, if you are providing breaking news on your homepage, it may not be advantageous to constantly update this information or assign your own people to gather news for your homepage. Instead, you can rely on a third party to provide your homepage with the latest news. You could call a third-party XML Web service that is especially designed to provide the news content that you are looking for and just call that information to its exposed XML Web service. You can then pull a set of news items in the form of XML and present it in your Web page in any manner that you'd like.

On the other end, you may have a specific functionality or service offering that you want to expose to the public or a set of clients. You may charge for this service or you may not. It really depends upon your business model. For instance, if you are a training organization, you may want to expose all your course offerings as an XML Web service to the public. Other sites or company Intranets could then put these class listings on their sites in their own formats.

Composition of XML Web Services

You now have some general idea of how you might use XML Web services. Visual Studio .NET and the Microsoft .NET platform make building and consuming XML Web services very easy. The next few chapters cover specifically how to build and consume these services within ASP.NET and your Windows Forms applications. Whether you are building or consuming XML Web services, you first need to understand the structure of XML Web services so that your first venture into this new application model will be successful.

Understanding a few pillars of XML Web services development makes this job a lot easier. Not all these specifications or technologies that are used to build and consume XML Web services are required, but you should review and understand everything before you start using XML Web services within any of your applications. Building XML Web services within the .NET environment gives you the following:

- An industry-standard way to represent data
- A way to transfer data in a common message format
- A way to describe an XML Web service to potential consumers
- A path to discovery of XML Web services on remote servers and local machines
- A way to find XML Web services

Now take a look at how each of these functions plays a role in XML Web services.

Data representation in XML Web services

Just as XML is tightly integrated throughout the .NET Framework, XML is the key technology used in Web services. Most of the Web services that are available today use XML for data representation as well as XML Schemas to describe data types. As you will see, using XML just makes sense.

Introducing XML

XML stands for e*Xtensible Markup Language* and, in its short lifetime, it has become the Internet standard in data representation.

XML came into its own when the W3C (*The World Wide Web Consortium*) realized that it needed to develop a markup language to represent data that could be used and consumed regardless of the platform. In 1998, XML came into being and was quickly hailed as the solution for data transfer across varying systems. Not only could XML be transported over HTTP, but it could also go through firewalls — making this markup language quite fluid.

XML Web services, as its name suggests, is highly dependent upon XML. Data is what makes the Internet world go around, and XML is an elementary method for representing and transporting data.

In the past, one way to package data for transport was to place the data within a comma-, tab- or pipe-delimited text file. Listing 3-1 shows an example of this:

Listing 3-1: An example of a pipe-delimited text file

```
Bill|Evjen|Programmer|03/08/1998|Seattle, Washington|2
```

These kinds of data representations are in use today. The individual pieces of data are separated by pipes, commas, tabs, or any other characters you want to use. Looking at this collection of items, it is hard to tell what the data represents. You might be able to get a better idea based upon the filename, but the meaning of the date and the number 2 is not evident.

On the other hand, XML relates data in a self-describing manner so that any user, technical or otherwise, can decipher the data. Listing 3-2 shows how the same piece of data is represented using XML:

Listing 3-2: XML file example

```xml
<?xml version="1.0" encoding="UTF-8" ?>
<Employee>
   <FirstName>Bill</FirstName>
   <LastName>Evjen</LastName>
   <JobTitle>Programmer</JobTitle>
   <StartDate>03/08/1998</StartDate>
   <WorkLocation>Seattle, Washington</WorkLocation>
   <NumDependents>2</NumDependents>
</Employee>
```

You can now tell, by just looking at the data in the file, what the data items mean and how they relate to one another. The data is laid out in such a simple format that it is quite possible for even a nontechnical person to understand the data.

After looking at this XML file, you may have noticed how similar XML is to HTML. Both markup languages are related, but HTML is used to markup text for presentation purposes; XML is used to mark up text for data representation purposes.

Both XML and HMTL have their roots in the Standard Generalized Markup Language (SGML), which was created in 1986. SGML is a more complex markup language that was also used for data representation. With the explosion of the Internet, the W3C realized that it needed a universal way to represent data that would be easier to use than SGML. That realization brought forth XML.

Advantages of using XML for data representation

XML has a distinct advantage over other forms of data representation. This markup language has become one of the most talked about languages on the Internet today. The following list presents some of the reasons XML has become as popular as it is today:

- XML is easy to read and understand.
- There are a large number of platforms that support XML and are able to manage it through an even larger set of tools that are available for XML data reading, writing, and manipulation.
- XML can be used across open standards that are available today.
- XML allows developers to create their own data definitions and models of representation.
- Because a large number of XML tools are available, XML is simpler to use than binary formats when sending complex data structures.

Understanding XML syntax

As I have stated, XML is a text-based markup language that is used to represent data as it moves from one platform to the next or from one application to another. XML was specifically designed to be easy to use and even easier to understand. In Listing 3-3, you take a look at another XML file and examine how the file is composed.

Listing 3-3: Painters.xml

```
<?xml version="1.0" encoding="UTF-8" ?>
<Artists>
   <Painter name="Vasily Kandinsky">
      <Painting>
         <Title>Composition No. 218</Title>
         <Year>1919</Year>
      </Painting>
   </Painter>
   <Painter name="Pavel Filonov">
      <Painting>
```

```
            <Title>Formula of Spring</Title>
            <Year>1929</Year>
        </Painting>
    </Painter>
    <Painter name="Pyotr Konchalovsky">
        <Painting>
            <Title>Sorrento Garden</Title>
            <Year>1924</Year>
        </Painting>
    </Painter>
</Artists>
```

XML was developed so that XML files would be easy to read and the data contained in the file would be easy to understand. Looking at the XML file in Listing 3-3, you can tell that it is data about painters and their paintings. It would definitely be more difficult to understand this data if the XML tags were not there.

Even though XML looks quite similar to HTML, the syntactical rules are different. HTML is a forgiving markup language. In HTML, if you don't have a closing tag here or there, sometimes the browsers are forgiving and render the page regardless. But XML is a different story. You have to be quite diligent to make sure that your XML code is compliant to the standards that are in place. Your XML documents need to be well-defined.

The very first line of the document is the XML declaration:

```
<?xml version="1.0" encoding="UTF-8" ?>
```

The `xml` word is a reserved keyword. You are specifying that this is an XML document and that you are running this document under version 1.0. This attribute will become more meaningful as future versions of XML are released. For the encoding type, you are assigning `UTF-8` as your specified choice. This is the default setting if none is specified.

In this example (Listing 3-3), your XML file uses angle brackets for building descriptive tags that are wrapped around the data that they are representing. You need to understand some important facts about the tags and how to use them within an XML document.

After your declaration, you have the root XML tag `<Artists>`. There can only be one root tag per XML document. You can tell by the file that the `<Artists>` tag is a container for a collection of painters in your document. The next sets of tags are the `<Painter>` tags. You can have as many of these sets of tags in the document as you wish. This tag is referred to as the child element. Notice that the `<Painter>` tag has an attribute associated with it, the name attribute. Contained within the `<Painter>` tag is the `<Painting>` element that contains descriptions of particular paintings from that particular painter.

Note, there are sets of rules that are used in the structure of the data. This makes it easy to pass data around, because the system that receives this file will understand what to do with it as long as it understands XML. To make everything work and enable XML documents to be easily understood by applications and systems, you need to follow certain XML grammar rules when composing your XML files. Here are some of the basic rules:

1. All tags must have an opening and closing tag. Therefore, unlike HTML where you can use single tags such as `<br>` or `<hr>` and others, in XML you always need to have a closing tag.

   For example:

   ```
   <Movie>Office Space</Movie>
   ```

2. All elements need to be properly nested. Therefore, if you open tag 1 and then tag 2, you cannot close tag 1 till you close tag 2.

   This code snippet shows the *incorrect* nesting of elements:

   ```
   <Cinema>
      <Movie>
      Office Space
      </Cinema>
   </Movie>
   ```

   This snippet shows the *correct* nesting:

   ```
   <Cinema>
      <Movie>Office Space</Movie>
   </Cinema>
   ```

3. All attribute values must be enclosed within quotation marks. Here's an example:

   ```
   <Book Title="Visual Basic .NET Bible">
   ```

4. XML is case-sensitive. Therefore, `<Book>` is not the same as `<book>`.

This was a really quick introduction to XML, but it is important to understand XML if you plan to work with XML Web services and even with the .NET Framework as a whole. XML is basically baked into the entire Framework, and you find it around every corner. So start breathing XML.

> **CROSS-REFERENCE:** For more detail on the basics of XML, see Appendix B.

XML Namespaces

Because developers are creating their own tag names in XML, using namespaces to define particular elements as their own is an important step. Namespaces are important because, if you are using two XML files within your application, there is a chance that the two files are using some of the same tags. Even though the tags have the same name, they might have different meanings. For instance, compare the two XML files in Listings 3-4 and 3-5.

Listing 3-4: Book.xml

```xml
<?xml version="1.0" encoding="UTF-8" ?>
<Book>
   <Title>Visual Basic .NET Bible</Title>
   <Price>44.99</Price>
   <Year>2002</Year>
```

```
<Book>
```

Now take a look at another XML file. You should be able to see right away where the problem lies.

Listing 3-5: Author.xml

```
<?xml version="1.0" encoding="UTF-8" ?>
<Author>
    <Title>Mr.</Title>
    <FirstName>Bill</FirstName>
    <LastName>Evjen</LastName>
<Author>
```

You should be able to see that there is a conflict with the `<Title>` tag. If you are using both of these XML files, you might be able to tell the difference between the tags by just glancing at them; but computers are unable to decipher the difference between the two tags with the same name.

The answer to this problem is to give the tag an identifier that enables the computer to tell the difference between the two tags. Do this is by using the XML namespace attribute, `xmlns`. Listing 3-6 shows you how you would differentiate between these two XML files by using XML namespaces.

Listing 3-6: Revised Book.xml using an XML Namespace

```
<?xml version="1.0" encoding="UTF-8" ?>
<Book xmlns="http://www.xmlws101.com/xmlns/book">
    <Title>Visual Basic .NET Bible</Title>
    <Price>44.99</Price>
    <Year>2002</Year>
<Book>
```

Notice that you now have added the XML namespace attribute to your root element `<Book>`. Now look at the second file (Listing 3-7).

Listing 3-7: Revised Author.xml using an XML Namespace

```
<?xml version="1.0" encoding="UTF-8" ?>
<Author xmlns="http://www.xmlws101.com/xmlns/author">
    <Title>Mr.</Title>
    <FirstName>Bill</FirstName>
    <LastName>Evjen</LastName>
<Author>
```

In this example, the `<Author>` element contains an XML namespace that uniquely identifies this XML tag and all the other tags that are contained within it. Note that you could have put an XML namespace directly in the `<Title>` tag if you wished. By putting the `xmlns` attribute in the root element, not only did you uniquely identify the root element, but you also identified all the child elements contained within the root element.

The value of the `xmlns` attribute is the *Universal Resource Identifier* (URI). It is not required that the URI be a Web site URL as shown in the example, but this is usually a good idea. The URI can be anything that you wish it to be. For example, it could just as easily be written as `xmlns="myData"` or `xmlns="12345"`. But with this kind of URI, you are not guaranteed any uniqueness, as another URI in another file elsewhere may use the same value. Therefore, it is common practice to use a URL, and this practice serves two purposes. First, it is guaranteed to be unique. A URL is unique, and using it as your URI ensures that your URI won't conflict with any other. The other advantage to using a URL as the URI is that it also identifies where the data originated.

You don't have to point to an actual file. In fact, it is usually better not to do that, but instead to use something like the following:

```
xmlns="http://www.xmlws101.com/[Namespace Name]"
```

If the XML file has an associated XSD file, another option is to point to this file. The XSD file defines the schema of the XML file. (XML schemas will be covered in the following section.)

The style of XML namespaces that you have used thus far is referred to as a *default namespace*. The other type of XML namespaces that is available for your use is a *qualified namespace*. To understand why you need another type of XML namespace, take a look at the example in Listing 3-8.

Listing 3-8: Author.xml using multiple XML namespaces

```
<?xml version="1.0" encoding="UTF-8" ?>
<Author xmlns="http://www.firstserver.com/xmlns/author">
   <Title xmlns="http://www.secondserver.com/title">Mr.</Title>
   <FirstName xmlns="http://www.thirdserver.com/fn">Bill</FirstName>
   <LastName xmlns="http://www.thirdserver.com/ln">Evjen</LastName>
<Author>
```

As you can see in this example, you used a number of different XML namespaces to identify your tags. First of all, your `<Author>` tag is associated with the XML namespace from the first server. The `<Title>` tag is associated with the second server, and the `<FirstName>` and `<LastName>` tags are associated with the third server. XML allows you to associate your tags with more than one namespace throughout your document.

The problem is that you might have hundreds or thousands of nodes within your XML document and, if one of the namespaces that is repeated throughout the document changes, you have a lot of changes to make throughout the document.

Using qualified namespaces enables you to construct the XML document so that if you need to make a change to a namespace that is used throughout the document, you only have to do it in one spot. The change will be reflected throughout the document. Take a look at Listing 3-9 to see an XML document that uses qualified namespaces.

Listing 3-9: Author.xml using qualified XML namespaces

```
<?xml version="1.0" encoding="UTF-8" ?>
<AuthorNames:Author
```

```
  xmlns:AuthorNames="http://www.firstserver.com/xmlns/author"
  xmlns:AuthorDetails="http://www.secondserver.com/xmlns/details">
    <AuthorNames:Title>Mr.</Title>
    <AuthorNames:FirstName>Bill</FirstName>
    <AuthorNames:LastName>Evjen</LastName>
    <AuthorDetails:Book>Visual Basic .NET Bible</Book>
<AuthorNames:Author>
```

In this document, you use an explicit declaration of the namespace. Explicit declarations of namespace prefixes use attribute names beginning with `xmlns:` followed by the prefix. So in the first node, you have explicitly declared two namespaces that you use later in the document.

```
xmlns:AuthorNames="http://www.firstserver.com/xmlns/author"
xmlns:AuthorDetails="http://www.secondserver.com/xmlns/details"
```

Notice that the declaration name follows a colon after `xmlns`. In this example, you declare two qualified namespaces: `AuthorNames` and `AuthorDetails`. Later, when you want to associate an element with one of these explicit declarations, you can use the shorthand (or prefix) to substitute for the full namespace. In your document, you do this by using `<AuthorNames:LastName>` and `<AuthorDetails:Book>`.

XML schemas

XML schemas, or XSD files, are used to define valid combinations of elements, attributes, and types that appear in a particular XML document. The importance of the XML Schema definition language (XSD) is to ensure that documents are valid and well-formed according to the rules that are laid out in the schema.

An XSD schema document is comprised of a top-level schema element. In the XSD file, you must declare the XML schema namespace after the XML document declaration.

```
<xsd:schema xmlns:xsd="http://www.w3.org/2001/XMLSchema">
```

The schema element is comprised of type definitions, as well as attribute and element declarations. Attributes and elements are the building blocks of XSD schemas. When you build your XSD schemas, you first classify the data types that you are going to assign to defined attributes and elements. *Elements* are the nodes that are used to describe your data. *Attributes* are the properties of the element. Look at this example:

```
<movie format="NTSC">Lawrence of Arabia</movie>
```

In this example, `<movie>` is the element and `format` is the attribute.

As I said earlier, elements are used to describe your data. In the preceding example, the element is informing you that the data contained within the nodes is a movie. There are two ways to declare your elements within XSD schemas. The first is by declaring your element as a *simple-type*. Simple-type definitions are used to put restrictions on the content of elements or attributes. For instance, you could construct an `<age>` element and force the element to always contain an integer. You specify that in your XSD file by doing the following:

```
<xsd:element name="age" type="xs:integer" />
```

In this example, you declare an element named `age` and force the type to be an integer. Therefore, the following code is valid:

```
<age>31</age>
```

That would also mean that by using the following code, you cause your XML document to be invalid:

```
<age>Thirty-one</age>
```

Attributes are constructed in a similar manner. Within your XSD file, you declare an attribute in the following manner:

```
<xsd:element name="movie">
   <xsd:complexType>
      <xsd:attribute name="format" type="xs:string" />
   </xsd:complexType>
</xsd:element>
```

With this type of construction, you can use your element `<movie>` with your newly declared attribute format.

```
<movie format="PAL">Close Encounters of the Third Kind</movie>
```

If you are going to expand the declaration of any element by declaring any associated attributes or child elements, you must declare a *complex type*. Complex types are element definitions that can contain other elements, attributes, and groups.

Before you create another complex type example, take a look at the simple XML document shown in Listing 3-10. This is the same document that you used in Listing 3-2, except you add an attribute to the `<Employee>` element. You also add a namespace to the main element that points to your soon-to-be created XML schema for this file.

Listing 3-10: Employee.xml

```
<?xml version="1.0" encoding="UTF-8" ?>
<Employee Sex="M" xmlns="http://www.ourserver.com/Employee.xsd">
   <FirstName>Bill</FirstName>
   <LastName>Evjen</LastName>
   <JobTitle>Programmer</JobTitle>
   <StartDate>03/08/1998</StartDate>
   <WorkLocation>Seattle, Washington</WorkLocation>
   <NumDependents>2</NumDependents>
</Employee>
```

Now take a look at how you construct the XSD file for this XML file (Listing 3-11).

Listing 3-11: XSD schema Employee.xsd based on Employee.xml

```
<?xml version=""1.0"" encoding=""UTF-8"" ?>
<xsd:schema xmlns:xsd="http://www.w3.org/2001/XMLSchema"">
   <xsd:element name=""Employee"">
      <xsd:complexType>
```

```
        <xsd:sequence>
          <xsd:element name=""FirstName"" type=""xsd:string"" />
          <xsd:element name="LastName" type="xsd:string" />
          <xsd:element name="JobTitle" type="xsd:string" />
          <xsd:element name="StartDate" type="xsd:string" />
          <xsd:element name="WorkLocation" type="xsd:string" />
          <xsd:element name="NumDependents" type="xsd:string" />
        </xsd:sequence>
        <xsd:attribute name="Sex" type="xsd:string" />
      </xsd:complexType>
    </xsd:element>
</xsd:schema>
```

The first line is your XML declaration node. You are declaring the version and encoding of your XML document. The next line is the root element and the schema declaration line where you include the namespace.

You then declare the only element that you are going to allow in the XML file, the `<Employee>` element. Because this element contains an attribute and a number of child elements, you need to use a complex type declaration. You start your complex type declaration with an assigned node and set all the element declarations in a specified sequence. After the sequence of elements, you declare one attribute and then close the complex type.

After this, the `Employee.xsd` file can validate the `Employee.xml` file, making sure that it follows the XML grammar rules that you have laid out. You will later find that XML schemas are an important part of XML Web services. Schemas allow you to provide valid results when you use XML to describe such items as data, service contracts, SOAP messages, and other XML-related items.

Creating an XML file in Visual Studio .NET

Before you go on to the other pillars of XML Web services, take a quick look at how to create and construct an XML file in Visual Studio .NET.

Not only is XML spread throughout the .NET Framework, it is also strongly supported in Visual Studio .NET. Visual Studio .NET contains an XML designer to quickly and efficiently build XML documents. Visual Studio .NET provides syntax checking so you can quickly tell if your XML documents are well-formed and valid. Visual Studio .NET also provides IntelliSense, which drops down valid subelements and attributes to enable you to build your documents quickly.

Take a look at how you can build an XML document within Visual Studio .NET:

1. First, open up a new ASP.NET Web Application. You do this by clicking the New Project button on the Start Page.
2. When you open this new Web application, right-click on the Project in the Solution Explorer.
3. Select Add ⇨ Add New Item.

4. You are now presented with the Add New Item dialog box. Select the XML file template. Name the file and select Open.

5. Now you need to start your XML file by typing the root node of your document. Type **<Employees>** and you see that after you type in the closing bracket, the XML designer automatically adds a closing </Employee> tag for you.

    Add some line spaces between the tags so that you can add some elements. Type in **<Employee>** for a single employee that you are adding to the XML document and then type in **<FirstName>** and add your first name between the tags.

6. Add **<LastName>** next and add your last name between the tags.

Now you have created a very basic XML file that has very limited information. Your XML file should look like the following:

```xml
<?xml version="1.0" encoding="utf-8" ?>
<Employees>
 <Employee>
   <FirstName>Bill</FirstName>
   <LastName>Evjen</LastName>
 </Employee>
</Employees>
```

If you have more records to add to the file, you can just continue to type in the elements and the data, but this could take a while. With Visual Studio .NET, it is quite simple to add more records to an XML file.

Click the data tab at the bottom of the designer and the program pulls up a screen that is quite similar to some database screens that you see in SQL Server or in Access. In the data mode, you simply enter the data directly into the text fields.

TIP: To quickly navigate between the fields in the data mode of the XML designer, just use the Tab key.

After you have entered a couple of other data items into your XML document, you might want to create an XML Schema for this document. This is also quite simple in Visual Studio .NET.

To create an XML Schema in Visual Studio .NET, simply click the XML menu and choose Create Schema. Visual Studio .NET automatically creates the XML Schema for you. Notice that a new file was created for you in the Solution Explorer. The XSD file that was created has the same name as the XML file from which you built the schema, but has an `.xsd` extension.

As you look at the original XML file, note that Visual Studio .NET added a namespace to your document. If you were following along in the example, the root element of your XML document should now include an XML namespace attribute as shown here:

```xml
<Employees xmlns="http://tempuri.org/XMLFile1.xsd">
```

This new namespace points to the newly created XSD file, `XMLFile1.xsd`. Take a look at the XSD file in Listing 3-12 and see what Visual Studio .NET created for you. Here is the IDE-created schema that was built from your XML document:

Listing 3-12: XSD schema XMLFile1.xsd based on XMLFile1.xml

```xml
<?xml version="1.0" ?>
<xs:schema id="Employees"
  targetNamespace="http://tempuri.org/XMLFile1.xsd"
  xmlns:mstns="http://tempuri.org/XMLFile1.xsd"
  xmlns="http://tempuri.org/XMLFile1.xsd"
  xmlns:xs="http://www.w3.org/2001/XMLSchema"
  xmlns:msdata="urn:schemas-microsoft-com:xml-msdata"
  attributeFormDefault="qualified" elementFormDefault="qualified">
    <xs:element name="Employees" msdata:IsDataSet="true"
  msdata:EnforceConstraints="False">
        <xs:complexType>
            <xs:choice maxOccurs="unbounded">
                <xs:element name="Employee">
                    <xs:complexType>
                        <xs:sequence>
                            <xs:element name="FirstName" type="xs:string"
                              minOccurs="0" />
                            <xs:element name="LastName" type="xs:string"
                              minOccurs="0" />
                        </xs:sequence>
                    </xs:complexType>
                </xs:element>
            </xs:choice>
        </xs:complexType>
    </xs:element>
</xs:schema>
```

Pretty outstanding and quite quick! You can see this XML code in the XSD file after you click the XML tab at the bottom of the designer. The XSD file opens up in the DataSet view. In this mode, you can work with your XSD file visually.

In the DataSet mode, you can add another element to the file. In the next available row, enter **EmployeeID** and tab to the next field. You are presented with a drop-down list of available types (see Figure 3-3). For your purposes, choose integer. After you have entered this information, click again on the XML tab at the bottom of the designer and notice that the newly added element has been added to the code and that the type you chose for the element is also specified.

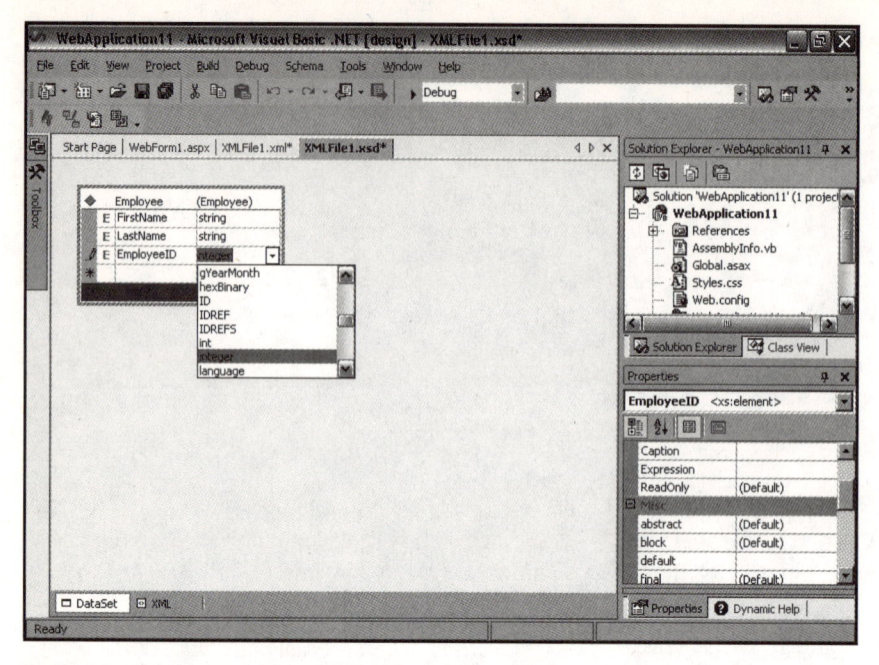

Figure 3-3: Visually creating your XSD file in Visual Studio .NET.

There is a reason for all this discussion about XML in the beginning of this book. XML is baked into the .NET Framework and is used throughout XML Web services. It is important to know the structure of XML and understand how data is packaged and sent when your XML Web service goes into action.

> **NOTE:** Even though I introduce you to many of the high points of XML in this book, for complete information on XML and XML schemas, be sure to visit the World Wide Web Consortium at www.w3c.com or take a look at the *XML Bible, 2nd Edition*, by Elliotte Rusty Harold, published by Hungry Minds, Inc.

Communicating data from an XML Web service

XML Web services (as the name implies) uses XML for data representation. This is done so that different systems and applications can quickly and easily share and consume this data. XML is a widely accepted way to represent data. XML is based upon standards, and any application or system that can take hold of an XML file and use it in some fashion is a candidate for dealing with an XML Web service.

To take advantage of XML's wide-spread acceptance, you need to be able to port XML data from point A to point B. XML Web services use HTTP, and occasionally SMTP, to transport XML data from one point to another. Study Figure 3-4 to understand how this works:

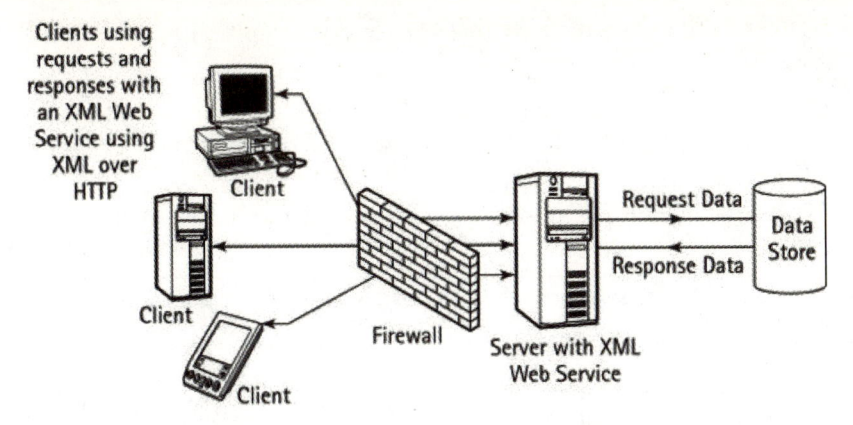

Figure 3-4: Various clients communicating with an XML Web service through a firewall using XML over HTTP.

One of the great advantages of XML Web services is that it transports XML data over HTTP. By transporting XML data in this manner, it is able to easily flow through firewalls without any hindrance. Firewalls already allow information from the Internet to flow freely through their walls.

As shown in Figure 3-4, by using an XML Web service, you are making a request from some sort of client. This request triggers a response from the server. The request message carries information about the function to be called and any parameters that are required by the function. After the server that hosts the XML Web service receives the request message from the client, it initiates the function and returns a response message that contains information returned by the function. This response message can be just a simple statement that some specific action was taken or it can contain a complete dataset. What you return is really up to you.

In the past it was quite possible to work with DCOM to port data from one point to another, but doing so required requests and responses riding on top of a proprietary communication protocol. This kind of architecture is not an effective way to provide data in a universal format. If your goal is to allow information to be sent and consumed regardless of the platforms used, DCOM does not achieve it.

By using XML Web services, it is possible to transmit these services over a couple of different protocols. XML Web services allow for the requests and responses to take place over HTTP-GET, HTTP-POST, and SOAP. I will present each of these protocols to give you a better idea of what protocol to use when building your XML Web services.

XML Web services via HTTP-GET and HTTP-POST

You can exchange messages using XML Web services via HTTP-GET and HTTP-POST. It is a simple and easy way to initiate actions and to receive simple information.

You may be quite familiar with these formats from using them in traditional client-server Web application development. In Active Server Pages 3.0, it was possible to send name/value pairs from one page to another by transmitting this information as querystrings that were attached directly to the URL. This is the protocol that is used when working with XML Web services using HTTP-GET.

For example, you could call XML Web service using HTTP-GET as shown in the following example. This code simulates a request to an XML Web service, passing in the ISBN number for a book in order to retrieve price information for that particular title.

```
http://www.hungryminds.com/bookinfo/bookprice.asmx/GetBookPrice?ISBN=0764548263
```

> **NOTE:** This is not an real XML Web service; therefore, you won't find it at this location. It is displayed here only for demonstration purposes.

After this request is sent to a server at the publishing company, ASP.NET on the server parses the name/value pairs that were sent in the URL string, creates a `BookInfo` object, and then calls the `GetBookPrice` method passing the method the singular parameter that it needs.

Figure 3-5 shows an example of calling an XML Web service by using HTTP-GET:

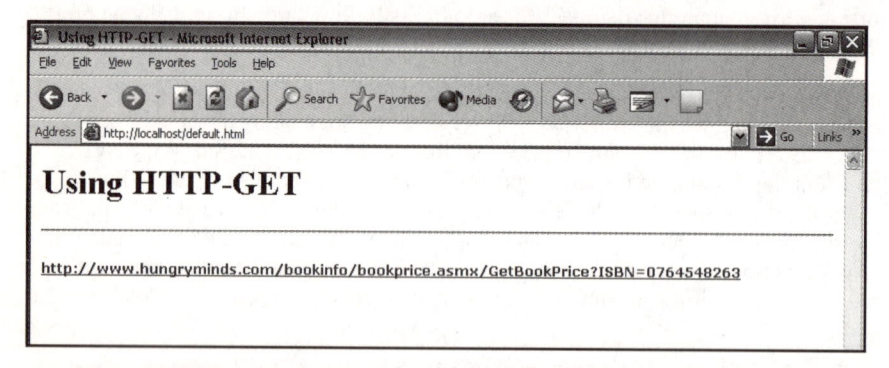

Figure 3-5: A sample Web page using HTTP-GET to invoke an XML Web service.

XML Web services also accept HTTP-POST requests. HTTP-POST also passes name/value pairs similar to HTTP-GET, but it holds these name/value pairs within the actual request header rather than as querystrings as is done with HTTP-GET.

Using this method, as opposed to HTTP-GET, enables you to transmit larger amounts of data because older browsers have a 255-character limit for URLs when using HTTP-GET. Using HTTP-POST, you can invoke the XML Web service from the form, and the form passes the name/value pairs to the server that hosts the XML Web service. Figure 3-6 shows an example of a form that invokes an XML Web service when the Submit button is clicked.

Chapter 3: Introduction to XML Web Services

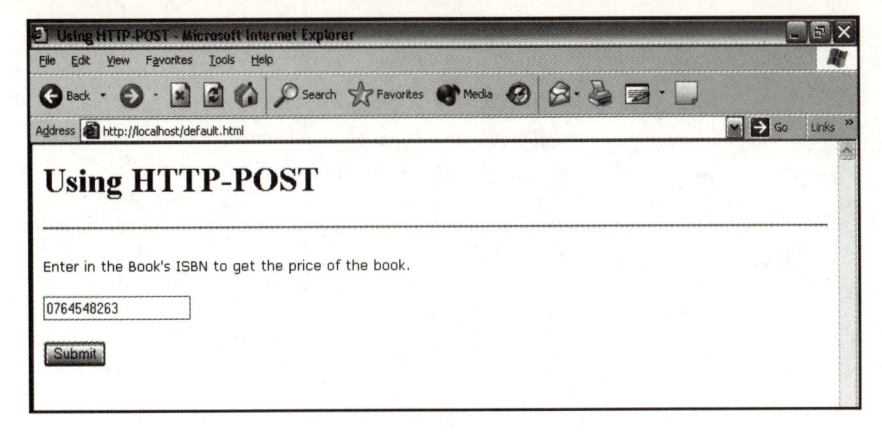

Figure 3-6: A sample Web page using HTTP-POST to invoke an XML Web service.

Remember that HTTP-GET and HTTP-POST are standard protocols that use HTTP for encoding and passing of name/value pairs. You will find it is simple and easy to use these protocols to invoke XML Web services.

> **CROSS-REFERENCE:** Chapter 6 shows you how to work with XML Web services in both HTTP-GET and HTTP-POST.

XML Web services via SOAP

The *Simple Object Access Protocol* (SOAP) is the third and most preferred way to deal with message-based communications over HTTP. There are many reasons to use SOAP as opposed to HTTP-GET and HTTP-POST when dealing with XML Web services.

The first reason for using SOAP as a protocol for dealing with XML Web services is that, by using SOAP, you are able to transmit more complex data structures. These include DataSets, or tables of data that have their relations in place. SOAP is a simple, lightweight XML-based protocol for exchanging structured and type information on the Web over HTTP.

SOAP uses HTTP-POST to transmit its SOAP message to the server as opposed to HTML forms, which use HTTP-POST to transmit name/value pairs within the request header. SOAP sends its request and response over HTTP within the payload section of HTTP-POST by enclosing a SOAP envelope. Listing 3-13 shows a simple SOAP request message that is transmitted over HTTP-POST.

Listing 3-13: SOAP request

```
POST /bookinfo/bookprice.asmx HTTP/1.1
Host: www.hungryminds.com
Content-Type: text/xml; charset=utf-8
Content-Length: length
SOAPAction: "http://tempuri.org/GetBookPrice"

<?xml version="1.0" encoding="utf-8"?>
```

```
<soap:Envelope xmlns:xsi="http://www.w3.org/2001/XMLSchema-instance"
 xmlns:xsd="http://www.w3.org/2001/XMLSchema"
 xmlns:soapenc="http://schemas.xmlsoap.org/soap/encoding/"
 xmlns:tns="http://tempuri.org/"
 xmlns:types="http://tempuri.org/encodedTypes"
 xmlns:soap="http://schemas.xmlsoap.org/soap/envelope/">
    <soap:Body
      soap:encodingStyle="http://schemas.xmlsoap.org/soap/encoding/">
        <tns:GetBookPrice>
            <ISBN xsi:type="xsd:integer">0764548263</ISBN>
        </tns:GetBookPrice>
    </soap:Body>
</soap:Envelope>
```

This request is sent to the XML Web service, and the SOAP response looks like the following (Listing 3-14):

Listing 3-14: SOAP response

```
HTTP/1.1 200 OK
Content-Type: text/xml; charset=utf-8
Content-Length: length

<?xml version="1.0" encoding="utf-8"?>
<soap:Envelope xmlns:xsi="http://www.w3.org/2001/XMLSchema-instance"
 xmlns:xsd="http://www.w3.org/2001/XMLSchema"
 xmlns:soapenc="http://schemas.xmlsoap.org/soap/encoding/"
 xmlns:tns="http://tempuri.org/"
 xmlns:types="http://tempuri.org/encodedTypes"
 xmlns:soap="http://schemas.xmlsoap.org/soap/envelope/">
<soap:Body
 soap:encodingStyle="http://schemas.xmlsoap.org/soap/encoding/">
    <tns:GetBookPriceResponse>
       <GetBookPriceResult href="#id1" />
    </tns:GetBookPriceResponse>
    <types:HMBookPrice id="id1" xsi:type="types:HMBookPrice">
       <BookPrice xsi:type="xsd:string">string</BookPrice>
    </types:HMBookPrice>
</soap:Body>
</soap:Envelope>
```

In these two code examples, the SOAP message is encapsulated within a SOAP envelope by using the `<soap:Envelope>` elements. Contained within the SOAP message are the SOAP body, `<soap:Body>`, and any optional headers, `<soap:header>`.

The great thing about using SOAP is that you can transmit anything that can be represented in XML. For this reason, SOAP is the preferred transfer protocol method when working with XML Web services.

> **CROSS-REFERENCE:** SOAP will be covered in detail in Part IV of this book. For the SOAP specification, you can visit the W3C Web site at `www.w3.org/TR/soap`.

Describing an XML Web service

When you find an XML Web service that you want to include in your application, you must figure out what parameters to pass to the service to make it work. After you pass the parameters to the XML Web service, you need to know what is returned so you can properly use the passed information within your own application. Without this information, using the Web service would prove rather difficult.

> **NOTE:** Finding existing XML Web services is covered later in this chapter.

Just as there are standard ways within XML Web services to represent data, as well as standard ways to move this data over the Internet, there is a standard way to get a description of the Web service that you are trying to consume. XML Web services use the Web Services Description Language (WSDL) to describe the Web service. WSDL is a language that uses XML to describe XML Web services and defines the format of messages the XML Web service understands.

> **CROSS-REFERENCE:** WSDL is covered in detail in Chapter 15 of this book. For the WSDL specification, visit the W3C Web site at `www.w3.org/TR/wsdl`.

Listing 3-15 is a sample WSDL file that describes a simple calculator XML Web service.

Listing 3-15: Sample WSDL file

```xml
<?xml version="1.0" encoding="utf-8"?>
<definitions xmlns:s="http://www.w3.org/2001/XMLSchema"
 xmlns:http="http://schemas.xmlsoap.org/wsdl/http/"
 xmlns:mime="http://schemas.xmlsoap.org/wsdl/mime/"
 xmlns:tm="http://microsoft.com/wsdl/mime/textMatching/"
 xmlns:soap="http://schemas.xmlsoap.org/wsdl/soap/"
 xmlns:soapenc="http://schemas.xmlsoap.org/soap/encoding/"
 xmlns:s0="http://tempuri.org/"
 targetNamespace="http://tempuri.org/"
 xmlns="http://schemas.xmlsoap.org/wsdl/">
  <types>
    <s:schema attributeFormDefault="qualified"
      elementFormDefault="qualified"
      targetNamespace="http://tempuri.org/">
      <s:element name="Calculator">
        <s:complexType>
          <s:sequence>
            <s:element minOccurs="1" maxOccurs="1" name="a"
              type="s:int" />
            <s:element minOccurs="1" maxOccurs="1" name="b"
              type="s:int" />
```

```xml
            </s:sequence>
          </s:complexType>
        </s:element>
        <s:element name="CalculatorResponse">
          <s:complexType>
            <s:sequence>
              <s:element minOccurs="0" maxOccurs="1"
                name="CalculatorResult" type="s:string" />
            </s:sequence>
          </s:complexType>
        </s:element>
        <s:element name="string" type="s:string" />
      </s:schema>
    </types>
    <message name="CalculatorSoapIn">
      <part name="parameters" element="s0:Calculator" />
    </message>
    <message name="CalculatorSoapOut">
      <part name="parameters" element="s0:CalculatorResponse" />
    </message>
    <message name="CalculatorHttpGetIn">
      <part name="a" type="s:string" />
      <part name="b" type="s:string" />
    </message>
    <message name="CalculatorHttpGetOut">
      <part name="Body" element="s0:string" />
    </message>
    <message name="CalculatorHttpPostIn">
      <part name="a" type="s:string" />
      <part name="b" type="s:string" />
    </message>
    <message name="CalculatorHttpPostOut">
      <part name="Body" element="s0:string" />
    </message>
    <portType name="Service1Soap">
      <operation name="Calculator">
        <input message="s0:CalculatorSoapIn" />
        <output message="s0:CalculatorSoapOut" />
      </operation>
    </portType>
    <portType name="Service1HttpGet">
      <operation name="Calculator">
        <input message="s0:CalculatorHttpGetIn" />
        <output message="s0:CalculatorHttpGetOut" />
      </operation>
    </portType>
    <portType name="Service1HttpPost">
      <operation name="Calculator">
        <input message="s0:CalculatorHttpPostIn" />
```

```xml
      <output message="s0:CalculatorHttpPostOut" />
    </operation>
</portType>
<binding name="Service1Soap" type="s0:Service1Soap">
  <soap:binding transport="http://schemas.xmlsoap.org/soap/http"
    style="document" />
  <operation name="Calculator">
    <soap:operation soapAction="http://tempuri.org/Calculator"
      style="document" />
    <input>
      <soap:body use="literal" />
    </input>
    <output>
      <soap:body use="literal" />
    </output>
  </operation>
</binding>
<binding name="Service1HttpGet" type="s0:Service1HttpGet">
  <http:binding verb="GET" />
  <operation name="Calculator">
    <http:operation location="/Calculator" />
    <input>
      <http:urlEncoded />
    </input>
    <output>
      <mime:mimeXml part="Body" />
    </output>
  </operation>
</binding>
<binding name="Service1HttpPost" type="s0:Service1HttpPost">
  <http:binding verb="POST" />
  <operation name="Calculator">
    <http:operation location="/Calculator" />
    <input>
      <mime:content type="application/x-www-form-urlencoded" />
    </input>
    <output>
      <mime:mimeXml part="Body" />
    </output>
  </operation>
</binding>
<service name="Service1">
  <port name="Service1Soap" binding="s0:Service1Soap">
    <soap:address
      location="http://localhost/webservice1/service1.asmx" />
  </port>
  <port name="Service1HttpGet" binding="s0:Service1HttpGet">
    <http:address
      location="http://localhost/webservice1/service1.asmx" />
```

```
    </port>
    <port name="Service1HttpPost" binding="s0:Service1HttpPost">
      <http:address
        location="http://localhost/webservice1/service1.asmx" />
    </port>
  </service>
</definitions>
```

Using this WSDL document, you are able to build a proxy class that exposes the methods of the XML Web service to your consuming application. There is a lot of code in this document, but it describes everything about the XML Web service, including the data types accepted and returned, as well as the different protocols that are used.

> **CROSS-REFERENCE:** More on UDDI can be found in Chapter 11.

Providing a means of discovery for your XML Web service

After you have built an XML Web service, you want users to be able to find your WSDL documents so that they can learn how to interact with your service. You must provide a way for users to discover your XML Web services by pointing users to your WSDL documents.

You may not always want to provide the means for users to find your XML Web service in order to consume the service. An XML Web service that is private does not need to have a discovery mechanism built into it. However, there must be a means for users to locate XML Web services that you do wish to provide to the public. You can provide a .disco file that points to any Web service description documents such as WSDL documents. (The .disco file has nothing to do with a popular dance from the 1970s, but instead refers to the discovery process used in finding XML Web services.)

An available .disco file, which is an XML document that consists of links to other resources that describe the XML Web service (such as any WSDL documents), enables programmatic discovery of an XML Web service. Listing 3-16 shows an example of the structure of a discovery document:

Listing 3-16: Example of a .disco file

```
<?xml version="1.0" encoding="utf-8" ?>
  <discovery xmlns:xsi="http://www.w3.org/2001/XMLSchema-instance"
    xmlns:xsd="http://www.w3.org/2001/XMLSchema"
    xmlns="http://schemas.xmlsoap.org/disco/">
  <contractRef
    ref="http://localhost/WebService1/Service1.asmx?wsdl"
    docRef="http://localhost/WebService1/Service1.asmx"
    xmlns="http://schemas.xmlsoap.org/disco/scl/"  />
  </discovery>
```

If you have a .disco file pointing to your WSDL file, users are able to use various tools or Visual Studio .NET to locate this Web service discovery document (DISCO). When you make a reference to a particular Web address, Visual Studio .NET interrogates the Web site using an algorithm designed to locate the DISCO file. The DISCO file then points to the WSDL document. Figure 3-7 shows how, by using the Add Web Reference dialog window in Visual Studio .NET, you can interact with your local server's DISCO files in order to find local XML Web services.

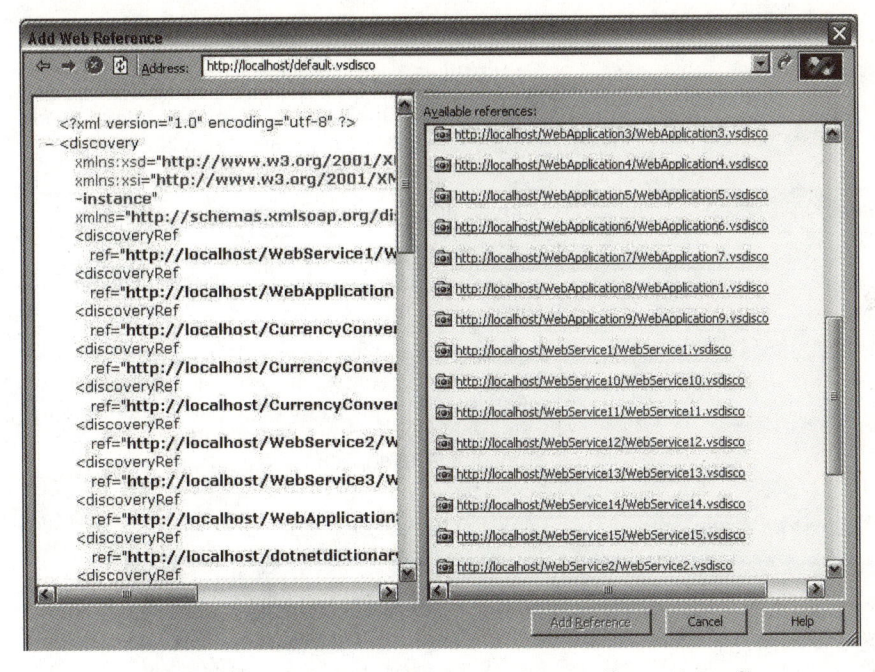

Figure 3-7: Using the Add Web Reference dialog window to interact with a `.disco` file.

Discovering an XML Web service provider

Let's say you're in the market to consume an XML Web service. You might need a mortgage calculator on your site. You decide that, instead of building this calculator yourself, you will take a look around and see if anyone is providing a mortgage calculator online exposed as an XML Web service that you can consume within your site.

What Internet sites provide a mortgage calculator as an XML Web service? That is your first question. How do you find a particular XML Web service among the billions of Web sites that are available on the Internet today? It could be a daunting task to manually search the Internet for such a service.

To accomplish this task, various companies such as Microsoft and IBM have worked to create an online search engine of Web services, the UDDI Web site located at www.uddi.org. Very similar to search engines on the Internet that search and locate particular Web site or pages, UDDI is there for searching through the growing list of Web services that are available for consumption.

Part II: The Basics of XML Web Services

The UDDI Web site shown in Figure 3-8 is a Web service in itself, and it uses UDDI (Universal Description, Discovery, and Integration) specifications to define a standard way to publish and discover information about XML Web services. The XML schemas associated with UDDI define four types of information that enable a developer to use a published XML Web service. Table 3-1 lists the types of information that UDDI provides.

TABLE 3-1 Types of Information Defined in UDDI

Information Provided	Description
Business Details	UDDI provides the business contact information for the person or company that is providing the particular Web service.
Service Detail	A name and description of the Web service.
Bindings	Details the specific access points for this service instance and allows display of additional instance-specific details.
Service Classifications	Classifications classify the field of operation of a business or a service (for example, a geographic location or an industry sector). These enable users of the registry to confirm the importance of a particular Web service.

Figure 3-8 shows the home page of the UDDI Web site at www.uddi.org:

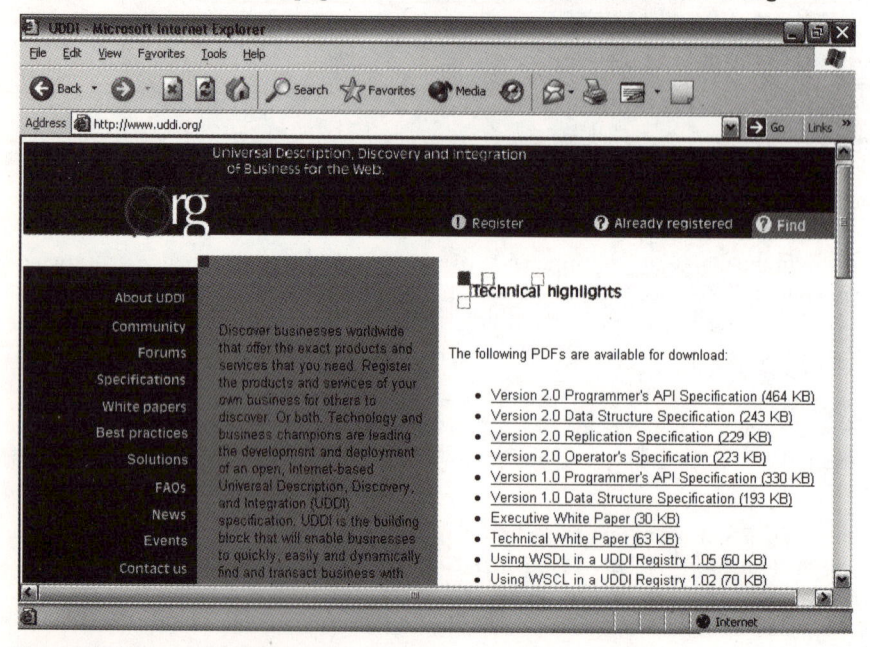

Figure 3-8: Homepage of UDDI.org.

UDDI.org is not the only way to publish and classify your XML Web services. There are other directories that have sprung up on the Internet, and I am sure that there will be plenty more as time goes by and the number of XML Web services grows. Presently, some of the better directories of Web services besides UDDI.org are `www.salcentral.com` and `www.xmethods.com`.

> **CROSS-REFERENCE:** UDDI is covered in detail in Chapter 16.

The Business of XML Web Services

XML Web services is such a new model for application development that many readers may be wondering how the services fit into their companies' business models. When it comes to a new technology, the big question is: How can I make money with this?

The money made using a new technology is gained by increased performance, more growth, faster transactions, or maybe the replacement of a human employee with an application. All these factors add to the net gain in the end.

XML Web services is no different and may do some of these things for your company or organization. However, there is also a new way for applications to communicate with one another under this new model. If your company is going to expose some new logic that it once sold in a different matter, you may wonder how you are going to get something in return for offering this service up on the Internet.

It is true that there is always going to be a plethora of free XML Web services that are going to give you free stock quotes, news items, or jokes of the day. But what if your company has some important and meaningful service to offer to the public? You don't want to give this out for free, but instead want to create a business model and actually provide another meaningful outlet for this service. You should look at some business models that fit in with the type of service that you offer.

Let's take a look at some of the potential revenue models that you can use when you have an XML Web service available for use.

First of all, you must have a Web service that is beneficial to users — one that they will actually want to pay to use. When companies are building application logic, they sometimes find it easier to procure the pieces of the application from another company than to build and maintain the entire application themselves.

For instance, you may want to have a text box on your Internet site that enables users to type in a company name and get the company's stock quote in return. In this case, it doesn't make much sense to have a database full of stock quotes that you will need to keep up to date for the end user. It makes a lot more sense to purchase this service from another company. The company that is providing the stock quotes transfers these quotes to you using XML Web services and charges you for access to the database.

If you are a company that approves credit applications for other companies, for instance, there may be a number of companies sending you their customers' applications for credit. Your company, as a service, looks over these applications and either approves or rejects them. In the past, you might have received these applications by mail, fax, or email. In any case, you used a human to transfer the data in one way or another to complete the approval process. Now, you want to use XML Web services for this credit-approval–process service that you offer to the public. But how do you charge for this service? There are a number of options and models that you can apply to your services.

In the XML Web services' world with UDDI (Universal Description, Discovery and Integration), WSDL (Web Services Description Language), and DISCO (Discovery of Web Services), it is quite simple to publish and offer your Web services to the public. Whether you charge for them or not is up to you.

There are some important reasons for charging, even if it isn't vital to your company's bottom line. You may be offering a Web service that needs to have the greatest possible uptime. If you are offering a Web service that only pushes out the joke of the day, it isn't vital that the Web service stay up and running. People's applications will still run just fine whether or not your service provides a joke. But on the other hand, if you are offering a service that is used as a core function within an application, having the service up and running could be vital. Charging for the service will ensure higher quality.

Charging a fee lessens the load, and you can spend some of the money gained on better equipment and on better connections in order to ensure uptime. There are a couple of models available for charging customers that want to use your Web service. Take a look at each of these models:

- *Lifetime Usage* — In this model, the customer pays a one-time fee to have access to your Web service for as long as it is in existence. This is an excellent model for Web services that are tied to a time-limited event. For instance, you are going to provide a Web service from the Masters Golf Tournament displaying an up-to-date score board. You are providing this service so that Internet sites can publish this information directly onto their own Web pages. You plan on charging for this service. This would be a good model for charging a one-time access fee. The event is limited, just over a long weekend, and customers can pay the one-time fee to receive the up-to-date score board throughout the event. After the event is over, the Web service stops.

- *Time-Limited Charge* — In this model, users pay to gain access to a Web service for a set period of time. For instance, one popular model charges users to gain access to the XML Web service on a monthly basis. Every month, their credit cards are charged a certain amount, and those users continue to gain access until they stop their accounts. Of course, the time limit doesn't have to be in monthly segments; it can be in weeks, quarters, or years. This is also called a subscription model, similar to how people purchase cable, magazines, and Internet access.

- *Per-Transaction Charge* — In this model, you charge your users for each and every time that they use your Web service. For instance, you may offer a service that the end user does not use every day or even every month. This service might make a good model for charging on every instance of use. The user signs up to use the service at the beginning, and you provide him with login credentials to your service. Thereafter, each time the user uses the service, his usage is recorded, and you can charge the user based upon the number of times he uses the service. Your charge may be pennies for use, or even dollars. It depends on the value your service offers.

- *Free* — As individuals, companies, and organizations start to experiment with the development of XML Web services, many will simply make their services available to the public free of charge. First of all, XML Web services are easy to build and develop and just as easy to publish and make available to the world. Providing free XML Web services from your company or organization also provides you with greater name recognition and will invariably point end users to other services that your company offers.

Think these models through, so that when you are finished building your XML Web services, you already know how you are going to allow access to this service. Think through what your service is offering and the level of quality that you want to maintain and choose wisely because this decision will have a direct impact on the overall success of your XML Web service.

You may not even have to figure out how you will make money from your XML Web services, if you are using them only within your own company. Many XML Web services will be developed only for use in networks within companies and organizations of all sizes. These XML Web services will be used to expose data to competing platforms and will allow different groups within the company to expose their own data islands to others. You may find that some of the first practical uses of XML Web services will be right within your own organization.

Summary

This chapter quickly touched on many facets of XML Web services. It also discussed the reasons you might want to build an XML Web service.

Microsoft's .NET Framework has brought us an outstanding platform to build and consume XML Web services. Because everything involved with XML Web services on the .NET platform deals with open standards such as XML, SOAP, WSDL, DISCO, and UDDI, the XML Web services that you build are guaranteed success in integrating with any platform or system that is able to consume XML over HTTP.

Visual Studio .NET makes the construction and consumption of XML Web services simple and straightforward. You will see this in action in the next few chapters as you build some sample XML Web services.

You may have noticed that this chapter did not focus on Visual Basic .NET or C#. XML Web services is a language-neutral technology. You can build and consume your XML Web services in any .NET-compliant language. In the end, however, when the XML Web service goes into action, it isn't relying on any of these languages, but instead is totally and completely using XML to do its magic!

Chapter 4

Building a Simple XML Web Service

No one knows what he can do till he tries.
Publilius Syrus, *Moral Sayings* (1st c. B.C.)

Enough talk about the philosophy behind building XML Web services and how this technology fits into the .NET Framework. Now is the time to build your first XML Web service and experience for yourself the ease of building distributed applications on the .NET platform. There is no type of learning like doing!

In this chapter, you learn exactly what is needed to build an XML Web service and you go through all the steps to build your own XML Web services. When you are finished, you will understand each of the steps involved and get a feel for the power of the .NET design tools that you use. *So let's get started!*

In this chapter, you learn the following:

- The requirements for building XML Web services
- How to use the .NET Framework SDK to build your first XML Web service
- How to test your XML Web service
- How to use Visual Studio .NET

Before you jump right in and start typing away, let's take a quick look at what you need to start building XML Web services today.

Requirements to Build XML Web Services

There are software and hardware requirements to build XML Web services. You need to make sure that everything is in place before you can actually start constructing your services. Here is a list of what you need to get started:

- An operating system that is capable of running IIS. You must have either Windows .NET Server, Windows XP Professional, Windows 2000 Advanced Server, Windows 2000 Professional, or Windows NT 4.0 (with service pack 6a or higher).
- You must install IIS on this operating system (if it is not already installed). Installing IIS will be covered in this chapter.

- A version of the .NET Framework. Install the .NET Framework on top of the operating system.
- It is highly suggested, but not required, that you install Visual Studio .NET. This is the IDE of the .NET Framework, and it makes building XML Web services seem like a breeze.

Setting Up Your Operating System with IIS

If you are running one of the operating systems mentioned in the preceding list, you must also have *Internet Information Server* (IIS) installed and running on the system so that the operating system will act as a server. Doing this allows you to program your XML Web services and test them within the confines of your own computer.

Not all operating systems come configured with IIS ready to go, but it is easy to install it. When you have it, you can turn your computer into a server and work through all the examples presented in this book.

If you are unsure whether your operating system is already configured to act as a server, open up Windows Explorer and look on your hard drive (usually Local Disk (C:)). Double-click this drive; if you see an `InetPub` folder with a `wwwroot` folder contained within, you already have IIS installed (an example of this is shown in Figure 4-1). If you don't see these two folders, you have to install IIS on your machine.

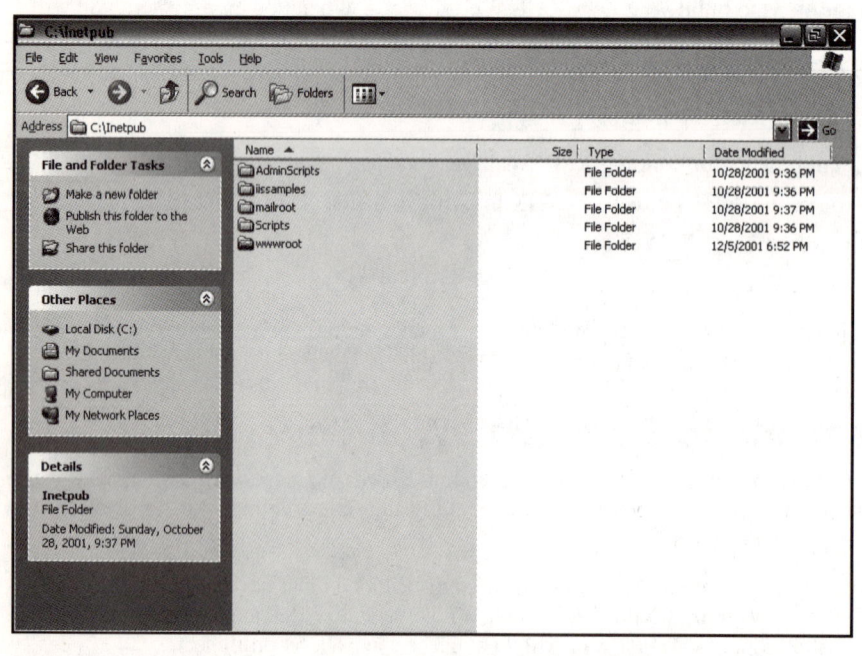

Figure 4-1: If you have the Inetpub folder on your computer, you have IIS installed.

If you don't find IIS on your computer, follow these installation instructions:

1. Pull up your Control Panel (Start ⇨ Settings ⇨ Control Panel).
2. Click Add/Remove Programs.
3. Click Add/Remove Windows Components, located on the left side of the dialog box.
4. The Windows Components Wizard displays (see Figure 4-2).

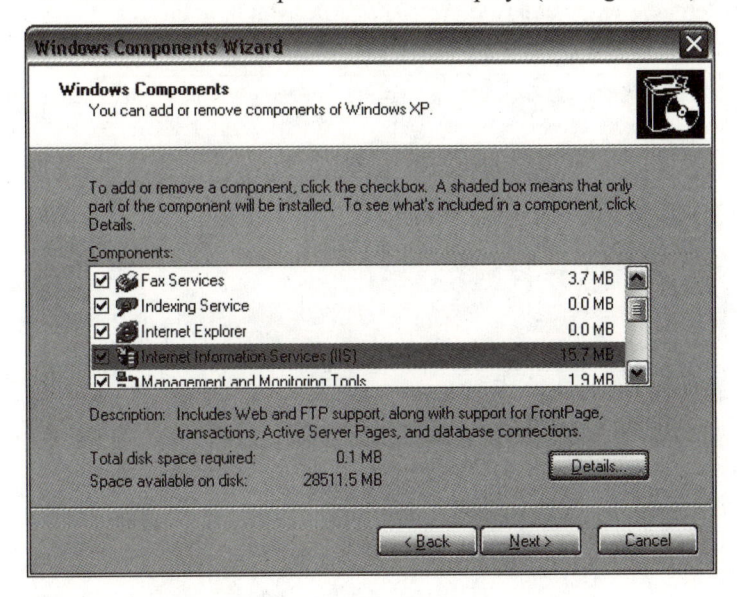

Figure 4-2: The Windows Components Wizard is used to install IIS.

5. Check the Internet Information Services (IIS) box.
6. Click Next (located at the bottom of the dialog box).

The wizard then installs IIS.

After you install IIS, go to your local hard drive and look for the `InetPub` folder. Double-click this folder; you will see the `wwwroot` folder. When you build Web pages, you place the files within the `wwwroot` folder. You can then gain access to the files through your browser, just as if you were surfing on the Internet.

Next you need to place one simple HTML file within the `wwwroot` folder and open your browser. Type the following URL: **http://localhost/default.html**. The name of the file is `default.html`. This will pull up the file in the browser window as if you were on the Internet. You are, in effect, because you make your HTTP request to a server (local server) and then IIS sends back an HTTP reply (to your browser).

Now you should have installed IIS along with Visual Studio .NET. If you have installed Visual Studio .NET, you have installed the .NET Framework on your machine as well. After this is installed, you are ready to start building some XML Web services!

Part II: The Basics of XML Web Services

Your First XML Web Service

Now you are ready to get cracking! To build your first XML Web service, you are not going to use Visual Studio .NET because you want to truly understand what is going on with XML Web services. It is important, therefore, that you build this first model from scratch. Don't worry; it's going to be easy. I promise!

Open Notepad (affectionately referred to as *Visual Notepad*). After you have this ready to go, study Listing 4-1 to see what the entire file should look like.

> **NOTE:** Remember that you can modify the code listings and use any language that is targeted at the .NET Framework for these examples.

Listing 4-1: Service1.asmx – Your first XML Web service

VB

```
<%@ WebService Language="VB" class="Calculator" %>

Imports System.Web.Services

Public Class Calculator

    <WebMethod()> Public Function Add(ByVal a As Integer,
            ByVal b As Integer) As Integer
        Return a + b
    End Function

    <WebMethod()> Public Function Subtract(ByVal a As
            Integer, ByVal b As Integer) As Integer
        Return a - b
    End Function

    <WebMethod()> Public Function Multiply(ByVal a As
            Integer, ByVal b As Integer) As Integer
        Return a * b
    End Function

    <WebMethod()> Public Function Divide(ByVal a As Integer,
            ByVal b As Integer) As Integer
        Return a / b
    End Function

End Class
```

C#

```
<%@ WebService Language="C#" class="Calculator" %>

using System.Web.Services;
```

Chapter 4: Building a Simple XML Web Service

```
class Calculator {

    [WebMethod]
    public int Add(int a, int b) {
        return a + b;
    }

    [WebMethod]
    public int Subtract(int a, int b) {
        return a - b;
    }

    [WebMethod]
    public int Multiply(int a, int b) {
        return a * b;
    }

    [WebMethod]
    public int Divide(int a, int b) {
        return a / b;
    }
}
```

After you type this code and save it to your system, take a quick look at what the code is doing. The first line of code in your XML Web service file is the page directive.

VB

```
<%@ WebService Language="VB" Class="Calculator" %>
```

C#

```
<%@ WebService Language="C#" Class="Calculator" %>
```

The page directive is always enclosed within a pair of <% tags and starts with an @ sign. The page directive is the place in your pages where you can put the page attributes. Page attributes are the page-wide settings that you wish to enact for your file. In this case, you are specifying that this page is going to be an XML Web service and that the language of the Web service is going to be either Visual Basic .NET (specified with VB) or C#. Specifying the WebService directive tells the compiler and the ASP.NET parser what type of component this will be so that it can be compiled correctly.

After the WebService directive, you import a namespace in order to work with XML Web services.

VB

```
Imports System.Web.Services
```

C#

```
using System.Web.Services;
```

The `System.Web.Services` namespace is made up of the classes that enable you to build and use XML Web services.

> **NOTE:** A namespace is the way in which .NET categorizes classes that are available for use within your applications. In order to gain access to the classes contained within the namespace, you have to first import that particular namespace into the your page. In the following example, you want to take advantage of the System.Web.Services namespace and, therefore, you import it into the page.

After importing the namespace, you define your class. Defining a class that contains methods that you want to expose as XML Web services is no different than defining a class that doesn't have these elements. In this example, you are building the traditional Calculator class. For your first XML Web service, building a calculator has become almost the standard, just as *Hello World!* has become the standard in traditional Web-application development.

After you build the class, you add the methods that will be needed in the class. Take a look at the first method in your Calculator class.

VB

```
<WebMethod()> Public Function Add(ByVal a As Integer, _
         ByVal b As Integer) As Integer
     Return a + b
End Function
```

C#

```
[WebMethod]
public int Add(int a, int b) {
     return a + b;
}
```

The first method here is the `Add()` method. Within this class, there are four methods, and you want to expose all four of these methods as Web methods that are accessible from the Calculator XML Web service. In .NET, this is as simple as adding an attribute in front of the method. In Visual Basic .NET, you do this by adding a `<WebMethod()>` attribute to the front of the method. In C#, you convert a regular method to a Web method by also using the Web method attribute, but C# encloses this attribute in square brackets: `[WebMethod]`.

Now that is pretty simple!

After you have typed in the file, save it to the `wwwroot` folder on your computer. Follow these steps to save your file:

1. Within the `wwwroot` folder, create a new folder called **TestWS**.
2. Save the file that you created in Notepad as **"Service1.asmx"** in the `TestWS` folder. Be sure to include the quotes when saving the file, otherwise Notepad won't save the file correctly.

Now that you have created your first XML Web service, see what you can do with it.

Chapter 4: Building a Simple XML Web Service   87

> **NOTE:** Although `.aspx` is the file extension for ASP.NET pages, XML Web services uses the file extension `.asmx` to instruct the ASP.NET parser that the file is an XML Web service.

Looking at Your First XML Web Service

Now that you have built an XML Web service, you have just exposed some application logic. Anyone who knows where your application logic resides is now able to consume and use this logic. Before you expose this logic to the public or to others within your network, it is always good to test it first.

XML Web services' Web interface: Testing your Web service

How do you look at an XML Web service? It is only XML being transported over HTTP. An XML Web service is just a class that has some of its methods exposed, so how do you view that in the browser? Well, actually, this process is one of the reasons why XML Web services on the .NET platform is so outstanding.

To view your XML Web service, open up Internet Explorer and direct the browser to the location of the service by the URL. If you saved the file according to the instructions, your XML Web service will be accessible at `http://localhost/TestWS/Service1.asmx`. Type that URL in the address bar and take a look at the results, shown in Figure 4-3.

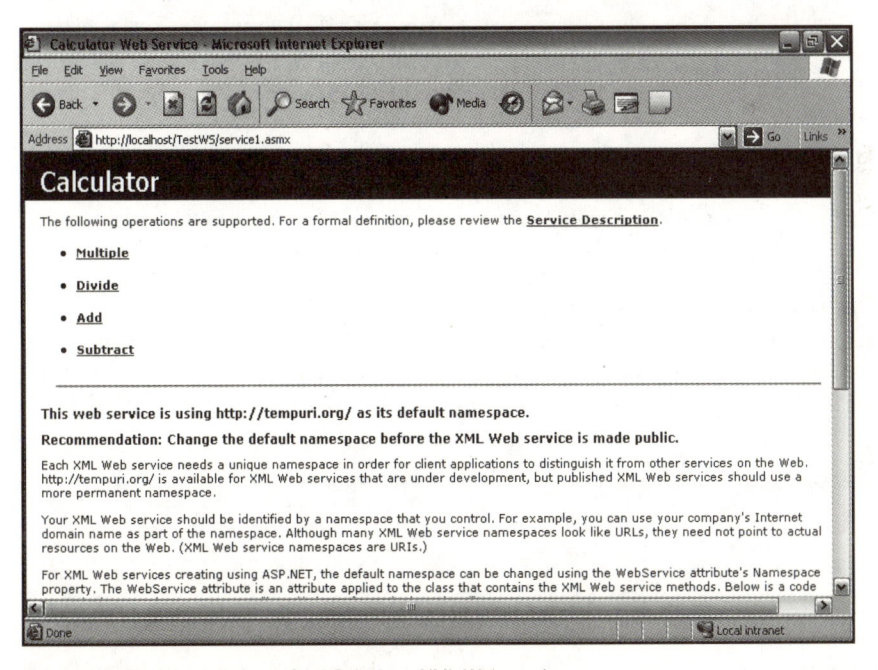

Figure 4-3: The Web interface of the Calculator XML Web service.

This is how .NET puts a face on your XML Web services. This Web interface is automatically created for you whenever someone pulls up the XML Web service in the browser.

> **CROSS-REFERENCE:** Chapter 6 shows you how to expand upon this page.

Understanding the XML Web service interface

The Web interface provides the name of your XML Web service as well as a list of all the available methods that the consumer can use. Figure 4-4 labels the parts of the Web interface.

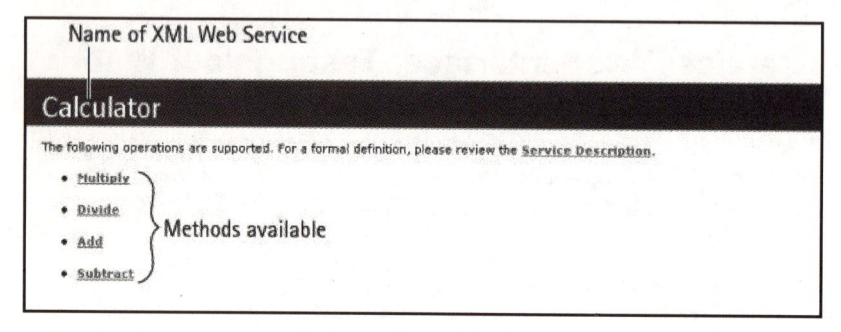

Figure 4-4: This figure shows some of the important parts of the Web Interface provided for your XML Web service.

The solid bar at the top of the page contains the title of the XML Web service. This is taken from the name of the class. You need to give your class a meaningful name so that when users view this page and are considering consuming your XML Web service, they can understand the basic functionality of the Web service by just reading the title of the service.

The Web interface also contains a bulleted list of all the methods that are exposed as Web methods. These are the methods that are available for users to openly consume. All the methods that are exposed as Web methods use the `WebMethod` attribute. In this example, you exposed all four of the methods, and they are all listed on the Web interface.

The WSDL document

In between the title and the bulleted list of methods that are available is a link to the *Web Services Description Language* (WSDL) document. The WSDL document is the interface to the XML Web service. Clicking the link pulls up a new page that shows you the complete WSDL document.

> **CROSS-REFERENCE:** WSDL will be covered extensively in Chapter 15.

The document is in XML and can be seen in Figure 4-5. By reviewing the WSDL document, you can tell how to consume the XML Web service. Click the back button on the browser and you are back on the Web interface page.

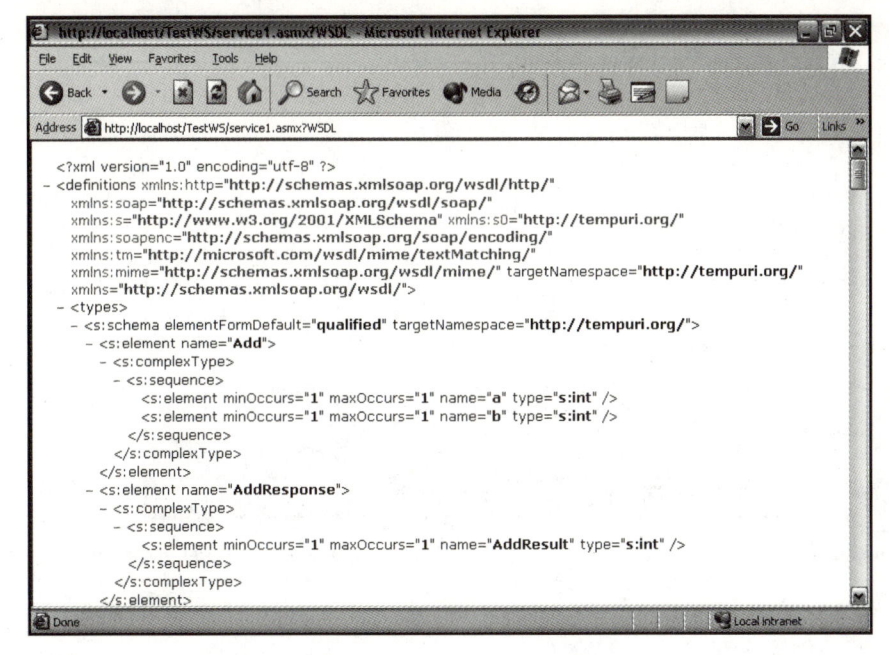

Figure 4-5: The WSDL document for the Calculator XML Web service.

Testing the WebMethod

Not only does this Web interface give a description of the interface and the methods that the XML Web service exposes, but it also gives you the ability to test your methods. Click one of the linked methods, and it will take you to a page where are able to test your method and see how it performs.

Figure 4-6 shows you the page that allows you to test the `Add()` method. At the top of the page is the title of the XML Web service and below that is the name of the Web method. In this case, you are going to look at the `Add()` method and test it to make sure that it does what you want it to do.

Underneath the WebMethod title is a form that allows you to invoke the method. Below that are instructions on how to send requests to the WebMethod from your own systems or applications by using SOAP, HTTP-GET, or HTTP-POST.

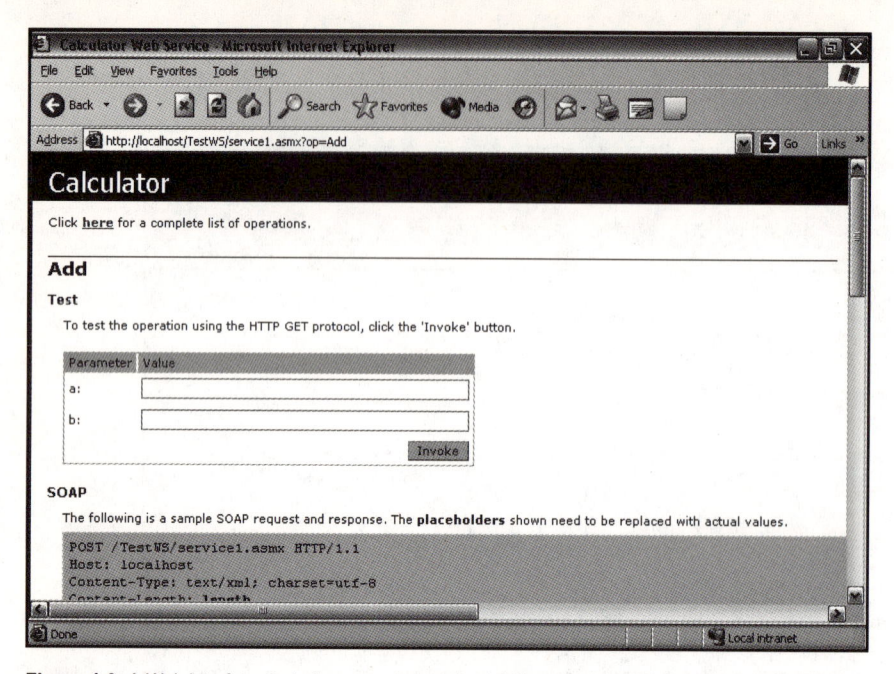

Figure 4-6: A Web interface that allows you to test the Add() method for the Calculator XML Web service.

Look back at the code for the `Add()` WebMethod, and remember that you required two parameters to be passed with the method.

VB

```
<WebMethod()> Public Function Add(ByVal a As Integer,
          ByVal b As Integer) As Integer
     Return a + b
End Function
```

C#

```
[WebMethod]
public int Add(int a, int b) {
     return a + b;
}
```

After looking over this code, note that you are passing in an integer value that you refer to as a and another integer value that you refer to as b. Therefore, in the test page, you see the two parameters listed a and b with empty text boxes next to them. Enter in values for a and b and click the Invoke button. By clicking the Invoke button, you are passing your two parameters into this remote WebMethod Add(), sending your parameters as XML over HTTP to the XML Web service. A listener then takes a hold of the parameters and passes them to the appropriate WebMethod. When the value is returned to the calling agent, the XML Web service passes the value (your answer) back to you as XML over HTTP.

Figure 4-7 shows the result after invoking the `Add()` method of your Calculator XML Web service.

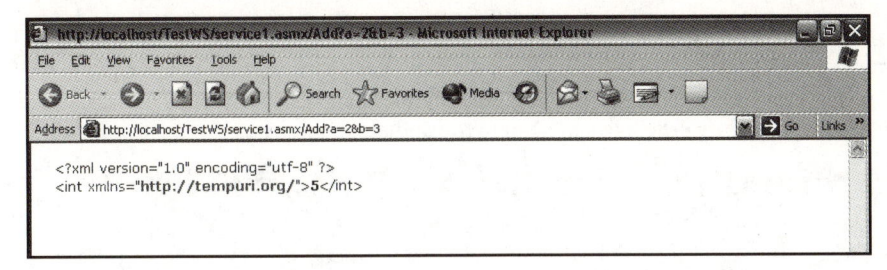

Figure 4-7: A view of the XML that is returned to you from the Add() WebMethod.

In this example, you gave parameter a the value of 2 and b a value of 3. The XML returned a value of 5.

That is pretty outstanding! You just built a simple XML Web service and then tested the `Add()` WebMethod to make sure that it would work. So when a user interacts with this Calculator XML Web service, he is basically doing the same thing that you just did in your Web interface. In the end, he will get back some XML that he can consume however he pleases. The more you get into all this, the more you will see the magic of XML Web services.

XML Web Services and Visual Studio .NET

You just built a simple calculator XML Web service with nothing more than Notepad, and it was fairly simple. In most cases, however, you won't be building such simple XML Web services, and you will need to rely on a more robust tool that will help you quickly construct the services. That is where Visual Studio .NET comes into the picture.

Visual Studio .NET is an outstanding tool for constructing XML Web services on the .NET platform. It was built to make the life of the developer easier and does a fine job of it. As you build more complex XML Web services throughout this book, you will see this more and more.

Your first XML Web service in Visual Studio .NET

Let's open up Visual Studio .NET and build a simple XML Web service to get a feel for the IDE. Follow these steps in building your XML Web service in Visual Studio .NET:

1. Open Visual Studio .NET by selecting Start ⇨ All Programs ⇨ Microsoft Visual Studio .NET ⇨ Microsoft Visual Studio .NET.

2. Click the New Project button to open the New Project dialog window, or select File ⇨ New ⇨ Project.

3. The New Project dialog window opens, and you can choose from a multitude of available projects. The left pane of this dialog window lists all the Project Types. These are organized by folders, and the first few folders are language specific. After you select one

of the language folders, you see in the right pane, labeled Templates, a list of projects that you can build that are specific to the language that you selected.

> **NOTE:** In Visual Studio .NET, the Visual Basic .NET and C# folders share the same projects and both offer the same RAD (Rapid Application Development) environment.

4. For the purposes of this example, you are going to build an ASP.NET Web service. Select that icon. Figure 4-8 shows the New Project dialog window.

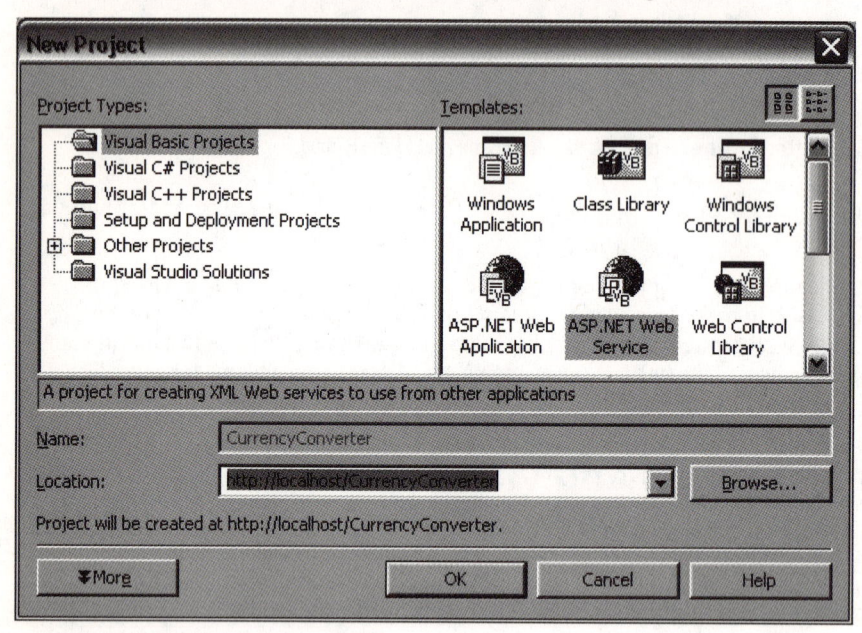

Figure 4-8: The New Project dialog window.

5. Change the name of the project from `WebService1` to **CurrencyConverter**.
6. Click OK.

After you click the OK button, Visual Studio .NET creates a solution for you called CurrencyConverter. (Figure 4-9 shows the Visual Studio .NET development environment after you start this project). Visual Studio .NET creates an application root for you on the Web and copies all the project files over to the Web server for you. If you are working with or debugging your files, you are working with the files directly on the Web server. If you are working with Visual Studio .NET for the first time, this is a good time to look at what is provided for you to build your XML Web services.

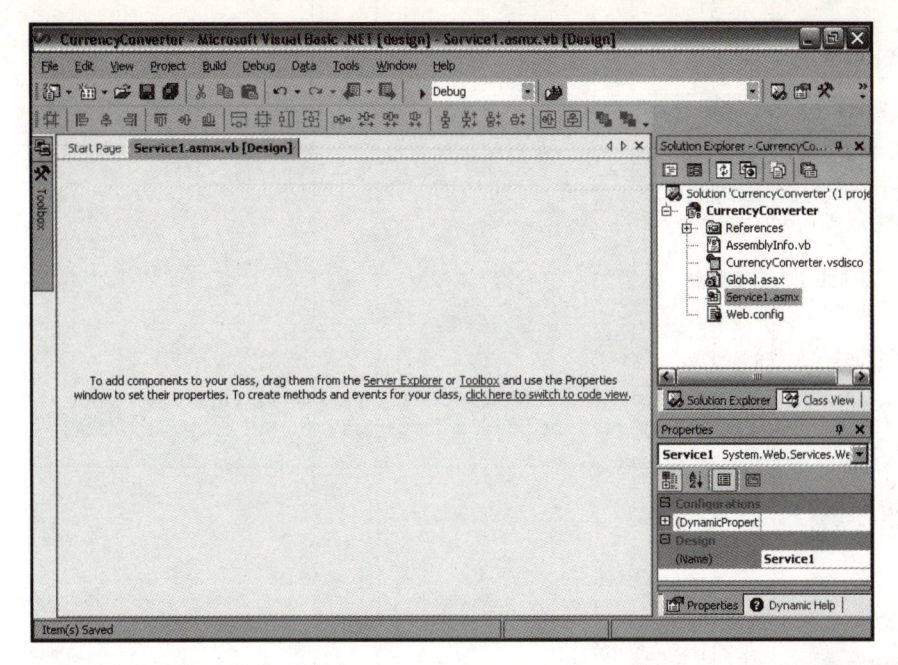

Figure 4-9: The Visual Studio .NET development environment after creating the CurrencyConverter ASP.NET Web service project.

The code window doesn't look as if you can enter code directly into it – and the fact is that you can't. What you are seeing in the code window is the design surface for the XML Web service. Visual Studio .NET introduces you to a visual design surface for the middle tier, although it is still possible to code your XML Web services into Visual Studio .NET. By using the design surface, you can drop and drag items from the Toolbox directly onto the design surface, select that item, and manipulate that item directly in the Properties window. You can easily get to the code window from this design surface either by clicking the link provided or by double-clicking the design surface itself.

The Solution Explorer window shows us you the files that make up your solution. Presently you only have one project within your solution, but you can create new projects within this solution very easily if you want. The Properties window allows you to change the properties settings of the items in your project.

Let's finish building your XML Web service in Visual Studio .NET:

1. Within the Properties window, change the name from `Service1` to **CurrencyConverter**. This changes the name of the class. Figure 4-10 shows the Properties window with this change in place.

2. Right-click the file `Service1.asmx` in the Solution Explorer and select Rename. Rename the file **Converter.asmx**.

Part II: The Basics of XML Web Services

Figure 4-10: The Properties window.

3. Right-click the design surface and select View Code (Figure 4-11). This causes a new page to open up. You are now presented with a file named `Converter.asmx.vb` or `Converter.asmx.cs`.

Figure 4-11: To change the the code view, right-click the design surface and select View Code.

If you have followed the steps thus far, you should have the code window open so that you can start coding directly to the XML Web service. In place of the sample XML Web service (Figure 4-12) that is commented out, add the method from Listing 4-2 to your class.

```
Imports System.Web.Services

<WebService(Namespace := "http://tempuri.org/")> _
Public Class Service1
    Inherits System.Web.Services.WebService

    Web Services Designer Generated Code

    ' WEB SERVICE EXAMPLE
    ' The HelloWorld() example service returns the string Hello World.
    ' To build, uncomment the following lines then save and build the project.
    ' To test this web service, ensure that the .asmx file is the start page
    ' and press F5.
    '
    '<WebMethod()> Public Function HelloWorld() As String
    '    HelloWorld = "Hello World"
    ' End Function

End Class
```

Figure 4-12: The initial XML Web service.

Chapter 4: Building a Simple XML Web Service

Your file should look somewhat like the code in Listing 4-2.

Listing 4-2: Converter.asmx

VB

```vb
Imports System.Web.Services

Public Class CurrencyConverter
    Inherits System.Web.Services.WebService

<WebMethod()> Public Function USDConvert(ByVal ConvertTo As _
            String, ByVal Amount As Double) As Double
        Dim USDollar As Double = 1
        Dim SecondCountryValue As Double

        Select Case (ConvertTo.ToUpper())
            Case ""USD"", "USA", "US"
                SecondCountryValue = 1
            Case "FIN", "FINLAND"
                SecondCountryValue = 6.6448
            Case "UK", "ENGLAND", "UNITED KINGDOM"
                SecondCountryValue = 0.686
            Case "CAN", "CANADA"
                SecondCountryValue = 1.603
            Case "GER", "GERMANY", "DEUTCHLAND"
                SecondCountryValue = 2.188
            Case "EURO"
                SecondCountryValue = 1.118
        End Select

        Return FormatCurrency(USDollar * SecondCountryValue * Amount)

    End Function

End Class
```

C#

```csharp
using System;
using System.Collections;
using System.ComponentModel;
using System.Data;
using System.Diagnostics;
using System.Web;
using System.Web.Services;

namespace CurrencyConverter
{
 /// <summary>
 /// USD to foreign currency converter.
 /// </summary>
```

```csharp
public class CurrencyConverter : System.Web.Services.WebService
{
 public CurrencyConverter()

 [WebMethod]
 public double USDConvert(string ConvertTo, double Amount)
 {
  double USDollar = 1;
  double SecondCountryValue = 1;

  switch (ConvertTo.ToUpper())
  {
   case "USD":
   {
    SecondCountryValue = 1;
    break;
   }
   case "FIN":
   {
    SecondCountryValue = 6.6448;
    break;
   }
   case "UK":
   {
    SecondCountryValue = 0.686;
    break;
   }
   case "CAN":
   {
    SecondCountryValue = 1.603;
    break;
   }
   case "GER":
   {
    SecondCountryValue = 2.188;
    break;
   }
   case "EURO":
   {
    SecondCountryValue = 1.118;
    break;
   }
  }

  return (USDollar * SecondCountryValue * Amount);
 }
}
```

Chapter 4: **Building a Simple XML Web Service** 97

One of the greatest advantages to coding your XML Web services in Visual Studio .NET is *IntelliSense*. IntelliSense is the drop-down list of code completion statements that you get as you type. This makes your coding experience just that much easier, and it actually speeds up development substantially.

After you get all this code into Visual Studio .NET. Save the code and press F5. Pressing F5 will start the build process. Visual Studio .NET begins compiling the code into a DLL. This DLL will be deployed to a server, and then a browser will automatically open the URL of the XML Web service.

Whenever an XML Web service URL is called without invoking a method, the .NET Framework will return the Web interface that is shown in Figure 4-13.

When the Web interface opens up, you can test the CurrencyConverter XML Web service.

Testing the CurrencyConverter XML Web service

Now that the Web interface of your CurrencyConverter XML Web service is open (Figure 4-13), you are able to look at the same items you saw when you were creating the XML Web service in Notepad earlier in this chapter.

For this XML Web service, you only have one method that is exposed. From this page, you can see the WSDL file for this particular XML Web service. You can also click the link of the WebMethod in order to test it.

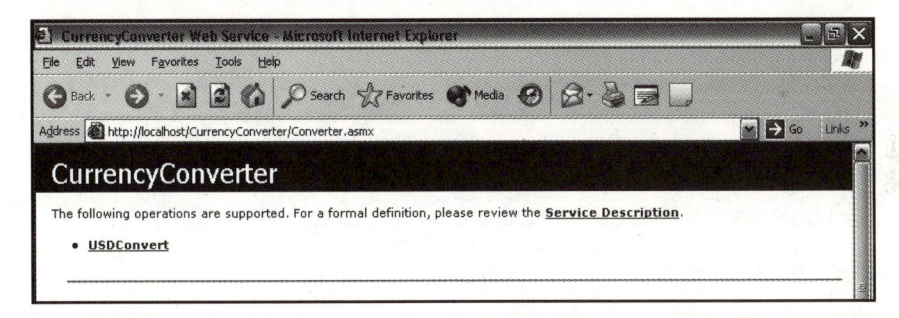

Figure 4-13: The Web interface for the CurrencyConverter XML Web service.

If you click the WebMethod `USDConvert`, you arrive on the page that allows for testing of the method (Figure 4-14). For this test, you convert the US Dollar to Finnish Marks, so you type **FIN** and specify that you want to convert **12** US Dollars.

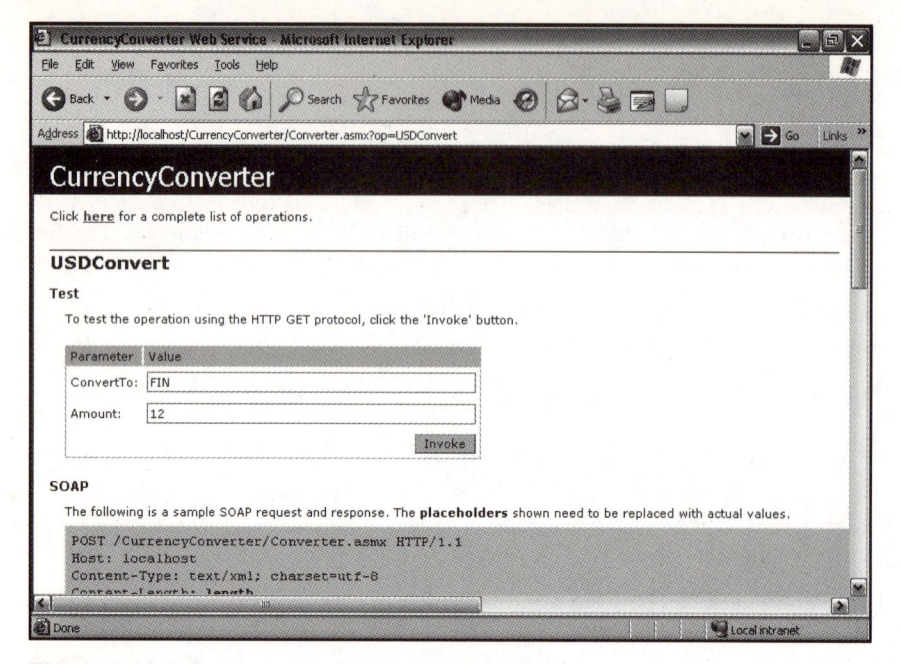

Figure 4-14: The test page of the USDConvert WebMethod.

After entering in the specified values, invoke the WebMethod and you will see an XML response (Figure 4-15).

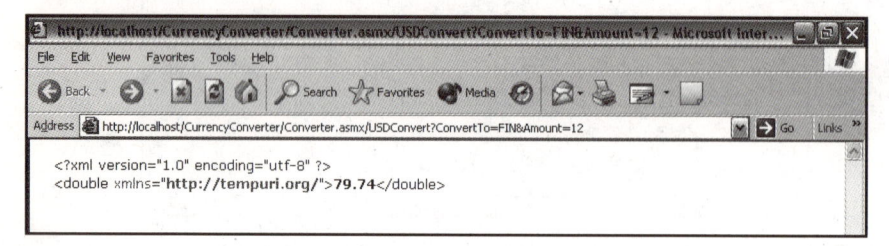

Figure 4-15: The XML response of the USDConvert WebMethod.

The value returned after the conversion comes to 79.74 Finnish Marks.

The test page, as I stated earlier, is one of the greatest features in building XML Web services on the .NET platform. The capability to quickly build and then test the WebMethods that you are exposing is a powerful tool.

By invoking the USDConvert WebMethod, you cause the browser to call the method by passing the function name and the parameter information through the URL. The response that you get back is XML – the *lingua franca* of the Internet and easily consumable by almost any platform.

Because you are using the .NET platform, you don't have to write any HTTP handling code or any XML formatting code to make this all work. The .NET Framework takes care of all this for you.

Building your Web services upon the .NET Framework means that you have full access to ASP.NET and the Common Language Runtime. This includes such features as the performance, state management, and authentication that are supported by ASP.NET.

Summary

In this chapter, you learned the basics of building your very first XML Web service. First, you built an XML Web service that exposed four WebMethods in Notepad. Then you built another XML Web service, but this time, you did it in Visual Studio .NET. As your XML Web services get more and more complicated, you will find it quite advantageous to use Visual Studio .NET. If, however, you are looking to take the hard road, it is possible to build everything from this book in Notepad, — much of that process is out of the scope of this book, but *it is possible!*

Building XML Web services upon the .NET platform ensures that they comply with today's Internet standards such as XML, SOAP, and WSDL. Following these standards allows for other platforms to interoperate with your XML Web services that are built upon .NET. As long as the client can send compliant SOAP messages following the rules set forth in the WSDL document that describes the XML Web service's interface, it is able to work with your XML Web service no matter in what platform it resides.

In the end, browsing XML is all well and good, but you are probably wondering how you are going to consume this XML and use it in the Windows Forms and Web Forms that you are building. You might also be wondering if it is possible to consume these XML Web services in your older Visual Basic 6.0 and Active Server Pages 3.0 applications. Chapter 5 addresses all these issues.

Chapter 5

Consuming XML Web Services

"When spider webs unite, they can tie up a lion."
Ethiopian Proverb

You don't have to build XML Web services to take advantage of what they offer. In fact, you may be interested only in how to *consume* XML Web services and use them in the applications that you are building today.

In this chapter, you work through some simple consumption scenarios that show you how to use these objects remotely in both your Windows Forms and Web Forms applications.

In the last chapter, I showed you how to build simple XML Web services and test them through a simple Web interface. What you got in return from the service was an XML stream of data. That may be all well and fine, but you want to use this XML data within the .NET applications that you are building today. I am going to show you the possibilities for doing this. After you are done with this chapter, you are going to be even *more* amazed at the power and ease with which you can use and build XML Web services on the .NET platform.

In this chapter, you will cover

- Understanding the consumption of XML Web services
- Using XML Web services with your Windows Forms
- Using XML Web services with your Web Forms
- Consuming an XML Web service from another XML Web service
- Consuming an XML Web service from a Visual Basic 6.0 Application
- Consuming an XML Web service from an ASP page

Understanding the Consumption of XML Web Services

What type of client application will you need to build in order to consume a remote XML Web service? This is an important question. Because of the many examples of XML Web services available on the Internet, you might think that XML Web services are only consumable via Web Forms or similar Web-based applications. However, XML Web services are accessible from *any* client application, as long as that application can consume XML that is transported via HTTP.

Don't let the name Web services fool you. You can just as easily consume and use the logic presented by an XML Web service in your Windows Forms applications as you can via your Web Forms. It is even possible to call and consume an XML Web service from another XML Web service. What is meant by *consumption* of an XML Web service? Consumption of an XML Web service is making a reference to a remote object that can be within your own network or half way around the world. After making a reference to this remote object, you can call and use the methods that the object exposes. You are *consuming* the object.

Why you would ever consume a distant object in a Windows Forms application? Traditionally, an application that resides on the desktop of a client computer usually performs simple to complex tasks (such as data entry) and interacts with an internal database or a remote database elsewhere on the network. As applications evolve, however, the demands on that client application also evolve.

For example, look at the Microsoft Money application shown in Figure 5-1. In the beginning of its life as an application, it had all the features that you would expect a home-finance application to have. As time went on, however, users started demanding more information that the application couldn't provide while it was just sitting on the desktop and grabbing information from an internal database.

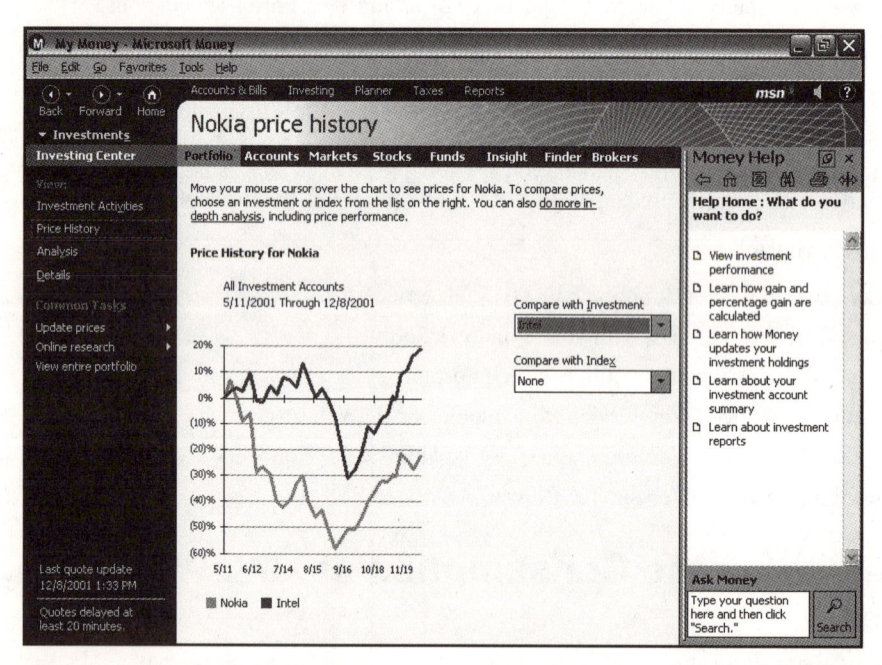

Figure 5-1: Microsoft Money using the Internet to provide more information to the user. This example shows Nokia's stock price history as compared to Intel's price history. This is not possible unless the application is tied to the Internet.

Users wanted stock quotes, charts, alerts, and current financial advice. So now this desktop application uses the Internet to transmit information and present it to the user. The application wouldn't be as valuable without its capability to receive up-to-date information that is transmitted across the Internet.

So, for the Windows Forms applications that you are building today, you may be required to provide information that is only accessible via the Internet. There is no better way than using today's standards, such as XML and SOAP, to access and present this information to your application.

You may find there are pieces of your applications that are easier to consume as an XML Web service than to build yourself. Sometimes it is easier to just buy a new house than to build one from the ground up.

Accessing an XML Web Service from a Windows Form

As I have mentioned, consuming an XML Web service into your Windows Forms applications is easy to do. Take a quick look at how to do this with the Calculator XML Web service that you built in the previous chapter. Follow these steps to create the Windows Form needed to consume the Calculator XML Web service:

1. Open Visual Studio .NET by clicking Start ⇨ All Programs ⇨ Microsoft Visual Studio .NET ⇨ Microsoft Visual Studio .NET.

2. Click the New Project button to open the New Project dialog window, or click File ⇨ New ⇨ Project (see Figure 5-2).

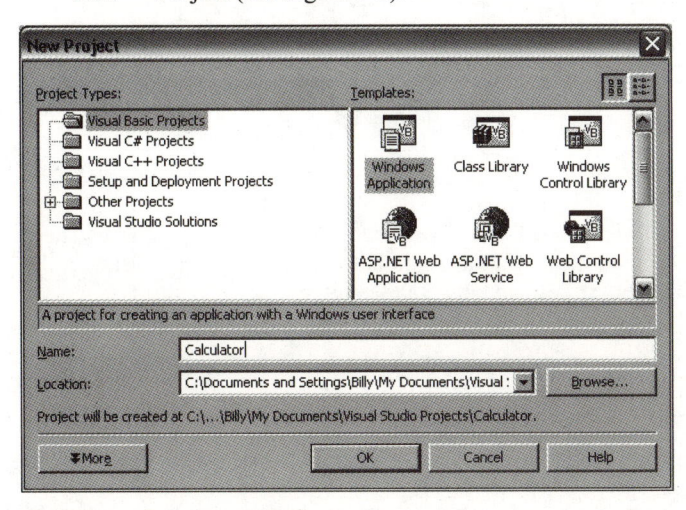

Figure 5-2: Selecting the Windows Application in order to consume the Calculator XML Web service.

3. Within the New Project dialog window, select the Windows Application template as shown in Figure 5-2. You can choose either Visual Basic .NET or C#; it won't make a difference.

4. After you have the application open, notice that there is already a form in place for you to start developing. Lay out the form using elements from the Toolbox so that it looks something like the form shown in Figure 5-3. You can do this by simply dragging and dropping the controls from the toolbox directly onto the form and then positioning them so that they are laid out properly.

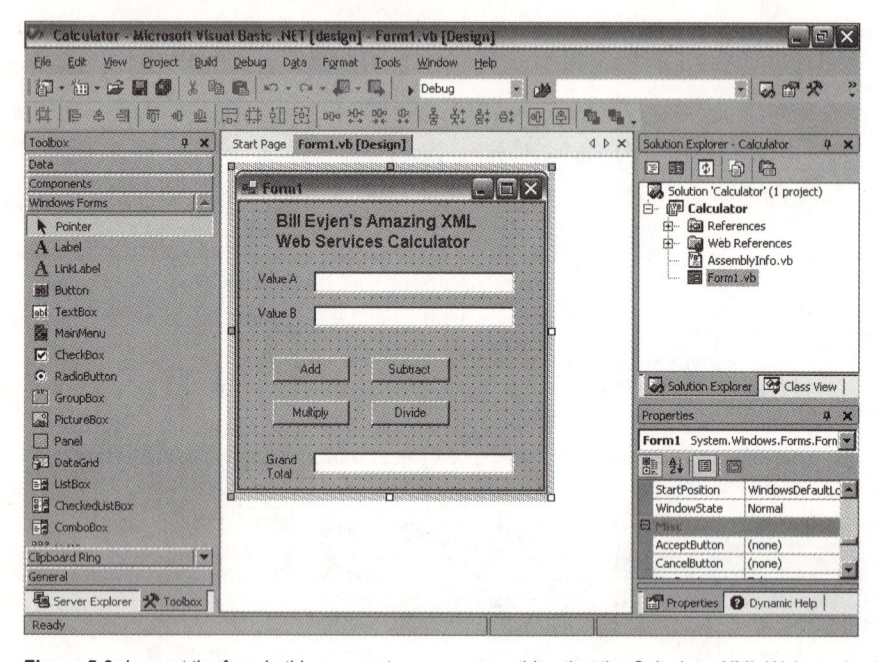

Figure 5-3: Lay out the form in this manner to access everything that the Calculator XML Web service has to offer.

5. Remember to make note of the name of each of the elements on the page. You also need to rename the Add button as `AddButton`, the Subtract button as `SubtractButton`, the Multiply button as `MultiplyButton`, and the Divide button as `DivideButton`.

6. After placing the three text boxes on your form, clear out the text values of each from the Properties window so that they are initially blank. You are now ready to deal with the remote XML Web service.

> **NOTE:** The basics on how to build a Windows Forms application are beyond the scope of this book. For more information on everything you need to know in building Windows Forms, please review the *Visual Basic .NET Bible* and the *C# Bible*, both by Hungry Minds, Inc.

The following are the steps to start consuming any particular XML Web service:

1. Discover the XML Web service that you need to use within your application.

2. Create a proxy class for your XML Web service within your application.
3. Make a reference to the proxy class in the client code by including its namespace.
4. Create an instance of the XML Web service proxy class in the client code.
5. Finally, access the WebMethods that the XML Web service has exposed.

Using Visual Studio .NET makes a lot of the steps listed here quite simple. The first trick is to discover the XML Web service that you want to consume. There are a number of directories available to the public where you can search for the particular XML Web service that you want.

Most notable is UDDI.org. UDDI is a way to search for XML Web services. Microsoft, IBM, and others started this service with the intention of providing one main search portal to find Web services. Other options include third-party directories such as `SalCentral.com` and `XMethods.com`.

Now start the discovery process on the Calculator XML Web service that you built in the previous chapter.

In order to access the Calculator XML Web service within the Calculator Windows Application, you make a *Web Reference* to it. In Visual Studio .NET it is very simple to do this. Right-click on the project name in the Solution Explorer window and select Add Web Reference (see Figure 5-4).

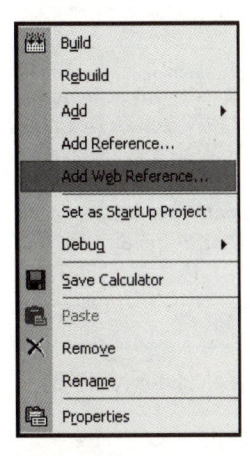

Figure 5-4: Adding a Web Reference to your project is as simple as right-clicking on your project name within the Solution Explorer.

After you choose to add a Web Reference to your project, you activate the Add Web Reference dialog window (Figure 5-5).

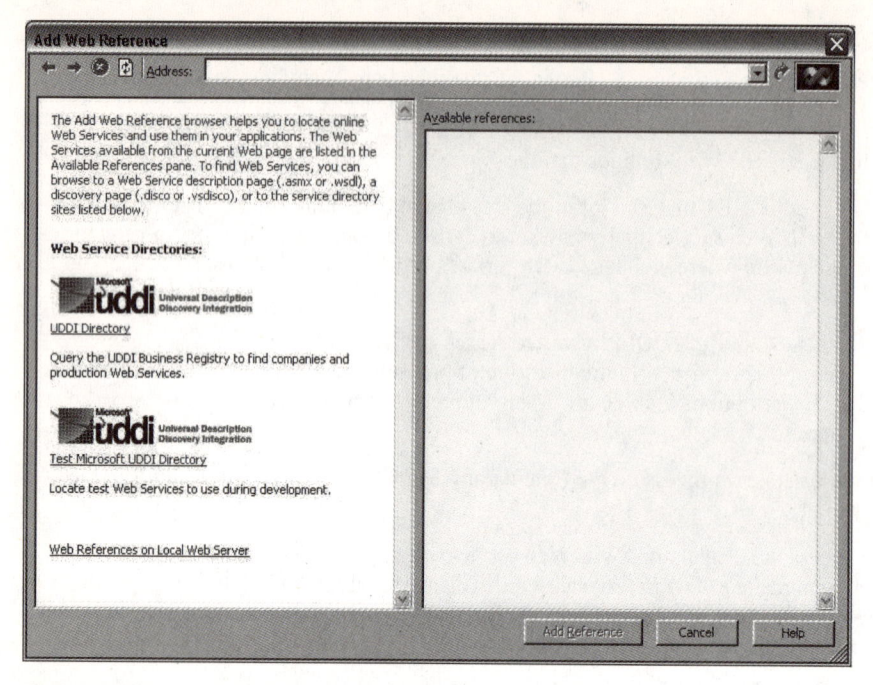

Figure 5-5: The Add Web Reference dialog window.

Using this dialog window, it is possible to search in a couple of different ways for potential XML Web services to consume. The first is by using the Microsoft UDDI Directory (located at `http://uddi.microsoft.com`). Another option is to use test XML Web services from the Test Microsoft UDDI Directory. A third option is to look for XML Web services that are located on your local server. A last option, which isn't listed in the left-pane window, is to type the direct path to the URL of the XML Web service in the address bar of the dialog window.

> **CROSS-REFERENCE:** These UDDI options are covered in Chapter 16.

For the purposes of this application, you make a direct reference to the Calculator XML Web service by typing the URL directly in the address bar. Type in **`http://localhost/TestWS/Service1.asmx`**, hit enter, and the XML Web service appears in the dialog window.

> **TIP:** If you clicked on the link *Web References on Local Web Server* and couldn't find the Calculator XML Web service, don't be alarmed! The reason that it didn't show up in the listing of XML Web services available on the local server is because you built that XML Web service from scratch, and you didn't build a discovery document (a .disco file) to go along with it so that Visual Studio could find it.

Figure 5-6 shows the Calculator XML Web service in the Add Web Reference dialog window.

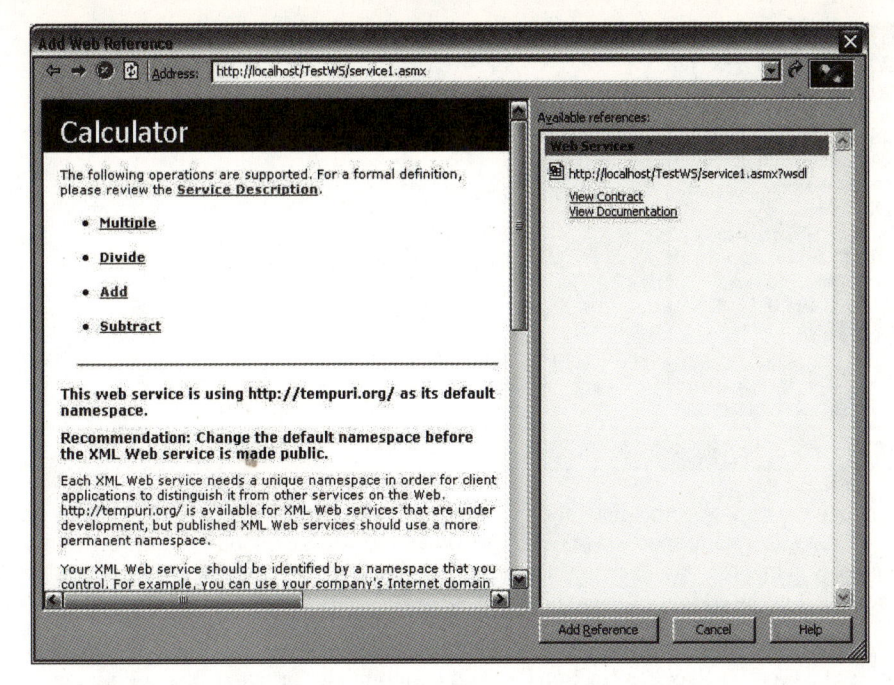

Figure 5-6: Your Calculator XML Web service as shown in the Add Web Reference dialog window.

From this dialog window you are able to view the details about the XML Web service and even test out the Web service. By clicking on the View Contract link, you can view the WSDL document that describes the interface to the XML Web service.

If you wish to add this service to your project (which you do), all you need to do is click the Add Reference button.

After you add the Calculator Web Reference to your project, Visual Studio .NET creates an XML Web service proxy class automatically and adds it to your Calculator project. Visual Studio .NET uses the WSDL description document to create a proxy class that exposes the methods of the XML Web service and handles the marshaling of appropriate arguments back and forth between the XML Web service and any application that you build. This is another reason to use Visual Studio .NET to build your XML Web services.

Notice the reference to the remote object, the Calculator XML Web service, in the Solution Explorer. Within the project you are working with, note a direct link to the server that is hosting the XML Web Server. In your case, it is the local server. This is shown in Figure 5-7.

108 Part II: **The Basics of XML Web Services**

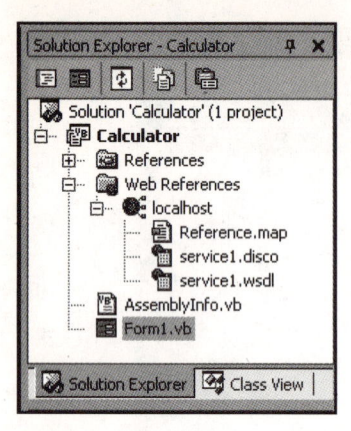

Figure 5-7: A reference in the Solution Explorer to the Calculator XML Web service.

This reference to the remote object now allows you to programmatically access this object over HTTP. To see how namespaces work in these situations, right-click on `localhost` and select Rename. Rename the reference to `CalcWebService`. Later, you will see how this name change is reflected in the coding of the application.

Now that you have made a reference to the Calculator XML Web service, write some code in order to access this service. Double-click on the Add button in the form and start coding the events behind each of the buttons on this code-behind page.

This action causes a new page within the code window to open, the *code-behind* page. The code-behind page is a separate page that allows you to place the business logic in a spot separate from the presentation code for your page. Notice that the Button click event is already in place for you, and you can start coding this event directly. When you have finished it, your code-behind page should look like the code from Listing 5-1.

Listing 5-1: Form1.vb and Form1.cs

VB

```
Public Class Form1
    Inherits System.Windows.Forms.Form

    Private Sub AddButton_Click(ByVal sender As System.Object, ByVal e As
 System.EventArgs) Handles AddButton.Click
        Dim ws As New CalcWebService.Calculator()
        Dim AddResult As Double
        AddResult = ws.Add(TextBox1.Text, TextBox2.Text)
        TextBox3.Text = AddResult
    End Sub

    Private Sub SubtractButton_Click(ByVal sender As
```

```vb
                System.Object, ByVal e As System.EventArgs) Handles
SubtractButton.Click
        Dim ws As New CalcWebService.Calculator()
        Dim SubtractResult As Double
        SubtractResult = ws.Subtract(TextBox1.Text, TextBox2.Text)
        TextBox3.Text = SubtractResult
    End Sub

    Private Sub MultiplyButton_Click(ByVal sender As
        System.Object, ByVal e As System.EventArgs) Handles
MultiplyButton.Click
        Dim ws As New CalcWebService.Calculator()
        Dim MultiplyResult As Double
        MultiplyResult = ws.Multiply(TextBox1.Text, TextBox2.Text)
        TextBox3.Text = MultiplyResult
    End Sub

    Private Sub DivideButton_Click(ByVal sender As System.Object, ByVal
e As
        System.EventArgs) Handles DivideButton.Click
        Dim ws As New CalcWebService.Calculator()
        Dim DivideResult As Double
        DivideResult = ws.Divide(TextBox1.Text, TextBox2.Text)
        TextBox3.Text = DivideResult
    End Sub
End Class
```

C#

```csharp
using System;
using System.Drawing;
using System.Collections;
using System.ComponentModel;
using System.Windows.Forms;
using System.Data;

namespace Calculator
{
  /// <summary>
  /// This Windows Application is to call the Calculator XML
      Web Service.
  /// </summary>
  public class Form1 : System.Windows.Forms.Form
  {
        private void AddButton_Click(object sender, System.EventArgs e)
        {
            CalcWebService.Calculator ws = new
CalcWebService.Calculator();
            double AddResult;
```

```csharp
            AddResult = ws.Add(int.Parse(textBox1.Text),
                            int.Parse(textBox2.Text));
            textBox3.Text = AddResult.ToString();
        }

        private void SubtractButton_Click(object sender, System.EventArgs e)
        {
            CalcWebService.Calculator ws = new CalcWebService.Calculator();
            double SubtractResult;
            SubtractResult = ws.Subtract(int.Parse(textBox1.Text),
                                    int.Parse(textBox2.Text));
            textBox3.Text = SubtractResult.ToString();
        }

        private void MultiplyButton_Click(object sender, System.EventArgs e)
        {
            CalcWebService.Calculator ws = new CalcWebService.Calculator();
            double MultiplyResult;
            MultiplyResult = ws.Multiply(int.Parse(textBox1.Text),
                                    int.Parse(textBox2.Text));
            textBox3.Text = MultiplyResult.ToString();
        }

        private void DivideButton_Click(object sender, System.EventArgs e)
        {
            CalcWebService.Calculator ws = new CalcWebService.Calculator();
            double DivideResult;
            DivideResult = ws.Divide(int.Parse(textBox1.Text),
                                int.Parse(textBox2.Text));
            textBox3.Text = DivideResult.ToString();
        }

    }
}
```

> **NOTE:** Some of the Visual Studio .NET generated C# code was removed from this code sample for clarity. The most important parts in the C# sample here are the button click events.

If you put all this C# code into the code-behind page and none of the buttons work, or if only one button works, redo the code behind by clicking one button at a time and putting in the code for just that particular button. Doing that for each button individually causes Visual Studio .NET to create the following code within the Windows Form Designer-generated code section:

```
this.AddButton.Click += new System.EventHandler(this.AddButton_Click);
```

In Visual Studio .NET, when you code your Windows Forms in C# and you click one of the buttons, Visual Studio .NET wires that button to the associated event handler in the Windows-generated code. Therefore, if you code this Windows Form in C#, click each of the buttons so that their click events are wired correctly. The reason that you do this in C# and not in Visual Basic .NET is that, in the initial design process, there were two separate teams working on this item, one for each language. Each team did the task in its own way.

Understanding the Code

Take a quick look at the code that you used in the Windows application for connecting to the Calculator XML Web service. It will help you understand a little better just what is going on and why.

With each of the button clicks, you invoke the XML Web service by instantiating an instance of the `CalcWebService.Calculator` proxy class.

VB

```
Dim ws As New CalcWebService.Calculator()
```

C#

```
CalcWebService.Calculator ws = new CalcWebService.Calculator();
```

You changed the name of the proxy class from `localhost` to `CalcWebService` in the beginning of this exercise. This change allows you to refer to the proxy class by any namespace that you choose. So instead of referring to the proxy class as `localhost.Calculator()`, you refer to it as `CalcWebService.Calculator()`.

Next you make a call to the `Add`, `Subtract`, `Multiply`, or `Divide` methods exactly as if you are making this call directly on the XML Web service itself. The main difference is that instead, you are making the call to the local proxy class, which is, in turn, making the appropriate calls to the Calculator XML Web service by packaging your request as SOAP and sending it to the appropriate destination for you.

VB

```
AddResult = ws.Add(TextBox1.Text, TextBox2.Text)
```

C#

```
AddResult = ws.Add(int.Parse(textBox1.Text), int.Parse(textBox2.Text));
```

In the end, you take the result of the XML Web service method call, place it inside your local variable, and assign that variable to a text box on the form.

VB

```
TextBox3.Text = AddResult
```

C#

```
textBox3.Text = AddResult.ToString();
```

Now you have just created a Windows Form that has all the Calculator Web service logic (as simple as it was), and imported that logic to use within itself. You did all this with very little code. Just think of the possibilities for your Windows Forms applications when the logic that you want to remotely call is more complicated than your simple Calculator Web service. As you develop more and more XML Web services for consumption, you see their power and utility within the programming models you work with.

Accessing an XML Web Service from a Web Form

You just saw how to consume an XML Web service from a Windows Form application. If you just jumped to this section of the chapter and skipped this first part, take note that if you get lost or need more clarification on any of the consumption issues mentioned here, you will probably find the explanation you're looking for in the earlier pages of this chapter.

As you will see, consuming an XML Web service in a Web Form is very similar to consuming one in a Windows Form. Before you work through an example of consuming an XML Web service in your Web Form, take a quick look at why you might want to consume an XML Web service in the Web applications that you are building today.

> **NOTE:** Because this is a book on XML Web services, I don't have a lot of time to go over all the basics of building Web Forms on the .NET platform. For more complete information on this issue, be sure to check out the *Visual Basic .NET Bible* and the *ASP.NET Bible*, both from Hungry Minds, Inc.

Browser-based applications have found the Web!

Web development has changed dramatically since people started doing static brochure sites in the mid-1990s. It has branched out to now include dynamic Internet applications. Until recently, companies often depended upon traditional Win16 and Win32 Visual Basic applications, as well as more complex C++ applications to deliver truly robust applications that end users could easily utilize in their day-to-day operations. Now these companies are turning to the Internet. The browser has actually turned out to be a great medium to deliver these robust applications.

If you think about it, it makes plenty of sense. Suppose you're a company that wants to build an application that 3,000 employees will use on a daily basis. You could build a Win32 Visual Basic application, but this requires you to install the application on every employee's computer (assuming that it has the proper hardware configurations needed to run the application). You must then train employees to use this new program. Beyond that, every time there is a bug fix or an upgrade to the application, someone needs to go out and apply these changes to each instance of the program. That can be a daunting task, even when done remotely!

This is exactly why Internet-based applications have become so popular and continue to increase in popularity every day.

Internet applications use the browser as the container of the application. This is a great advantage. Most computers out there have a browser installed, and most users know how to use a browser (greatly reducing any training that may be required). Using the browser also makes obsolete the need to install the program (or any upgrades) on users' computers. Users always see the latest and greatest version of the application because there is only one instance of the application sitting on the server.

As time goes on, these Internet applications become more and more robust and allow parties to work with each other in ways they never dreamed of in the past. Even with these changes in application development underway, there is still a need on the Web for brochure, commercial, and informative sites. Some sites require only a simple form, whereas others may connect to a simple database table to provide up-to-date information. The great thing about all this is that these sites can use the same advantages of .NET development that the largest browser-based applications use.

Why use XML Web services with Web Forms?

XML Web services are going to be heavily involved with Web application development as the applications that you are building in the browser evolve. Web application development has changed dramatically over the years and as it has changed and evolved, so have the technologies that you use to develop applications on top of this platform.

Using XML Web services is the next step in the fast evolution of Web applications and, as you work through some of these examples, you will quickly see why.

When developers sit down to write a new application for the Web, in many cases, they have trouble using the pieces that they have written in the past within the current application that they are building. Web-application development is customized to the overall application requirements and usually requires heavy changes in order to make it fit elsewhere. You may work with some models that allow you to get closer to the holy grail of programming — *code reuse* — but these models have been painfully developed over time and usually still require substantial work to completely integrate them into the current applications that you are developing.

XML Web services are services that are available now for you to use within your Web applications. These XML Web services, in many cases, make up the building blocks of your applications and bring your applications to the next step in their development. These pieces of logic, which are callable remotely from other providers, enable you to develop certain pieces of the application yourself, while allowing you to purchase or freely consume other pieces that may be difficult or impossible to develop on your own.

This kind of model allows businesses to focus on their core business and to outsource (in a sense) the pieces of logic that are not part of what they do. Because XML Web services enable you to obtain certain pieces of logic without building them yourself, all that you need to be concerned about, from a developer's standpoint, is how to integrate this service into your current environment.

Look at another example. Say you're a developer who works for a company that sells custom-built airplanes. One day the vice-president of the company wants the company Web site to display a box on the front page that contains aviation news. You probably can do this easily. What if he said, however, that he wanted these few lines to be linked to the full story, but he didn't want the user to be taken off of the company's Web site to read the story? And what if he also wanted the news feed to be filtered for certain topics? Now it's getting a little trickier.

XML Web services were built with this kind of model in mind. As you are already aware, the provider of an XML Web service is just providing pure data, and this data is formatted using XML. This formatted data is then sent to the requester, and the requester can use this data in whatever manner he sees fit. So if the requester of the data wants to place the data on the front page of his Web site, or if he wants to filter the data before using it, so be it. It is easy and simple to do.

You may find that getting some of the building blocks of your applications for the Web will be more desirable as the XML Web services model advances. You may also find core functionality within your own company that you want to expose to selected customers or to the public at large for free (as a promotional service) or for a set price. Exposing these functionalities or services as XML Web services will create a new revenue model for your company or organization, or a new way of communicating with your customers or peers.

Building an ASP.NET Web application

Now you venture on and build a Web Form that consumes an XML Web service, but this time, you will change things around and consume an *actual* remote XML Web service (one that is residing on an actual remote server and not on the localhost).

The XML Web service that you can consume in your Web Form can be found at the following location:

`www.xmlws101.com/xmlws/EnglishGermanDictionary.asmx`

As you might be able to tell from the descriptive URL, this XML Web service is an English-German-English Dictionary XML Web service. Follow these steps to consume the EnglishGermanEnglishDictionary XML Web service:

1. Open Visual Studio .NET by clicking Start ⇨ All Programs ⇨ Microsoft Visual Studio .NET ⇨ Microsoft Visual Studio .NET.
2. Click the New Project button to open the New Project dialog window, or select File ⇨ New ⇨ Project.
3. Within the New Project dialog window, select the ASP.NET Web Application template (see Figure 5-8). You can choose to use either Visual Basic .NET or C#. As I said before, it won't make a difference.
4. Click OK.

Now Visual Studio .NET creates a virtual root for you. The name is shown after the forward-slash, `EnglishGermanDictionary`.

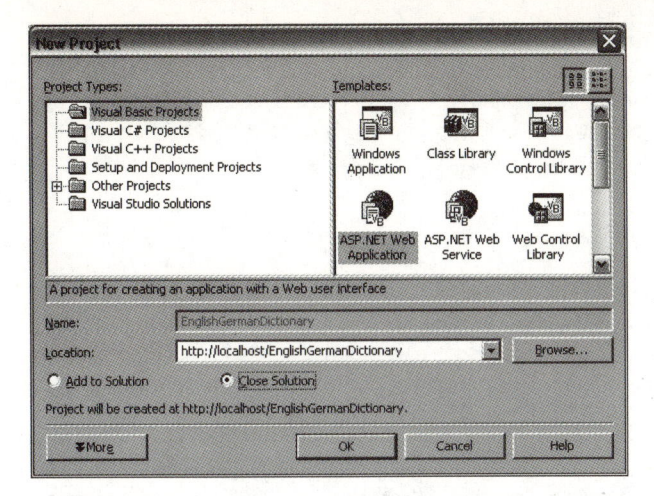

Figure 5-8: Creating a Web Form to consume your XML Web service.

Within the Solution Explorer, notice that Visual Studio .NET also created a number of different files for you (Figure 5-9). The file that you want to concentrate on is the WebForm1.aspx file. This is the file in which you create the Web Interface to the XML Web service.

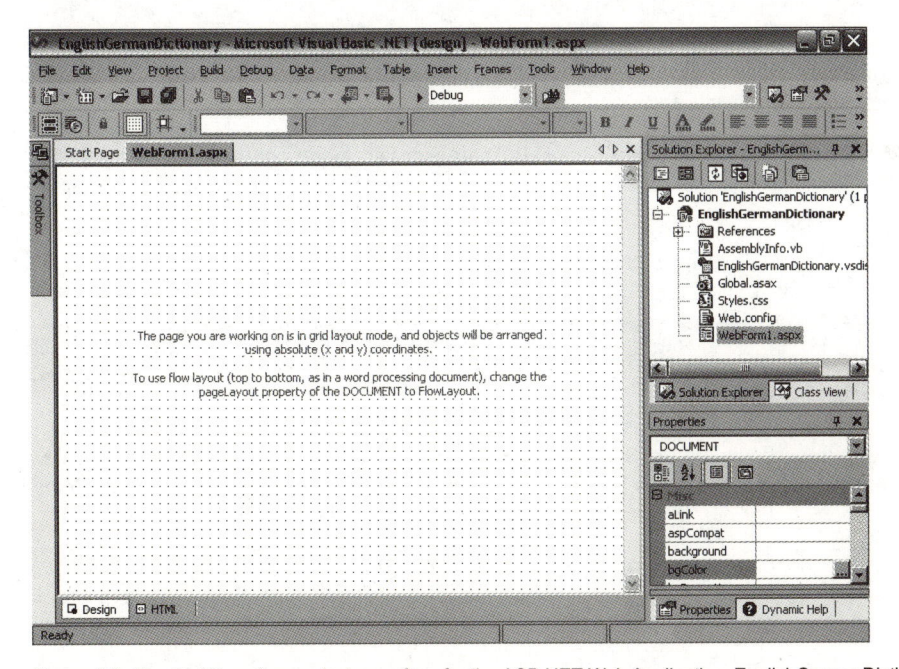

Figure 5-9: The WebForm1.aspx design surface for the ASP.NET Web Application, EnglishGermanDictionary.

Presently the `WebForm1.aspx` file is in the grid-layout mode. Click anywhere in the code window, and you are able to change the properties for the page in the Properties window. Scroll down until you see the `pageLayout` property. Click in the `GridLayout` box and you see a drop-down list. Change the page to a `FlowLayout` (see Figure 5-10).

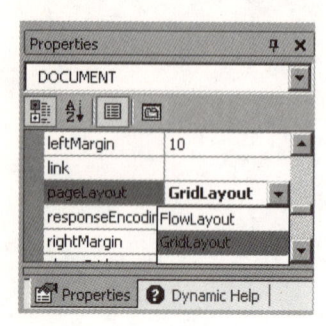

Figure 5-10: Changing the pageLayout property from GridLayout to FlowLayout.

`GridLayout` is quite similar to what Visual Basic 6.0 developers use when developing their Windows applications. `GridLayout` uses X-Y positioning to place controls on the page. `FlowLayout` is similar to what ASP developers use. It employs standard HTML methods to break apart controls on the page. You can use the mode you are comfortable with, but just be aware that this is a changeable property.

Within the Solution Explorer, change the name of the `WebForm1.aspx` file to `EnglishGerman.aspx`. After this is all done, you are ready to start laying the elements on the design surface.

You don't need to design your pages by just dropping and dragging controls onto the page. Instead, you can switch to the code view of the page and code the controls directly into the page.

For this example, you'll work in the Design mode. Open the Toolbox and drag over a DropDownList Web control.

> **NOTE:** For these examples, you are working with the controls under the Web Forms tab in the Toolbox, although it is quite possible to work with the HTML controls under the HTML tab.

If you make sure the DropDownList control is highlighted, you see the properties of this control in the Properties window. Scroll down to the Misc section of the properties available for this control and click the Items box. Click the button that shows up after you do this. You'll notice that a new dialog box appears, the ListItem Collection Editor, as shown in Figure 5-11.

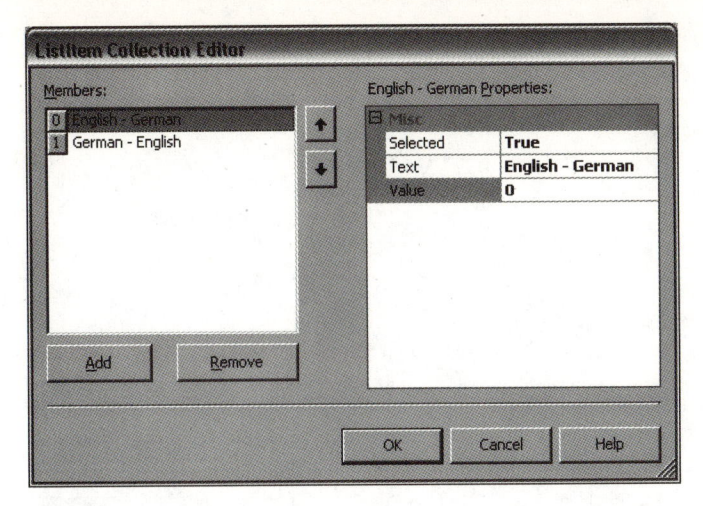

Figure 5-11: Creating a DropDownList control.

This editor allows you to add elements to the DropDownList control. Click the Add button twice to add two items. Highlight the `ListItem 0` and change its properties to the following in the right pane of the editor:

Selected: **True**
Text: **English-German**
Value: **0**

For the second ListItem, change the properties to the following:

Selected: **False**
Text: **German-English**
Value: **1**

Next put a Textbox, a Button, and a Label control in your form. Your code for this page should look somewhat like Listing 5-2.

Listing 5-2: EnglishGerman.aspx

```
<%@ Page Language="vb" AutoEventWireup="false"
    Codebehind="EnglishGerman.aspx.vb"
    Inherits="EnglishGermanDictionary.WebForm1"%>

<HTML>
  <HEAD>
     <title>English - German Dictionary</title>
        <meta name="GENERATOR" content="Microsoft Visual
          Studio.NET 7.0">
        <meta name="CODE_LANGUAGE" content="Visual Basic
          7.0">
        <meta name="vs_defaultClientScript"
```

```
            content="JavaScript">
        <meta name="vs_targetSchema"
            content="http://schemas.microsoft.com/
            intellisense/ie5">
</HEAD>
<body>
    <form id="Form1" method="post" runat="server">
        <P><STRONG><FONT face="Verdana" size="2">Choose a
        dictionary<BR>
        </FONT></STRONG>
        <asp:DropDownList id="DropDownList1" runat="server">
            <asp:ListItem Value="0" Selected="True">
            English - German</asp:ListItem>
            <asp:ListItem Value="1">
            German - English</asp:ListItem>
        </asp:DropDownList></P>
        <P><STRONG><FONT face="Verdana" size="2">
        Type in your word to translate</FONT><BR>
        <asp:TextBox id="TextBox1" runat="server"
         Width="243px"></asp:TextBox></STRONG></P>
        <STRONG><P>
        <asp:Button id="Button1" runat="server"
         Text="Translate"></asp:Button></P>
        <P>
        <asp:Label id="Label1"
        runat="server"></asp:Label></P>
        </STRONG>
    </form>
</body>
</HTML>
```

NOTE: In this code sample, some of the attribute values will be different if you are using C# as the language of your ASP.NET Web Application.

Your page should look like Figure 5-12.

Now that you have this code in place, you make a reference to the remote XML Web service on the Internet. You do this as you did for the Windows application earlier in this chapter.

Right-click on the project in the Solution Explorer window and select Add Web Reference. In the address bar of the Add Web Reference dialog window, type in the location of the remote .asmx file, www.xmlws101.com/xmlws/EnglishGermanDictionary.asmx. Press Return and you should find the EnglishGermanEnglishDictionary XML Web service. Click the Add Reference button and this adds this remote reference to your project so that you are able to remotely call the methods of this object as if it were on your local machine. Rename the reference whatever you choose. In my example, I named it `Translator`.

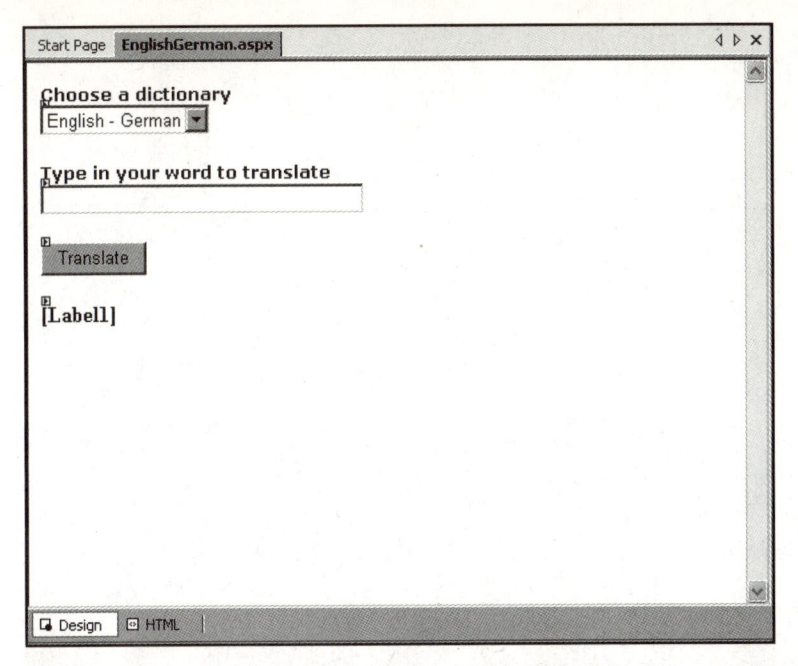

![Screenshot of EnglishGerman.aspx design view showing a dropdown "Choose a dictionary" with "English - German" selected, a textbox labeled "Type in your word to translate", a "Translate" button, and [Label1].]

Figure 5-12: The code window showing the Web Form that will integrate with your EnglishGermanDictionary XML Web service.

After you have everything in place, double-click the Button control on the design page. The code in Listing 5-3 shows what this code-behind page should look like when it is completed.

Listing 5-3: EnglishGerman.aspx.vb and EnglishGerman.aspx.cs

VB

```
Public Class WebForm1
    Inherits System.Web.UI.Page
    Protected WithEvents DropDownList1 As
System.Web.UI.WebControls.DropDownList
    Protected WithEvents TextBox1 As System.Web.UI.WebControls.TextBox
    Protected WithEvents Button1 As System.Web.UI.WebControls.Button
    Protected WithEvents Label1 As System.Web.UI.WebControls.Label

    Private Sub Button1_Click(ByVal sender As System.Object,
                ByVal e As System.EventArgs) Handles Button1.Click
        Dim EG As New Translator.EnglishGermanEnglishDictionary()

        If DropDownList1.SelectedItem.Value = 0 Then
            Label1.Text = EG.EnglishGermanDictionary(TextBox1.Text)
        Else
            Label1.Text = EG.GermanEnglishDictionary(TextBox1.Text)
```

```
            End If
    End Sub
End Class
```

C#

```csharp
using System;
using System.Collections;
using System.ComponentModel;
using System.Data;
using System.Drawing;
using System.Web;
using System.Web.SessionState;
using System.Web.UI;
using System.Web.UI.WebControls;
using System.Web.UI.HtmlControls;

namespace EnglishGermanDictionary1
{
    public class WebForm1 : System.Web.UI.Page
    {
        protected System.Web.UI.WebControls.TextBox TextBox1;
        protected System.Web.UI.WebControls.DropDownList DropDownList1;
        protected System.Web.UI.WebControls.Button Button1;
        protected System.Web.UI.WebControls.Label Label1;

        private void Button1_Click(object sender, System.EventArgs e)
        {
            Translator.EnglishGermanEnglishDictionary EG =
              new Translator.EnglishGermanEnglishDictionary();

            if (DropDownList1.SelectedItem.Value == "0")
            {
                Label1.Text = EG.EnglishGermanDictionary(TextBox1.Text);
            }
            else
            {
                Label1.Text = EG.GermanEnglishDictionary(TextBox1.Text);
            }

        }
    }
}
```

There are two methods in this service: `EnglishGermanDictionary` and `GermanEnglishDictionary`. The user determines which one is called by selecting from the DropDownList control. Depending on the dictionary method called, the word that is typed by the user is passed into the method call, and the XML Web service gives back the translated word.

This is a pretty simple example, but shows you how to consume an XML Web service within your Web Forms.

From One XML Web Service to Another

Now you know how to consume an XML Web service from a Windows Form and a Web Form. Another way that you will frequently consume XML Web services is from another XML Web service.

As you have seen, XML Web services are a great way to consume business logic and expose data from competing systems. Sometimes you may want to return some data or logic from a system, but you won't have the resources necessary to return everything you need without drawing on a second system. In a case like this, it makes sense to consume another XML Web service, distinct from the XML Web service that you are writing. Figure 5-13 shows an example of this.

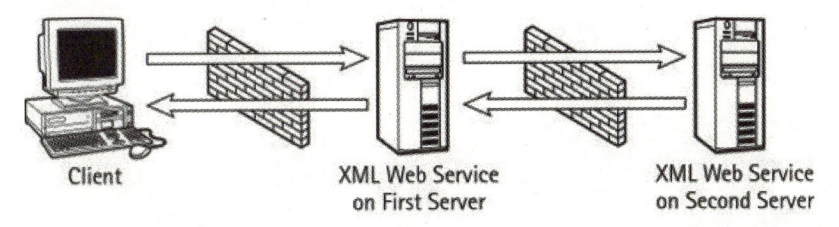

Figure 5-13: In this example, the first XML Web service needs to get information from another XML Web service before it can return any information to the client.

For example, suppose you are supplying an XML Web service that provides users with information on available tee times for the golf course that you own (just imagine!). Users can access your XML Web service and get a schedule of all the available tee times for the week. But then suppose the users started demanding an extra feature from your XML Web service: They also want to know the weather forecast for the specific time of the tee off. How would you go about this? It would probably be too much for you to start building applications that produce up-to-date weather forecasts; therefore, you might find it easier to consume another XML Web service that provides forecasts. You are able to take the particular data you need from the second XML Web service and plug that into the XML data that you are passing to your users. In this case, you put forecasts next to all the available tee times, thereby increasing the functionality of your own particular XML Web service.

A simple example: The first XML Web service

Take a look at a quick and simple example of how to consume another XML Web service from a your XML Web service.

Just for example's sake, use for your main XML Web service the one that comes commented in the code when you first pull up a new XML Web service project, the Hello World example. (See Listing 5-4.)

Part II: The Basics of XML Web Services

Listing 5-4: Your main XML Web service

VB

```
Imports System.Web.Services

<WebService()> _
Public Class Service1
    Inherits System.Web.Services.WebService

    <WebMethod()> Public Function HelloWorld() As String
        Return "Hello World"
    End Function

End Class
```

C#

```
using System;
using System.Collections;
using System.ComponentModel;
using System.Data;
using System.Diagnostics;
using System.Web;
using System.Web.Services;

namespace FirstWebService
{
  public class Service1 : System.Web.Services.WebService
  {
        [WebMethod]
        public string HelloWorld()
        {
               return "Hello World";
        }
  }
}
```

A simple example: The second XML Web service

Now take a look at the second XML Web service that you want to merge in with the first one (Listing 5-5).

Listing 5-5: Your second XML Web service

VB

```
Imports System.Web.Services

<WebService()> _
Public Class Service2
```

```
        Inherits System.Web.Services.WebService

        <WebMethod()> Public Function AnnounceTime() As DateTime
            Return System.DateTime.Now()
        End Function

End Class
```

C#

```csharp
using System;
using System.Collections;
using System.ComponentModel;
using System.Data;
using System.Diagnostics;
using System.Web;
using System.Web.Services;

namespace AnnounceTime
{
  public class Service2 : System.Web.Services.WebService
  {
        [WebMethod]
        public DateTime AnnounceTime()
        {
            return System.DateTime.Now;
        }
  }
}
```

Now you have two XML Web services. You want to add to the first example, where you simply return a Hello World string, the system time from your second XML Web service. Doing this is rather simple. Just reference another XML Web service as you would if you were using a Windows Form or Web Form. You do this by right-clicking on the project and choosing to Add Web Reference. Go through the dialog and find the XML Web service that you want to consume. It is a good idea to always rename these references within the Solution Explorer so that they make sense to you within your own solution.

After you have made this reference, you are ready to consume the second XML Web service into your first one (see Listing 5-6).

Listing 5-6: Consuming the second XML Web service into the Hello World XML Web service

VB

```
Imports System.Web.Services

<WebService()>
Public Class Service1
    Inherits System.Web.Services.WebService
```

```
    <WebMethod()> Public Function HelloWorld() As String
        Dim ST As New DateTimeFromSystem.Service2()
        Return "Hello World. The time from the 2nd XML Web Service is " _
            & ST.AnnounceTime()
    End Function

End Class
```

C#

```
using System;
using System.Collections;
using System.ComponentModel;
using System.Data;
using System.Diagnostics;
using System.Web;
using System.Web.Services;

namespace FirstWebService
{
  public class Service1 : System.Web.Services.WebService
  {
        [WebMethod]
        public string HelloWorld()
        {
            DateTimeFromSystem.Service2 ST = new
                DateTimeFromSystem.Service2();
            return "Hello World. The time from the
                2nd XML Web Service is " +
                ST.AnnounceTime();
        }
  }
}
```

This was a quick example to show you that just as you can consume XML Web services in both Windows Forms and Web Forms, you can also use this consumption model to your advantage and consume a service in any of the XML Web services that you create. You are also not limited to referencing just one XML Web service at a time. You can reference an unlimited number (but this would, of course, affect performance).

Consuming an XML Web Service from a Visual Basic 6.0 Application

Can you consume something from .NET, such as a .NET-generated XML Web service, into an older technology that is not .NET-enabled such as a Visual Basic 6.0 application? You sure can!

There are literally millions of applications that are built using VB6, and they are not going to disappear for a long time to come. You may be doing new VB6 development, altering a VB6 application, or extending one of these applications, and you want to use the capabilities for consuming an XML Web service just as you would with a .NET application.

Why you would want to do this? After you have worked with XML Web services (and as more XML Web services come to the market), you will find a definite value in their consumption. You don't want to be limited to only the technology that you are working with. From what was said in earlier chapters, you know that the platform and the technologies used have little to do with the capability to use XML Web services. As long as the platform and/or the application can consume XML over HTTP, you are able to work with the Web services that are generated on the .NET platform.

Of course, it isn't as easy to consume an XML Web service in a Visual Basic 6.0 application as it is in a Windows Forms application, but the capability to do it is there. You start by consuming a simple XML Web service into a Visual Basic 6.0 application. You can work with the XML Web service that was shown in Listing 5-6.

I won't go through everything you need to do in order to build a Visual Basic 6.0 application. I will show you enough so that when you are building these kinds of applications, you will be able to easily follow the code examples and use them to consume an XML Web service.

Open up a Standard EXE project in Visual Basic and you are presented with a form. All you need to do to this form is to add a button; so add a button to the form and give it the caption: "Click me to invoke the XML Web service."

The next step is to add a reference to the executable. To do this, click Project ⇨ References and you are presented with the References dialog window. You want to make a reference to the Microsoft XML, v3.0 library by checking the check box for this (Figure 5-14) and then clicking OK.

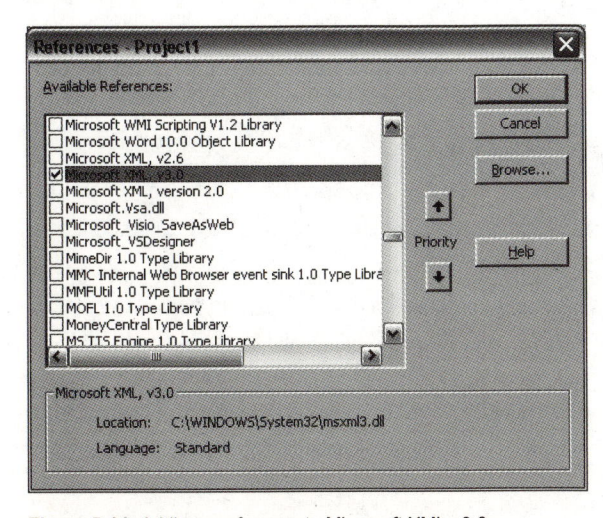

Figure 5-14: Adding a reference to Microsoft XML v3.0.

Now double-click the button on your form and type in the code from Listing 5-7 for that button click.

Listing 5-7: Your Visual Basic 6.0 form to invoke an XML Web service

```
Private Sub Command1_Click()
    Dim myXMLDoc As MSXML2.DOMDocument

    Set myXMLDoc = New DOMDocument
    myXMLDoc.async = False
    Dim XMLwsURL As String
    XMLwsURL = "http://localhost/XMLWS101/Service1.asmx/HelloWorld?"

    myXMLDoc.Load (XMLwsURL)
    Dim XMLMessage As String
    XMLMessage = myXMLDoc.Text
    MsgBox (XMLMessage)

    Set myXMLDoc = Nothing
End Sub
```

> **NOTE:** Replace `XMLWS101` in the URL with the name of your project from the XML Web service that you are calling.

This is a simple example, but shows you what you need to do in order to consume an XML Web service into a Visual Basic 6.0 application.

Quickly review the code in order to get a better understanding of what is going on. In the first bit of code, you call an object.

```
Dim myXMLDoc As MSXML2.DOMDocument
```

By doing this, you are creating an object that will house the in-memory XML document from the XML Web service response. In the next few lines of code, you get ready to send your request.

```
Set myXMLDoc = New DOMDocument
myXMLDoc.async = False
Dim XMLwsURL As String
XMLwsURL = "http://localhost/XMLWS101/Service1.asmx/HelloWorld?"
```

After you establish the object that you will be using, you set the asynchronous property of the object to *False*. This will cause the XML document to be loaded completely before the rest of the code is processed. Then you create a string that points to the location of the XML Web service.

After this is done, you can then load the response and use it however you wish.

```
myXMLDoc.Load (XMLwsURL)
Dim XMLMessage As String
XMLMessage = myXMLDoc.Text
```

```
MsgBox (XMLMessage)
```

In the first line of code, you load the XML into the temporary in-memory location so that you can use it. You then create a spot to place this XML by creating a string and placing the text of the XML document into this string. After this, you simply output the string to a message box.

Now take a look at another example, where instead of just simply invoking an XML Web service, you pass some parameters to it and get back something that is based upon those parameters. For this example, start a new form and place two text boxes and a Submit button on it. For this form, you interact with the CurrencyConverter XML Web service that you created in Chapter 4 (Listing 4-2). Your form should look like the one in Figure 5-15.

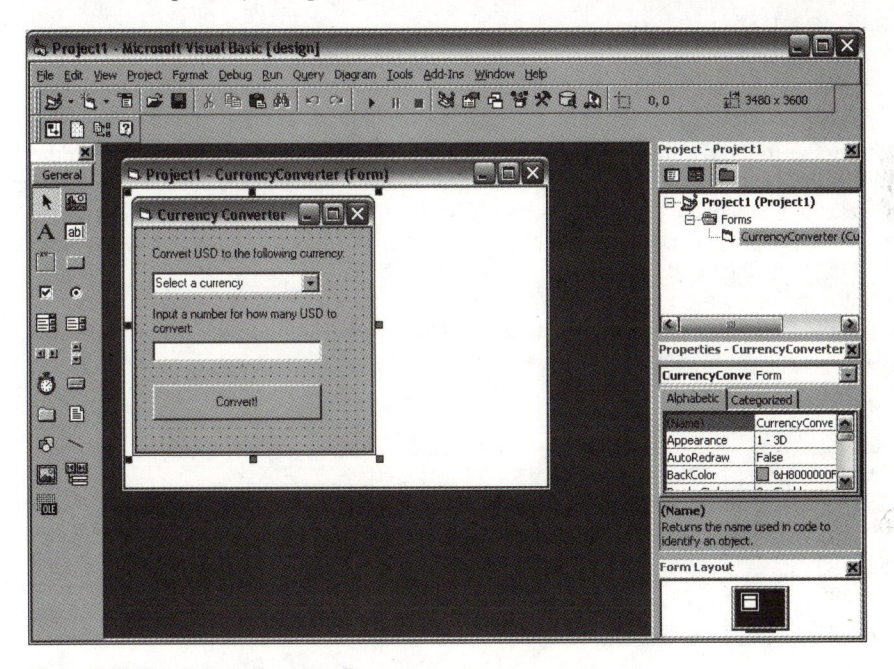

Figure 5-15: The CurrencyConverter Form.

The combo box should have the following items for the drop-down box: USD, FIN, UK, CAN, GER, and EURO. The text box passes the number of US Dollars that you want to convert. Your button-click code should look like Listing 5-8.

Listing 5-8: Passing parameters from a Visual Basic 6.0 application to an XML Web service

```
Private Sub Command1_Click()
    Dim myXMLDoc As MSXML2.DOMDocument
    
    Set myXMLDoc = New DOMDocument
    myXMLDoc.async = False
    Dim XMLwsURL As String
```

```
    Dim CurrencyConvert As String
    Dim CurrencyValue As String
    CurrencyConvert = Combo1.Text
    CurrencyValue = Text1.Text
    XMLwsURL = "http://localhost/CurrencyConverter/
             Converter.asmx/USDConvert?ConvertTo=" & CurrencyConvert
             & "&Amount=" & CurrencyValue & ""

    myXMLDoc.Load (XMLwsURL)
    Dim XMLMessage As String
    XMLMessage = myXMLDoc.Text
    MsgBox (XMLMessage)

    Set myXMLDoc = Nothing
End Sub
```

This is very similar to the first example except you are passing a couple of arguments that the XML Web service uses to calculate its operation. You take the value of the combo box and the value of the text box and place those values into querystrings of the XML Web service URL. You call using HTTP-GET to pass the values, and based upon that, you get an XML document in return that contains the logic that was performed upon the values that you passed. You gave the `ConvertTo` parameter the value that was passed from the combo box and the `Amount` parameter got the value that was passed from the text box. After running this application, you should see results similar to those shown in Figure 5-16.

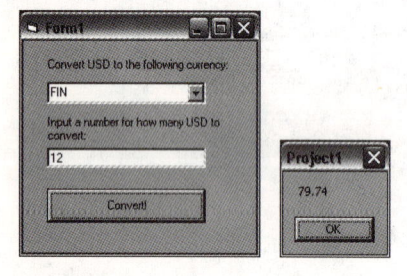

Figure 5-16: Running your Visual Basic 6.0 project to interact with the CurrencyConverter XML Web service.

Just as in the previous Visual Basic 6.0 example, you took the returned XML document and loaded this into the message box.

There really is so much you can do with XML Web services and applications that use an older technology, such as Visual Basic 6.0, even if it isn't .NET-enabled! So even if you are working with VB6 applications, don't feel that you are restricted from using these great new tools of a distributed application environment.

Consuming an XML Web Service from an Active Server Pages Application

Just as VB6 applications can consume .NET-generated XML Web services, classic Active Server Pages (ASP) can also consume your XML Web services.

There are millions, if not billions, of classic ASP pages on the Internet today. These pages will slowly move to ASP.NET pages, but it will take time. Some of these pages won't be converted at all; if you are working with classic ASP, it will sometimes be to your benefit to consume an XML Web service just as it would in ASP.NET.

It isn't as easy to consume XML Web services in classic ASP as it is in ASP.NET, but it isn't too difficult either. In order to get an idea of how to do this, go directly to a code example. In Listing 5-9, you work with the XML Web service that you created in Listing 5-6. It returns a Hello World and the server time just like the Visual Basic 6.0 application that you created.

> **NOTE**: I am just going to show examples of how to consume XML Web services in ASP using VBScript, even though you can easily use JScript.

Listing 5-9: A simple XML Web service call from a classic Active Server Pages page

```
<html>
<head>
  <title>XML Web Service into ASP</title>

  <%
    Dim myRequest, myXMLDoc, XMLwsURL
    Set myRequest = Server.CreateObject("MSXML2.XMLHTTP")
    Set myXMLDoc = Server.CreateObject("MSXML.DOMDocument")

    myXMLDoc.Async = False
    XMLwsURL = "http://localhost/XMLWS101/Service1.asmx/HelloWorld?"
    myRequest.Open "GET", XMLwsURL, False
    myRequest.Send()

    myXMLDoc.load(myRequest.responseXML)
    Dim XMLMessage
    XMLMessage = myXMLDoc.text

    Set myRequest = Nothing
    Set myXMLDoc = Nothing
  %>
</head>

<body>

    Here is the XML Response:
    <p>
```

```
    <b><% Response.Write XMLMessage %></b>
    </p>

</body>
</html>
```

> **NOTE:** Once again, replace `XMLWS101` with the name of the Hello World project that you created earlier.

This is a simple example, similar to the one you called from the Visual Basic 6.0 application, but it shows you what to do to consume an XML Web service into a classic ASP page. Even though it is similar to what you did in the VB6 application, there are some differences that you should note.

Go through the code in order to get a better understanding of what is going on. In the first bit of code, you create a couple of objects.

```
Dim myRequest, myXMLDoc, XMLwsURL
Set myRequest = Server.CreateObject("MSXML2.XMLHTTP")
Set myXMLDoc = Server.CreateObject("MSXML.DOMDocument")
```

The first object here, `myRequest`, is a server-side object that can make POST and GET requests over HTTP. The second object that you create here, `myXMLDoc`, is an object that houses the in-memory XML document from the XML Web service response. In the next few lines of code, you get ready to send your request.

```
myXMLDoc.Async = False
XMLwsURL = "http://localhost/XMLWS101/Service1.asmx/HelloWorld?"
```

After you establish the object that you will be using, you set the asynchronous property of the object to False. This causes the XML document to be loaded completely before the rest of the code is processed. Next you create a string which points to the location of the XML Web service. After the XML Web service file (`.asmx`), you then refer to the WebMethod that you want to call by name. In this case, it is the `HelloWorld` method. After this, you open a connection to the XML Web service and send the request with the following lines of code:

```
myRequest.Open "GET", XMLwsURL, False
myRequest.Send()
```

What you are doing here on your ASP page is using the XMLHTTP object (MSXML2.XMLHTTP) to send an arbitrary HTTP request in order to receive a response. You are only passing three arguments here, but there are more options available to you. Here is the structure of the available arguments:

```
oXMLHttpRequest.open(Method, Url, Async, User, Password)
```

Table 5-1 describes each of these arguments.

Table 5-1: The Open Method Arguments

Argument	Description
Method	A string value that represents the HTTP method used to open the connection, such as `GET`, `POST`, `PUT`, or `PROPFIND`. This is a required parameter.

Argument	Description
Url	A string value that represents the requested URL. This must be an absolute URL, such as `"http://Myserver/Mypath/MyWebService.asmx/MethodName"`. This is a required parameter.
Async	A Boolean value that indicates whether the call is asynchronous. The default is True, which means that the call is returned immediately. A setting of False means that no other code will be processed until the call is complete. This is an optional parameter.
User	The name of the user for authentication. If this parameter is Null ("") or missing and the site requires authentication, the component displays a logon window. This is an optional parameter.
Password	The password for authentication. This parameter is ignored if the user parameter is Null ("") or missing. This is an optional parameter.

When all the arguments are in place, you simply send the request. After this is done, you can then load the response and use it however you wish.

```
myXMLDoc.load(myRequest.responseXML)
Dim XMLMessage
XMLMessage = myXMLDoc.text
```

In the first line of code, you load the XML into the temporary in-memory location so that you can use it. You then create a spot to place this XML by creating a string and placing the text of the XML document into this string. After this, you simply output the string to the browser.

```
<% Response.Write XMLMessage %>
```

A more complicated example

The previous example works well if you are returning a single value or statement within an XML file, but what if you are returning a large XML document? You then must be able to parse this XML in your ASP page and use it somehow.

Say that you have a large XML file that you want to access through your ASP page that has a `Customer` node for your best client and related `Order` nodes showing what that customer has bought from your company. Instead of showing the entire XML document, I will just show the `Customer` node along with one `Order` node. The actual XML document is a data representation of the customer along with all the orders that she has made. Therefore this document would have a single `Customers` node along with an indefinite number of `Orders` nodes. Look at Listing 5-10.

Listing 5-10: Your sample XML document

CUSTOMERS NODE

```
<Customers diffgr:id="Customers1" msdata:rowOrder="0">
   <CustomerID>ALFKI</CustomerID>
   <CompanyName>Alfreds Futterkiste</CompanyName>
   <ContactName>Maria Anders</ContactName>
   <ContactTitle>Sales Representative</ContactTitle>
   <Address>Obere Str. 57</Address>
   <City>Berlin</City>
   <PostalCode>12209</PostalCode>
   <Country>Germany</Country>
   <Phone>030-0074321</Phone>
   <Fax>030-0076545</Fax>
</Customers>
```

ORDERS NODE

```
<Orders diffgr:id="Orders1" msdata:rowOrder="0">
   <OrderID>10643</OrderID>
   <CustomerID>ALFKI</CustomerID>
   <EmployeeID>6</EmployeeID>
   <OrderDate>1997-08-25T00:00:00.0000000-05:00</OrderDate>
   <RequiredDate>1997-09-22T00:00:00.0000000-05:00</RequiredDate>
   <ShippedDate>1997-09-02T00:00:00.0000000-05:00</ShippedDate>
   <ShipVia>1</ShipVia>
   <Freight>29.46</Freight>
   <ShipName>Alfreds Futterkiste</ShipName>
   <ShipAddress>Obere Str. 57</ShipAddress>
   <ShipCity>Berlin</ShipCity>
   <ShipPostalCode>12209</ShipPostalCode>
   <ShipCountry>Germany</ShipCountry>
</Orders>
```

This data is being sent from my local XML Web service CustomerOrders, and I am pulling this data from the SQL Northwind database. All this data in the XML file relates to the customer ALFKI (as you will see in the ASP code). Even though there is only one Orders node showing, in the actual document there are six orders altogether.

If you are sent this XML document with the request, what can you do with it? You want a list of all the orders placed by customer ALFKI. Take a look at the code in Listing 5-11 to see how to do this.

Listing 5-11: CustomerOrders.asp

```
<html>
<head>
   <title>CustomerOrders XML Web Service into ASP</title>

   <%
```

```
        Dim myRequest, myXMLDoc, XMLwsURL
        Set myRequest = Server.CreateObject("MSXML2.XMLHTTP")
        Set myXMLDoc = Server.CreateObject("MSXML.DOMDocument")


        myXMLDoc.Async = False
        XMLwsURL = "http://localhost/XMLws101/
                Service1.asmx/CustomersOrders?CustID=ALFKI"
        myRequest.Open "GET", XMLwsURL, False
        myRequest.Send()

        myXMLDoc.load(myRequest.responseXML)

        Dim nodeCustomer, nodeOrder
        Set nodeCustomer =
myXMLDoc.documentElement.selectNodes("//CustomerID")
        Set nodeOrders = myXMLDoc.documentElement.selectNodes("//OrderID")

        NumOrderNodes = nodeOrders.Length
    %>

</head>

<body>

    Our Customer ALFKI:
    <p><b><% Response.Write nodeCustomer(0).Text %></b><p>
    <p>Orders in the system:<br>
    <%
        For i=0 to NumOrderNodes -1
            Response.Write nodeOrders(i).Text & " "
        Next
    %>

</body>
</html>
```

It was a little more complicated, but actually pretty easy, to consume the entire XML document and use only the pieces of the document that you want. In the end you should have an ASP page that looks like Figure 5-17:

134 Part II: The Basics of XML Web Services

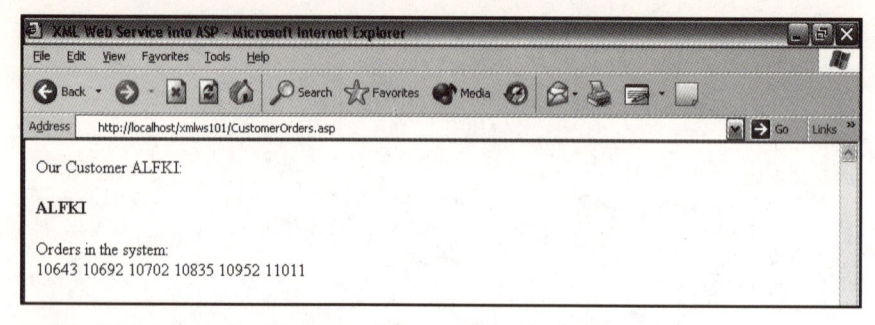

Figure 5-17: Consuming an XML Web service in an ASP 3.0 application.

Examining the code

Run through the code to get a better understanding of the new pieces to this page. First, note that you are passing the `CustomerID` as a querystring to the XML Web service. You could easily build an application that dynamically feeds in the `CustomerID`.

```
XMLwsURL = "http://localhost/XMLws101/
           Service1.asmx/CustomersOrders?CustID=ALFKI"
```

So, you are passing the XML Web service the `CustomerID` of `ALFKI`, and the CustomerOrders XML Web service is then going to the SQL Northwind database and pulling out the data that is related to this particular customer. Because you get back such a large amount of data, you are forced to parse through this XML to get the pieces that you need.

```
Dim nodeCustomer, nodeOrder
Set nodeCustomer = myXMLDoc.documentElement.selectNodes("//CustomerID")
Set nodeOrders = myXMLDoc.documentElement.selectNodes("//OrderID")
```

Note what is going on in these few lines of code. First, you are selecting the `CustomerID` and the `OrderID` nodes from the XML document. By doing this, you are selecting each and every `<CustomerID>` and `<OrderID>` node in the document. These are then populated into `nodeCustomer` and `nodeOrders` as arrays of nodes.

> **NOTE:** When selecting nodes, remember that the name of the node you specify is case-sensitive and calling `//CustomerID` is not the same as calling `//Customerid`. If you call `//Customerid`, you won't receive anything in return.

After specifying the nodes that you are searching for in the document, you need to find the length of the array for the `OrdersID` collection of nodes.

```
NumOrderNodes = nodeOrders.Length
```

Now you are ready to input the name of the customer as it is specified in the `CustomerID` node of the XML document. Also, because you know that there is more than one order in the XML document, you need to loop through the orders and specify each node individually.

```
Our Customer ALFKI:
<p><b><% Response.Write nodeCustomer(0).Text %></b><p>
```

```
<p>Orders in the system:<br>
<%
   For i=0 to NumOrderNodes -1
      Response.Write nodeOrders(i).Text & " "
   Next
%>
```

After this ASP page is generated, it calls the XML Web service and returns a complete list of orders for the customer Alfki.

> **NOTE:** Arrays are zero-based. Therefore, `nodeCustomers(0)` is the first item in the array and `nodeCustomers(1)` is the second item in the array.

Summary

Not only are XML Web services easy to build, as you saw in Chapter 4, but they are just as easy to consume in your applications. You went through several scenarios for consuming XML Web services in Windows Forms, Web Forms, other XML Web services, and even applications that were not .NET enabled, such as Visual Basic 6.0 and ASP applications.

You should now realize that it doesn't matter what platform the application resides on, or if it is made specifically for .NET. The applications that you want to use for consuming XML Web services only need to be able to connect to XML and then know what to do with it. If the applications that you are working with today are able to perform this type of functionality, these applications are able to work with XML Web services.

You looked at simple ways of working with XML Web services within your applications. As you work through the chapters of this book, you look at more complicated scenarios. In the next chapter, you take a look at some of the items that you need to know to build better XML Web services. By the end of that chapter, you will have a better understanding of all the building blocks of this great transport protocol.

Part III

Building XML Web Services

Chapter 6: XML Web Services Architecture

Chapter 7: The Visual Part of XML Web Services

Chapter 8: State Management

Chapter 9: Proxies

Chapter 6

XML Web Services Architecture

Always design a thing by considering it in its next larger context – a chair in a room, a room in a house, a house in an environment, an environment in a city plan.
Eliel Saarinen, Time Magazine, July 2, 1956

Chapter 3 covered the foundations of XML Web services such as data representation, communication of data, data description, and discovery. You learned that all these pillars depend heavily upon XML. In this chapter, you are going to dig a little deeper into the architecture of XML Web services to learn how and when you will use this new model of distributed application development.

In this chapter, you go over some of the architecture basics of XML Web services. You also look closely at the wire formats that XML Web services use to transport the data and at some different ways in which these services interact with the applications that you are building today.

The Architecture Basics of XML Web Services

You can easily understand why XML Web services were created. There are many systems and platforms out there on the Internet, and there are even more applications that reside on these systems and platforms. These are built using more programming languages than one cares to imagine. The world is moving to an environment where people demand that their applications, systems, and platforms evolve and, eventually, enable communication with the system next door. Businesses want to share information with their customers, but they don't want to go through the nightmare of painfully transferring information and data in each and every instance. People have started saying, "There must be a better way!"

This is why XML Web services came on the scene as quickly as they did. They enable differing platforms and applications to work with one another. They do this, as you learned in earlier chapters, by using standard protocols that are not owned or controlled by any one commercial enterprise. Therefore, all platforms have access to the means of communication to implement and use them to advantage.

You already looked at how all this is done, but now take a closer look at how the entire process works. It is important to understand all the steps and processes involved when an XML Web service is called into action.

The process of working with an XML Web service

The XML Web services infrastructure provides everything you need in order to fully utilize all that XML has to offer. The infrastructure includes the means to locate the XML Web service that you need. It also gives you the means to describe an XML Web service to others so that they may use it. Additionally, it provides standard wire formats that comply with open standards so that there are no hindrances to consumption of the Web service. Figure 6-1 shows how to work with an XML Web service.

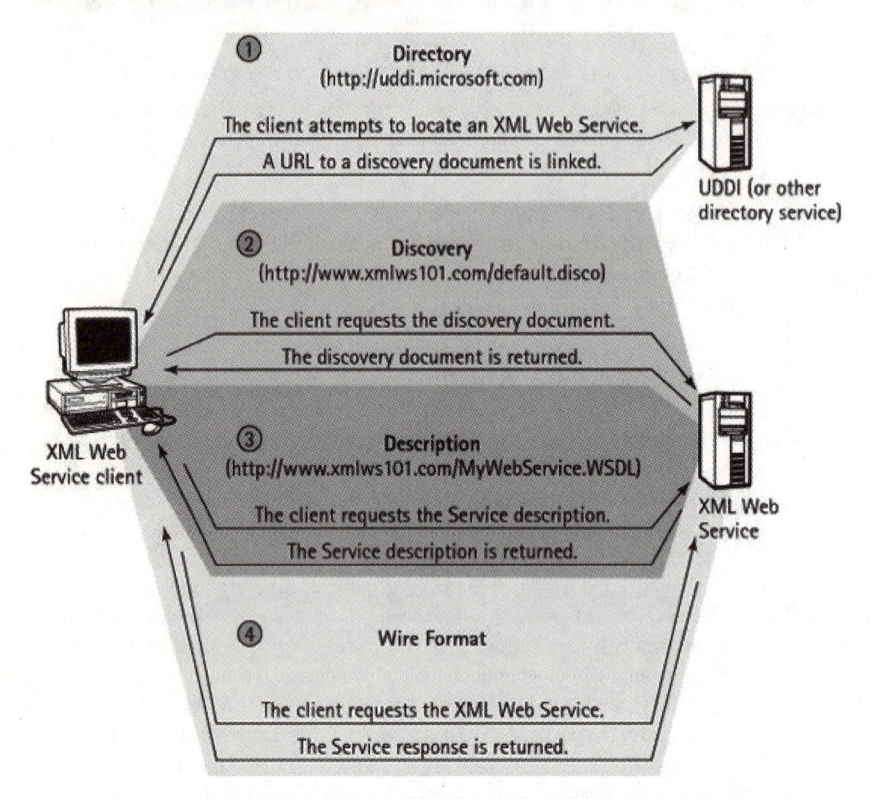

Figure 6-1: This diagram shows the process of working with an XML Web service.

You may recall from Chapter 3 that the first step is to find the XML Web service that you need. There are a number of options for accomplishing this. You may already know where the XML Web service resides because you have used it in the past or because its location was given to you. Another option is to use some sort of directory to find the XML Web service that you are looking for. There are a number of directories available, the most notable being UDDI.org. You may also have access to a UDDI directory within your internal network where you can search for XML Web services.

After the search phase, there is the discovery phase where you discover the actual XML Web service you are looking for in order to make a reference to it. Chapter 3 introduced the disco document to handle this task. The third phase is the description phase, in which you obtain a full description of the XML Web service that you want to consume. This description explains what you need to communicate to the XML Web service and what it will return to you. The final stage is where you actually invoke the XML Web service over a selected protocol to get back a response.

In order for XML Web services to truly be interoperable, they need to be *loosely coupled*. Loosely coupled systems can work with each other by using open standards that are easily available to all platforms and systems. This is the opposite of *tightly coupled* systems, which depend upon some proprietary means to communicate and require significantly more effort to integrate. If you ensure that each of the four steps that I just described are loosely-coupled systems, you also ensure that XML Web services succeed in making all your different applications, devices, and systems work with one another.

Declaring an XML Web service

When you build an XML Web service on the .NET platform, you must declare to the system that it is about to deal with is an XML Web service.

The first thing that sets an XML Web service apart is the file extension. This file extension is .asmx. Next, place a simple declaration at the top of the page. It declares that the file is an XML Web service and must be treated differently by ASP.NET.

```
<%@ WebService Language="C#" Class="MyClass" %>
```

This is one of the simplest declarations possible. The declaration of an XML Web service in this page directive, like classic ASP, uses the symbols `<%` and `%>` to open and close the declaration. Within the `@ WebService` directive, there are four possible attribute/value pairs that you can use. The two attributes shown above, `Language` and `Class`, are required. The other available attributes include `CodeBehind` and `Debug`.

The `Language` attribute is where you specify the language that the XML Web service uses when it compiles. You specify your choice within quotes, and you can choose either `VB` (for Visual Basic .NET), `C#`, `JS` (for JScript .NET), or `J#`. If you are using any third-party languages, you can plug in the language specification here as well.

The next attribute is the `Class` attribute. This is a required attribute and specifies the class that is used to define the methods and data types visible to the XML Web service clients. The class that you are using for your XML Web service can either be inline (in the same .asmx file as the `@ WebService` directive) or can be located elsewhere. If the class is inline, you simply specify the name of the class used.

VB

```
<%@ WebService Language="VB" Class="Calculator" %>
Imports System.Web.Services
Public Class Calculator
   <WebMethod()> Public Function Add(ByVal a As Integer, _
       ByVal b As Integer) As Integer
       Return a + b
```

```
        End Function
End Class
```

C#

```
<%@ WebService Language="C#" Class="Calculator" %>
using System.Web.Services;
class Calculator {
    [WebMethod] public int Add(int a, int b) {
        return a + b;
    }
}
```

In both these code examples, the class you want to work with for your XML Web service is within the same file as your declaration. You simply specify the name of the class as the value of the attribute. In this case it is `Calculator`.

Specifying the class name in the `@ WebService` directive causes the named class to be compiled the first time the Web class is invoked.

You can also declare a class that is located elsewhere than within the same file. To do this, import into your project the class that you want to point to for your Web service. You then need to place this file within your project. After it is imported into your project, place the class inside the `bin` folder. You can only point to class files that are in this folder. If you do not see the folder, press the *Show All Files* button in the Solution Explorer. After the class file that you are going to use is in place, reference this file within the `@ WebService` directive of your `.asmx` file.

```
<%@ WebService Language="VB" Class="ClassFileName.Calculator" %>
```

In this example, this is the only line of code that you need in the `.asmx` file. Instead of an inline class, you are pointing to a class called `Calculator` in a particular class filename.

Just as when you build an `.aspx` page in ASP.NET, when you build XML Web services you have the option of splitting your `.asmx` page into two separate elements: a visual page that allows dragging and dropping of elements, and a code-behind page. In the `.aspx` model, pages can be split using a presentation page and a code-behind page. When building an XML Web service, you also have the choice of a visual designer or a code-behind model; however, the XML Web services visual designer page is not used for building any visual piece to the Web service. The visual designer is simply another tool for writing the code for the Web service. XML Web services do not have any real visual representations except for the test page that is generated automatically by the .NET Framework. XML Web services are not meant to be accessed in any visual manner, but instead, are meant to be consumed by applications or platforms that, in some cases, provide the interface themselves.

By using the visual designer and code-behind model, you can easily and quickly build your XML Web services with various data components and other available system components. To use the code-behind model, you declare in the `@ WebService` directive the location of your code-behind page.

```
<%@ WebService Language="vb" Codebehind="Service1.asmx.vb"
```

```
Class="WebService1.Service1" %>
```

You will notice that the code-behind file is a compiled file and, therefore, takes either the `.vb` or `.cs` extension.

The last attribute you can use in the `@ WebService` directive is the `Debug` attribute. This is an optional attribute that takes a setting of either `True` or `False`. If `Debug` is set to `True`, your XML Web service will be compiled with debug symbols. If `Debug` is set to `False`, then of course, it won't be.

Data types

When sending XML Web service requests by HTTP-GET or HTTP-POST, you are basically sending name/value pairs. When using SOAP, your data types are correlated to data types that can be serialized into XML. The data types that you are using in the .NET Framework are serialized into the simple data types that are allowed in an XML Schema definition language (XSD) schema. Often, the data types that you are using in the .NET Framework have a corresponding data type in XML. For instance, the `int` in the .NET Framework corresponds with the `int` in XML. However, sometimes there isn't a corresponding data type. For example, in the case of the data type `NOTATION`, the data type is the type `string`. The following table (Table 6-1) shows the mapping of data types between XML and the .NET Framework.

Table 6-1   XSD to .NET Data Type Mappings

XSD Data Type	.NET Data Type
anyURI	String
base64Binary	Array of Byte objects
boolean	Boolean
byte	SByte
date	DateTime
dateTime	DateTime
decimal	Decimal
double	Double
ENTITY	String
ENTITIES	String
float	Single
gDay	String
gMonth	String
gMonthDay	String

XSD Data Type	.NET Data Type
gYear	String
gYearMonth	String
hexBinary	Array of Byte objects
ID	String
IDREF	String
IDREFS	String
int	Int32
integer	String
language	String
long	Int64
Name	String
NCName	String
negativeInteger	String
NMTOKEN	String
NMTOKENS	String
normalizedString	String
nonNegativeInteger	String
nonPositiveInteger	String
NOTATION	String
positiveInteger	String
QName	XmlQualifiedName
recurringDate	String
duration	String
string	String
short	Int16
time	DateTime
token	String
unsignedByte	Byte
unsignedInt	UInt32
unsignedLong	UInt64

XSD Data Type	.NET Data Type
unsignedShort	UInt16

Defining methods

When building methods in an XML Web service, note that not all methods contained within an `.asmx` or class file are automatically made accessible as callable WebMethods.

In fact, any method contained within these files needs to have the WebMethod attribute preceding the method declaration. That means that you can have as many methods as you want contained within your class, but the only ones that will be made accessible to call across the HTTP wire will be the methods to which you have applied this attribute. Listing 6-1 illustrates this concept.

Listing 6-1: Service1.asmx.vb and Service1.asmx.cs

VB

```
Imports System.Web.Services

<WebService()> _
Public Class HumanYearsToDogYears
    Inherits System.Web.Services.WebService

    Private Function ConvertHumanToDog(ByVal HumanYears As Integer) _
      As Integer
        HumanYears = HumanYears * 7
        Return HumanYears
    End Function

    <WebMethod()> Public Function HumanYearsToDogYears(ByVal HumanYears _
      As Integer) As Integer
        Dim DYValue As Integer
        DYValue = ConvertHumanToDog(HumanYears)
        Return DYValue
    End Function

End Class
```

C#

```
using System;
using System.Collections;
using System.ComponentModel;
using System.Data;
using System.Diagnostics;
using System.Web;
using System.Web.Services;
```

```
namespace WebService1
{
 public class HumanToDogYears : System.Web.Services.WebService
 {
  public HumanToDogYears()
  {
   InitializeComponent();
  }

  private int ConvertHumanToDog(int HumanYears)
  {
   HumanYears = (HumanYears * 7);
   return HumanYears;
  }

  [WebMethod]
  public int HumanYearsToDogYears(int HumanYears)
  {
   int DYValue;
   DYValue = ConvertHumanToDog(HumanYears);
   return DYValue;
  }
 }
}
```

In the preceding code examples, the `CovertHumanToDog` function is private and only accessible to the code within the class. By having a WebMethod attribute only in front of the `HumanYearsToDogYears` function, you make this method the only one that is accessible to the user who consumes this XML Web service.

Transport Protocols

The reason that XML Web services are so much more powerful than prior ways of calling remote objects, such as DCOM, is that XML Web services use standard wire formats such as HTTP. Because you are building interoperable Web services, your format must be one that is easily accessible and consumable by the largest number of platforms.

DCOM uses a binary protocol that consists of a method-request layer riding on top of a proprietary communication protocol. One of the problems with using DCOM and similar methods for calling remote objects is that a server's firewalls usually get in the way.

Most servers have firewalls that block certain traffic. Usually, the server's network administrator locks down every open port in order to protect the server. So, when you work with DCOM, you often have to convince others to open ports so that you can make the necessary remote calls.

With all these closed ports, however, there is one port that usually remains open — *port 80*. Port 80 is so special and usually open because this is the port that is used for HTTP, or in other words, *surfing the Web*. You will find that most servers and the people working on those servers want to have access to the Internet, so in almost every case you will find port 80 open for business.

This is why XML Web services have such a distinct advantage over the other means of calling remote objects. XML Web services transmit information as pure ASCII text over HTTP, the same as when HTML is called over HTTP. When a person on a server calls another remote server for a Web page, he is getting back HTML (ASCII text) over HTTP. XML is the same. XML is just a file of ASCII text that is comprised of textual data with a bunch of markup tags in place to describe the data. This is why XML Web services are so powerful and why this new way of making remote object calls is getting so much attention.

XML Web services can use three different wire-formats as transport protocol: HTTP-GET, HTTP-POST, or SOAP.

HTTP-GET

HTTP-GET has been used for quite a while as a way to transmit data over HTTP. You might have used it when building Active Server Pages. Basically HTTP-GET uses a series of request headers that transmit a definition of whatever the client is requesting. In response, it returns a series of HTTP response headers.

HTTP-GET passes parameters of the request along in the URL of the requesting page. These parameters are attached to the end of the URL and consist of a collection of name/value pairs. This attachment is referred to as querystrings. You might have used querystrings as a means of passing data from one page to the next in some of your Web applications.

Understanding querystrings

QueryStrings are simple and easy to use to pass data from one page to the next within a Web application. QueryStrings are a collection of name/value pairs that are appended onto the URL to be passed to the next page or a remote object.

Here is how the URL looks when passing the name of a user from one page to the next:

```
http://www.hungryminds.com?username=Bill
```

In this example you appended a variable called `username` and gave it a value of `Bill`. You did this by ending the URL string with a question mark, followed by the variable name.

It is possible to pass more than one name/value pair along with the URL by separating the name/value pairs with an ampersand (`&`). For example, if you were passing the username and the employee's ID number, you could do it in the following manner:

```
http://www.hungryminds.com?username=Bill&EmployeeID=9040777
```

Using HTTP-GET with XML Web services

You can use HTTP-GET to call a remote method and pass the method the parameters it needs directly in the URL. To do this, either find or deploy your own XML Web service and then link to the service from the URL in the address bar of your browser.

Part III: Building XML Web Services

You then need to gain access to the XML Web service by linking to it in the following manner:

```
http://servername/vdir/webservicename.asmx/Methodname?name=value
```

You can see this in action by calling the simple `Add` WebMethod that is part of the Calculator XML Web service that you built in Chapter 4. You can create a page that contains a hyperlink to the method that you want to call. Contained within the URL of the link are the values that you need to pass to the `Add` method. The code in Listing 6-2 shows how to quickly and easily access an XML Web service using HTTP-GET.

Listing 6-2: Calling your Calculator XML Web service's Add method

```
<HTML>
 <HEAD>
  <title>WebForm1</title>
 </HEAD>
 <body>
  <form id="Form1" method="post" runat="server">
   <asp:HyperLink id="HyperLink1" runat="server"
   NavigateUrl="http://localhost/Calculator/Service1.asmx/Add?a=5&b=5"
   Font-Bold="True" Font-Names="Verdana" Font-Size="X-Small">
   http://localhost/Calculator/service1.asmx/Add?a=5&b=5
   </asp:HyperLink>
  </form>
 </body>
</HTML>
```

NOTE: The method name that you refer to in your URL is case-sensitive. Therefore, `Add` and `add` are not the same methods.

Figure 6-2 shows how your page will look with the embedded link to your XML Web service.

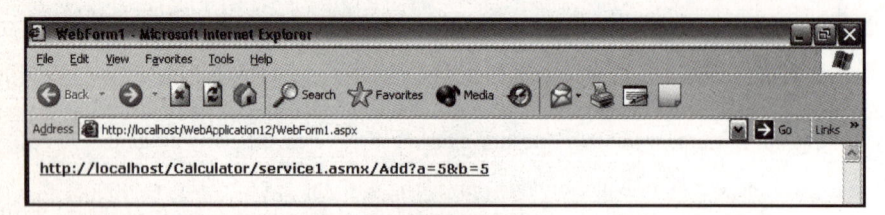

Figure 6-2: Using HTTP-GET to interact with an XML Web service.

Clicking on the link calls the method that follows the `.asmx` extension in the URL, in this case, `/Add`. Following the method name, you insert the name/value pairs that are the parameters needed by the `Add` method, in this case, an integer value for `a` and another for `b`. With this full construction, you have an address for the XML Web service, the method that you are calling, and the parameters that the method needs in order to get back a return.

In return, you get back an XML file with the value in place as shown in the following code:

```
<?xml version="1.0" encoding="utf-8" ?>
<int xmlns="http://tempuri.org/">10</int>
```

You can now use this XML in your applications as you see fit, whether they are ASP, VB6, or any .NET application. Using HTTP-GET is a quick and easy way to access XML Web services. There are, however, problems with this scenario. You can easily see what you are passing and so can everyone else. For security purposes, this might not be the best way to do things.

HTTP-POST

Very much like HTTP-GET, HTTP-POST works by sending name/value pairs to the XML Web service that you are calling. Therefore, you are limited by not being able to send complex data types as you can with SOAP. Unlike HTTP-GET, HTTP-POST sends these name/value pairs in the request header so they are not open to view. HTTP-GET sends the parameters in the URL and, therefore, they are open for the public to see.

In order for you to work with HTTP-POST, you must have an HTML page with a form in it. Listing 6-3 gives you a quick look at a simple form that will interact with your Calculator XML Web service.

Listing 6-3: Interacting with an XML Web service via HTTP-POST

```
<HTML>
 <HEAD>
    <title>Using HTTP-POST</title>
 </HEAD>
 <body>
  <form method="post"
        action="http://localhost/TestWS/Service1.asmx/Add">
    <P>
     <input type="text" name="a"></P>
    <P>
     <input type="text" name="b"></P>
    <P>
     <input type=submit value=Add></P>
  </form>
 </body>
</HTML>
```

The attributes of the `<Form>` tag are important. First, the `method` attribute needs to be set to POST. The second attribute is the `action` attribute. The `action` attribute specifies where the form will post the name/value pairs that are generated. In this case, you need to specify the location of the Calculator XML Web service. After the extension .asmx, specify the method that you are going to call. In this case, it is /Add because you are calling the Add() WebMethod, but it could just as easily be /Subtract, /Multiply, or /Divide.

The form elements that collect the information that you pass on as parameters need to have a `name` attribute. The value of the `name` attribute must be the name of the parameters that the XML Web service is requesting. To determine the name of the parameters that you are going to pass to a Web service, study the WSDL document. Look at the Calculator XML Web service's WSDL document at `http://localhost/TestWS/Service1.asmx?wsdl`. Scroll down the document a bit and look at what the `Add()` WebMethod is asking for. The code in Listing 6-4 is from the WSDL document of the Calculator XML Web service.

Listing 6-4: Part of the WSDL document from the Calculator XML Web service

```
<s:element name="Add">
   <s:complexType>
      <s:sequence>
         <s:element minOccurs="1" maxOccurs="1" name="a" type="s:int" />
         <s:element minOccurs="1" maxOccurs="1" name="b" type="s:int" />
      </s:sequence>
   </s:complexType>
</s:element>
```

In this WSDL document, the `Add` method is asking for just two parameters, `a` and `b`, both of the type integer.

Running your POST sample, you get an XML response from the XML Web service as shown in the following code:

```
<?xml version="1.0" encoding="utf-8" ?>
<int xmlns="http://tempuri.org/">10</int>
```

This is a quick and convenient way to pass information to an XML Web service to get back some simple results. Using HTTP-POST is also a bit better than using HTTP-GET because HTTP-GET limits the number of characters that can be sent to the XML Web service. The URL of an HTTP-GET call can only handle 255 characters; this seriously limits the scope of the name/value pairs that you can use. If you use HTTP-POST, you can place as many name/value pairs as you need. In addition, because these name/value pairs are stored in the request header, they are hidden from the user.

As you work with XML Web services more and more, you may want to pass more complex data structures. These types of transactions are presently only possible using SOAP. So, take a quick look at SOAP and how you can use it with XML Web services.

SOAP

SOAP is XML and is a lightweight protocol for exchanging more complex data structures over HTTP. You also gain the ability to specify types in SOAP, something that isn't possible when using HTTP-GET or HTTP-POST. Using SOAP as the transport protocol is the default way in which the .NET applications communicate with XML Web services.

> **CROSS-REFERENCE:** SOAP will be covered extensively in Part IV of this book. You can also find more information on SOAP at `www.w3c.org/TR/soap`.

A SOAP message is made up of three main parts — the *SOAP envelope*, the *SOAP header*, and the *SOAP body*.

Chapter 6: XML Web Services Architecture

The SOAP envelope defines the overall framework of the SOAP message and forms the root element of the packet that is sent. The SOAP envelope encapsulates the SOAP message, including any headers and the body.

The SOAP header is an optional element that enables you to place information that you wouldn't put in the body part of the SOAP packet, such as authentication, transaction management, and more.

The SOAP body is where all the action is and is where the information is passed to the XML Web service. The code in Listing 6-5 shows an ASP.NET Web application that calls your Calculator XML Web service's `Add()` method.

Listing 6-5: AddMethod.aspx

```
<%@ Page Language="vb" AutoEventWireup="false"
    Codebehind="WebForm1.aspx.vb"
    Inherits="WebApplication1.WebForm1"%>
<HTML>
 <HEAD>
  <title>SOAP AddMethod</title>
 </HEAD>
 <body>
  <form id="Form1" method="post" runat="server">
   <P>
    <asp:TextBox id="TextBox1" runat="server"></asp:TextBox></P>
   <P>
    <asp:TextBox id="TextBox2" runat="server"></asp:TextBox></P>
   <P>
    <asp:Button id="Button1" runat="server"
Text="Add"></asp:Button></P>
   <P>
    <asp:Label id="Label1" runat="server"></asp:Label></P>
  </form>
 </body>
</HTML>
```

The code-behind page that calls the Calculator's Add method is shown in Listing 6-6:

Listing 6-6: AddMethod.aspx (NOTE: Only part of the file is displayed)

VB

```
Private Sub Button1_Click(ByVal sender As System.Object, ByVal e As
            System.EventArgs) Handles Button1.Click
  Dim CalcWS As New Calc.Calculator()
  Label1.Text = CalcWS.Add(TextBox1.Text, TextBox2.Text)
End Sub
```

C#

```
private void Button1_Click(object sender, System.EventArgs e)
{
```

```
    CalcWS.Calculator ws = new CalcWS.Calculator();
    label1.Text = CalcWS.Add(int.Parse(textbox1.Text),
int.Parse(textbox2.Text));
}
```

In this example, you created an ASP.NET application, and within this application you created an instance of the Calculator class and called the `Add()` method directly from your code. The call to the `Add()` method is quite simple because the class takes care of marshaling the call over SOAP for you. It then takes what is sent back to you in return, deserializes this data, and gets it back as an object.

The SOAP request that is sent to the Calculator XML Web service looks like the code in Listing 6-7:

Listing 6-7: The SOAP request

```
POST /TestWS/Service1.asmx HTTP/1.1
Host: localhost
Content-Type: text/xml; charset=utf-8
Content-Length: {length}
SOAPAction: "http://www.xmlws101.com/Add"

<?xml version="1.0" encoding="utf-8"?>
<soap:Envelope xmlns:xsi="http://www.w3.org/2001/XMLSchema-instance"
 xmlns:xsd="http://www.w3.org/2001/XMLSchema"
 xmlns:soap="http://schemas.xmlsoap.org/soap/envelope/">
  <soap:Body>
    <Add xmlns="http://www.xmlws101.com">
      <a>5</a>
      <b>10</b>
    </Add>
  </soap:Body>
</soap:Envelope>
```

Right away you will notice that your SOAP request is simply an ASCII file as specified by the `Content-Type` value of `text/xml`. Encapsulating the SOAP body is the SOAP envelope. The envelope is specified by the element `<soap:Envelope>`. Within the `<soap:Envelope>` element are various namespace attributes. The SOAP envelope contains only the SOAP body because the example does not have a SOAP header. The SOAP body is specified with a `<soap:Body>` element.

The `<soap:Body>` element encapsulates the parameters that you are passing as XML elements.

```
<Add xmlns="http://www.xmlws101.com">
    <a>5</a>
    <b>10</b>
</Add>
```

Here you are specifying the method that you are working with and the parameters that are required by this method. The parameter names are turned into elements that contain the values that you are passing between the elements. So, for instance, for the `a` parameter, you are passing the value of `5`; and for the `b` parameter, you are passing the value of `10`.

In return you get back a SOAP response that the application deserializes and turns into an object (see Listing 6-8).

Listing 6-8: The SOAP response

```
HTTP/1.1 200 OK
Content-Type: text/xml; charset=utf-8
Content-Length: {length}

<?xml version="1.0" encoding="utf-8"?>
<soap:Envelope xmlns:xsi="http://www.w3.org/2001/XMLSchema-instance"
 xmlns:xsd="http://www.w3.org/2001/XMLSchema"
 xmlns:soap="http://schemas.xmlsoap.org/soap/envelope/">
  <soap:Body>
    <AddResponse xmlns="http://www.xmlws101.com">
      <AddResult>15</AddResult>
    </AddResponse>
  </soap:Body>
</soap:Envelope>
```

As in the SOAP request, you are dealing with a text file as specified in the `Content-Type`. Just as with the SOAP request, the response has a SOAP envelope and a SOAP body. The body of the SOAP packet contains the response from the `Add` method.

```
<AddResponse xmlns="http://www.xmlws101.com">
  <AddResult>15</AddResult>
</AddResponse>
```

The response is always constructed as an element with the method's name immediately followed by the word `Response`. For instance, we are working with the `Add()` method and, therefore, the element that contains the response is the `<AddResponse>` element. This element in the example contains a value of `15`.

SOAP uses the payload section of the HTTP-POST to hold the encoded SOAP envelope as it is transmitted over HTTP. The fact that you can build a complex data structure to send over HTTP gives SOAP a distinct advantage over using HTTP-GET and HTTP-POST.

> **CROSS-REFERENCE:** When working with DataSets, you can, without any problem, use SOAP to send multiple tables with all the table relations in place to the XML Web service. Chapter 19 covers this topic in more detail.

XML Web Services in a Multitiered Development Environment

It is true that people can develop their applications however they see fit, but there are certain recommendations usually adhered to. One notable standard is that application developers should provide a multitiered environment, otherwise known as an *n-tiered* development environment.

In this model, most systems will separate client/server applications into three areas, *presentation*, *business logic*, and the *data store*. Figure 6-3 shows how this environment is structured.

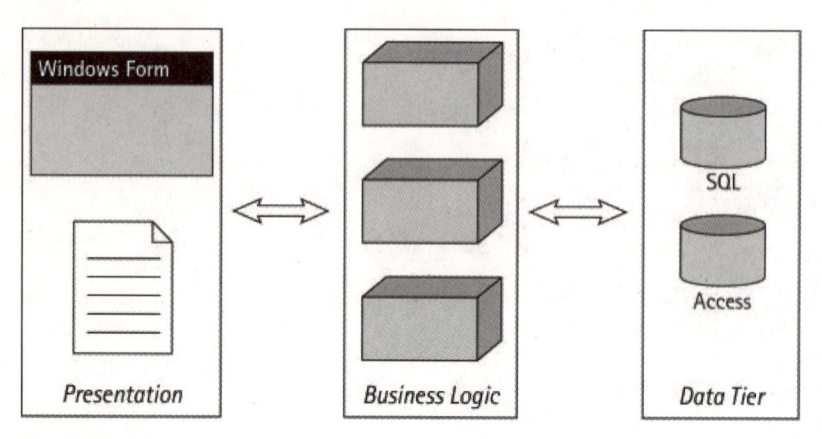

Figure 6-3: *N-Tiered* structure.

The presentation layer in the n-tiered model is meant to provide all the graphical user interfaces (GUI) that the user encounters when dealing with the application. This layer not only provides the GUI for the user, but enables the user to input and manipulate data on the client.

The business logic layer lies between the presentation layer and the data layer. The business logic captures the rules that govern application processing and connects the user to the data stores that are in place.

The data layer houses all the data stores that are in use for the application. Examples of data stores in place might be SQL Server, Oracle, Microsoft Access, or just XML files.

As XML Web services progress, they will address all these tiers. You will be building and consuming XML Web services that work in all three tiers of your application.

Presentation layer

So far in this book, you have been working with XML Web services to provide some sort of business logic and to return the results of that logic. Although it is possible and quite beneficial to build XML Web services that will expose data or logic, you will also find it easy and advantageous to provide the presentation interface of that logic as well. Let's start off with a general example to give you an understanding of how this works.

In this example, you have an XML Web service that provides a random image of a book cover that users can use directly in the presentation layer of their applications. Listing 6-9 gives you a look at the simple XML Web service that does this.

Listing 6-9: Random image XML Web service

VB

```vb
Imports System.Web.Services

<WebService()> Public Class Service1
  Inherits System.Web.Services.WebService

  <WebMethod()> Public Function DotNetBookOfTheDay() As String
    Dim RN As New Random()
    Dim ResultString As String

    Select Case RN.Next(4)
      Case 0
        ResultString =
            "<img src='http://server/images/BookImage001.gif'>"
      Case 1
        ResultString =
            "<img src='http://server/images/BookImage002.gif'>"
      Case 2
        ResultString =
            "<img src='http://server/images/BookImage003.gif'>"
      Case 3
        ResultString =
            "<img src='http://server/images/BookImage004.gif'>"
      Case 4
        ResultString =
            "<img src='http://server/images/BookImage005.gif'>"
    End Select

    Return ResultString

  End Function

End Class
```

C#

```csharp
using System;
using System.Collections;
using System.ComponentModel;
using System.Data;
using System.Diagnostics;
using System.Web;
using System.Web.Services;

namespace BookImage
{
 public class Service1 : System.Web.Services.WebService
```

```
{
  [WebMethod]
  public string DotNetBookOfTheDay()
  {
   Random RN = new Random();
   string ResultString = "";

   switch (RN.Next(4))
   {
     case 0:
     {
       ResultString = "<img
src='http://server/images/BookImage001.gif'>";
       break;
     }
     case 1:
     {
       ResultString = "<img
src='http://server/images/BookImage002.gif'>";
       break;
     }
     case 2:
     {
       ResultString = "<img
src='http://server/images/BookImage003.gif'>";
       break;
     }
     case 3:
     {
       ResultString = "<img
src='http://server/images/BookImage004.gif'>";
       break;
     }
     case 4:
     {
       ResultString = "<img
src='http://server/images/BookImage005.gif'>";
       break;
     }
   }

   return ResultString;
  }
 }
}
```

This is a pretty simple example to show you that not only can you return some logic (as in previous examples), but you can also return raw HTML so that others may incorporate this into their Web pages. This little XML Web service, when invoked, will provide the HTML

`<img>` tag that points to a random image. In order to get the random number, you use the `Random` class to generate a number between 0 and 4. Then depending on the number generated, you send back the associated `<img>` tag. Figure 6-4 shows the XML that is returned from this Web service.

```
<?xml version="1.0" encoding="utf-8" ?>
<string xmlns="http://tempuri.org/"><img src='http://server/images/BookImage004.gif'></string>
```

Figure 6-4: HTML returned within an XML file.

So now take a quick look at how you would go about consuming this directly into the presentation layer of your ASP.NET application (see Listings 6-10 and 6-11).

Listing 6-10: RandomImage.aspx

```
<%@ Page Language="vb" AutoEventWireup="false"
Codebehind="RandomImage.aspx.vb"
    Inherits="WebApplication1.WebForm1"%>

<HTML>
 <HEAD>
   <title>Random Image</title>
 </HEAD>
 <body>
   <form id="Form1" method="post" runat="server">
     <asp:Literal id="Literal1" runat="server"></asp:Literal>
   </form>
 </body>
</HTML>
```

Listing 6-11: RandomImage.aspx.vb and RandomImage.aspx.cs (partial code)

VB

```
Private Sub Page_Load(ByVal sender As System.Object, ByVal e As
        System.EventArgs) Handles MyBase.Load
    Dim ImgURL As New DotNetImage.Service1()
    Literal1.Text = ImgURL.DotNetBookOfTheDay()
End Sub
```

C#

```
private void Page_Load(object sender, System.EventArgs e)
{
```

```
    DotNetImage.Service1 ImgURL = new DotNetImage.Service1();
    Literal1.Text = ImgURL.DotNetBookOfTheDay();
}
```

As you can tell from this example, you are consuming the raw HTML of the `<img>` tag directly into the presentation layer by using the ASP.NET Literal control. On the page load event, you then assign the output of the `DotNetBookOfTheDay` XML Web service to the `Text` attribute of the Literal control. For clarity's sake, I renamed the client-side proxy to `DotNetImage` from `localhost`.

The point of this example is that you can output to the clients certain items that they can include in their presentation layers. The HTML string can be as long as you need it to be and can even include dynamically created tables with links, images, or whatever you want to expose.

Business layer

The business layer in an n-tiered application houses all the business logic that the application might need. You have already seen examples of how this works within the XML Web services model. For example, even the simple `Add()` WebMethod that added up two numbers is a piece of business logic that is kept in the business layer of your application.

There is no practical need for developers to reinvent the wheel each time they build a new application. There may be pieces of logic available from a third party or business partner that are importable. As you have read in previous chapters, it is an easy thing to expose and consume logic through the XML Web services model. You might expose various calculators (such as financial or mortgage calculators) or just the joke of the day.

As you build pieces of logic within your applications today, whenever you build a valuable piece of logic, ask yourself if this is a piece of logic that you would benefit by exposing as an XML Web service internally or externally.

Data layer

There will be plenty of XML Web services whose only purpose is to expose a data store. A data store is any container of data, whether that container is SQL Server, Oracle, Microsoft Access, or any text-based files (such as XML files).

If you simply want to expose the data to be used elsewhere, by far the best way to do this is by using XML Web services.

Often, one entity wants to expose some data to another, and it turns out to be a daunting task. The reason is that the entities use different platforms that don't talk well to each other. XML Web services answers this, as you have learned, by using standard protocols such as XML to port information from one system to another. So if you are in a company or corporation that has multiple platforms and you need data that resides on a different platform than your host application, using Web services may be the answer.

Chapter 6: XML Web Services Architecture 159

How can you expose your data to the general public without having to go through extreme measures and personal customizations? Using XML Web services as the interface to your data stores may be the answer.

Listing 6-12 offers an example of exposing an XML file as an XML Web service.

Listing 6-12: XMLDataStore.asmx.vb and XMLDataStore.asmx.cs

VB

```vb
Imports System.Web.Services

<WebService()> _
Public Class Service1
    Inherits System.Web.Services.WebService

    <WebMethod()> Public Function GetCustomers() As DataSet
        Dim myDataSet As New DataSet()

     myDataSet.ReadXml("http://localhost/XMLDataStore/GetCustomers.xml")

        Return myDataSet
    End Function

End Class
```

C#

```csharp
using System;
using System.Collections;
using System.ComponentModel;
using System.Data;
using System.Diagnostics;
using System.Web;
using System.Web.Services;

namespace XMLDataStore
{
 public class Service1 : System.Web.Services.WebService
 {

  [WebMethod]
  public DataSet GetCustomers()
  {
   DataSet myDataSet = new DataSet();
   myDataSet.ReadXml("http://localhost/XMLDataStore/GetCustomers.xml");

   return myDataSet;
  }
 }
}
```

In this example, you are simply taking an XML file and exposing this data store to anyone who wants to consume this XML Web service. This is a simple way to generically open a data store. You do not have to worry about cross-platform issues or any tough logistical issues to expose this data. Now anyone who wants to consume this data simply makes a reference to it in his own applications and he can call this data over the wire as if it were a local data store.

The same simplicity applies to exposing data from larger and more complex data stores such as SQL Server. You can expose entire databases, selected tables, or even just certain queries through XML Web services. This will enable you to share data company-wide or worldwide very simply and with little development time.

Summary

In this chapter, you took a look at some of the basics of building XML Web services such as declaring your XML Web services, defining methods, and understanding data types. You also learned the different transport protocols that XML Web services use.

Remember that your transport protocol, whether it is HTTP-GET, HTTP-POST, or SOAP, depends on the type and structure of the data that you want to expose. SOAP has a distinct advantage over the other types of transport protocols in that it enables you to send more complex data structures across the wire.

Finally, you looked at how XML Web services can play a role in tiered application development and provide the building blocks needed for the presentation layer, business logic layer, and the data layer.

The next chapter covers the `WebMethod` and `WebService` properties and how to customize the interface to your XML Web services.

Chapter 7

The Visual Part of XML Web Services

It is easy to be beautiful; it is difficult to appear so.
Frank O'Hara, *Meditations in an Emergency* (1967)

After users find your XML Web services, they are going to want to learn what your Web service offers quickly. There are some simple things you can do to make this easy for anyone interested in consuming your service.

This chapter covers

- How to use a WebService attribute to improve your XML Web service
- Using the WebMethod properties
- Customizing the Web interface
- Configuring the test page

Working with the WebService Attribute

As users come to your ASP.NET test page, you want to give them as much information as possible so they can decide if the XML Web service you are providing is what they are looking for. This information also enables these potential users to better understand what is input into the service and what is outputted. Users are able to look at the WSDL description document, but that document isn't always sufficient to answer their questions.

The WSDL gives users the name of the necessary variables and their types as well as the types that are returned from the XML Web service. Sometimes, a user might understand the concept of the Web service that he wants to consume, but for the life of him, he cannot understand the meaning of one of the variables that he must provide. For instance, although the XML Web service developer gives the variable named `NumDaysSec34`, the consumer might not have any idea what is required — even if he knows that it is of the type integer. In this area, you, as a XML Web services developer, can make the lives of consumers easier and guarantee their success. Just follow the simple suggestions that are explained in this chapter. Doing this will provide more documentation for the end users and give them fewer headaches when dealing with the XML Web services that you develop. One of the things that you can do to make the lives of end users easier is to use the `WebService` attribute in your XML Web services. This is an optional attribute, but one that I would highly recommend.

When users find your XML Web service (or if they are invited to view the Web service), there usually isn't much to see. The only page that they can view is the ASP.NET XML Web service test page. Figure 7-1 shows an example of an XML Web service test page.

![Figure 7-1 screenshot of EnglishGermanEnglishDictionary Web Service test page in Internet Explorer showing supported operations GermanEnglishDictionary and EnglishGermanDictionary, along with namespace recommendation text.]

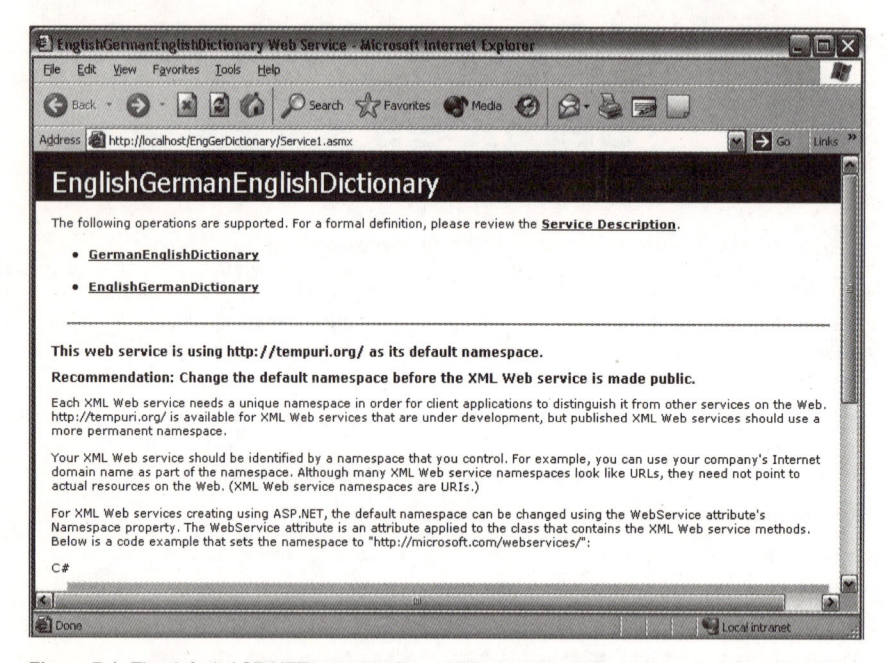

Figure 7-1: The default ASP.NET test page for an XML Web service.

The WebService attribute and the Namespace property

The page in Figure 7-1 displays the name of the class as well as the two methods that can be called from the XML Web service. Below this is a lot of information that you didn't put into the interface. It is warning information from the .NET Framework suggesting that you give your XML Web service a namespace.

By default, when you build an XML Web service, it does not have a namespace. Instead, it uses `http://tempuri.org` as the XML Web service's namespace. This is meant to be a temporary namespace and should be replaced with a more meaningful and original namespace, such as the URL where you are hosting the XML Web service. For instance, for this EnglishGermanEnglishDictionary XML Web service, you only need to add the namespace `http://www.xmlws101.com/xmlws` to give it a unique identifier.

This test page displays instructions on how to add the namespace to an XML Web service written both in Visual Basic .NET and in C#.

Directly before a class declaration in your XML Web service, you can add an optional and recommended `WebService` attribute. The `WebService` attribute has a number of other possible settings. You define a namespace for your XML Web service with a `WebService` attribute, as shown in Listing 7-1.

Listing 7-1: Adding a namespace to an XML Web service

VB

```
<WebService(Namespace:="http://microsoft.com/webservices/")>
Public Class MyWebService
    ' implementation
End Class
```

C#

```
[WebService(Namespace="http://microsoft.com/webservices/")]
public class MyWebService {
    // implementation
}
```

As the preceding code illustrates, in Visual Basic .NET you declare a `WebService` attribute for a class in between arrow brackets, with the namespace inside opening and closing parenthesis. In C#, you declare the `WebService` attribute within square brackets and also with an opening and closing parenthesis. All the WebService's definitions are placed in between the parenthesis.

Notice how the two languages define their properties within the `WebService` attribute. Visual Basic .NET uses a colon and an equal sign to set the property.

```
Namespace:="http://microsoft.com/webservices/"
```

C# uses just an equal sign to assign the properties within the `WebService` attribute values.

```
Namespace="http://microsoft.com/webservices/"
```

After placing the `WebService` attribute along with the `Namespace` property assignment within your XML Web service, you won't be warned any longer and the ASP.NET test page for your XML Web service will now end with a listing of the available methods. This gives a much cleaner look to your test page.

The Description property

One of the first things you can do to make your XML Web services' ASP.NET test pages more descriptive and easier for the end user to understand is to provide a description of the entire XML Web service. This description is included in the beginning of the test page of your XML Web service. Figure 7-2 shows this description as part of the test page.

164 Part III: **Building XML Web Services**

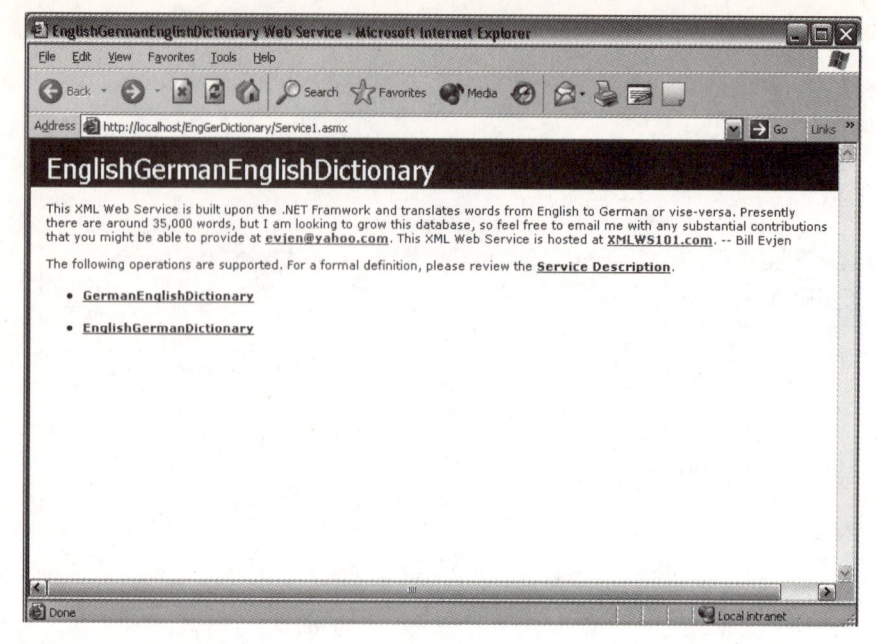

Figure 7-2: Your XML Web service with both the Namespace and Description properties.

Now I have added a description that even contains some links. This is quite easy to do, as the code in Listing 7-2 illustrates.

Listing 7-2: Using the Description property

VB

```
<WebService(Namespace:="http://www.xmlws101.com/xmlws", _
 Description:="This XML Web service is built upon the .NET " & _
 "Framwork and translates words from English to German or " & _
 "vise-versa. Presently there are around 35,000 words, " & _
 "but I am looking to grow this database, so feel free " _
 "to email me with any substantial contributions that you " & _
 "might be able to provide at <a href='mailto:evjen@yahoo.com'>" & _
 "evjen@yahoo.com</a>. " & _
 "This XML Web service is hosted at " & _
 "<a href='http://www.xmlws101.com/' target='_blank'>" & _
 "XMLWS101.com</a>. -- Bill Evjen")>
Public Class EnglishGermanEnglishDictionary
    ' implementation
End Class
```

C# (Minus most of the description)

```
[WebService(Namespace="http://www.xmlws101.com/xmlws", _
 Description="This XML Web service is built upon the .NET Framwork …")]
public class EnglishGermanEnglishDictionary {
   // implementation
}
```

You can see how easy it is to add HTML code directly into the description. My suggestion is to use the description spot to include any or all the following information:

- Contact information (name and e-mail)
- Link to the hosting site
- Link to a separate ASP.NET Help page that contains instructions on how to consume the XML Web service
- The full description and purpose of the XML Web service

The Name property

The `Name` property within the `WebService` attribute is used to give your XML Web service a unique name. When the end user goes to the test page of the XML Web service, by default the name of the XML Web service class is the name that is used in the banner of the test page.

In this case, the name EnglishGermanEnglishDictionary is self-explanatory, but it doesn't look too presentable. Therefore, you can use the `Name` property to change the title of your XML Web service.

VB

```
Name:="English-German-English Dictionary"
```

C#

```
Name="English-German-English Dictionary"
```

> **NOTE:** Remember that multiple properties need to be separated by a comma.

Figure 7-3 shows how this change looks in the test page.

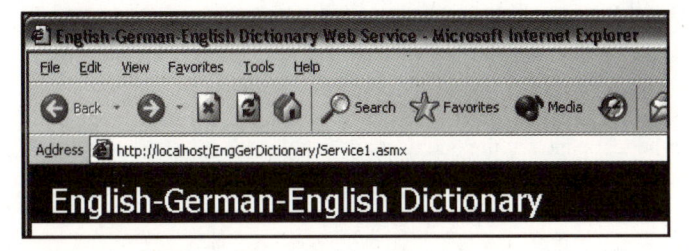

Figure 7-3: Changing the title of your XML Web service test page.

After making all those additions by using the `WebService` attribute, notice that you customized the test page a lot more and made it easier for the end user to understand. If you look at the WSDL document from the Service Description link on the test page, notice that the changes are also reflected at the bottom of this document.

```
<service name="English-German-English_x0020_Dictionary">
  <documentation>This XML Web service is built upon the .NET Framwork
  and translates words from English to German or vise-versa. Presently
  there are around 35,000 words, but I am looking to grow this
  database, so feel free to email me with any substantial contributions
  that you might be able to provide at
  <a href='mailto:evjen@yahoo.com'>evjen@yahoo.com</a>. This XML Web
  Service is hosted at <a href='http://www.xmlws101.com/'
  target='_blank'>XMLWS101.com</a>. -- Bill Evjen</documentation>
  <port name="English-German-English_x0020_DictionarySoap"
    binding="s0:English-
    German-English_x0020_DictionarySoap">
    <soap:address
      location="http://localhost/EngGerDictionary/Service1.asmx" />
  </port>
  <port name="English-German-English_x0020_DictionaryHttpGet"
    binding="s0:English-German-English_x0020_DictionaryHttpGet">
    <http:address
      location="http://localhost/EngGerDictionary/Service1.asmx" />
  </port>
  <port name="English-German-English_x0020_DictionaryHttpPost"
    binding="s0:English-German-English_x0020_DictionaryHttpPost">
    <http:address
      location="http://localhost/EngGerDictionary/Service1.asmx" />
  </port>
</service>
```

Working with the WebMethod Attribute

You learned in early chapters how easy it is to convert regular methods to XML Web services. These methods become consumable pieces of logic accessible via standard protocols when a single attribute is put in front of them.

You have already been doing this throughout the book. By simply placing a `<WebMethod()>` or `[WebMethod()]` attribute in front of a method, you have easily opened up your method for others to consume it.

Just as with the `WebService` attribute, the `WebMethod` can take a number of different properties in order to change the test page for the end users. It enables them to better understand what each of the available methods does and what they can expect in return from these methods.

The Description property

The `Description` property in the WebMethod attribute is exactly the same as the `Description` property that is used in the `WebService`'s attribute, except that it provides a description for each of the methods in the XML Web service to which it is applied. The following code applies a description to one of the methods of the EnglishGermanEnglishDictionary XML Web service.

VB

```
<WebMethod(Description:="Converts English words to German.")>
Public Function EnglishGermanDictionary(ByVal EnglishWord As String)
   As String
      ' code here
End Function
```

C#

```
[WebMethod(Description="Converts English words to German.")]
public string EnglishGermanDictionary(string EnglishWord) {
    // code here
}
```

By providing this description, you can make it easier for the developer that wants to consume this XML Web service. Not only do you provide a description of what the method does, but you also describe what the method takes. It is quite easy to figure out what method type should be inputted into the XML Web service, but the description is also a good spot to provide some explanation of what is needed and how it might affect the entire return of the Web service.

Figure 7-4 show what your XML Web service looks like after you have applied descriptions to all the available methods.

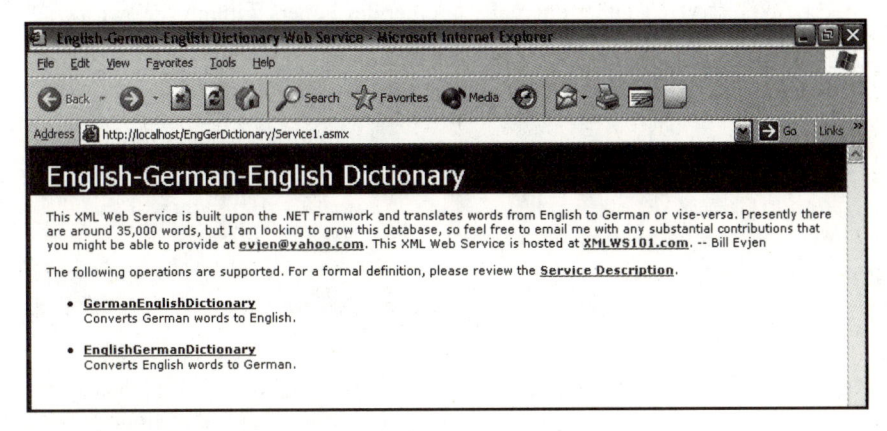

Figure 7-4: Adding desciptions to your methods.

Now your ASP.NET test page is becoming a little more helpful to the end user.

The MessageName property

You changed the name in the banner earlier by using the `Name` property within the `WebService` attribute. By default the banner in the ASP.NET test page displayed the name of the class, and you changed it to something a little more understandable.

It is also possible to change the names of the methods that you will expose as XML Web services by using the `MessageName` property. This will change the way the name appears in the ASP.NET test page for your XML Web service.

To change how the name appears, use the following code in the `WebMethod` attribute:

VB

```
MessageName:="EnglishGermanDictionary / English-German Converter"
```

C#

```
MessageName="EnglishGermanDictionary / English-German Converter"
```

This will change the name of the method in the ASP.NET test page and make it a little more understandable for the end user.

> **NOTE:** If you don't include the function name somewhere in the `MessageName` property, you might be making it difficult for the consumer of your XML Web service. Changing the name here will not change this value in the IntelliSense of the end user, and he may have a hard time finding the method if he doesn't know its name.

Customizing the ASP.NET Test Page

The ASP.NET test page that is provided with the .NET Framework is a great page on which to present your XML Web services, either internally to other developers within your own organization or to the public. You can use any of the features discussed so far to modify the test page so that it is a more descriptive for the end user. It is also possible to customize this page beyond what you can do by changing the `WebService` and `WebMethod` attributes.

Included in the .NET Framework is an `.aspx` page that is used to display the XML Web service test page. You can find the page at `Windows\Microsoft.NET\Framework\vX.X.XXXX\CONFIG`. Here you will find the file `DefaultWsdlHelpGenerator.aspx`.

> **NOTE:** Be sure to make a copy of this file so that you can always go back to the original if needed.

This is an ASP.NET page that is written in ASP.NET and C#. In the layout of the page, the ASP.NET Repeater control is used. Modifying this page enables you to customize the page however you see fit. Add a company logo or do whatever is needed to give it the look and feel that you require.

Disabling the Test Page

You will not always want end users to be able to test your XML Web services from this test page. If you don't, it's possible to turn off the capability to test the XML Web service from the generated `.aspx` file.

In order to do this you need to add a configuration setting into the `Web.Config` file that's located in the root of your XML Web service. Open the file and add the following code so that it's contained within the `<system.web>` elements.

```
<webServices>
   <protocols>
      <remove name="HttpGet" />
   </protocols>
</webServices>
```

This removes the HTTP-GET functionality from your XML Web service. This is the main protocol that is used when testing XML Web services from the ASP.NET test page. When this protocol is turned off from the `Web.Config` file, users are still able to view the ASP.NET test page, but they aren't able to test the XML Web service from that page. This is shown in Figure 7-5.

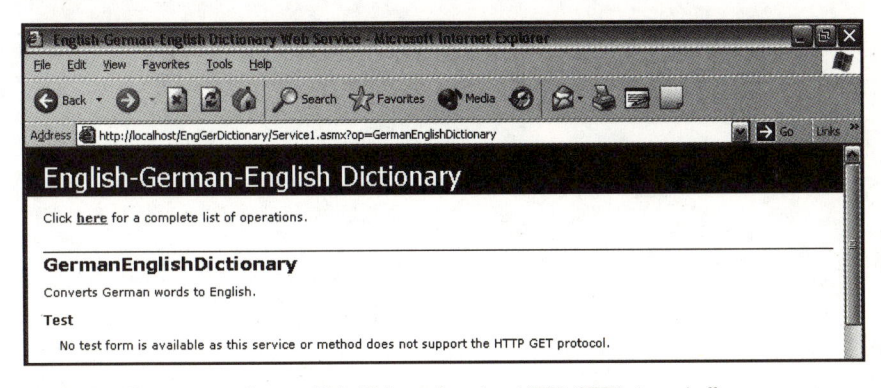

Figure 7-5: The test page for your XML Web service when HTTP-GET is turned off.

Now that you have removed the capability for the end user to access the XML Web service using HTTP-GET, not only is it removed from the test page, but it is also removed from the WSDL file. Configuring the preceding example this way means that the end user is only able to access the EnglishGermanEnglishDictionary XML Web service from either HTTP-POST or SOAP.

Summary

This was a short chapter, but an important step in the construction of your XML Web services. In your XML Web services, the end user cannot always open the hood and take a look around. It is, therefore, imperative that you provide end users with as much information as possible so that they truly understand your XML Web service and that they understand what the XML Web service needs in order to work properly.

Remember that, after building your XML Web services, you should provide descriptions and even links to ASP.NET pages that might show the end user how to consume your service. Doing so will more effectively ensure the success of the XML Web services that you build.

Chapter 8
State Management

Memory is the thing you forget with.
Alexander Chase, *Perspectives* (1966)

Developing applications on the Internet provides some special challenges. One of the major obstacles is persisting state throughout the application.

The Internet is *stateless* by nature. The whole thing basically works with HTTP requests and responses. The server receives an HTTP request for a particular page and sends the calling application the requested page or information, otherwise known as a response. The server sending the response does not keep track of who made the request. Every request is equal in the server's eyes.

When the same calling application makes a second request, the server gives it the second piece of information but still does not house any information about this calling application. The server doesn't know that this application is the same one that just recently requested the first piece of logic.

This creates a problem if you want your XML Web service to remember information about the calling application. Remembering the calling application and being able to make a distinction between requests allows end users to work through an application in a continuous manner. You may want your service to retain certain information: who the users are, their preferences, or any other pertinent information about them as they makes multiple requests. You do this by using varying techniques that you can apply throughout the Web service's code.

ASP.NET offers some new features and techniques to apply when working with state management. You might have used many of these techniques with Web applications that you developed in the past.

This chapter covers

- Understanding state
- Using sessions
- Working with the `Application` object
- Using cookies when you consume an XML Web service
- Working with the ViewState when you consume an XML Web service

Understanding State in .NET

If you are working with state management in your XML Web services, it is important to fully understand state as it works within .NET as a whole. XML Web services technology is part of ASP.NET and, therefore, has access to state management just as any ASP.NET application does. You might also build .NET applications that need to maintain state on the client-side in order to work with a particular XML Web service. Take a close look at how you can manage state in different ways in ASP.NET and XML Web services.

You can turn on the capability to use the ASP.NET `HTTPSessionState` object as simply as you add a property setting to the `WebMethod` attribute for a method in your XML Web service. You do this by adding the `EnableSession` property to the `WebMethod` attribute. Listing 8-1 shows an example of this.

Listing 8-1: Using sessions with XML Web services

VB

```
Imports System.Web.Services

Public Class Service1
    Inherits WebService

    <WebMethod(EnableSession:=True)> _
    Public Function SessionCounter() As Integer

        If Session("Counter") Is Nothing Then
            Session("Counter") = 1
        Else
            Session("Counter ") = CInt(Session("Counter ")) + 1
        End If

        Return CInt(Session("Counter"))

    End Function
End Class
```

C#

```
using System.Web.Services;

public class Service1: WebService {
  [WebMethod(EnableSession=true)]
    public int SessionCounter() {
        if (Session["Counter"] == null) {
           Session["Counter"] = 1;
        }
        else {
           Session["Counter"] = ((int) Session["Counter"]) + 1;
        }
```

Chapter 8: **State Management** 173

```
        return ((int) Session["Counter"]);
    }
}
```

You will notice that the `EnableSession` property takes a Boolean value. The default is that `EnableSession` is `false`. Using this property will allow access to ASP.NET intrinsics such as the `Session` and `Application` objects.

If you compile and run the preceding XML Web service, you are shown the XML Web service's test page where you can invoke the `SessionCounter` method. Because you are not passing any parameters to the method, you are given only an Invoke button. Clicking this button fires up a request to the XML Web service, and the returned XML is shown in a new browser window. Repeatedly hitting the URL of your XML Web service and invoking the `SessionCounter()` WebMethod causes the number that is passed back in the XML file to increment by one each time the method is invoked. Figure 8-1 shows an example of this.

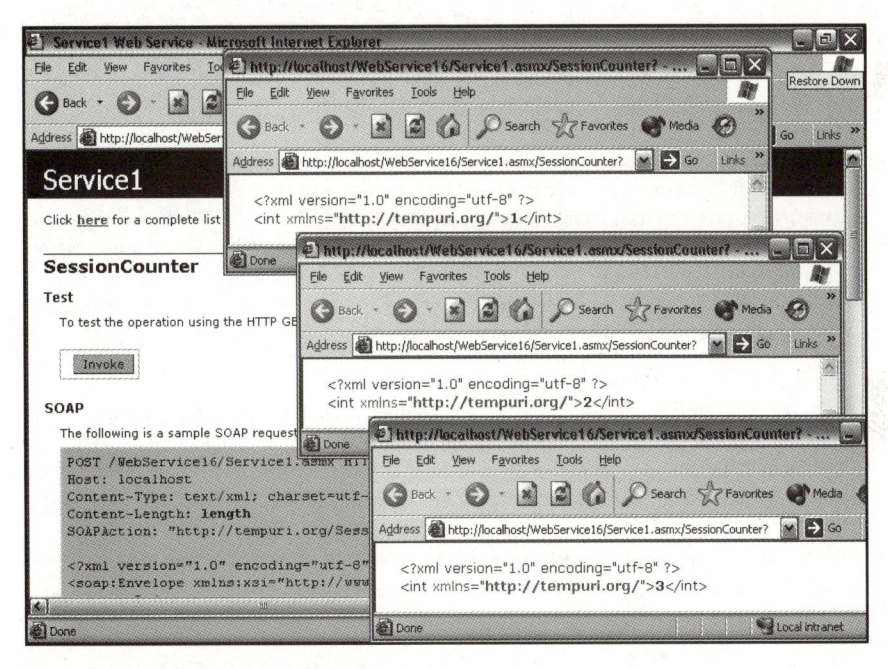

Figure 8-1: Using sessions in an XML Web service.

You can see that the Web service is now keeping track of the successive calls from the same user (namely you).

Understanding Sessions

Sessions within an XML Web service enable users to easily maintain application state. Sessions will remain with the user as he works through repeated calls to an XML Web service for a defined period of time.

Sessions are easily created, and it is just as easy to retrieve information from them. Use the following code to create a session for the user or calling application that can be accessed later in the XML Web service or to assign a value to an already established session.

VB

```
Session("EmployeeID") = Value1
```

C#

```
Session["EmployeeID"] = Value1;
```

This will assign what was placed in `Value1` to the `EmployeeID` session. To retrieve this information from the session and then use it in your code, do the following:

VB

```
Value2 = Session("EmployeeID")
```

C#

```
Value2 = Session["EmployeeID"];
```

In ASP.NET, session timeout is similar to what it was in classic ASP — a session would timeout on the user after 20 minutes. If the user opened a page within a Web application (thereby creating a session) and then walked away for a cup of coffee, when the user came back to the page 40 minutes later, the session wouldn't be there. You could get around this by going into the server and changing the time allotted to the session timeout property, but this was cumbersome and required that you stop the server and then start it again for the changes to take effect. In addition, because sessions are resource intensive, you wouldn't want to store too many sessions for too long.

With ASP.NET, and XML Web services, it is now possible to change the session timeout property quite easily. On the application level, it is now stored in the `web.config` file. The `machine.config` file stores the default timeout setting for the entire server. By changing the setting in the `web.config` file, you can effectively change the timeout property of sessions within the application. The great thing about changing this property within this XML application file is that the server does not have to be stopped and started for the changes to take effect. After the `web.config` file is saved with its changes, the changes take effect immediately.

The part of the `web.config` file that deals with session state management is the `sessionState` node.

```
<sessionState
   mode="InProc"
   stateConnectionString="tcpip=127.0.0.1:42424"
   sqlConnectionString="data source=127.0.0.1;user id=sa;password="
   cookieless="false"
   timeout="20" />
```

Chapter 8: State Management

The `sessionState` node of the `web.config` file is where session state is managed. The property that you are concerned with now is the `timeout` property.

The `timeout` property is set to `20` (the default setting). This setting represents minutes of time. Therefore, if you want the users' sessions to last for one hour, you set the timeout property to `60`.

> **NOTE:** If you are integrating classic ASP with XML Web services that you are building with ASP.NET, be aware that even though the two technologies run side by side on the same server, they do not share `Session` or `Application` objects. It is impossible to pass these objects from one technology to the other.

Running sessions in-process

Presently, the default setting for sessions in ASP.NET stores the sessions in the *in-process* mode. This is the same as in classic ASP. Running sessions in-process means that the sessions are stored in the same process as the ASP.NET worker process. Therefore, if IIS is shut down and then brought back up again, all sessions are destroyed and unavailable to users. On mission-critical Web applications, this can be a nightmare.

In order to run the sessions in-process, set the mode property in the `sessionState` node to `InProc`. Running sessions in-process will provide the application with the best possible performance.

Table 8-1 describes all the session modes available.

Table 8-1:   Session State Modes

Mode	Description
InProc	Session state is in-process with the ASP.NET worker process. Running sessions `InProc` is the default setting.
Off	Session state is not available.
StateServer	Session state is using an out-of-process server to store state.
SQLServer	Session state is using an out-of-process SQL Server to store state.

Running sessions out-of-process

It is possible to run sessions out-of-process. Running a session out-of-process allows IIS to be stopped and then restarted while maintaining the user's sessions.

Along with the .NET Framework is a Windows service called *ASPState*. This service enables you to run sessions out-of-process, but it has to be started in order to use it to manage sessions.

Part III: Building XML Web Services

To start the ASPState service, open the *Command Prompt* (Start ⇨ Programs ⇨ Accessories ⇨ Command Prompt). On the Command Prompt line type the following command:

```
CD \WINDOWS\Microsoft.NET\Framework\v1.0.3512
```

Next, press Enter. This changes the directory of the command prompt. After typing that line in the command prompt, type

```
net start aspnet_state
```

This turns on the session out-of-process capabilities, as shown in Figure 8-2.

> **NOTE:** The path shown above is for Windows XP Professional. If you are on a different operating system, the path could be different. Also, take a look at the path within Windows Explorer and view the version of the .NET Framework that you are running. The preceding example uses Version 1.0.3512, but you are most likely running a different version and you need to change the command appropriately. If you have more than one version folder, choose the latest version.

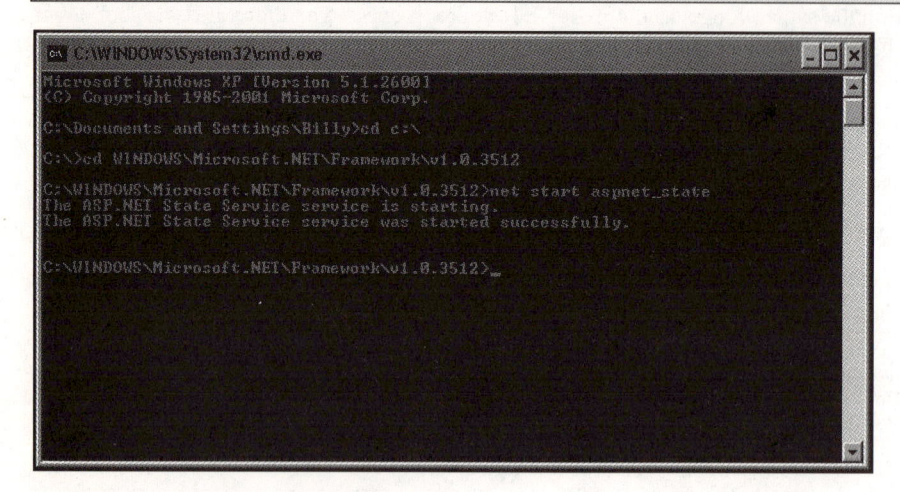

Figure 8-2: Turning on the ASP.NET State Service.

It is also possible to turn on the ASP.NET State Service through the Services console. In Windows XP, open the console by selecting Start ⇨ Control Panel ⇨ Performance and Maintenance ⇨ Administrative Tools ⇨ Services. In Windows 2000, open the console by selecting Start ⇨ Settings ⇨ Control Panel ⇨ Administrative Tools ⇨ Services. You are presented with a list of services available on the server. In Windows XP, you can start or stop the ASP.NET State Service by clicking the appropriate link. In Windows 2000, right-clicking on the ASP.NET State Service enables you to either stop or start the service (see Figure 8-3).

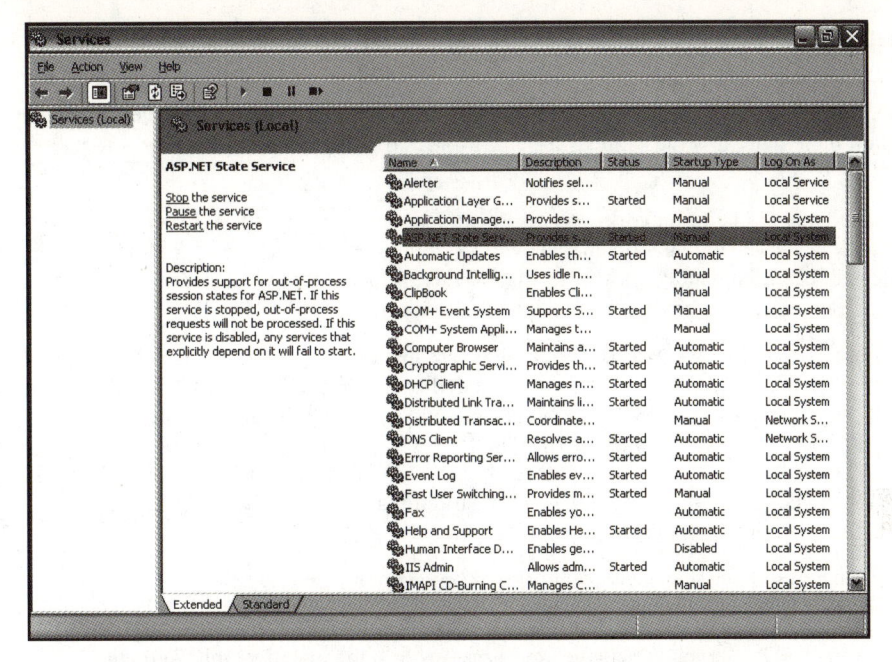

Figure 8-3: Starting the ASP.NET State Service from the Services console in Windows XP.

Once the out-of-process mode is enabled, you can change the settings in the `sessionState` node of the `web.config` file so that all the users' sessions are run in this manner. You do this by setting the `mode` to `StateServer`.

```
<sessionState
  mode="StateServer"
  stateConnectionString="tcpip=127.0.0.1:42424"
  sqlConnectionString="data source=127.0.0.1;user id=sa;password="
  cookieless="false"
  timeout="20" />
```

Now the user can turn IIS off and then on again and his sessions will remain intact, although doing this is a little more resource intensive than running the sessions in-process.

If the mode is set to `StateServer`, the server looks to the `stateConnectionString` property to assign the sessions to a specified server and port. In this case, which is the default setting, it is set to the local server. You can easily change this so that the sessions are stored on a completely separate server.

Running sessions out-of-process is a great new advantage with ASP.NET that isn't available in classic ASP. This is a great tool when running Web applications in a Web farm where you are unsure which server the user will navigate to. This gives you the ability to move users from one server to another and yet maintain their state.

Maintaining sessions on SQL Server

Another option to run sessions out-of-process is to employ SQL Server to store the user sessions. Storing sessions in SQL Server also enables users to move from one server to another and maintain their state. It is the same as the `StateServer` mode, but instead stores the sessions in SQL Server.

If you installed the .NET Framework, you also installed a miniversion of SQL Server on your server. This SQL Server-lite version enables you to store your sessions to use for state management. It is recommended, however, that you use a full-blown version of SQL Server, such as SQL Server 2000. This is a more dependable solution.

The first thing to do in order to use SQL Server as a repository of your sessions is to create the database within SQL that ASP.NET can use. Included in the version folder of ASP.NET (found at `C:\WINDOWS\Microsoft.NET\Framework\v1.0.XXXX`) are two scripts that work with SQL Server session management. The first is the install script, `InstallSqlState.sql`. This is a script that instructs SQL Server which database tables and procedures to create. You can look at the script instructions, which are quite readable, by opening up the script in Notepad.

If you ever wish to remove these tables and stored procedures from SQL Server, use the uninstall script, `UninstallSqlScript.sql`.

If you wish to use SQL Server to manage your sessions, run the install script. To do this, open up the command prompt again and navigate to the version folder of ASP.NET that you are running. On the command line, type

```
OSQL -S localhost -U sa -P <InstallSqlState.sql
```

The OSQL utility enables you to enter Transact-SQL statements, system procedures, and script files. This utility uses ODBC to communicate with the server. Running this command creates the tables and procedures needed to run the SQL Server session management option. The notation `-S` in the command line is specifying the location of the server that is to be used. In this case, you are using `localhost`, meaning your local server.

The notation `-U` means the SQL Server's assigned username to gain access. In this case, it is just the typical `sa`.

The notation `-P` is for the SQL Server's password, if required. In this case, it isn't required. Therefore, you leave it blank.

Following the SQL Server's setting specifications, you then specify the script that you wish to install, `InstallSqlState.sql`. This installs what is necessary to run SQL Server session management.

After you have created the tables and procedures necessary, change the `sessionState` node of the `web.config` file.

```
<sessionState
   mode="SQLServer"
   stateConnectionString="tcpip=127.0.0.1:42424"
```

```
    sqlConnectionString="data source=127.0.0.1;user id=sa;password="
    cookieless="false"
    timeout="20" />
```

To use SQL Server to manage sessions, the mode of the `sessionState` node needs to be set to `SQLServer`. After the mode is set to `SQLServer`, ASP.NET then looks to the `sqlConnectionString` property to find the SQL Server to connect to. The value of this property should be set so that the `data source` is the server where the SQL and any needed login information are located.

Deciding on the state of sessions

The mode you choose for running sessions within your XML Web service makes a considerable difference in the performance, functionality, and reliability of your Web application.

Which mode should you choose? The following list summarizes the best conditions for each option:

- **InProc:** This option is similar to the way it is done in classic ASP. The session is run in the same process as the ASP.NET worker process. Therefore, this option should be used when maintaining sessions is not mission-critical to the application. This option has the best performance possible out of all the choices.
- **StateServer:** This Windows Service option runs the sessions out-of-process and is, therefore, best when used on multiple servers or when sessions need to be maintained if IIS is stopped and then restarted. This option provides better performance than the other out-of-process option, SQLServer.
- **SQLServer:** This out-of-process option is the most reliable choice because the sessions are stored directly in SQL Server. Even though this is the most reliable choice, this option ranks worst in performance.

Cookieless session state

All the options mentioned so far also allow you to set the sessions so that they employ a cookieless option. This is for visitors to your site who choose to have cookies disabled in their browsers. You enable the cookieless-session-state environment by setting the `cookieless` property in the `sessionState` node of the `web.config` file to `true`, as shown here:

```
<sessionState
    mode="StateServer"
    stateConnectionString="tcpip=127.0.0.1:42424"
    sqlConnectionString="data source=127.0.0.1;user id=sa;password="
    cookieless="True"
    timeout="20" />
```

ASP.NET embeds the user's session directly into the URL. When a user calls an XML Web service with a URL, the URL is rendered to contain the user's session ID in the middle of the URL itself.

Part III: Building XML Web Services

For an example of this, use the same session counter method that you used earlier in this chapter and change the `web.config` file so that the `cookieless` property is set to `True`. Figure 8-4 shows an example of running the same XML Web service with this setting in place.

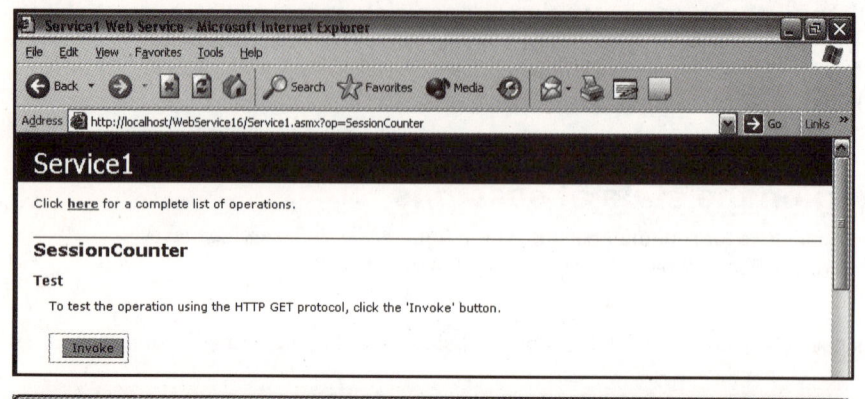

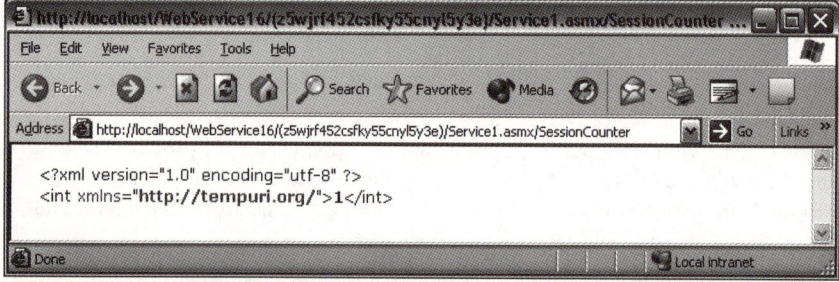

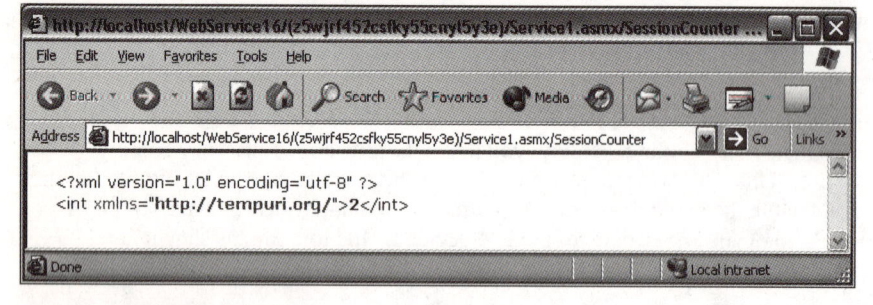

Figure 8-4: Cookieless session state.

The URL in the browser's address box now contains the session ID right in the middle:

```
http://localhost/WebService16/(z5wjrf452csfky55cnyl5y3e)/
Service1.asmx/SessionCounter
```

Because you set the `web.config` file to perform cookieless sessions, it gave the user a session ID of `(z5wjrf452csfky55cnyl5y3e)`. ASP.NET uses this to identify the user on any subsequent XML Web service requests. The drawback is that the user could change the contents of his session, thus destroying the session.

Using the Application Object in XML Web Services

Just as you can use the `Session` object, you are able to use the `Application` object within your XML Web services. The `Application` object is a shared container for managing state within your XML Web services. This object enables you to store variables or object references that are available to all the visitors to the XML Web service for the life of the Web service. Unlike the `Session` object, the `Application` object can only run in-process, meaning that it can only run in the same process as ASP.NET. This means that if the ASP.NET is shutdown for any reason, all `Application` data is lost.

Even though there are some limitations when compared to `Session` objects, you will find that there will be many benefits to using `Application` within your XML Web services. Take a quick look at how to use an `Application` within your code.

Very much like working with sessions, working with an `Application` is easy. First of all, to create an `Application`, you just assign a value to the `Application` object as shown here:

VB

```
Application("City") = "Helsinki"
```

C#

```
Application["City"] = "Helsinki";
```

It is also just as easy to assign a variable the value of the `Application` object as shown in the following code:

VB

```
Dim ProgramCity As String = Application("City")
```

C#

```
string ProgramCity = Application["City"];
```

You probably noticed that this syntax is the same as the syntax you use with sessions. There is, however, a big difference between the two that you should always be aware of. Because the `Application` object is an *application-wide* object that is accessible by all users of your XML Web service, two users could simultaneously attempt to update the same `Application` object. To resolve such possible conflicts, ASP.NET has provided two methods — `Lock()` and `UnLock()`.

The idea is to lock down the `Application` while the first user is updating it. This prevents a second user from changing any information before the first user has had the chance to make her changes. After the first user is finished making the update to the `Application`, the `Application` is unlocked, thereby allowing the second user to make his own changes. See how this is done in Listing 8-2.

To show the differences between `Session` and `Application`, build an XML Web service that uses both to keep track of the number of times that the XML Web service is accessed. Keep in mind that the `Session` is *per user,* and that the `Application` is for the XML Web service as a whole and will continue to keep on counting the numbers of hits regardless of the number of different users or applications that are hitting the service.

Listing 8-2: The Application object and the Session object compared

VB

```
Imports System.Web.Services

<WebService(Namespace:="http://www.xmlws101.com")> _
 Public Class Application_VS_Session
    Inherits System.Web.Services.WebService

    <WebMethod(Description:="Number of times this XML Web service has
               been accessed as a whole.")> _
      Public Function ApplicationHits() As Integer
      If Application("ApplicationHitsCount") Is Nothing Then
          Application.Lock()
          Application("ApplicationHitsCount") = 1
          Application.UnLock()
      Else
          Application.Lock()
          Application("ApplicationHitsCount") = _
              CInt(Application("ApplicationHitsCount")) + 1
          Application.UnLock()
      End If
      Return CInt(Application("ApplicationHitsCount"))
    End Function

    <WebMethod(Description:="Number of times a single user has accessed
               this XML Web service.", EnableSession:=True)> _
      Public Function SessionHits() As Integer
      If Session("SessionHitsCount") Is Nothing Then
          Session("SessionHitsCount") = 1
      Else
          Session("SessionHitsCount") =
              CInt(Session("SessionHitsCount")) + 1
      End If
      Return CInt(Session("SessionHitsCount"))
    End Function
End Class
```

C#

```
using System;
using System.Collections;
using System.ComponentModel;
```

```csharp
using System.Data;
using System.Diagnostics;
using System.Web;
using System.Web.Services;

namespace WebService1
{
 [ WebService(Namespace="http://www.xmlws101.com") ]
   public class Application_VS_Session : System.Web.Services.WebService
 {
   [ WebMethod(Description="Number of times this XML Web service has been
              accessed as a whole.") ]
   public int ApplicationHits()
   {
    if (Application["ApplicationHitsCount"] == null)
    {
     Application.Lock();
     Application["ApplicationHitsCount"] = 1;
     Application.UnLock();
    }
    else
    {
     Application.Lock();
     Application["ApplicationHitsCount"] =
          ((int) Application["ApplicationHitsCount"]) + 1;
     Application.UnLock();
    }
    return  (int) Application["ApplicationHitsCount"];
   }

   [ WebMethod(Description="Number of times a single user has accessed
              this XML Web service.",EnableSession=true) ]
   public int SessionHits()
   {
    if (Session["SessionHitsCount"] == null)
    {
     Session["SessionHitsCount"] = 1;
    }
    else
    {
     Session["SessionHitsCount"] =
         ((int) Session["SessionHitsCount"]) + 1;
    }
    return  (int) Session["SessionHitsCount"];
   }

 }
}
```

After you have you typed all the code, press F5 to build and deploy your XML Web service and you will be presented with two available methods. The first is the `SessionHits` method. Test this out first. Go to the test page of the `SessionHits` method and invoke this method. You get back an integer: 1. Close this XML document and invoke the method again, and you now get back the number 2. The method is counting the number of times that you, as a user, have accessed this method.

Now do the same thing to the other method, `ApplicationHits`. Open the test page to this method and invoke it the same as you did `SessionHits`. Close the XML document and invoke the method one more time. Now you have accessed each of these methods twice.

To see the differences between `Applications` and `Sessions`, close all the test pages and, within Visual Studio .NET, deploy the XML Web service again by pressing F5. This time you are a second user, according to ASP.NET.

Now, open up the `SessionHits` test page and invoke the method again. This time notice that you are given the number 1 because this is the first time that you have accessed this method as this particular user.

Now pull up the `ApplicationHits` method. This is the first time that this particular user has accessed this method. Invoke the method and you get back the number 3. It has kept record of the total number of hits to the method regardless of the user. It is a global variable that is saved for any user that can access it and saved for the lifetime of the XML Web service.

Now, change something in the XML Web service file and recompile. This causes the old XML Web service to be killed and a new one to be put into its place, thereby creating a new XML Web service. If you go back to the `ApplicationHits` method and invoke it, you will notice that the count has once again started at the beginning.

One important difference between `Session` and `Application` that you can see in the code is that the Application object does not require the `EnableSession` property to be set in the `WebMethod` attribute. Notice that in the `ApplicationHits` method you do not set the `EnableSession` property to `True` as you do in the `SessionHits` method. The reason for this is that any class deriving from `WebService` automatically has access to the `Application` object.

Another thing to note is that you lock your `Application` before you make a change to it to avoid concurrency issues. You do this with the `Lock()` method that is available with the `Application` object. After you are done making the necessary changes, you use the `UnLock()` method to open it up to any other users. If you do not use the `UnLock()` method, the .NET Framework does the unlock for you when the request completes, when the request times out, or when an unhandled error occurs during request execution and causes the request to fail. This automatic unlocking prevents the application from deadlocking.

> **NOTE:** Locking and unlocking the `Application` can really slow up an XML Web service if this `Application` is accessed frequently. Once you lock an `Application`, you are blocking other users from using the same object until it is freed. In most cases, this delay may not be appropriate.

Using Cookies along with the Consumption of XML Web Services

Cookies are key/value pairs that are stored on the client computer. Using cookies to persist information is a simple and easy option in ASP.NET if you need to maintain state when working with XML Web services. Cookies are passed along with the HTTP request to the server and are used to identify the user upon receipt.

Advantages to using cookies

There are advantages to using cookies within your ASP.NET Web applications to store simple data. First, cookies don't require server resources because none of the cookies are stored on the server. Second, you can set cookies to expire when the browser is shut down or at any date in the future. Therefore, it's possible for the application to remember the user if he returns weeks or months later.

Disadvantages to using cookies

There are also some negatives to using cookies. One negative is that cookies need to be small. You cannot send large amounts of data to the clients to store on their machines. Generally, there's a 4,096-byte limit to the size of a cookie, limiting the types of data that you can store. For some applications, cookies can cause some serious security risks. It is easy for knowledgeable users to change cookies. This can be a major problem if you're using cookies to help users gain access to private information.

I know of a financial institution that was storing each user's account number as a cookie on the client's machine. The application that displayed information about the users' accounts used this cookie to give a user access to his account. You can see the problem here. All you had to do was change the numbers in the cookie and you were in someone else's account.

Listings 8-3 and 8-4 show an example of working with cookies and XML Web services within the same application. In order for this application to work, you need to make a reference to the Calculator XML Web service that you built earlier.

Listing 8-3: Creating and displaying cookies (WebForm1.aspx)

```
<%@ Page Language="vb" AutoEventWireup="false"
    Codebehind="WebForm1.aspx.vb"
    Inherits="CookieApp.WebForm1"%>
<HTML>
 <HEAD>
  <title>WebForm1</title>
 </HEAD>
 <body>
  <form id="Form1" method="post" runat="server">
   <P><FONT face="Verdana" size="2">
   <STRONG>Enter two numbers and press the Add
    button.</STRONG></FONT></P>
   <P>
    <asp:TextBox id="TextBox1" runat="server"></asp:TextBox></P>
```

```
  <P>
    <asp:TextBox id="TextBox2" runat="server"></asp:TextBox></P>
  <P>
    <asp:Button id="Button1" runat="server"
Text="Add"></asp:Button></P>
  <P>
    <asp:Label id="Label1" runat="server"
      Visible="False"></asp:Label></P>
  <P>
    <asp:Label id="Label2" runat="server"></asp:Label></P>
  </form>
 </body>
</HTML>
```

Listing 8-4: The code-behind page (WebForm1.aspx.vb and WebForm1.aspx.cs)

VB

```vb
Public Class WebForm1
    Inherits System.Web.UI.Page
    Protected WithEvents TextBox1 As System.Web.UI.WebControls.TextBox
    Protected WithEvents TextBox2 As System.Web.UI.WebControls.TextBox
    Protected WithEvents Label1 As System.Web.UI.WebControls.Label
    Protected WithEvents Label2 As System.Web.UI.WebControls.Label
    Protected WithEvents Button1 As System.Web.UI.WebControls.Button

    Private Sub Page_Load(ByVal sender As System.Object, _
                    ByVal e As System.EventArgs) Handles MyBase.Load
        Dim MyCookie1 As HttpCookie
        Dim sysNull As System.DBNull
        MyCookie1 = Request.Cookies("CalcWS")

        If Not MyCookie1 Is sysNull Then
          Label1.Visible = True
          Label1.Text = "You last accessed this XML Web service on: " & _
              MyCookie1.Item("LastAccessed").ToString()
        End If

    End Sub

    Private Sub Button1_Click(ByVal sender As System.Object, _
                    ByVal e As System.EventArgs) Handles Button1.Click
        Dim MyCookie As HttpCookie

        MyCookie = New HttpCookie("CalcWS")
        Dim ws As New CalculatorWS.Calculator()
        Label2.Text = ws.Add(CInt(TextBox1.Text), CInt(TextBox2.Text))

        MyCookie.Values.Add("LastAccessed", Date.Now)
        Response.AppendCookie(MyCookie)
    End Sub
```

End Class

C#

```csharp
using System;
using System.Collections;
using System.ComponentModel;
using System.Data;
using System.Drawing;
using System.Web;
using System.Web.SessionState;
using System.Web.UI;
using System.Web.UI.WebControls;
using System.Web.UI.HtmlControls;

namespace CookieApp
{
 public class WebForm1 : System.Web.UI.Page
 {
  protected System.Web.UI.WebControls.TextBox TextBox1;
  protected System.Web.UI.WebControls.TextBox TextBox2;
  protected System.Web.UI.WebControls.Button Button1;
  protected System.Web.UI.WebControls.Label Label1;
  protected System.Web.UI.WebControls.Label Label2;

  private void Page_Load(object sender, System.EventArgs e)
  {
   HttpCookie MyCookie1 = Request.Cookies["CalcWS"];

   if (MyCookie1 != null)
   {
    Label1.Visible = true;
    Label1.Text = "You last accessed this XML Web service on: " +
                  MyCookie1["LastAccessed"].ToString();
   }
  }

  private void Button1_Click(object sender, System.EventArgs e)
  {
   HttpCookie MyCookie = new HttpCookie("CalcWS");

   CalculatorWS.Calculator ws = new CalculatorWS.Calculator();
   Label2.Text = ws.Add(Int32.Parse(TextBox1.Text),
                        Int32.Parse(TextBox2.Text)).ToString();

   MyCookie.Values.Add("LastAccessed", (DateTime.Now).ToString());
   Response.AppendCookie(MyCookie);
  }
 }
```

In this example, you placed a cookie on the client's machine whenever he accessed the Calculator Web service (Figure 8-5). So, the second time the client hit the XML Web service, he was posted a message indicating the last time he accessed the `Add` method. You will find that using cookies along with the consumption of XML Web services is a good and easy way to maintain state in your applications.

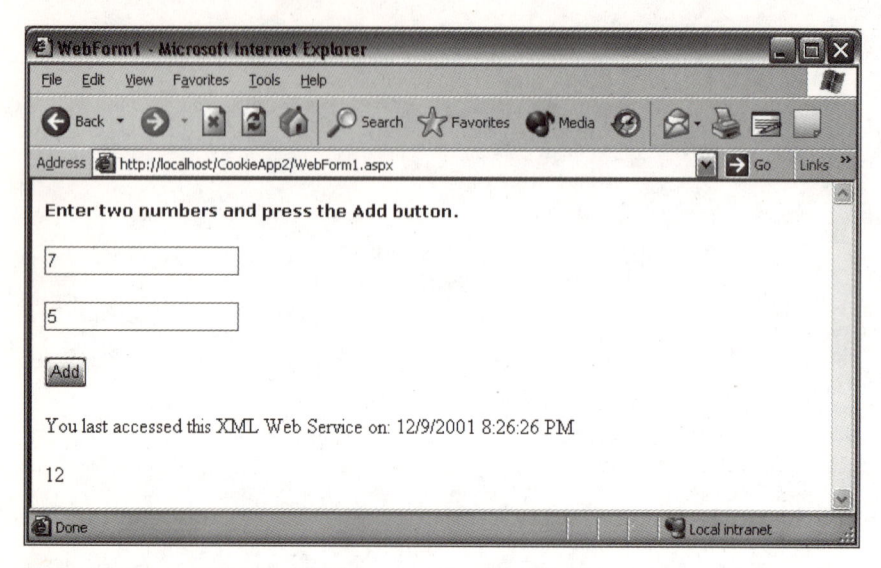

Figure 8-5: Using cookies along with the consumption of an XML Web service.

Using ViewState along with the Consumption of XML Web Services

ViewState is another ASP.NET feature that isn't available in ASP 3.0. With ViewState, you can easily maintain the state of your controls between round trips to the server. ASP.NET requires this capability because you can program your Web Forms with multiple round trips to the server. It's possible to program your Web controls so that each control forces the page to make a round trip to the server every time the control is changed in order to perform an event.

As the page makes this trip to the server and back, it remembers the state of each control, including the controls to which you bind XML Web services, and it populates each control's status back into the control as the page is redrawn. It does this by including a hidden form field element within your form page. If you look at the source of your Web Form page, notice that there's a ViewState model right at the beginning of the form. Listing 8-5 displays the beginning of a Web Form.

Listing 8-5: ViewState of a Web Form

```
<html>
  <head>
       <title>ViewState Display</title>
  </head>

  <body>
  <form name="Form1" method="post" action="WebForm1.aspx"
  language="javascript" onsubmit="ValidatorOnSubmit();"
  id="Form1">

<input type="hidden" name="__VIEWSTATE"
 value="dDwtMTA3MTIxNjQxMTt0PDtsPGk8Mj47PjtsPHQ8O2w8aTwyNj47Pj
 tsPHQ8cDxwPGw8VGV4dDtWaXNpYmxlOz47bDxXZWxjb21lIHRvIHRoZSBncm9
 1cCFcPGJyXD4xO288dD47Pj47Pjs7Pjs+Pjs+" />
```

This unreadable mess within the hidden form field shows the state of all the controls on the Web Form page. Instead of listing the state of the controls directly, this information is put into a format that's not readable to you and me, but is readable by the ASP.NET parser.

The parser takes this data and repopulates that page's controls. This is wonderful because this task usually required a lot of coding in ASP 3.0. However, you can probably tell that it takes some processing on the server to persist this state and to repopulate the controls after the page is redrawn.

Toggling ViewState on and off

Keeping the ViewState functionality on isn't always a priority with every Web Form you create. For this reason, you can turn off the ViewState, thus saving server resources and increasing the speed of your application. You can turn this functionality off in two ways. The first is to disable ViewState on the page level, and the other is to disable it on the control level. To disable ViewState for the entire page, turn off this functionality within the page directive.

To turn off the ViewState functionality for the entire page, just add the following attribute to the page directive at the top of the page:

```
<%@ Page EnableViewState="False" %>
```

It's also possible to disable ViewState on the control level. If maintaining a control's state is not an important feature of that control, turn it off. This mildly increases the performance of the page overall. To turn off ViewState for a control, add the `EnableViewState` attribute to the control:

```
<asp:Label id="Label1" Runat="Server" EnableViewState="False" />
```

> **TIP:** Paying attention to which pages and controls are ViewState-enabled leads to better overall application performance.

Extending ViewState

There are times when you might want to include user-specific information in your Web Forms that needs to be carried across server round trips but is beyond the state of the control. In this case, it's possible to piggyback onto the ViewState functionality. In a sense, you're adding your own set of name/value pairs to ViewState. Listing 8-6 shows a simple example of using this functionality to incorporate a page-count function.

Listing 8-6: Adding onto ViewState

VB

```
<html>
  <head>
    <title>ViewState Example</title>

    <script language="vb" runat="server">
        Sub Page_Load(sender As Object, e As EventArgs)
            If not Page.IsPostBack Then
                    ViewState("PageCount") = 1
            Else
                    ViewState("PageCount") += 1
            End If
        End Sub
    </script>

  </head>
  <body>
  <form id="form1" runat="server">
    The ViewState("PageCount") is equal to:
    <%= ViewState("PageCount") %>
    <p><asp:button id="button1" runat="server"
        text="Cause PostBack" /></p>
  </form>
  </body>
</html>
```

C#

```
<html>
 <head>
  <title>ViewState Example</title>
  <script language="c#" runat="server">
        private void Page_Load(object sender, System.EventArgs e)
        {
            if (!IsPostBack)
            {
                ViewState["PageCount"] = 1;
            }
            else
```

```
            {
                ViewState["PageCount"] = (int) ViewState["PageCount"] + 1;
            }
        }
    </script>
</head>
<body>
    <form id="form1" runat="server">
      The ViewState["PageCount"] is equal to:
      <%= ViewState["PageCount"] %>
      <p><asp:button id="button1" runat="server"
          text="Cause PostBack" /></p>
    </form>
</body>
</html>
```

In the past, you performed this operation either by using sessions or making your own hidden tags within the code. Using this ViewState functionality is a great way to keep data relatively private and to pass it with the ease of sessions.

In this example, when the page is first drawn, you create a name/value pair named `PageCount` and give it a value of 1:

```
ViewState("PageCount") = 1
```

It's possible to create as many name/value pairs as you want, but in this case, you've only created one.

In the example page, you also refer to the name/value pair by calling it in much the same way that you created it. Within the body part of the page, you print the `ViewState("PageCount")` directly onto the screen. Another option would be to create a Label control and set the `Text` property of the control as follows:

```
Label1.Text = ViewState("PageCount")
```

Clicking the Button control causes the page to postback, and your code adds 1 to the value of `PageCount`.

```
ViewState("PageCount") += 1
```

Both cookies and ViewState are quick and easy ways to maintain state while working with applications in the .NET Framework that work with the XML Web services you consume.

Summary

The Internet has produced some great applications, but it has also made the development of these applications difficult. Because the Internet is a disconnected environment, (meaning that the only *real* time that you are connected to an application or remote server is when you are making a request or getting a response), it is quite difficult at times to maintain state on it. However, ASP.NET and, in turn, XML Web services have answered this difficulty with a number of solutions that, if used properly, can quickly make you forget about the disconnected world in which you work and play.

In this chapter, you took a look at how state works in XML Web services and in the applications that consume them. You took a look at the `Session` object, the `Application` object, as well as cookies and ViewState.

In the next chapter, you look at how to work with proxies in XML Web services.

Chapter 9

Proxies

Utility is the great idol of the age,
to which all powers must do service and all talents swear allegiance.
Schiller, *On the Aesthetic Education of Man* (1795)

So far, as you have worked through the chapters and consumed the XML Web services that you have created, you haven't been aware of all that is going on behind the scenes. Communication with the XML Web service is possible because you are working with a proxy class that handles many of the difficulties involved in this communication.

In this chapter, you take a look at the proxy class and how it works within the XML Web services model. This chapter discusses the following:

- Building a proxy class with Visual Studio .NET
- Using wsdl.exe to create, compile, and configure proxy classes
- Modifying the proxy class

How XML Web Services Are Consumed

As you are quite aware from Chapter 5, which covered consuming XML Web services, it is extremely easy to consume XML Web services within the .NET Framework. In that chapter, you learned how to simply and easily consume XML Web services in all sorts of different applications. You probably noticed that it is easier to consume the XML Web services in .NET applications than it is to consume them in a Visual Basic 6.0 or in an Active Server Pages application. The .NET Framework creates a proxy class that does all the hard work for you.

You usually have to go through the following steps in order to consume the XML Web service into an XML Web service client:

- Find the XML Web service using UDDI or some other means.
- Review the WSDL document that describes the XML Web service.
- Make a Web reference to the WSDL document and create a proxy class.
- In the XML Web service client, create a reference to the proxy classs.
- Call the XML Web service's methods through the proxy class.

You may have already consumed a large number of XML Web services in various clients, but you probably don't remember creating a proxy class and using this proxy class in any way. That is what makes working with the .NET Framework so outstanding when dealing with XML Web services. You don't need to know all the underlying details of what is happening if you choose not to; but, if you wish, you can see what is going on and directly manipulate all the activity.

> **NOTE:** XML Web service clients can be Windows Forms, Web Forms, and even other XML Web services. Any application, platform, method, or device that can consume XML over HTTP can consume XML Web services and, therefore, be an XML Web service client.

Before I discuss what a proxy class is, think about what it would be like if you didn't have these classes to work with in your applications. As you recall, XML Web services use SOAP over HTTP in the requests and responses that are going back and forth. Can you imagine the increased difficulty if you had to build your own SOAP packet and take care of the transportation communications in order to make a SOAP request to the XML Web service? Also, when a SOAP response packet was sent back to your XML Web service client, you would need to dissect that SOAP packet in order to use it within your application. All these transactions are taken care of for you by the .NET Framework.

A *proxy class* is a local class that mimics the interface of the XML Web service that it references. The proxy class exposes all the WebMethods of the XML Web service and allows you to call these methods locally. After a method is called, the proxy class takes care of marshaling the arguments back and forth across HTTP using SOAP. This proxy class, in essence, builds the messages that you are sending to an XML Web service and parses the messages that are received back from the Web service. If you had to write this code yourself, it would be very time-consuming.

For instance, you might have an ASP.NET Web application that you want to consume the Calculator XML Web service that you have been using throughout the book. This XML Web service client, the ASP.NET Web application, needs to have a reference to this remote object, the Calculator XML Web service.

After this reference is made, a proxy class is generated and the calling application is then able to work through the proxy class as if it were working directly with the XML Web service. So, when the `Add()` method that is in the proxy class is called, the proxy class, in turn, constructs the SOAP packet for you and sends the request over HTTP. This proxy class maps to the operations that are exposed by the XML Web service and hides all these construction and parsing details within its implementation. Upon receipt of the response SOAP packet, the proxy class returns the result as an XML file. Not bad, eh? The following diagram (Figure 9-1) shows this visually.

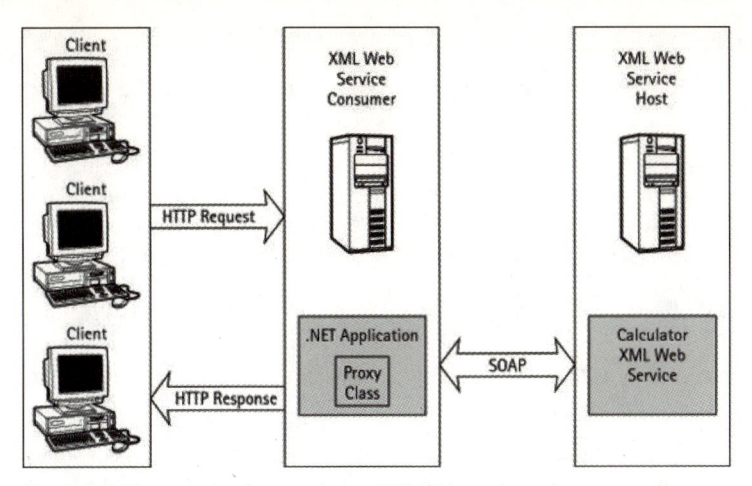

Figure 9-1: The process of consuming an XML Web service using a proxy class.

Creating Proxies

You have probably already become accustomed to all the outstanding wizards and tools that are in the .NET Framework and Visual Studio .NET. They eliminate much of the mundane work associated with building the plumbing. As you might expect, it is no different when dealing with the proxies that you need to interface with the XML Web services you want to consume. In order to create a proxy class for your XML Web service client, you need to do one of the following:

- Create a Web Reference within Visual Studio .NET, thereby creating a proxy class.
- Use the wsdl.exe utility that is available in the .NET Framework.

The focus is on these two methods because they are the most common ways to create the proxy class for your .NET applications. However, there are other ways in which to create a proxy class. You might also use the Microsoft SOAP Toolkit or create the proxy class from scratch.

Using Visual Studio .NET to Create a Proxy Class

Like many other tasks, using Visual Studio .NET to create a proxy class is fairly straightforward and easy. All you want to do is create a client that makes a reference to the remote object, the Calculator XML Web service.

Visual Basic 6.0 developers are familiar with this process of creating a reference to an object within the project. In Visual Basic 6.0, it is as simple as selecting Project ⇨ Add Reference. This step enables you to add a reference to one of the many available objects at your disposal.

By making this reference, you set up the capability to use *early-binding* with this object. For instance, in one of the earlier examples, you made a reference to the Microsoft XML v3.0 DLL within a Visual Basic 6.0 form. By making this reference, you make an early-bind to this object, and you are then able to able to make reference to the object in the following manner:

```
Dim myXMLDoc As MSXML2.DOMDocument
```

By early-binding, you can achieve statement completion. That means, after you type in **MSXML** and hit the period, IntelliSense kicks in and provides you with a drop-down list of available items.

The other option, of course, is *late-binding* by making reference to the object at runtime. This is not as desirable because it taxes the system. It is always preferable to make any object calls by early-binding. If you use late-binding to make the call, do so in the following manner:

```
Dim ourLateBoundObject as Object
ourLateBoundObject = CreateObject("MSXML2.DOMDocument")
```

Doing this late-bound, you do not create the object until runtime and, therefore, you don't have statement completion to help you along the way.

Now, go back to the process of creating an XML Web service client so that you can consume an XML Web service. Just as Visual Basic 6.0 made an early-bound reference to an object, the .NET application that wants to consume a remote object (an XML Web service) is early-binding to this XML Web service class.

In this example, there is no need to show the code, but Figure 9-2 shows the ASP.NET Web application. This application will consume the `Multiply()` method from the Calculator XML Web service.

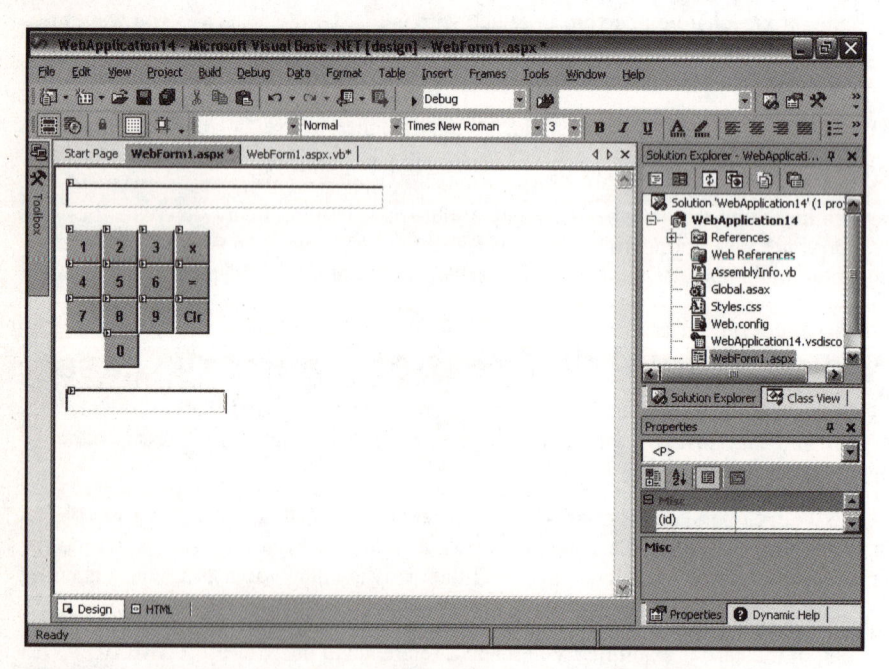

Figure 9-2: An XML Web service client that will consume the Calculator XML Web service.

Now that you have your application in place, you need to make a reference to the remote object, the Calculator XML Web service, so that you can get at the `Multiply` method. Visual Studio .NET makes this easy for you. All you have to do is right-click on the project in the Solution Explorer and select Add Reference (Figure 9-3).

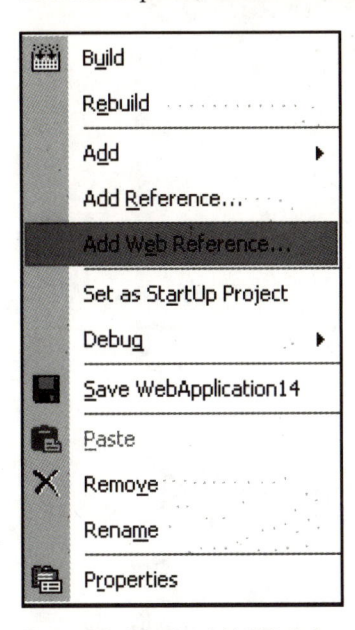

Figure 9-3: Selecting Add Web Reference to make a reference to the Calculator XML Web service.

After you choose to add a reference in Visual Studio .NET, you are given the Add Web Reference dialog box. This box enables you to point to a particular `.asmx` file in order to make the reference. If you don't know the location of the file, or if you don't even know the particular XML Web service that you want, you are given a couple of options to find what you are looking for. Besides typing in the location of the XML Web service directly in the address bar, you have the option of searching for XML Web services from Microsoft's UDDI registry. This registry allows you to search for particular XML Web services based upon any number of factors, such as the company's name, location, business type, or the functionality of the XML Web service that you are looking for.

The other option from the Add Web Reference dialog box is to search for local XML Web services on your particular server. If you know the location of the `.asmx` file, you can type it directly into the address bar and hit Enter. After you have done this, the test page for that particular XML Web service shows up in the dialog window (see Figure 9-4).

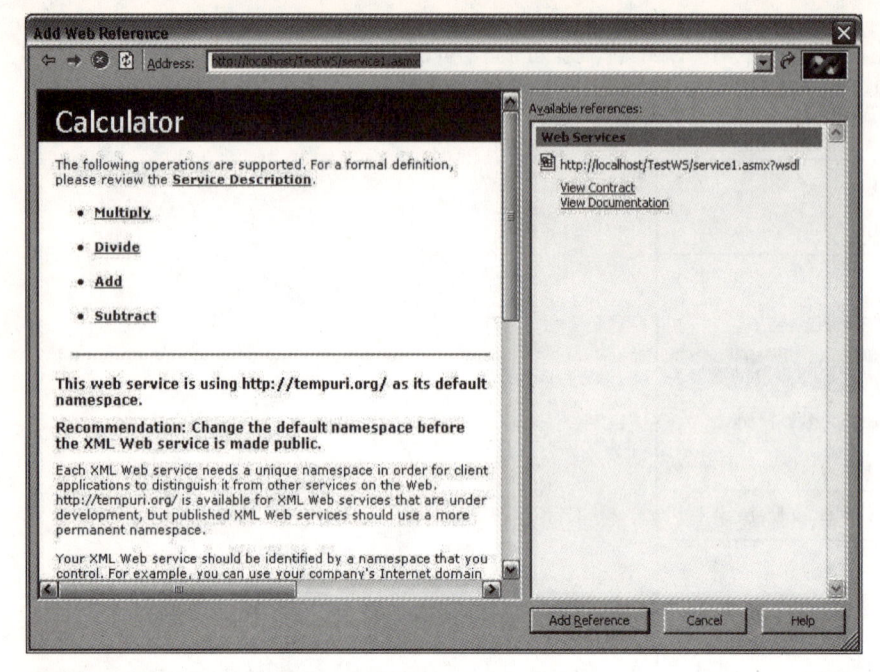

Figure 9-4: The Add Web Reference dialog window.

At this point you can examine the WSDL document, and you can also test the individual methods of the XML Web service directly from this dialog window. After you have located the XML Web service and it appears in the dialog window, the Add Reference button at the bottom of the dialog window is enabled and you can make a reference to this remote object.

After you click the Add Reference button in this dialog window, Visual Studio .NET goes through a number of steps. Visual Studio .NET opens up the WSDL document of the Calculator XML Web service and, based upon this document, creates a local proxy class directly in the project from which it was called. By doing this, Visual Studio .NET has inferred a local copy of all the exposed methods from the Calculator XML Web service and made them available for you to call directly from your code after you make an instance of the object.

> **NOTE:** You can add a Web reference from any Visual Studio .NET project written in any language.

Note that you aren't limited to making references only to `.asmx` files. With such a limitation, you could only work with other XML Web services. But there are many other Web services available on other platforms, and it is possible to work with all these Web services as well, as long as there is a WSDL document to point to in this dialog window. If the Web service has a WSDL document, Visual Studio .NET can analyze this document and create the appropriate proxy class (as long as there aren't any errors in the WSDL document).

Results from making a reference in Visual Studio .NET

Now you have made a reference to the Calculator XML Web service; and Visual Studio .NET, in return, has reviewed and validated the WSDL document. Next Visual Studio .NET made a proxy class directly in your project. Notice that the Web Reference folder in your project has expanded and is either showing `localhost` (meaning that the XML Web service is local on your server), or it shows the root URL where the XML Web service is located (but backwards!), for example `com.xmlws101.www`.

The name of this reference is important, and so my recommendation is to change the name to something more meaningful. To do this, right-click on the name and choose Rename.

> **TIP:** Renaming your reference will help you understand your code a little better, especially if you are consuming multiple XML Web services.

This name is how you make reference to the Web service in your code. For example, the following code shows how you reference this XML Web service if you don't change the name of the reference:

VB

```
Dim ws As New localhost.Calculator()
```

C#

```
localhost.Calculator ws = new localhost.Calculator();
```

If you are making a reference to an XML Web service that is located on a remote server and you don't change the name of the reference, your code looks like the following:

VB

```
Dim ws As New com.xmlws101.www.Calculator()
```

C#

```
com.xmlws101.www.Calculator ws = new com.xmlws101.www.Calculator();
```

In the preceding code examples, you are creating an instance of the proxy to gain programmatic access to the methods of the XML Web service.

So what did Visual Studio .NET actually create for you in your project? If you click the plus sign next to the `localhost` reference, you notice three files contained within this folder: `Reference.map`, `service1.disco`, and `service1.wsdl`. Click the Show All Files button at the top of the Solution Explorer and a plus sign appears next to the `Reference.map` file. Expanding this exposes the `Reference.vb` or `Reference.cs` file — this is the proxy class that Visual Studio .NET created for you (see Figure 9-5).

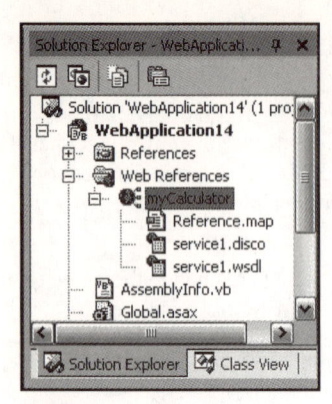

Figure 9-5: The files created for you when Visual Studio .NET makes a reference to an XML Web service. This reference was renamed to `myCalculator`.

Now take a look at the `Reference.vb` and the `Reference.cs` files, shown in Listing 9-1.

Listing 9-1: The Reference.vb and Reference.cs files

VB

```
'------------------------------------------------------------------
' <autogenerated>
'   This code was generated by a tool.
'   Runtime Version: 1.0.3512.0
'
'   Changes to this file may cause incorrect behavior and will be lost if
'   the code is regenerated.
' </autogenerated>
'------------------------------------------------------------------

Option Strict Off
Option Explicit On

Imports System
Imports System.ComponentModel
Imports System.Diagnostics
Imports System.Web.Services
Imports System.Web.Services.Protocols
Imports System.Xml.Serialization


'
'This source code was auto-generated by Microsoft.VSDesigner, Version
'1.0.3512.0.
'
Namespace localhost

    '<remarks/>
    <System.Diagnostics.DebuggerStepThroughAttribute(),  _
     System.ComponentModel.DesignerCategoryAttribute("code"),  _
```

```
System.Web.Services.WebServiceBindingAttribute(Name:="CalculatorSoap",
    [Namespace]:="http://www.xmlws101.com/")> _
   Public Class Calculator
       Inherits System.Web.Services.Protocols.SoapHttpClientProtocol

       '<remarks/>
       Public Sub New()
           MyBase.New
           Me.Url = "http://localhost/testws/service1.asmx"
       End Sub

       '<remarks/>

<System.Web.Services.Protocols.SoapDocumentMethodAttribute
 ("http://www.xmlws101.com/Add",
 RequestNamespace:="http://www.xmlws101.com/",
 ResponseNamespace:="http://www.xmlws101.com/",
 Use:=System.Web.Services.Description.SoapBindingUse.Literal,
 ParameterStyle:=System.Web.Services.
 Protocols.SoapParameterStyle.Wrapped)> _
   Public Function Add(ByVal a As Integer, ByVal b As Integer) As Integer
           Dim results() As Object = Me.Invoke("Add",
               New Object() {a, b})
           Return CType(results(0),Integer)
   End Function

   '<remarks/>
   Public Function BeginAdd(ByVal a As Integer, ByVal b As Integer, ByVal
       callback As System.AsyncCallback, ByVal asyncState As Object) As
       System.IAsyncResult
           Return Me.BeginInvoke("Add", New Object() {a, b}, callback,
               asyncState)
   End Function

   '<remarks/>
   Public Function EndAdd(ByVal asyncResult As System.IAsyncResult) As
        Integer
           Dim results() As Object = Me.EndInvoke(asyncResult)
           Return CType(results(0),Integer)
       End Function
    End Class
End Namespace
```

C#

```
//------------------------------------------------------------------
// <autogenerated>
// This code was generated by a tool.
```

```
// Runtime Version: 1.0.3512.0
//
// Changes to this file may cause incorrect behavior and will be lost if
// the code is regenerated.
// </autogenerated>
//------------------------------------------------------------------------

//
// This source code was auto-generated by Microsoft.VSDesigner, Version
// 1.0.3512.0.
//
namespace WebApplication1.localhost {
    using System.Diagnostics;
    using System.Xml.Serialization;
    using System;
    using System.Web.Services.Protocols;
    using System.ComponentModel;
    using System.Web.Services;


    /// <remarks/>
    [System.Diagnostics.DebuggerStepThroughAttribute()]
    [System.ComponentModel.DesignerCategoryAttribute("code")]

[System.Web.Services.WebServiceBindingAttribute(Name="CalculatorSoap",
    Namespace="http://www.xmlws101.com/")]
    public class Calculator :
    System.Web.Services.Protocols.SoapHttpClientProtocol {

        /// <remarks/>
        public Calculator() {
            this.Url = "http://localhost/testws/service1.asmx";
        }

        /// <remarks/>
[System.Web.Services.Protocols.SoapDocumentMethodAttribute
 ("http://www.xmlws101.com/Add",
 RequestNamespace="http://www.xmlws101.com/",
 ResponseNamespace="http://www.xmlws101.com/",
 Use=System.Web.Services.Description.SoapBindingUse.Literal,
 ParameterStyle=System.Web.Services.
 Protocols.SoapParameterStyle.Wrapped)]
        public int Add(int a, int b) {
            object[] results = this.Invoke("Add", new object[] {
                        a,
                        b});
            return ((int)(results[0]));
        }
```

```
            /// <remarks/>
            public System.IAsyncResult BeginAdd(int a, int b,
            System.AsyncCallback callback, object asyncState) {
                return this.BeginInvoke("Add", new object[] {
                        a, b}, callback, asyncState);
            }

            /// <remarks/>
            public int EndAdd(System.IAsyncResult asyncResult) {
                object[] results = this.EndInvoke(asyncResult);
                return ((int)(results[0]));
            }
    }
}
```

> **NOTE:** I removed three of the methods from the proxy class (`Subtract`, `Multiply`, and `Divide`) in order to shorten the file. I also formatted it a bit for clarity.

You may have realized that the language that you are using in your .NET application will be the language that is used for your proxy class. The proxy class defines methods that represent the actual methods exposed by an XML Web service and, now that you have this proxy class within your .NET application, you are capable of calling the XML Web service methods as if the XML Web service were a locally available component.

The other option for finding your proxy class is to look for it from the path: `C:\Inetpub\wwwroot\[projectname]\Web References\localhost\Reference.vb` as shown in Figure 9-6.

> **NOTE:** `localhost` is the name of the reference. You might have changed this name and, in effect, changed the path.

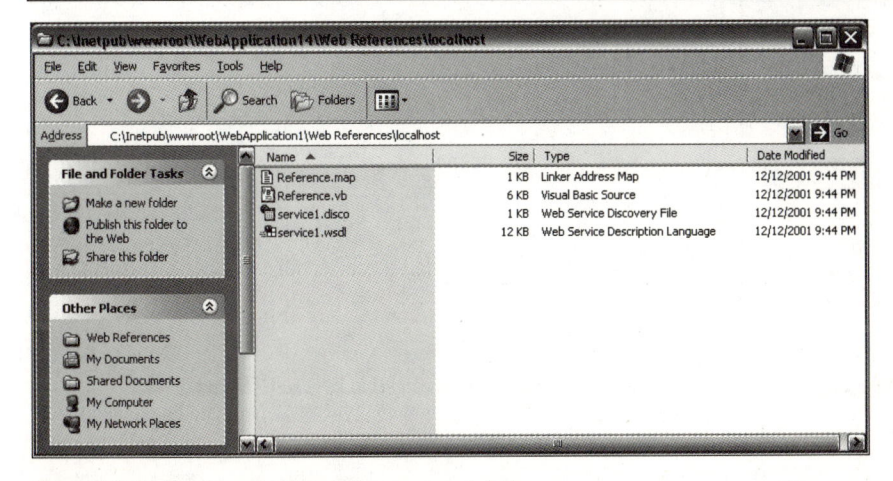

Figure 9-6: Finding the proxy class in the `Inetpub` folder.

204 Part III: Building XML Web Services

Now you have seen the ease with which you can easily create proxy classes to interact with remote XML Web services if you are using Visual Studio .NET. Visual Studio .NET is really built for this type of functionality and makes it easy for you to consume these services. Without this tool, you would have to build this proxy class yourself.

Updating a project's Web reference

People often change the Web services that they have put out there for others to consume. Some just expose additional methods, but others may dramatically change their Web services in such a way that you are in danger of breaking your application if you continue consuming the changed services.

A Web service author can break his Web service by simply adding an additional argument. If he adds an additional argument, the next time that your application calls that Web service, your call fails because you lack the proper arguments. If this happens, there are a couple of easy steps that you can take to get back on your feet.

The first option is to delete the reference to the Web service and to remove this reference from your code. You will definitely have to do this if the Web service is no longer available for you to consume. This is as simple as right-clicking on the reference to the Web service within the Solution Explorer window and selecting Delete.

If the Web service has changed in such a manner that your proxy class no longer represents it, you need to change your proxy class so that it can represent the new Web service along with all the changes that have taken place. You have two options. The first option is to delete your reference to this Web service and create a new one. This, in effect, also creates a new proxy class in your project. The other option is to right-click on the Web service reference within the Solution Explorer window and select Update Web Reference (see Figure 9-7).

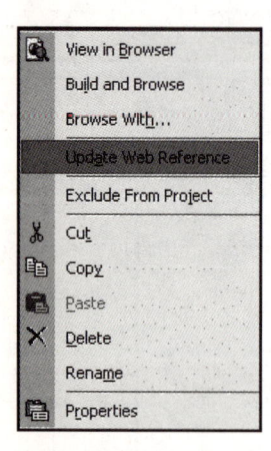

Figure 9-7: Regenerating the proxy class within the project by selecting Update Web Reference.

By updating the Web reference, Visual Studio .NET re-creates the proxy class, replacing this new proxy class with the old one.

Visual Studio .NET makes it quite simple to create proxy classes to use within your applications. As easy as it is to create a proxy class using Visual Studio .NET, there may be occasions where you will be unable to use Visual Studio .NET. (For instance, you may be creating a proxy class on a server that doesn't have Visual Studio .NET on it, or you may be working with the server remotely.) In this case, the .NET Framework provides a command-line tool called `wsdl.exe` that you can use to create your proxy classes.

wsdl.exe

As you have learned, proxies are necessary to build applications that can interact with an XML Web service. Visual Studio .NET makes this easy for you because it builds the proxy class under the covers. You don't have to know anything about it to use it. But as you are about to learn, sometimes you want to get in there and tweak the way the proxy class is generated. As with most underlying technologies that the .NET Framework provides, you can choose to have items and processes created for you or you can get in there and structure the items and processes yourself.

As I showed you in the first part of this chapter, Visual Studio .NET provides you with a one-click proxy class generator. By default, Visual Studio .NET will create a proxy class in the language of the calling application, and it will also generate the proxy class to operate based upon SOAP calls.

Also included in the Framework is a utility that allows for command-line proxy class generation. This tool is `wsdl.exe` and can be found at `C:\Program Files\Microsoft Visual Studio .NET\FrameworkSDK\Bin`.

Follow these steps to create your own proxy from the wsdl.exe tool.

1. Select Start ⇨ Run.
2. Open up a command prompt by typing in **cmd**.
3. Change directories until you are at the directory where wsdl.exe is located. (Please note that you can change directories by using the `cd` command. For instance, `cd ../` will move up one directory.) From the `c:>` prompt, if you type **cd Program Files/ Microsoft Visual Studio .NET/FrameworkSDK/Bin,** you are in the correct directory.
4. After you are in the directory of wsdl.exe, type in the following command: **wsdl http://localhost/TestWS/service1.asmx?wsdl**
5. Press Enter. After pressing Enter, you get the proxy class that you need to build an XML Web service client that can interact with this Web service, and it is generated at the specified location. Figure 9-8 shows an example of the work that results from using these steps.

206   Part III: **Building XML Web Services**

Figure 9-8: Creating a proxy class using the wsdl.exe tool.

Now if this is the tough way, life is getting easier! You have very easily created a proxy class using the `wsdl.exe` tool. As it says, the `wsdl.exe` tool created and saved the proxy class, `Calculator.cs`, in the same folder where it resides. It named the file based upon the name of the class of the XML Web service, and it created the proxy class in the default language of C#.

The syntax for creating proxy classes on the command line is as follows:

```
wsdl [options] [URL Path ]
```

The command that you gave `wsdl.exe` in order to create `Calculator.cs` didn't point at the URL of the Web service, but instead pointed at the WSDL document of the XML Web service. If the XML Web service was created using the .NET Framework, the WSDL document is an autogenerated document. Therefore, to point at this document, you only have to use the URL of the XML Web service followed by `?wsdl`.

> **NOTE:** You aren't limited to pointing the `wsdl.exe` tool at WSDL documents. You can also point it at a discovery document (`.disco`) or at a XSD Schema (`.xsd`) to create a proxy class.

Before you specify the path in the command line of the WSDL document, you can provide a number of different options that will customize the proxy class a little more to your liking. For example, you might need this proxy class in Visual Basic .NET and not just in C#, the default language that `wsdl.exe` uses in the created proxy class. If you do, use the following command:

```
wsdl /language:VB http://localhost/TestWS/service1.asmx?wsdl
```

Running this command creates a Visual Basic .NET proxy class in the same directory that you can use in your applications to call the Calculator XML Web service.

Table 9-1 covers the commands that are at your disposal for creating proxies.

Table 9-1: wsdl.exe Options

Command	Short Command	Description
/appsettingurlkey:key	/urlkey:key	Specifies the configuration key to use when reading the default value for the URL property when generating the code of the proxy class.
/appsettingbaseurl:baseurl	/baseurl:baseurl	Specifies the base URL to use when calculating the URL fragment. If you are going to use this command option, it needs to be used along with /appsettingurlkey.
/domain:domain	/d:domain	Specifies the domain name that needs to be used when working with a server that requires authentication.
/language:language	/l:language	Specifies the language to use when generating the proxy class. The value options include Visual Basic .NET (VB), C# (CS), and JScript .NET (JS).
/namespace:namespace	/n:namespace	Specifies the name of the namespace to be used in the proxy class.
/nologo		Specifies that there shouldn't be a Microsoft banner at the top of the proxy class.
/out:filename	/o:filename	Specifies the name of the file for the proxy class. Use the appropriate file extension based upon the language that is used in the generated proxy class.
/password:password	/p:password	Specifies the password that is required when connecting to a server that requires authentication.

Command	Short Command	Description
/protocol:protocol		Specifies the protocol that needs to be used for the proxy class. You can choose from either SOAP (default), HttpGet, HttpPost, or a custom protocol specified in the configuration file.
/proxy:URL		Specifies the URL of the proxy server to use for HTTP requests. The default setting is to use the system proxy setting.
/proxydomain:domain	/pd:domain	Specifies the domain to use when connecting to a proxy server that requires authentication.
/proxypassword:password	/pp:password	Specifies the password that might be needed to connect to a proxy server that requires authentication.
/proxyusername:username	/pu:username	Specifies the username that might be needed to connect to a proxy server that requires authentication.
/server		Generates an abstract class for an XML Web service based on the contracts. The default is to generate client proxy classes.
/username:username	/u:username	Specifies the username that is required when connecting to a server that requires authentication.
/?		Displays a list of available option commands.

You will find that using the wsdl.exe tool is quite beneficial in a lot of situations. When you need to create a proxy class that uses a protocol other than SOAP, it is an invaluable tool. Because Visual Studio .NET generates the proxy class using SOAP as the default protocol, you need to create a proxy class by hand or by using this tool if you want your XML Web service client to use either HTTP-GET or HTTP-POST.

For example, to create a proxy class named HappyProxy.vb that uses HTTP-GET for the protocol, you use the following command options:

```
wsdl /l:VB /o:HappyProxy.vb /protocol:HTTPGet
http://localhost/TestWS/service1.asmx?wsdl
```

Using these commands to generate the proxy class gives you a proxy class like the one shown in Listing 9-2:

Listing 9-2: HappyProxy.vb (partial code)

```
'
'This source code was auto-generated by wsdl, Version=1.0.3512.0.
'

'<remarks/>
<System.Diagnostics.DebuggerStepThroughAttribute(),  _
 System.ComponentModel.DesignerCategoryAttribute("code")>  _
Public Class Calculator
    Inherits System.Web.Services.Protocols.HttpGetClientProtocol

    '<remarks/>
    Public Sub New()
        MyBase.New
        Me.Url = "http://localhost/testws/service1.asmx"
    End Sub

    '<remarks/>
    <System.Web.Services.Protocols.HttpMethodAttribute
      (GetType(System.Web.Services.Protocols.XmlReturnReader),
      GetType(System.Web.Services.Protocols.UrlParameterWriter))>  _
    Public Function Add(ByVal a As String, ByVal b As String) As
    <System.Xml.Serialization.XmlRootAttribute("int",
      [Namespace]:="http://www.xmlws101.com", IsNullable:=false)> Integer
        Return CType(Me.Invoke("Add", (Me.Url + "/Add"), New Object()
           {a, b}),Integer)
    End Function

    '<remarks/>
    Public Function BeginAdd(ByVal a As String, ByVal b As String,
       ByVal callback As System.AsyncCallback,
       ByVal asyncState As Object) As
       System.IAsyncResult
        Return Me.BeginInvoke("Add", (Me.Url + "/Add"), New Object()
           {a, b}, callback, asyncState)
    End Function

    '<remarks/>
    Public Function EndAdd(ByVal asyncResult As System.IAsyncResult)
         As Integer
        Return CType(Me.EndInvoke(asyncResult),Integer)
    End Function
```

You will notice that this proxy class is quite different from the proxy classes that are generated by Visual Studio .NET. One of the main differences is that instead of inheriting from `System.Web.Services.Protocols.SoapHttpClientProtocol`, the proxy class inherits from `System.Web.Services.Protocols.HttpGetClientProtocol`.

Compiling the proxy class

Now that you have created a proxy class using `wsdl.exe`, you need to compile this class in order to use it in your XML Web service client. Therefore, the .NET Framework provides you with a compiler for each of the targeted .NET languages. This book focuses on the Visual Basic .NET and C# compilers that come with the Framework.

To compile the proxy class that was generated for you, place the proxy class in the same folder as the compilers, located at `C:\WINDOWS\Microsoft.NET\Framework\v1.0.3512`. Here you find both the Visual Basic .NET compiler, `vbc.exe`, and the C# compiler, `csc.exe`. After your proxy class is in place, pull up a command prompt and navigate to that particular folder. After everything is in place, you can run the following commands to compile the proxy class.

VB

```
vbc /t:library /r:system.web.services.dll /r:system.xml.dll
/r:system.dll
/out:c:\inetpub\wwwroot\bin\CalculatorProxy.dll HappyProxy.vb
```

C#

```
csc /t:library /r:system.web.services.dll /r:system.xml.dll
/r:system.dll
/out:c:\inetpub\wwwroot\bin\CalculatorProxy.dll HappyProxy.cs
```

After running this command at the command prompt, you have a compiled proxy class in the `bin` directory of your XML Web service client. In order to gain access to this class, it is important to place the compiled proxy class in the `bin` directory and not elsewhere in the application.

Table 9-2 describes all the possible options to use with the command line compilers in compiling your proxy classes.

Table 9-2: vbc.exe and csc.exe Compiler Options

Option	Purpose
`@ (Specify Response File)`	Specifies a response file.
`/?`	Displays the compiler options. This command is the same as specifying the `/help` option. When using this option, no compilation occurs.

Option	Purpose
`/addmodule`	Causes the compiler to make all type information from the specified file(s) available to the project you are currently compiling.
`/baseaddress`	Specifies the base address of a DLL.
`/bugreport`	Produces a file that includes information that makes it easy to report a bug.
`/checked`	Specifies whether integer arithmetic that overflows the bounds of the data type will cause an exception at runtime. C# only.
`/codepage`	Specifies the code page to use for all source code files in the compilation. C# only.
`/debug`	Produces debugging information.
`/define` or `/d`	Defines symbols for conditional compilation.
`/delaysign`	Specifies whether the assembly will be fully or partially signed. VB only.
`/doc`	Processes the documentation comments to an XML file. C# only.
`/filealign`	Specifies the size of sections in the output file. C# only.
`/fullpaths`	Specifies the absolute path to the file in compiler output. C# only.
`/help`	Displays compiler options. This command is identical to specifying the `/?` option. When using this option, no compilation occurs.
`/imports`	Imports a namespace from a specified assembly. VB only.
`/incremental`	Enables incremental compilation of source code files. C# only.
`/keycontainer`	Specifies a key container name for a key pair to give an assembly a strong name. VB only.
`/keyfile`	Specifies a file containing a key or key pair to give an assembly a strong name. VB only.
`/lib`	Specifies the location of assemblies referenced via `/reference`. C# only.

Option	Purpose
`/libpath`	Specifies the location of assemblies referenced via the `/reference` option. VB only.
`/linkresource` or `/linkres`	Creates a link to a managed resource.
`/main`	Specifies the class that contains the `Sub Main` procedure to use at startup.
`/nologo`	Suppresses compiler banner information.
`/nostdlib`	Does not import standard library (`mscorlib.dll`). C# only.
`/noconfig`	Does not compile with the global or local versions of `csc.rsp`. C# only.
`/nowarn`	Suppresses the compiler's capability to generate warnings. VB only.
`/optimize`	Enables/disables code optimization.
`/optioncompare`	Determines whether string comparisons should be binary or use locale-specific text semantics. VB only.
`/optionexplicit`	Requires explicit declaration of variables. VB only.
`/optionstrict`	Enforces strict language semantics. VB only.
`/out`	Specifies an output file.
`/quiet`	Prevents the compiler from displaying code for syntax-related errors and warnings. VB only.
`/recurse`	Searches for source files to compile in subdirectories.
`/reference` or `/r`	Imports metadata from an assembly.
`/removeintchecks`	Disables integer overflow checking. VB only.
`/resource` or `/res`	Embeds a managed resource in an assembly.
`/rootnamespace`	Specifies a namespace for all type declarations.
`/target:exe` or `/t:exe`	The executable file is created with a `.exe` extension. This option is the default when no /target option is specified.

Option	Purpose
`/target:library` or `/t:library`	The dynamic-link library file is created with a `.dll` extension.
`/target:module` or `/t:module`	The output file is created with an extension of `.netmodule`.
`/target:winexe` or `/t:winexe`	The executable file is created with a `.exe` extension. A Windows program is one that provides a user interface from either the Services Framework class library or with the Win32 APIs.
`/unsafe`	Compiles code that uses the unsafe keyword. C# only.
`/utf8output`	Displays compiler output using UTF-8 encoding.
`/verbose`	Outputs extra information during compilation. VB only.
`/warnaserror`	Promotes warnings to errors.
`/win32icon`	Inserts a `.ico` file into the output file.
`/win32resource`	Inserts a Win32 resource into the output file.

Configuring wsdl.exe

As newer versions of the .NET Framework come onto the scene, you may find yourself with multiple versions of the Framework on your server. Each new version of the .NET Framework does not simply overwrite the previous one, but instead is placed so that both versions are able to run together on the same machine. Therefore, if you have applications that run on a particular version of the Framework, they won't break simply because a newer version comes out. You'll see evidence of this by looking in `C:\WINDOWS\Microsoft.NET\Framework`. There you may find one or more versions of the Framework.

The `wsdl.exe` utility is configured to run off only one of these versions of the Framework, and if you wish to modify this version, you need to manually change the configuration. Fortunately, this is quite easy.

At `C:\Program Files\Microsoft Visual Studio .NET\FrameworkSDK\Bin` you find an xml file called `wsdl.exe.config`. This is the configuration file of the `wsdl.exe` utility. There isn't much code to it, as shown in Listing 9-3:

Listing 9-3: wsdl.exe.config

```
<?xml version ="1.0"?>
<configuration>
    <startup>
        <requiredRuntime version="v1.0.3512" />
    </startup>
</configuration>
```

The `<requiredRuntime>` element specifies the version of the common language runtime that should run `wsdl.exe`. In this case it is Version `1.0.3512`.

Examining and Modifying the Proxy Class

The proxy class is an important part of anything you build that needs to consume a Web service. It is true that you might not ever have to get down into the proxy class code and see what is going on there. You may never need to modify what the proxy class does. In most cases, you will just let it be while it does its magic. Despite that, take a look at what it contains.

Open up a proxy class that has been generated for you or take a look at some of the code samples from this chapter. The proxy class in this chapter has been generated for us from the traditional Calculator XML Web service. Therefore, as you would expect, there are methods for `Add()`, `Subtract()`, `Multiply()`, and `Divide()`.

There is a lot more as well. For instance, if you look at the `Add()` method that is available, there is also a `BeginAdd()` and an `EndAdd()` method. The proxy class exposes both synchronous and asynchronous methods for each of the Web service methods that are in the XML Web service.

If you are invoking this XML Web service synchronously, you use the `Add()` method. If you invoke the XML Web service using the `BeginAdd()` and `EndAdd()` methods, then you are working with the XML Web service asynchronously.

> **CROSS-REFERENCE:** Invoking asynchronous XML Web services will be covered in Chapter 25.

There are a number of things that you can do with the proxy class. In the end, it is just a class that has been generated for you so that you don't have to generate it yourself. In most cases, the default proxy class will be just fine, but there will be times when you need to change some of the code in this class, recompile it, and use this newer version for your XML Web service client. You can also change some of the settings within the proxy class at runtime within the code of your application.

The URL property

In the proxy class that was generated for you from the Calculator XML Web service, there are some lines of code in the class that point at the location of the XML Web service that is being invoked (Listing 9-4).

Listing 9-4: The proxy class (partial code)

VB

```
Public Sub New()
    MyBase.New
    Me.Url = "http://localhost/TestWS/service1.asmx"
End Sub
```

C#

```
public Calculator() {
    this.Url = "http://localhost/TestWS/service1.asmx";
}
```

If you want to point to a different Web service by changing the value of the URL at runtime, you do so by implementing the code from Listing 9-5 in your XML Web service client.

Listing 9-5: The XML Web service client code (partial code)

VB

```
Dim ws As New myCalculator.Calculator()
ws.Url = "http://localhost/TestWS/SecondWebService.asmx"
```

C#

```
myCalculator.Calculator ws = new myCalculator.Calculator();
ws.Url = "http://localhost/TestWS/SecondWebService.asmx";
```

If you make this change at runtime, the XML Web service client uses the same proxy on the XML Web service located at `http://localhost/TestWS/SecondWebService.asmx` instead of the one at the location that is specified in the proxy class.

NOTE: In order to change the URL of the Web service that you are invoking at runtime, the new XML Web service that you are pointing to needs to implement the same service description that the proxy class was generated from.

The Timeout property

When making synchronous calls to a Web service, you can use the Timeout property to modify the default timeout for how long your client application is willing to wait to invoke the Web service. Some Web services take time, due to network traffic or based upon how busy a particular Web service is; it might, therefore, be beneficial to set the timeout property to account for this.

You can implement the Timeout property in your client application code using the code in Listing 9-6.

Listing 9-6: Using the Timeout property in an XML Web service client (partial code)

VB

```
Dim ws As New myCalculator.Calculator()
ws.Timeout = 60000
```

C#

```
myCalculator.Calculator ws = new myCalculator.Calculator();
ws.Timeout = 60000;
```

The value of the Timeout property is in milliseconds; 60000 milliseconds are equal to 60 seconds or 1 minute.

Summary

The .NET Framework and Visual Studio .NET both provide outstanding tools to build a proxy class for you. If it weren't for these tools, programmers would have to spend a lot of time building plumbing that would be prone to errors. This chapter covered some of the basics in building and constructing proxies to use within your XML Web service clients and discussed some of the different ways to modify the behavior of the tools used in generating the proxy classes.

The next chapter covers the XML Web service classes that are provided with the .NET Framework. These classes are the main reasons why building XML Web services on the .NET platform is so simple and easy.

Part IV

XML Web Services Description and Discovery

Chapter 10: WSDL

Chapter 11: UDDI

Chapter 12: Disco

Chapter 10
WSDL

> *There's nothing the world loves more than a ready-made description.*
> W. Somerset Maugham, *Mrs. Dot* (1912)

As you learned in the early chapters of this book, in order for others to be able to interact with the XML Web services that you build and in order for you to interact with Web services in your client applications, there must be some sort of description of these Web services.

This description is provided by a *Web Services Description Language* (*WSDL*) document. This file is also known as a *Wiz-dull*, but I will leave what you call it up to you. This document describes the Web service and can be used by a calling application.

In this chapter, you learn

- The basics of WSDL documents
- The structure of WSDL documents

Introduction to the WSDL Document

You have already interacted with many WSDL documents in the XML Web service clients that you have built so far in this book. In Chapter 9, whenever you built a proxy class, either with Visual Studio .NET or with the command-line proxy class generator, `wsdl.exe`, you were interacting with the Web service's WSDL file in order to generate the proxy class.

The WSDL document is an important part of any XML Web service. This document describes to the end user, the consumer of your Web service, what parameters need to be passed into the XML Web service. It also tells users what they should expect to get in return.

Version 1 of the Web Service Description Language was finished in the fall of 2000 by a group of companies, including Microsoft and IBM, to help define the Web services that people were building on their systems. The whole concept of Web services demands interoperability; therefore, it made sense for system competitors to sit down together to figure out how their respective Web services would describe themselves to client applications, regardless of their platforms. Luckily these companies realized that the best way to achieve the goal of interoperability is to have just one standard in place. Consequently, they have worked together on a standard description of Web services that we can all use — WSDL.

In the beginning this wasn't so. At first, both IBM and Microsoft introduced their own Web service description languages. IBM called its language NASSL, or the *Network Accessibility*

Service Specification Language. Microsoft also had a version called SCL, or the *Service Contract Language*. Both these languages described the Web services on their respective systems, but these two languages were not able to understand one another. Therefore, people on a Microsoft system were unable to understand NASSL, and people on any IBM or Java system were unable to understand SCL. The difficulties that ensued caused both companies to see the light and to come together to develop WSDL.

WSDL took hold and has now gone on to Version 1.1, which was submitted to the World Wide Web Consortium (www.w3c.org) in March of 2001.

The following diagram (Figure 10-1) shows how WSDL stacks in with the rest of the XML Web service technology pillars discussed so far.

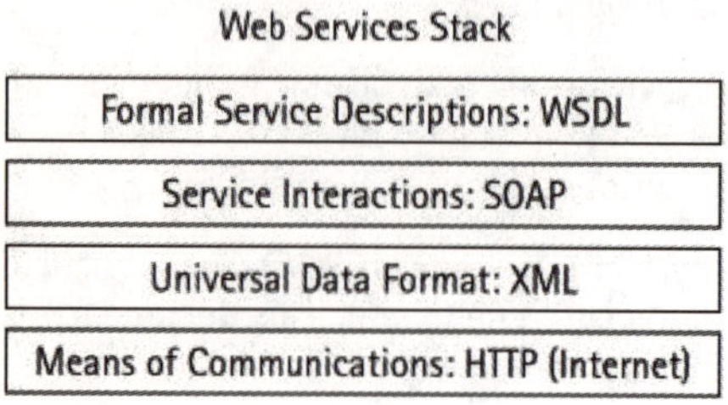

Web Services Stack

Formal Service Descriptions: WSDL
Service Interactions: SOAP
Universal Data Format: XML
Means of Communications: HTTP (Internet)

Figure 10-1: WSDL, an important pillar in the Web services stack.

You will be building XML Web service clients that must know how to interact with the XML Web service they are trying to invoke. You provide this information by using the formal service description, WSDL. (There are informal ways to describe the interface of an XML Web service. Probably one of the most informal ways is to call the end user on the telephone and describe the service to her verbally. Other ways include building an HTML Web page that describes what parameters the end user should pass into the Web service and what she should expect in return. You can see that you don't absolutely need a WSDL document to describe the XML Web services that you are building, and neither do you absolutely need one to consume a Web service. If the user knows, by some other means, what parameters the Web service takes and what types of information it gives back, he won't need to interact with a WSDL document if he doesn't want to.)

A good reason for you to interact with a WSDL document is that WSDL provides you, and all the other end users out there in the world, with the standard way to write the interface to the Web service. There won't be huge variations among Web service descriptions. By having a standard in place, it is possible to build tools that can interact with these WSDL documents. These tools know what to expect from the documents and, therefore, perform as they are intended to perform. You saw an example of this in Chapter 9 in the section on proxies. In that chapter, the .NET Framework built a complete proxy class for you based solely on the WSDL document. If that WSDL document didn't follow the standards, the tools would have had a lot of problems interacting with the document. As a result, you might have ended up building that proxy class by hand.

If you have WSDL documents associated with the XML Web services that you build, it is easier for others to consume them. So if you want to create a successful XML Web service, it is always beneficial to create this document describing your XML Web service's interface.

WSDL documents are written in WSDL (of course), an XML grammar that is used for describing a Web service in terms of the messages it accepts and generates for the end user. Before you go any further, take a look at a sample WSDL document. To find a WSDL document, pull up the test page of any XML Web service and you'll notice a link to the service description on the page (see Figure 10-2). This service description is the WSDL document.

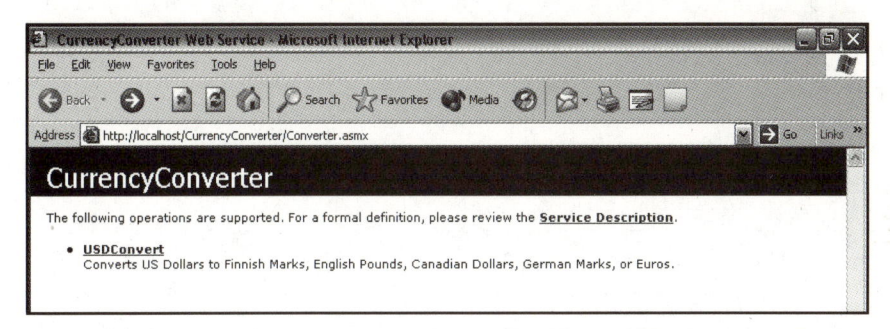

Figure 10-2: The test page of the XML Web service has a link to the WSDL file embedded in it.

Listing 10-1 shows a complete WSDL document based upon the CurrencyConverter XML Web service that you built in Chapter 4.

Listing 10-1: The WSDL document from the CurrencyConverter XML Web service

```xml
<?xml version="1.0" encoding="utf-8"?>
<definitions xmlns:http="http://schemas.xmlsoap.org/wsdl/http/"
 xmlns:soap="http://schemas.xmlsoap.org/wsdl/soap/"
 xmlns:s="http://www.w3.org/2001/XMLSchema"
 xmlns:s0="http://www.xmlws101.com"
 xmlns:soapenc="http://schemas.xmlsoap.org/soap/encoding/"
 xmlns:tm="http://microsoft.com/wsdl/mime/textMatching/"
 xmlns:mime="http://schemas.xmlsoap.org/wsdl/mime/"
 targetNamespace="http://www.xmlws101.com"
 xmlns="http://schemas.xmlsoap.org/wsdl/">
  <types>
    <s:schema elementFormDefault="qualified"
      targetNamespace="http://www.xmlws101.com">
      <s:element name="USDConvert">
        <s:complexType>
          <s:sequence>
            <s:element minOccurs="0" maxOccurs="1" name="ConvertTo"
              type="s:string" />
            <s:element minOccurs="1" maxOccurs="1" name="Amount"
              type="s:double"
              />
```

```xml
        </s:sequence>
      </s:complexType>
    </s:element>
    <s:element name="USDConvertResponse">
      <s:complexType>
        <s:sequence>
          <s:element minOccurs="1" maxOccurs="1"
            name="USDConvertResult"
            type="s:double" />
        </s:sequence>
      </s:complexType>
    </s:element>
    <s:element name="double" type="s:double" />
  </s:schema>
</types>
<message name="USDConvertSoapIn">
  <part name="parameters" element="s0:USDConvert" />
</message>
<message name="USDConvertSoapOut">
  <part name="parameters" element="s0:USDConvertResponse" />
</message>
<message name="USDConvertHttpGetIn">
  <part name="ConvertTo" type="s:string" />
  <part name="Amount" type="s:string" />
</message>
<message name="USDConvertHttpGetOut">
  <part name="Body" element="s0:double" />
</message>
<message name="USDConvertHttpPostIn">
  <part name="ConvertTo" type="s:string" />
  <part name="Amount" type="s:string" />
</message>
<message name="USDConvertHttpPostOut">
  <part name="Body" element="s0:double" />
</message>
<portType name="CurrencyConverterSoap">
  <operation name="USDConvert">
    <documentation>Converts US Dollars to Finnish Marks, English
      Pounds, Canadian Dollars, German Marks, or Euros.</documentation>
    <input message="s0:USDConvertSoapIn" />
    <output message="s0:USDConvertSoapOut" />
  </operation>
</portType>
<portType name="CurrencyConverterHttpGet">
  <operation name="USDConvert">
    <documentation>Converts US Dollars to Finnish Marks, English
      Pounds, Canadian Dollars, German Marks, or Euros.</documentation>
    <input message="s0:USDConvertHttpGetIn" />
    <output message="s0:USDConvertHttpGetOut" />
```

```xml
    </operation>
  </portType>
  <portType name="CurrencyConverterHttpPost">
    <operation name="USDConvert">
      <documentation>Converts US Dollars to Finnish Marks, English
        Pounds, Canadian Dollars, German Marks, or Euros.</documentation>
      <input message="s0:USDConvertHttpPostIn" />
      <output message="s0:USDConvertHttpPostOut" />
    </operation>
  </portType>
  <binding name="CurrencyConverterSoap" type="s0:CurrencyConverterSoap">
    <soap:binding transport="http://schemas.xmlsoap.org/soap/http"
      style="document" />
    <operation name="USDConvert">
      <soap:operation soapAction="http://www.xmlws101.com/USDConvert"
        style="document" />
      <input>
        <soap:body use="literal" />
      </input>
      <output>
        <soap:body use="literal" />
      </output>
    </operation>
  </binding>
  <binding name="CurrencyConverterHttpGet"
   type="s0:CurrencyConverterHttpGet">
    <http:binding verb="GET" />
    <operation name="USDConvert">
      <http:operation location="/USDConvert" />
      <input>
        <http:urlEncoded />
      </input>
      <output>
        <mime:mimeXml part="Body" />
      </output>
    </operation>
  </binding>
  <binding name="CurrencyConverterHttpPost"
   type="s0:CurrencyConverterHttpPost">
    <http:binding verb="POST" />
    <operation name="USDConvert">
      <http:operation location="/USDConvert" />
      <input>
        <mime:content type="application/x-www-form-urlencoded" />
      </input>
      <output>
        <mime:mimeXml part="Body" />
      </output>
    </operation>
```

```xml
    </binding>
    <service name="CurrencyConverter">
      <port name="CurrencyConverterSoap"
       binding="s0:CurrencyConverterSoap">
        <soap:address
         location="http://localhost/CurrencyConverter/Converter.asmx"
         />
      </port>
      <port name="CurrencyConverterHttpGet"
       binding="s0:CurrencyConverterHttpGet">
        <http:address
         location="http://localhost/CurrencyConverter/Converter.asmx"
         />
      </port>
      <port name="CurrencyConverterHttpPost"
       binding="s0:CurrencyConverterHttpPost">
        <http:address
         location="http://localhost/CurrencyConverter/Converter.asmx"
         />
      </port>
    </service>
</definitions>
```

So there you have it, a WSDL document. It is important that you become familiar with a WSDL document so that you can read it to determine what the XML Web service needs to run effectively. You might be wondering why you need to do this if the .NET Framework and Visual Studio .NET can so easily build the proxy class that interacts with the XML Web service. There are actually a lot of reasons why you want to know how a WSDL file works.

The first reason is that, when dealing with a Web service, you might not always have access to either Visual Studio .NET or the command-line proxy generator, wsdl.exe. In this case, you benefit by being able to open up the WSDL document and understand what is going on.

The second reason is that, if you are building an XML Web service, you may not always want to use the autogenerated WSDL document. You might, instead, want to modify the WSDL document so that it is more appropriate. In this case, understanding how the file works saves you a lot of headaches.

A third reason is that some users who want to consume your XML Web service are on different platforms. Because WSDL is XML and is, therefore, platform independent, these users will be able to understand, using this document, what is going on in your XML Web service. They can then build client applications that can consume your service.

One of the biggest reasons to know how a WSDL file works is that (as all programmers should know) developers are not always perfect. There are, most likely, WSDL documents out there that have errors in them. If this is the case, you want to be able to open up the WSDL document and find the error so that you can modify the document and use it in your applications. So, enough reasons . . . read on.

Structure of WSDL Documents

The code from Listing 10-1 shows a complete WSDL document based on one of the XML Web services that you built in Chapter 4, the CurrencyConverter XML Web service. When looking over this code, note that the WSDL document is just a list of definitions using XML grammar.

This grammar is used to describe the protocols that are needed to communicate with the Web service, the Web service's interface, and the location of the Web service. The grammar of WSDL describes message network endpoints or ports. The diagram in Figure 10-3 shows the message structure of a WSDL document.

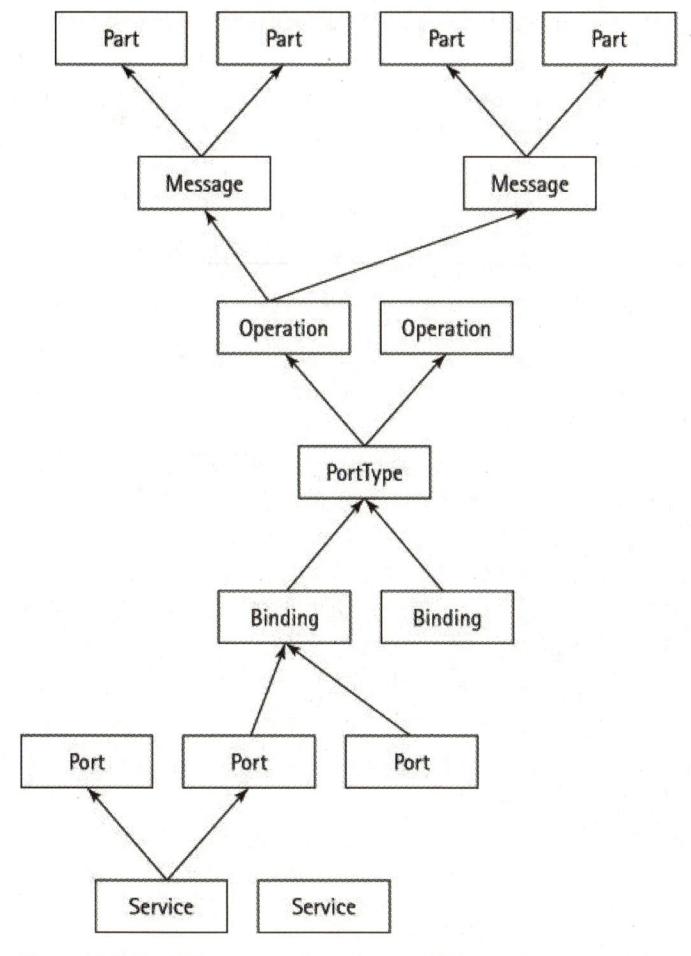

Figure 10-3: The XML grammar that is used in WSDL to define endpoints.

Starting from the bottom of the diagram in Figure 10-3, in the first level of the WSDL document are the *services*. Each service description refers to the Web service that the end user wants to invoke within his client applications. The service includes all the available methods that the creator of the Web service has exposed or the collection of available endpoints. Beyond this is the *port*. The port is referenced from the service and points to the network address of an endpoint and all the bindings that the endpoint adheres to. For example, an XML Web service that hasn't been altered in any manner will have a port description of all the bindings that it adheres to such as SOAP, HTTP-POST, and HTTP-GET. The *binding* describes the transport and encoding particulars for a *portType*. The portTypes refer to the operations anticipated by a particular endpoint type, without any specifics relating to transport or encoding. The *operation* details all the messages that are involved in dealing with the service at the endpoint. For instance, an XML Web service that returns a value after a request entails two messages, a request and a response. Each *message* makes a reference to XSD Schemas to detail the different parts of the message. Each piece of data that makes up part of a message is referred to as a *part*.

Take a look at the code from the WSDL document and go over each of the parts of the document in order to better understand what is going on.

<definitions>

The WSDL document contains a root element, just like other XML documents. Directly preceding the start of the <definitions> element is the XML namespace.

```
<?xml version="1.0" encoding="utf-8"?>
```

This specifies what the WSDL document truly is — an XML file. The next line in the WSDL document is the root element, <definitions>. The following code shows the <definitions> element for your WSDL file.

```
<definitions xmlns:http="http://schemas.xmlsoap.org/wsdl/http/"
 xmlns:soap="http://schemas.xmlsoap.org/wsdl/soap/"
 xmlns:s="http://www.w3.org/2001/XMLSchema"
 xmlns:s0="http://www.xmlws101.com"
 xmlns:soapenc="http://schemas.xmlsoap.org/soap/encoding/"
 xmlns:tm="http://microsoft.com/wsdl/mime/textMatching/"
 xmlns:mime="http://schemas.xmlsoap.org/wsdl/mime/"
 targetNamespace="http://www.xmlws101.com"
 xmlns="http://schemas.xmlsoap.org/wsdl/">
</definitions>
```

The <definitions> element includes a number of namespaces. Table 10-1 describes some of the namespaces that you might see in WSDL documents.

Table 10-1: WSDL Namespaces

prefix	namespace URI	definition
wsdl	http://schemas.xmlsoap.org/wsdl/	WSDL namespace for WSDL framework.
soap	http://schemas.xmlsoap.org/wsdl/soap/	WSDL namespace for WSDL SOAP binding.
http	http://schemas.xmlsoap.org/wsdl/http/	WSDL namespace for WSDL HTTP GET & POST binding.
mime	http://schemas.xmlsoap.org/wsdl/mime/	WSDL namespace for WSDL MIME binding.
soapenc	http://schemas.xmlsoap.org/soap/encoding/	Encoding namespace as defined by SOAP 1.1.
soapenv	http://schemas.xmlsoap.org/soap/envelope/	Envelope namespace as defined by SOAP 1.1.
xsi	http://www.w3.org/2000/10/XMLSchema-instance	Instance namespace as defined by XSD.
xsd	http://www.w3.org/2000/10/XMLSchema	Schema namespace as defined by XSD.
tns	(various)	The "this namespace" (tns) prefix is used as a convention to refer to the current document.

Along with these namespaces, you also have the option (not shown in this example) of using the attribute name within the <definitions> element. If you use this example, the name attribute could take the following form:

```
<definitions name="CurrencyConverter" ...
```

This really doesn't have any purpose except to provide some sort of lightweight description for any user who might be looking at the WSDL document and trying to figure out the overall purpose of the Web service that he is trying to consume. Another optional element that is used in the example is `targetNamespace`. This attribute, when used, defines the namespace for each of the items in the WSDL document. This means that all the elements contained within this WSDL file belong to this namespace, much the same as a `targetNamespace` declaration in an XSD file. Along with the `targetNamespace` are a number of other namespaces for HTTP-POST, HTTP-GET, and SOAP binding, as well as for MIME.

<types>

In the WSDL example from the CurrencyConverter XML Web service, you defined a couple of types.

```xml
<types>
  <s:schema elementFormDefault="qualified"
    targetNamespace="http://www.xmlws101.com">
    <s:element name="USDConvert">
      <s:complexType>
        <s:sequence>
          <s:element minOccurs="0" maxOccurs="1" name="ConvertTo"
            type="s:string" />
          <s:element minOccurs="1" maxOccurs="1" name="Amount"
            type="s:double"
            />
        </s:sequence>
      </s:complexType>
    </s:element>
    <s:element name="USDConvertResponse">
      <s:complexType>
        <s:sequence>
          <s:element minOccurs="1" maxOccurs="1" name="USDConvertResult"
            type="s:double" />
        </s:sequence>
      </s:complexType>
    </s:element>
    <s:element name="double" type="s:double" />
  </s:schema>
</types>
```

The information within the `<types>` element includes the type definitions that are needed in the message exchange. In order to define these types, you should use the XML Schema Definition Language (XSD). The XSD language was described in detail in Chapter 3.

XSD is used to provide the most interoperability possible to a Web service by using a language that is widely accepted as the standard way of describing types within XML documents.

The code example starts with the definition of the types that are required for the `USDConvert` method. The first is the `ConvertTo` parameter, which is of type `string`. The second parameter is the `Amount` parameter, which is of type `double`. It is possible to fully describe various complex types and the sequence of these types using XSD within the `<types>` element of the WSDL document.

In the end, what's being returned is a single item of the type `double`. This message is defined by `USDConvertResult`. Notice that the inbound message has the same name as the method that it is exposing (in this case, `USDConvert`), and the outbound message has the same name as the method, but with the word `Result` appended to it (in this case, `USDConvertResult`).

The diagram in Figure 10-4 shows a map of the available types at your disposal.

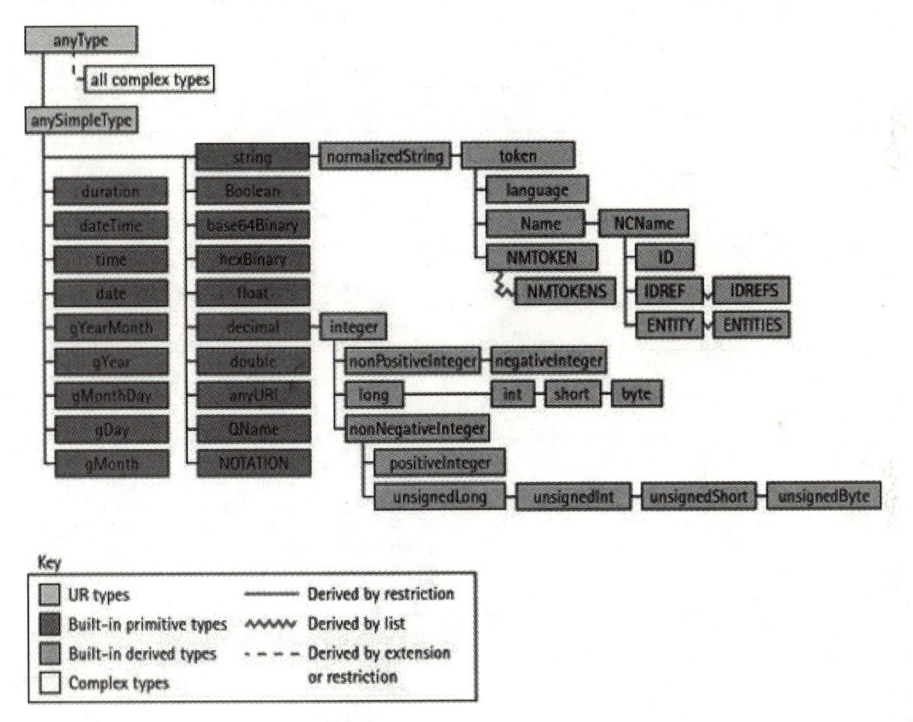

Figure 10-4: The available types from XSD to define the types within your WSDL document.

There are a number of different types that you can use within the WSDL file to describe the information that you are requiring from the user and also for the types of data that you are going to return to the end user. Table 10-2 shows you how the XSD data types relate to the data types that are provided by the .NET Framework.

Table 10-2: XSD Data Types Compared to .NET Data Types

XML Schema (XSD) type	.NET Framework type
anyURI	System.Uri
base64Binary	System.Byte[]
Boolean	System.Boolean
Byte	System.SByte
Date	System.DateTime
dateTime	System.DateTime
decimal	System.Decimal
Double	System.Double
duration	System.TimeSpan
ENTITIES	System.String[]
ENTITY	System.String
Float	System.Single
gDay	System.DateTime
gMonthDay	System.DateTime
gYear	System.DateTime
gYearMonth	System.DateTime
hexBinary	System.Byte[]
ID	System.String
IDREF	System.String
IDREFS	System.String[]
int	System.Int32
integer	System.Decimal
language	System.String
long	System.Int64
month	System.DateTime
Name	System.String
NCName	System.String
negativeInteger	System.Decimal

XML Schema (XSD) type	.NET Framework type
NMTOKEN	System.String
NMTOKENS	System.String[]
nonNegativeInteger	System.Decimal
nonPositiveInteger	System.Decimal
normalizedString	System.String
NOTATION	System.String
positiveInteger	System.Decimal
QName	System.Xml.XmlQualifiedName
short	System.Int16
string	System.String
time	System.DateTime
timePeriod	System.DateTime
token	System.String
unsignedByte	System.Byte
unsignedInt	System.UInt32
unsignedLong	System.UInt64
unsignedShort	System.UInt16

As you can see from the diagram and the table provided, there are a large number of types at your disposal.

> **TIP:** If you are going to be passing back an undefined type, be sure to use the type `anyType` in the following manner: `type="s:anyType"`. This represents a parameter of any type.

\<message\>

Messages consist of one or more parts. The sample WSDL document uses a number of different `<message>` elements.

```
<message name="USDConvertSoapIn">
  <part name="parameters" element="s0:USDConvert" />
</message>
<message name="USDConvertSoapOut">
  <part name="parameters" element="s0:USDConvertResponse" />
</message>
<message name="USDConvertHttpGetIn">
  <part name="ConvertTo" type="s:string" />
```

```
      <part name="Amount" type="s:string" />
</message>
<message name="USDConvertHttpGetOut">
   <part name="Body" element="s0:double" />
</message>
<message name="USDConvertHttpPostIn">
   <part name="ConvertTo" type="s:string" />
   <part name="Amount" type="s:string" />
</message>
<message name="USDConvertHttpPostOut">
   <part name="Body" element="s0:double" />
</message>
```

You see all the type definitions that play a role in the data that is being transported back and forth across the wire, but the `<message>` element is the piece of the pie that packages this up. The `<message>` element is protocol independent and is really only concerned with the message and all the parts of the message that are going to be sent and received.

The `<message>` element can have a single attribute, the `name` attribute. The `name` attribute is just that — *a name*. It doesn't really have any special meaning except that it provides a unique identifier among all messages defined within the enclosing WSDL document. In this example, all the messages have the name of the method, plus the protocol of the part. You can give the `<message>` elements whatever name that you choose, because WSDL makes no distinction on the name that is used, just as long as there are no naming conflicts among the messages.

You can think of the `<part>` elements as the payload of the messages. By looking at the `<message>` example that is laid out, you can see that there is a message for each request and response for each of the three different protocols. The HTTP-GET and HTTP-POST messages each contain two `<part>` elements that relate to the types of information that are sent into the Web service, whereas the response information contains a single `<part>` element.

The SOAP `<part>` elements used in this code example are interesting. If you use SOAP, the `<part>` elements basically correspond to the SOAP request or response. These `<part>` elements do not contain the parameter type definitions like the other `<part>` elements do, but instead point to the type definitions that were defined in the `<type>` element earlier. Going back to this definition, you will see a type definition for `USDConvert` and `USDConvertResponse`.

<portType>

The job of the `<portType>` element is to define all the operations that can be used. A port type is a set of certain abstract operations and the abstract messages involved.

The WSDL document example has a number of different `<portType>` definitions. The following code reviews these listings.

```
<portType name="CurrencyConverterSoap">
   <operation name="USDConvert">
      <documentation>Converts US Dollars to Finnish Marks, English
      Pounds, Canadian Dollars, German Marks, or Euros.</documentation>
```

```
      <input message="s0:USDConvertSoapIn" />
      <output message="s0:USDConvertSoapOut" />
    </operation>
  </portType>
  <portType name="CurrencyConverterHttpGet">
    <operation name="USDConvert">
      <documentation>Converts US Dollars to Finnish Marks, English
        Pounds, Canadian Dollars, German Marks, or Euros.</documentation>
      <input message="s0:USDConvertHttpGetIn" />
      <output message="s0:USDConvertHttpGetOut" />
    </operation>
  </portType>
  <portType name="CurrencyConverterHttpPost">
    <operation name="USDConvert">
      <documentation>Converts US Dollars to Finnish Marks, English
        Pounds, Canadian Dollars, German Marks, or Euros.</documentation>
      <input message="s0:USDConvertHttpPostIn" />
      <output message="s0:USDConvertHttpPostOut" />
    </operation>
  </portType>
```

The `<portType>` element can take a single attribute, the `name` attribute. This attribute provides you with a unique identifier for the `<portType>` element, so that this `<portType>` is set out from the other `<portType>` elements.

A single Web service can support a number of different protocols. The structure of the data depends on the protocol that you use to invoke the Web service. Because of this, you need a way to map from the operations to the endpoints from which they can be accessed. The `<portType>` element takes care of this mapping.

There is a `portType` definition for each of the protocols available to you for this XML Web service. There are individual `portType` definitions for using SOAP, HTTP-POST, and HTTP-GET. The operation name is the method available from this Web service. If there were other methods available to you, there would be additional `<operation>` elements defined as well.

For each `<operation>` element, there is a `<documentation>` element. This element is discussed later in the chapter. The other elements that you can use within the `<operation>` element include `<input>`, `<output>`, and `<fault>`. Each `<operation>` can contain only one of each of these available elements. There can only be one input into a Web service, just as there can only be one output. Each of these three elements has a `name` and a `message` attribute.

The `<input>` element specifies the request to a Web service. The `<output>` element specifies the response of the Web service. The `<fault>` element details any error messages that may be output by the Web service.

\<binding\>

Now that you have definitions in place for the different logical ports at your disposal, you need to define how the end user will bind to a port where the operation is obtainable. You do this by using the `<binding>` element. The following code is one of the three `<binding>` elements that is used in the sample WSDL document.

```
<binding name="CurrencyConverterSoap" type="s0:CurrencyConverterSoap">
  <soap:binding transport="http://schemas.xmlsoap.org/soap/http"
    style="document" />
  <operation name="USDConvert">
    <soap:operation soapAction="http://www.xmlws101.com/USDConvert"
      style="document" />
    <input>
      <soap:body use="literal" />
    </input>
    <output>
      <soap:body use="literal" />
    </output>
  </operation>
</binding>
```

The `<binding>` that is shown in this example is using SOAP. The other two bindings that are in the main WSDL document include `<binding>` definitions for both HTTP-POST and HTTP-GET.

The `<binding>` element contains a `name` attribute. This attribute's value is the name of the Web service class with the word SOAP attached to the end of it. The `<binding>` element also contains a `type` attribute. This attribute is a reference to the `<portType>` name attribute that was used earlier.

\<soap:binding\>

This example shows that a number of different elements are enclosed within the `<binding>` element. The first is the `<soap:binding>` element. By using this `<soap:binding>` element, you are specifying that this protocol is bound to the SOAP specification that uses a SOAP packet for transport. The SOAP packet is made up of the Envelope, Header, and Body. The `<soap:binding>` element can contain two attributes. The first is the `transport` attribute. The `transport` attribute, a URI, specifies the protocol that is going to be used in transporting the SOAP packet. The value of this attribute in the example is http://schemas.xmlsoap.org/soap/http. This `transport` value is specifying that the SOAP packet will be transported over HTTP.

The `style` attribute allows you to specify one of the two available binding styles at your disposal. The optional values are `rpc` and `document`. The preceding example is using the `style` attribute with the value of `document`. A setting of `document` means that the SOAP will be transported using a single document message. Using `rpc` means that the SOAP message will be sent using an RPC-oriented operation. RPC messages are made up of parameters and return values. If a `style` value isn't specified, assume that `document` is the `style` setting.

<soap:operation>

Contained within the <operation> element is a <soap:operation> element. The <operation> element is associated with each of the available methods from the Web service. The <soap:operation> element is used to show how the operation should be bound. In this case, it is to the SOAP protocol. The soapAction attribute specifies the value of the SOAPAction header for this operation.

The style attribute is the same as it is in the <soap:body> element. The possible values of this attribute include both rpc and document.

The <soap:operation> element can take up to one <input> and one <output> element. Each <input> and <output> element can contain either a <soap:body>, <soap:header> or a <soap:headerfault>. The sample WSDL document that is used in this chapter contains only a <soap:body> element for both the <input> and <output> elements.

<soap:body>

The <input> or <output> element can contain a <soap:body> element. This indicates that the message parts are part of the SOAP Body element. There are a number of available attributes that can be used within the <soap:body> element.

In the example used in this chapter, the <soap:body> contains a use attribute. The use attribute specifies whether the message parts are being encoded. The possible values of the use attribute include encoded or literal. The value of encoded means that a URI is used to determine how the message is mapped to the SOAP body. If encoded is set as the value, there needs to be an encodingStyle attribute. The value of the encodingStyle attribute is a list of URIs, each divided by a single space. The URIs signify encoding used within the message, and they are ordered from the most restrictive to the least restrictive.

If literal is used as the value of the use attribute, the message parts represent a concrete schema definition. When this value is set to literal, the message parts are sent literally and not altered in the process.

<service>

The <service> element contains the endpoints for the Web service. The following code demonstrates this.

```
<service name="CurrencyConverter">
  <port name="CurrencyConverterSoap"
   binding="s0:CurrencyConverterSoap">
    <soap:address
     location="http://localhost/CurrencyConverter/Converter.asmx"
     />
  </port>
  <port name="CurrencyConverterHttpGet"
   binding="s0:CurrencyConverterHttpGet">
    <http:address
     location="http://localhost/CurrencyConverter/Converter.asmx"
     />
```

```
    </port>
    <port name="CurrencyConverterHttpPost"
     binding="s0:CurrencyConverterHttpPost">
      <http:address
       location="http://localhost/CurrencyConverter/Converter.asmx"
       />
    </port>
</service>
```

In this example, there are three ports or endpoints for the Web service. There is one available port for each of the protocols: SOAP, HTTP-GET, and HTTP-POST. The `binding` attribute in the `<port>` element points to the associated `<binding>` element. Contained within the `<port>` element is an `<http:address>` child element that specifies the URI of the endpoint.

Like the other elements that are part of the WSDL document, the `<port>` element can also take a name attribute that allows it to have a unique identifier in order to differentiate itself from the other `<port>` elements.

<imports>

Although not shown in the example, it is also possible to use the `<imports>` element within a WSDL document. Using the `<imports>` element enables you to associate a namespace with a document location. The following code shows this:

```
<definitions>
     <imports namespace="uri" location="uri"/>
</definitions>
```

Basically you can actually import parts of another WSDL document directly into the WSDL document that you are working with. For instance, if you have a type definition in a separate file, your file should look like Listing 10-2:

Listing 10-2: The <types> section in its own WSDL file

```
<types>
  <s:schema elementFormDefault="qualified"
   targetNamespace="http://www.xmlws101.com">
    <s:element name="USDConvert">
      <s:complexType>
        <s:sequence>
          <s:element minOccurs="0" maxOccurs="1" name="ConvertTo"
            type="s:string" />
          <s:element minOccurs="1" maxOccurs="1" name="Amount"
            type="s:double"
            />
        </s:sequence>
      </s:complexType>
    </s:element>
    <s:element name="USDConvertResponse">
      <s:complexType>
```

```
            <s:sequence>
              <s:element minOccurs="1" maxOccurs="1" name="USDConvertResult"
                type="s:double" />
            </s:sequence>
          </s:complexType>
        </s:element>
        <s:element name="double" type="s:double" />
      </s:schema>
</types>
```

You can now import this `.wsdl` file directly into the WSDL document that you are working on. The following partial code example shows how this is done.

Listing 10-3: A WSDL document containing an imported type definition

```
<?xml version="1.0" encoding="utf-8"?>
<definitions xmlns:http="http://schemas.xmlsoap.org/wsdl/http/"
 xmlns:soap="http://schemas.xmlsoap.org/wsdl/soap/"
 xmlns:s="http://www.w3.org/2001/XMLSchema"
 xmlns:s0="http://www.xmlws101.com"
 xmlns:soapenc="http://schemas.xmlsoap.org/soap/encoding/"
 xmlns:tm="http://microsoft.com/wsdl/mime/textMatching/"
 xmlns:mime="http://schemas.xmlsoap.org/wsdl/mime/"
 targetNamespace="http://www.xmlws101.com"
 xmlns="http://schemas.xmlsoap.org/wsdl/">

  <import namespace="http://www.xmlws101.com"
    location="http://localhost/SomeLocation/TypeDefinition.wsdl" />

  <message name="USDConvertSoapIn">
    <part name="parameters" element="s0:USDConvert" />
  </message>
```

This will cause the types that are defined in a separate WSDL document to be planted in the spot where the `<import>` element is located. You may have pieces of a WSDL document that are easy to carve off and use numerous times in other WSDL documents.

The `<import>` element takes two attributes. The first is the `namespace` attribute and the second is the `location` attribute. The `location` attribute specifies the location of the actual file that you want to import into the WSDL document.

Using the `<import>` element properly enables you to separate your WSDL documents into reusable blocks that can be used when needed.

<documentation>

As discussed earlier in the book, it is not always possible for the end user to figure out what is going on in a particular Web service by just looking at the WSDL file or the test page that is automatically generated by .NET. One option to understand it better is to use the `WebService` and `WebMethod` properties to fully describe the XML Web service. You can use these properties to help others understand what is meant by the argument `CityDays2002` in your method. The end user might be able to tell that the `CityDays2002` takes an integer, but he might not know the actually meaning of the argument. Even after testing it on the test page, he may be no closer to figuring it out.

It is always best to give as much information as possible if you want users to consume your Web services with a smile. Do this by providing documentation notes within your WSDL files, as well by using the `<documentation>` element.

The `<documentation>` element is allowed anywhere within the WSDL document. I advise you to use this element to place documentation information in as many places as possible to make it easier for end user to consume your Web services.

For instance, in the example used throughout this chapter, the `<documentation>` element is placed within the `<operation>` element in order to give the end user more information about what the operation actually does. The following code shows an example of this:

```
<operation name="USDConvert">
    <documentation>Converts US Dollars to Finnish Marks, English Pounds,
    Canadian Dollars, German Marks, or Euros.</documentation>
    <input message="s0:USDConvertSoapIn" />
    <output message="s0:USDConvertSoapOut" />
</operation>
```

As you look at this operation, you can see it is somewhat self-explanatory. Because you know a little more about this particular operation, you also know how to work more effectively with the Web service you are looking to consume.

Summary

The Web Services Description Language is a new XML-based language that is used to describe not only XML Web services on a .NET platform, but also Web services on every other platform. WSDL is not a Microsoft technology, even though Microsoft (along with other companies) had a hand in its creation.

Now that you know how a WSDL document is constructed, you will be better able to discern the structure of a Web service from these documents, even if the Web service and its associated WSDL document is on a platform other than a .NET platform.

Chapter 11
UDDI

They are ill discoverers that think there is no land, when they see nothing but sea.
Francis Bacon, *The Advancement of Learning* (1605)

UDDI has one of those long names that is easy to turn into an acronym; therefore, most people will always refer to this technology as the chapter is titled, UDDI. But if you want to impress your friends, you can use the name in the long form – *Universal Description, Discovery, and Integration*.

UDDI is a way to publish your XML Web services so that others can find them. It is also possible, using UDDI, to find other Web services that you can consume in your client applications. This chapter takes a close look at the following:

- Understanding UDDI and why you need it
- The UDDI API specification
- Using the Microsoft UDDI SDK

Why Do You Need UDDI?

There are standards in place for how Web services are transported across the wire. Also, there are standards set in place for the description of a Web service so that consumers of that Web service are better able to use it in their applications. Why is everything based upon these standards? If Web services are going to be truly interoperable, there must be a set of rules defining how certain steps are taken in their use, deployment, and consumption.

Most of the standards for use of XML Web services are based upon XML – and UDDI is no different. Figure 11-1 shows you how UDDI is placed in the Web service's stack. This stack was first shown in Chapter 10 where WSDL was discussed.

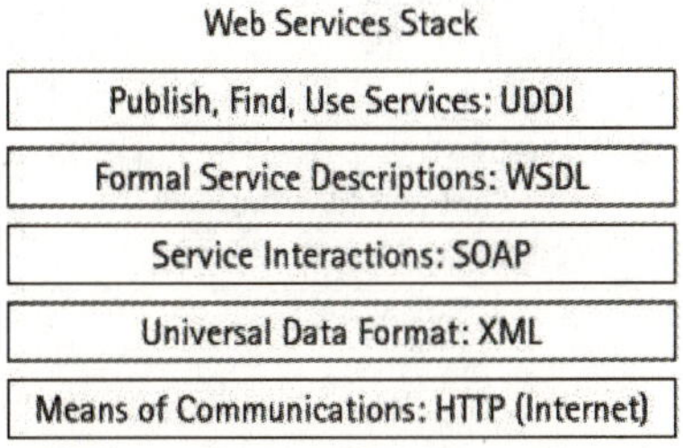

Web Services Stack

| Publish, Find, Use Services: UDDI |
| Formal Service Descriptions: WSDL |
| Service Interactions: SOAP |
| Universal Data Format: XML |
| Means of Communications: HTTP (Internet) |

Figure 11-1: The Web services Stack with UDDI at the top.

The first layer is the means of communication, which is a ubiquitous communication model. This is what the Internet offers us. On top of this is a method for sending structured data over HTTP. The structured data uses XML and SOAP. WSDL describes the services that are offered, whereas UDDI is a way to look up these services in a formalized manner. By using UDDI, you are better equipped to publish, find, or consume these services.

For instance, if you have built an XML Web service, this Web service transports its information using HTTP and XML. Because of this, any consumer who can receive XML is able to consume your Web service. You can also add a description to your Web service in WSDL. This description makes it easier for the end user to understand what is needed to consume your Web service. Even if you have completed all these steps, you still may not see much traffic to your Web service because users have no easy way to find your Web service. You must tell them about it or put something in place to help end users search for and find it. UDDI is there to fill this gap. UDDI can be thought of as the Yellow Pages of Web services. As with WSDL, Microsoft does not own this technology. UDDI is built upon standards developed by IBM, Microsoft, Ariba, and others as a way for individuals, organizations, and companies to publish their Web services in a virtual directory. This technology was started by these companies to address the service discovery problem, and they made a point of developing this technology on industry standards such as XML, HTTP, TCP/IP, and SOAP.

The end user finds your XML Web services by finding your service's description document. WSDL and UDDI work closely together and neither would be effective without the presence of the other. For instance, what is the purpose of a description document if no one is able to find this document, and what is the purpose of a registry where you can search for services if there are no standard descriptions in place to search?

What is UDDI?

UDDI can be thought of as a large registry on the Internet that is run by Microsoft and IBM so that developers can publish their Web services and users can find them and then consume them. There is a lot more to UDDI than that, however. UDDI is a means of defining a standard way to publish and discover information about Web services. You can access a lot of the functionality that UDDI provides programmatically because UDDI is basically a Web service itself. By using a set of SOAP-based XML API calls, it is possible to interact with UDDI at both design-time and runtime.

To transport its messages across the wire, UDDI uses SOAP (*Simple Object Access Protocol*). There are also APIs in place for both inquiring and publishing. These APIs consist of 40 SOAP-compliant requests and responses. Because UDDI is also a Web service, it has some WSDL documents associated with it. There is a WSDL document for publishing to the UDDI registry programmatically, located at `www.uddi.org/wsdl/publish_v1.wsdl`. There is also a WSDL document in place for inquiring about Web services that are available. This document is also available programmatically by making a reference to the document and creating a proxy class for it. The WSDL document for inquiring is located at `www.uddi.org/wsdl/inquire_v1.wsdl`.

Presently, UDDI is at Version 2. This version of the specification was released in June of 2001. Even though there is a newer version available, there are still many public repositories using Version 1.

> **NOTE:** For complete information on UDDI and for current news on the status of UDDI, visit the UDDI Web site at www.uddi.org.

The Shared UDDI Business Registry

UDDI is basically a shared implementation of a Web service that is based upon UDDI technologies. This Web service, the *UDDI Business Registry*, is shared among companies such as Microsoft, IBM, Hewlett-Packard, and SAP. Although there is more than one UDDI Business Registry, the policy of these companies ensures that if a user registers once, he is registered everywhere. Each of these companies has a Web interface to this Business Registry on its own site where you can register your Web services. Figures 11-2 and 11-3 show the Microsoft and IBM UDDI sites, respectively. The Microsoft UDDI site can be found at uddi.microsoft.com and the IBM UDDI site can be found at www.ibm.com/services/uddi.

Figure 11-2: The Microsoft UDDI site at http://uddi.microsoft.com. From here, you can publish or find Web services.

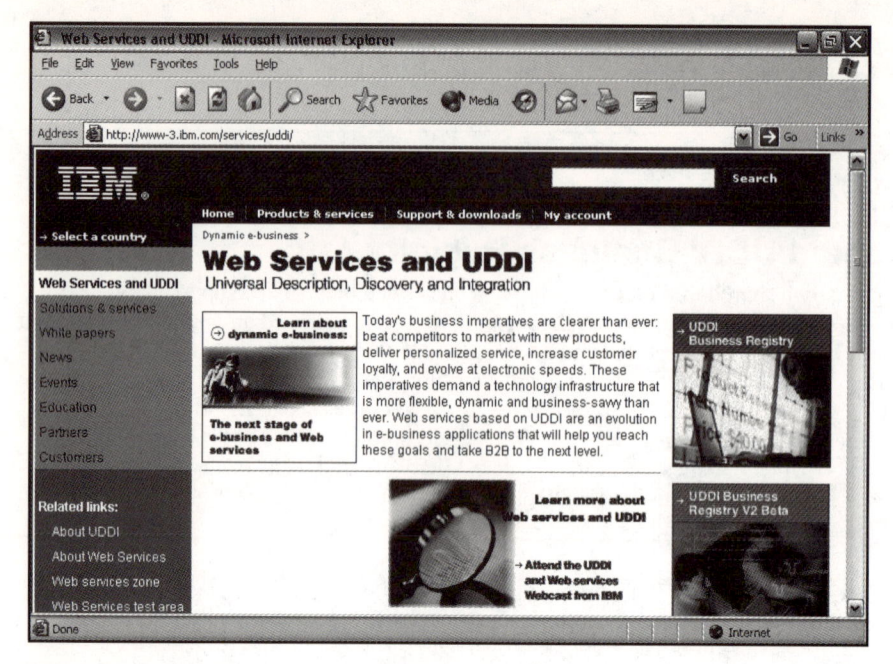

Figure 11-3: The IBM UDDI site located at www.ibm.com/services/uddi.

An example

From either of the sites shown in the preceding figures, it is possible to search for and publish information about Web services. For example, suppose that you are a company that sells air filters for cars, and you have built an XML Web service that enables your customers to order these air filters. You built the XML Web service and have a description in place for it, but now you need a way for people out there on the Internet to find your Web service. In order to do this, you register your XML Web service on the Microsoft UDDI site. A few days later, one of your customers is on the IBM UDDI site and does a search for your XML Web service. He will find it there, including the reference to the WSDL file. He can then make a reference to this WSDL file and bind to your Web service.

Information replication

Microsoft, IBM, Hewlett-Packard, and SAP (Ariba dropped out) are all considered *operator nodes* because they are hosting the main Business Registry. These companies have made it easy for all of us because they are sharing the registry information with each other. This is done so that you, as a Web service owner, only have to register once on one of these nodes and, within 24 hours, the information you have put into the registry is replicated to the other nodes. Figure 11-4 shows an example of this replication model.

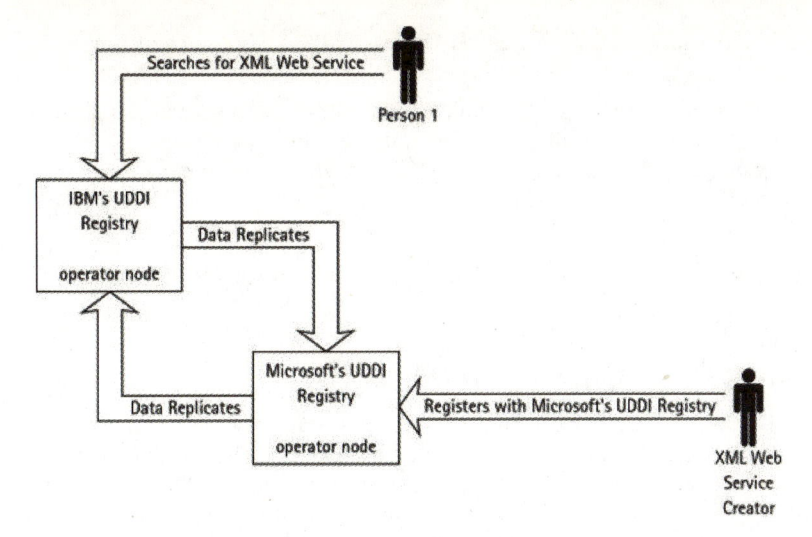

Figure 11-4: The UDDI information replication model.

The data replication functionality can take 24 hours to complete, but you can be assured that by registering on one of the operator nodes your service information is replicated to the other nodes. If you make changes to your XML Web service, you must also make those changes on the operator node with which you originally registered the Web service. With this data replication going on, your changes will also be replicated to the other nodes within 24 hours.

If all these companies basically have the same registry for the services that people and companies are providing, how do you choose which registry to work from? Well, it really doesn't matter which registry you use to publish your XML Web services. The main difference between the registries is how they provide access to the registry itself. Of course, if you are providing company and service information to a registry, you need to be authorized and authenticated to be able to update your information. The different operator nodes use different ways in which to do this. Microsoft, for example, uses Microsoft Passport for all authorizations and authentications to access the UDDI registry.

Information types

You can publish or find much more information on the UDDI registry other than just a simple link to a WSDL document. The information that is provided from UDDI consists of three categories of information: *White pages*, *Yellow pages*, and *Green pages*. Each one of these categories has its own specific niche describing the services provided and the companies that are providing them.

- *White pages* – This category includes generic business contact information, such as the service provider's address, as well as Web and e-mail addresses. This section provides the end user with a general description of the company.

- *Yellow pages* – This category includes information on how the company that is providing the services is categorized based upon standard categorizations that are in use today. Some of these categorizations include NAICS, UNSPSC, SIC, and geographic taxonomies. These categorizations will be discussed in the next section of this chapter.

- *Green pages* – This section provides the technical information that programmers need in order to consume the Web services that are listed in the registry. These pages include references to specifications for the listed Web services as well as the pointers to the WSDL files. It enables the programmer to make a simple reference to the file and bind to the Web service.

Using these categories, you can easily publish or find information about any Web service in the registry.

Publishing Services with UDDI

It is quite easy to publish information to the UDDI registry. The UDDI registry allows you to publish information about a business and the services that this business offers, including XML Web services. For each business and service that is placed within the registry, there is a unique identifier associated with that business or service. After you have information about your businesses and services in the registry, others can then search for them based upon various search criteria. Therefore, it is important to provide as much information as possible about businesses and services that are placed into the registry.

You will be able to categorize each business and service that is placed within the registry. The available categorizations include NAICS, UNSPSC, ISO 3166 Geographic Taxonomy, SIC, GeoWeb Geographic Classification, and the UDDI Types Taxonomy. You should provide a classification for each business and service that you put into the registry. Table 11-1 shows available UDDI categorizations.

Table 11-1: Available UDDI Categorizations

Categorization	Description
North American Industry Classification System (NAICS)	This classification system is specific to the United States, Canada, and Mexico. It is used to classify business into specific industries. NAICS was developed jointly by these countries in 1997 to provide new comparability in statistics about business activity across North America. This classification system was developed to replace SIC. Listed here is a sample classification for beverage manufacturing and some of its subcategories. 3121 Beverage Manufacturing 31211 Soft Drink and Ice Manufacturing 312111 Soft Drink Manufacturing 312112 Bottled Water Manufacturing 312113 Ice Manufacturing 31212 Breweries 31213 Wineries 31214 Distilleries

Categorization	Description
Universal Standard Products and Services Codes (USPSC)	The Universal Standard Products and Services Classification (UNSPSC) is an open global coding system that classifies products and services. The UNSPSC is used extensively around the world in the electronic catalogs, search engines, procurement application systems, and accounting systems. This classification system currently covers 56 industry segments including electronics, chemical, medical, educational services, automotive, and fabrications. The UNSPSC code covers any product or service that can be bought or sold. It includes 12,000 codes covering everything from pencils to computers and from accountancy to cleaning services. For example, the classification for Educational and Training Services is 86.00.00.00.00. A child to this classification is Specialized educational services with a classification code of 86.13.00.00.00. Directly below this is Fine Arts with a classification of 86.13.15.00.00 and below this is Sculpture with a classification of 86.13.15.03.00.
ISO 3166 Geographic Taxonomy	This is a classification that is meant to describe the physical location of the service or business in the UDDI registry. This geographic taxonomy can be used to classify services or businesses down to the state or province. This is a broad classification, and that is why Microsoft is pushing the GeoWeb Geographic Classification in place of the ISO 3166 Geographic Taxonomy. The classification of US-MO is a classification for a business or service that is geographically located in the state of Missouri in the United States.
Standard Industrial Classification (SIC)	This is the older classification system that was used by the United States. SIC was started in the 1930s and has been replaced by NAICS. SIC has considerably fewer divisions for classifications than NAICS. The classification for *Automotive Repair, Services, And Parking* is 75 and going one level lower, the classification for *Passenger Car Rental* is 7514.
GeoWeb Geographic Classification	This geographic classification system provides more direct information on where a particular business or service resides. Whereas the ISO 3166 Geographic Taxonomy gets down to the state or province level, the GeoWeb Geographic Classification reaches the city level. For instance, the classification for St. Charles, Missouri, USA, North America, World is `517027`.
UDDI Types Taxonomy	This taxonomy exists to classify tModel and service information.

Keeping these classifications in mind, you can go through the process of registering a business and a service with UDDI. As discussed, there are registries at both Microsoft and IBM. For the examples in this book, you will use the registry at Microsoft. To make this even better, both IBM and Microsoft have a test registry where you can work with a UDDI registry just like the original one. The test UDDI registry allows you to play with it so that you can better understand how everything works. You will be working with the Microsoft Test UDDI Registry at `test.uddi.microsoft.com`. The test registry is there to enable you to practice using UDDI for publishing and consuming services. It gives you a way to go in and fiddle around without really putting out any false or erroneous information. Even though the UDDI registry enables you to access all the functionality of publishing and finding services programmatically through XML and SOAP, both IBM and Microsoft provide a Web interface as well so that you can access all this functionality from a Web browser. First, look at how to access the UDDI registry through these Web interfaces.

NOTE: The test registries that are used by both IBM and Microsoft are *not* replicated.

Registering

The first step is to register yourself so that you can start putting your businesses and services in the registry. Before you can do this, however, you need to get a Passport account to give you authentication and authorization to access the registry. After you have been authenticated, you are given a registration page (Figure 11-5).

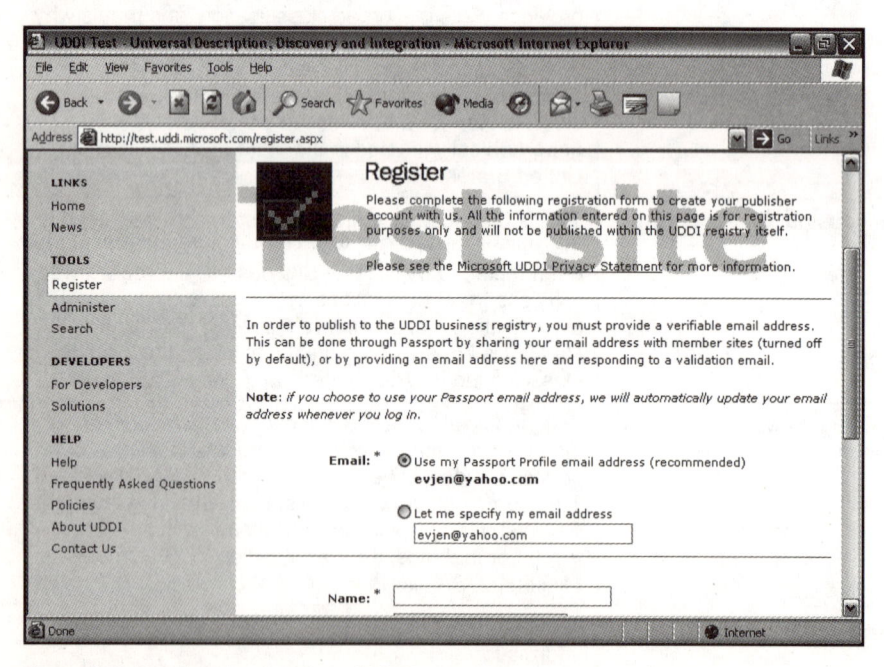

Figure 11-5: Registering on the Microsoft UDDI test registry.

You can tell right away that you are working on the test site by the large words: "Test site" over the background of the page. On the site, you are asked for your basic contact information. After registering your basic contact information, you are asked on the next page for the name and description of the business that you are registering with UDDI. For each business that you register in the UDDI registry, you provide the following information:

- Business details
- Contacts
- Services
- Identifiers
- Business classifications
- Discovery URLs

Business Detail

The Business Detail section enables you to enter a name and a description for your business. Figure 11-6 shows an example of this from the Microsoft Test UDDI Registry.

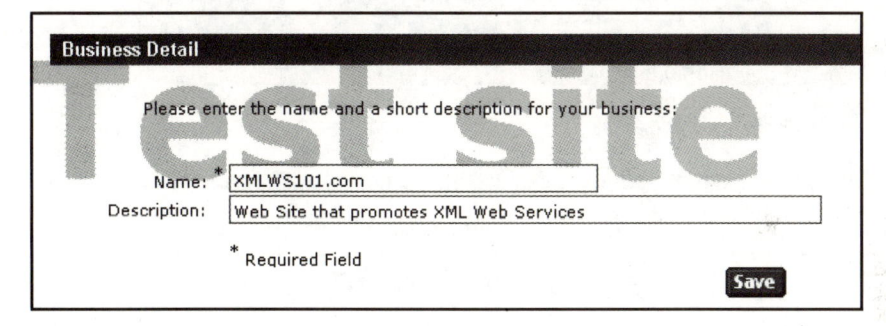

Figure 11-6: Providing information on your business.

Contacts

After you enter the basic details about your business, you are asked to provide the contact information for your business. You can add any number of contacts for this business in the registry. Figure 11-7 shows the page that allows you to enter your contact information.

Contacts are pretty simple, and you should enter all the contacts possible for the business.

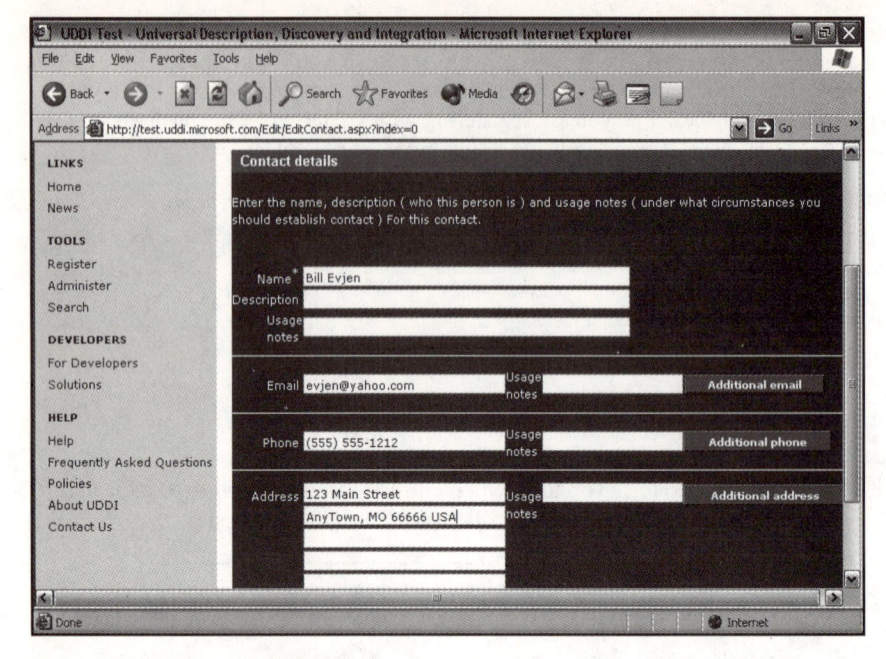

Figure 11-7: Adding contacts for the business.

After you have entered in the appropriate contact information, the information will be presented on your business page. See Figure 11-8.

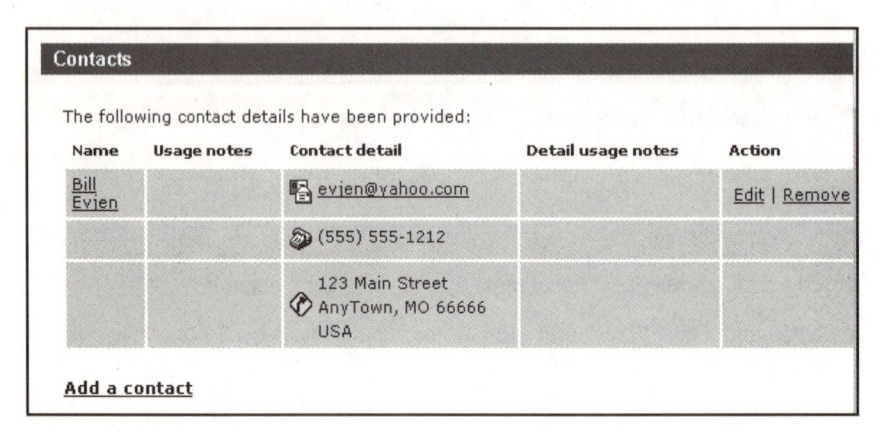

Figure 11-8: The contact information.

Services

The Services section of the registry enables the business to expose all the services that it offers. You want to put your XML Web services in this section. What you are describing in this section of the registry is all the `tModels` that your company exposes. The `tModels` are basically type models. The `tModel` is a generic metadata structure to uniquely represent any concept or construct. The `tModel` also includes interface protocol definitions. If you are dealing with XML Web services, a `tModel` is the same as a WSDL file. Other options for what a `tModel` represents include XML Schemas (XSD documents), namespaces, or categorization schemas. In the case of an XML Web service, because `tModels` are associated with a WSDL file, the `tModel` shows all the operations that are available from that Web service. When inputting the services, you can provide service details as well as the classifications of these services. Service details include the specifics of these applications as well as interfaces and location of the services. First, you will be asked to enter the name of the service and a description of the service (Figure 11-9).

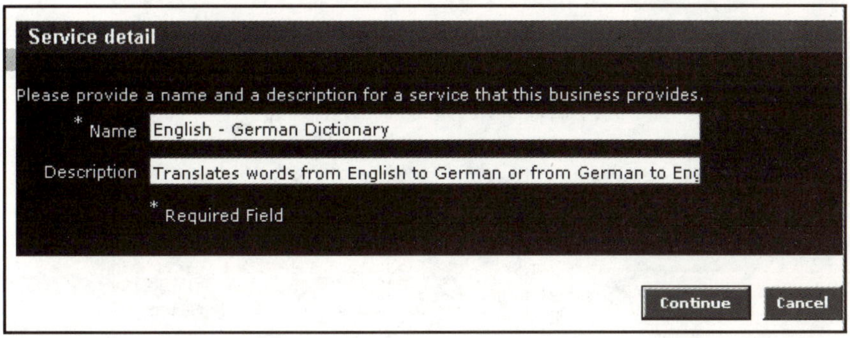

Figure 11-9: Entering the service details.

When searching for a Web service, some individuals search for services by particular classifications or geographic locations. Therefore, it is vital that you classify not only the business that you register with UDDI, but also classify the services that you are offering. Table 11-1 described the different types of classifications available, and it is important to use as many of those classifications as possible (see Figure 11-10). In the end, this assists others to find your service and decide if it is what they are looking for.

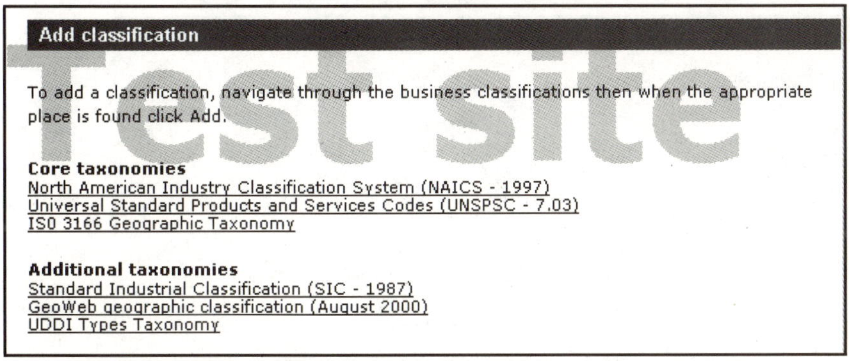

Figure 11-10: Adding a classification to your XML Web service.

After you have all the classifications in place for your XML Web service, you can see the classifications laid out for you in a table (Figure 11-11).

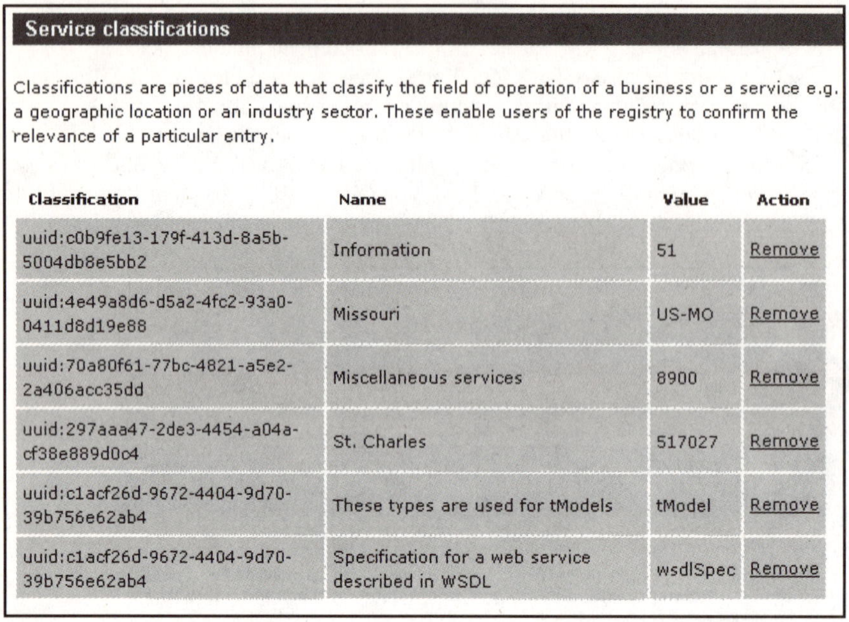

Service classifications

Classifications are pieces of data that classify the field of operation of a business or a service e.g. a geographic location or an industry sector. These enable users of the registry to confirm the relevance of a particular entry.

Classification	Name	Value	Action
uuid:c0b9fe13-179f-413d-8a5b-5004db8e5bb2	Information	51	Remove
uuid:4e49a8d6-d5a2-4fc2-93a0-0411d8d19e88	Missouri	US-MO	Remove
uuid:70a80f61-77bc-4821-a5e2-2a406acc35dd	Miscellaneous services	8900	Remove
uuid:297aaa47-2de3-4454-a04a-cf38e889d0c4	St. Charles	517027	Remove
uuid:c1acf26d-9672-4404-9d70-39b756e62ab4	These types are used for tModels	tModel	Remove
uuid:c1acf26d-9672-4404-9d70-39b756e62ab4	Specification for a web service described in WSDL	wsdlSpec	Remove

Figure 11-11: The classifications set in place for the EnglishGermanEnglishDictionary XML Web service.

As you can see, each classification has a unique identifier as well as a classification name and values. You can also remove a particular classification from the list. After you have put in your description and your classifications for a particular service, you can put in the binding information to the service. In this case, you want to make a binding reference to your XML Web services access point, the .asmx file. Figure 11-12 shows an example of this.

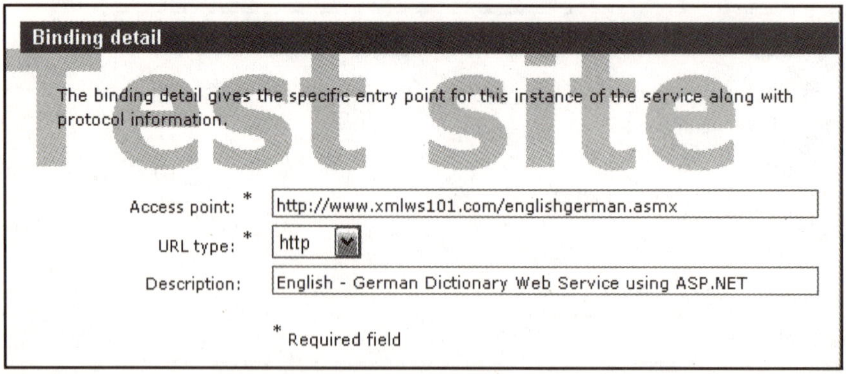

Binding detail

The binding detail gives the specific entry point for this instance of the service along with protocol information.

Access point: * http://www.xmlws101.com/englishgerman.asmx
URL type: * http
Description: English - German Dictionary Web Service using ASP.NET

* Required field

Figure 11-12: Providing the access point of the XML Web service.

> **NOTE:** You are able to list up to four services for your business entity.

Identifiers

Using identifiers, you can describe how your business is unique by using custom classifications as name/value pairs. You can also use specific classifications that might be a little more obscure than the classifications already provided. Figure 11-13 shows the page that allows for identifiers to be entered for your particular business.

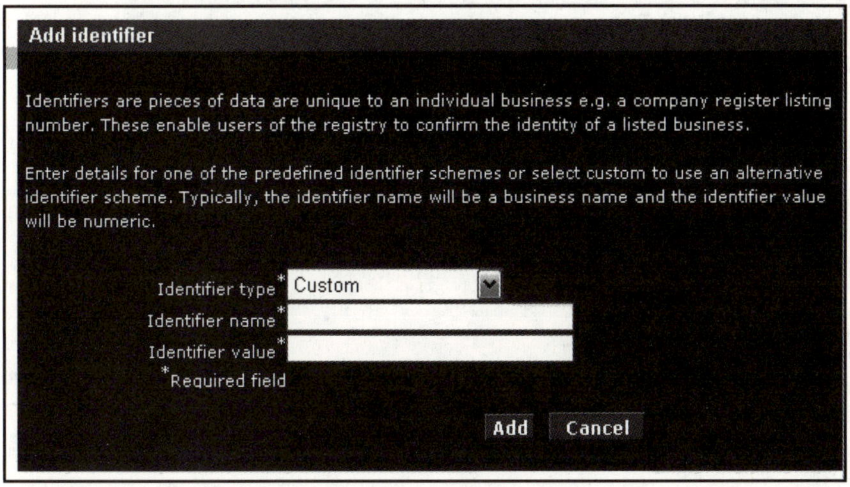

Figure 11-13: UDDI provides you with the ability to add unique identifiers for your business.

The identifier types that you can put into the registry include a *D-U-N-S Number*, *Thomas Supplier ID,* and a *RealNames Keyword*. The other option is to include a Custom identifier. This could be anything that you want, including ISBN numbers, Store IDs, or anything that uniquely identifies or classifies your organization.

Business Classifications

Identifying your business with specific classifications is much the same process as you used when you classified the services that you were offering. You can classify your business with any of the available classifications from Table 11-1 in this chapter.

Discovery URLs

This section provides the capability to add links to other related resources within your organization or elsewhere. It is fairly simple and straightforward to enter URLs associated with your business as shown in the following diagram (Figure 11-14).

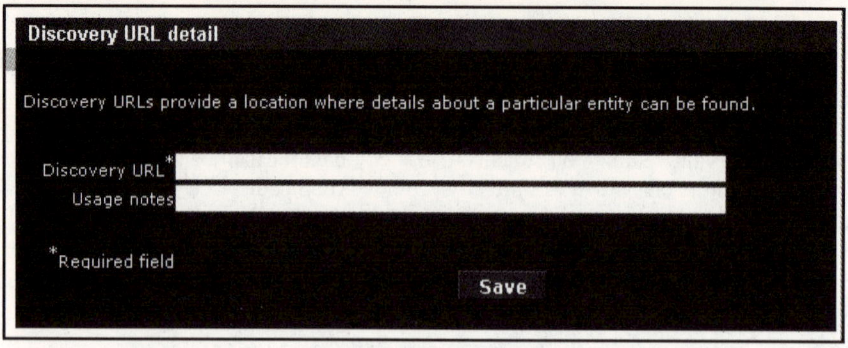

Figure 11-14: Providing links to relevant sites that are associated with your business.

Publishing your business and service information is a pretty straightforward process when using one of the available UDDI Business Registries. You can quickly and easily publish your business information as well as all the information for an end user to find your XML Web service so that he is then able to bind to it and consume it.

Registering capabilities

The UDDI Business registry allows you to easily publish information about your business and the services that your business offers by using the Web interface to the service through the Microsoft or IBM UDDI site. It is free, but there are limitations to the amount of information that you can put into the registry.

Everyone who signs up on the registry is given a Level 1 publisher account. This specific designation allows you to publish the following:

- 1 business entity
- 4 business services
- 2 binding templates
- 10 tModels

If you need to publish more than this, you must contact the UDDI administrators at uddiask@microsoft.com. If given permission, you can get a Level 2 publisher account. A Level 2 publisher account is meant for large organizations, marketplaces, or service providers that provide registration services on behalf of multiple businesses.

Finding Services with UDDI

As a programmer, you not only publish your Web service to the UDDI Business registry, but you also use this registry to find Web services that you can use in your applications. To search for Web services in the UDDI registry, you don't go through the same authentication and authorization process as you did when you published your services. You are allowed to freely search for Web services from any of the available registries. For the purposes of this demonstration, instead of using the Test UDDI Business Registry, use the real Microsoft Business Registry at uddi.microsoft.com.

On the main page of the Microsoft UDDI Business Registry, there is a single text box where you can search for services based upon the name of the business. By clicking on the Advanced Search option, you also have the option of searching by business location, tModel by name, business identifier, discovery URL, GeoWeb Taxonomy, NAICS codes, SIC codes, UNSPSC codes, ISO 3166 Geographic Taxonomy, and by RealNames keywords. You can see an example of a search in Figure 11-15.

After typing in a search parameter, you are presented with a paged-list of available services. For instance, searching for weather as the name of the `tModel`, you will be presented with a number of options. Some may be Web services that you can consume, whereas some of the listings might not have anything to do with Web services.

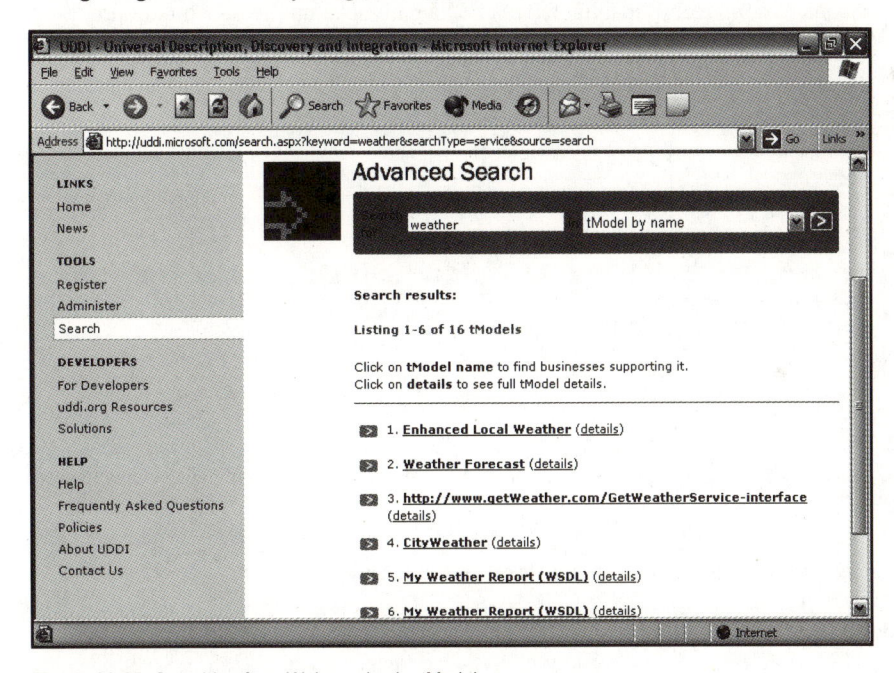

Figure 11-15: Searching for a Web service by tModel name.

After viewing the details of a service, you see the description page covered earlier in this chapter. Here you will find all the information about the service, including information about the business that is offering the service. Most important, you can tell if the service offered is a Web service and if there is an associated WSDL that you can bind to in order to consume the Web service in your application. After you have found a WSDL file of a service that you want to consume, just copy the link to the WSDL document and then back in your application, make a Web Reference, and use this link to the WSDL document within the Add Web Reference dialog window.

UDDI API Specification

By understanding the underlying UDDI API specification, you gain the knowledge to programmatically interact with a UDDI registry in either publishing or consuming Web services. It is even possible, if you license this UDDI specification, to build your own registries that are compatible with the UDDI specifications.

UDDI data structure

UDDI uses XML and SOAP to a great extent, and like all XML documents, it has an underlying data structure specification (an XML Schema document). You can actually find the XSD file, uddi_v2.xsd, that describes this data structure at www.uddi.org/specification.html.

This XSD document defines five specific types of data that make up the registration process. The following diagram (Figure 11-16) shows the data structures involved and how they relate to one another.

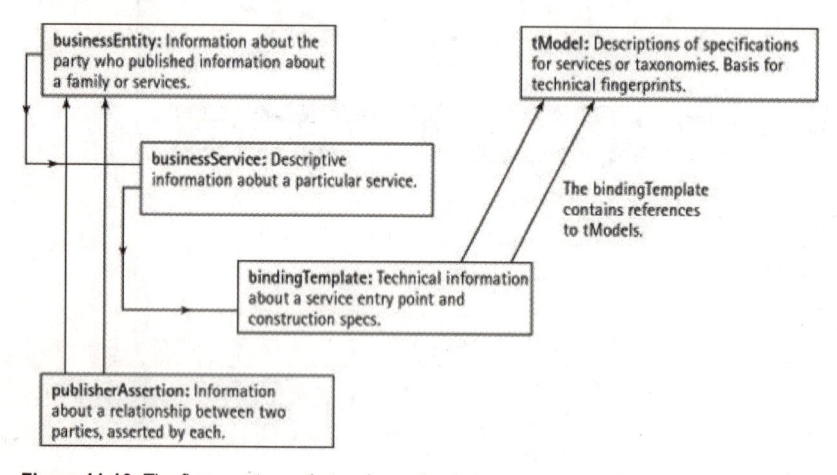

Figure 11-16: The five core types that make up the data structure specification.

The five data structure types that makes up the data structure specification include business information (businessEntity), information on the services provided (businessService), the binding information (bindingTemplate), the specification pointers and unique identifiers (tModel), and the information about the relationships between business entities (publisherAssertions).

Each piece of information in the specification is assigned a unique identifier when the information is saved to the UDDI registry. You can use this unique key as a reference to the particular piece of information. Each unique identifier is a *Universally Unique ID* (UUID). This UUID is a hexadecimal string, generated by a specific algorithm that is guaranteed to be unique.

businessEntity

The `businessEntity` contains information about the business, such as the business name, description, contact information, and information on the services that the business is offering. The `businessEntity` can be thought of as a top-level structure to the XML document. The following code sample (Listing 11-1) shows the structure that the `businessEntity` follows.

Listing 11-1: businessEntity specification

```
<element name = "businessEntity">
 <complexType>
  <sequence>
   <element ref = "discoveryURLs" minOccurs = "0"/>
   <element ref = "name" maxOccurs = "unbounded"/>
   <element ref = "description" minOccurs = "0" maxOccurs =
    "unbounded"/>
   <element ref = "contacts" minOccurs = "0"/>
   <element ref = "businessServices" minOccurs = "0"/>
   <element ref = "identifierBag" minOccurs = "0"/>
   <element ref = "categoryBag" minOccurs = "0"/>
  </sequence>
  <attribute ref = "businessKey" use = "required"/>
  <attribute ref = "operator"/>
  <attribute ref = "authorizedName">
 </complexType>
</element>
```

The `businessEntity` element breaks down into the following subelements:

- `businessKey` — The `businessKey` is an attribute that is used to provide a unique identifier for the business or entity. This UUID is assigned to the element at the moment the registering business saves its information to the registry.

- `authorizeName` — The `authorizeName` is an attribute of type `string` that is used to provide the name of the individual that registered the business into the registry.

- `operator` — The `operator` is another attribute of type string that is used to provide the name of the operator node that was used to publish the information into the registry.

- `discoveryURLs` — The `discoveryURLs` is an optional list of URLs that point to alternate, file-based service discovery mechanisms.

- `name` — The `name` element is a required element that provides the name of the business or entity.

- `description` — The `description` element enables you to provide a business description. Using the attribute `xmlns:lang="en"` within the `description` element allows you to specify the language of the description. Also by using this attribute, you can have other language values. You cannot have more than one `description` element unless it has another language value assigned to it.

- `contacts` — The `contacts` element is an optional element that enables you to provide a list of contact information.

256 Part IV: XML Web Services Description and Discovery

- **businessServices** – The businessServices element is an optional element that allows you to add one or more logical business service descriptions.

- **identifierBag** – The identifierBag element is an optional element that enables you to add a list of name-value pairs that can be used to record identifiers for a businessEntity.

- **categoryBag** – The categoryBag element is an optional element that allows you to add a list of name-value pairs that are used to tag a businessEntity with specific taxonomy information.

All these elements are used for identification purposes and allow other parties to search for your services or for your business based upon what is input. Listing 11-2 is a code sample using the businessEntity element:

Listing 11-2: businessEntity code example

```
<businessEntity businessKey="566874G4-6E17-1342-EA4136E876732ED0"
 operator="">
  <name>John Wiley</name>
  <description xml:lang="en">A computer book publisher</description>
  <contacts>
     <contact>
        <description xml:lang="en">Website Administrator</description>
        <personName>Henri Franklin</personName>
        <phone>800-555-1212</phone>
        <email>hfranklin@wiley.com</email>
        <address>
           <addressLine>123 Any Street</addressLine>
           <addressLine>AnyTown, MO 12345</addressLine>
        </address>
     </contact>
  </contacts>
</businessEntity>
```

Although not all the elements are used, this shows you how to use the businessEntity element to report to the UDDI registry all the description and contact information for a particular business.

businessService

The businessService describes the exposed services from a particular business or entity. For the topic that is being discussed here, the services exposed are the Web services from a particular organization.

In this section, you can assign classifications to a particular Web service and associate the Web service to a particular business and binding information (see Listing 11-3).

Listing 11-3: businessService specification

```
<element name = "businessService">
 <complexType>
  <sequence>
   <element ref = "name" maxOccurs = "unbounded"/>
   <element ref = "description" minOccurs = "0" maxOccurs =
   "unbounded"/>
   <element ref = "bindingTemplates"/>
   <element ref = "categoryBag" minOccurs = "0"/>
  </sequence>
  <attribute ref = "serviceKey" use = "required"/>
  <attribute ref = "businessKey"/>
 </complexType>
</element>
```

The `bindingService` element contains the following subelements:

- `businessKey` – The key for the business entity that contains this service.
- `serviceKey` – The `serviceKey` attribute provides a unique key for a particular `businessService`. This key is assigned to the service at the moment the service is registered in the registry.
- `name` – The `name` element is a required element that gives the service a human-readable name. Within this element, it is possible to use the `xmlns:lang="en"` attribute to specify a particular language that the name adheres to.
- `description` – The `description` element is an optional element that provides a description of the element. With this element, it is possible to use the `xmlns:lang="en"` attribute to specify a particular language that the description adheres to.
- `bindingTemplates` – The `bindingTemplates` element holds the technical service description information related to a given business-service family.
- `categoryBag` – The `categoryBag` element is an optional element that allows you to add a list of name-value pairs that are used to tag a `businessService` with specific taxonomy information.

The `businessService` element and all of its subelements provide the end user with a unique key and description for any service that a particular business or entity offers.

bindingTemplate

The `bindingTemplate` element describes for the end user all the technical information that he needs to know in order to bind to a particular service. This element supports naming a particular Web service and providing a URL associating the Web service to a specific access point or the option of pointing to a different `bindingTemplate`. The code in Listing 11-4 shows the `bindingTemplate` specification.

Listing 11-4: bindingTemplate specification

```
<element name = "bindingTemplate">
 <complexType>
    <sequence>
      <element ref = "description" minOccurs = "0" maxOccurs =
      "unbounded"/>
         <choice>
            <element ref = "accessPoint" minOccurs = "0"/>
            <element ref = "hostingRedirector" minOccurs = "0"/>
         </choice>
      <element ref = "tModelInstanceDetails"/>
    </sequence>
    <attribute ref = "bindingKey" use = "required"/>
    <attribute ref = "serviceKey"/>
 </complexType>
</element>
```

Of all the elements in the UDDI data structure, this one will be the most interesting to you when you wish to consume the Web service in your client application. This is the element where you find the information that you need in order to bind to the WSDL file. The bindingTemplate will provide the link to the WSDL file.

Within the bindingTemplate are the following subelements:

- bindingKey – The bindingKey attribute is a unique key for a particular bindingTemplate. This unique key is generated when the bindingTemplate is generated for the first time.
- serviceKey – The key for the businessService element that contains this bindingTemplate.
- description – The description element is an optional element that provides a description of the element. With this element, it is possible to use the xmlns:lang="en" attribute to specify a particular language that the description adheres to.
- accessPoint – The accessPoint element is the pointer to the URL of the WSDL file. This element points to the access point of a particular service. Valid access points can include e-mail addresses (mailto), URLs (http), secure URLs (https), a File Transfer Protocol address (ftp), a fax number (fax), and even a phone number (phone).
- hostingRedirector – The hostingRedirector element gives you the ability to point the access point to another bindingTemplate. This binding template is used when you have not expressed an access point using the accessPoint element.
- tModelInstanceDetails – The tModelInstanceDetails provides a container for one or more tModelInstanceInfo structures. The tModel acts as a technical fingerprint for the Web service.

tModel

One of the goals of UDDI is to make the descriptions rich enough that the end user will easily be able to figure out how to interact with the Web service. In order to do this, you must be able to describe to the end user everything that he needs to know in order to bind and consume your Web service. It is the job of the tModel to describe how your Web service behaves, what conventions it follows, and the standards with which the Web service is compliant.

The tModel takes the form of metadata (data about the Web service) and also has a unique identifier attached to it. Even though the tModel can be used to describe almost anything, it has been developed to provide information on two particular items:

- Sources for determining compatibility
- Keyed namespace references

The information that makes up the tModel is quite simple. It has a key and a name value. Along with these is an optional description. You can also add a URL to learn more information on a particular Web service. The code sample in Listing 11-5 shows the tModel specification:

Listing 11-5: tModel specification

```
<element name = "tModel">
 <complexType>
  <sequence>
   <element ref = "name"/>
   <element ref = "description" minOccurs = "0" maxOccurs =
   "unbounded"/>
   <element ref = "overviewDoc" minOccurs = "0"/>
   <element ref = "identifierBag" minOccurs = "0"/>
   <element ref = "categoryBag" minOccurs = "0"/>
  </sequence>
  <attribute ref = "tModelKey" use = "required"/>
  <attribute ref = "operator"/>
  <attribute ref = "authorizedName"/>
 </complexType>
</element>
```

The following subelements are within the tModel element:

- tModelKey – The tModelKey attribute is a unique key that is associated with identifying a particular tModel. This is generated when the tModel is registered in the UDDI registry.
- authorizeName – The authorizeName attribute is the recorded name of the individual that published the tModel data.
- operator – The operator is another attribute of type string that is used to provide the name of the operator node that was used to publish the information into the registry.
- name – The name element is a required element that gives the tModel a human-readable name. Within this element, it is possible to use the xmlns:lang="en" attribute to specify a particular language that the name adheres to.

- **description** – The `description` element is an optional element that provides a description of the `tModel`. With this element, it is possible to use the `xmlns:lang="en"` attribute to specify a particular language that the description adheres to.

- **overviewDoc** – The `overviewDoc` element is used to reference remote descriptive information or instructions related to the `tModel`. You can use this element to point to any descriptive URL for the Web service.

- **identifierBag** – The `identifierBag` element is an optional element that allows you to add a list of name-value pairs that can be used to record identifiers for a `tModel`.

- **categoryBag** – The `categoryBag` element is an optional element that allows you to add a list of name-value pairs that are used to tag a `tModel` with specific taxonomy information.

publisherAssertion

As more and more companies start using UDDI for registering their Web services, many large organizations will have multiple `businessEntity` registrations in the system. This requires a way to make an assertion about the relationship between two or more registrations.

To eliminate the possibility of one company making a false claim about a relationship in the registry, the `publisherAssertion` only works if both parties publish their connected relationship. If only one of the parties publishes an assertion of a relationship, this information is ignored. The `publisherAssertion` element has been added to Version 1 of the UDDI specification.

The code sample in Listing 11-6 shows the `publisherAssertion` specification.

Listing 11-6: publisherAssertion specification

```
<element name = "publisherAssertion">
 <complexType>
  <sequence>
    <element ref = "fromKey"/>
    <element ref = "toKey"/>
    <element ref = "keyedReference"/>
  </sequence>
 </complexType>
</element>
```

Within the `publisherAssertion` element are the following subelements:

- **fromKey** – The `fromKey` element is a unique key reference to the first `businessEntity` for which the assertion is made.

- **toKey** – The `toKey` element is a unique key reference to the second `businessEntity` for which the assertion is made.

- **keyedReference** – The `keyedReference` element designates the relationship type for which the assertion is made.

As an example of this issue, suppose the publishing company John Wiley has a registration of a particular service that it offers on the UDDI registry, and another company, XYZ Wholesale Booksellers, also has a particular service that it offers on the registry. XYZ Wholesale Booksellers would be unable to associate the two services unless John Wiley confirmed the association by also providing a reference to it within its own registration.

The UDDI programming model

The UDDI specification enables you to interact with two available APIs in a request/response model. The two APIs that are at your disposal as a programmer include a Publisher and an Inquiry API. The Publisher API allows you to publish services to a UDDI registry, and the Inquiry API enables you to programmatically inquire about available services.

Publisher APIs

The Publishing APIs simply enable you to programmatically save and delete the five data types that are made available to you through the UDDI data specification. The following table (Table 11-2) is a description of the available Publisher API functions.

Table 11-2: Publisher API Functions

Function	Description
add_publisherAssertions	This call is used to add relationship assertions to an existing set of assertions.
delete_binding	This call is used to remove an existing bindingTemplate from the bindingTemplates collection that is part of the specified businessService structure.
delete_business	This call is used to delete any registered businessEntity information from the registry.
delete_publisherAssertions	This call is used to delete certain publisher assertions from the assertion collection controlled by a specific publisher account.
delete_service	This call is used to delete an existing businessService from the businessServices collection that is part of a specified businessEntity.
delete_tModel	This call is used to hide registered information about a tModel. If you hide a tModel in this way, it is still usable for the purpose of referencing and will be accessible via the get_tModelDetail message, but it is simply hidden from find_tModel result sets. There is no way to actually cause a tModel to be deleted. The only way to delete is to petition the administration of the registry.

Function	Description
discard_authToken	This call is used to inform an Operator Node Site that a previously provided authentication token is no longer valid and should be deemed invalid if used after this message is received and until such time as an authToken value is recycled or reactivated at an operator's discretion. See get_authToken.
get_assertionStatusReport	This call is used to get a status report containing publisher assertions and status information. This report is useful to help an administrator manage active and tentative publisher assertions. Publisher assertions are used in UDDI to manage publicly visible relationships between businessEntity structures. Relationships are a feature that help manage complex business structures that require more than one businessEntity or more than one publisher account to manage parts of a businessEntity. This returns an assertionStatusReport that includes the status of all assertions made involving any businessEntity controlled by the requesting publisher account.
get_authToken	This call is used to request an authentication token from an Operator Site. Authentication tokens are required if you plan on using any of the functions from the publisher APIs. This function serves as the program's equivalent of a login request.
get_publisherAssertions	This call is used to get a list of active publisher assertions that are controlled by an individual publisher account. Returns a publisherAssertions message that contains all publisher assertions associated with a specific publisher account. Publisher assertions are used to control publicly visible business relationships.
get_registeredInfo	This call is used to request an abbreviated summary of all information currently administered by a given individual.
save_binding	This call is used to register new bindingTemplate information or update existing bindingTemplate information. Use this to control information about technical capabilities exposed by a registered business.

Function	Description
`save_business`	This call is used to register new businessEntity information or update existing businessEntity information. Use this when you wish to control the overall information about the entire business. Of the APIs that are able to save information, this one has the broadest effect. In UDDI V2, a feature is introduced that allows `save_business` to be used to reference a businessService that is parented by another businessEntity.
`save_service`	This call is used to register or update complete information about a businessService exposed by a specified businessEntity.
`save_tModel`	This call is used to register or update complete information about a tModel.
`set_publisherAssertions`	This call is used to save the complete set of publisher assertions for an individual publisher account. Replaces any existing assertions, and causes any old assertions that are not reasserted to be removed from the registry. Publisher assertions are used to control publicly visible business relationships.

The Publisher APIs at your disposal enable you to update and publish information to the UDDI registry. If you are going to make any changes to anything in the registry, you first have to be authenticated and authorized to make those changes by using the `get_authToken` call. Then you will be able to use this function as a parameter to any subsequent Publisher API function calls. After you are finished making any necessary changes, you need to use the `discard_authToken` function call to get rid of your authorization token. All these Publisher APIs can be invoked using SOAP from the UDDI registry.

Inquiry APIs

Not quite as big as the Publisher APIs, there is also a list of available Inquiry APIs that you can use to inquire about businesses and the services that they offer. Table 11-3 describes each of the Inquiry APIs at your disposal.

Table 11-3: Inquiry API Functions

Function	Description
find_binding	Used in locating specific bindings within a registered businessService. This function will return a bindingDetail message.
find_business	Used in locating information about one or more businesses. Returns a businessList message.
find_relatedBusinesses	Used in locating information about businessEntity registrations that are related to a specific business entity whose key is passed in the inquiry call. The Related Businesses feature is used to manage registration of business units and, subsequently, relate them based on organizational hierarchies or business partner relationships. Returns a relatedBusinessesList message.
find_service	Used in locating specific services within a registered businessEntity. Returns a serviceList message.
find_tModel	Used in locating one or more tModel information structures. Returns a tModelList structure.
get_bindingDetail	Used in getting full bindingTemplate information suitable for making one or more service requests. Returns a bindingDetail message.
get_businessDetail	Used in getting the full businessEntity information for one or more businesses or entities. Returns a businessDetail message.
get_businessDetailExt	Used in getting extended businessEntity information. Returns a businessDetailExt message.
get_serviceDetail	Used in getting full details for a given set of registered businessService data. Returns a serviceDetail message.
get_tModelDetail	Used in getting full details for a given set of registered tModel data. Returns a tModelDetail message.

All these Inquiry APIs support finding specific or full details about businesses or entities that are providing services through the UDDI registry. You can use the Inquiry APIs to find business contact information, lists of all the available services that they are exposing, or even links to the WSDL documents that you will need in order to bind to the services that they are exposing.

As an example, note how to use the `find_business` method call to find a business (Listing 11-7).

Listing 11-7: Using the find_business method call to find John Wiley

```
<?xml version="1.0" encoding="UTF-8" ?>
   <Envelope xmlns="http://schemas.xmlsoap.org/soap/envelope/">
      <Body>
         <find_business generic="2.0" xmlns="urn:uddi-org:api_v2">
            <name>John Wiley</name>
         </find_business>
      </Body>
</Envelope>
```

In this example, you requested the business name `John Wiley` using the `find_business` method call.

> **NOTE:** This example uses Version 2 of UDDI; at present, most UDDI registries are still using Version 1.

Using the Microsoft UDDI SDK

To avoid the complications of working with the UDDI APIs, Microsoft has provided the UDDI Software Development Kit. The UDDI SDK provides managed wrappers for the UDDI APIs so that you actually have to know very little about SOAP in order to publish or inquire about UDDI registry information.

By going to the UDDI MSDN page at `msdn.microsoft.com/uddi`, you can get the latest version of the UDDI SDK. As of this writing, the latest version is 1.75. This version of the UDDI SDK contains a class library that can be used to write client applications that can programmatically access any of the nodes from the UDDI specification.

> **NOTE:** You need to be running the .NET Framework in order to take advantage of the UDDI SDK. Also the UDDI SDK is meant to be run on the .NET Framework using tools like Visual Studio .NET. There is no support for using the UDDI SDK v1.75 with Visual Studio 6.0. If you want to use the UDDI SDK with Visual Studio 6.0, you need to download the UDDI SDK v1.52.

The UDDI SDK will be installed at `C:\Program Files\Microsoft UDDI SDK`. The UDDI SDK installs three items: The first is a .NET assembly, `Microsoft.Uddi.Sdk.dll`. This is installed to the Global Assembly Cache.

> **NOTE:** If you're unable to have this UDDI DLL in the Global Assembly Cache for any reason, just place it in the `bin` directory of your application.

The second item installed is `uddi.net.sdk.chm`, a help file. The last item installed is a folder containing samples that you can learn from.

The UDDI sample application

The UDDI SDK also comes with a sample application that can be loaded by choosing Start ⇨ All Programs ⇨ Microsoft UDDI SDK ⇨ UDDI Explorer .NET Sample. This will cause Visual Studio .NET to open a sample C# application that you can use to inquire about UDDI entries from a listing of different options. Pressing F5 and running the application will open up a simple Windows Form where you can select the operator node that you wish to inquire from and the name of the company or `tModel` that you want to search for.

For example, typing in **Microsoft** will provide you with a number of options that are then displayed in the text box (Figure 11-17).

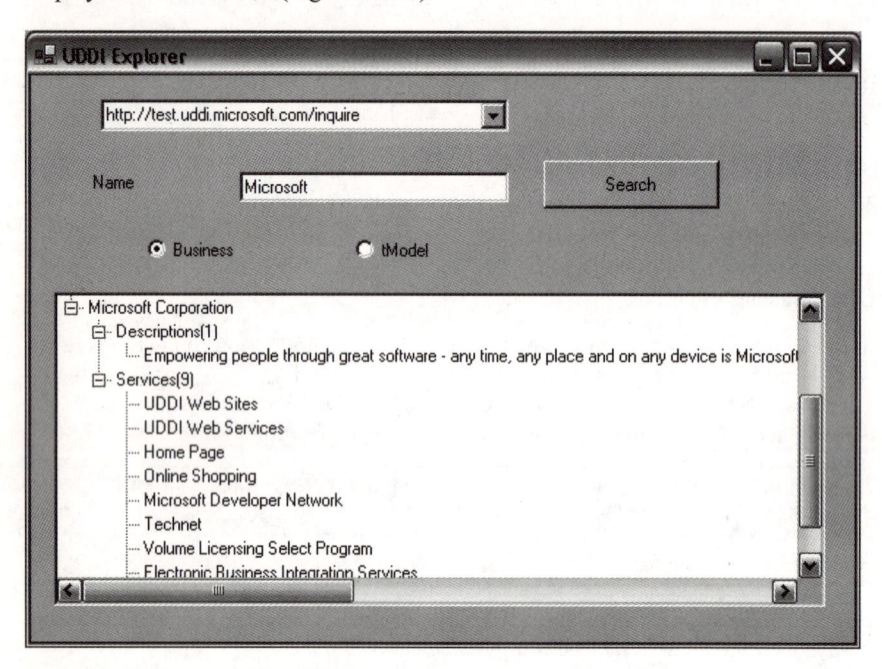

Figure 11-17: Using the sample UDDI Explorer to search for a business name.

This sample application is a good resource for understanding how to use the UDDI classes within your code.

Using the UDDI classes

The UDDI classes that are provided with the UDDI SDK are a powerful way to gain access to the Publishing and Inquiry UDDI APIs. These classes are all housed within the `Microsoft.UDDI` namespace. What makes it so easy to use these UDDI classes is that all the UDDI data structures that were discussed earlier in this chapter are represented as .NET classes along with many different properties.

Table 11-4 describes the `Microsoft.UDDI` namespace and the classes from the namespace that are at your disposal.

Table 11-4: Microsoft.UDDI Namespace

Namespace	Description
`Microsoft.UDDI`	This namespace includes the classes that map to the UDDI SOAP APIs.
`Microsoft.UDDI.Api`	Includes base classes and utility classes for the other namespaces.
`Microsoft.UDDI.Authentication`	Includes a class to denote an authentication token as well as classes for getting and discarding a token.
`Microsoft.UDDI.Binding`	Includes classes that represent binding template elements.
`Microsoft.UDDI.Business`	Includes classes that represent business entity elements.
`Microsoft.UDDI.Service`	Includes classes that represent business service elements.
`Microsoft.UDDI.ServiceType`	Includes classes that represent `tModel`, `tModelInstanceDetail`, and `tModelInstanceCollection` elements.

To make use of these UDDI classes within your client applications, you need to make a reference to the UDDI DLL. In order to do this, follow these steps:

1. Right-click on the project name within the Solution Explorer and select Add Reference.
2. In the Add Reference dialog window, scroll down until you find the `Microsoft.UDDI.SDK` reference. Highlight this option and click Select. After this is done, click OK. This is shown in Figure 11-18.

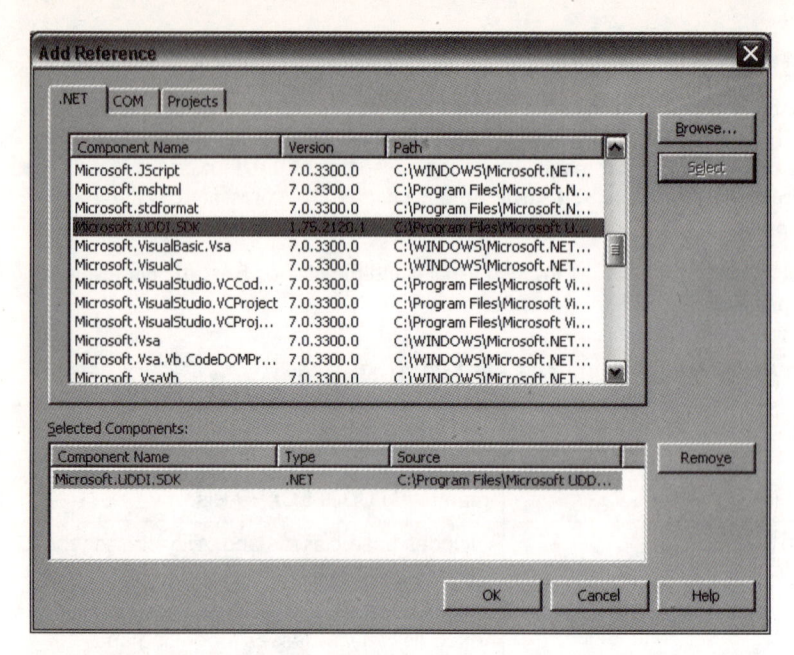

Figure 11-18: Adding the Microsoft.UDDI.SDK to the project by making a reference to it.

Now that you have made a reference to this DLL, you see it listed in the References folder within the Solution Explorer, as shown in Figure 11-19.

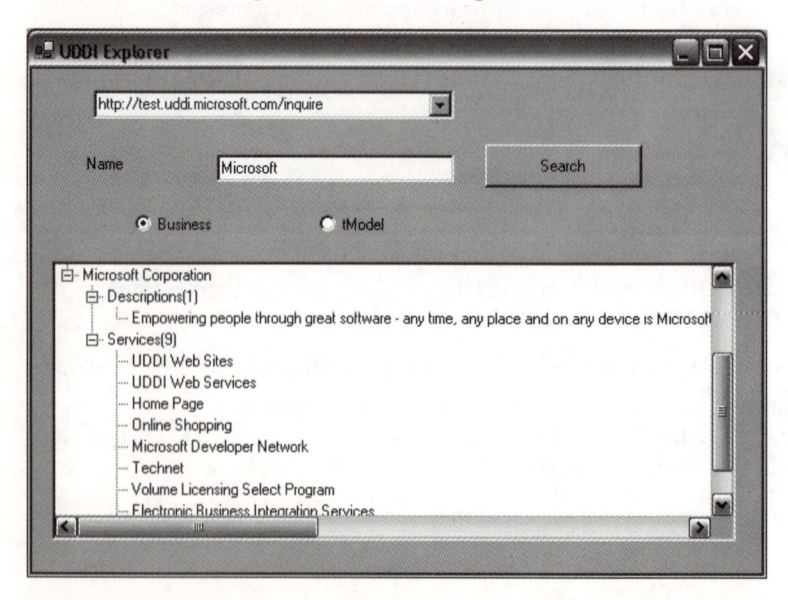

Figure 11-19: The reference in the Solution Explorer to the UDDI SDK DLL.

After this, you can easily make a reference to the objects within the classes by importing the appropriate namespaces into your pages.

Publishing to the UDDI registry using the UDDI SDK

Publishing your UDDI information programmatically is quite simple. There will be instances when you will prefer this way of registering with UDDI rather than using the Microsoft Web interface to the UDDI registry. For instance, if your application registers various XML Web services in the UDDI registry as part of an automatic installation process, you can automate it by providing the UDDI registration programmatically.

Authenticating and authorizing yourself to register

Before you publish anything to the UDDI registry, you first need to be authenticated and authorized. To get authenticated and authorized, you must have a Microsoft Passport login and password. After you have a Passport login in place, import in the `Microsoft.UDDI` namespace into your page or application. After that, test the process of being authenticated using the code in Listing 11-8:

Listing 11-8: Getting authenticated on the UDDI registry programmatically

VB

```
Publish.Url = "https://test.uddi.microsoft.com/publish"
Publish.User = strYourLogin
Publish.Password = strYourPassword

Literal1.Text = "Authenticated and authorized!"
```

C#

```
Publish.Url = "https://test.uddi.microsoft.com/publish";
Publish.User = strYourLogin;
Publish.Password = strYourPassword;

Literal1.Text = "Authenticated and authorized!";
```

Using this code in the `Page_Load` event of an ASP.NET Web Application gives you a notice after you have successfully put a proper value as the password into the registry. Be sure to put a Literal Web control on the `.aspx` page.

Notice that you are using the Microsoft Test UDDI registry using HTTPS. It is better to test all this on the test registry, as opposed to practicing your programming skills on the actual registry. Now that you are authenticated and authorized to proceed, the UDDI registry has given you an authentication token that you can use to publish your information to the registry.

Publishing a tModel

As easy as it was to get yourself authenticated and authorized to use the UDDI registry, it is just as simple to publish a `tModel` to your registration. Remember that you are allowed up to 10 `tModels` for every business entity.

Part IV: XML Web Services Description and Discovery

Before you actually get to the point where you use a `bindingTemplate` to associate a `tModel` with a `businessService`, you need to create the `tModel`. The code in Listing 11-9 shows you how to publish a `tModel` to your registration. Put this code after your authentication and authorization code.

Listing 11-9: Publishing a tModel to the UDDI registry

VB

```
Dim stm As New SaveTModel()
stm.TModels.Add()
stm.TModels(0).Name = "Name of tModel goes here."
stm.TModels(0).Descriptions.Add("en", "This is the description")
stm.TModels(0).OverviewDoc.OverviewURL =
  "http://www.mySite.com/myWsdlFile.wsdl"
stm.TModels(0).CategoryBag.Add("uddi-org:types", "wsdlSpec",
                    "uuid:c1acf26d-9672-4404-9d70-39b756e62ab4")

Dim myTModelKey As String = ""

Try
   Dim tmd As TModelDetail = stm.Send()
   myTModelKey = tmd.TModels(0).TModelKey

   Literal1.Text = "Success! Here is my TModelKey value: " + myTModelKey
Catch ue As UddiException
   Literal1.Text = ue.Message
Catch ue2 As Exception
   Literal1.Text = ue2.Message
End Try
```

C#

```
SaveTModel stm = New SaveTModel();
stm.TModels.Add();
stm.TModels[0].Name = "Name of tModel goes here.";
stm.TModels[0].Descriptions.Add("en", "This is the description");
stm.TModels[0].OverviewDoc.OverviewURL =
                    "http://www.mySite.com/myWsdlFile.wsdl";
stm.TModels[0].CategoryBag.Add("uddi-org:types", "wsdlSpec",
                    "uuid:c1acf26d-9672-4404-9d70-39b756e62ab4");

string myTModelKey = "";

try
{
   TModelDetail tmd = stm.Send();
   myTModelKey = tmd.TModels[0].TModelKey;

   Literal1.Text = ("Success! Here is my TModelKey value: " +
```

```
            myTModelKey);
}
catch (UddiException ue)
{
   Literal1.Text = ue.Message;
   return;
}
catch (Exception ue2)
{
   Literal1.Text = ue2.Message;
   return;
}
```

Using this code after the authentication and authorization code, you can publish a `tModel` to the UDDI registry. In the beginning of the code, you are providing a name and description of the `tModel` that you are creating. You also make a reference to the WSDL file, specifying the file location by using the `OverviewDoc.OverviewURL` property. After this, you specify a single classification for this particular tModel, although you can have more than one classification if you want to. At a minimum, you should classify your XML Web service using the UDDI taxonomy stating that this is a specification for a Web service (`wsdlSpec`). After this `tModel` is registered in the UDDI registry, a unique identifier is created for you that represents this particular `tModel`, and that key is displayed to the page using a Literal Web control.

Publishing a businessEntity, businessService, and a bindingTemplate

After creating a `tModel`, you can create a business entry. You are allowed to have one business entry per registration unless you are given special permission by the folks at UDDI to become a Level 2 registrant. Level 2 registrants can have more than one business registration. Creating a `businessEntity` with which your Web service will be associated is fairly simple and straightforward. After your `businessEntity` is in place, you can associate a service with this business. After the service is in place, you populate the binding information and associate the `tModel` that was created earlier to this particular service. The code in Listing 11-10 is used following the `tModel` code in the `Page_Load` event of the ASP.NET Web application. For this example, you add a second Literal Web control to the `.aspx` page.

Listing 11-10: Publishing a businessEntity, businessService, bindingTemplate to the UDDI registry

VB

```
'Create businessEntity
Dim sb As New SaveBusiness()
sb.BusinessEntities.Add()
sb.BusinessEntities(0).Name = "Your business name goes here."
sb.BusinessEntities(0).Descriptions.Add("en", "The business desc. goes
  here.")

'Create businessService
```

```
sb.BusinessEntities(0).BusinessServices.Add()
sb.BusinessEntities(0).BusinessServices(0).Name = "My XML Web service"
sb.BusinessEntities(0).BusinessServices(0).Descriptions.Add("en", "The
  service description goes here.")

'Create bindingTemplate
sb.BusinessEntities(0).BusinessServices(0).BindingTemplates.Add()
sb.BusinessEntities(0).BusinessServices(0).BindingTemplates(0).
  Descriptions.Add("en", "The binding description goes here.")
sb.BusinessEntities(0).BusinessServices(0).BindingTemplates(0).
  AccessPoint.Text = "http://www.myServer.com/myWebService.asmx"
sb.BusinessEntities(0).BusinessServices(0).BindingTemplates(0).
  AccessPoint.URLType = Api.URLTypeEnum.Http

'Create tModelInstanceInfo
sb.BusinessEntities(0).BusinessServices(0).BindingTemplates(0).
  TModelInstanceDetail.TModelInstanceInfos.Add()
sb.BusinessEntities(0).BusinessServices(0).BindingTemplates(0).
  TModelInstanceDetail.TModelInstanceInfos(0).
  Descriptions.Add("en", "The description goes here.")
sb.BusinessEntities(0).BusinessServices(0).BindingTemplates(0).
  TModelInstanceDetail.TModelInstanceInfos(0).
  TModelKey = myTModelKey

Try
   Dim bd As New BusinessDetail()
   bd = sb.Send()

   Literal2.Text = bd.ToString()
Catch ue As UddiException
   Literal2.Text = ue.Message
Catch ue2 As Exception
   Literal2.Text = ue2.Message
End Try
```

C#

```
//Create businessEntity
SaveBusiness sb = New SaveBusiness();
sb.BusinessEntities.Add();
sb.BusinessEntities[0].Name = "Your business name goes here.";
sb.BusinessEntities[0].Descriptions.Add("en", "The business desc. goes
  here.");

//Create businessService
sb.BusinessEntities[0].BusinessServices.Add();
sb.BusinessEntities[0].BusinessServices[0].Name = "My XML Web service";
sb.BusinessEntities[0].BusinessServices[0].Descriptions.Add("en", "The
  service description goes here.");
```

```
//Create bindingTemplate
sb.BusinessEntities[0].BusinessServices[0].BindingTemplates.Add();
sb.BusinessEntities[0].BusinessServices[0].BindingTemplates[0].
   Descriptions.Add("en", "The binding description goes here.");
sb.BusinessEntities[0].BusinessServices[0].BindingTemplates[0].
   AccessPoint.Text = "http://www.myServer.com/myWebService.asmx";
sb.BusinessEntities[0].BusinessServices[0].BindingTemplates[0].
   AccessPoint.URLType = Api.URLTypeEnum.Http;

//Create tModelInstanceInfo
sb.BusinessEntities[0].BusinessServices[0].BindingTemplates[0].
   TModelInstanceDetail.TModelInstanceInfos.Add();
sb.BusinessEntities[0].BusinessServices[0].BindingTemplates[0].
   TModelInstanceDetail.TModelInstanceInfos[0].
   Descriptions.Add("en", "The description goes here.");
sb.BusinessEntities[0].BusinessServices[0].BindingTemplates[0].
   TModelInstanceDetail.TModelInstanceInfos[0].
   TModelKey = myTModelKey;

try
{
   BusinessDetail bd = New BusinessDetail();
   bd = sb.Send();

   Literal2.Text = bd.ToString();
}
catch (UddiException ue)
{
   Literal2.Text = ue.Message;
   return;
}
catch (Exception ue2)
   Literal2.Text = ue2.Message;
   return;
}
```

After creating a business description, you can create a service along with the service description that is associated with this particular business. After the service and the service description are in place, you provide the binding information for that service. Then using the tModelInstanceInfo, you associate this particular bindingTemplate with the tModel that you created in the first part of the Page_Load event by assigning it the myTModelKey value.

There is a lot to UDDI, but both Microsoft and IBM have made it easy for you to register the services that your business offers. In addition to this public registry, Microsoft now provides the means to have your own private UDDI registries using the Windows .NET Servers.

Windows .NET Servers

The new Windows .NET Servers have built-in native UDDI support, providing you with a UDDI registry for your own private use. The Windows .NET Standard Server, Enterprise Server, and Datacenter Server have this built-in support for UDDI, whereas the Windows .NET Server is the only server in the family without built-in UDDI support.

If you have your own private UDDI registry within your business or organization, you are able to share Web service descriptions throughout your organization and, at the same time, keep these descriptions out of the public eye. For larger organizations, there will be many internal Web services that are used company-wide, but are not meant for the general public. This private UDDI registry enables you to propagate this description information.

The UDDI registry is not only for internal use; you can use this private registry for an extranet as well. The following diagram (Figure 11-20) shows a sample private UDDI registry.

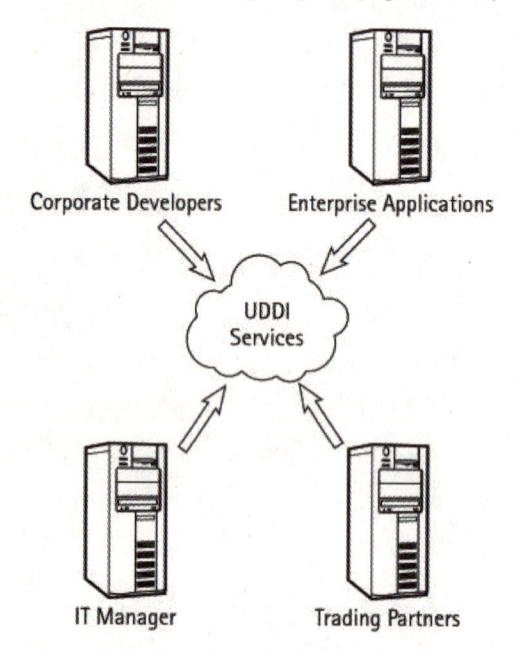

Figure 11-20: Everyone is able to view the internal Web service using the Windows .NET Server's UDDI registry.

Using the registry in this kind of scenario, you will find that your developers will be more efficient. They will have the ability to share and reuse Web services easily because they are able to find them quickly. This registry gives developers the ability to broadcast the Web services that they have constructed company-wide. You can open the registry for your customers as well, through an extranet of some kind. This will enable your customers to access the registry to find Web services that you wish to make available to them.

Summary

UDDI is a pillar in the XML Web services model that enables you to publish your XML Web services for others to consume, as well as to find Web services that you can use within your client applications. Only in its second version, UDDI has, in this short time, become the standard way to publish and inquire about XML Web services.

As time goes on, you will find more and more applications and platforms that will have UDDI support built right in. One example of this is the next generation of servers that is available from Microsoft, the Windows .NET Servers with native UDDI support built right into the product.

Like a lot of the other pieces of the XML Web services model, UDDI is built upon open standards such as XML and SOAP. Like the other technologies that are used in the Web services model, UDDI is transparent and there are plenty of tools in place that can do much of the plumbing work for you if you choose.

Chapter 12

Disco

The process of discovery is very simple.
An unwearied and systematic application of known laws
to nature causes the unknown to reveal themselves.
Henry David Thoreau, *A Week on the Concord and Merrimack Rivers* (1849)

If, as you open up this chapter, you are wondering what a popular dance from the 1970s has to do with XML Web services, you will probably be disappointed to learn that the answer is, "Very little." Most programmers I know have little time for disco dancing. Instead, Disco (in Microsoft terminology) has to do with the *disco*very of Web services.

So far in this book, you have learned how to describe your XML Web services using WSDL and how to publish these services to a globally accessible registry. In this chapter, you will learn about Web services discovery. Web services discovery is the process by which you can locate a Web service, as well as its descriptions, in order to interact with it.

This chapter addresses

- Understanding `.disco` files
- Working with `.vsdisco` files
- Using Disco.exe in the discovery process

The Discovery Step

The discovery process is an important step for both the consumer of an XML Web service and the publisher of the service. The creator of the XML Web service designed it to be consumed by a company or the general public. For the consumer, the person who is building an XML Web services client application, the discovery process is one of the first and most important steps in the entire process. He wants to find the Web service that will provide whatever he needs in his application. Choosing the incorrect Web service can spell disaster for the client application. It is even worse if the user cannot find an XML Web service that can do what he needs done. The entire discovery process is important for both parties.

After reading the chapters on WSDL and UDDI, you may wonder why you need another way to find an XML Web service. Even though ASP.NET can automatically create a WSDL file for a Web service, and the developer can also go to the UDDI registry and publish a Web service for the world to see, you still need the discovery process. You need it because not everyone takes the steps to publish information on all Web services. Therefore, there must be a way for you, as a consumer, to discover XML Web services and to locate WSDL files at known endpoints.

The .NET Framework has provided you with a discovery model (Disco) that you can use to do this. By using Disco, you can catalog all the Web services available at a particular endpoint and then locate the WSDL files for these particular Web services.

The Disco File

The Disco file is automatically generated by ASP.NET for any XML Web service that you build upon the .NET platform. It is also possible to create your own Disco files if you choose.

The purpose of the Disco file, as it relates to an XML Web service, is to provide a means of discovering the details about a particular XML Web service. The Disco file provides *static discovery* to find XML Web service details. Static discovery is a means of obtaining the discovery document in order to interpret its contents. You can use static discovery when you know the location of an XML Web service discovery document (.disco file).

Viewing the .disco file that describes your own XML Web service is as simple as viewing the WSDL file. To view the .disco file for any XML Web service built upon the .NET platform, simple add a ?disco to the end of the file address.

```
http://localhost/TestWS/Service1.asmx?disco
```

This causes ASP.NET to dynamically create a .disco file for that particular XML Web service. Doing this to the Calculator XML Web service (demonstrated throughout this book) gives you the .disco file shown in Figure 12-1.

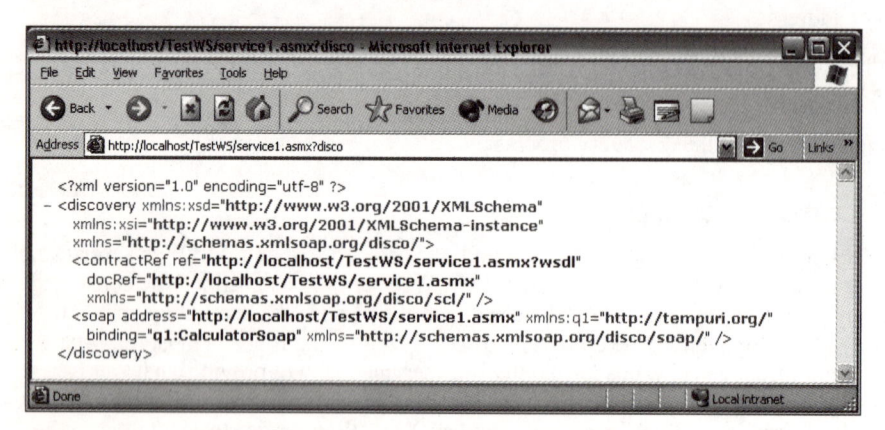

Figure 12-1: Viewing the Disco file for the Calculator XML Web service.

This Disco file describes the XML Web service's WSDL location. The Disco file is created dynamically by ASP.NET. It is possible for you to create your own Disco files and put them wherever you choose, even on a separate server.

These Disco files can be used to point to a particular XML Web service (as shown in Figure 12-1) or even to point to other discovery documents. You will have one Disco file for each XML Web service that you create in ASP.NET.

You can use this Disco file as a link to your XML Web service by using it as a discovery link within UDDI. The end user, the XML Web service consumer, can then use this link within the Add Web Reference dialog window. This dialog window accepts `.disco` files and, after the files are accepted, Visual Studio .NET creates the proxy class based on the information contained within the file.

> **NOTE:** Disco is a Microsoft technology and is currently not supported by any other Web service's platform other than the ASP.NET Web services platform in the .NET Framework. There is nothing within the Disco files, however, that has to be run on the .NET platform; therefore, it is possible for Web service developers on other platforms to create Disco files that point to the discovery of their Web services. Disco is based upon XML and, therefore, any platform that can work with XML is able to work with Disco.

The Disco file structure

This Disco file is simple and easy to understand. Like most of the technologies that deal with XML Web services, Disco is a technology that uses XML. Disco uses an XML grammar to provide discovery information regardless of the platform performing the discovery.

Just like other technologies that are built using XML, Disco starts off with an XML declaration:

```
<?xml version="1.0" encoding="utf-8" ?>
  <discovery xmlns:xsd="http://www.w3.org/2001/XMLSchema"
   xmlns:xsi="http://www.w3.org/2001/XMLSchema-instance"
   xmlns="http://schemas.xmlsoap.org/disco/">
    <contractRef ref="http://localhost/TestWS/service1.asmx?wsdl"
     docRef="http://localhost/TestWS/service1.asmx"
     xmlns="http://schemas.xmlsoap.org/disco/scl/" />
    <documentRef ref="http://localhost/TestWS/Service2.asmx?disco" />
    <schemaRef ref="http://localhost/TestWS/myXSDfile.xsd" />
    <soap address="http://localhost/TestWS/service1.asmx"
     xmlns:q1="http://tempuri.org/" binding="q1:CalculatorSoap"
     xmlns="http://schemas.xmlsoap.org/disco/soap/" />
  </discovery>
```

After this, the Disco file is made up of five parts:

- `<discovery>` - Header
- `<contractRef>` - Contract
- `<discoveryRef>` - Discovery
- `<schemaRef>` - Schema
- `<soap>` - Soap Binding

Take a quick look at these different sections of the Disco file.

<discovery>

The `<discovery>` element is the root element of the Disco file. It is also a mandatory element used to specify any namespaces that are used throughout the Disco file.

```
<discovery xmlns:xsd="http://www.w3.org/2001/XMLSchema"
 xmlns:xsi="http://www.w3.org/2001/XMLSchema-instance"
 xmlns="http://schemas.xmlsoap.org/disco/">
```

In this example, the `<discovery>` element contains a mandatory reference to the discovery namespace at `http://schemas.xmlsoap.org/disco/`. This is not an actual file endpoint, but a unique namespace identifier. The namespace also indicates that this Disco file conforms to the XML Disco standard.

This root discovery document and any referenced discovery documents that are contained within it make up the catalog of XML Web services available at this endpoint.

<contractRef>

The `<contractRef>` element is used to define the location of the WSDL files. If you are looking for WSDL files, this is the element that you use. This example has a single `<contractRef>` element.

```
<contractRef ref="http://localhost/TestWS/service1.asmx?wsdl"
 docRef="http://localhost/TestWS/service1.asmx"
 xmlns="http://schemas.xmlsoap.org/disco/scl/" />
```

Using the attribute `ref`, the `<contractRef>` element specifies the location of the WSDL document. Recall that the WSDL document is used to describe the XML Web service and all the available methods at the disposal of the end user. The end user can look at the parameters these methods take, including their types, and can also learn what to expect in return from the XML Web service, including the types returned.

> **CROSS-REFERENCE:** WSDL is covered in Chapter 10.

Currently, you are only able to specify WSDL documents within the `ref` attribute because other description types are not supported within this attribute. This singular support level is evident with the `xmlns` attribute that points at the Service Contract Language namespace.

In this example, the `docRef` attribute points to the actual XML Web service file `http://localhost/TestWS/service1.asmx`. ASP.NET, with its autogeneration of the Disco file, will always use the `docRef` attribute to point to the `.asmx` file of the XML Web service, although this attribute is not a requirement. The `docRef` is just what you might think; it is a reference document. Therefore, any appropriate file can be a reference document.. This personalization of the `docRef` attribute is only possible, however, if you create your own Disco files. If you choose to do this, you may point the `docRef` to other Help documents or to those that give more information on your XML Web service.

The autogenerated Disco file from ASP.NET will always contain just one `<contractRef>` element. If you are building your own Disco file, however, you can have as many `<contractRef>` elements as you choose. Using multiple `<contractRef>` elements will enable you to point to additional resources in order to provide a richer discovery for the end user.

<discoveryRef>

The `<discoveryRef>` element provides linkage to additional discovery documents. This can be a powerful tool, creating a tree-like structure to facilitate the discovery of XML Web services. Therefore, search engine spiders and applications built on discovery models are able to peruse these discovery documents, linking onto other discovery documents in an effort to catalog them. The `<discoveryRef>` element is structured as shown:

```
<documentRef ref="http://localhost/TestWS/Service2.asmx?disco" />
```

The `<discoveryRef>` is not used in the autogenerated version of an XML Web service's Disco document, but it can be used in the version that you create yourself. The `<documentRef>` element contains a single attribute, `ref`. The `ref` attribute's value is used to point to another Disco file. When you use this capability to point to other Disco files, you are not limited to a single `<documentRef>` element, but your Disco files can have multiple Disco references. You will see an example of this later in the chapter.

<schemaRef>

The `<schemaRef>` element is used to specify an XML Schema Definition (XSD), which describes the different data types that are being returned by the XML Web service. An example of the `<schemaRef>` element is as follows:

```
<schemaRef ref="http://localhost/TestWS/myXSDfile.xsd" />
```

Just like the `<discoveryRef>` element, the `<schemaRef>` element is not used in the autogenerated version of the XML Web service's Disco document, but it can be used in the version that you create for yourself. The `<schemaRef>` element also contains the attribute `ref`. The `ref` attribute's value is used to point to the XSD file.

<soap>

The `<soap>` element shows you some of the information that is available from the WSDL file regarding binding. The following code offers an example of the `<soap>` element in the Disco file:

```
<soap address="http://localhost/TestWS/service1.asmx"
     xmlns:q1="http://tempuri.org/" binding="q1:CalculatorSoap"
     xmlns="http://schemas.xmlsoap.org/disco/soap/" />
```

In this example, there are a couple of namespace references. The first is a reference to a SOAP namespace, `http://schemas.xmlsoap.org/disco/soap/`. It specifies that this element adheres to SOAP as used in Disco. The second is the namespace that is used in the XML Web service. Because there isn't one assigned for this particular XML Web service, the `<soap>` element uses the temporary URI namespace, `http://tempuri.org/`.

In addition to these namespace declarations, there are two additional attributes, `address` and `binding`. The `address` attribute points to the XML Web service that it refers to. The `binding` attribute points to the SOAP binding information that is taken from the WSDL file.

Putting it within the Disco file is a quicker way for discoverers to find information about the XML Web service in question.

Creating your own .disco file

The easiest way to create your own `.disco` file is to do so in Visual Studio .NET, although you could also create it with Notepad and save your filename with a `.disco` file extension. If you plan to build the file within Visual Studio .NET, add a new file to your ASP.NET Web service project. Choose the Static Discovery File from the Add New Item dialog window, as shown in Figure 12-2.

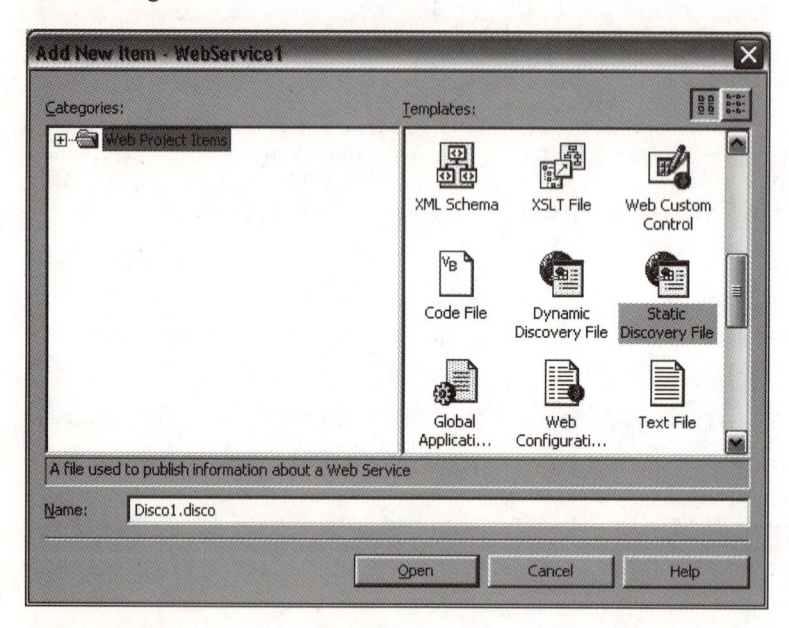

Figure 12-2: Creating your own .disco file in Visual Studio .NET. Choose the Static Discovery File from the Add New Item dialog window.

After you have added a .disco file to your project, you will be presented with the file in the code window of Visual Studio .NET (Figure 12-3).

```
1  <?xml version="1.0" encoding="utf-8" ?>
2  <discovery xmlns="http://schemas.xmlsoap.org/disco/">
3  </discovery>
4
```

Figure 12-3: The .disco file that is added to a project within Visual Studio .NET.

This file contains only the `<xml>` tag along with the document's root element, the `<discovery>` element. You create the rest of the document, using any of the elements that were described earlier. After it is created, you can use this file as the discovery document for your XML Web services.

The great thing about creating your own `.disco` files is that you can make the file much more descriptive than is possible with the autogenerated Disco file. For instance, with your own created `.disco` file, you can add multiple `<contractRef>` elements, which are used to provide descriptions of the XML Web services by locating WSDL files. You can also have multiple `<discoveryRef>` elements within your self-created `.disco` files. Using the `<discoveryRef>` to point to another discovery document gives users multiple Web services discovery. For example, if a single Web service referenced two other Web services that each referenced two other Web services, the discovery method would be outstanding. Figure 12-4 shows an example of this tree-like discovery model.

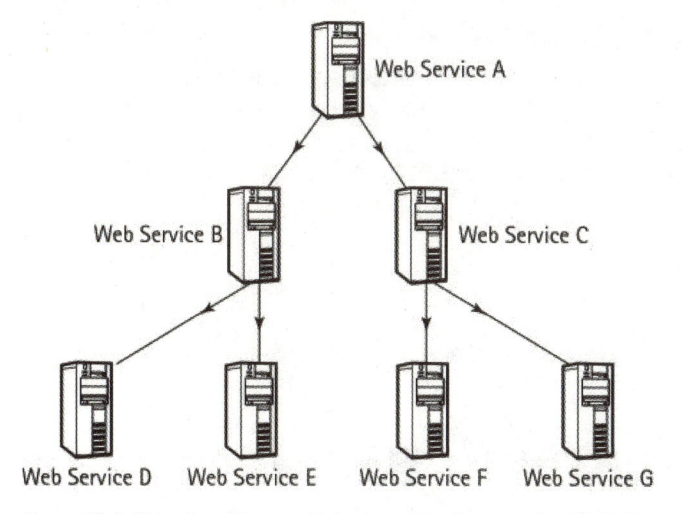

Figure 12-4: Using the <discoveryRef> element to discover other Disco files.

Figure 12-4 demonstrates discovery of Web services that are located on separate servers. All these Web services can also be located on the same server.

To create a Disco file, use the following code:

```
<?xml version="1.0" encoding="utf-8" ?>
<discovery xmlns:xsd="http://www.w3.org/2001/XMLSchema"
 xmlns:xsi="http://www.w3.org/2001/XMLSchema-instance"
 xmlns="http://schemas.xmlsoap.org/disco/">
  <contractRef ref="http://localhost/WebService1/service1.asmx?wsdl"
    docRef="http://localhost/WebService1/service1.asmx"
    xmlns="http://schemas.xmlsoap.org/disco/scl/" />
  <discoveryRef ref="http://localhost/TestWS/service1.asmx?disco" />
</discovery>
```

This Disco file is used as a discovery document for a Web service at /WebService1/service1.asmx. In this code, the Disco document is also expanded a bit, and there is an additional reference to another discovery document for a totally different Web service using the <discoveryRef> element.

So, in an XML Web service client application, when you add a Web reference, add it to this newly created .disco file. Typing the address of the document in the address bar of the Add Web Reference dialog window will give you the following result (shown in Figure 12-5):

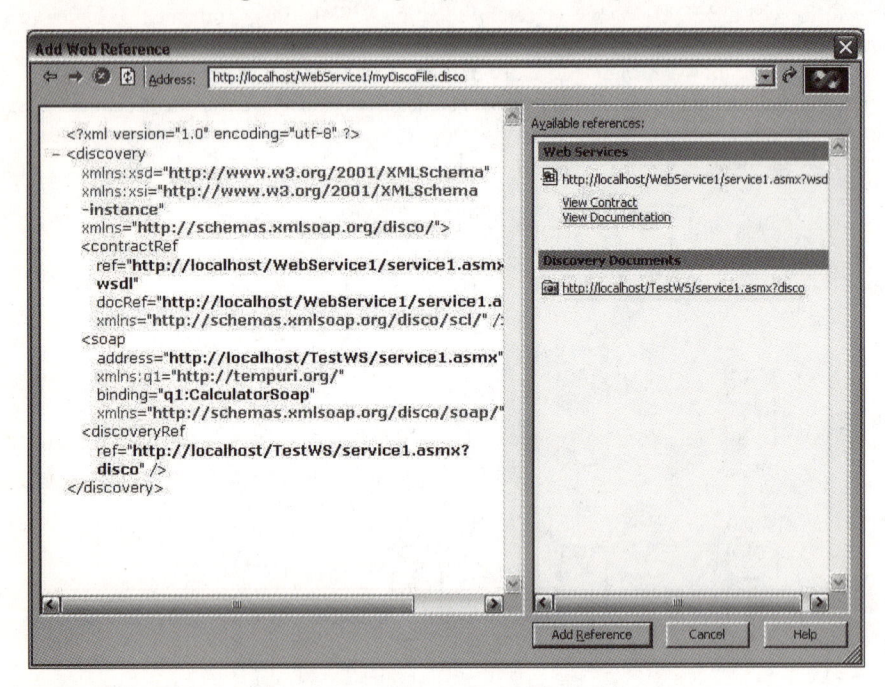

Figure 12-5: Calling a created Disco file in the Add Web Reference dialog window.

In the Add Web Reference dialog window, you can see the Disco document in the left pane. The right pane displays the available references. The first reference is the one specified in this particular Disco file. The second Web reference is a totally different Disco file that is associated with a different Web service. You created this reference using the <discoveryRef> element. Any additional references that you add to the Disco file using this element will show up under the Discovery Documents heading in the list of available references.

After you have created a Disco file, save the file and put it wherever you choose. It doesn't matter where the file is located; it can even be on a separate server from that of the XML Web service it represents. The only requirement is that the Disco file be located in a place where the end user can gain access to it through the browser or through Visual Studio .NET.

The .vsdisco File

So far you have seen that using `.disco` files is a fairly simple and straightforward way to discover XML Web services. This method of discovering XML Web services is known as static discovery. Static discovery is possible when you know the address of the XML Web service that you are interested in discovering. This may not always be the case. If you do not know the address, you may want to use *dynamic discovery*.

Dynamic discovery is best used when you don't know the particular endpoint of a certain XML Web service, but you do know the endpoint of the Web service provider. Dynamic discovery uses a document other than `.disco` for discovery. Instead of the `.disco` document, when using dynamic discovery you are interacting with `.vsdisco` files that, in turn, catalog all the available XML Web services in a particular project or Web site. The diagram in Figure 12-6 illustrates this:

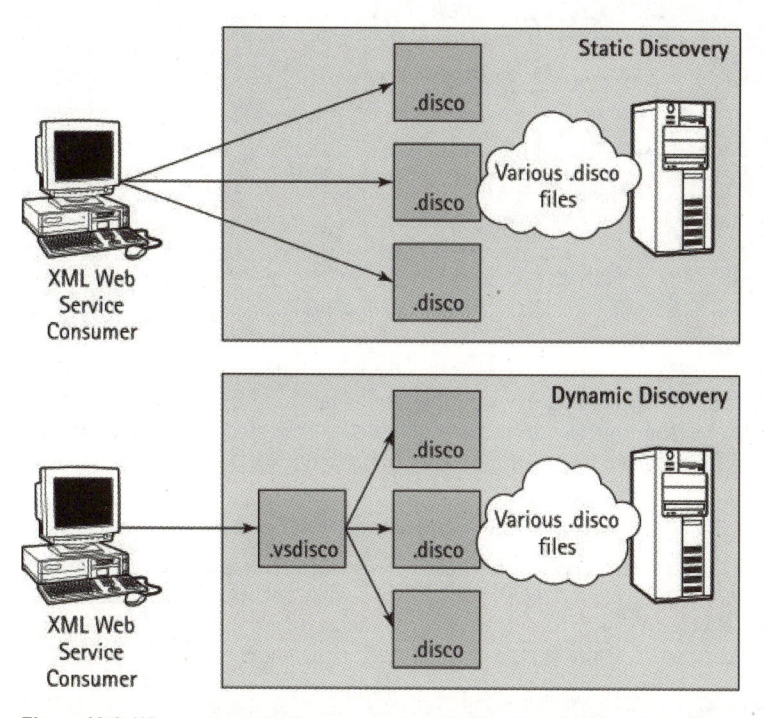

Figure 12-6: When using static discovery, you are looking at each of the .disco files separately. With dynamic discovery, you are using one file to find all the available .disco documents.

By default, when the .NET Framework is installed, the capability to access your `.vsdisco` file is turned off. This is done for security reasons and you can easily change it; although, in most cases, you want to have dynamic discovery disabled.

In order to enable dynamic discovery on a server that hosts XML Web services, you need to make a change within the `machine.config` file. This file controls configuration settings for everything that resides on the server as a whole. You can find the `machine.config` file at C:\Windows\Microsoft.NET\Framework\v1.0.*XXXX*\CONFIG\machine.config.

Within this file, find the following piece of code:

```
<httpHandlers>
 <!--<add verb="*" path="*.vsdisco"
   type="System.Web.Services.Discovery.DiscoveryRequestHandler,
   System.Web.Services, Version=1.0.3300.0, Culture=neutral,
   PublicKeyToken=b03f5f7f11d50a3a" validate="false"/>-->
 <add verb="*" path="trace.axd"
   type="System.Web.Handlers.TraceHandler"/>
 <add verb="*" path="*.aspx" type="System.Web.UI.PageHandlerFactory"/>
 <add verb="*" path="*.ashx" type="System.Web.UI.SimpleHandlerFactory"/>
 <add verb="*" path="*.asmx"
   type="System.Web.Services.Protocols.WebServiceHandlerFactory,
   System.Web.Services, Version=1.0.3300.0, Culture=neutral,
   PublicKeyToken=b03f5f7f11d50a3a" validate="false"/>
 <add verb="*" path="*.rem"
   type="System.Runtime.Remoting.Channels.Http.
   HttpRemotingHandlerFactory, System.Runtime.Remoting,
   Version=1.0.3300.0, Culture=neutral, PublicKeyToken=b77a5c561934e089"
   validate="false"/>

 <!-- THERE IS A LOT MORE LISTED HERE THAT I REMOVED -->

</httpHandlers>
```

The `<httpHanders>` section of the `machine.config` file takes care of all the file types that can be viewed from the server. Notice that the very first one is the `.vsdisco` file, and the reason that access to the `.vsdisco` file is disabled is that it is commented out. So to enable dynamic discovery on the server as a whole, you simply remove the starting and ending comments and resave the file.

Creating a `.vsdisco` file is just as easy as creating the .disco file. When you create a project using Visual Studio .NET, it creates a `[ProjectName].vsdisco` file for you automatically within the root directory of your project. Using dynamic discovery is a means of letting ASP.NET iterate through a hierarchy of folders in order to locate any XML Web services that might be there. A sample `.vsdisco` file is shown in the following code:

```
<?xml version="1.0" encoding="utf-8" ?>
<dynamicDiscovery xmlns="urn:schemas-dynamicdiscovery:disco.2000-03-17">
    <exclude path="_vti_cnf" />
    <exclude path="_vti_pvt" />
    <exclude path="_vti_log" />
    <exclude path="_vti_script" />
    <exclude path="_vti_txt" />
    <exclude path="Web References" />
</dynamicDiscovery>
```

The root element of the `.vsdisco` file is the `<dynamicDiscovery>` element. Contained within this element are any number of `<exclude>` elements. The `<exclude>` element is used to keep ASP.NET from searching through specific paths. You block a specific path by including this relative location as the value of the path attribute.

For an example of how this works, create a new Web service, `Service1.asmx`, and uncomment out the *Hello World* example within the function. Save the file and then create a second XML Web service, `Service2.asmx`, again uncommenting out the Hello World example.. Now you should have one project with two XML Web services. There will already be a single `.vsdisco` document within the root directory of the Web service that was created when the project was originally created. Next, make a Web reference to the particular `.vsdisco` file that is contained within this project. It makes sense to call the reference from a separate project, but just for demonstration sake, you can do it here. If you type the address of the `.vsdisco` file in the address bar of the Add Web Reference dialog window, you are presented with two available choices to reference. This is shown in Figure 12-7.

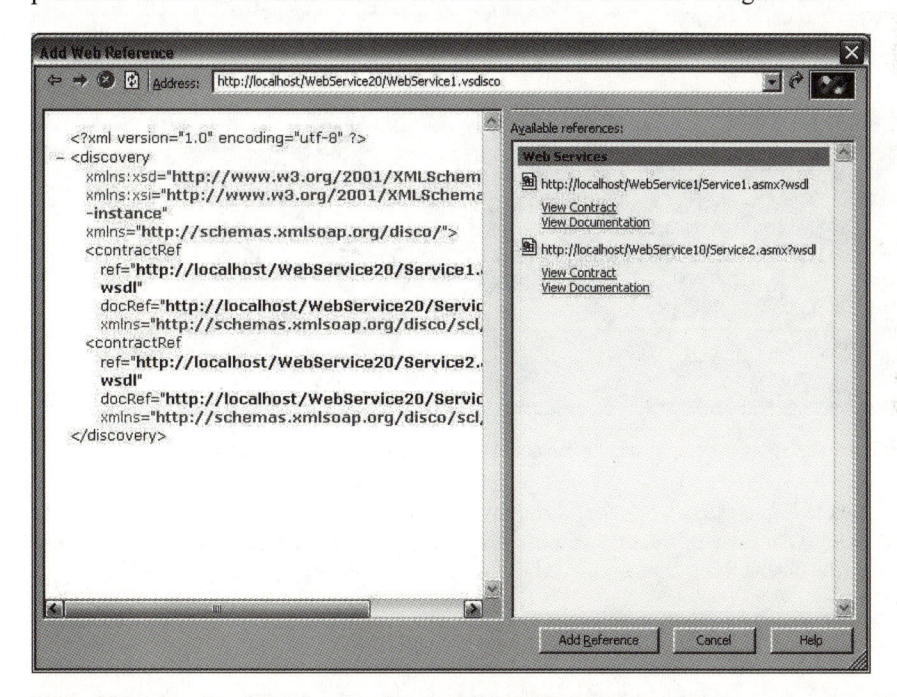

Figure 12-7: Using the .vsdisco file to discover multiple XML Web services at once.

Using the `.vsdisco` properly, you can create references to all your available XML Web services in one file, making it quite easy for others to discover all that you have available.

Using Disco.exe

You can use a Microsoft Web services discovery tool within the .NET Framework called Disco.exe to discover the endpoints of Web services and save these discovery documents on your local hard drive.

To use the tool, open the command prompt and go to the directory where the Disco executable is located. You will find this in `C:\Program Files\Microsoft Visual Studio .NET\FrameworkSDK\Bin`. After you are in the proper directory, you can use Disco.exe to copy the discovery documents to your local hard drive by using the following syntax:

```
disco [options] URL
```

For instance, if you start with the location of a known Disco file on your local server without using any options, you use the following command:

```
disco http://localhost/TestWS/Service1.asmx?disco
```

Figure 12-8 shows an example of this.

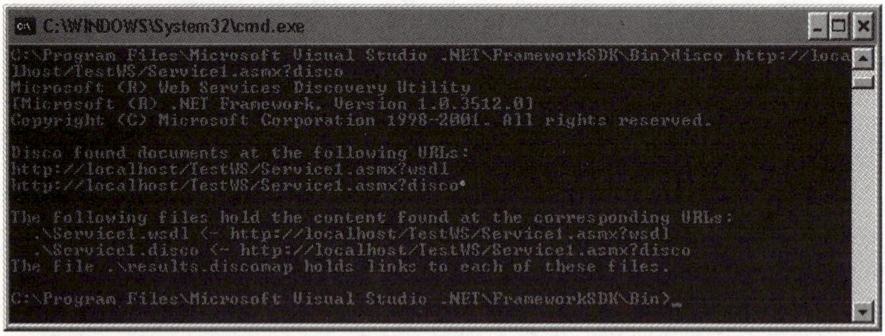

Figure 12-8: Using Disco.exe to discover information about a particular XML Web service.

Running this executable causes the .NET Framework to examine the disco file that you point it to. You then receive a copy of the `.disco` file, the `.wsdl` file, and an additional file — the `.discomap` file. These three files are saved in the same directory.

The `.discomap` file is a rundown of the information found by Disco.exe in its search. In the preceding example, the `.discomap` file contains the following information:

```
<?xml version="1.0" encoding="utf-8"?>
<DiscoveryClientResultsFile xmlns:xsd="http://www.w3.org/2001/XMLSchema"
 xmlns:xsi="http://www.w3.org/2001/XMLSchema-instance">
  <Results>
    <DiscoveryClientResult
     referenceType="System.Web.Services.Discovery.ContractReference"
     url="http://localhost/TestWS/Service1.asmx?wsdl"
     filename="Service1.wsdl" />
    <DiscoveryClientResult
```

```
        referenceType="System.Web.Services.Discovery.
        DiscoveryDocumentReference"
        url="http://localhost/TestWS/Service1.asmx?disco"
        filename="Service1.disco" />
    </Results>
</DiscoveryClientResultsFile>
```

This file points to both the `.disco` and `.wsdl` files that were found in the discovery process. The preceding example was done without using any of the options available for you to use when discovering these files.

Table 12-1 describes the options that you can use with the Disco executable to fine-tune the discovery process.

Table 12-1 Disco.exe Options

Option	Description

`/domain:domain`
or
`/d:domain`
	Specifies the domain name to use when connecting to a proxy server that requires authentication.

`/nosave`	Does not save the discovered documents or results (`.wsdl`, `.xsd`, `.disco`, and `.discomap` files) to disk. The default is to save these documents.
`/nologo`	Suppresses the Microsoft startup banner display.

`/out:directoryName`
or
`/o:directoryName`
	Specifies the output directory in which to save the discovered documents. The default is the current directory.

`/password:password`
or
`/p:password`
	Specifies the password to use when connecting to a proxy server that requires authentication.

`/proxy:URL`	Specifies the URL of the proxy server to use for HTTP requests. The default is to use the system proxy setting.

`/proxydomain:domain`
or
`/pd:domain`
	Specifies the domain to use when connecting to a proxy server that requires authentication.

`/proxypassword:password`
or
`/pp:password`
	Specifies the password to use when connecting to a proxy server that requires authentication.

Option	Description

`/proxyusername:username`
or
`/pu:username`
	Specifies the username to use when connecting to a proxy server that requires authentication.

`/username:username`
or
`/u:username`
	Specifies the username to use when connecting to a proxy server that requires authentication.

`/?`	Displays command syntax and options for using Disco.exe.

You can use these options to manipulate how Disco.exe functions. For instance, if you wish to save the results to a specified directory, use the following syntax:

```
disco /out:myDiscoDirectory http://localhost/TestWS/Service1.asmx?disco
```

This command saves the files to the directory titled `myDiscoDirectory` instead of to the same directory in which Disco.exe is located.

If you need a username and password to gain access to a server where the Disco file of a particular Web service is located, use the following command:

```
disco /username:myLogin /password:myPassword /out:myDiscoDirectory
http://localhost/TestWS/Service1.asmx?disco
```

So far, I have discussed a number of different standards at your disposal. These technologies, such as UDDI, WSDL, and Disco are built upon the base standard of XML and are used to further expand the capabilities of the XML Web services that you build or consume. By following the rules that are set forth with these new languages, you make it easier for others to consume and use the XML Web services that you build.

Summary

This chapter looked at the discovery process using `.disco` and `.vsdisco` files. It discussed the important role that these files play in your ASP.NET Web service projects. If used correctly, these files can be powerful tools for the end user to discover the XML Web services that you build.

One of the great features of these files is the capability to link together discovery documents so that end users or applications can greatly expand their discovery process.

Finally, the chapter examined the Disco executable and how you can use this file in discovering Web services.

Part V

All About SOAP

Chapter 13: SOAP

Chapter 14: Advanced SOAP

Chapter 15: Global XML Web Services Architecture

Chapter 13
SOAP

*Two prisoners whose cells adjoin communicate with each other by knocking on the wall.
The wall is the thing which separates them but is also their means of communication.*
Simone Weil, *Gravity and Grace* (1947)

This chapter focuses on the principal language that XML Web services speak as they transmit their information over the wire. XML Web services use SOAP, or *Simple Object Access Protocol*, for transmitting messages. In this chapter, you look at the structure of SOAP and different ways you can use SOAP with your XML Web services and the applications you build that consume these SOAP messages.

More specifically, this chapter will cover the following points:

- The basics of SOAP.
- Why you need SOAP.
- The SOAP specification.
- The data types provided by SOAP.
- The Microsoft SOAP Toolkit.

SOAP and XML Web Services

Simple Object Access Protocol is an XML-based technology. It is used as a common message format in the transmission of messages from an XML Web service to any endpoint that is able to consume and understand these SOAP messages. This functionality is an important pillar in the XML Web services model.

Figure 13-1 shows a visualization of the XML Web services model, indicating where SOAP is used in this model. The first step in consumption of an XML Web service is the initial discovery of the service using a directory such as the UDDI registry. In the UDDI registry, you find the WSDL document that you can use to create a proxy class that enables you to communicate with the XML Web service. This communication uses SOAP.

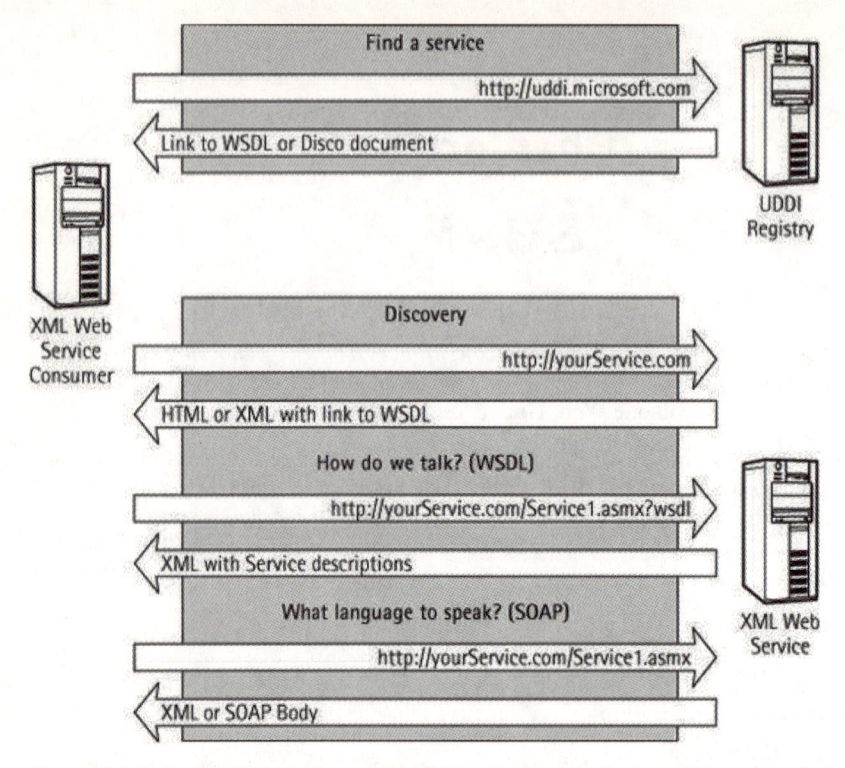

Figure 13-1: In the XML Web services model, SOAP is the language that is used for communication.

Why SOAP?

SOAP is not the only means of communication available for a Web service in this multiplatform world. In fact, there are Web services on non-.NET platforms that use other means, including XML-RPC, and ebXML, to structure the messages sent from the Web services that sit on those platforms.

The .NET platform uses SOAP as its common message format in the exchange of information packets from one point to another. SOAP is a lightweight XML format that is platform-neutral. This means that if your platform or calling application can consume XML over HTTP, you can work with the SOAP packets that are sent and received across the wire. That's the miracle of SOAP.

You can build or consume XML Web services on the .NET platform without understanding the structure of SOAP or even knowing that it is used as the communication protocol. Still, it is a good idea to understand exactly what SOAP is. Understanding the structure of the SOAP packets that are sent across the wire will help you if you wish to extend them in order to enhance the performance of your XML Web services.

SOAP Basics

SOAP 1.1 was developed in March of 2000 and was accepted as a note by the W3C on May 8, 2000. The companies that worked on the development of SOAP include Microsoft, DevelopMentor, IBM, Lotus, and UserLand Software. Presently, the W3C is working on Version 1.2 of SOAP, but at this time, SOAP 1.1 is the latest complete specification. The biggest change from Version 1.0 to 1.1 is that SOAP 1.1 now allows SOAP packets to be sent not only via HTTP, but also via FTP and SMTP.

> **NOTE:** The actual SOAP specification can be found at `www.w3c.org/tr/soap`.

SOAP is not a proprietary technology, run or controlled by Microsoft or IBM. It is, instead, an open standard. Therefore, you know you can use SOAP on almost any platform as long as the platform can work with XML.

SOAP and XML

Like a lot of the technologies used in working with XML Web services, SOAP is an XML-based technology. SOAP uses an XML grammar for a number of reasons:

- XML is an open standard.
- XML is workable on most platforms.
- There is tremendous industry support for XML.
- XML is very human-friendly.
- There are a number of applications and parsers already available that deal with XML.

The industry support and momentum behind XML make this technology the natural choice on which to base SOAP. Also, the simplicity of SOAP makes this technology considerably easier to work with than others, such as CORBA and DCOM, that provided similar functionality.

SOAP over HTTP

Businesses constantly need to share data among departments or with other companies. Often the data must travel from one database to another between incompatible platforms. SOAP technology is the glue between these systems. This technology bridges the gap between these platforms. When a company or department needs data from another location, the first question is not, "What platform is the data on?" but instead, "Can you send me that data as SOAP?"

These differing platforms are connected to each other via HTTP. HTTP is the string, or the web, which connects all these systems and platforms. Most systems, applications, and platforms are connected to the outside world in order to gain access to the Internet. The Internet has become a powerful means of human-to-human communication. It is becoming an even stronger force for machine-to-machine communication. These machines communicate with one another via HTTP.

Putting SOAP on top of HTTP is powerful. SOAP allows you to send data that is a lot more complex and meaningful than the name/value pairs that you can send using HTTP-GET or

HTTP-POST. Also, if you are going to send complex data from one machine to another, you have the problem of firewalls to deal with. Almost all machines or servers are behind a firewall of some kind. If you have a server that isn't behind a firewall, you are just asking for some malicious person to come in and mess with your machine and its contents. Firewalls, basically, block all entrances to the server. If the entrances to a server are blocked, however, how can anyone use SOAP to communicate with a machine?

Communication is possible because one of the doors to this server is usually open. Port 80 on almost every server is used for access to the Internet. SOAP rides along (using HTTP) right through this open door to the server. Because SOAP is just a set of ASCII characters, it cannot harm the receiving server, so the information is let in without any problems.

An example of a request/response SOAP message

Before you go into the SOAP specification, take a quick look at a typical SOAP message. The SOAP message that is sent from the client is a SOAP *request*. The XML Web services client makes a request of the XML Web service. Listing 13-1 shows a typical SOAP request.

Listing 13-1: A typical SOAP request using a simple Add() method

```
POST /TestWS/service1.asmx HTTP/1.1
Host: localhost
Content-Type: text/xml; charset=utf-8
Content-Length: xxx
SOAPAction: "http://www.xmlws101.com/Add"

<?xml version="1.0" encoding="utf-8"?>
<soap:Envelope xmlns:xsi="http://www.w3.org/2001/XMLSchema-instance"
 xmlns:xsd="http://www.w3.org/2001/XMLSchema"
 xmlns:soap="http://schemas.xmlsoap.org/soap/envelope/">
  <soap:Body>
    <Add xmlns="http://www.xmlws101.com/">
      <a>6</a>
      <b>5</b>
    </Add>
  </soap:Body>
</soap:Envelope>
```

The receiving XML Web service has a listener in place, accepts this SOAP message, dissects it, and then sends back a response based upon the information received. Listing 13-2 shows a response.

Listing 13-2: A typical SOAP response from a simple Add() method

```
HTTP/1.1 200 OK
Content-Type: text/xml; charset=utf-8
Content-Length: xxx

<?xml version="1.0" encoding="utf-8"?>
<soap:Envelope xmlns:xsi="http://www.w3.org/2001/XMLSchema-instance"
```

```
  xmlns:xsd="http://www.w3.org/2001/XMLSchema"
  xmlns:soap="http://schemas.xmlsoap.org/soap/envelope/">
  <soap:Body>
    <AddResponse xmlns="http://www.xmlws101.com/">
      <AddResult>11</AddResult>
    </AddResponse>
  </soap:Body>
</soap:Envelope>
```

This is a simple example. The return from the XML Web service is just a single value (11). This is all well and good, but you really see the true value of SOAP when you send more complex data either in the request or response message.

Listing 13-3 is an example of a complex piece of data that is being sent across the wire as SOAP. This is data from two tables using the Northwind database in SQL 2000: the Customers table and the Orders table.

Listing 13-3: Complex data sent in the SOAP response to the client

```
HTTP/1.1 200 OK
Server: Microsoft-IIS/5.1
Date: Mon, 31 Dec 2001 03:49:39 GMT
Cache-Control: private, max-age=0
Content-Type: text/xml; charset=utf-8
Content-Length: 7013

<?xml version="1.0" encoding="utf-8"?>
<soap:Envelope xmlns:soap="http://schemas.xmlsoap.org/soap/envelope/"
 xmlns:xsi="http://www.w3.org/2001/XMLSchema-instance"
 xmlns:xsd="http://www.w3.org/2001/XMLSchema">
 <soap:Body>
 <GetCustomersResponse xmlns="http://tempuri.org/">
  <GetCustomersResult>
  <xs:schema id="ExampleDataset"
   targetNamespace="http://www.tempuri.org/ExampleDataset.xsd"
   xmlns:mstns="http://www.tempuri.org/ExampleDataset.xsd"
   xmlns="http://www.tempuri.org/ExampleDataset.xsd"
   xmlns:xs="http://www.w3.org/2001/XMLSchema"
   xmlns:msdata="urn:schemas-microsoft-com:xml-msdata"
   attributeFormDefault="qualified"
   elementFormDefault="qualified">
     <xs:element name="ExampleDataset" msdata:IsDataSet="true">
       <xs:complexType>
         <xs:choice maxOccurs="unbounded">
           <xs:element name="Customers">
             <xs:complexType>
               <xs:sequence>
                 <xs:element name="CustomerID" type="xs:string" />
                 <xs:element name="CompanyName" type="xs:string" />
                 <xs:element name="ContactName" type="xs:string"
```

```xml
          minOccurs="0" />
        <xs:element name="ContactTitle" type="xs:string"
          minOccurs="0" />
        <xs:element name="Address" type="xs:string" minOccurs="0"
         />
        <xs:element name="City" type="xs:string" minOccurs="0" />
        <xs:element name="Region" type="xs:string" minOccurs="0"
         />
        <xs:element name="PostalCode" type="xs:string"
          minOccurs="0" />
        <xs:element name="Country" type="xs:string" minOccurs="0"
         />
        <xs:element name="Phone" type="xs:string" minOccurs="0"
         />
        <xs:element name="Fax" type="xs:string" minOccurs="0" />
      </xs:sequence>
    </xs:complexType>
  </xs:element>
  <xs:element name="Orders">
    <xs:complexType>
      <xs:sequence>
        <xs:element name="CustomerID" type="xs:string"
          minOccurs="0" />
        <xs:element name="EmployeeID" type="xs:int"
          minOccurs="0" />
        <xs:element name="Freight" type="xs:decimal"
          minOccurs="0" />
        <xs:element name="OrderDate" type="xs:dateTime"
          minOccurs="0" />
        <xs:element name="OrderID" msdata:AutoIncrement="true"
            type="xs:int" />
        <xs:element name="RequiredDate" type="xs:dateTime"
          minOccurs="0"
         />
        <xs:element name="ShipAddress" type="xs:string"
          minOccurs="0" />
        <xs:element name="ShipCity" type="xs:string"
          minOccurs="0" />
        <xs:element name="ShipCountry" type="xs:string"
          minOccurs="0" />
        <xs:element name="ShipName" type="xs:string"
          minOccurs="0" />
        <xs:element name="ShippedDate" type="xs:dateTime"
          minOccurs="0"
         />
        <xs:element name="ShipPostalCode" type="xs:string"
          minOccurs="0"
         />
        <xs:element name="ShipRegion" type="xs:string"
```

```xml
              minOccurs="0" />
            <xs:element name="ShipVia" type="xs:int" minOccurs="0"
              />
          </xs:sequence>
        </xs:complexType>
      </xs:element>
    </xs:choice>
  </xs:complexType>
  <xs:unique name="Constraint1" msdata:PrimaryKey="true">
    <xs:selector xpath=".//mstns:Customers" />
    <xs:field xpath="mstns:CustomerID" />
  </xs:unique>
  <xs:unique name="Orders_Constraint1"
   msdata:ConstraintName="Constraint1"
   msdata:PrimaryKey="true">
    <xs:selector xpath=".//mstns:Orders" />
    <xs:field xpath="mstns:OrderID" />
  </xs:unique>
  <xs:keyref name="CustomersOrders" refer="Constraint1">
    <xs:selector xpath=".//mstns:Orders" />
    <xs:field xpath="mstns:CustomerID" />
  </xs:keyref>
 </xs:element>
</xs:schema>
<diffgr:diffgram xmlns:msdata="urn:schemas-microsoft-com:xml-msdata"
 xmlns:diffgr="urn:schemas-microsoft-com:xml-diffgram-v1">
  <ExampleDataset xmlns="http://www.tempuri.org/ExampleDataset.xsd">
    <Customers diffgr:id="Customers1" msdata:rowOrder="0">
      <CustomerID>ALFKI</CustomerID>
      <CompanyName>Alfreds Futterkiste</CompanyName>
      <ContactName>Dieter Utrecht</ContactName>
      <ContactTitle>Sales Representative</ContactTitle>
      <Address>Obere Str. 57</Address>
      <City>Berlin</City>
      <PostalCode>12209</PostalCode>
      <Country>Germany</Country>
      <Phone>030-0074321</Phone>
      <Fax>030-0076545</Fax>
    </Customers>
    <Orders diffgr:id="Orders1" msdata:rowOrder="0">
      <CustomerID>ALFKI</CustomerID>
      <EmployeeID>6</EmployeeID>
      <Freight>29.46</Freight>
      <OrderDate>1995-09-25T00:00:00.0000000-05:00</OrderDate>
      <OrderID>10643</OrderID>
      <RequiredDate>1995-10-23T00:00:00.0000000-05:00</RequiredDate>
      <ShipAddress>Obere Str. 57</ShipAddress>
      <ShipCity>Berlin</ShipCity>
      <ShipCountry>Germany</ShipCountry>
```

```xml
            <ShipName>Alfreds Futterkiste</ShipName>
            <ShippedDate>1995-10-03T00:00:00.0000000-05:00</ShippedDate>
            <ShipPostalCode>12209</ShipPostalCode>
            <ShipVia>1</ShipVia>
         </Orders>
         <Orders diffgr:id="Orders2" msdata:rowOrder="1">
            <CustomerID>ALFKI</CustomerID>
            <EmployeeID>3</EmployeeID>
            <Freight>1.21</Freight>
            <OrderDate>1996-05-09T00:00:00.0000000-05:00</OrderDate>
            <OrderID>11011</OrderID>
            <RequiredDate>1996-06-06T00:00:00.0000000-05:00</RequiredDate>
            <ShipAddress>Obere Str. 57</ShipAddress>
            <ShipCity>Berlin</ShipCity>
            <ShipCountry>Germany</ShipCountry>
            <ShipName>Alfred's Futterkiste</ShipName>
            <ShippedDate>1996-05-13T00:00:00.0000000-05:00</ShippedDate>
            <ShipPostalCode>12209</ShipPostalCode>
            <ShipVia>1</ShipVia>
         </Orders>
       </ExampleDataset>
     </diffgr:diffgram>
    </GetCustomersResult>
   </GetCustomersResponse>
 </soap:Body>
</soap:Envelope>
```

This is a great example of the power of using SOAP and XML as the communication vehicle for your XML Web services. The XML Web service that built the SOAP response for this example took data from one table, related data from another (the customer's orders), and then put all that data in a dataset that was serialized into XML and sent using SOAP over HTTP. This would not have been possible using name/value pairs as in HTTP-GET or HTTP-POST. In this case, you have all the data, along with an inline XSD document that describes the structure of the data. All the data's relations are in place, so it is possible to relate the customer and the orders from the customer within this one data file.

> **CROSS-REFERENCE:** Part VII of this book covers working with datasets and SQL Servers along with your XML Web services.

Now that you have a basic introduction to SOAP, take a quick look at some of the details of the SOAP specification.

The SOAP Specification

SOAP was developed to be simple. It is a lightweight protocol that is used in the communication of messages from one point to another. It works in a decentralized and distributed environment, typically using HTTP as its mode of transport. As mentioned earlier, the last complete SOAP specification was Version 1.1. Presently, SOAP is now under the control of the XML Protocols working group, which is working on Version 1.2 of the specification. The .NET Framework (including ASP.NET and the requests and responses from XML Web services) abides by Version 1.1 of the SOAP specification.

The SOAP specification is made up of the following parts, covered in this chapter and the following one:

- A description of the SOAP envelope and how to package SOAP so that it can be sent over the wire using HTTP
- The encoding rules for SOAP messages
- A definition of the protocol binding between SOAP and HTTP
- The capability to use SOAP for RPC-like binding

One of the more important aspects of the SOAP specification is the makeup of the SOAP message or SOAP packet. You must understand the structure of this packet in order to extend and mold it within your own XML Web services.

You can start by taking a closer look at the SOAP message and all its parts.

The SOAP Message

The SOAP message is simple, and it was meant to be just that. The SOAP message is what is sent over the wire using HTTP, with or without the HTTP Extension Framework (HTTP-EF). SOAP messages are meant to be one-way. There is nothing built into these messages that warrants any response. SOAP does not contain any built-in functions or methods that cause specific events to be initiated. The SOAP message is XML, and XML is simply used as a way of marking up data.

The problem is that XML Web services require a request and response action to take place. SOAP gets around this problem by sending the SOAP message within the HTTP request and response messages.

The typical SOAP message consists of a SOAP Envelope, Header, and Body section. The SOAP Envelope is a mandatory element that is the root element of the entire package. Within the SOAP Envelope element is an optional Header element and a mandatory Body element. Figure 13-2 shows an example of the structure of a SOAP message.

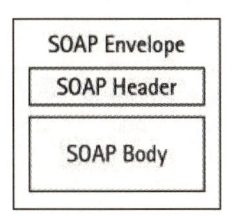

Figure 13-2: The SOAP Envelope holding SOAP Header and Body elements.

Because this entire message is an XML document, it has a single root element (the SOAP Envelope element), just like any typical XML document.

SOAP Envelope

Listing 13-4 shows a typical SOAP Envelope.

Listing 13-4: The SOAP Envelope

```
<?xml version="1.0" encoding="utf-8"?>
<soap:Envelope xmlns:xsi="http://www.w3.org/2001/XMLSchema-instance"
 xmlns:xsd="http://www.w3.org/2001/XMLSchema"
 xmlns:soap="http://schemas.xmlsoap.org/soap/envelope/">
  <soap:Body>
     <!-- The message contents go here. -->
  </soap:Body>
</soap:Envelope>
```

The SOAP Envelope is specified as the root element and is qualified by using the SOAP namespace `http://schemas.xmlsoap.org/soap/envelope/`. This element, qualified by this namespace in the code, is expressed as `<soap:Envelope>`.

The SOAP Envelope namespace that is used in this message is the required namespace for Version 1.1 of the SOAP specification. If your SOAP message does not have this required namespace, the message fails and is considered invalid.

Your SOAP Envelopes can contain additional namespaces if you so choose. There is a single attribute available to the SOAP Envelope, `encodingStyle`. The `encodingStyle` attribute can actually be used in any of the elements contained within the SOAP message. You will typically use it, however, within the SOAP Envelope. Typically the SOAP message is serialized according to the SOAP schema, located at `http://schemas.xmlsoap.org/soap/envelope`, but it is possible to specify a completely different serialization encoding by assigning a different value to the `encodingStyle` attribute.

You can also have additional attributes within the SOAP Envelope, but these need to be namespace qualified in order to be valid.

SOAP Header

The SOAP Header element is an optional element used to provide information that is related to what is contained within the SOAP Body element. The convenient thing about the SOAP Header is that you are not required to inform the end user beforehand about the information you place there. Basically, the SOAP Header is used to transmit supporting information about the payload that is contained within the SOAP Body.

For instance, you can use the SOAP Header for any of the following:

♦ Authentication

♦ Transaction management

♦ Payment

Of course, you can use SOAP Headers for any number of things, but these points give you a general idea of what you can do with them. Listing 13-5 shows a typical SOAP Header.

Listing 13-5: The SOAP Header

```xml
<?xml version="1.0" encoding="utf-8"?>
<soap:Envelope xmlns:xsi="http://www.w3.org/2001/XMLSchema-instance"
 xmlns:xsd="http://www.w3.org/2001/XMLSchema"
 xmlns:soap="http://schemas.xmlsoap.org/soap/envelope/">
  <soap:Header>
    <MyHeader xmlns="http://www.xmlws101.com">
      <Username>Admin</Username>
      <Password>MyPassword</Password>
    </MyHeader>
  </soap:Header>
  <soap:Body>
    <MyWebMethod xmlns="http://www.xmlws101.com" />
  </soap:Body>
</soap:Envelope>
```

In this example, the SOAP request requires credentials to be sent in with the SOAP message in order to authenticate the user before a SOAP response can be issued. As you can see, this can be quite a powerful tool.

> **CROSS-REFERENCE:** An example of how to use this type of security model within your XML Web services is discussed in Chapter 16.

The SOAP Header element is a child element to the SOAP Envelope element. Because there is a required sequence of elements, if there is a SOAP Header contained within the SOAP message, the SOAP Header must come directly after the SOAP Envelope element but before the SOAP Body element.

There are a number of available attributes that can be used within the SOAP Header. The first optional element is the `encodingStyle` attribute. As you may remember, this attribute can be used within any element of the SOAP message. Typically you won't have this element contained within the SOAP Header, but that option is there.

The SOAP Header can also contain an `actor` and a `mustUnderstand` attribute. Look at each of these attributes.

actor attribute

When SOAP messages are sent from one point to another, a SOAP message may come in contact with a number of SOAP intermediaries along the way. A SOAP intermediary is an application that is capable of both receiving and sending SOAP messages as it comes into contact with them.

The SOAP Header that you include along with the SOAP message might, in some cases, be intended for one of these SOAP intermediaries and not for the final receiver of the SOAP message. If this is the case, it is possible to use the `actor` attribute within the SOAP Header element to specify that the enclosed Header element is intended only for only one of the SOAP intermediaries that the SOAP message comes in contact with. After it is received by the SOAP intermediary, the SOAP Header will not be forwarded with the rest of the SOAP message.

To specify that the SOAP Header is intended for the first SOAP intermediary that the SOAP message comes into contact with, the value of the `actor` attribute needs to be the URI

http://schemas.xmlsoap.org/soap/actor/next

If you wish to give the SOAP Header to a SOAP intermediary other than the first one, the value of the `actor` attribute needs to be the URI of the intended location.

mustUnderstand attribute

The SOAP `mustUnderstand` attribute is an optional attribute that enables you to specify whether the end user can ignore the SOAP Header. The person who receives the SOAP Header is specified in the `actor` attribute.

The value of the `mustUnderstand` attribute is either 0 or 1. If the value is set to 1, the recipient of that SOAP Header element *must* process the SOAP Header or fail the entire message. A value of 0 means that the recipient is not required to process the SOAP Header.

SOAP Body

The SOAP Body element is required within your SOAP message. The SOAP Body is the main part of the message, where the data part of the message is housed. The SOAP Body contains data that is specific to the method call such as the method name and all the input and output parameters that are sent to the XML Web service. Your XML Web service uses the SOAP Body to return data to the client. The SOAP Body can also contain any error information that is sent back from the XML Web service.

SOAP Body Request

If there is a SOAP Header element contained within the SOAP Envelope, the SOAP Body needs to come directly after the SOAP Header element.

The request payload that is sent in the SOAP Body maps directly to a method and the arguments that are required for the method. For example, your simple Calculator `Add()` method looks like the following:

```
<WebMethod()> Public Function Add(ByVal a As Integer,
                                  ByVal b As Integer) As Integer
    Return a + b
End Function
```

Therefore, the SOAP Body request maps directly to this method and the parameters that are required for this particular method.

```
<soap:Body>
  <Add xmlns="http://www.xmlws101.com/">
    <a>6</a>
    <b>5</b>
```

```
    </Add>
</soap:Body>
```

As you can tell from the preceding code example, the method and its parameters are serialized into XML, and the method name is now the first child element of the <soap:Body> element. The parameters of the method are also serialized into XML and the first parameter, a, is turned into an <a> element just as the b parameter is converted into a <b> element.

SOAP Body response

The XML Web service also returns a SOAP Body response that is serialized into XML just as the request is.

```
<soap:Body>
  <AddResponse xmlns="http://www.xmlws101.com/">
    <AddResult>11</AddResult>
  </AddResponse>
</soap:Body>
```

In the case of the response SOAP Body message, the method name is turned into an element bearing the same name, but with the word Response tacked onto it. The result that is returned is encased within the <AddResult> element, which is the method name with the word Result appended to it.

SOAP Fault

As you probably are quite aware, programmers are not perfect beasts, and there are bound to be problems within some of the XML Web services that you are trying to consume. When errors happen, it is essential that you know that the error occurred and that the error message is communicated to you in some manner.

This is where the SOAP Fault element comes into play. The SOAP Fault is contained within the SOAP body and is sent in the payload if an error occurs. The XML Web services that are built using the .NET Framework do this automatically, and as a developer, you don't have to do anything special in order to make it happen. The client consuming your Web service can then take this information and use it to display the message in some format so that the end user has an understanding of some of the issues that he is facing.

For instance, if you send in a SOAP message with the mustUnderstand attribute set to True, but the SOAP packet receiving the request doesn't understand the SOAP Header, you get a faultcode 200 error. The SOAP packet that is returned to you looks like the following:

```
<soap:Envelope xmlns:xsi="http://www.w3.org/2001/XMLSchema-instance"
 xmlns:xsd="http://www.w3.org/2001/XMLSchema"
 xmlns:soap="http://schemas.xmlsoap.org/soap/envelope/">
  <soap:Body>
    <soap:Fault>
      <faultcode>200</faultcode>
      <faultstring>
        Unrecognized 'causality' header
```

```
        </faultstring>
        <runcode>No</runcode>
    </soap:Fault>
  </soap:Body>
</soap:Envelope>
```

You will notice that the `<soap:fault>` element is contained within the `<soap:Body>` element.

faultcode

As a child of the `<soap:fault>` element, the `<faultcode>` element is used to give the error number, and thereby inform you about the type of error. The preceding example shows a `faultcode` of 200. Table 13-1 provides a brief description of all the `faultcodes` that you might encounter.

Table 13-1: Faultcode Possible Errors

Name	Description
Version Mismatch	The call used an invalid namespace for the SOAP Envelope element.
Must Understand	The SOAP Header element had a `mustUnderstand` attribute set to True and the processing endpoint did not understand it or didn't obey the processing instructions.
Client	The receiver didn't process the request because the request was improperly constructed or is malformed in some way.
Server	The receiving application faulted when processing the request because of the processing engine and not due to any fault of the sender or the composition of the message sent.

As you can tell by the numbers in the returned SOAP message in last code example and the unreadable error message, the `<faultcode>` element was intended for use by software to provide an algorithmic mechanism for identifying the fault. This `<faultcode>` element is a required element whenever there is a `<soap:fault>` element sent in the SOAP payload.

faultstring

The `<faultstring>` element provides a human-readable version of an error report. This element contains a string value that briefly describes the error encountered. This element will always be contained within the `<soap:fault>` element.

faultactor

The `<faultactor>` element describes the point in the process where the fault occurred. This is identified by the URI of the location where the fault was generated. This is meant for situations where the SOAP message is being passed among a number of SOAP intermediaries and, therefore, the location where the fault occurred must be identified. This is a required element within the `<soap:fault>` element *only* if the fault occurred within one of the SOAP intermediaries. If the fault occurred at the endpoint, the endpoint is not required to populate this element, although it can do so.

detail

The detail element carries application-specific error information related to the SOAP Body element. The fault elements previously described are, in most cases, enough for disclosing the error information. It is always good, however, to have more than enough information when you are trying to debug something. The `<detail>` element can be used to provide that extra bit of information that can assist in the debug process. For instance, you can carry the line in the code where the error occurred.

SOAP Encoding

Along with the programming language you use to build your XML Web services, you are passing some specific data types from your application, whether it is written in Visual Basic .NET, C#, or some other .NET-compliant language. That data is being sent across the wire as a SOAP message. Therefore, the data type that is sitting on the SOAP payload needs to maintain its specified data type so that the data on the other end can be used correctly. For instance, if your method returns an integer of 22, the value that is received on the other end must remain an integer of 22 and not become a string value of "22". Changes in value would make dealing with XML Web services quite difficult.

SOAP does maintain data types as it takes data and moves it from one point to another. The process of converting the data types from the application code to a data type that SOAP recognizes is called *SOAP encoding*.

The types that are serialized into SOAP are the same types that are specified in the XML Schema specification found at www.w3.org/TR/xmlschema-2. These data types are pretty standard, and most of the data types that you want to pass into SOAP can be serialized in a manner that works for you. So, for example, you are easily able to serialize primitive types such as String, Char, Byte, Boolean, Int16, Int32, Int64, UInt16, UInt32, UInt64, Single, Double, Guid, Decimal, DateTime (as XML's timeInstant), DateTime (as XML's date), DateTime (as XML's time), and XmlQualifiedName (as XML's QName).

Take a look at a code example, along with what is returned from that function, and how it is serialized into XML.

The following Visual Basic .NET WebMethod returns a simple string:

```
<WebMethod()> Public Function GetString() As String
    Dim myString As String = "This is a string."
    Return myString
End Function
```

What you get back in return is the string serialized into XML, shown below:

```
<?xml version="1.0" encoding="utf-8" ?>
<string xmlns="http://tempuri.org/">This is a string.</string>
```

This Visual Basic .NET WebMethod returns an integer:

```
<WebMethod()> Public Function GetInteger() As Integer
    Dim myInt As Integer = 5
    Return myInt
End Function
```

What you get back in return is an integer that has been serialized into XML:

```
<?xml version="1.0" encoding="utf-8" ?>
<int xmlns="http://tempuri.org/">5</int>
```

Now take a look at a WebMethod in Visual Basic.NET that returns a DateTime value:

```
<WebMethod()> Public Function GetDateTime() As DateTime
    Dim myDateTime As DateTime = DateTime.Now
    Return myDateTime
End Function
```

In return you see the following:

```
<?xml version="1.0" encoding="utf-8" ?>
<dateTime xmlns="http://tempuri.org/">2001-12-31T16:56:37.6928848-
 06:00</dateTime>
```

For the last example of serializing data types into XML from your code, take a look at an example of a WebMethod that returns an array of integers:

```
<WebMethod()> Public Function GetIntArray() As Integer()
    Dim I As Integer
    Dim A(4) As Integer
    For I = 0 To 4
        A(I) = I * 10
    Next
    Return A
End Function
```

This array of integers that is returned is then serialized into XML for you by the ASP.NET Web service.

```
<?xml version="1.0" encoding="utf-8" ?>
<ArrayOfInt xmlns:xsd="http://www.w3.org/2001/XMLSchema"
 xmlns:xsi="http://www.w3.org/2001/XMLSchema-instance"
 xmlns="http://tempuri.org/">
  <int>0</int>
  <int>10</int>
  <int>20</int>
  <int>30</int>
  <int>40</int>
</ArrayOfInt>
```

Not only are these primitive types easily serialized into SOAP, but complex data structures and hierarchies are also easily serialized. You saw an example in the beginning of this chapter. A complete dataset was represented within a SOAP message. In the beginning of the SOAP Body element, an inline XSD document defined all the types that were used throughout in the SOAP payload. Whenever a dataset is returned from an XML Web service, an XSD document is attached to the dataset. The capability to attach an XSD document that can create these definitions is a powerful tool and enables you to send complex data structures that the consuming application can easily understand.

Probably one of the best things about serializing your data in SOAP is that ASP.NET takes care of this serialization for you, and therefore you don't need to know anything about the serialization process and the type conversion that is taking place. It does it all for you. It just makes it that simple. Another SOAP miracle.

Watching SOAP Messages

So far, you have seen several examples of how the SOAP message is constructed. In the next part of this chapter, you are going to start working with extending and manipulating the SOAP messages that are sent to your XML Web service. In order to do this, you need to be able to view the SOAP messages as they are sent back and forth across the wire.

You already know how to view the payload of the SOAP message that was sent from an XML Web service. For instance, if you invoke the CurrencyConverter XML Web service, you see the following results for the XML Web service test page:

```
<?xml version="1.0" encoding="utf-8" ?>
<double xmlns="http://www.xmlws101.com">111.8</double>
```

What you see here is the SOAP payload that has been serialized into XML. But this may not be what you want to see. You might instead need to see the entire SOAP message — including the entire SOAP Envelope as shown here in Listing 13-6.

Listing 13-6: The SOAP response message sent back from the CurrencyConverter XML Web service

```
<?xml version="1.0" encoding="utf-8" ?>
<soap:Envelope xmlns:soap="http://schemas.xmlsoap.org/soap/envelope/"
 xmlns:xsi="http://www.w3.org/2001/XMLSchema-instance"
 xmlns:xsd="http://www.w3.org/2001/XMLSchema">
  <soap:Body>
    <USDConvertResponse xmlns="http://www.xmlws101.com">
      <USDConvertResult>111.8</USDConvertResult>
    </USDConvertResponse>
  </soap:Body>
</soap:Envelope>
```

If you want to view the entire SOAP Envelope, how do you go about that? Well, actually it is fairly simple, but you must take a few steps to set it up.

The Microsoft SOAP Toolkit

To view SOAP messages as they are sent back and forth across the wire, you must download the Microsoft SOAP Toolkit from Microsoft's MSDN site at `http://msdn.microsoft.com/soap`. After you install the toolkit, you find a number of applications available for dealing with Web services from Visual Basic 6.0. This toolkit enables you to create, consume, and debug Web services from Visual Basic 6.0.

Out of all these great tools, you need only one at the moment — that is the Trace Utility. You can use the Trace Utility within the SOAP Toolkit to trace the SOAP messages as they are being sent and received by an XML Web services client application.

Using the Trace Utility

You must take a few steps in order to use the Trace Utility. First, you need to have an XML Web service that you can consume. For the sake of this example, you can consume the CurrencyConverter XML Web service that you built earlier in the book.

Next, you need to build an application that consumes this XML Web service and is able to make a request of the XML Web service that causes the Web service to issue a response. Follow these steps for your XML Web service client application:

1. In the design mode, place two text boxes on the page. Underneath the text boxes, place a Button control, followed by a Label control. You should now have four controls on your page: `TextBox1`, `TextBox2`, `Button1`, and `Label1`.

2. Make a Web reference to the CurrencyConverter XML Web service using the Add Web Reference dialog window. To do this, right-click on the project name within the Solution Explorer and choose Add Web Reference. Type in the address of the .asmx file of the XML Web service that you want to consume and click Add Reference when this button becomes highlighted.

3. Click on the Show All Files button at the top of the Solution Explorer window.

4. Open the Web References folder (this folder is represented with a tiny globe in the Solution Explorer).

5. Expand the plus sign next to the `Reference.map` file and you will see the `Reference.vb` or the `Reference.cs` file (shown in Figure 13-3).

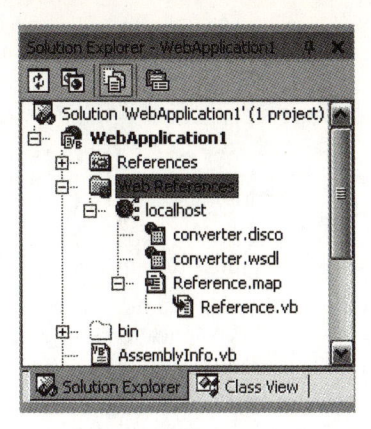

Figure 13-3: Finding the Reference.vb file with the Solution Explorer.

6. The `Reference.vb` or `Reference.cs` file is the proxy class that was generated for you by Visual Studio .NET. It takes care of marshaling the SOAP messages back and forth across the wire for you. In order to work with the Microsoft SOAP Toolkit's Trace Utility, you need to manipulate this file so that the SOAP messages are sent through the same port as the Trace Utility. If you are running the Trace Utility to monitor a local XML Web service, in most cases you must set the Trace Utility to monitor port 8080. Open the `Reference.vb` or `Reference.cs` file to tell the proxy class to send the SOAP messages through port 8080 so that the Trace Utility can monitor these messages for you.

7. You only need to make one change within the proxy class in order to instruct the proxy class to use port 8080. Scroll down part way till you see the following lines of code:

VB From the Reference.vb file.

```
Public Sub New()
    MyBase.New
    Me.Url = "http://localhost/currencyconverter/converter.asmx"
End Sub
```

C# From the Reference.cs file.

```
public CurrencyConverter() {
    this.Url = "http://localhost/currencyconverter/converter.asmx";
}
```

8. Change the code by inserting the port number that you want the proxy class to use when marshaling the SOAP messages. This is shown in the following code:

VB

```
Public Sub New()
    MyBase.New
    Me.Url = "http://localhost:8080/currencyconverter/converter.asmx"
End Sub
```

C#

```
public CurrencyConverter() {
    this.Url = "http://localhost:8080/currencyconverter/converter.asmx";
}
```

> **NOTE:** Your XML Web service's path might be different from the one listed in the code.

9. Save the file and choose Build ⇨ Build Solution so that this file is recompiled.
10. Now you are completely finished with the proxy class, but before you run the XML Web service client application, you need to start up the Trace Utility application by choosing Start ⇨ All Programs ⇨ Microsoft SOAP Toolkit ⇨ Trace Utility.
11. From the Trace Utility application, choose File ⇨ New ⇨ Formatted Trace.
    What opens up next is the Trace Setup window that enables you to specify the local port number that you will use, as well as the destination host and port number. This dialog window is shown in Figure 13-4.

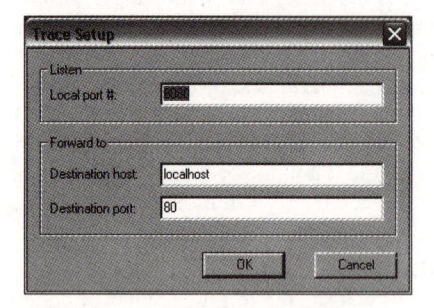

Figure 13-4: The Trace Setup dialog window.

Next, go back to the XML Web service client application that you are building in order to consume the CurrencyConverter XML Web service.

12. In the design mode, double-click on the button and add the following code to the button click.

VB

```
Dim ws as New localhost.CurrencyConverter()
Label1.Text = ws.USDConvert(TextBox1.Text, TextBox2.Text)
```

C#

```
localhost.CurrencyConverter ws = new localhost.CurrencyConverter();
Label1.Text = ws.USDConvert(TextBox1.Text,
                            double.Parse(TextBox2.Text)).ToString();
```

13. Press F5 to compile and run the code.

Now both your XML Web service client application and the Trace Utility from the Microsoft SOAP Toolkit should be open. Enter the information that is needed in the text boxes and then invoke the XML Web service by clicking the button. After you click the button, the result of the XML Web service is returned and the value is placed into the Label control.

Now comes the interesting part. If you go back to the Trace Utility, you see that there is an entry in the left pane of the application. 127.0.0.1 is your local IP address. Expand the plus sign next to this IP address and you see Message #1. Highlight Message #1 and you see the SOAP messages show up in the other two panes within the utility. Figure 13-5 shows what the Trace Utility should look like after you have taken these steps.

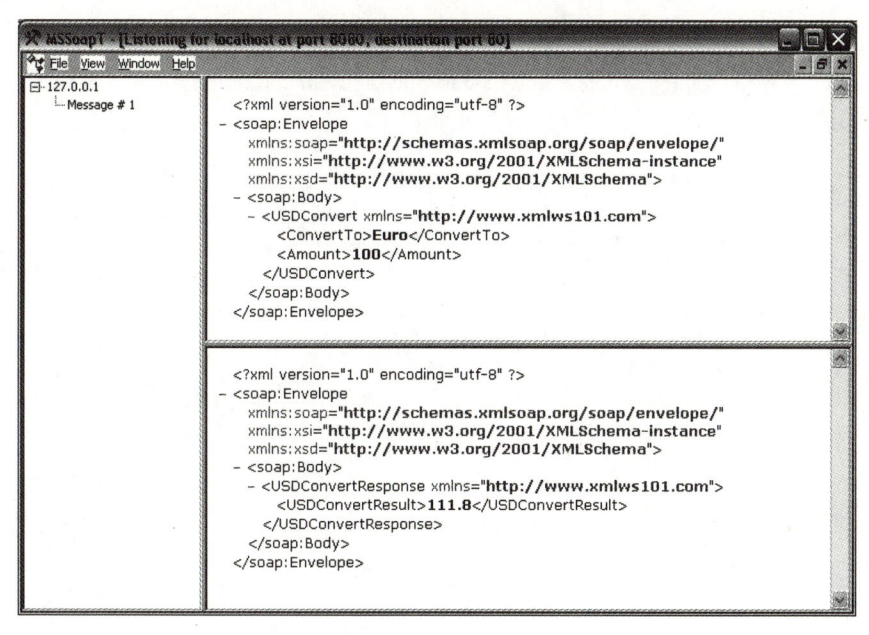

Figure 13-5: The Trace Utility from the Microsoft SOAP Toolkit showing both the request and response SOAP messages.

After completing these steps, you can now watch the SOAP messages that are sent to and from your XML Web services. This will be quite beneficial for debugging and for forming your SOAP messages. You will learn techniques to do this in the next chapter.

There are other tools you can use to watch SOAP packets as they move across the wire, but the Microsoft SOAP Toolkit will take care of most of your needs. If you are looking for other projects that perform functions similar to the Trace Utility, check out the various trace tools provided at www.pocketsoap.com.

Summary

SOAP is a powerful tool, in the sense that it is uses an XML grammar and is a platform-independent language. Platform independence is a required element of the XML Web services model if Web services are truly going to live up to their purpose — a means of moving logic and data across the Internet regardless of the platform making the call.

Because SOAP is a lightweight technology that doesn't require a lot of verbose language attached to the data moving across the wire, it has become the standard way in which Web services work. Whether you are working on a UNIX platform building Java Web services or working on Windows 2000 building C# Web services, all Web services models use SOAP for transmitting messages across HTTP.

This chapter covered the basics of SOAP, the data types that are used, and how to look at the SOAP packets as they move across the wire. You will need to understand all these facets as you move onto the next chapter, where you will start playing with and modifying the SOAP packets.

Chapter 14
Advanced SOAP

"It is a bad plan that admits of no modification."
Publilius Syrus, *Moral Sayings* (1st c. B.C.)

In the last chapter, you learned about the main structure of SOAP, otherwise known as Simple Object Access Protocol. There is a lot more to SOAP than what is automatically generated for you by ASP.NET. You can do a lot with the SOAP messages that you send and receive in order to greatly enhance the capabilities of your XML Web services.

This chapter covers some of the ways that you can modify, customize, and enhance SOAP messages.

The following topics are covered in this chapter:

- Building XML Web services that interact with SOAP Headers
- Building XML Web service clients that send SOAP Headers
- Validating SOAP Headers
- Using SOAP extensions
- Using different SOAP Body formats
- Modifying the XML output of a SOAP Body

Working with SOAP Headers

As you have learned, the SOAP message is made up of a single SOAP Envelope that contains a SOAP Body. The SOAP Body carries the SOAP payload. You also have the option to include a SOAP Header. The SOAP Header can contain information that is not directly related to any of the methods and parameters that are carried in the SOAP Body, but instead can be used for anything from registration to authentication purposes. It is really up to you, as the developer of the XML Web service, to decide what type of information the XML Web service consumer needs so that you can place it within the SOAP Header.

The SOAP specification doesn't make any rules about what the SOAP Header must contain, and this lack of restriction makes the SOAP Header a powerful tool.

Say that you have built this great XML Web service, but for some reason, you want to collect the names and e-mail addresses of all the people who are using your XML Web service. You can do this by forcing the XML Web service consumer to put her name and e-mail address in the SOAP Header of the SOAP message sent to the XML Web service.

To do this, you want the SOAP Header that the client sends to the XML Web service to look like the following:

```xml
<soap:Header xmlns:soap="http://schemas.xmlsoap.org/soap/envelope/">
    <myHeader xmlns="http://www.xmlws101.com">
        <Name>Bill Evjen</Name>
        <EmailAddress>evjen@yahoo.com</EmailAdress>
    </myHeader>
</soap:Header>
```

This SOAP Header can be as simple or as complex as you make it, and it is possible to either require consumers of an XML Web service to pass appropriate values back in the header, or simply make the values optional.

Building XML Web services that accept SOAP Headers

If you want your Web service to accept SOAP Headers, the first step is to import a namespace that you need to access from the Web service.

VB

```vb
Imports System.Web.Services.Protocols
```

C#

```csharp
using System.Web.Services.Protocols;
```

The next step is to create a class within your XML Web service that derives from the `SoapHeader` class. The `SoapHeader` class will serialize the payload of the `<soap:header>` element into XML for you. You also need to define the input parameters that are part of the SOAP Header. Listing 14-1 shows this code.

Listing 14-1: The SOAPHeader class

VB

```vb
Public Class myHeader
    Inherits SoapHeader

    Public Name As String
    Public EmailAddress As String
End Class
```

C#

```csharp
public class myHeader : SoapHeader
{
    public string Name;
    public string EmailAddress;
}
```

The variables that you create within this class are the names used for the elements within the SOAP Header, so it is important to give the variables meaningful names.

Next, turn your attention to the class that makes up your XML Web service. Listing 14-2 addresses this.

Listing 14-2: A WebMethod that works with SOAP Headers

VB

```
<WebService(Namespace:="http://www.xmlws101.com/")> _
Public Class AddWithHeader
    Inherits System.Web.Services.WebService

    Public GetClientInfo As myHeader

    <WebMethod(), SoapHeader("GetClientInfo")> _
    Public Function Add(ByVal a As Integer, ByVal b As Integer) _
                   As String
        Dim Result As Integer
        Dim myMessage As String

        Result = a + b
        myMessage = "Hello " + GetClientInfo.Name _
            + ". The result of your addition is: " + Result.ToString() _
            + "<br>Your email address is: " + GetClientInfo.EmailAddress

        ' You could put the name and email address into a database here.

        Return myMessage
    End Function

End Class
```

C#

```
public class AddWithHeader : System.Web.Services.WebService
  {
  public myHeader GetClientInfo;

  [WebMethod()]
  [SoapHeader("GetClientInfo")]
  public string Add(int a, int b)
  {
   int result;
   string myMessage;

   result = a + b;
   myMessage = "Hello " + GetClientInfo.Name
           + ". The result of your addition is: " + result.ToString()
           + "<br>Your email address is: "
```

```
            + GetClientInfo.EmailAddress;

    // You could put the name and email address into a database here.

    return myMessage;
  }
}
```

Within the `WebService` class, declare a public member, `GetClientInfo`, of the type that represents the SOAP Header class — in this case, the `myHeader` class. After this declaration, you add an additional attribute to the WebMethod that has the capability to accept SOAP Headers. Set the `MemberName` property of the `SoapHeader` class to the name of the public member of the type `myHeader` that was just declared. After this is in place, the `Add()` XML Web service method specifies the `myHeader` member as the `MemberName` property to receive the contents of `myHeader` SOAP headers passed into the XML Web service method.

After you have done this, you can refer to the properties that are available to the `GetClientInfo` member. In this case, the `Name` and `EmailAddress` properties are available from IntelliSense within Visual Studio .NET.

After you have created this XML Web service that can accept SOAP Headers, notice that the WSDL document reflects this (see Listing 14-3).

Listing 14-3: The partial WSDL document from the XML Web service that accepts the Name and EmailAddress SOAP Headers

```
<types>
 <s:schema elementFormDefault="qualified"
  targetNamespace="http://tempuri.org/">
   <s:element name="Add">
     <s:complexType>
       <s:sequence>
         <s:element minOccurs="1" maxOccurs="1" name="a" type="s:int" />
         <s:element minOccurs="1" maxOccurs="1" name="b" type="s:int" />
       </s:sequence>
     </s:complexType>
   </s:element>
   <s:element name="AddResponse">
     <s:complexType>
       <s:sequence>
         <s:element minOccurs="0" maxOccurs="1" name="AddResult"
           type="s:string" />
       </s:sequence>
     </s:complexType>
   </s:element>
   <s:element name="myHeader" type="s0:myHeader" />
     <s:complexType name="myHeader">
       <s:sequence>
         <s:element minOccurs="0" maxOccurs="1" name="Name"
           type="s:string" />
```

```
            <s:element minOccurs="0" maxOccurs="1" name="EmailAddress"
              type="s:string" />
          </s:sequence>
        </s:complexType>
      </s:schema>
    </types>
```

Not only does the WSDL document describe the parameters and types that are inputted and outputted from the XML Web service, but it also describes the parameters and the parameter types that are accepted in the SOAP Header.

The end user can also see a description of these SOAP Headers on the XML Web service test page that is automatically generated in ASP.NET for the Web service. This page gives an example of the structure of the SOAP message that includes a description of the SOAP Header.

Now that everything is in place on the side of the XML Web service, you can build an XML Web service client application that will be able to pass in a SOAP Header to this Web service.

Building XML Web Service clients that pass SOAP Headers

If you have an XML Web service that accepts SOAP Headers, you can simply create values for each of the SOAP Header elements needed within the SOAP Header.

The first step in creating an XML Web service client application is to make a Web reference to the XML Web service. After this is done, you see the `localhost` reference within the Web Reference folder in the Solution Explorer. For this example, you are creating an ASP.NET Web Application. You can just as easily do this in a Windows Application.

NOTE: Be sure to modify the proxy class that is generated for you (as explained in Chapter 13) so that you can view the SOAP Envelope within the Trace Utility.

After this is done, place a Label control on the design page and use the code in Listing 14-4 to create the `Page_Load` event.

Listing 14-4: The Page_Load event of your XML Web service client application

VB

```
Private Sub Page_Load(ByVal sender As System.Object, ByVal e As _
                  System.EventArgs) Handles MyBase.Load
    Dim ws As New localhost.AddWithHeader()
    Dim wsHeader As New localhost.myHeader()

    wsHeader.Name = "Bill Evjen"
    wsHeader.EmailAddress = "evjen@yahoo.com"

    ws.myHeaderValue = wsHeader
    Label1.Text = ws.Add(5, 6)
End Sub
```

C#

```
private void Page_Load(object sender, System.EventArgs e)
{
 localhost.Service1 ws = new localhost.AddWithHeader();
 localhost.myHeader wsHeader = new localhost.myHeader();

 wsHeader.Name = "Bill Evjen";
 wsHeader.EmailAddress = "evjen@yahoo.com";

 ws.myHeaderValue = wsHeader;
 Label1.Text = ws.Add(5,6);
}
```

In this code example, you first create an instance of the proxy class for the `AddWithHeader` class, as well as an instance of the class that works with the SOAP Header. Then you assign values to each available property within the `myHeader` class. In this example, both the `Name` and `EmailAddress` properties get an assigned value. This value will be serialized into XML by the `SoapHeader` class.

After the properties of the SOAP Header are assigned, the SOAP Header's values are assigned to the XML Web service. The final line is used to call the `Add()` method with pre-assigned values. When this method is called, the header information is sent as part of the SOAP request.

Running this application will produce the following result in the browser:

Hello Bill Evjen. The result of your addition is: 11
Your email address is: evjen@yahoo.com

If you change the proxy class so that it runs through a port that lets you watch the SOAP message with the Trace Utility, you can see the new message there. The request and response SOAP Envelopes for this transaction are shown in Listings 14-5 and 14-6.

Listing 14-5: The SOAP request

```xml
<?xml version="1.0" encoding="utf-8" ?>
<soap:Envelope xmlns:soap="http://schemas.xmlsoap.org/soap/envelope/"
 xmlns:xsi="http://www.w3.org/2001/XMLSchema-instance"
 xmlns:xsd="http://www.w3.org/2001/XMLSchema">
  <soap:Header>
    <myHeader xmlns="http://tempuri.org/">
      <Name>Bill Evjen</Name>
      <EmailAddress>evjen@yahoo.com</EmailAddress>
    </myHeader>
  </soap:Header>
  <soap:Body>
    <Add xmlns="http://tempuri.org/">
      <a>5</a>
      <b>6</b>
    </Add>
  </soap:Body>
</soap:Envelope>
```

Listing 14-6: The SOAP response

```
<?xml version="1.0" encoding="utf-8" ?>
<soap:Envelope xmlns:soap="http://schemas.xmlsoap.org/soap/envelope/"
 xmlns:xsi="http://www.w3.org/2001/XMLSchema-instance"
 xmlns:xsd="http://www.w3.org/2001/XMLSchema">
  <soap:Body>
    <AddResponse xmlns="http://tempuri.org/">
      <AddResult>Hello Bill Evjen. The result of your addition is:
        11<br>Your email address is: evjen@yahoo.com
      </AddResult>
    </AddResponse>
  </soap:Body>
</soap:Envelope>
```

Requiring and not requiring SOAP Headers

If you build into your XML Web service the fact that it accepts headers (shown in the code examples above), all SOAP headers are required by default. A user who tries to consume this XML Web service without passing in the SOAP Header encounters an error and is unable to consume the XML Web service until this requirement is met.

This might not, however, always be what you want to happen. You might want to give the end user the option of putting in the SOAP Header, or if he chooses not to, still allowing him to proceed with the consumption of the XML Web service. In the end, you want him to be able to consume your XML Web service.

You allow the user to bypass this requirement by setting the `Required` property of the `SoapHeader` attribute to `False`, as shown in Listing 14-7.

Listing 14-7: Not requiring a SOAP Header

VB

```
<WebMethod(), SoapHeader("GetClientInfo"), Required:=False> _
   Public Function Add(ByVal a As Integer, ByVal b As Integer) As String
     Dim Result As Integer
     Dim myMessage As String

     Result = a + b

     If Not (GetClientInfo Is Nothing) Then
        myMessage = "Hello " + GetClientInfo.Name _
           + ". The result of your addition is: " + Result.ToString() _
           + "<br>Your email address is: " + GetClientInfo.EmailAddress
     Else
        myMessage = "Hello" _
           + ". The result of your addition is: " + Result.ToString()
     End If
```

```
        Return myMessage
    End Function

End Class
```

C#

```
[WebMethod()]
[SoapHeader("GetClientInfo"), Required=false]
    public string Add(int a, int b)
    {
      int result;
      string myMessage;

      result = a + b;

      if (GetClientInfo != null)
      {
         myMessage = "Hello " + GetClientInfo.Name
            + ". The result of your addition is: " + result.ToString()
            + "<br>Your email address is: "
            + GetClientInfo.EmailAddress;
      }
      else
      {
         myMessage = "Hello"
            + ". The result of your addition is: " + result.ToString();
      }

      return myMessage;
    }
}
```

With the `Required` setting set to `False`, the end user will not be required to pass in a SOAP Header. As an XML Web services developer, you can change how the Web service is processed based upon whether the end user passed in information or not.

SOAP Header direction

By default, SOAP Headers are sent from the XML Web service client to the XML Web service. The SOAP Header in this situation moves in a single direction. It is possible, however, to change the direction of the SOAP Header so that it can go in either direction, or even both ways if you require it.

To specify the direction of the SOAP Header, you provide the `Direction` property to the `SoapHeader` attribute. Table 14-1 describes each of the possible values of the `Direction` property.

Table 14-1: The Direction Property Values

Value	Description
In	This is the default setting. `In` means that the direction of the SOAP Header is going from the XML Web service client to the XML Web service (*into the Web service*).
Out	A setting of `Out` means that the direction of the SOAP Header is the reverse of the default and is moving from the XML Web service to the XML Web service Client (*out of the Web service*).
InOut	A value of `InOut` means that the SOAP Header will move in both directions.

For example, suppose you have a SOAP message that you want to send out with a SOAP Header that includes your name, e-mail address, and the version number of the XML Web service that the SOAP Header represents. In order to do this, you change the direction of the SOAP Header so that it goes from the XML Web service to the XML Web service client. Listing 14-8 shows an example of this.

Listing 14-8: Sending a SOAP Header from an XML Web service to a consuming application

VB

```
Imports System.Web.Services
Imports System.Web.Services.Protocols

Public Class myHeader
    Inherits SoapHeader

    Public Name As String
    Public EmailAddress As String
    Public Version As String
End Class

<WebService(Namespace:="http://www.xmlws101.com/")> _
Public Class AdditionCalculator
    Inherits System.Web.Services.WebService

    Public ReturnMyInfo As myHeader

    <WebMethod(), SoapHeader("ReturnMyInfo", _
      Direction:=SoapHeaderDirection.Out)> _
    Function Add(ByVal a As Integer, ByVal b As Integer) As String

        ReturnMyInfo = New myHeader()
        ReturnMyInfo.Name = "Bill Evjen"
        ReturnMyInfo.EmailAddress = "evjen@yahoo.com"
```

```
            ReturnMyInfo.Version = "v1.0"

        Return Convert.ToString(a + b)
    End Function

End Class
```

C#
```
using System;
using System.Collections;
using System.ComponentModel;
using System.Data;
using System.Diagnostics;
using System.Web;
using System.Web.Services;
using System.Web.Services.Protocols;

namespace WebService1
{
 /// <summary>
 /// This XML Web Service returns a SOAP Header to the client.
 /// </summary>
 ///

 public class myHeader : SoapHeader
 {
  public string Name;
  public string EmailAddress;
  public string Version;
 }

 [WebService(Namespace="http://www.xmlws101.com")]
 public class AdditionCalculator : System.Web.Services.WebService
 {
  public myHeader ReturnMyInfo;

  [WebMethod]
  [SoapHeader("ReturnMyInfo", Direction=SoapHeaderDirection.Out)]
  public string Add(int a, int b)
  {
   myHeader ReturnMyInfo = new myHeader();
   ReturnMyInfo.Name = "Bill Evjen";
   ReturnMyInfo.EmailAddress = "evjen@yahoo.com";
   ReturnMyInfo.Version = "v1.0";

   return Convert.ToString(a + b);
  }
 }
}
```

The direction of the SOAP Header specifies it is to be sent from the XML Web service. This is done by specifying the value of the `Direction` property to be `SoapHeaderDirection.Out`. Because of this, when a consumer of this particular XML Web service makes a typical request, the end user expects to see a SOAP message returned with a SOAP Header included (Listing 14-9).

Listing 14-9: The SOAP response with a SOAP Header included

```
<?xml version="1.0" encoding="utf-8" ?>
<soap:Envelope xmlns:soap="http://schemas.xmlsoap.org/soap/envelope/"
 xmlns:xsi="http://www.w3.org/2001/XMLSchema-instance"
 xmlns:xsd="http://www.w3.org/2001/XMLSchema">
  <soap:Header>
    <myHeader xmlns="http://www.xmlws101.com/">
      <Name>Bill Evjen</Name>
      <EmailAddress>evjen@yahoo.com</EmailAddress>
      <Version>v1.0</Version>
    </myHeader>
  </soap:Header>
  <soap:Body>
    <AddResponse xmlns="http://www.xmlws101.com/">
      <AddResult>11</AddResult>
    </AddResponse>
  </soap:Body>
</soap:Envelope>
```

As the XML Web service developer, you can probably think of better things to include in your SOAP Headers. The point here is that these SOAP Headers don't have to be specific to the logic that is provided by the Web service itself. They can be basically anything your heart desires.

Validating SOAP Header information

If you are asking for SOAP Header information from the consumers of your XML Web service, in some cases you are going to want to validate the data that is being sent to you in the SOAP Header payload. For instance, you might run the data received through some sort of comparative logic to see if it is the information that you are looking for. If it isn't, you can then return a SOAP Fault to the consumer.

As an example, look at how you would validate some simple data that is sent by an XML Web service client to your XML Web service. In order to validate data within your XML Web service, you work with the `MustUnderstand` property of the `SoapHeader` class.

MustUnderstand

An XML Web service client has the capability to specify instructions to the XML Web service. She can specify that, in order to process the entire SOAP message sent by the client, the Web service *has to* understand the SOAP Header payload. This is done with the code shown in Listing 14-10:

Listing 14-10: Validating SOAP Header data within an XML Web service

VB

```vb
Imports System.Web.Services
Imports System.Web.Services.Protocols
Imports System.Text.RegularExpressions

Public Class myHeader
    Inherits SoapHeader

    Public Name As String
    Public EmailAddress As String
End Class

<WebService(Namespace:="http://www.xmlws101.com/")> _
 Public Class AddCalculator
    Inherits System.Web.Services.WebService

    Public GetClientInfo As myHeader

    <WebMethod(), SoapHeader("GetClientInfo")> _
    Public Function Add(ByVal a As Integer, ByVal b As Integer) _
                    As String
        GetClientInfo.MustUnderstand = True

        Dim EmailRegex As Regex = New Regex("([\w-]+@([\w-]+\.)+[\w-]+)")
        Dim M As Match = EmailRegex.Match(GetClientInfo.EmailAddress)

        If M.Success Then
            GetClientInfo.DidUnderstand = True
        Else
            GetClientInfo.DidUnderstand = False
        End If

        Dim Result As Integer
        Dim myMessage As String

        Result = a + b
        myMessage = "Hello " + GetClientInfo.Name _
            + ". The result of your addition is:" + Result.ToString() _
            + "<br>Your email address is: " + GetClientInfo.EmailAddress

        Return myMessage
    End Function

End Class
```

C#

```csharp
using System;
using System.Collections;
using System.ComponentModel;
using System.Data;
using System.Diagnostics;
using System.Web;
using System.Web.Services;
using System.Web.Services.Protocols;
using System.Text.RegularExpressions;

namespace WebService1
{
 /// <summary>
 /// This XML Web Service checks if the SOAP Header is valid.
 /// </summary>
 ///

 public class myHeader : SoapHeader
 {
  public string Name;
  public string EmailAddress;
 }


[WebService(Namespace="http://www.xmlws101.com")]
 public class AdditionCalculator : System.Web.Services.WebService
 {
  public myHeader GetClientInfo;

  [WebMethod]
  [SoapHeader("GetClientInfo")]
  public string Add(int a, int b)
  {
   GetClientInfo.MustUnderstand = true;

   Regex EmailRegex = new Regex("([\\w-]+@([\\w-]+\\.)+[\\w-]+)");
   Match M = EmailRegex.Match(GetClientInfo.EmailAddress);

   if (M.Success)
   {
    GetClientInfo.DidUnderstand = true;
   }
   else
   {
    GetClientInfo.DidUnderstand = false;
   }
```

```
    int Result;
    string myMessage;

    Result = a + b;
    myMessage = "Hello " + GetClientInfo.Name
      + ". The result of your addition is:" + Result.ToString()
      + "<br>Your email address is: " + GetClientInfo.EmailAddress;

    return myMessage;
  }
 }
}
```

Because this simple XML Web service does not contain a `Required:=False` SoapHeaderAttribute, the client is required to send in a SOAP Header along with her SOAP request. This is a great feature if you want to collect certain related information. You need to ensure, however, that you are collecting *valid* information. If you want to ensure that you do not even process an XML Web service unless the information within the SOAP Header is correct, you set the `MustUnderstand` property to `True`.

VB

```
GetClientInfo.MustUnderstand = True
```

C#

```
GetClientInfo.MustUnderstand = true;
```

Within the XML Web service, it is possible to override the `MustUnderstand` property, setting it to `True`. By overriding this property within the XML Web service, you specify whether the WebMethod did or did not understand the SOAP Header that was sent in. You do this by setting the `DidUnderstand` property to either `False` or `True`. (Note that clients can also require that SOAP Headers be understood.)

In the previous example, the XML Web service takes an e-mail address from the SOAP Header and checks the validity of this address using a regular expression. If the Web service finds it to be a valid e-mail address, the `DidUnderstand` property is set to `True`. If it finds that the consumer of the XML Web service sent something other than an e-mail address within the `<EmailAddress>` element of the SOAP Header, the `DidUnderstand` property is set to `False`.

If the `DidUnderstand` property is set to `False`, the XML Web service will not be processed and the end user will receive a SOAP Fault message within the SOAP Body. An example of this is shown in Listings 14-11 and 14-12.

Listing 14-11: The SOAP request with an improper e-mail address in the SOAP Header

```
<?xml version="1.0" encoding="utf-8" ?>
<soap:Envelope xmlns:soap="http://schemas.xmlsoap.org/soap/envelope/"
 xmlns:xsi="http://www.w3.org/2001/XMLSchema-instance"
 xmlns:xsd="http://www.w3.org/2001/XMLSchema">
  <soap:Header>
    <myHeader xmlns="http://www.xmlws101.com/">
      <Name>Bill Evjen</Name>
      <EmailAddress>I'm not giving it to you</EmailAddress>
    </myHeader>
  </soap:Header>
  <soap:Body>
    <Add xmlns="http://www.xmlws101.com/">
      <a>5</a>
      <b>6</b>
    </Add>
  </soap:Body>
</soap:Envelope>
```

Listing 14-12: A SOAP Fault message that is sent from the XML Web service

```
<?xml version="1.0" encoding="utf-8" ?>
<soap:Envelope xmlns:soap="http://schemas.xmlsoap.org/soap/envelope/">
  <soap:Body>
    <soap:Fault>
      <faultcode>soap:MustUnderstand</faultcode>
      <faultstring>System.Web.Services.Protocols.SoapHeaderException:
       SOAP header myHeader was not understood. at
       System.Web.Services.Protocols.SoapHeaderHandling.
       EnsureHeadersUnderstood (SoapHeaderCollection headers) at
       System.Web.Services.Protocols.SoapServerProtocol.
       WriteReturns(Object[] returnValues, Stream outputStream) at
       System.Web.Services.Protocols.WebServiceHandler.
       WriteReturns(Object[] returnValues) at
       System.Web.Services.Protocols.WebServiceHandler.Invoke()
       at System.Web.Services.Protocols.
       WebServiceHandler.CoreProcessRequest()
      </faultstring>
    </soap:Fault>
  </soap:Body>
</soap:Envelope>
```

As you can tell, the response is a SOAP Fault message with a `faultcode` specifying that the XML Web service didn't process the input because of a `MustUnderstand` error. It is very easy to build validation of your SOAP Headers into your XML Web services. You will find this valuable when working with authentication and authorization within your XML Web services. This will be discussed in Chapter 16.

SOAP Header exceptions

If you want to customize the error messages that are received on the consumer's end, you can use the `SoapHeaderException` class. This enables you to provide the end user with more error information so that he can figure out how to interact with your Web service. This will be covered in detail in Chapter 20, which discusses errors and exception handling.

SOAP Extensions

As mentioned earlier, in most cases, you are going to want to let ASP.NET do its trick and take care of all the SOAP messaging for you. There are going to be moments, however, when you want to intercept SOAP message and work with the SOAP message before it is sent past certain points.

In .NET, there are specific points in the short life of a SOAP message being sent and received when you are able to jump in and interact with it. The following diagram (Figure 14-1) shows you where, in the process of sending a SOAP message, you can work with it.

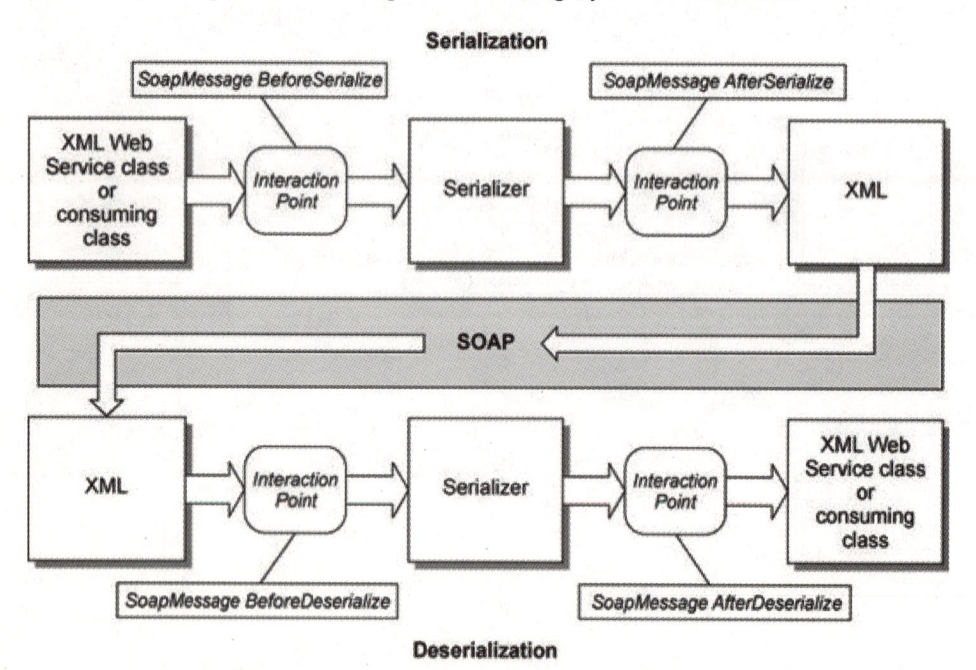

Figure 14-1: The four points to interact with a SOAP message as it is being sent.

Chapter 14: **Advanced SOAP**

Serialization is the process whereby an object is converted into a format that enables it to be readily transported. In this case, the format is XML. When you serialize an object within ASP.NET in the context of XML Web services, it is formatted into XML and then sent via a SOAP packet. In the SOAP packet, the XML payload can be deserialized. The process of *deserialization*, as you would expect, is the conversion of an XML payload back into the object that was originally sent.

ASP.NET provides these means of interacting with the SOAP message process before or after serialization and deserialization in order for you to be able to inspect or modify the SOAP message. The capability to inspect the SOAP message throughout its journey gives you quite a bit of power. On either the client or server, you can manipulate SOAP messages to perform specific actions based upon items found in the SOAP payload. These points of interaction include `BeforeSerialize`, `AfterSerialize`, `BeforeDeserialize`, and `AfterDeserialize`.

For an example of this process, you are going to build an XML Web service that will write the SOAP messages to a text file as they are being sent and received. In order to perform this type of functionality in the XML Web service, all you need to do in the XML Web service itself is to apply a SOAP extension attribute to the WebMethod that you are going to interact with. Look at Listing 14-13.

Listing 14-13: Referring to the SOAP extensions by using an attribute within the WebMethod

VB

```
<WebMethod(), TraceExtension(Filename:="c:\myTextFile.txt")> _
Public Function Add(ByVal a As Integer, ByVal b As Integer) As Integer
    Return a + b
End Function
```

C#

```
[WebMethod]
[TraceExtension(Filename="c:\\myTextFile.txt")]
public int Add(int a, int b)
{
    return a + b;
}
```

If you can't find the `TraceExtension` attribute in the .NET Framework SDK, don't worry — it's not there. In fact, it's not supposed to be there; it's a custom attribute that you can add to a WebMethod yourself.

Unfortunately it isn't as simple to add this attribute to the WebMethod. In order to accomplish this, you have to build a class that you can place within the `bin` folder of your application. After this step is taken, you are able to refer to the class by specifying the class name as an attribute to the method to which you want to apply the class.

In reality, the first step is to create a couple of classes. You need one class that derives from `System.Web.Services.Protocols.SoapExtension` and another class that derives from `System.Web.Services.Protocols.SoapExtensionAttribute`. So, open up your XML Web service project from within Visual Studio .NET and add a class file to your project. Name the file whatever you choose.

Take a look at the code (shown in Listing 14-14) that you put into this file for the `TraceExtensionAttribute` class.

Listing 14-14: The TraceExtensionAttribute class

VB

```
Imports System
Imports System.Web.Services
Imports System.Web.Services.Protocols
Imports System.IO

<AttributeUsage(AttributeTargets.Method)> _
Public Class TraceExtensionAttribute
    Inherits SoapExtensionAttribute

    Private TraceFileName As String = "c:\myTextFile.txt"
    Private TracePriority As Integer

    Public Overrides ReadOnly Property ExtensionType() As Type
        Get
            Return GetType(TraceExtension)
        End Get
    End Property

    Public Overrides Property Priority() As Integer
        Get
            Return TracePriority
        End Get
        Set
            TracePriority = value
        End Set
    End Property

    Public Property Filename() As String
        Get
            Return TraceFileName
        End Get
        Set
            TraceFileName = value
        End Set
    End Property
End Class
```

C#

```csharp
using System;
using System.Web.Services;
using System.Web.Services.Protocols;
using System.IO;

[AttributeUsage(AttributeTargets.Method)]
public class TraceExtensionAttribute : SoapExtensionAttribute {

    private string TraceFileName = "c:\\myTextFile.txt";
    private int TracePriority;

    public override Type ExtensionType {
        get { return typeof(TraceExtension); }
    }

    public override int Priority {
        get { return TracePriority; }
        set { TracePriority = value; }
    }

    public string Filename {
        get {
            return TraceFileName;
        }
        set {
            TraceFileName = value;
        }
    }
}
```

In order to create your own user-defined attribute to apply to your WebMethod, you first create a class that derives from the `SoapExtensionAttribute` class. Before this, you apply an `AttributeUsage` attribute to the `TraceExtensionAttribute` class. The `AttributeTargets` property specifies that this custom attribute is designed for a method. Within the class itself are the property definitions that the custom attribute can take. In this case, you get the value of the property `Filename`.

Listing 14-15 creates another class within the same file that inherits from `SoapExtension`. This class will grab the SOAP message that is sent to the XML Web service after serialization and write this SOAP message to a text file. The SOAP message that is returned will be read right after is it is deserialized and recorded into the same text file that the end user specifies.

Listing 14-15: The class that provides all the functionality for the SOAP attribute

VB

```
Public Class TraceExtension
    Inherits SoapExtension

    Private OldStream As Stream
    Private NewStream As Stream
    Private FileName As String

    Public Overloads Overrides Function GetInitializer(methodInfo As _
       LogicalMethodInfo, attribute As SoapExtensionAttribute) As Object
        Return CType(attribute, TraceExtensionAttribute).Filename
    End Function

    Public Overloads Overrides Function GetInitializer(WebServiceType _
       As Type) As Object
        Return WebServiceType.GetType().ToString() & ".txt"
    End Function

    Public Overrides Sub Initialize(initializer As Object)
        FileName = CStr(initializer)
    End Sub

    Public Overrides Sub ProcessMessage(message As SoapMessage)
        Select Case message.Stage

            Case SoapMessageStage.BeforeSerialize

            Case SoapMessageStage.AfterSerialize
                WriteOutput(message)

            Case SoapMessageStage.BeforeDeserialize
                WriteInput(message)

            Case SoapMessageStage.AfterDeserialize

        End Select
    End Sub

    Public Overrides Function ChainStream(stream As Stream) As Stream
        OldStream = stream
        NewStream = New MemoryStream()
        Return NewStream
    End Function

    Public Sub WriteOutput(message As SoapMessage)
        NewStream.Position = 0
```

```vb
        Dim fs As New FileStream(FileName, FileMode.Append, _
            FileAccess.Write)
        Dim w As New StreamWriter(fs)
        w.WriteLine("------------------------------ SOAP RESPONSE AT " _
            + DateTime.Now.ToString())
        w.Flush()
        Copy(m_newStream, fs)
        fs.Close()
        NewStream.Position = 0
        Copy(NewStream, OldStream)
    End Sub

    Public Sub WriteInput(message As SoapMessage)
        Copy(OldStream, NewStream)
        Dim fs As New FileStream(FileName, FileMode.Append, _
            FileAccess.Write)
        Dim w As New StreamWriter(fs)
        w.WriteLine(vbCrLf + _
            "*************************************************")
        w.WriteLine(vbCrLf + _
            "------------------------------ SOAP REQUEST AT " _
            + DateTime.Now.ToString())
        w.Flush()
        NewStream.Position = 0
        Copy(NewStream, fs)
        fs.Close()
        NewStream.Position = 0
    End Sub

    Sub Copy(fromStream As Stream, toStream As Stream)
        Dim reader As New StreamReader(fromStream)
        Dim writer As New StreamWriter(toStream)
        writer.WriteLine(reader.ReadToEnd())
        writer.Flush()
    End Sub
End Class
```

C#

```csharp
public class TraceExtension : SoapExtension {

  Stream oldStream;
  Stream newStream;
  string filename;

  public override object GetInitializer(LogicalMethodInfo methodInfo,
    SoapExtensionAttribute attribute) {
      return ((TraceExtensionAttribute) attribute).Filename;
  }
```

```
public override object GetInitializer(Type WebServiceType) {
    return WebServiceType.GetType().ToString() + ".txt";
}

public override void Initialize(object initializer) {
    filename = (string) initializer;
}

public override void ProcessMessage(SoapMessage message) {
    switch (message.Stage) {

    case SoapMessageStage.BeforeSerialize:
        break;

    case SoapMessageStage.AfterSerialize:
        WriteOutput( message );
        break;

    case SoapMessageStage.BeforeDeserialize:
        WriteInput( message );
        break;

    case SoapMessageStage.AfterDeserialize:
        break;

    }
}

public override Stream ChainStream( Stream stream ){
    oldStream = stream;
    newStream = new MemoryStream();
    return newStream;
}

public void WriteOutput( SoapMessage message ){
    newStream.Position = 0;
    FileStream fs = new FileStream(filename, FileMode.Append,
        FileAccess.Write);
    StreamWriter w = new StreamWriter(fs);
    w.WriteLine("-------------------------------- SOAP RESPONSE AT " +
        DateTime.Now);
    w.Flush();
    Copy(newStream, fs);
    fs.Close();
    newStream.Position = 0;
    Copy(newStream, oldStream);
}
```

```
public void WriteInput( SoapMessage message ){
    Copy(oldStream, newStream);
    FileStream fs = new FileStream(filename, FileMode.Append,
        FileAccess.Write);
    StreamWriter w = new StreamWriter(fs);
    w.WriteLine("\n************************************************");
    w.WriteLine("\n------------------------------- SOAP REQUEST AT " +
        DateTime.Now);
    w.Flush();
    newStream.Position = 0;
    Copy(newStream, fs);
    fs.Close();
    newStream.Position = 0;
}

void Copy(Stream from, Stream to) {

    TextReader reader = new StreamReader(from);
    TextWriter writer = new StreamWriter(to);
    writer.WriteLine(reader.ReadToEnd());
    writer.Flush();
}
}
```

This second class is defining the class that is initiated from the SOAP attribute. The `GetInitializer` function grabs the value of the `Filename` property, which is the filename and path that the result set will be saved to.

The most important function in this class is the `ProcessMessage` method. The `ProcessMessage` is called at all stages for SOAP extensions in which the SOAP extensions are applied to both an XML Web service and an XML Web service client. Within the `ProcessMessage` method are the `SoapMessageStage` enumerations. Table 14-2 provides a brief description of each of these enumerations.

Table 14-2: SoapMessageStage Enumerations

SoapMessageStage Enumeration	*Description*
`SoapMessageStage.BeforeSerialize`	This stage occurs just prior to the SOAP message being serialized.
	If this method is being performed on the client, this occurs directly after the client has invoked the Web service but before the object has been serialized into XML.
	If this method is being performed on the server where the XML Web service is hosted, this stage occurs directly after the invocation of the WebMethod but directly before the result is serialized into XML.
`SoapMessageStage.AfterSerialize`	This stage occurs just after the SOAP message is serialized.
	If this method is being performed on the client, this occurs directly after the client has invoked the Web service and the results have been serialized into XML but directly before the SOAP message has been sent across the wire to the Web service.
	If this method is being performed on the server where the XML Web service is hosted, this stage occurs directly after the invocation of the WebMethod and the results have been serialized into XML but directly before the SOAP message has been sent back over the wire to the client.
`SoapMessageStage.BeforeDeserialize`	This stage occurs just before the SOAP message is deserialized.
	If this method is being performed on the client, this occurs directly after the client has received the SOAP message from the Web service but before the message has been deserialized.
	If this method is being performed on the server where the XML Web service is hosted, this stage occurs directly after the invocation of the WebMethod but directly before the result is serialized into XML.

SoapMessageStage Enumeration	Description
`SoapMessageStage.AfterDeserialize`	This stage occurs directly after the SOAP message is deserialized.
	If this method is being performed on the client, this occurs directly after the client has received the SOAP message from the Web service but before the client takes the object.
	If this method is being performed on the server where the XML Web service is hosted, this stage occurs directly after the deserialization of the SOAP message to an object, but prior to the WebMethod performing any action on the object.

In addition to the `ProcessMessage` method, there are additional methods for writing the input and output SOAP messages to a text file. After all the code is in place, simply follow these steps in order to use your new custom attribute, the SOAP extension:

1. Save the class file.
2. Place the class file in the `bin` directory of your project. Make sure that it is the same project as the one that holds your XML Web service.
3. Go to your XML Web service and give the WebMethod that will record the traffic of the `TraceExtension` attribute.

VB

```
<WebMethod(), TraceExtension(Filename:="c:\myTextFile.txt")> _
```

C#

```
[WebMethod]
[TraceExtension(Filename="c:\\myTextFile.txt")]
```

4. To cause the custom attribute to work, you need to create an ASP.NET Web Application or a Windows Application to consume this XML Web service because you must work with SOAP messages in order to be able to process the messages that are sent across the wire. Using HTTP-GET or HTTP-POST does not give you this capability and also prevents the XML Web service from the ASP.NET test page from initiating the custom attribute. For this example, create an ASP.NET Web Application.
5. Put a literal control on your ASP.NET page and, in the code-behind, call the XML Web service just as you normally would. In fact, invoke it a couple of times.

Go to the root directory of your system and look for the file `myTextFile.txt` (see Figure 14-2).

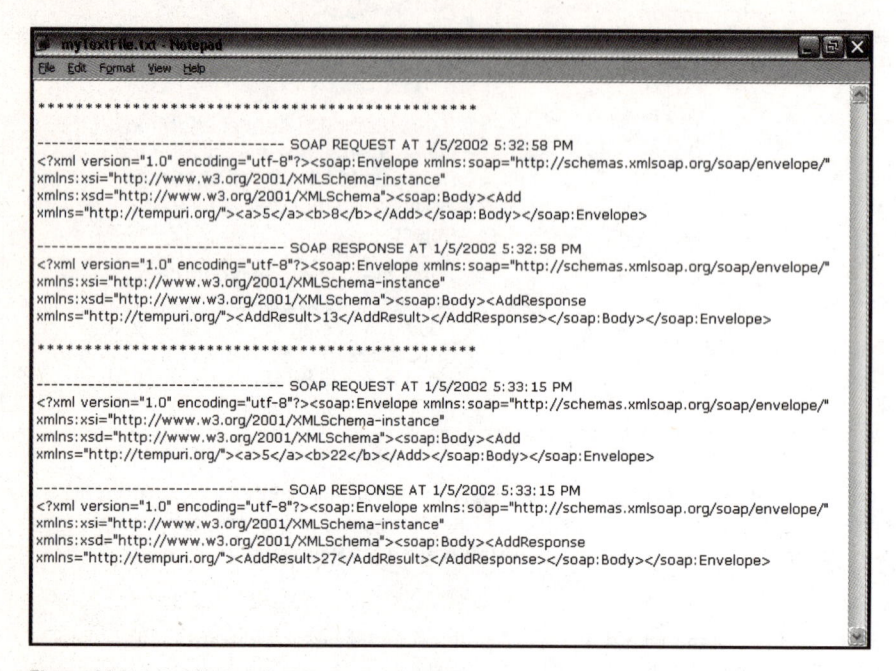

```
---------------------------- SOAP REQUEST AT 1/5/2002 5:32:58 PM
<?xml version="1.0" encoding="utf-8"?><soap:Envelope xmlns:soap="http://schemas.xmlsoap.org/soap/envelope/"
xmlns:xsi="http://www.w3.org/2001/XMLSchema-instance"
xmlns:xsd="http://www.w3.org/2001/XMLSchema"><soap:Body><Add
xmlns="http://tempuri.org/"><a>5</a><b>8</b></Add></soap:Body></soap:Envelope>
---------------------------- SOAP RESPONSE AT 1/5/2002 5:32:58 PM
<?xml version="1.0" encoding="utf-8"?><soap:Envelope xmlns:soap="http://schemas.xmlsoap.org/soap/envelope/"
xmlns:xsi="http://www.w3.org/2001/XMLSchema-instance"
xmlns:xsd="http://www.w3.org/2001/XMLSchema"><soap:Body><AddResponse
xmlns="http://tempuri.org/"><AddResult>13</AddResult></AddResponse></soap:Body></soap:Envelope>

---------------------------- SOAP REQUEST AT 1/5/2002 5:33:15 PM
<?xml version="1.0" encoding="utf-8"?><soap:Envelope xmlns:soap="http://schemas.xmlsoap.org/soap/envelope/"
xmlns:xsi="http://www.w3.org/2001/XMLSchema-instance"
xmlns:xsd="http://www.w3.org/2001/XMLSchema"><soap:Body><Add
xmlns="http://tempuri.org/"><a>5</a><b>22</b></Add></soap:Body></soap:Envelope>
---------------------------- SOAP RESPONSE AT 1/5/2002 5:33:15 PM
<?xml version="1.0" encoding="utf-8"?><soap:Envelope xmlns:soap="http://schemas.xmlsoap.org/soap/envelope/"
xmlns:xsi="http://www.w3.org/2001/XMLSchema-instance"
xmlns:xsd="http://www.w3.org/2001/XMLSchema"><soap:Body><AddResponse
xmlns="http://tempuri.org/"><AddResult>27</AddResult></AddResponse></soap:Body></soap:Envelope>
```

Figure 14-2: A text file that displays the trace output.

As you can tell from this example, it is quite easy to interact with the SOAP messages as they are moved around on the wire, either before they are serialized or directly after. This opens the door to your XML Web services and allows you to extend the functionality of your services. As time goes on, there will be some pretty outstanding SOAP extensions, many available from third parties, for use within your XML Web services.

> **CROSS-REFERENCE:** Working with SOAP extensions is covered in detail in Chapter 17.

The Formatting of SOAP

As you are already aware, XML Web services deal quite heavily with XML. Within the SOAP Body is a XML payload for the entire SOAP message that is sent to and from the XML Web service. What you may not be aware of is that XML encoding within this SOAP message is not strictly defined.

Within SOAP Specification 1.1 (`www.w3.org/TR/2000/NOTE-SOAP-20000508`), Sections 5 and 7 discuss the different encoding types that are available to use within SOAP. There are two available encoding types that SOAP can use with Web services:

- Document encoding
- RPC encoding

XML Web services for ASP.NET can use either of these encoding types. Therefore, it is possible to use either RPC encoding or document encoding for the XML that is transported within your SOAP message. By default, XML Web services in .NET use document encoding.

If an XML Web service is using the default setting, document encoding, for the XML payload, not only does this Web service send out all SOAP messages using this encoding type, but it accepts only SOAP messages that abide by this encoding type. Therefore, regardless of the platform that is sending the message, the SOAP requests must be encoded so that the XML Web service accepts them.

The .NET Framework provides you with the attributes and settings that you can apply in your code so you are able to encode the XML within your SOAP messages in either format. However, it is not the role of the XML Web service developer to adapt the SOAP message to the proper encoding. It is the responsibility of the XML Web service consumer to encode his messages in the proper format in order to interact with the Web service that he is trying to consume.

Document encoding

Document encoding is the default encoding that is used for any XML Web service built with ASP.NET. You don't have to apply any attributes or settings in order to make this your encoding choice. Basically, in document encoding, the XML is formatted according to an XSD schema. These schemas are specified in the WSDL documents, and consumers of the XML Web service need to abide by these schemas in order for their SOAP requests to be processed.

RPC encoding

The RPC encoding format is used in many Web services that reside on non-Microsoft platforms. This encoding type is also used in the Microsoft SOAP Toolkit and with .NET Remoting. XML that is RPC encoded is set to conform to Section 7 of the SOAP specification. In fact, some people refer to this encoding style as "Section 7 encoding."

In RPC encoding, the root element of the XML document is named after the WebMethod, and all the elements contained within this root element refer to the parameters that the WebMethod accepts. Therefore, in the typical `Add()` method example used throughout the book, the SOAP request and response messages look like Listings 14-16 and 14-17:

Listing 14-16: An RPC encoded SOAP request

```
POST /WebService21/Service1.asmx HTTP/1.1
Host: localhost
Content-Type: text/xml; charset=utf-8
Content-Length: length
SOAPAction: "http://tempuri.org/Add"

<?xml version="1.0" encoding="utf-8"?>
<soap:Envelope xmlns:xsi="http://www.w3.org/2001/XMLSchema-instance"
```

Part V: All About SOAP

```
  xmlns:xsd="http://www.w3.org/2001/XMLSchema"
  xmlns:soapenc="http://schemas.xmlsoap.org/soap/encoding/"
  xmlns:tns="http://tempuri.org/"
  xmlns:types="http://tempuri.org/encodedTypes"
  xmlns:soap="http://schemas.xmlsoap.org/soap/envelope/">
  <soap:Body
    soap:encodingStyle="http://schemas.xmlsoap.org/soap/encoding/">
    <tns:Add>
      <a xsi:type="xsd:int">int</a>
      <b xsi:type="xsd:int">int</b>
    </tns:Add>
  </soap:Body>
</soap:Envelope>
```

Listing 14-17: An RPC encoded SOAP response

```
HTTP/1.1 200 OK
Content-Type: text/xml; charset=utf-8
Content-Length: length

<?xml version="1.0" encoding="utf-8"?>
<soap:Envelope xmlns:xsi="http://www.w3.org/2001/XMLSchema-instance"
  xmlns:xsd="http://www.w3.org/2001/XMLSchema"
  xmlns:soapenc="http://schemas.xmlsoap.org/soap/encoding/"
  xmlns:tns="http://tempuri.org/"
  xmlns:types="http://tempuri.org/encodedTypes"
  xmlns:soap="http://schemas.xmlsoap.org/soap/envelope/">
  <soap:Body
    soap:encodingStyle="http://schemas.xmlsoap.org/soap/encoding/">
    <tns:AddResponse>
      <AddResult xsi:type="xsd:int">int</AddResult>
    </tns:AddResponse>
  </soap:Body>
</soap:Envelope>
```

As you can plainly see, this is quite a different structure than you have been used to seeing thus far. If you want to use the RPC-encoded format for your XML Web services, it is actually quite simple to implement.

In order to change the encoding style from document encoding to RPC encoding, you apply the `SoapRpcService` or the `SoapRpcMethod` attributes to your XML Web service or the methods contained therein.

> **NOTE:** Document encoding uses the `SoapDocumentService` and `SoapDocumentMethod` attributes. They can be applied in exactly the same manner as the `SoapRpcService` and the `SoapRpcMethod` attributes.

To change the encoding style of the entire XML Web service to RPC encoding, you apply the `SoapRpcService` attribute to the class, as shown in Listing 14-18.

Listing 14-18: Changing the entire Web service to RPC encoding

VB

```
<WebService(), SoapRpcService()> Public Class Calculator
```

C#

```
[WebService]
[SoapRpcService] public class Calculator
```

Putting this attribute in front of the class declaration causes every WebMethod within that class to send and require receipt of all SOAP messages in the RPC-encoding style.

If you only require a specific method, not the entire class, to be RPC encoded, you use the `SoapRpcMethod` attribute in conjunction with the WebMethod that you want to encode, as in Listing 14-19.

Listing 14-19: Changing the WebMethod to RPC encoding

VB

```
<WebMethod(), SoapRpcMethod()> Public Function DoSomething() As Integer
```

C#

```
[WebMethod]
[SoapRpcMethod] public int DoSomething()
```

This code causes only this particular WebMethod to be RPC encoded. Even if there were an encoding setting at the class level, you could override this setting at the method level by using the `SoapRpcMethod` attribute.

Therefore, it would be possible to use the `SoapRpcService` attribute at the class level and then apply the `SoapDocumentMethod` attribute to one of the available WebMethods. Doing this causes this particular WebMethod to use the standard document-encoding style.

Using both RPC and document encoding

Many different end users will consume Web services in the virtual world. The value of Web services is that they enable disparate systems to interoperate.

If you have an XML Web service that you know is going to be consumed by a wide variety or a large number of end users, it makes sense for you to offer your Web service in both the document-encoding and the RPC-encoding styles. Even though it is possible for the end users, the consumers of your XML Web service, to change how they send SOAP messages to your XML Web service, they can't always do this easily.

To make it easier for all users, you can offer the service in both formats. One option is to have a completely separate `.asmx` file that is offered for each encoding style. People who want RPC encoding pull up the first `.asmx` page, and those who want document encoding use the second `.asmx` page.

344   Part V: All About SOAP

Another option is to have two WebMethods on the same page that offer the same functionality but in different encoding styles. Listing 14-20 illustrates this option.

Listing 14-20: Using both RPC and document encoding in the same XML Web service

VB

```
Imports System.Web.Services
Imports System.Web.Services.Protocols
Imports System.Web.Services.Description

<WebService(Namespace:="http://www.xmlws101.com/")> _
 Public Class Calculator
    Inherits System.Web.Services.WebService

    <WebMethod()> Public Function Add_DocEncoding(ByVal a As Integer,
          ByVal b As Integer) As Integer
        Return a + b
    End Function

    <WebMethod(), SoapRpcMethod()> _
     Public Function Add_RpcEncoding(ByVal a As Integer,
          ByVal b As Integer) As Integer
        Return a + b
    End Function

End Class
```

C#

```
using System.Web.Services;
using System.Web.Services.Protocols;
using System.Web.Services.Description;

[WebService(Namespace="http://www.xmlws101.com/")]
public class Calculator
{
    [WebMethod]
    public int Add_DocEncoding(int a, int b)
    {
        return a + b;
    }

    [WebMethod]
    [SoapRpcMethod]
    public int Add_RpcEncoding(int a, int b)
    {
        return a + b;
    }
}
```

In this XML Web service, when the user logs onto the Web service test page, he finds two available WebMethods waiting for him. From there, he is able to choose the encoding style that best fits his needs.

Client-side RPC SOAP message generation

What do you change if you are building an XML Web service client application that is going to consume a Web service that uses RPC encoding? The answer is really nothing at all. You still do everything as you always did.

When you make a Web reference within Visual Studio .NET, a proxy class is created for you within your application. If the Web service, from which this proxy class was generated, needs SOAP messages that are encoded in RPC, this is specified in the WSDL document. The proxy class will be appropriately generated. Therefore, you only have to create the proxy class and invoke the Web service as you normally would. ASP.NET takes care of all the encoding and marshaling of the SOAP messages for you, as shown in Listing 14-21.

Listing 14-21: A snippet taken from a Visual Basic .NET proxy class that is structured to marshal SOAP messages using a RPC-encoding style

```
<System.Web.Services.Protocols.SoapRpcMethodAttribute
("http://tempuri.org/Add", RequestNamespace:="http://tempuri.org/",
ResponseNamespace:="http://tempuri.org/")> _
Public Function Add(ByVal a As Integer, ByVal b As Integer) As Integer
    Dim results() As Object = Me.Invoke("Add", New Object() {a, b})
    Return CType(results(0),Integer)
End Function
```

Shaping the XML

The XML payload that is contained in the SOAP Body of the SOAP message being sent across the wire is serialized from an object. This serialization process is controlled by the `XmlSerializer` class from the `System.XML.Serialization` namespace.

The `XmlSerializer` class completely takes care of the serialization and deserialization processes for you, and in most cases you won't ever have to worry about the details of this process. There are moments, however, when you are going to want to shape the XML to your own specifications.

If you want to change the output of the XML contained within the SOAP Body, you can use two available sets of attributes. One of the sets is available for HTTP-GET and HTTP-POST calls, and the other is used for SOAP calls. Table 14-3 lists the available attributes.

Table 14-3: Available Attributes for XML Serialization

Used for HTTP-GET and HTTP-POST	Used for SOAP
XmlAnyAttributeAttribute	
XmlAnyElementAttribute	
XmlArrayAttribute	
XmlArrayItemAttribute	
XmlAttributeAttribute	SoapAttributeAttribute
XmlChoiceIdentifierAttribute	
XmlElementAttribute	SoapElementAttribute
XmlEnumAttribute	SoapEnumAttribute
XmlIgnoreAttribute	SoapIgnoreAttribute
XmlIncludeAttribute	SoapIncludeAttribute
XmlRootAttribute	
XmlTextAttribute	
XmlTypeAttribute	SoapTypeAttribute

There is no problem applying both of these attribute styles at the same time. This will not cause any errors.

To show you how you can change the XML so that it better suits your needs, Listing 14-22 shows an XML Web service where all the XML is generated automatically by the `XmlSerializer` class.

Listing 14-22: Returning an instance of a class from an XML Web service

VB

```
Imports System.Web.Services

<WebService(Namespace:="http://www.xmlws101.com/")> _
Public Class BaseballTeams
    Inherits System.Web.Services.WebService

    Public Class BB_Teams
        Public Part As String
        Public Year As Integer
        Public Teams() As String
    End Class

    <WebMethod()> Public Function GetTeams() As BB_Teams
```

```
            Dim bbt As New BB_Teams()
            bbt.Part = "AL"
            bbt.Year = 2002

            ReDim bbt.Teams(5)
            bbt.Teams(0) = "Seattle Mariners"
            bbt.Teams(1) = "New York Yankees"
            bbt.Teams(2) = "Chicago White Sox"
            bbt.Teams(3) = "Anaheim Angels"
            bbt.Teams(4) = "Baltimore Orioles"

            Return bbt
        End Function

End Class
```

C#

```
using System;
using System.Collections;
using System.ComponentModel;
using System.Data;
using System.Diagnostics;
using System.Web;
using System.Web.Services;

namespace WebService1
{
 public class BaseballTeams : System.Web.Services.WebService
  {
   public class BB_Teams
    {
     public string Part;
     public int Year;
     public string[] Teams;
    }

   [WebMethod]
   public BB_Teams GetTeams()
    {
     BB_Teams bbt = new BB_Teams();
     bbt.Part = "AL";
     bbt.Year = 2002;

     bbt.Teams = new string[5];

     bbt.Teams[0] = "Seattle Mariners";
     bbt.Teams[1] = "New York Yankees";
     bbt.Teams[2] = "Chicago White Sox";
```

```
      bbt.Teams[3] = "Anaheim Angels";
      bbt.Teams[4] = "Baltimore Orioles";

      return bbt;
    }
  }
}
```

What is returned to you from the `XmlSerializer` class is an XML document where the class name is the root element of the document. Beyond that, each of the definitions in this class constitutes a subelement. So, when this XML Web service is invoked, you see the results shown in Listing 14-23:

Listing 14-23: The returned XML document from the class

```
<?xml version="1.0" encoding="utf-8" ?>
<BB_Teams xmlns:xsd="http://www.w3.org/2001/XMLSchema"
 xmlns:xsi="http://www.w3.org/2001/XMLSchema-instance"
 xmlns="http://www.xmlws101.com/">
  <Part>AL</Part>
  <Year>2002</Year>
  <Teams>
      <string>Seattle Mariners</string>
      <string>New York Yankees</string>
      <string>Chicago White Sox</string>
      <string>Anaheim Angels</string>
      <string>Baltimore Orioles</string>
  </Teams>
</BB_Teams>
```

This return document from the XML Web service might suit your needs, but there are times when you want to rename some the elements, or even make one of the elements an attribute of the root element. In this case, you can apply attributes to the element declarations in your XML Web service.

The first step is to import the `System.XML.Serialization` namespace into your XML Web service. This will enable you to work with the `XmlSerializer` class. After this is done, you can apply the attributes that modify the output of the XML (see Listing 14-24).

Listing 14-24: Modifying the output of the XML using the XmlSerializer class

VB

```
Imports System.Web.Services
Imports System.Xml.Serialization

<WebService(Namespace:="http://www.xmlws101.com/")> _
Public Class BaseballTeams
    Inherits System.Web.Services.WebService

    <XmlRoot("Baseball_Teams")> Public Class BB_Teams
```

```vb
            <XmlElement("League"), SoapElement("League")> _
            Public Part As String
            <XmlAttributeAttribute(), SoapAttributeAttribute()> _
            Public Year As Integer
            Public Teams() As String
        End Class

        <WebMethod()> Public Function GetTeams() As BB_Teams
            Dim bbt As New BB_Teams()
            bbt.Part = "AL"
            bbt.Year = 2002

            ReDim bbt.Teams(5)
            bbt.Teams(0) = "Seattle Mariners"
            bbt.Teams(1) = "New York Yankees"
            bbt.Teams(2) = "Chicago White Sox"
            bbt.Teams(3) = "Anaheim Angels"
            bbt.Teams(4) = "Baltimore Orioles"

            Return bbt
        End Function

End Class
```

C#

```csharp
using System;
using System.Collections;
using System.ComponentModel;
using System.Data;
using System.Diagnostics;
using System.Web;
using System.Web.Services;
using System.Xml.Serialization;

namespace WebService1
{
 public class BaseballTeams : System.Web.Services.WebService
  {
   [XmlRoot("Baseball_Teams")]public class BB_Teams
   {
    [XmlElement("League")]
    [SoapElement("League")]
    public string Part;
    [XmlAttributeAttribute]
    [SoapAttributeAttribute]
    public int Year;
    public string[] Teams;
   }
```

```
[WebMethod]
public BB_Teams GetTeams()
{
  BB_Teams bbt = new BB_Teams();
  bbt.Part = "AL";
  bbt.Year = 2002;

  bbt.Teams = new string[5];

  bbt.Teams[0] = "Seattle Mariners";
  bbt.Teams[1] = "New York Yankees";
  bbt.Teams[2] = "Chicago White Sox";
  bbt.Teams[3] = "Anaheim Angels";
  bbt.Teams[4] = "Baltimore Orioles";

  return bbt;
 }
}
}
```

In this example, the root element is changed from `BB_Teams` (the name of the class) to something a little more understandable, `Baseball_Teams`. You can do this by using the `<XmlRoot>` attribute. The value given in this attribute is the new assigned name for the root element of the XML document.

Renaming elements is just as easy. By using the `<XmlElement>` and the `<SoapElement>` attributes, subelements to the root element are easily renamed. This example uses both the `<XmlElement>` and the `<SoapElement>` so that these changes are in place regardless of the wire format used for invocation. Therefore, if you use HTTP-POST, you get back the same XML document that you get if you use SOAP.

In the code example above, one of the declarations is assigned as an attribute to the root element using the `<XmlAttributeAttribute>` and the `<SoapAttributeAttribute>` elements.

Listing 14-25 shows you the XML document that is returned after running this example:

Listing 14-25: The returned XML document after shaping the XML

```
<?xml version="1.0" encoding="utf-8" ?>
<Baseball_Teams xmlns:xsd="http://www.w3.org/2001/XMLSchema"
 xmlns:xsi="http://www.w3.org/2001/XMLSchema-instance" Year="2002"
 xmlns="http://www.xmlws101.com/">
   <League>AL</League>
   <Teams>
      <string>Seattle Mariners</string>
      <string>New York Yankees</string>
      <string>Chicago White Sox</string>
      <string>Anaheim Angels</string>
```

```
    <string>Baltimore Orioles</string>
  </Teams>
</Baseball_Teams>
```

Using the `XmlSerializer` class, it is very simple to change the XML output from your XML Web services to a format that a consuming application might require or into a format that is more understandable.

Summary

In this chapter, you covered a lot of ground. Working with SOAP to make it to do what you want could be the subject of a whole book by itself. This chapter covered some of the common ways in which you might change the SOAP that is being sent from one place to another.

Working with SOAP Headers is an entirely new model of how to add data that might not be directly related to the SOAP message payload itself. SOAP Headers are a powerful addition to the SOAP message, and you will see more about them in Chapter 17.

Another powerful way to work with SOAP messages from ASP.NET is to extend your SOAP using SOAP extensions. This chapter covered some simple ways of using SOAP extensions to give you a glimpse of the power involved. You can use this knowledge to develop SOAP extensions for use with your own XML Web services or as a third party-tool that you might provide to the rest of the programming community.

You also explored the different ways in which the XML payload in SOAP messages is encoded, and how to work with and change the encoding styles of your XML Web services. Finally, this chapter demonstrated how to change and shape the XML output from your XML Web services and give them the shape that works best for you.

In the next chapter, you take a look at further extensions to SOAP that have recently been introduced, Global XML Web Services Architecture.

Chapter 15

Global XML Web Services Architecture

Growth is the only evidence of life.
John Henry Newman, *Apologia pro Vita Sua* (1864)

This is the forward-thinking chapter of the book. Now that you have read a couple of chapters on SOAP and what you can do with SOAP, you probably have questions about certain capabilities of SOAP and about how XML Web services deals with this transport language.

For instance, you might be wondering what you would do to get a SOAP packet from point A to point Z if you had to route it through 24 points in between. You might also be wondering about security. When applications provide credentials to your XML Web service, how can you tell if the responses truly are what they say they are?

These points are addressed in a collection of draft proposals from Microsoft and IBM that is referred to as the Global XML Web Services Architecture (GXA).

In this chapter, you will learn about the concepts behind these proposals, including

- Why GXA?
- WS-Inspection
- WS-License
- WS-Referral
- WS-Routing
- WS-Security
- What the future holds for XML Web services

Looking into the Crystal Ball

As you have seen throughout the book, XML Web services is a powerful new application model. With this new model, we make as big of a jump as we did going from the mainframe world to the client/server world (maybe bigger!). XML Web services enables applications and data stores to go beyond their initial purposes. As was demonstrated and discussed in this book, XML Web services provides some of the following capabilities:

- A new and quick way to expose data stores to disparate systems
- A way to quickly expand an application's capabilities
- A simple way to expose common logic
- A system in which you are able to easily integrate with partners and customers
- New revenue models
- New ways for advertising and promotion

I could add many additional points, but let's stick with these right now. The main idea is that XML Web services changes everything. The introduction of this technology by the major players of the tech world changes many of the ways in which systems, applications, and devices function.

The future of XML Web services has been discussed in earlier chapters. The conclusion is that because all major devices and applications of the future will be connected to each other, they must be able to interact in ways that are easy to understand and to use methods that are easy to consume. XML has been the key to both these goals. XML is easy to understand and, because it is purely text-based, it is generally simple and easy to consume.

XML Web services technology today is new — *very new*. Being new, it is still immature, even if it is ready to play hardball. All the potential of this new technology is not realized in the first version, but it will definitely be realized in future releases.

This slow realization of potential is the case with most technologies. Just look at Visual Basic .NET today. When Visual Basic was first introduced, it was rudimentary. Today Visual Basic .NET is a true object-orientated language that is on par with C# and J#. Change happens over time and takes many iterations of a technology. You can be sure that Visual Basic .NET will continue to evolve as time goes on.

XML Web services is just the same as any other first iteration of a concept. Although it is an outstanding solution to many problems, XML Web services still has a lot of evolving to do. Microsoft and others see this and are working toward providing this technology with the tools it needs to grow adequately and provide end users and developers with new solutions.

GXA Specifications

As the Web services' model grows in popularity, applications and developers are digging deep into the technology and demanding more from it. Microsoft and IBM, in talking with their customers, critics, and the development community at large, are working to add to Web services' capabilities.

XML Web services are built upon a base of standards such as XML, SOAP, UDDI, and WSDL. Using these standards as the base of the pyramid, Microsoft and IBM are adding to this base to enable users to develop more complex Web services that contain higher levels of security, the capability for routing, and the capability for transitioning within Web services. Any extensions that are built upon the present base of technologies must also be non-proprietary, thus allowing easy access to the disparate systems and applications using these technologies.

Both Microsoft and IBM introduced the idea of this designed expansion of the standards for Web services at a W3C workshop in April of 2001. The expansion of the standards for Web services is referred to as the Global XML Web Services Architecture (GXA). At the present time, five specifications are included in the GXA with the promise of more to come. These five specifications are WS-Inspection, WS-License, WS-Referral, WS-Routing, and WS-Security. The pyramid structure they form is shown in Figure 15-1.

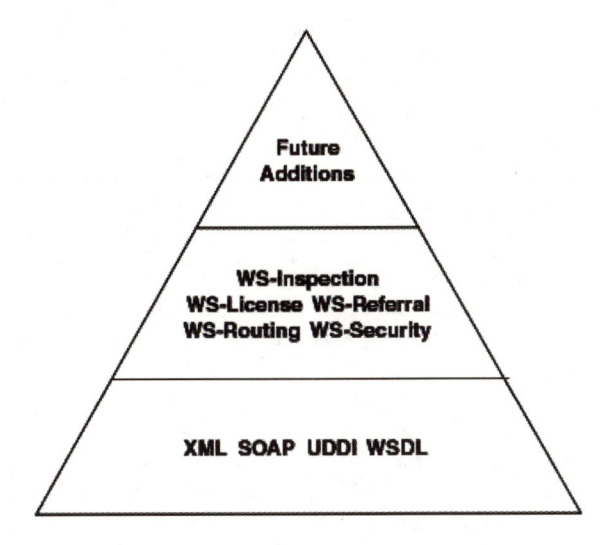

Figure 15-1: The Web services pyramid of technologies.

All these new proposals play an important role in the expansion and growth of Web services' technical capabilities. WS-Inspection is a means by which end users can inspect locales for any available Web services. WS-Referral is used in conjunction with WS-Routing for routing XML Web services from one point to another. WS-Security is used to greatly enhance the security model that underlies Web services. Finally, WS-License describes license types that are placed inside of the WS-Security credentials section.

As I cover these specifications in this chapter, remember that they are *draft* specifications and will most likely change before release of the finished product. The specifications are released before the finished product mainly so that the development community can review them and suggest changes to the governing boards that control the specifications.

Is GXA Necessary?

Yes (to put it simply). Just remember — *change is a good thing!* Technologies evolve, usually for the better. Web services is no different, and even though it is fairly new, its evolution is underway.

As applications and devices evolve and become more integrated, more demands will be placed upon Web services to change. GXA is the first step in this direction. Its specifications are needed to address some of the issues in the current Web services model. Look at each of these specifications and how they play a role in the future development of XML Web services.

WS-Inspection

The Web Services Inspection protocol (WS-Inspection) was introduced by Microsoft and IBM in November of 2001 to help the end user seek out available Web services from known endpoints. Presently, an end user may know about a Web Service that resides on Company XYZ's Web server. He may not, however, know the location of the WSDL document or the exact filename and location of the Disco file. What can he do? Currently, not much. He must contact Company XYZ and ask about the Web Service. Even if Disco files were predictable and easy to find, only Microsoft uses Disco files. He wouldn't be able to find this technology on other Web services' platforms.

WS-Inspection was developed in order to address this issue of discovery. With this specification, you will be able to place discovery documents that either contain links to other discovery means (such as Disco files) or contain direct references to the WSDL documents that are contained on the server in question.

WSIL documents

How does WS-Inspection do this? Well, for one thing, these WS-Inspection documents will always have a predictable filename — `inspection.wsil`. For another, you can place multiple copies of WSIL documents throughout the system in any folder where you expect people to look for Web services directly related to that particular folder.

For instance, you may have an `inspection.wsil` document in the root directory of your Web site that points to additional WSIL documents in your sales and service folders. The following diagram (Figure 15-2) shows an example of this scenario.

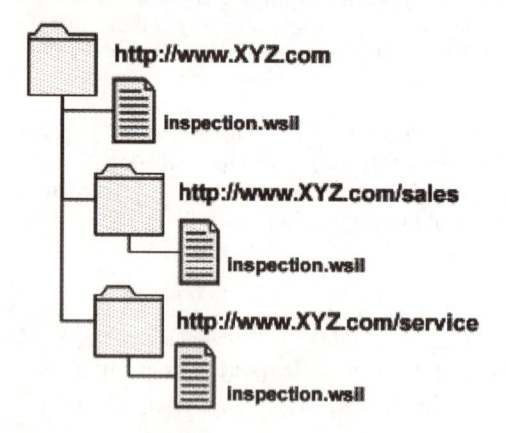

Figure 15-2: Multiple WSIL documents in one solution.

With this standard name in place, individuals can use www.XYZ.com/inspection.wsil to locate any Web services that they might want to consume.

The specification has been proposed. When it is implemented, will you be required to create WSIL documents and place them in strategic areas? In my opinion, you won't have to. Do you have to create WSDL and Disco documents yourself within .NET? You certainly can, but you can also choose to use the tools that automatically create these documents for you. In some cases, as is the case with a WSDL document, the document is automatically generated each time the user makes a request for this document. A WSIL document might also be created dynamically whenever the user requests it. This would guarantee that the Web Service or other discovery document is still at the specified location.

The composition of a WSIL document

WSIL documents are made from XML using a specified schema. A WSIL document is basically a mini-description of any available Web services or any additional discovery documents and is very lightweight in nature. One WSIL can reference additional WSIL documents so there is no need for duplicate service descriptions. WSIL documents are designed to be easy to build and quite easy to understand, even to the human eye.

Using the proposed specification, WSIL documents are to be constructed as shown in Listing 15-1.

Listing 15-1: A WSIL document

```xml
<?xml version="1.0"?>
<inspection xmlns="http://schemas.xmlsoap.org/wsil/"
            xmlns:wsiluddi="http://schemas.xmlsoap.org/wsil/uddi/">
  <service>
    <abstract>A stock quote service with two descriptions</abstract>
    <description referencedNamespace="http://schemas.xmlsoap.org/wsdl/"
                 location="http://example.com/stockquote.wsdl"/>
    <description referencedNamespace="urn:uddi-org:api">
      <wsiluddi:serviceDescription
                 location="http://www.example.com/uddi/inquiryapi">
        <wsiluddi:serviceKey>
                 4FA28580-5C39-11D5-9FCF-BB3200333F79
        </wsiluddi:serviceKey>
      </wsiluddi:serviceDescription>
    </description>
  </service>
  <service>
    <description referencedNamespace="http://schemas.xmlsoap.org/wsdl/"
                 location="ftp://anotherexample.com/tools/calculator.wsdl"/>
  </service>
  <link referencedNamespace="http://schemas.xmlsoap.org/wsil/"
        location="http://example.com/moreservices.wsil"/>
</inspection>
```

The root element is the `<inspection>` element. Any related schema definitions are located here. Within the `<inspection>` element you can place any number of `<service>` elements. Each `<service>` element is an individual description of a particular Web Service that is located on the server.

> **NOTE:** Even though the specification mentions that you are pointing to description documents that are located on the same server as the WSIL document, nothing prevents you from describing and referring to descriptions documents for Web services that are located other servers, even if they aren't your own.

The `<abstract>` element enables you provide a description of the Web Service that is meant for a human to read. This element is a good place to describe, briefly but thoroughly, the Web Service and its functionality.

The `<description>` element is meant for applications to read. The description document can either provide you with the WSDL binding information or the UDDI binding information. You can provide both of these descriptions at the same time for a single service, as shown in the preceding example. UDDI points to additional information about the Web Service, including the location of the WSDL document. A `<description>` element might also point to the WSDL document directly. Use this document with Visual Studio .NET to create a proxy class so that you can consume the Web Service from your application.

In the preceding example, this WSIL document points to two Web services. The first provides stock quotes, and the description information is pointing to information that is stored in the UDDI registry. The second Web Service in this WSIL document is a Calculator Web Service, and the description information is pointing to a WSDL document.

In addition to the `<service>` elements that point to particular Web services, there is a `<link>` element that is used at the bottom of the document. This element refers to any additional discovery documents that might be located elsewhere. It is possible to have multiple `<link>` elements in the WSIL document along with any number of `<service>` elements. These elements make up the complete inspection document.

In addition to referencing other discovery documents directly in a WSIL document, you can reference a WSIL document from an HTML page. You can do this using the HTML Meta tag. The value of the `name` attribute within the `<META>` tag must be set to `serviceInspection` and the `content` value is the location of the WSIL document. This is demonstrated in Listing 15-2.

Listing 15-2: Making a reference to a WSIL document in an HTML page

```
<!DOCTYPE HTML PUBLIC "-//W3C//DTD HTML 4.0 Transitional//EN">
<HTML>
  <HEAD>
    <META name="serviceInspection" content="myServices.wsil">
    <META name="serviceInspection"
            content="http://www.myPartnersServices.wsil">
    <META name="serviceInspection"
            content="ftp://www.AnotherPartnerServices.wsil">
  </HEAD>
  <BODY>
      <!-- Body section here -->
  </BODY>
</HTML>
```

This functionality is useful on the default page of a Web site so that others can easily find your WSIL documents. This is just another method and can be used in conjunction with the methods found in the WSIL document itself.

The idea behind this demonstration is to make theWSIL document easy to construct and even easier to find. Therefore, after this specification is in place, you will be able to search for Web services from Microsoft by looking at www.microsoft.com/inspection.wsil.

> **NOTE:** Because this specification hasn't been implemented as of yet, you will not find this URL anywhere on the Microsoft servers.

WS-Routing

The Web Service Routing protocol (WS-Routing) is a SOAP-based protocol that is used to route SOAP packets from one point to another over HTTP, TCP, or some other transport protocols. It is especially designed to use when you must route the SOAP packet through several points before it reaches its final destination.

To accomplish this, the path that the SOAP message needs to travel is specified in the SOAP Header along with the SOAP message. Therefore, when a SOAP message is sent, the message path will also be connected to this message.

For example, you want to get a message from point A to point D, but in order to do this, you must route the SOAP message through points B and C along the way.

The diagram in Figure 15-3 illustrates this situation.

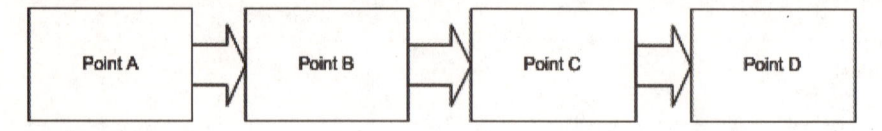

Figure 15-3: The SOAP message being routed from point A to point D.

In Figure 15-3, point A is the initial SOAP sender. This is where the WS-Routing information is placed into the SOAP header and then sent on its way. Points B and C are the routing points, known as either the SOAP nodes or SOAP routers. When they receive a SOAP message with a WS-Routing specification about the final destination, these two points forward this message onto the next point. Point D is the ultimate receiver of the SOAP message that is specified in the SOAP Header.

Contained within the SOAP Header itself is a forward message path, an optional reverse path, and the points through which the message must be routed. The entire message path can be described directly in the SOAP Header and doesn't need to be included elsewhere. These paths can be created dynamically at runtime as well.

A sample SOAP message used for the situation shown in the preceding diagram looks like Listing 15-3:

Listing 15-3: A WS-Routing example

```
<S:Envelope xmlns:S="http://schemas.xmlsoap.org/soap/envelope/">
   <S:Header>
      <m:path xmlns:m="http://schemas.xmlsoap.org/rp/">
         <m:action>http://www.im.org/chat</m:action>
         <m:to>soap://D.com/some/endpoint</m:to>
         <m:fwd>
            <m:via>soap://B.com</m:via>
            <m:via>soap://C.com</m:via>
         </m:fwd>
         <m:rev>
            <m:via/>
         </m:rev>
         <m:from>mailto:evjen@yahoo.com</m:from>
         <m:id>uuid:78b9f5d0-23fb-4a45-b02b-3e743641c2d8</m:id>
      </m:path>
   </S:Header>
   <S:Body>
      ...
   </S:Body>
</S:Envelope>
```

You were introduced to SOAP Headers in the previous chapter. Within this section of the SOAP message, using WS-Routing, you will be able to specify the entire message path.

Within the SOAP Header, the main element `<path>` specifies that the SOAP Header contains a message path.

The `<x:action>` element is similar to the SOAPAction HTTP header field that is in the SOAP request, `SOAPAction: "http://www.xmlws101.com/Add"`. The `<action>` element, in most cases, points to the method and the location for which the message is intended.

The `<x:to>` element is used to describe the location of the final recipient of the message, whereas the `<x:fwd>` element is meant to describe all the points through which the message will be forwarded. In this case, it is forwarded through two separate points, point B and point C. These points are specified using the `<x:via>` element within the `<x:fwd>` element.

This WS-Routing SOAP Header in this example also specifies a return path for the message. So using these descriptions, you can specify not only message instructions, but also a return path. In this case, the return path specification is small — just an `<x:via />` element, which instructs the end service that the return path of the SOAP message is the reverse of the one it took to get there.

The `<x:from>` element is used to specify the sender of the message. This can be an application or even a human being. In most cases, the `<x:from>` element contains an e-mail address of the person who is originally responsible for sending the SOAP message. It is important that you never use this `<x:from>` element's value as a means of authentication. This information isn't secure because it is easily changeable at any point along the path to its final destination.

You are required to use the `<x:id>` to provide the SOAP message with a unique identifier. This message must always be unique whether the message is being sent or received.

As the Web services' model expands and developers start demanding more from their XML Web services, routing is going to become a more important issue.

WS-Referral

The Web Services Referral protocol (WS-Referral) is a SOAP-based way of providing instructions on how SOAP messages should be routed. This specification only refers to the strategies that are to be used for the routing. It does not do the actual routing. The actual routing is taken care of by the WS-Routing protocol. WS-Referral only creates the message paths that are used within the SOAP Header. These message paths can be either static paths or created dynamically.

WS-Referral can make insertions, deletions, or queries to a SOAP router. The SOAP router is the point that takes SOAP messages and forwards them on to the next message path specified in the SOAP Header.

This specification that works in conjunction with WS-Routing is based upon an XML structure that describes the referral information and has similarities to a simple language. Not only a description of data, WS-Referral has a simple logic that is used to determine which paths to use for the SOAP messages that come its way.

The logic within WS-Referral might be described as follows:

*for any SOAP actor name that comes
my way that matches any of the SOAP actors
that are described in the **for** element*

*if the conditions that are specified in the **if** element
are met, then the statement is satisfied*

*then go via one of the specified SOAP routers that
are contained within the **go** element*

In code, this logic would look like Listing 15-4.

Listing 15-4: A WS-Referral example

```
<r:ref xmlns:r="http://schemas.xmlsoap.org/ws/2001/10/referral">
 <r:for>
  <r:prefix>soap://b.org</r:prefix>
 </r:for>
 <r:if/>
 <r:go>
  <r:via>soap://c.org</r:via>
 </r:go>
 <r:refId>mid:1234@some.host.org</r:refId>
</r:ref>
```

The `<x:prefix>` element that is contained within the `<x:for>` element is used to make a reference to the SOAP actor. If the SOAP actor of the SOAP message being sent into the SOAP router matches this value, the `<x:go>` element specifies the next SOAP router to which the SOAP message will be sent. This information is then input into the SOAP Header in the WS-Routing information, as shown in Listing 15-5.

Listing 15-5: The WS-Referral's change to the SOAP Header

```
<S:Envelope xmlns:S="http://www.w3.org/2001/09/soap-envelope">
 <S:Header>
  <m:path xmlns:m="http://schemas.xmlsoap.org/rp/">
   <m:action>http://www.notification.org/update</m:action>
   <m:to>soap://b.org/service/</m:to>
   <m:fwd>
    <m:via>soap://c.org</m:via>
   </m:fwd>
   <m:from>soap://a.org</m:from>
   <m:id>mid:1001@a.org</m:id>
  </m:path>
 </S:Header>
 <S:Body>
  ...
 </S:Body>
</S:Envelope>
```

The WS-Referral changes the SOAP message by adding the entire `<x:fwd>` element, as well as the `<x:via>` element that is contained within the `<x:fwd>` element.

WS-Routing and WS-Referral, used together, promise to be great tools for getting a SOAP message from one point to another when routing is required before the message reaches its final destination.

WS-Security

Security is an important word in technology. One of the first questions that people ask when they hear about a new technology is whether it is safe to use. Web services' designers have looked at security very closely, and they have addressed security concerns in a draft that describes the Web Services Security protocol (WS-Security).

This new protocol will allow you to work with credential exchange (for example, exchanging Kerberos tickets), deal with message integrity, and provide message confidentiality. This functionality is stored within the SOAP Header of the SOAP message.

Credential exchange

WS-Security will enable two entities to exchange their security credentials. The WS-Security protocol does not specify the type of credentials to be exchanged, but instead it allows any type of credentials to be used. WS-License, discussed next, describes how many of the common credential types can be used in conjunction with WS-Security. There can be multiple credentials within one SOAP message, but it is recommended that all credentials abide by the WS-License specification.

Message integrity

Because it is possible to send messages through multiple routers and, in effect, bounce messages from here to there before they reach their final destination, you must ensure the messages are not tampered with in transit. As messages move from one SOAP router to another, these SOAP nodes can make additions or subtractions from messages. This could sometimes harm the integrity of the message. Using WS-Security to check for message tampering will become more important as the routing of messages becomes more commonplace.

Message confidentiality

One of the more important functions that you will want to apply to your SOAP messages is the capability to encrypt either all or part of a message. When your messages are zipping across the virtual world, there is the chance that they might be intercepted and opened for viewing.

For this reason, you will often find it beneficial to somehow scramble the contents of a message. When it reaches the intended receiver, he can use your encryption key and descramble the message to read the contents.

WS-License

The Web Service License protocol (WS-License) is a set of common license types that you can use in conjunction with WS-Security. WS-Security is a protocol that is used specifically for transmitting SOAP messages across the wire securely and verifying a message's integrity. WS-License, as a piece of this, shows how to encode credentials for use within WS-Security.

You can use the WS-License specification for defining encoding license formats for X.509 certificates or Kerberos tickets, as well as when passing arbitrary credentials. WS-License specifies this information in the `<wssec:credentials>` element that is contained within the SOAP Header.

Within the `<wssec:credentials>` element, you will use `<wslic:abstractCredential>`, `<wsil:abstsractLicense>`, `<wsil:binaryLicense>`, and the `<wsil:binaryCredential>` elements.

To understand the proposed WS-License structure, take a look at the following example:

```xml
<?xml version="1.0" encoding="utf-8"?>
<S:Envelope xmlns:S=http://schemas.xmlsoap.org/soap/envelope/
            xmlns:xsd=http://www.w3.org/2001/XMLSchema
            xmlns:xsi=http://www.w3.org/2001/XMLSchema-instance>
    <S:Header>
        <m:path xmlns:m="http://schemas.xmlsoap.org/rp">
            <m:action>http://tickers-r-us.org/getQuote</m:action>
            <m:to>soap://tickers-r-us.org/stocks</m:to>
            <m:from>mailto:johnsmith@isps-r-us.com</m:from>
            <m:id>uuid:84b9f5d0-33fb-4a81-b02b-5b760641c1d6</m:id>
        </m:path>
        <wssec:credentials xsi:type="wslic:CREDENTIALS"
            xmlns:wssec="http://schemas.xmlsoap.org/ws/2001/10/security"
            xmlns:wslic="http://schemas.xmlsoap.org/ws/2001/10/license">
            <wslic:binaryLicense
                    wslic:valueType="wslic:x509v3"
                    xsi:type="xsd:base64Binary">
MIIEZzCCA9CgAwIBAgIQEmtJZc0rqrKh5i2ksE9pjzANBgkqhkiG9w0BAQQFADCBzDEXM
BUGA1UEChMOVmVyaVNpZ24sIEluYy4xHzAdBgNVBAsTFlZlcmlTaWduIFRydXN0IE5ldH
dvcmsxRjBEBgNVBAsTPXd3dy52ZXJpc2lnbi5jb20vcmVwb3NpdG9yeS9SUEEgSW5jb3J
dnJyukFGNr6nORGjNIz/MnzHavmAMEdY7rnSoEFuuckrPxe6OJkyjbmjVz7Vq4vG1rtnn
qDIU2LhvNYLS2VlBVB1Clp/uSaEzWMgRnSNBe8DQveqD6a3gUACyZ6XVe3u
            </wslic:binaryLicense>
        </wssec:credentials>
    </S:Header>
    <S:Body>
        <tru:StockSymbol xmlns:tru="http://tickers-r-
            us.org/payloads">QQQ</tru:StockSymbol>
    </S:Body>
</S:Envelope>
```

I took a lot of the binary code out of this example, but you get the idea. One of the more important lines from this example is the line that specifies the encoding specification that is used:

```
<wslic:binaryLicense wslic:valueType="wslic:x509v3"
     xsi:type="xsd:base64Binary">
```

The `valueType` is given the value of `wslic:x509v3`, which is a description for an X.509 certificate. A value of `wslic:Kerberos` is a description for using a Kerberos ticket.

This WS-License specification was developed with the intention of working within the WS-Security specification and, therefore, is limited in nature.

The Future of XML Web Services

The future of Web services looks strong. Just the fact that some of the world's fiercest competitors are sitting at a table together and discussing how they can best play with each other in this arena is simply amazing! The key to the success of the Web services technology, regardless of the platform and development tools used in its construction, is that it is built using open standards.

XML, SOAP, UDDI, and WSDL are excellent tools to build upon. Using these standards as the foundation of Web services, the Global XML Web Services Architecture can extend the capability and the functionality of all Web services and, more specifically, the XML Web services that are built upon the .NET Framework using ASP.NET.

This chapter is a look into the future of Web services. None of this is set in stone, and you can be assured that some information you were given in this chapter will change. You can also be assured that the functionality provided for you by Web services will only continue to gain ground.

Microsoft and IBM, the authors of the Global XML Web Services Architecture, will continue to release additional specifications. These additions will be a part of the GXA. Both these companies have research and development divisions that are working on new specifications as you read this book.

REFERENCE: You will find more information on GXA by searching for it at `msdn.microsoft.com`.

Summary

How will Microsoft implement the new GXA specifications? I don't know. Because the GXA is presently in the draft phase, GXA is not implemented in the first version of Visual Studio .NET. It may be included in future service packs or in the next version of Visual Studio .NET. We all have to wait and see when this will come about.

One thing is sure, Microsoft will make it easy to use and implement the GXA within your XML Web services and within the .NET applications that interact with them. Look at how easy it is to deal with SOAP, WSDL, and even Disco documents within Visual Studio .NET today. You can assume that it will be just as easy to create WS-Inspection documents and integrate these other technologies within your SOAP Headers. Wait and see.

As you learned in this chapter, XML Web services and the technologies that it is built upon are growing fast. XML Web services is being developed to answer many of the issues that companies and organizations faced in the past when trying to communicate through disparate systems. Global XML Web Services Architecture has been proposed to greatly extend and enhance the functionality of this new model.

WS-Inspection will be used to provide a more logical means of finding XML Web services at known servers and Web sites. WS-Referral and WS-Routing will be used to help with the hop, skip, and jump that some Web services must do. Finally, WS-Security and WS-License will be used to provide encryption protection to the SOAP messages that you send.

Part VI

Security

Chapter 16: General Security Issues

Chapter 17: Advanced Security

Chapter 16

General Security Issues

Protect your bagels, put lox on them.
Sign at Bagel Connection, New Haven CT

At some time, you may want to create some sort of restricted access for an XML Web service that you have built. There is no real built-in support for security in the SOAP protocol. You must depend on security measures that can be implemented either on the system where the XML Web service is hosted or within the application itself. The next two chapters present you with a number of measures you can use if you want to implement security within your XML Web service. Some of these measures you can use by themselves and others you can use in unison.

In this chapter, you will look at the following items:

- Understanding authentication and authorization
- Looking at the `web.config` file
- IIS security
- ASP.NET security
- Accessing user properties

Using Security with XML Web Services

Some XML Web services don't require much in the way of security. If you have a simple XML Web service that is converting temperatures from Celsius to Fahrenheit, it might not be critical to build elaborate security measures around it.

However, if you have an XML Web service that exposes critical data or one that people pay to gain access to you must think through the possible security options at your disposal. You can then apply one or more of the possible choices in order to protect your information and systems.

Just like other applications on a system, XML Web services can be implemented so that only authorized users receive access to its data or logic. Security measures within XML Web services are similar, in some ways, to security for applications that you have built in the past: You must apply an authorization and authentication process. There is one big difference between security for XML Web services and that for other applications, such as Web sites. When you apply authentication and authorization to a Web site, you are authorizing actual people or end users. With XML Web services, you are applying authentication and authorization to computers, applications, or businesses that want to access your XML Web service instead of to end users.

As you have learned so far in this book, a Web service call is simply an HTTP request and response. Therefore, an XML Web service has all the HTTP security mechanisms available including Basic, Digest, and Windows authentication.

Before you learn about the different ways in which you can apply security to your XML Web services, you should have a good understanding of both authentication and authorization. All security models are based upon these two principles.

Authentication

Authentication is the process of determining the identity of the end user (or consuming application) based upon credentials that the end user presents. As the reviewer of these credentials, you need to be able to validate these credentials against some source.

There are many different modes of authentication to use within your applications. These modes include basic authentication, digest authentication, forms authentication, Passport, Integrated Windows authentication (such as NTLM or Kerberos), or authentication methods that you develop yourself.

One of the more standard ways to authenticate users is to ask for a login and password. For instance, if you're building an XML Web service for a select group that wants to allow only members to have access, you can authenticate each user by requiring every member to use a login and password to access the XML Web service. Another method you can use is to designate a one-word password that everyone uses to gain access. Either way is fine, as long as the user is authenticated.

You should never authorize an end user to proceed to the resource if you haven't applied an authentication program to the process. There are different means of obtaining this authentication, as you will see shortly in this and the next chapter. Some of them are better than others. The ones you use within your applications should directly reflect the level of security that you want to achieve. Keep in mind is that usually developing more security for your applications results in an associated hit in performance and an increased chance of errors.

Authorization

Authorization is the process of determining whether a consuming application or end user, after its credentials have been authenticated, is allowed to have access to specific points of your application. You might have exposed a large number of WebMethods in your XML Web service. You can require the authenticated application to belong to a category of users in order to gain access to certain specific WebMethods.

If you do this, you then categorize your authenticated end users into roles or groups and provide access to specific points based upon those roles.

For an example of authorization in action, imagine a large building with many floors. Each employee at this large building is provided with an access key to the building. The process of the employee using a key to access the building is a means of authentication in action. Each employee can't just go to any floor in the building that he chooses, however; he can only go to the floors of the building where he has authorization. This is the authorization process.

web.config

The `web.config` file is a powerful new addition to building ASP.NET applications. This XML-based file is at your disposal for configuring your ASP.NET applications. Within this file you apply authentication and authorization settings.

> **CROSS-REFERENCE:** The `web.config` file is covered in more detail in Chapter 21.

There are many elements within the `web.config` file that are used to apply application settings, but the ones that you need to focus on in this chapter are the `<authentication>` and the `<authorization>` elements.

<authentication> node

The `<authentication>` node allows you to directly control all the authentication aspects of your application. The following code shows the structure of the `<authentication>` node:

```
<authentication mode="Windows|Forms|Passport|None">

   <forms name="name" loginUrl="url"
       protection="All|None|Encryption|Validation"
       timeout="30" path="/" >

       <credentials passwordFormat="Clear|SHA1|MD5">
           <user name="username" password="password" />
       </credentials>

   </forms>

   <passport redirectUrl="internal"/>

</authentication>
```

When you're developing applications for the Internet, often you don't want to allow every public user to gain access. You want to build an authentication system so users can identify themselves before entering the application. You can build an XML Web service that checks for names in a database before allowing users to continue. ASP.NET gives you a number of different authentication options.

Notice that four possible choices are used in determining the mode of authentication. The default setting is `Windows`.

```
<authentication mode="Windows|Forms|Passport|None">
```

It's possible to configure ASP.NET authentication in the four modes listed in Table 16-1.

Table 16-1: Authentication Modes

Authentication Provider	Description
`Windows`	Windows authentication is used together with IIS authentication. Authentication is performed by IIS in the following ways: basic, digest, or Integrated Windows Authentication. When IIS authentication is complete, ASP.NET uses the authenticated identity to authorize access.
`Forms`	Requests that are not authenticated are redirected to an HTML form using HTTP client-side redirection. The user provides his login information and submits the form. If the application authenticates the request, the system issues a form that contains the credentials or a key for reacquiring the identity.
`Passport`	A centralized authentication service provided by Microsoft that offers a single login and core profile services for member sites.
`None`	No authentication mode in place.

<authorization> node

The `<authorization>` node works with the `<authentication>` node in the `web.config` file to apply an authorization model to your ASP.NET applications. The following code shows the structure of the `<authorization>` node:

```
<authorization>

    <allow users="comma-separated list of users"
        roles="comma-separated list of roles"
        verb="comma-separated list of verbs" />

    <deny users="comma-separated list of users"
        roles="comma-separated list of roles"
        verb="comma-separated list of verbs" />

</authorization>
```

The `<authorization>` node allows for two subnodes, `<allow>` and `<deny>`. You can allow individual users by using the `users` attribute and separating the values with a comma. It's also possible to allow groups or members by using the `roles` attribute:

```
<allow users="Bill, Dave, Fred" roles="Admins" />
```

The `<deny>` sub node works in the same way, except it denies users access. For either the `<allow>` or `<deny>` node, an asterisk means to apply that particular functionality to all users. A question mark applies that functionality to all anonymous users. So if you wanted to allow all users access to your resource, but at the same time deny anonymous users, here's how it would look:

```
<allow users="*" />
<deny users="?" />
```

The `verb` attribute allows you to specify the HTTP transmission methods that are used for allowing or denying users to the resource. The values of the `verb` attribute include GET, POST, HEAD, and DEBUG.

Authentication for XML Web Services

The first step on your way to securing your XML Web service and the exposed methods that it offers is to apply an authentication model. In most cases, this is the toughest part of the security model. At times, it is difficult to be sure if users are passing in the correct credentials and if they are truly who they say they are.

In order to provide authentication, one of your best bets is to look to the system (the Windows operating system), IIS, the .NET Framework, and the common language runtime (CLR). You can use any of these items to help give you the security that you require in your applications.

IIS Authentication

Internet Information Services (IIS) authentication is one possibility for authenticating end users or the consuming applications that want to gain access to your XML Web service. Using IIS or Windows-based authentication is usually a good way to authenticate your end users because it is fully integrated within the Windows operating system. IIS supports a number of different models for authentication that are built right in. These include

- Integrated Windows authentication
- Basic authentication
- Digest authentication
- Anonymous authentication
- Certificates

Take a closer look at some of the main authentication models.

Integrated Windows authentication

Integrated Windows authentication was previously known as NTLM or Windows NT Challenge/Response authentication. Integrated Windows authentication has limited uses within your XML Web services. Integrated Windows authentication requires that the consumer of the XML Web service have proxy classes that are created with either Wsdl.exe or with Visual Studio .NET.

An additional problem when using this model is that Integrated Windows authentication does not work over HTTP proxy connections. You must open a port in addition to port 80 because Integrated Windows authentication does not use port 80. Therefore, this model is best suited for Intranet environments where the consuming application resides on the same domain as the XML Web service.

If you are using this authentication model, Integrated Windows authentication has the client prove its identity by sending a hash of its credentials to the server that is hosting the XML Web service. Along with Microsoft's Active Directory, the client can use Kerberos if it is using Microsoft Internet Explorer 5 or a higher version.

If you set the `<authentication>` element to use `Windows` authentication for its authentication model, Integrated Windows authentication becomes the default setting.

Basic authentication

Basic authentication is another means of providing a login and password in order to become authenticated. The plus about Basic authentication is that it is part of the HTTP specification and, therefore, is supported by most browsers. Unfortunately, Basic authentication passes the login and passwords as clear text and, therefore, can be read if intercepted.

In order to change the authentication mode from Integrated Windows authentication to Basic, use the following steps. (Note that these steps apply to Windows XP. Other operating systems may differ.)

1. Click Start ⇨ Control Panel ⇨ Performance and Maintenance ⇨ Administrative Tools ⇨ Internet Information Services. You are presented with IIS (shown in Figure 16-1).

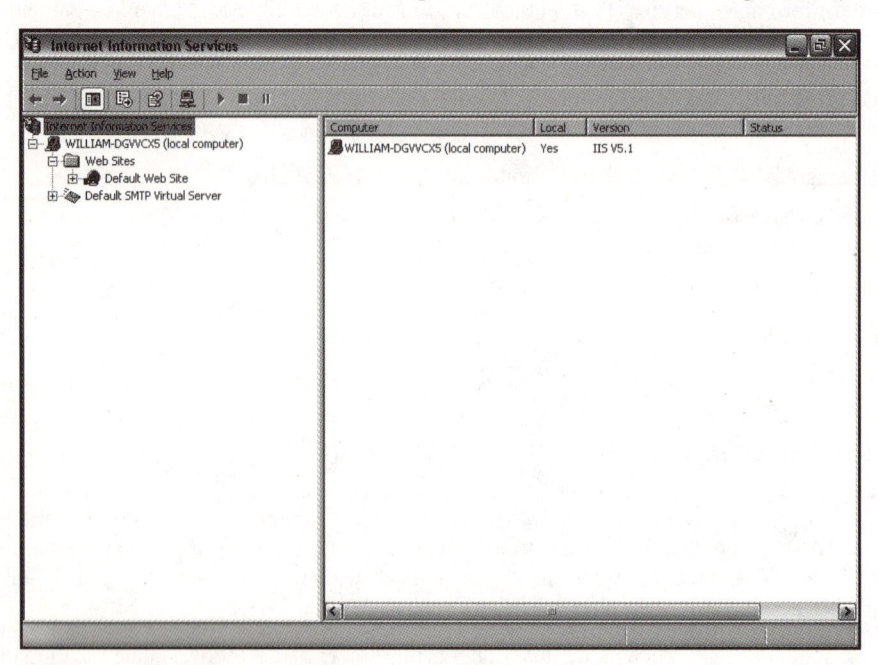

Figure 16-1: Internet Information Services.

Chapter 16: **General Security Issues** 375

2. Within Internet Information Services, open the Default Web Site tree and you find a list of all the ASP.NET applications that you have created. Select the ASP.NET application for the mode of authentication you want to apply.
3. Right-click on the selected application and choose Properties.
4. Select the Directory Security tab.
5. Click the Edit button in the Anonymous Access and Authentication control box. The Authentication Methods dialog window appears (Figure 16-2).

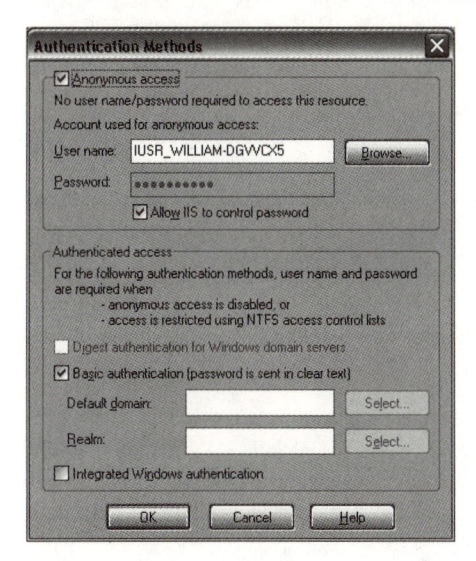

Figure 16-2: Changing the authentication mode in the Authentication Methods dialog window.

6. Uncheck the Integrated Windows Authentication check box.
7. Check the Basic Authentication check box.
8. Apply changes by clicking OK. You are given a warning about using clear text passwords at this point.

After you apply these settings, your XML Web service uses Basic authentication instead of Integrated Windows authentication.

Digest authentication

Digest authentication is the latest authentication model to be introduced. This authentication model alleviates the Basic authentication problem of passing the credentials as clear text.

Digest authentication uses an encryption algorithm to encrypt the credentials before they are sent to the server. In order to use Digest authentication, you are required to have a Windows domain controller. One of the main problems with Digest authentication is that it is not supported on all platforms and requires browsers that abide by the HTTP 1.1 specification.

You can change from Integrated Windows authorization to Digest in the same way as you change to Basic authentication, except that you check the Digest authentication check box if it is enabled.

Working with users and groups

Windows-based authentication that uses either Basic, Digest, or Windows Integrated authentication occurs between the Windows server and the client's browser. Windows-based authentication goes to IIS to provide the authentication module. This kind of authentication is quite useful in an intranet environment, where you can let the server deal with the authentication process.

Windows-based authentication, such as Integrated Windows authentication, first tries to use the user's credentials from the domain login. If this fails, a dialog box pops up so the user can re-enter his login information. When Windows-based authentication is used, the user's password isn't passed from the client to the server. If a user has logged on to a local computer as a domain user, the user won't need to be authenticated again when accessing a network computer in that domain.

The next step is to configure the sample XML Web service so that it uses a Windows-based authentication system. Before doing so, play around a little with creating users and groups. You can utilize these users and groups to give only the people that you specify in your `web.config` file access to the XML Web service

Creating users

The process of creating users on a server is simple and straightforward. Before declaring users within your `web.config` file, create some users on the server to whom you give access to the XML Web service.

Follow these steps to create users on the local server:

1. Within Windows XP Professional, open up the Computer Management utility by clicking Start ➪ Control Panel ➪ Performance and Maintenance ➪ Administrative Tools ➪ Computer Management. (You can also open the utility by right-clicking on the My Computer icon on your desktop and choosing Manage.)

> **NOTE:** The Computer Management utility manages and controls resources on the local or remote servers. There are many things that you can do within the Computer Management utility to control your system.

2. Open the Local Users and Groups branch. After expanding this branch, two folders are displayed, Users and Groups.

3. Right-click on the Users folder and select New User, as shown in Figure 16-3. The New User dialog box appears (see Figure 16-4).

Chapter 16: General Security Issues 377

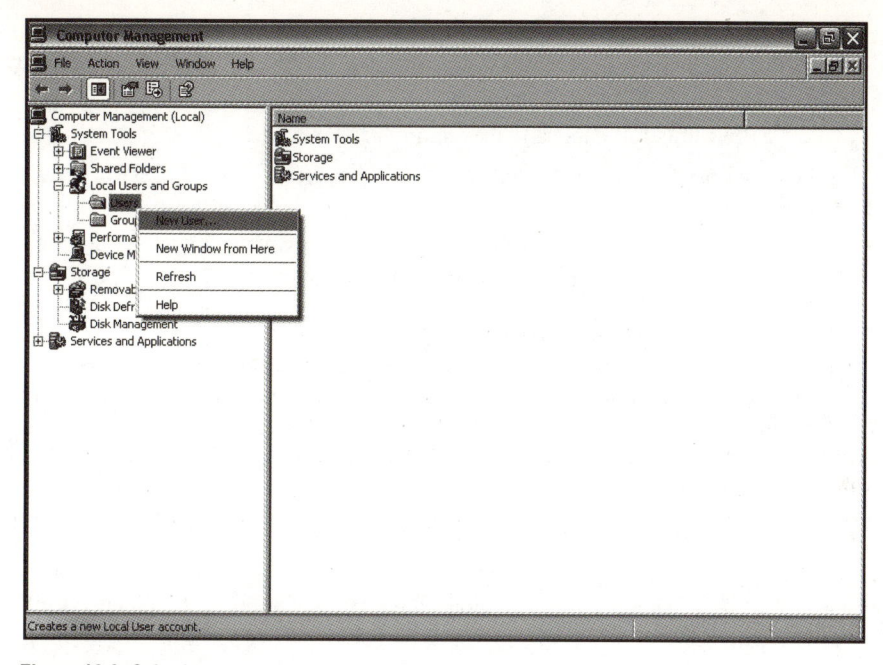

Figure 16-3: Selecting a new user.

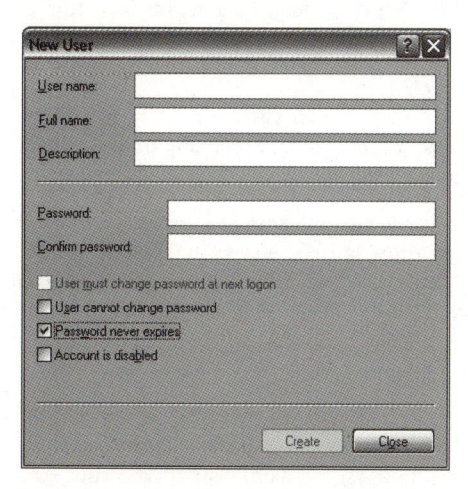

Figure 16-4: Assign a user using the New User dialog window.

4. Because you are dealing with both applications that will consume your XML Web service and human beings who are going to log into your system, you want to uncheck the *User must change password at next login* check box. An application will have a hard time doing this task. Also, you want to check the Password Never Expires check box so

that the consuming application of your XML Web service won't hit an error when it comes time to change the password.

5. Give the user (the consuming application) a name, such as **XYZdivision**. You can provide the division's full name and description here as well.

6. Give the user a password. For this example, I use the ultra top secret password — **password**.

7. After you've filled in all the necessary information, click Create. Your user now appears in the list of users in the Computer Management utility.

Authenticating and authorizing a user

Next, arrange for IIS to authenticate users (after you provide the authorizations based upon these authentications) by changing the appropriate application settings in the `web.config` file. You find this file within the root directory of your application. After it's open, navigate down to the `<authentication>` node. Directly after the closing of this node, place the following element:

```
<identity impersonate="true" />
```

This element doesn't need to be directly after the `<authentication>` node, but it's shown that way here for file readability. These elements are related in terms of the functionality you're working with now.

This code changes the `impersonate` attribute to `true` so that you don't have to deal with authentication and authorization issues in the ASP.NET application code. Instead, you're relying on IIS to authenticate the user and pass an authenticated token to the ASP.NET application or, if it's unable to authenticate the user, pass an unauthenticated token.

Next, change the `<authorization>` node to suit your needs. The authorization element allows for two subelements, `<allow>` and `<deny>`. You can have as many of these two subelements within the authorization element as you see fit.

Both the `<allow>` and `<deny>` nodes can contain the attributes `users`, `roles`, and `verbs`. The attribute `users` specifies individual users to allow or deny access to the application; `roles` is for groups, and `verbs` specifies how the user came to the application. (Groups are discussed in the next section.) This chapter doesn't show any examples using the `verbs` attribute, but basically you can allow or deny users based on whether they came to the application using `GET`, `POST`, `HEAD`, or `DEBUG` methods.

For example, you've created the user, XYZdivision, and now you want to allow XYZdivision to access the XML Web service. Before you can do that, deny access to all users. Add the `<identity impersonate="true" />` line of code, as you were instructed earlier, and change the `<authorization>` node so that it reads as follows:

```
<authorization>
  <deny users="*" />
</authorization>
```

A "*" refers to all users, and a "?" refers to anonymous users. So you just instructed the application to deny all users, even if they're authenticated.

Next, type in the URL of the XML Web service that you applied this to. If you are authenticated or if there isn't an authentication model in place, you get the XML Web service test page. But instead, you're asked to log on to the application, even though nobody is allowed (see Figure 16-5). You're given three chances to type in your login information.

Figure 16-5: The authentication and authorization process to log on to the XML Web service test page.

Because you're not letting any user access the XML Web service, after the third try, you're informed that you are denied access (see Figure 16-6).

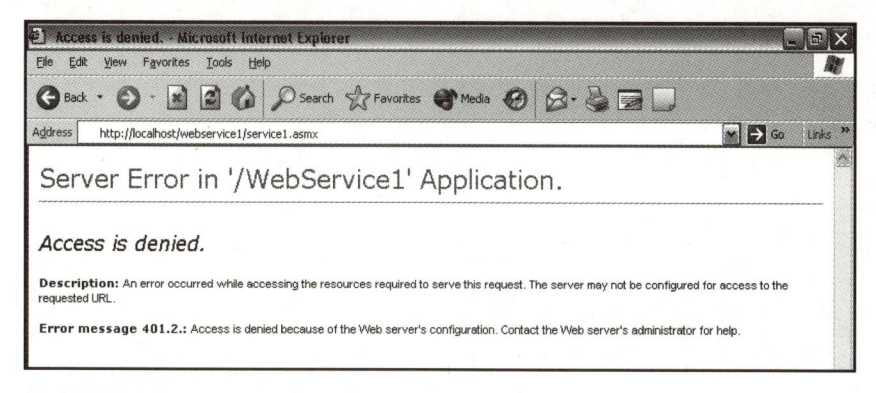

Figure 16-6: Access denied.

You've now successfully locked out everyone, but this is not likely to be what you want. You'll tend to want to let people into the application, even if it's only yourself.

Back in the `web.config` file, within the `<authorization>` node, you can allow your user XYZdivision to access the application by adding an `<allow>` subnode to the document:

```
<authorization>
  <allow users="william-dgvvcx5\XYZdivision" />
  <deny users="*" />
</authorization>
```

Remember to replace `william-dgvvcx5` with the name of your own computer domain. Remember that if you changed the `web.config` file to allow XYZdivision, you have to be logged into the computer as XYZdivision.

> **TIP**: To add multiple users, separate them with commas.

Creating groups

Creating groups is just as easy as creating users:

1. Open up the Computer Management utility by right-clicking the My Computer icon on your desktop and choosing Manage.

2. Right-click the Groups folder under Local Users and Groups. Select New Group. You're presented with the New Group dialog box, shown in Figure 16-7.

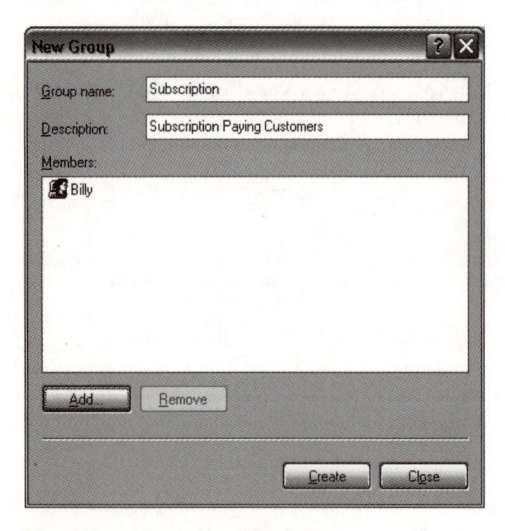

Figure 16-7: New Group dialog window.

3. Give your group a descriptive name and a description.

4. To add members to the group, click the Add button and select a user from the list. Select as many members for the group as you wish. After you're finished, click the Create button.

Authenticating and authorizing a group

Now you're going to change the settings in the `web.config` file to authorize your group to access the application. IIS authenticates your user and makes sure that the user belongs to the group.

For example, say you've created the user, XYZdivision, and added XYZdivision to the group Subscription. You now want to allow Subscription to access the XML Web service. Add the `<identity impersonate="true" />` line of code as you were instructed earlier, and change the `<authorization>` node so that it reads as follows:

```
<authorization>
  <allow roles="william-dgvvcx5\Subscription" />
  <deny users="*" />
</authorization>
```

Remember to change the domain name so that it's the same as the domain name on your computer. If you are not part of a domain, you need to include the computer name. You can add more groups to the list by separating them with commas.

When XYZdivision's consuming application logs on to the site, the server authenticates XYZdivision, checks that it is a member of the Subscription group, and then grants the application access to the XML Web service.

Consuming an XML Web service that requires Windows-based authentication

For an example of how to consume an XML Web service that uses Windows-based authentication, set up your XML Web service so that it uses Basic authentication. Next, start a new ASP.NET Web application. Be sure that you have configured the `web.config` file to include the users that you want to gain access to the XML Web service.

For this example, I am consuming a simple *Hello World* XML Web service. Make a Web reference to the XML Web service. Notice that you are required to provide credentials even to make a Web reference to the XML Web service that you are trying to consume if a Windows-based authentication model in enabled. See Figure 16-8.

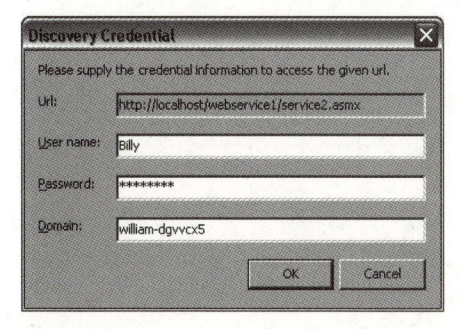

Figure 16-8: The Discovery Credential dialog window. You are required to fill this out in order to make a Web reference if a Windows-based authentication model is enabled.

Then on your ASP.NET page, include just a single Label control. You use this control to print out the result, whether it is *Hello World* or some type of error. Listing 16-1 is the code of the application that will provide credentials and consume the XML Web service.

Listing 16-1: Consuming an XML Web service that requires credentials

VB

```vb
Imports System.Net

Public Class WebForm1
    Inherits System.Web.UI.Page
    Protected WithEvents Label1 As System.Web.UI.WebControls.Label

    Private Sub Page_Load(ByVal sender As System.Object, ByVal e As _
                    System.EventArgs) Handles MyBase.Load
        Dim ws As New localhost.Service1()
        Dim myCredentials As New NetworkCredential("william-
                dgvvcx5\Billy", "password")

        ws.Credentials = myCredentials

        Try
            Label1.Text = ws.HelloWorld()
        Catch we As WebException
            Label1.Text = "Failed! " & we.Message
        End Try

    End Sub

End Class
```

C#

```csharp
using System.Net;

namespace WebApplication1
{
 public class WebForm1 : System.Web.UI.Page
  {
   protected System.Web.UI.WebControls.Label Label1;

    private void Page_Load(object sender, System.EventArgs e)
    {
     localhost.Service1 ws = new localhost.Service1();
     NetworkCredential myCredentials = new NetworkCredential
        ("william-dgvvcx5\\Billy", "password");

     ws.Credentials = myCredentials;
```

```
      try
      {
        Label1.Text = ws.HelloWorld();
      }
      catch (WebException we)
      {
        Label1.Text = "Failed! " + we.Message;
      }
    }
  }
}
```

In the consuming application, import the `System.Net` namespace in order to use the `NetworkCredential` class. This class takes the username, password, and a possible domain.

After you have tested this with proper credentials, try passing in the incorrect credentials. You will get the following error:

```
Failed! The request failed with HTTP status 401: Access Denied.
```

Authentication on individual XML Web services

It is possible to provide an authentication and authorization model for specific files within your application. If you have an ASP.NET application that contains multiple `.asmx` files, you can identify specific files that you want users to be authenticated against.

For instance, within the `web.config` file, you can allow everyone to gain access to every file in the application. You do this by placing your new code within the `<configuration>` element, but after the `</system.web>` closing tag. Your `web.config` file then looks like the code in Listing 16-2:

Listing 16-2: A sample web.config file that provides security to one individual XML Web service

```
<configuration>
   <system.web>
      <!-- Your regular web.config file goes here -->
   </system.web>

   <!-- This is where you put your custom settings -->

   <location path="Service2.asmx">
      <system.web>
         <authentication mode="Windows" />
         <authorization>
            <allow roles="william-dgvvcx5\Subscription" />
            <deny users="*" />
         </authorization>
      </system.web>
   </location>
</configuration>
```

If you structure your `web.config` file in this format, every `.asmx` file is open for use, except for `Service2.asmx`. This one XML Web service requires credentials to be passed to it in order for a user to consume it.

The other great thing about this setup is that you can apply a completely different authentication and authorization model to a separate XML Web service that resides in the same application by adding an additional `<location>` element.

The `<location>` element takes a single attribute `path`. You can assign either a file or a folder as the value of the `path` attribute. If you assign a folder as the value, every file within this folder will then be under the authentication and authorization rules that you define with that particular `<location>` element.

ASP.NET Authentication

There are additional authentication models that have been made available in ASP.NET. Forms-based authentication uses HTML forms to authenticate the user, whereas Passport authentication uses Microsoft Passport in its authentication process. The big disadvantage to both of these authentication models is that they are not truly designed for use with XML Web services.

Form authentication is a popular way to authenticate and authorize users. It provides them with access to application resources by having them type their credentials into HTML forms. When a user attempts to enter the application unauthenticated, he's redirected to a specified login page. Here he can type in his username and password to get authenticated. After he's authenticated, the user receives an HTTP cookie to use for subsequent requests.

Passport is a popular centralized authentication service that is provided by Microsoft. This service offers a single login mechanism for participating member Web sites.

Presently, neither Forms nor Passport authentication are ideal tools for authenticating users or for consuming applications to gain access to your XML Web services. Both of these models require some sort of human interaction. It is possible, however, to play with the proxy class of the consuming application in order to provide workarounds to these models. However, there are better paths for authentication and authorization than these. As you will see in the next chapter, using SOAP Headers and SOAP extensions is more practical.

What does the future hold for these models? Is it possible that, in the future versions of .NET, it will be easier to use Forms and Passport authentication for your XML Web services? This is most likely, but we will have to wait and see.

Authorization for XML Web Services

After authentication, authorization is the process of applying rules to determine if the identified user is allowed access to specific methods or pieces of logic in the XML Web service.

You have already seen a little bit of authorization played out in this chapter. It is difficult to separate authentication and authorization because they work hand-in-hand.

So for instance, you already used authorization based upon the users and groups that were in IIS and provided or denied access based upon their roles. That is a type of authorization. You were able to control the authorization from the `web.config` file where you specified the rules of authorization using the `<allow>` and `<deny>` elements within the `<authorization>` element.

The entire concept behind this type of authorization is called *Role-Based Security*. You are dictating access rights based upon the role of the consumer of your XML Web service.

Context.User

You can use the `Context` property along with the `User` object within your XML Web service in order to make access decisions based upon information that the object provides. Using this object, you can find specific information about the user or consuming application that is logged onto your XML Web service.

Context.User.Identity

Using the `Identity` property, you can gain access to the user's name, his authentication type, and whether he is authenticated. The code in Listing 16-3 shows how to use this object. To get the desired results, set up an authentication model by building your `web.config` file to allow specific users to gain access to the XML Web Service, as shown earlier in the chapter.

Listing 16-3: Identifying the user's name and authentication type

VB

```
Imports System.Web.Services

<WebService(Namespace := "http://www.xmlws101.com/")> _
Public Class Service1
    Inherits System.Web.Services.WebService

   <WebMethod()> Public Function HelloUser() As String
        Dim identityUser As String
        identityUser = "Hello " & Context.User.Identity.Name
        identityUser += ". You are using " & _
          Context.User.Identity.AuthenticationType & " authentication."

        Return identityUser
    End Function

End Class
```

C#

```
using System;
using System.Collections;
using System.ComponentModel;
using System.Data;
using System.Diagnostics;
```

```
using System.Web;
using System.Web.Services;

namespace WebService
{
 public class Service1 : System.Web.Services.WebService
 {

  [WebMethod]
  public string HelloUser()
  {
    string identityUser;

    identityUser = "Hello " + Context.User.Identity.Name;
    identityUser += ". You are using " +
       Context.User.Identity.AuthenticationType + " authentication.";

    return identityUser;
  }
 }
}
```

Running this code will give you the results shown in Figure 16-9.

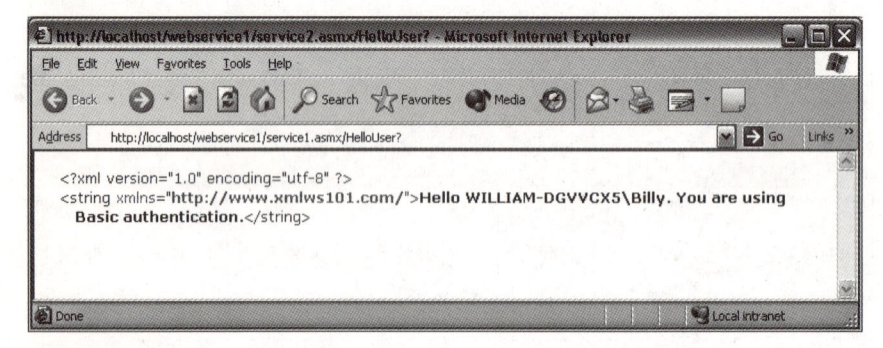

Figure 16-9: Checking the user's name and type of authentication that was given by working with the User object.

With `Context.User.Identity`, you can check if the user or consuming application is authenticated. You can allow people to use your XML Web service, but provide a higher level of functionality or support based on whether the user is authenticated. (See Listing 16-4.)

Listing 16-4: Checking if the user is authenticated

VB

```
If Context.User.Identity.IsAuthenticated = True Then
   Return "You are authenticated!"
Else
   Return "You are not authenticated!"
End If
```

C#

```
If (Context.User.Identity.IsAuthenticated == true)
{
   return "You are authenticated!";
}
else
{
   return "You are not authenticated!";
}
```

Using what is returned from these properties, you can perform conditional logic within your XML Web service to alter the level of functionality provided. For example, if you are providing stock charts, you could provide real-time charts for authenticated users and delayed charts for users that are not authenticated.

Context.User.IsInRole

The `User` object also contains an `IsInRole` method that allows you to find the specific role that the user or consuming application holds. Based on this role, you can decide in your code what kind of actions to perform.

Earlier in this chapter, you learned how to create groups and assign users to specific groups. Using these groups, you can build your code around the user's group. For instance, you probably have a group called Administrators on your system. Make sure you are part of this group and then build an XML Web service that looks out for users that fill this specific role, as shown in Listing 16-5.

Listing 16-5: Finding out what role the user plays

VB

```
Imports System.Web.Services

<WebService(Namespace:="http://www.xmlws101.com/")> _
Public Class Service1
    Inherits System.Web.Services.WebService

   <WebMethod()> Public Function HelloUser() As String
       Dim userRoles As String

     If Context.User.IsInRole("BUILTIN\Administrators") Then
         userRoles = "You are an administrator"
     ElseIf Context.User.IsInRole("william-dgvvcx5\Happy People") Then
         userRoles = "You are a happy person"
     ElseIf Context.User.IsInRole("william-dgvvcx5\Trouble Makers") Then
         userRoles = "You are a trouble maker"
     Else
         userRoles = "You are not part of any role"
     End If
```

```
            Return userRoles
        End Function

End Class
```

C#

```csharp
using System;
using System.Collections;
using System.ComponentModel;
using System.Data;
using System.Diagnostics;
using System.Web;
using System.Web.Services;

namespace WebService
{
 public class Service1 : System.Web.Services.WebService
 {

  [WebMethod]
  public string HelloUser()
  {
   string userRoles;

   if (Context.User.IsInRole("BUILTIN\\Administrators"))
   {
    userRoles = "You are an administrator";
   }
   else if (Context.User.IsInRole("william-dgvvcx5\\Happy People"))
   {
    userRoles = "You are a happy person";
   }
   else if (Context.User.IsInRole("william-dgvvcx5\\Trouble Makers"))
   {
    userRoles = "You are a trouble maker";
   }
   else
   {
    userRoles = "You are not part of any role";
   }
   return userRoles;
  }
 }
}
```

Here you use the `IsInRole` method of the `User` object to check if the authenticated user belongs to a specific group. If you are using one of the Windows operating systems built-in roles, use `BUILTIN`; if you are using a role that you have specifically created, use the domain name of your system (in my case, `william-dgvvcx5`).

Using System.Security.Principal

You can use the `System.Security.Principal` namespace to gain access to the `WindowsGeneric` and `WindowsPrincipal` objects. These will enable you to find even more information about the particular user logged on to your XML Web service.

WindowsBuiltInRole enumeration

Using this namespace, you can use the `WindowsBuiltInRole` enumeration to check if the user is part of any Windows built-in role. This is similar to what you did with the User object, but this enumeration maps more directly to the Windows groups in your system.

In order to use this enumeration, be sure to import the `System.Security.Principal` namespace into your XML Web service class. You then use this enumeration in the following manner, shown in Listing 16-6:

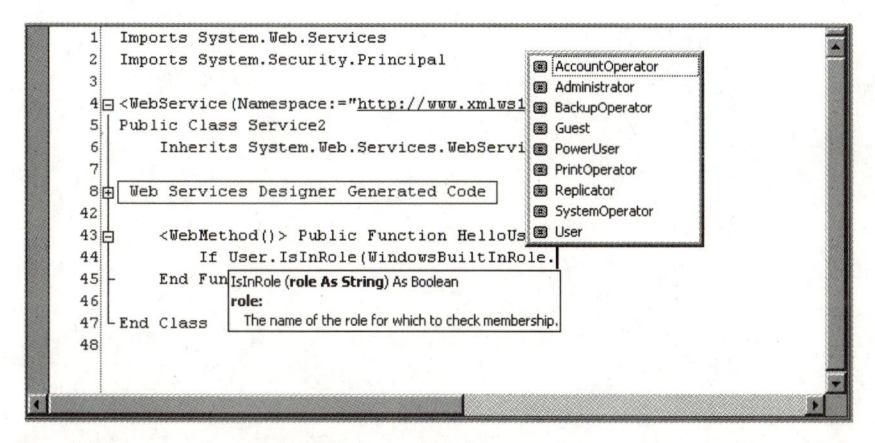

Listing 16-6: Using the WindowsBuiltInRole enumeration

VB

```
If Users.IsInRole(WindowsBuiltInRole.Administrator) Then
    ' Do something
End If
```

C#

```
If (Users.IsInRole(WindowsBuiltInRole.Administrator))
{
    // Do something
}
```

The great thing about using this enumeration is that, within Visual Studio .NET, you are provided with IntelliSense on the specific system roles that are in your domain, as shown in Figure 16-10.

Figure 16-10: Using the WindowsBuiltInRole enumeration.

Accessing additional user properties

When you use Windows authentication, you can use the `WindowsIdentity` object to find more information about the user logged on to your XML Web service. Knowing more about your users gives you more control over access to the code within your service.

The code example in Listing 16-7 shows you how to use this object to learn more about the user that is logged on to your XML Web service.

Listing 16-7: Using the WindowsIdentity object

VB

```
Imports System.Web.Services
Imports System.Security.Principal

<WebService(Namespace:="http://www.xmlws101.com/")> _
Public Class Service1
    Inherits System.Web.Services.WebService

    <WebMethod()> Public Function HelloUser() As String

      Dim currentUserID As WindowsIdentity = currentUserID.GetCurrent()

        Dim returnString As String

        returnString = "Hello " + currentUserID.Name.ToString() + "<br>"
        returnString += "Authentication Type: " +
            currentUserID.AuthenticationType.ToString() + "<br>"
        returnString += "IsAnonymous: " +
            currentUserID.IsAnonymous.ToString() + "<br>"
        returnString += "IsAuthenticated: " +
            currentUserID.IsAuthenticated.ToString() + "<br>"
        returnString += "IsGuest: " + currentUserID.IsGuest.ToString() +
            "<br>"
        returnString += "IsSystem: " + currentUserID.IsSystem.ToString()

        Return returnString
    End Function

End Class
```

C#

```
using System;
using System.Collections;
using System.ComponentModel;
using System.Data;
using System.Diagnostics;
using System.Web;
using System.Web.Services;
using System.Security.Principal;
```

```
namespace WebService
{
 public class Service1 : System.Web.Services.WebService
 {

  [WebMethod]
  public string HelloUser()
  {
    WindowsIdentity currentUserID = WindowsIdentity.GetCurrent();

    string returnString;

    returnString = "Hello " + currentUserID.Name.ToString() + "<br>"
       + "Authentication Type: "
       + currentUserID.AuthenticationType.ToString() + "<br>"
       + "IsAnonymous: "
       + currentUserID.IsAnonymous.ToString() + "<br>"
       + "IsAuthenticated: "
       + currentUserID.IsAuthenticated.ToString() + "<br>"
       + "IsGuest: " + currentUserID.IsGuest.ToString() + "<br>"
       + "IsSystem: " + currentUserID.IsSystem.ToString();


    return returnString;
  }
 }
}
```

Using the `WindowsIdentity` object in this manner allows you to gain additional information about the user that is logged on to the system, and produces the following result (Figure 16-11) if consumed in an ASP.NET Web Application.

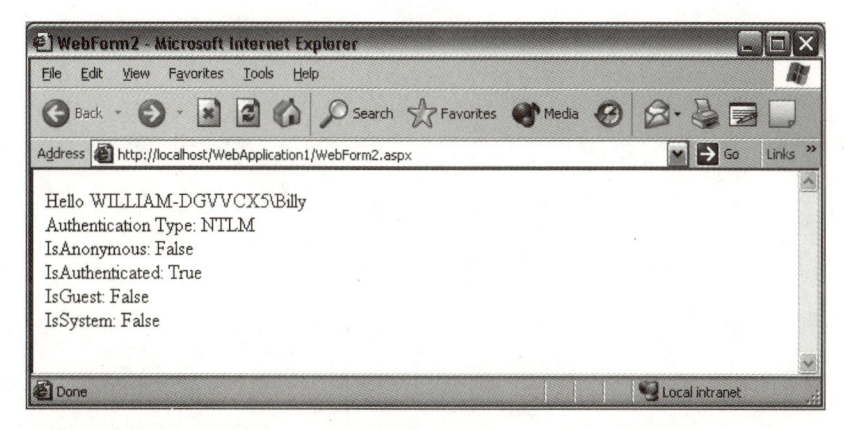

Figure 16-11: Using the WindowsIdentity object to find additional information about the user.

The code in Listing 16-7 imports the `System.Security.Principal` namespace at the top of the page and then creates an instance of the `WindowsIdentity` object. You relate the current user session to this object. After this, you display information about the current user's credentials, such as if the user is authenticated, anonymous, a guest account, or a system account, as well as the authentication type and login name.

Summary

This chapter covered some of the basics of security and how to apply both authentication and authorization to your XML Web services. You learned about some of the various authentication and authorization models at your disposal, such as Basic, Digest, and Windows Integrated Authentication. The chapter also covered how to use authentication properties within your applications and how to authorize users and groups based upon these properties.

In most situations, security in Web applications is very important. Sometimes you want to lock down applications and keep them off-limits to all but certain selected individuals. Authentication and authorization of users is a vital step in this process, and it's possible to authenticate in a number of different ways. This chapter showed you a couple of the more basic ways, but you should explore other opportunities that are available.

In the next chapter, you will learn about how to apply security using SOAP and how to apply encryption to the data that you send through your XML Web service.

Chapter 17
Advanced Security

There is one safeguard generally known to the wise,
which is an advantage and security to all.
What is it? Distrust.
Demosthenes, Greek orator (c. 384-322 B.C.)

As you may have noted in the last chapter, using IIS-based authentication has its limitations. In some cases, if you use certain authentication and authorization mechanisms to achieve system security, you limit the reach of your XML Web service. Sometimes, these mechanisms only authenticate users on the same operating system or even within the same domain.

The security measures shown in this chapter do not limit you to particular domains or to certain types of systems. These measures are considered *application security*. With application security, you let the application, not the system, take care of authenticating and authorizing of the user supplying the credentials. In many cases, you verify a user's credentials against a database or an XML file. The methods described in this chapter enable you to do just that. This chapter covers the following information:

♦ Sending credentials via SOAP Headers

♦ Using SOAP extensions for security

♦ Encrypting SOAP messages

Security via SOAP Headers

If I could recommend only one way in which to apply an authentication and authorization mechanism to your XML Web service, I would recommend using SOAP Headers. The SOAP Header is sent along with the SOAP message. SOAP Headers enable you to require consumers of your XML Web service to pass their credentials to your service.

As you learned in Chapter 14, SOAP Headers are a separate part of the SOAP message that really don't have anything to do with the actual SOAP message. You are able to include in the SOAP Header almost any kind of XML data that you wish to include. The definitions of the structure of the SOAP Header are flexible and, therefore, give you a lot of room to play. You can use this storage container that is sent along with the SOAP message to house the consuming application's credentials.

Using the SOAP Header, you require the consumers of your XML Web service to pass their login credentials (usually a login and password) directly in the SOAP Header payload. Then your XML Web service can verify these credentials by performing its own custom authentication. In Listing 17-1, you can see how to build an XML Web service that requires a login and password to get at the WebMethod that is exposed.

Listing 17-1: An XML Web service that requires a SOAP Header for authentication

VB

```
Imports System.Web.Services
Imports System.Web.Services.Protocols

Public Class AuthenticationHeader
    Inherits SoapHeader

    Public Login As String
    Public Password As String
End Class

<WebService(Namespace:="http://www.xmlws101.com/")> _
Public Class AccountBalance
    Inherits System.Web.Services.WebService

    Public GetClientInfo As AuthenticationHeader

    <WebMethod(), SoapHeader("GetClientInfo")> _
    Public Function GetBalance(ByVal AccNum as Integer) As Double
        GetClientInfo.MustUnderstand = True

        If GetClientInfo.Login = "user12345" _
            and GetClientInfo.Password = "password" Then
                GetClientInfo.DidUnderstand = True
        Else
                GetClientInfo.DidUnderstand = False
        End If

        ' You could connect to the DB now to get the account balance.
        Dim AcctBalance as Double = 124.25

        Return AcctBalance
    End Function

End Class
```

C#

```
using System;
using System.Collections;
using System.ComponentModel;
using System.Data;
using System.Diagnostics;
```

```
using System.Web;
using System.Web.Services;
using System.Web.Services.Protocols;

namespace WebService1
{

 public class AuthenticationHeader: SoapHeader
 {
  public string Login;
  public string Password;
 }

 [WebService(Namespace="http://www.xmlws101.com")]
 public class AccountBalance: System.Web.Services.WebService
 {
  public AuthenticationHeader GetClientInfo;

  [WebMethod]
  [SoapHeader("GetClientInfo")]
  public double GetBalance(int AcctNum)
  {
   GetClientInfo.MustUnderstand = true;

   if (GetClientInfo.Login == "user12345" &&
       GetClientInfo.Password == "password")
   {
    GetClientInfo.DidUnderstand = true;
   }
   else
   {
    GetClientInfo.DidUnderstand = false;
   }

   double AcctBalance;
   AcctBalance = 124.25;

   return AcctBalance;
  }
 }
}
```

In order to use SOAP Headers for authentication, you import the
`System.Web.Services.Protocol` namespace into your XML Web service. After this, you create the class `AuthenticationHeader`. This class derives from `SoapHeader`.

```
Public Class AuthenticationHeader
    Inherits SoapHeader

    Public Login As String
    Public Password As String
End Class
```

Then, within the WebService, you add a field of type `AuthenticationHeader` to the class that implements the `AccountBalance` class.

```
Public GetClientInfo As AuthenticationHeader
```

After this, you apply the `SoapHeader` to the `GetBalance` WebMethod, giving it a reference of `GetClientInfo`.

```
<WebMethod(), SoapHeader("GetClientInfo")>
```

Within the WebMethod itself, you force a requirement (by using the `MustUnderstand` property) that your WebMethod has to understand the SOAP Header that is passed to it.

```
GetClientInfo.MustUnderstand = True
```

After you have specified that the WebMethod is *required* to understand the SOAP Header that is passed to it, you assign the `DidUnderstand` property to either `True` or `False` depending on whether the end user passed in the correct information. In this case, `True` means he passed in the correct login credentials.

If you set the `DidUnderstand` property to `False`, the rest of the method is not processed and the end user receives a SOAP Fault.

Now that you have the XML Web service in place, it is vital that you change the `web.config` file in order to disable any other type of authentication mode that is specified in this document so that you can use custom authentication (see Listing 17-2).

Listing 17-2: Allowing custom authentication in the web.config file

```
<?xml version="1.0" encoding="utf-8" ?>
<configuration>
   <system.web>
      <authentication mode="None" />

      <!-- The rest of the web.config file -->

   </system.web>
</configuration>
```

Your XML Web service should now be in place with the proper SOAP Header definitions established. After you have changed your `web.config` file by specifying that no authentication is to be processed by the system (because you are doing this at the application level), you are ready for others to consume the WebMethod that you have exposed.

Consuming an XML Web service with an authentication SOAP Header

Imagine that an end user has found your XML Web service and she wants to consume this powerful piece of logic that provides the customers' account balances.

The first step in the entire process is for the end user to locate the WSDL document so that she can create a proxy class that will allow her to communicate with your XML Web service. The WSDL document in Listing 17-3 contains a description of the SOAP Header authentication that is required in order for her to get back a value from your XML Web service.

Listing 17-3: A piece of the WSDL document that specifies the SOAP Header required

```
<s:element name="AuthenticationHeader" type="s0:AuthenticationHeader" />
<s:complexType name="AuthenticationHeader">
   <s:sequence>
     <s:element minOccurs="0" maxOccurs="1" name="Login"
        type="s:string" />
     <s:element minOccurs="0" maxOccurs="1" name="Password"
        type="s:string" />
   </s:sequence>
</s:complexType>
```

After finding the WSDL document, the end user just needs to make a Web reference to the XML Web service, create a proxy class, and then use the code in Listing 17-4 to access the XML Web service programmatically. She gets an actual account balance after providing valid login credentials. In the following code example (Listing 17-4), the `localhost` Web reference was renamed to `Finance`. Assume, for demonstration purposes, that there is a simple ASP.NET page in place with a single Label control on the page with the ID of `Label1`.

Listing 17-4: Consuming the AccountBalance XML Web service

VB

```
Public Class WebForm1
    Inherits System.Web.UI.Page

    Private Sub Page_Load(ByVal sender As System.Object, ByVal e As
                   System.EventArgs) Handles MyBase.Load

       Dim ws As New Finance.AccountBalance()
       Dim wsAuth As New Finance.AuthenticationHeader()

       wsAuth.Login = "user12345"
       wsAuth.Password = "password"

       ws.AuthenticationHeaderValue = wsAuth

       Label1.Text = ws.GetBalance(1234).ToString()
```

```
    End Sub

End Class
```

C#

```csharp
using System;
using System.Collections;
using System.ComponentModel;
using System.Data;
using System.Drawing;
using System.Web;
using System.Web.SessionState;
using System.Web.UI;
using System.Web.UI.WebControls;
using System.Web.UI.HtmlControls;

namespace WebApplication1
{
 public class WebForm1 : System.Web.UI.Page
 {
   protected System.Web.UI.WebControls.Label Label1;

   private void Page_Load(object sender, System.EventArgs e)
   {
     Finance.AccountBalance ws = new Finance.AccountBalance();
     Finance.AuthenticationHeader wsAuth =
       new Finance.AuthenticationHeader();

     wsAuth.Login = "user12345";
     wsAuth.Password = "password";

     ws.AuthenticationHeaderValue = wsAuth;

     Label1.Text = ws.GetBalance(1234).ToString();
   }
 }
}
```

After this is all in place, view it in action using the SOAP Toolkit Trace Utility. Redo the Reference.vb or the Reference.cs file so that the SOAP request and response messages run through port 8080.

> **CROSS-REFERENCE:** Using the SOAP Toolkit Trace Utility to monitor SOAP messages is covered in Chapter 13.

After you have compiled and run the application, you should see your SOAP messages within the SOAP Toolkit Trace Utility, as in Figure 17-1.

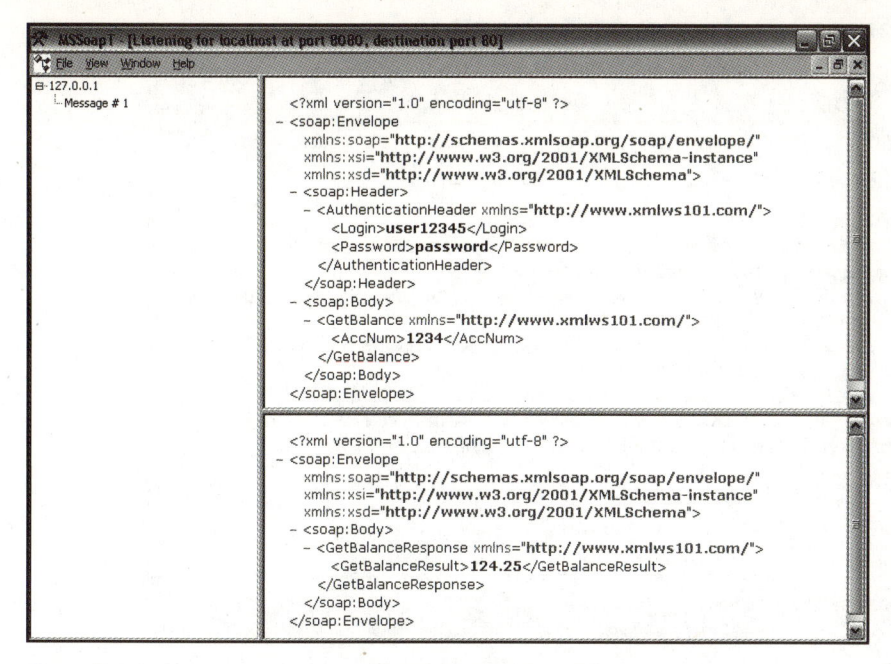

Figure 17-1: Monitoring the SOAP message using the SOAP Toolkit Trace Utility.

The end user sends in an appropriate SOAP message with a SOAP Header (using the `<AuthenticationHeader>` element) containing the proper credentials. These are accepted in the Web service itself. A response SOAP message that contains the payload the end user is looking for is then returned.

You have successfully created an XML Web service that requires credentials in order to return a response. You have also created an XML Web service client that passes in the credentials in the format required by the XML Web service. Now, try running the consuming application again — but this time, do so without proper credentials.

For example, if you change the login to something that the XML Web service doesn't recognize, you get back a SOAP Fault, or an error that informs you that you were unable to process the XML Web service (Figure 17-2).

Using SOAP Headers for the process of authentication and authorization is ideal and very simple to implement. You might be wondering about the security behind SOAP Headers and if it is safe to send credentials within a SOAP Header. It is true that someone could intercept your SOAP message as it is sent across the wire and read the values that are within the SOAP Header itself, thereby getting hold of the login and password to your XML Web service. As you will learn later in this chapter, however, you can encrypt this data so that even if someone does get his hands on your SOAP envelope, he won't understand its vital contents.

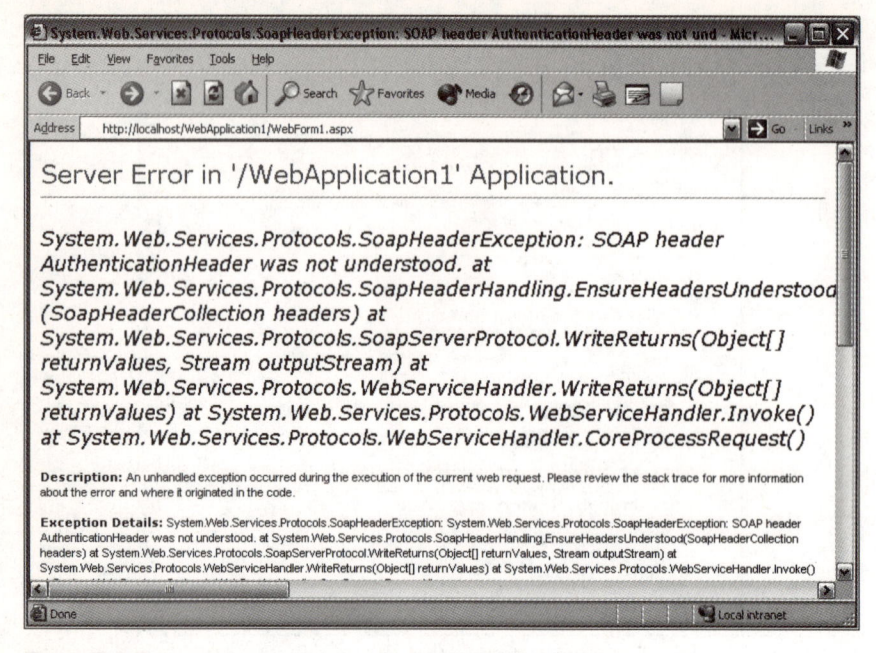

Figure 17-2: The message received when the credentials are not correct.

Verifying credentials against a data source

The preceding example showed how to authenticate a user by login and password inline. In most cases, however, you are going to want to authenticate consumers of your XML Web service against a data source.

In later chapters, I show you how to work with databases and ADO.NET along with your XML Web services. In this example, I show you how to validate consumers of your XML Web service against an XML file.

The first item that you need is an XML file from which you authenticate users, as shown in Listing 17-5.

Listing 17-5: XML file that holds consumers' credentials

```
<?xml version="1.0" encoding="utf-8" ?>
<GetBalanceUsers>
 <XYZdivision>pass1</XYZdivision>
 <ABCcompany>pass2</ABCcompany>
 <HappyPerson>pass3</HappyPerson>
 <TroubledPerson>pass4</TroubledPerson>
 <Admin>pass5</Admin>
</GetBalanceUsers>
```

This XML file holds all the credentials of the users who will have access to the `ValidateUser` WebMethod. Each user has his login represented by an element, and within that element is his password, `<login>password</login>`. Listing 17-6 shows you how to take the SOAP Header credentials that the end user will pass into the Web service and validate these credentials against the sample XML file.

Listing 17-6: Authenticating users from an XML file in your XML Web service

VB

```vb
Imports System.Web.Services
Imports System.Web.Services.Protocols
Imports System.Xml

Public Class AuthenticationHeader
    Inherits SoapHeader

    Public Login As String
    Public Password As String
End Class

<WebService(Namespace:="http://www.xmlws101.com/")> _
Public Class SimpleAuthenticate
    Inherits System.Web.Services.WebService

    Public UserCredentials As AuthenticationHeader

    <WebMethod(), SoapHeader("UserCredentials")> _
    Public Function ValidateUser() As String
        UserCredentials.MustUnderstand = True

        Dim returnString As String

        Dim myXmlPath As String = Server.MapPath("ValidUsers.xml")
        Dim myXmlDoc As New XmlDocument()

        Try
            myXmlDoc.Load(myXmlPath)
        Catch err As Exception
            returnString = "ERROR: " & err.Message & "<br>" _
                & err.Source & "."
        End Try

        Dim WsUser As XmlNodeList
        WsUser = myXmlDoc.GetElementsByTagName(UserCredentials.Login)

        If Not (WsUser Is Nothing) Then
          If UserCredentials.Password = WsUser.ItemOf(0).InnerXml Then
                UserCredentials.DidUnderstand = True
            Else
```

402 Part VI: Security

```
                UserCredentials.DidUnderstand = False
          End If
        End If

        returnString = "You are a valid user"

        Return returnString
    End Function

End Class
```

C#

```csharp
using System;
using System.Collections;
using System.ComponentModel;
using System.Data;
using System.Diagnostics;
using System.Web;
using System.Web.Services;
using System.Web.Services.Protocols;
using System.Xml;

namespace WebService1
{

 public class AuthenticationHeader: SoapHeader
 {
  public string Login;
  public string Password;
 }

 [WebService(Namespace="http://www.xmlws101.com")]
 public class SimpleAuthenticate: System.Web.Services.WebService
 {
  public AuthenticationHeader UserCredentials;

  [WebMethod]
  [SoapHeader("UserCredentials")]
  public string ValidateUser()
  {
   UserCredentials.MustUnderstand = true;

   string returnString;

   string myXmlPath = Server.MapPath("ValidUsers.xml");
   XmlDocument myXmlDoc = new XmlDocument();

   try
```

```
   {
      myXmlDoc.Load(myXmlPath);
   }
   catch (Exception err)
   {
      returnString = "ERROR: " + err.Message + "<br>" + err.Source &
".";
   }

   XmlNodeList WsUser;
   WsUser = myXmlDoc.GetElementsByTagName(UserCredentials.Login);

   if (WsUser != null)
   {
      if (UserCredentials.Password == WsUser.Item(0).InnerXml)
      {
         UserCredentials.DidUnderstand = true;
      }
      else
      {
         UserCredentials.DidUnderstand = false;
      }
   }

   returnString = "You are a valid user";

   return returnString;
  }
 }
}
```

Using this example, an XML file (`ValidateUsers.xml`) is loaded. The XML is searched for a particular node that matches the end user's login passed in by the SOAP Header. After this is found, the inner XML (the text between the XML tags) is compared to the password that was also passed through the SOAP Header. If both the login and password match, then (within the WebMethod) you programmatically assign the fact that the SOAP Header was understood. You do this by using `DidUnderstand=True`. Otherwise, you assign the fact that it wasn't understood by using `DidUnderstand=False`.

Using SOAP Extensions for Encryption

The data that is sent to and from XML Web services sometimes contains information that should remain private. With SOAP messages going back and forth across the Internet, some SOAP messages might be grabbed as they travel from one SOAP router to another. You definitely do not want some of this data exposed to people or applications for which the message payload was not intended. For instance, you do not want your credit card number, medical information, or bank account information floating around in cyberspace without any protection. You can protect this data by putting it (in a sense) under lock and key.

With XML Web services, the lock is *encryption* or *cryptography,* and the key is the public or private key used for encrypting and decrypting the information in the SOAP message.

One way to encrypt your SOAP messages is to use your XML Web services over HTTPS. This is a secure method that encrypts the *entire* SOAP message. Therefore, the HTTP header and the entire SOAP message, including any headers, are encrypted before they are sent across the wire. This format is secure and safe, but it taxes the server and makes the SOAP message dependent upon HTTP for message transport.

Using Secure Sockets Layer (SSL) over HTTPS for XML Web services is the same as using it for any Web application. You must get a certificate and install it on your server. You then force SSL usage on your XML Web services by using a URL with HTTPS.

Partial Encryption Using DES

Instead of taking the route of using SSL over HTTPS, you might want to encrypt the body of the SOAP message. To see an example of this, you can build an XML Web service that encrypts its return payload using *Data Encryption Standard* (DES).

DES is a popular U.S. government algorithm, developed in the 1970s, which is used to encrypt and decrypt data. The algorithm is designed to encipher and decipher blocks of data consisting of 64 bits under control of a 64-bit key. The key consists of 64 binary digits (0's or 1's) of which 56 bits are generated randomly and then are used directly by the algorithm. The other 8 bits, which are not used by the algorithm, are used for error detection.

Using DES, the person who encrypts the message has to have the same key as the person who decrypts the message. So in the end, one copy of the key locks up the message and another copy of the key unlocks it. The consumer of your XML Web service must have the algorithm key to unlock the encrypted message.

With the release of the .NET Framework, you have a namespace (or a collection of classes) that gives you direct access to encrypting and decrypting functionality: `System.Security.Cryptography`.

In order to see the entire process of encrypting and decrypting the body of a SOAP message, you can play the roles of both the XML Web service creator and of the consumer. To do this you must complete the following tasks:

- Creating a SOAP extension class in C# – `EncryptionEngine`.
- Creating an XML Web service that uses the EncryptionEngine SOAP extension.
- Creating an XML Web service consumer that consumes the encrypted SOAP message.

Creating the SOAP extension

The first step is to create a SOAP extension that you can use in an XML Web service.

> **CROSS-REFERENCE:** SOAP extensions are covered more fully in Chapter 14.

SOAP extensions enable you to jump in and intercept the message at a specific point, such as directly before it is serialized into XML and sent across the wire. In this case, you want to establish a SOAP extension that takes the response from the XML Web service. Immediately before the SOAP response is sent to the end user, this SOAP extension class will encrypt the message. The encryption ensures that, should the message be intercepted along the wire, any person or application viewing the message won't understand it — unless they are smart enough to break the encryption code.

Before you can build the XML Web service, you must build the SOAP extension that allows for encryption of the SOAP response. To do this, create a new class file in Visual Studio .NET and use the code in Listing 17-7 to create the SOAP extension in C#. Even though you are creating this SOAP extension in C#, you can use this class file in your Visual Basic .NET XML Web service applications. This is shown in the following examples.

Listing 17-7: Building a SOAP extension that will encrypt the SOAP response

C#

```
using System;
using System.IO;
using System.Xml;
using System.Text;
using System.Web.Services;
using System.Web.Services.Protocols;
using System.Security.Cryptography;

namespace Encryption {

[AttributeUsage(AttributeTargets.Method)]
public class EncryptionEngineAttribute : SoapExtensionAttribute
{
 private int priority;
 private EncryptMode encryptionMode = EncryptMode.None;
 private DecryptMode decryptionMode = DecryptMode.None;
 private Target target = Target.Method;

 public override Type ExtensionType
 {
  get { return typeof(EncryptionEngine); }
 }

 public override int Priority
 {
  get { return priority; }
  set { priority = value; }
 }

 public EncryptMode Encrypt
 {
  get { return encryptionMode; }
```

```csharp
    set { encryptionMode = value; }
  }

  public DecryptMode Decrypt
  {
    get { return decryptionMode; }
    set { decryptionMode = value; }
  }

  public Target Target
  {
    get { return target; }
    set { target = value; }
  }
}

public enum DecryptMode
{ None, Response, Request }

public enum EncryptMode
{ None, Response, Request }

public enum Target
{ Envelope, Body, Method }

public class EncryptionEngine : SoapExtension
{
  Stream oldStream;
  Stream newStream;
  DecryptMode decryptMode;
  EncryptMode encryptMode;
  Target target;

  private Byte[] key = {0x01, 0x23, 0x45, 0x67, 0x89, 0xab, 0xcd, 0xef};
  private Byte[] IV  = {0x13, 0x34, 0x56, 0x78, 0x90, 0xab, 0xcd, 0xef};

  public override object GetInitializer(LogicalMethodInfo methodInfo,
      SoapExtensionAttribute attribute)
  {
    return attribute;
  }

  public override object GetInitializer(Type t)
  {
    return typeof(EncryptionEngine);
  }

  public override void Initialize(object initializer)
  {
```

```csharp
    EncryptionEngineAttribute attribute =
        (EncryptionEngineAttribute) initializer;

    // Find the mode we should be in
    decryptMode = attribute.Decrypt;
    encryptMode = attribute.Encrypt;
    target = attribute.Target;
    return;
}

public override void ProcessMessage(SoapMessage message)
{
    switch (message.Stage)
    {
        case SoapMessageStage.BeforeSerialize:
            break;

        case SoapMessageStage.AfterSerialize:
            Encrypt();
            break;

        case SoapMessageStage.BeforeDeserialize:
            Decrypt();
            break;

        case SoapMessageStage.AfterDeserialize:
            break;

        default:
            throw new Exception("invalid stage");
    }
}

public override Stream ChainStream( Stream stream )
{
    oldStream = stream;
    newStream = new MemoryStream();
    return newStream;
}

private void Decrypt()
{
    MemoryStream decryptedStream = new MemoryStream();

    if ((decryptMode == DecryptMode.Request) ||
        (decryptMode == DecryptMode.Response))
    {
        TextReader reader = new StreamReader(oldStream);
        TextWriter writer = new StreamWriter(decryptedStream);
```

Part VI: Security

```
   writer.WriteLine(reader.ReadToEnd());
   writer.Flush();

   decryptedStream = DecryptSoap(decryptedStream);

   Copy(decryptedStream, newStream);
  }
  else
  {
   Copy(oldStream, newStream);
  }

  newStream.Position = 0;
 }

 private void Encrypt()
 {
  newStream.Position = 0;

  if ((encryptMode == EncryptMode.Request) ||
      (encryptMode == EncryptMode.Response))
   newStream = EncryptSoap(newStream);

  Copy(newStream, oldStream);
 }

 private byte[] CovertStringToByteArray(string s)
 {
  char[] c = {' '};
  string[] ss = s.Split(c);

  byte[] b = new byte[ss.Length];

  for(int i=0; i<b.Length; i++)
  {
   b[i] = Byte.Parse(ss[i]);
  }

  return b;
 }

 private byte[] Decrypt(string stringToDecrypt)
 {
  DESCryptoServiceProvider des = new DESCryptoServiceProvider();
  byte[] inputByteArray = CovertStringToByteArray(stringToDecrypt);

  MemoryStream ms = new MemoryStream();
  CryptoStream cs = new CryptoStream(ms, des.CreateDecryptor( key, IV
),
```

```
        CryptoStreamMode.Write);

  cs.Write(inputByteArray, 0, inputByteArray.Length);
  cs.FlushFinalBlock();

  return ms.ToArray();
}
private byte[] Encrypt(string stringToEncrypt)
{
  DESCryptoServiceProvider des = new DESCryptoServiceProvider();

  byte[] inputByteArray = Encoding.UTF8.GetBytes(stringToEncrypt);

  MemoryStream ms = new MemoryStream();
  CryptoStream cs = new CryptoStream(ms, des.CreateEncryptor( key, IV ),
        CryptoStreamMode.Write);

  cs.Write(inputByteArray, 0, inputByteArray.Length);
  cs.FlushFinalBlock();

  return ms.ToArray();
}
public MemoryStream EncryptSoap(Stream streamToEncrypt)
{
  streamToEncrypt.Position = 0;
  XmlTextReader reader = new XmlTextReader(streamToEncrypt);
  XmlDocument dom = new XmlDocument();
  dom.Load(reader);

  XmlNamespaceManager nsmgr = new XmlNamespaceManager(dom.NameTable);
  nsmgr.AddNamespace("soap",
        "http://schemas.xmlsoap.org/soap/envelope/");
  XmlNode node = dom.SelectSingleNode("//soap:Body", nsmgr);
  node = node.FirstChild.FirstChild;

  byte[] outData = Encrypt(node.InnerText);

  StringBuilder s = new StringBuilder();

  for(int i=0; i<outData.Length; i++)
  {
    if(i==(outData.Length-1))
      s.Append(outData[i]);
    else
      s.Append(outData[i] + " ");
  }
```

```csharp
    node.InnerText = s.ToString();

    MemoryStream ms = new MemoryStream();
    dom.Save(ms);
    ms.Position = 0;

    return ms;
}

public MemoryStream DecryptSoap(Stream streamToDecrypt)
{
    streamToDecrypt.Position = 0;
    XmlTextReader reader = new XmlTextReader(streamToDecrypt);
    XmlDocument dom = new XmlDocument();
    dom.Load(reader);

    XmlNamespaceManager nsmgr = new XmlNamespaceManager(dom.NameTable);
    nsmgr.AddNamespace("soap",
        "http://schemas.xmlsoap.org/soap/envelope/");
    XmlNode node = dom.SelectSingleNode("//soap:Body", nsmgr);
    node = node.FirstChild.FirstChild;

    byte[] outData = Decrypt(node.InnerText);

    string sTmp = Encoding.UTF8.GetString(outData);

    node.InnerText = sTmp;

    MemoryStream ms = new MemoryStream();
    ms.Position = 0;
    dom.Save(ms);
    ms.Position = 0;

    return ms;
}

void Copy(Stream from, Stream to)
{
    TextReader reader = new StreamReader(from);
    TextWriter writer = new StreamWriter(to);
    writer.WriteLine(reader.ReadToEnd());
    writer.Flush();
}
}
}
```

Okay, that is a lot of code for an example, but it shows you the hardest part of the entire process. Note the important parts of this code. To initiate the class, you need to import the

System.Security.Cryptography namespace. This namespace enables you to perform all the magic you need.

You now declare three properties that you use with this SOAP extension: Encrypt, Decrypt, and Target.

```
public enum DecryptMode
{ None, Response, Request }

public enum EncryptMode
{ None, Response, Request }

public enum Target
{ Envelope, Body, Method }
```

Notice that each property has a set of possible values. The most interesting one is the Target property. It allows you to specify Envelope, Body, or Method as the value. This specification enables you to select the part of the SOAP message that gets encrypted. For instance, if you want to encrypt the entire SOAP message, you use a value of Envelope with the Target property.

Within the SOAP extension document, note that two byte arrays are declared within the ExtensionEngine class. These byte arrays hold the encryption and decryption keys.

```
private Byte[] key = {0x01, 0x23, 0x45, 0x67, 0x89, 0xab, 0xcd, 0xef};
private Byte[] IV  = {0x13, 0x34, 0x56, 0x78, 0x90, 0xab, 0xcd, 0xef};
```

The consumers of your XML Web service need these all-important keys to decrypt the SOAP response. How can they get the keys? It is actually easy. You simply provide the consumers of your XML Web service with the SOAP extension class file so that they can use it within their applications to decrypt the SOAP responses from your XML Web service. Therefore, any person who has this class file will be able to decrypt your SOAP messages as long as the keys remain the same.

Next in the class file is the ProcessMessage method. This is a required method of the SOAP extension class. Within this method you simply call the Encrypt() method after the SOAP message has been serialized and the Decrypt() method after the SOAP message has been deserialized.

Both the encryption and decryption methods cipher or decipher the message whether it is a request or a response message. This enables the consumer of the XML Web service not only to decode SOAP responses from the Web service, but also to send encoded message to the XML Web service.

Using the SOAP EncryptionEngine extension in an XML Web service

Now that you have your class file all ready, saved, and compiled, create a new XML Web service and place the EncryptionEngine.cs class file within the bin directory of your XML Web service project. It doesn't matter if your XML Web service project is in Visual

Basic .NET, a C# class file will work just fine within the application. All you have to do, in this case, is make a reference to the DLL where this encryption class is located.

Even though this class is in C# and you might be building your XML Web service in Visual Basic .NET, don't worry. If you want to use this encryption class file within a Visual Basic .NET application, make a reference to it in your project. You can create a C# Class Library called `Encryption` and put the C# `EncryptionEngine.cs` file in it. After compiling the class library, you are ready to return to the XML Web service that you are creating in Visual Basic .NET and make a reference to the Encryption DLL. Take the following steps to make a reference to the DLL:

1. Right-click on the References folder within the Solution Explorer.
2. Select Add Reference.
3. You see the Add Reference dialog window. Click the Projects tab.
4. Click the Browse button and look for the `Encryption.dll` file that you just created. If you don't find it under the `Inetpub` folder, look under the `My Documents/Visual Studio Projects` folder.
5. Click Open.
6. You will now see the `Encryption.dll` file as a selected reference, as shown in Figure 17-3. Click OK.

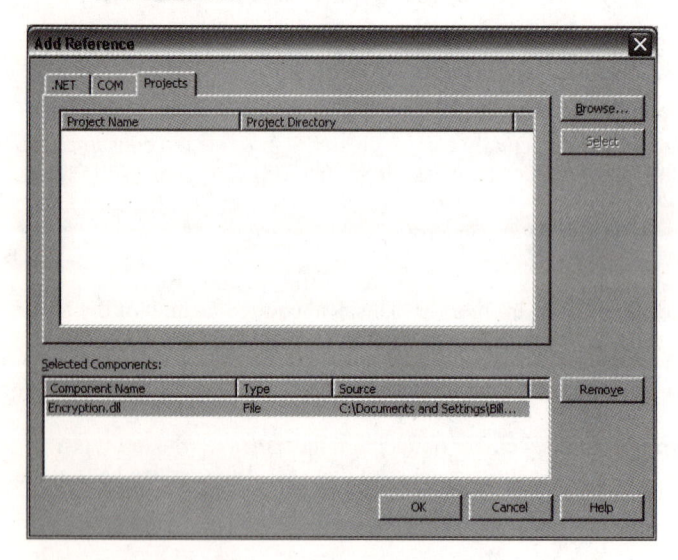

Figure 17-3: Making a reference to the Encryption.dll file.

You can use this class file by simply making a reference to the `Encryption` namespace within your code.

Building the rest of your XML Web service consumer

After the encryption class file is in place, you can use encryption to encode the payloads of SOAP messages that are sent from your XML Web service. You can now include all sorts of top-secret information within your XML Web service, providing it only to select individuals. You give your key to these people so that they will be able to consume your XML Web service and unlock the data that is contained within it.

You can now build an XML Web service (Listing 17-8) that provides a top-secret family recipe for an apple cake that you only want select individuals to consume (the XML Web service that is). You have decided to encrypt the SOAP message payload in order to prevent just anyone from seeing what is inside.

Listing 17-8: The XML Web service that uses the SOAP EncryptionEngine extension

VB

```vb
Imports System.Web.Services
Imports Encryption

<WebService(Namespace := "http://www.xmlws101.com/")> _
Public Class Service1
   Inherits System.Web.Services.WebService

   <WebMethod(), EncryptionExtension(Encrypt:=EncryptMode.Response)> _
   Public Function GetAppleCake() As String
     Return "Tuija's Apple Cake - 200 grams margarine. 2 dl sugar. " & _
     "3 eggs. 3 dl flour. 1 tsp vanilla. 1 tsp baking powder. " & _
     "1 tsp cinnamon. 3 apples cut in pieces. Melt margarine in " & _
     "microwave. Add sugar and stir. Add eggs one at a time " & _
     "beating well. Stir in flour, baking powder, vanilla, " & _
     "cinnamon and apples. Bake at 375 for 50-55 minutes. " & _
     "Serve with whipped cream or with vanilla ice cream. "
   End Function

End Class
```

C#

```csharp
using System;
using System.Collections;
using System.ComponentModel;
using System.Data;
using System.Diagnostics;
using System.Web;
using System.Web.Services;

namespace WebService1
{
 public class Service1 : System.Web.Services.WebService
 {
```

```
    [WebMethod]
    [EncryptionEngine(Encrypt=EncryptMode.Response)]
    public string GetAppleCake()
    {
      return "Tuija's Apple Cake - 200 grams margarine. 2 dl sugar. " +
        "3 eggs. 3 dl flour. 1 tsp vanilla. 1 tsp baking powder. " +
        "1 tsp cinnamon. 3 apples cut in pieces. Melt margarine in " +
        "microwave. Add sugar and stir. Add eggs one at a time " +
        "beating well. Stir in flour, baking powder, vanilla, " +
        "cinnamon and apples. Bake at 375 for 50-55 minutes. " +
        "Serve with whipped cream or with vanilla ice cream. ";
    }
  }
}
```

If the EncryptionEngine class is in the bin folder or if you have made a reference to the Encryption DLL and imported the Encryption namespace into your application, you can use your custom attributes for any WebMethods that you develop. For this example, the EncryptionEngine WebMethod is set to encrypt the SOAP response of the GetAppleCake() method.

Consuming the XML Web service

Now, put on a different hat and pretend that you are the XML Web service consumer and you have built a .NET application that needs to consume this XML Web service. To do this, you must make some sort of arrangement with the XML Web service provider to consume the Web service and invoke the GetAppleCake() method. If you don't, you just get back the encoded message. This arrangement can be made by signing up for the service in some manner or by being a partner or customer of the XML Web service provider. You can also go the XML Web service provider's Web site, pay for admission to the XML Web service and, in return, receive the class file that contains the key needed to consume the Web service. No matter how you do it, in the end, you need a copy of the class file (ExtensionEngine.cs).

After you have the class file that enables you to apply decryption to the message, you place this file within the bin directory of your application or make a reference to the class file. After you do this, make a Web reference to the XML Web service and open up the proxy class that is created for you. Then within this proxy class, simply add an extension to the class that calls the GetAppleCake() method, as shown in Listing 17-9.

Listing 17-9: Altering the proxy class (Note: The entire proxy class is not shown)

VB

```
<System.Web.Services.Protocols.SoapDocumentMethodAttribute
 ("http://www.xmlws101.com/GetAppleCake",
   RequestNamespace:="http://www.xmlws101.com/",
   ResponseNamespace:="http://www.xmlws101.com/",
   Use:=System.Web.Services.Description.SoapBindingUse.Literal,
   ParameterStyle:=System.Web.Services.Protocols.
   SoapParameterStyle.Wrapped),
```

Chapter 17: Advanced Security

```
    EncryptionEngine(Decrypt:=DecryptMode.Response)> _
    Public Function GetAppleCake() As String
        Dim results() As Object = Me.Invoke("GetAppleCake", New
           Object(-1) {})
        Return CType(results(0), String)
    End Function
```

C#

```
[System.Web.Services.Protocols.SoapDocumentMethodAttribute
 ("http://www.xmlws101.com/GetAppleCake",
  RequestNamespace="http://www.xmlws101.com/",
  ResponseNamespace="http://www.xmlws101.com/",
  Use=System.Web.Services.Description.SoapBindingUse.Literal,
  ParameterStyle=System.Web.Services.Protocols.
  SoapParameterStyle.Wrapped)]
[EncryptionEngine(Decrypt=DecryptMode.Request)]
public string GetAppleCake() {
    object[] results = this.Invoke("GetAppleCake", new object[0]);
        return ((string)(results[0]));
}
```

With the `EncryptionEngine` attribute in place in the client code, you are specifying that the SOAP message needs to be decrypted upon receipt. After the SOAP message is received, this custom attribute will, in turn, call functionality in the `ExtensionEngine` class file and decrypt the message to plain text.

After this, build an application (just as you normally would) that calls and consumes the `GetAppleCake()` method.

If you set up the SOAP Toolkit's Trace Utility to watch the SOAP messages come and go across the wire, you see that the encrypted response looks like the message shown in Listing 17-10.

Listing 17-10: The encrypted SOAP response

```
<?xml version="1.0" encoding="utf-8" ?>
<soap:Envelope xmlns:soap="http://schemas.xmlsoap.org/soap/envelope/"
 xmlns:xsi="http://www.w3.org/2001/XMLSchema-instance"
 xmlns:xsd="http://www.w3.org/2001/XMLSchema">
  <soap:Body>
    <GetAppleCakeResponse xmlns="http://www.xmlws101.com/">
      <GetAppleCakeResult>243 40 251 23 245 144 190 235 91 237 248 138
         34 75 178 187 190 127 211 12 186 1 103 106 161 228 211 147 59
         194 65 130 164 149 36 151 248 108 188 40 210 53 206 159 204 104
         5 105 244 59 178 235 181 49 40 223 60 121 244 43 215 70 22 122
         94 15 124 245 227 143 134 175 231 188 180 51 85 19 105 77 30 44
         193 14 47 103 52 92 34 246 234 132 61 206 153 225 229 133 163
         221 252 45 145 45 13 246 130 164 246 159 190 89 169 221 105 154
         238 19 183 245 182 218 240 33 171 105 7 200 16 196 203 129 251
         40 67 226 208 230 49 115 91 220 12 34 222 164 14 127 224 98 176
```

```
            211 58 249 133 224 166 86 98 7 37 68 236 33 163 152 34 165 69
            203 187 95 191 210 91 199 226 36 85 44 51 200 113 202 138 117
            184 111 152 169 119 116 209 183 252 196 217 172 36 19 138 249
            159 188 31 231 181 178 17 13 128 30 137 46 100 7 85 153 236 236
            114 197 175 34 69 23 119 156 16 37 36 117 0 163 229 189 65 67
            254 83 140 233 4 116 119 3 111 139 255 137 227 252 31 99 185 185
            75 89 8 187 52 152 59 172 218 125 165 107 83 158 191 235 155 49
            169 159 68 51 127 216 3 231 0 166 30 166 18 101 123 236 210 30
            172 18 154 10 157 35 130 135 159 109 79 192 238 195 173 228 188
            130 49 43 250 91 45 169 119 14 251 119 192 143 228 196 204 35 55
            63 31 129 4 50 178 217 54 173 163 138 252 135 123 64 177 186 235
            176 102 155 84 99 200 148 226 134 41 225 175 43 194 224 209 85
            189 83 9 118 39 185 80 247 44 85 52 98 220 188 246 69 231 99 18
            115 13 106</GetAppleCakeResult>
        </GetAppleCakeResponse>
    </soap:Body>
</soap:Envelope>
```

This worked because the key, the `ExtensionEngine` class file, was at both ends. If the consumer of this XML Web service (or someone who intercepted this SOAP message along its route) got this message and didn't have the key, he would simply see the encrypted data. Without the key, it is rather difficult to decipher the message.

Summary

This chapter covered some of the more advanced ways to apply security to your XML Web services. You saw how to use SOAP Headers in order to pass credentials to the XML Web service for authentication and authorization of the consumer.

You also learned about using SOAP extensions for encrypting the SOAP message. The example used DES encryption to encode the SOAP message before it was sent across the wire. This required the consumer of the XML Web service to have a key furnished by the XML Web service provider to decrypt the message as it was received.

The examples in this chapter demonstrate that security can be used individually or in unison. For instance, for even greater security, you can use SOAP Headers for login credentials and also apply encryption to the returned message.

The next two chapters take a look at ADO.NET and how to use this new technology along with your XML Web services.

Part VII

ADO.NET and XML Web Services

Chapter 18: Working with ADO.NET

Chapter 19: XML Web Services and ADO.NET

Chapter 18

Working with ADO.NET

Data is what distinguishes the dilettante from the artist.
George V. Higgins, *Guardian*, (London, June 17, 1988)

XML Web Services do more than provide remote application logic. One of the main functions of XML Web Services is to provide access to data. XML Web services can perform this function even for platforms and applications that are incompatible with the system where the data is stored. This is possible because XML Web Services can expose this data as XML.

This means XML Web Services can be used to share and port data between these incompatible systems within companies or between companies and their partners or customers.

Building XML Web Services on the .NET platform gives you access to ADO.NET and all the classes that this new data-access technology provides.

This chapter covers the following basics of ADO.NET:

- Introduction to ADO.NET
- Common data techniques
- Understanding the DataSet
- Using the DataAdapter

ADO.NET and XML

.NET has introduced a new way to access data: XML. XML is the strength behind data in .NET, and ADO.NET is built to use XML to its fullest advantage. Visual Studio .NET, the new development tool for .NET, makes it quite easy for you to work with ADO.NET and to manipulate the XML as it is being sent to and from the database. Within this new tool are a number of new wizards and designers that make it easy to provide your XML Web Services with data-access capabilities.

ADO.NET is a completely different model than ADO. ADO.NET knows how to take data from a data store, serialize it into XML, and then populate a data store from XML.

XML has become the standard that is used for representing data. This makes XML Web Services powerful as they pass application logic and data across the Internet. Using this standard ensures compliance with other systems and applications. So, when Microsoft started developing .NET, it knew that it also had to develop a new data-access technology to take advantage of this data-representation standard.

ADO.NET addresses a couple of the most common data-access strategies that are used for applications today. When classic ADO was developed, many applications could be connected to the data store almost indefinitely. Today, with the explosion of the Internet as the means of data communication, a new data technology is required to make data accessible and updateable in a disconnected architecture.

The first of these common data-access scenarios is one in which a user must locate a collection of data and iterate through this data just a single time. This is a popular scenario for Web pages. When a request for data from a Web page that you have created is received, you can simply fill a table with data from a data store. In this case, you go to the data store, grab the data that you want, send the data across the wire, and then populate the table. In this scenario, the goal is to get the data in place as fast as possible.

The second way to work with data in this disconnected architecture is to grab a collection of data and use this data separately from the data store itself. This could be on the server or even on the client. Even though the data is disconnected, you want the ability to keep the data (with all of its tables and relations in place) on the client side. Classic ADO data was represented by a single table that you could iterate through; but ADO.NET can be a reflection of the data store itself, with tables, columns, rows, and relations all in place. When you are done with the client-side copy of the data, you can persist the changes that you made in the local copy of data directly back into the data store. The technology that gives you this capability is the DataSet, which will be covered shortly.

Although classic ADO was geared for a two-tiered environment (client-server), ADO.NET addresses a multitiered environment. ADO.NET is easy to work with because it has a unified programming model. This unified programming model makes working with data on the server the same as working with data on the client. Because the models are the same, you find yourself more productive when working with ADO.NET.

NOTE: Remember that in .NET, data is XML and XML is data.

ADO.NET Architecture

The central piece in ADO.NET is the DataSet. The DataSet is a powerful new XML-based way to represent disconnected data. As you will see in the next chapter, you can return a complete DataSet, along with all its tables and relations, from an XML Web Service. The power behind a DataSet is that, because it is built to be disconnected, you can limit the database connections to the data store.

Figure 18-1 is a diagram of how data in .NET is built to move from the data store to the client. Starting on the right side of the diagram, note that data is generally housed in some sort of data store. This data store can be a Microsoft SQL Server database, a Microsoft Access database, or even an XML file.

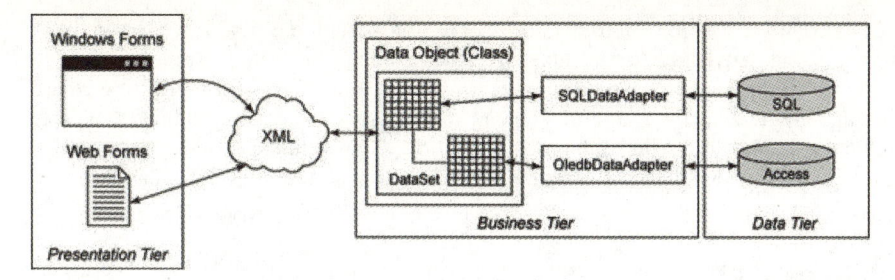

Figure 18-1: The ADO.NET architecture showing how the this new data access technology works with a distributed environment.

> **NOTE:** The examples in this chapter and Chapter 19, demonstrating ADO.NET, concentrate primarily on working with SQL Server.

A DataAdapter takes hold of the data and moves it from the data store to the DataSet. The DataAdapter is the firehose connection from the data store to the DataSet. Because there are different types of data stores, there are different types of DataAdapters. You need to choose the DataAdapter appropriate to the type of data store to which you are connecting. The DataAdapter then populates the DataSet with the data that is taken from the one of the data stores.

Interestingly, when populating a DataSet, you are not required to do so from just one particular data store. You can populate the DataSet from multiple tables within the same database or even from completely unrelated data stores. In the example shown in the diagram above (Figure 18-1), the DataSet is populated from an Access table using the OleDbDataAdapter and a SQL database using a SqlDataAdapter.

In the next step, the DataSet serializes its data into XML. It then can send the data to any type of presentation client, such as a Windows Form, a Web Form, or any other client application. All these clients use XML in the same manner, so the XML from the DataSet doesn't have to be modified to work with a particular client.

After the client is done with the data and wants to persist the changed data back into the data store, this XML data is sent back into a DataSet. From the DataSet, new DataAdapters are created to populate the associated data stores with the changed data.

The DataSet

Probably the most revolutionary thing about ADO.NET is the DataSet. You can think of the DataSet as the container for data. It is composed of a collection of table objects, with columns, rows, and relations all in place. This is a dramatic change from ADO, where data could be represented as a single table, whose rows you could iterate through one at a time. In fact, the change from ADO to ADO.NET is so dramatic that it is almost impossible to compare the two.

The DataSet is a miniature database in its own right. A DataSet is completely unaware of where the data that it holds came from (remember, it got there from the DataAdapter). The

DataSet is a disconnected collection of data. A user can work with it on the server or on the client before it is populated back to the data store. That is one of the new and revolutionary powers of the DataSet. You can have a collection of data sit in a client-side application where the client can manipulate the data for hours on end without once connecting to the data source. After the client is done with the data that it is using, it can then populate the data source with the changes that were made client-side. Figure 18-2 shows the structure of the DataSet.

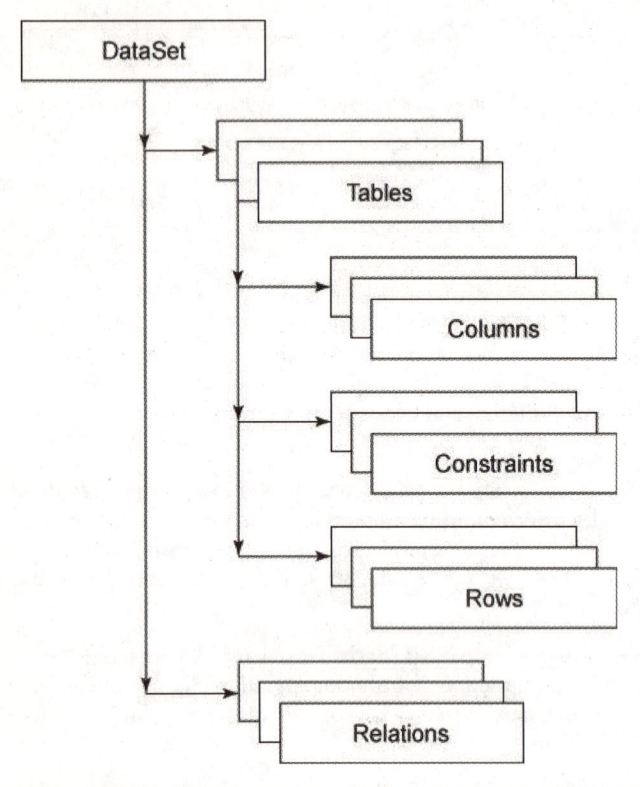

Figure 18-2: The DataSet is made up of tables, columns, constraints, rows, and relations.

DataSet

The DataSet, which is an in-memory cache of data retrieved from a database, is made up of DataTables, DataColumns, DataRows, DataConstraints, and DataRelations. The DataSet object sits at the root of the DataSet and handles all the serialization and deserialization of XML that goes to and from this data container. After it is serialized, this data and any associated schemas can be easily transported across HTTP to consuming clients.

DataTable

The DataTable is a central object within the DataSet. Each DataSet can contain one or more DataTable objects. You create DataTable objects with a DataAdapter, each representing a logical table of data. The DataTable is made up of a Columns collection along with a Constraints collection. These two items define the DataTable schema.

DataColumn

The DataColumn object is part of the DataTable and specifies the column names and data types that make up the DataTable. The DataColumn, along with the DataConstraint, is used as a building block for creating the schema of the DataTable. For each DataColumn, there can be an associated DataType, which enables you to specify the data type required for that column. For example, you can specifically state that the column can only contain integers, strings, or decimals. Much of the functionality that you can assign to the DataColumn is similar to that of SQL Server. You can state whether the column allows null values, if it is unique, and even if it is an auto-incrementing column.

DataConstraint

The DataConstraint enables developers to specify constraints to be enforced on particular DataColumns within the DataTable. A constraint on a piece of data ensures that a specified action will occur if a related field or column changes.

DataRow

The DataRow and DataColumn are the main components of a DataTable. A DataTable can be made up of zero or more DataRows. These DataRows are the pieces that make up the data contained within the DataTable. You have a lot of power in dealing with DataRows, such as the ability to add, edit, and delete rows that are contained within the DataTable.

DataRelation

The DataRelation object exists directly off of the root DataSet object. It's used to relate two or more DataTables to each other through the DataColumn objects. For instance, a DataSet can contain two DataTables, one for Customers and another for Orders. The DataRelation object is the piece that relates the customers with the orders that they've made.

The Typed DataSet

As powerful as the DataSet is, it still has some limitations. The DataSet is created at runtime. It accesses particular pieces of data by making certain assumptions. Take a look at how you would normally access a specific field in a DataSet that is *not* strongly typed (Listing 18-1).

Listing 18-1: Accessing a field in a DataSet

VB

```
ds.Tables("Customers").Rows(0).Columns("CompanyName") = "XYZ Company"
```

C#

```
ds.Tables["Customers"].Rows[0].Columns["CompanyName"] = "XYZ Company";
```

The preceding code looks at the Customers table, the first row (remember, everything is zero-based now) in the column CompanyName and assigns the value of XYZ Company to the field. This is pretty simple and straightforward, but it is based upon assumptions and is generated at runtime. The "Customers" and "CompanyName" words are string literals in this line of code. If they are spelled wrong or if these items aren't in the table, an error will occur at runtime.

Listing 18-2 shows you how to assign the same value to the same field but using a typed DataSet.

Listing 18-2: Accessing a field in a typed DataSet

VB

```
ds.Customers(0).CompanyName = "XYZ Company"
```

C#

```
ds.Customers[0].CompanyName = "XYZ Company";
```

Now the table name and the field to be accessed are not treated as string literals, but instead are encased in an XML Schema and a class that is generated from the DataSet class. When you create a typed DataSet, you are creating a class that implements the tables and fields based upon the schema used to generate the class. Basically, the schema is coded into the class.

As you compare the two examples, you see that a typed DataSet is easier to read and understand. It is less error-prone, and errors are realized at compile time as opposed to runtime.

In the end, typed DataSets are optional and you are free to use either style as your code.

The DataAdapter

The DataAdapter is responsible for the communications between the DataSet and the data stores. There are different DataAdapters at your disposal; your choice depends on the type of data store that you are interacting with. Currently, there are DataAdapters for connecting to SQL, Ole DB, and ODBC. It is best to use the SQL DataAdapter when working with SQL Server because this DataAdapter uses native SQL drivers and, therefore, performs better than the Ole DB DataAdapter. You can use the Ole DB DataAdapter when working with Microsoft Access or an Oracle database.

The DataAdapter connects to the data source as well as supplies all the commands for updating, inserting, and deleting records from the data store. You can also connect the operations of the DataAdapter to any stored procedures that you have.

Finally, the DataAdapter also handles mapping the column names in the data store to the column names that are in the DataSet. This means you don't have to mirror the names from the data store in your DataSet. If you have column names that are not very friendly to the general public in your data store, you can have your DataSet substitute different column names in your code. These become the column headers in any displayed data. By using the DataAdapter, you can then map these DataSet columns to the appropriate columns from the data store.

The following diagram (Figure 18-3) shows you the structure of the DataAdapter.

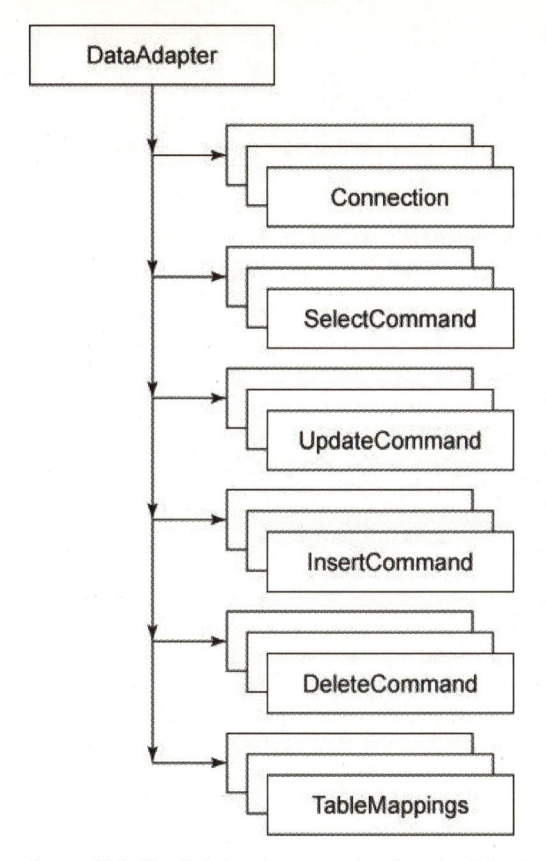

```
                    DataAdapter
                         |
                         +----> Connection
                         |
                         +----> SelectCommand
                         |
                         +----> UpdateCommand
                         |
                         +----> InsertCommand
                         |
                         +----> DeleteCommand
                         |
                         +----> TableMappings
```

Figure 18-3: The DataAdapter moves data from the data store to the DataSet and back.

The DataAdapter was built for speed. Its main job is to funnel data from the data store straight to the DataSet or to takes changes from the DataSet and apply these changes to the data store. Therefore, it does not keep an in-memory copy of the data. It is only the transport mechanism.

Common ADO.NET Tasks

There are around 3,400 classes in the .NET Framework, and several of these classes deal with data access. The two namespaces most frequently used are the `System.Data.SQLClient` and the `System.Data.OleDb` namespaces.

If you are going to use any of the classes that are contained within any of these namespaces, you must import these namespaces into your classes. For instance, if you are going to populate a DataSet from both SQL Server and from an Access table, you want to import the following into your file:

VB

```
Imports System.Data
Imports System.Data.SqlClient
Imports System.Data.OleDb
```

C#

```
using System.Data;
using System.Data.SqlClient;
using System.Data.OleDb;
```

The following section takes a look at some of the steps in the process of exposing data from specific data stores. In Chapter 19, you will build XML Web Services that will expose this data.

> **TIP:** Be forewarned that most of the tasks shown in the following examples can be done in a couple of ways within .NET if you are using Visual Studio .NET to build your applications. One way is by coding the tasks yourself. The other option is to use the wizards that are provided with Visual Studio .NET to take care of the coding tasks for you. Some examples of these wizards are shown in the next chapter.

Connecting to a data source

Connecting to a data source is probably the most common task in working with data. This example and the ones that follow assume that you have a SQL Server database. In order to connect to your SQL Server database, you use the `SQLConnection` class. This is shown in Listing 18-3.

Listing 18-3: Connecting to a SQL Database

VB

```
Dim conn as SqlConnection
conn = New
    SqlConnection("Server=localhost;uid=sa;pwd=;database=Northwind")

conn.Open()
```

C#

```
SqlConnection conn;
conn = new
    SqlConnection("Server=localhost;uid=sa;pwd=;database=Northwind");

conn.Open();
```

To make this connection work, be sure that the proper namespaces are imported before you start working with any of the classes that work with SQL. The first step in creating a connection is to create an instance of the `SqlConnection` class and assign it to `conn`. This `SqlConnection` class is initialized after you pass in the connection string as a parameter to the class. In this case, you are connecting to the Northwind database that resides on your local machine using the system administrator's login credentials.

Whenever you are done with your connection to the data source, be sure that you close the connection by using `conn.Close()`. .NET will not implicitly release the connections for you when they fall out of scope.

Reading data

After the connection to the data source is open and ready to use, you probably want to read the data from the data source. If you do not want to manipulate the data, but simply want to read it or transfer it from one spot to another, you should use the `DataReader` class.

In the following example (Listing 18-4), you use the `GetData()` function to provide a list of company names from the SQL Northwind database.

Listing 18-4: Reading the data from a SQL data base using the DataReader class

VB

```
Public Function GetData() As String
    Dim conn As SqlConnection
    Dim cmd As SqlCommand
    Dim cmdString As String = "Select CompanyName from Customers"
    conn = New _
        SqlConnection("Server=localhost;uid=sa;pwd=;database=Northwind")
    cmd = New SqlCommand(cmdString, conn)
    conn.Open()

    Dim myReader As SqlDataReader
    Dim returnData As String
    myReader = cmd.ExecuteReader(CommandBehavior.CloseConnection)

    While myReader.Read()
        returnData += myReader("CompanyName") & "<br>"
    End While

    conn.Close()
    Return returnData
End Function
```

C#

```
public string GetData()
{
    SqlConnection conn;
    SqlCommand cmd;
    string cmdString = "Select CompanyName from Customers";
    conn = new
        SqlConnection("Server=localhost;uid=sa;pwd=;database=Northwind");
    cmd = new SqlCommand(cmdString, conn);
```

```
    conn.Open();

    SqlDataReader myReader;
    string returnData = "";

    myReader = cmd.ExecuteReader(CommandBehavior.CloseConnection);

    while (myReader.Read())
        {
                returnData += myReader["CompanyName"] + "<br>";
        }

    conn.Close();
    return returnData;
}
```

In this example, you create an instance of both the `SqlConnection` and the `SqlCommand` classes. Then before you open the connection, you simply pass the `SqlCommand` class a SQL command selecting specific data from the Northwind database. After your connection is opened (based upon the commands passed in), you create a `DataReader`. To read the data out of the database, you need to iterate through the data using the `DataReader` by using the `while myReader.Read()` command. After this is done and the string is built, the connection is closed and the string is returned from the function.

Inserting data

When working with data, you often need to insert the data into the data source. This data may have been passed to you by the end user through the XML Web Service, or it may be data that you generated within the logic of your class. Listing 18-5 shows you how to do this.

Listing 18-5: Inserting data into SQL Server

VB

```
Public Sub InsertData()
    Dim conn As SqlConnection
    Dim cmd As SqlCommand
    Dim cmdString As String = "Insert Customers (CustomerID,
        CompanyName, ContactName) Values ('BILLE', 'XYZ Company', 'Bill
        Evjen')"
    conn = New
        SqlConnection("Server=localhost;uid=sa;pwd=;database=Northwind")
    cmd = New SqlCommand(cmdString, conn)
    conn.Open()

    cmd.ExecuteNonQuery()
    conn.Close()
End Sub
```

Chapter 18: Working with ADO.NET

C#

```csharp
public void InsertData()
{
    SqlConnection conn;
    SqlCommand cmd;
    string cmdString = "Insert Customers (CustomerID, CompanyName,
        ContactName) Values ('BILLE', 'XYZ Company', 'Bill Evjen')";
    conn = new
        SqlConnection("Server=localhost;uid=sa;pwd=;database=Northwind");
    cmd = new SqlCommand(cmdString, conn);
    conn.Open();

    cmd.ExecuteNonQuery();
    conn.Close();
}
```

Inserting data into SQL is pretty straightforward and simple. Using the SQL command string, you can insert specific values for specific columns. The actual insertion is initiated using the `cmd.ExecuteNonQuery()` command. This command is used to execute a command on the data when you don't need to get anything in return.

Updating data

In addition to inserting new records into a database, you frequently update existing rows of data in a table. Imagine a table where you can update multiple records at once. In the example in Listing 18-6, you want to update an employee table by putting a particular value in the `emp_bonus` column if the employee has been at the company for five years or longer.

Listing 18-6: Updating data in SQL Server

VB

```vb
Public Function UpdateEmployeeBonus() As Integer
    Dim conn As SqlConnection
    Dim cmd As SqlCommand
    Dim RecordsAffected as Integer
    Dim cmdString As String = "UPDATE Employees SET emp_bonus=1000 WHERE
        yrs_duty>=5"
    conn = New
        SqlConnection("Server=localhost;uid=sa;pwd=;database=Northwind")
    cmd = New SqlCommand(cmdString, conn)
    conn.Open()

    RecordsAffected = cmd.ExecuteNonQuery()
    conn.Close()

    Return RecordsAffected
End Function
```

C#

```csharp
public int UpdateEmployeeBonus()
{
    SqlConnection conn;
    SqlCommand cmd;
    int RecordsAffected;
    string cmdString = "UPDATE Employees SET emp_bonus=1000 WHERE
        yrs_duty>=5";
    conn = new
        SqlConnection("Server=localhost;uid=sa;pwd=;database=Northwind");
    cmd = new SqlCommand(cmdString, conn);
    conn.Open();

    RecordsAffected = cmd.ExecuteNonQuery();
    conn.Close();

    return RecordsAffected;
}
```

This update function changes the value of the `emp_bonus` field to `1000` if the employee has been with the company for more than five years. This is done with the SQL command string. The great thing about these update capabilities is that you can capture the number of records that were updated by assigning the `ExecuteNonQuery()` command to the `RecordsAffected` variable, which is then returned by the function.

Deleting data

Along with reading, inserting, and updating data, you sometimes need to delete data from the data source. Deleting data is a simple process of using the SQL command string to your advantage and using the `ExecuteNonQuery` command as you did in the update example. See Listing 18-7 for an illustration of this.

Listing 18-7: Deleting data from SQL Server

VB

```vb
Public Function DeleteEmployee() As Integer
    Dim conn As SqlConnection
    Dim cmd As SqlCommand
    Dim RecordsAffected as Integer
    Dim cmdString As String = "DELETE Employees WHERE LastName='Evjen'"
    conn = New
        SqlConnection("Server=localhost;uid=sa;pwd=;database=Northwind")
    cmd = New SqlCommand(cmdString, conn)
    conn.Open()

    RecordsAffected = cmd.ExecuteNonQuery()
    conn.Close()
```

```
        Return RecordsAffected
End Function
```

C#

```csharp
public int DeleteEmployee()
{
    SqlConnection conn;
    SqlCommand cmd;
    int RecordsAffected;
    string cmdString = "DELETE Employees WHERE LastName='Evjen'";
    conn = new
        SqlConnection("Server=localhost;uid=sa;pwd=;database=Northwind");
    cmd = new SqlCommand(cmdString, conn);
    conn.Open();

    RecordsAffected = cmd.ExecuteNonQuery();
    conn.Close();

    return RecordsAffected;
}
```

Just as you did for the update function, you can assign the `ExecuteNonQuery()` command to an integer variable and return the number of records deleted.

Populating a DataSet

As you learned in the early part of this chapter, a DataSet is an important part of ADO.NET and is basically an in-memory view of the data that is disconnected. Creating a DataSet that can be sent to the client is an easy process. When the DataSet is created, one or more DataTables are created along with it. Listing 18-8 shows you how to create a DataSet with a single DataTable.

Listing 18-8: Creating and filling a DataSet from SQL Server

VB

```vb
Public Function GetDataSet() As DataSet
    Dim conn As SqlConnection
    Dim myDataAdapter As SqlDataAdapter
    Dim myDataSet As DataSet
    Dim cmdString As String = "Select * from Customers"
    conn = New
        SqlConnection("Server=localhost;uid=sa;pwd=;database=Northwind")
    myDataAdapter = New SqlDataAdapter(cmdString, conn)

    myDataSet = New DataSet()
    myDataAdapter.Fill(myDataSet, "Companies")

    Return myDataSet
End Function
```

C#

```
public DataSet GetDataSet()
{
    SqlConnection conn;
    SqlDataAdapter myDataAdapter;
    DataSet myDataSet;
    string cmdString = "Select * from Customers";
    conn = new
        SqlConnection("Server=localhost;uid=sa;pwd=;database=Northwind");
    myDataAdapter = new SqlDataAdapter(cmdString, conn);

    myDataSet = new DataSet();
    myDataAdapter.Fill(myDataSet, "Companies");

    return myDataSet;
}
```

You can see in the preceding code that this operation is different from previous examples. No `SqlCommand` object is created and used. Also, no connection is opened to the data source anywhere in the code. Instead of seeing a `conn.Open()` in the code, a `SqlDataAdapter` is created, and this object takes care of opening and closing the connection to the SQL Server for you.

After the `SqlDataAdapter` is created, it uses the connection and command strings to connect to the SQL database and carry out the command. Then the `SqlDataAdapter` fills a DataSet.

```
myDataAdapter.Fill(myDataSet, "Companies");
```

This `SqlDataAdapter` fills the `myDataSet` DataSet and, more specifically, fills a new table, `Companies`, with the results from the command string.

Summary

This chapter described the main pieces of ADO.NET to give you an idea of some of the basic methods for moving and manipulating data with this new data-access technology. ADO.NET is truly revolutionary. If you understand only a single piece of ADO.NET and what it offers you as a developer, I advise you to focus on and completely understand the DataSet. The DataSet is the key to this new technology, and it will most likely herald a new wave of functionality for applications yet to be created.

This chapter took a look at some of the basics of ADO.NET and provided overviews of the DataSet and the DataAdapter. Later in the chapter, you were exposed to some of the common tasks that you can perform using this new technology.

In the next chapter, you learn how to integrate ADO.NET with your XML Web Services, as well as how to use some of the new wizards and tools that Visual Studio .NET provides to quickly build your .NET applications.

Chapter 19

XML Web Services and ADO.NET

>To write it, it took three months;
>to conceive it three minutes;
>to collect the data in it — all my life.
>F. Scott Fitzgerald (1896–1940), U.S. author.
>*A letter to the Booksellers' Convention*, April 1920.

In the last chapter, you learned some of the basics of working with ADO.NET. You were introduced to the DataSet and the DataAdapter, as well as to the basics of working with data in your .NET applications. In this chapter, you learn to go one step further and take advantage of the new tools that ADO.NET offers for use within your XML Web services.

The fact that ADO.NET is tightly intertwined with XML is of great benefit to you as you build your XML Web services, because these also depend on XML for applications and message transport.

This chapter covers the following topics:

- Using Visual Studio .NET's data wizards
- Passing complex types

Visual Studio .NET's Data Wizards

Chapter 18 covered how to construct a DataSet and to fill it with data using the DataAdapter. In the examples, you built the code yourself. Although you can always do this, you also have the option of building data access into your XML Web services using some of the wizards from Visual Studio .NET.

The following example, which is a lengthy one, shows you how to build an XML Web service that returns a DataSet that gets its data from two separate tables. Through this example, you will discover several different wizards in Visual Studio .NET that you can work with when using ADO.NET.

Visual Studio .NET's Component Designer

When you open up a new XML Web service application in Visual Studio .NET, the first page that is displayed is the `Service1.asmx.vb [Design]` or the `Service1.asmx.cs [Design]` page. This is shown in Figure 19-1.

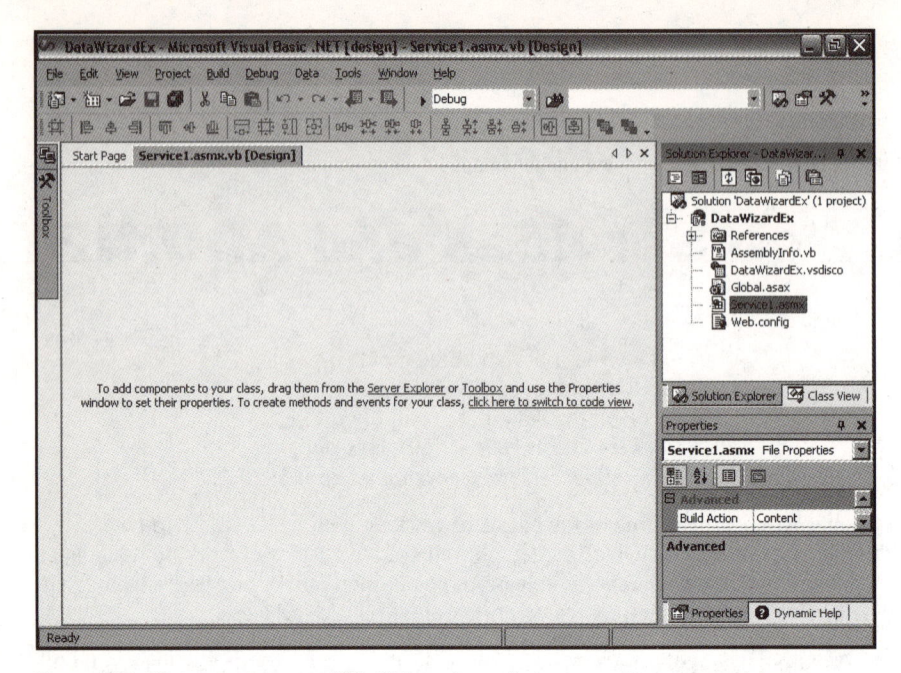

Figure 19-1: When you start a new XML Web service project, you see the component designer.

Just as Visual Basic developers, at one point, were given the tools that enabled them to perform Rapid Application Development (RAD development) on the presentation layer, Visual Studio .NET now brings RAD development to the middle tier. This is what you see on the first page of your XML Web service. You cannot type code directly onto this page.

This page is referred to as the *Component Designer*. This is the design surface for any non-visual components that you incorporate within your XML Web service. Just as you can drag and drop controls onto a design surface for any Windows Forms or Web Forms application, the Component Designer enables you to drag and drop components onto this surface.

A component doesn't appear visually in your applications, but there is a visual representation of the component that sits on the design surface. Highlighting the component allows you to modify its settings and properties in the Properties window.

What can you drag and drop onto this surface? In the following examples, you see how to work with `SqlConnection` and `SqlDataAdapter` objects on this design surface. If you open up the Toolbox window, and click the Data tab, you see a larger list of components that can be used on this design surface (Figure 19-2). From this Data section in the Toolbox window, you are able to work with the OleDbDataAdapter, SqlDataAdapter, DataSets, and DataViews among other objects.

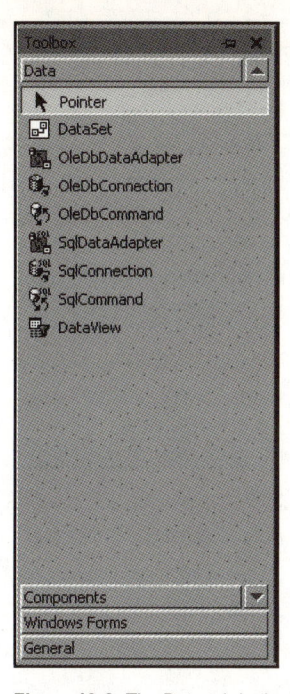

Figure 19-2: The Data tab in the Toolbox window.

Creating a connection to the data source

Just as in code, one of the first things you do when working with data is make a connection to the data source. Visual Studio .NET provides a visual way to make connections to your data stores. In this case, you make a connection to the Northwind database in SQL Server.

When you open the Server Explorer, you notice a section for data connections (Figure 19-3).

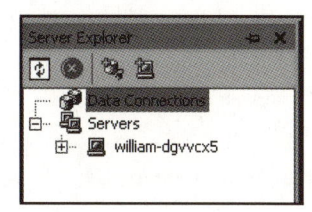

Figure 19-3: The Data Connections are displayed in the Server Explorer.

The steps to create a data connection to the Northwind database in SQL Server are pretty straightforward. Right-click on Data Connections and choose Add Connection. You are presented with the Data Link Properties dialog. This dialog, by default, asks for a connection to SQL Server. If you are going to connect to a different source, such as Microsoft Access, simply click on the Provider tab and change the provider.

> **NOTE:** If you are making a connection to Microsoft Access, you choose the Microsoft Jet 4.0 OLE DB Provider.

Figure 19-4 shows the Data Link Properties dialog and the settings that you need in order to connect to your local SQL Server.

If you are connecting to a SQL Server that resides on your `localhost`, you want to put a period (.) in the box that asks you to select or enter a server name. Put in your login credentials for SQL Server and then select the database that you wish to make the connection to by using the drop-down list.

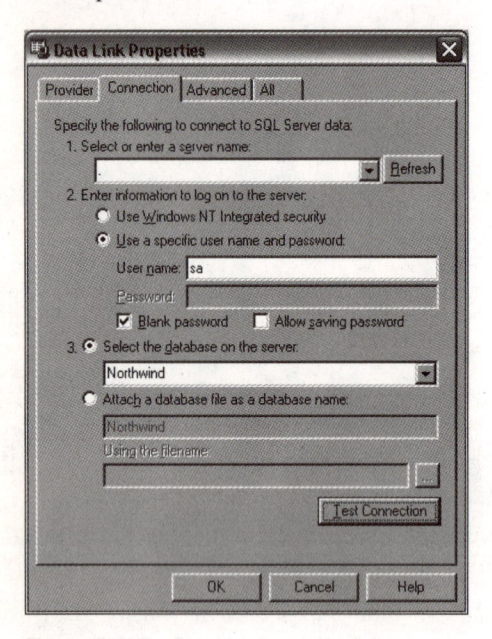

Figure 19-4: The Data Link Properties dialog.

From this dialog, you can also test the connection to make sure that everything works properly. If everything is in place, you get a confirmation. Clicking OK will cause a connection to appear in the Solution Explorer.

Expanding this connection, you find a way to access the data source just as you would by using the SQL Server Enterprise Manager (Figure 19-5).

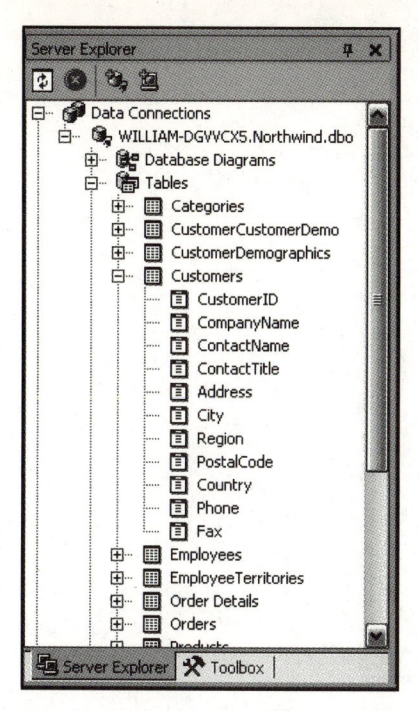

Figure 19-5: Viewing the Northwind database through the Server Explorer.

From here, you can work with the database and view information about all the tables and fields that are contained within the database. More specifically, you can view and work with Database Diagrams, Tables, Views, Stored Procedures, and Functions.

After you have run through this wizard, you have a connection to the Northwind database that can be used by any components that you place on the Component Designer.

The DataAdapter Wizard

The goal of this example is to return a DataSet to the end user through an XML Web service. To accomplish this, you have to incorporate a DataAdapter to extract the data from the data source and to populate the DataSet before passing it on.

Because this example uses the Northwind database, you need to drag and drop a SqlDataAdapter onto the XML Web service's design surface. Dragging and dropping a SqlDataAdapter onto your design surface causes a wizard to appear, as shown in Figure 19-6.

Because you want this XML Web service to return to the consumer a DataSet that contains two DataTables — one for the `Customers` table and another for the `Orders` table — you have to go through this process twice.

Figure 19-6: The Data Adapter Configuration Wizard.

Remember that the job of the SqlDataAdapter object is to make the connection to the specified table as well as to perform all the select, update, insert, and delete commands that are required. For this example, you simply want the SqlDataAdapter to make the select call and then later to update any changes that are made back to the SQL Server.

As you work through the wizard, you come to a screen that asks how you want to query the database (Figure 19-7). You have three options: using SQL statements, using stored procedures that have already been created, or building brand-new stored procedures directly from this wizard.

For this example, choose Use SQL statements. Selecting this option brings you to a text box where you can write your own SQL statement if you wish.

Chapter 19: XML Web Services and ADO.NET 439

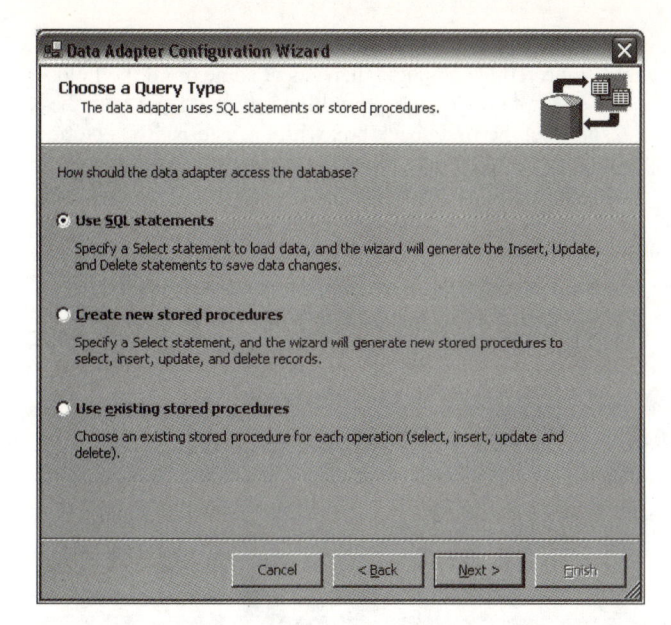

Figure 19-7: Choosing a type of query that you want to perform against the Northwind database.

The great thing about this process is that, after you create a SQL select command, the DataAdapter wizard also creates the associated insert, update, and delete commands for you. You also have the option of building your queries using the Query Builder. This enables you to graphically design the query yourself. If this option is selected, you can choose from a list of tables in the Northwind database. For the first SqlDataAdapter, choose `Customers`. For the second SqlDataAdapter choose `Orders`. You make your selection by clicking the Add button and then closing the dialog window (see Figure 19-8).

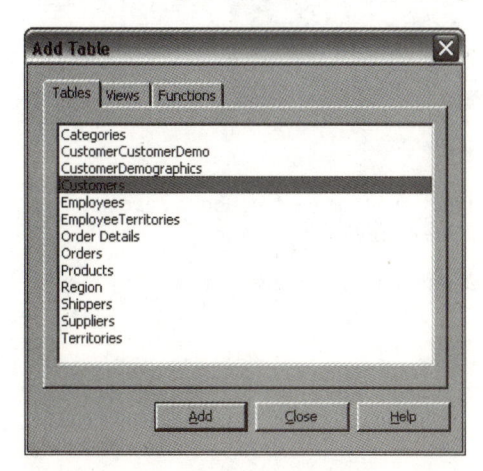

Figure 19-8: Selecting the tables to be part of your query.

After you close the Add Table dialog, you see a visual representation of the table that you selected in the Query Builder dialog (Figure 19-9). You can then select some or all the fields to be returned from the query. For this example, you want everything returned from both the `Customers` and the `Orders` table, so select the first check box with the asterisk (*). Notice that the query listed in this dialog now says `SELECT * FROM Customers`. After the word *Customers*, add text to the query so that it looks like the following:

```
SELECT Customers.* FROM Customers WHERE (CustomerID LIKE @Customer)
```

With this query, you specify that you want to return the customer information when the `CustomerID` fits the parameter that you pass into the query from your code (using `@Customer`).

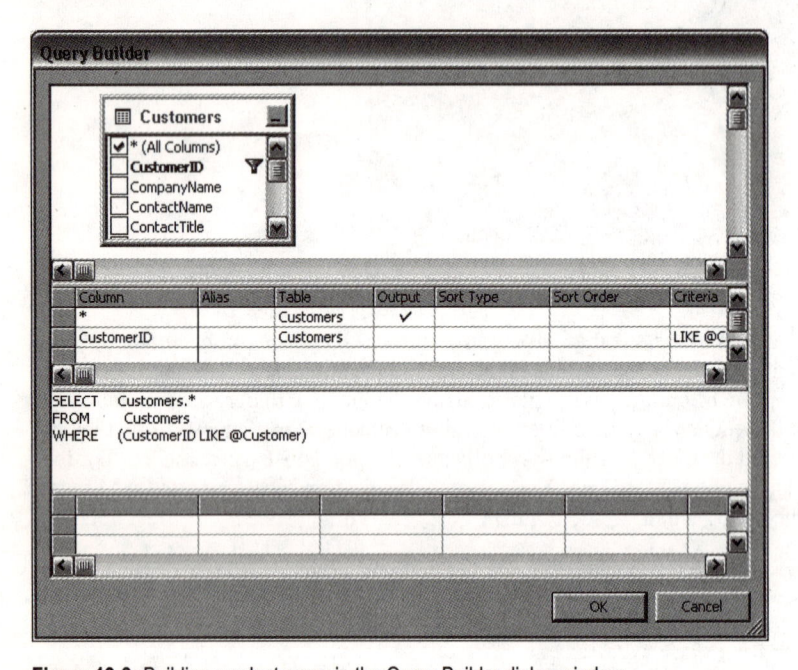

Figure 19-9: Building a select query in the Query Builder dialog window.

After your query is in place, simply click OK and then click the Next button to have not only the select query, but also the insert, update, and delete queries generated for you.

Figure 19-10 shows you the final page after all the queries have been generated.

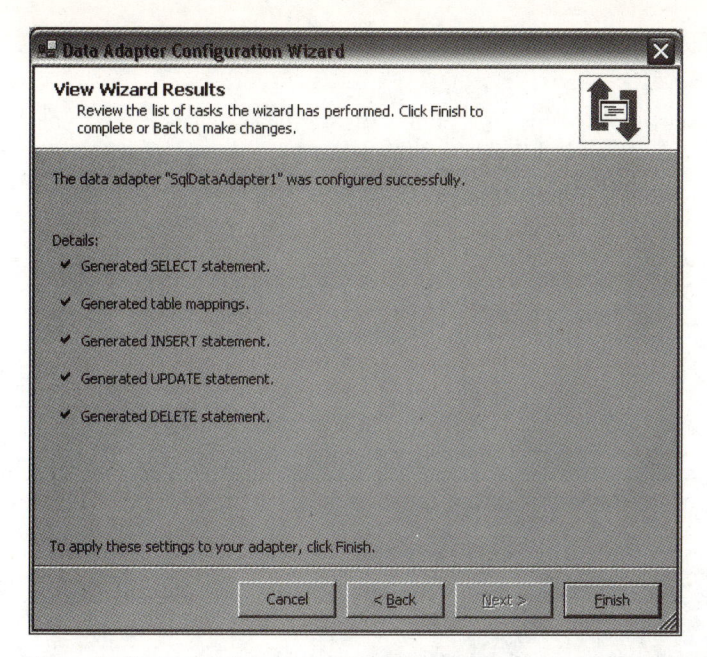

Figure 19-10: The DataAdapter wizard completes the process and builds all the required statements.

After you reach this point, you can either click the Back button to return to one of the prior steps in order to change a setting or the query itself, or you can click the Finish button to apply everything to your DataAdapter. After you are finished using the wizard, notice there is a visual representation of the SqlDataAdapter that you just created (see Figure 19-11). Along with that is a SqlConnection object. The DataAdapter and the Connection objects that are shown on the design surface are also labeled with their IDs. Therefore, in your code, you can address this SqlDataAdapter that you just built by referring to it as `SqlDataAdapter1`. The second DataAdapter that queries the Orders table is then shown and referred to as `SqlDataAdapter2`.

Figure 19-11: The visual representation of the created objects on the Component Designer.

After you have the two DataAdapters in place, the next step is to highlight each DataAdapter and change the way the fields are mapped from the SQL Server Northwind database to the DataSet that is going to be sent to the client, who will consume this DataSet as an XML Web service. To do this, highlight the DataAdapter, as shown in Figure 19-11. You will find a setting named Table Mappings in the Properties window of Visual Studio .NET. Click the button that is within the Table Mapping's field and you are presented with the Table Mappings dialog (Figure 19-12).

The Table Mappings dialog shows you many items of the DataSet you can change. First, you can change the name of the DataSet table, the table that the SQL table will map to. In this case, you want it to be the `Customers` table.

In the main window of the Table Mappings dialog, you see a list of columns from the table in SQL Server and how they map over to the columns in the DataSet. They will appear in the very same form when this dialog is initialized. Because consumers of this DataSet can use the column names in their pages and within their code, you might want to think about changing the visual presentation of the names within the DataSet. Changing them to something that is a little more presentable to the general public is usually a good idea.

The example in Figure 19-12 shows how some of the column names represented in the DataSet have been changed. After everything is the way you want it, click OK.

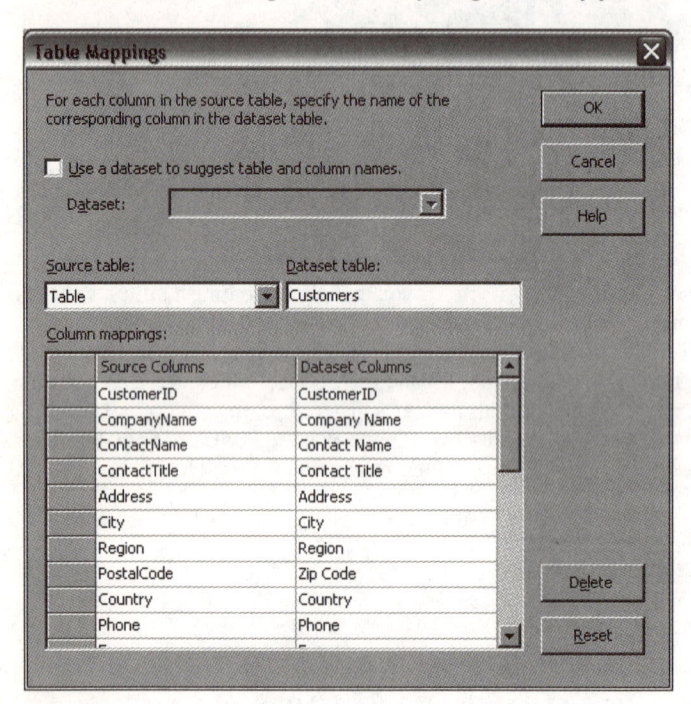

Figure 19-12: Mapping the fields from the database to the DataSet.

In the end, Visual Studio .NET has taken care of a lot of the coding for you. You can see the results of this by switching to the code-behind view for your XML Web service and expanding the `Web Services Designer Generated Code` section. Here you find the two created SqlDataAdapters as well as a connection object and all the queries to the data from the Customers and Orders tables of the Northwind database. Also in place is a generic DataSet.

You'll see in a minute how this DataSet outputs its two tables of data from queries based on a CustomerID.

Again, this isn't the only way to complete all these tasks. It is possible to code all this functionality yourself, but Visual Studio .NET does a good job of producing the code without disturbing any existing code. It does this by changing only the code in this one section of the document, the Web Services Designer-Generated Code section.

Creating a typed DataSet

This example would work fine just as it is, but (as you learned in the last chapter) ADO.NET also enables you to work with a typed DataSet. With ADO.NET, the DataSet is constructed to be a generic DataSet that is defined at runtime. A typed DataSet is based upon a class that contains definitions of all the tables, fields, and relations within the DataSet. This allows you to take advantage of a richer programming model.

Creating a DataSet from the DataAdapters that are on the design surface is simple when using Visual Studio .NET. Simply right-click on the design surface and select Generate DataSet. You are given the Generate Dataset dialog (Figure 19-13). From this dialog, you can create your typed DataSet.

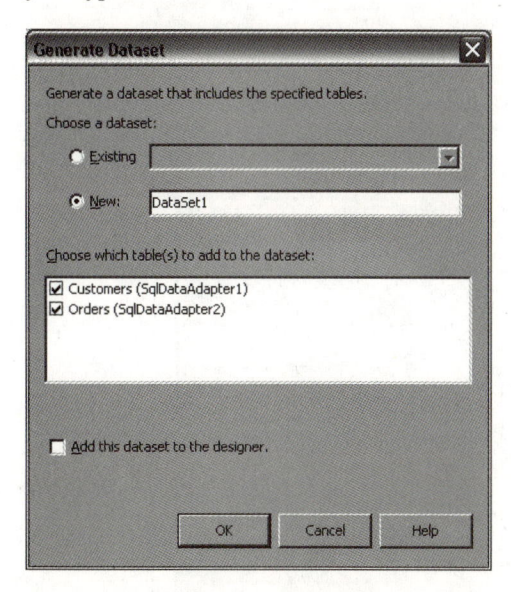

Figure 19-13: Creating a typed DataSet that contains two DataTables.

Within this dialog, you see the two SqlDataAdapters that were created earlier. By default, you select both to be included in the typed DataSet. Your other task is to specify the name of the DataSet. The name that you choose for the DataSet is also the name of the class that is created.

After you click OK, you will notice that Visual Studio .NET has created an XSD file within the Solution Explorer that has the same name as your DataSet (Figure 19-14).

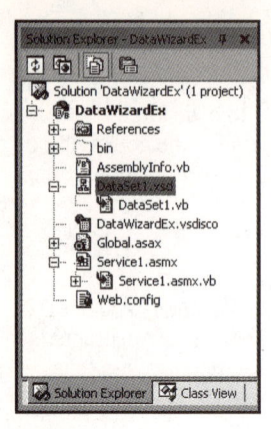

Figure 19-14: An XSD file and a class file that represents the typed DataSet.

If you click the Show All Files button in the Solution Explorer and open the typed DataSet's class file, you see that this class inherits from the DataSet. The file is actually quite large and would take a lot of effort to create on your own.

If you open the `DataSet1.xsd` file, you find yourself in one of the XML designers provided by Visual Studio .NET. This yellow design surface is the *Schema Designer* (Figure 19-15). The Schema Designer enables you to construct XSD documents visually by dragging and dropping items onto the design surface.

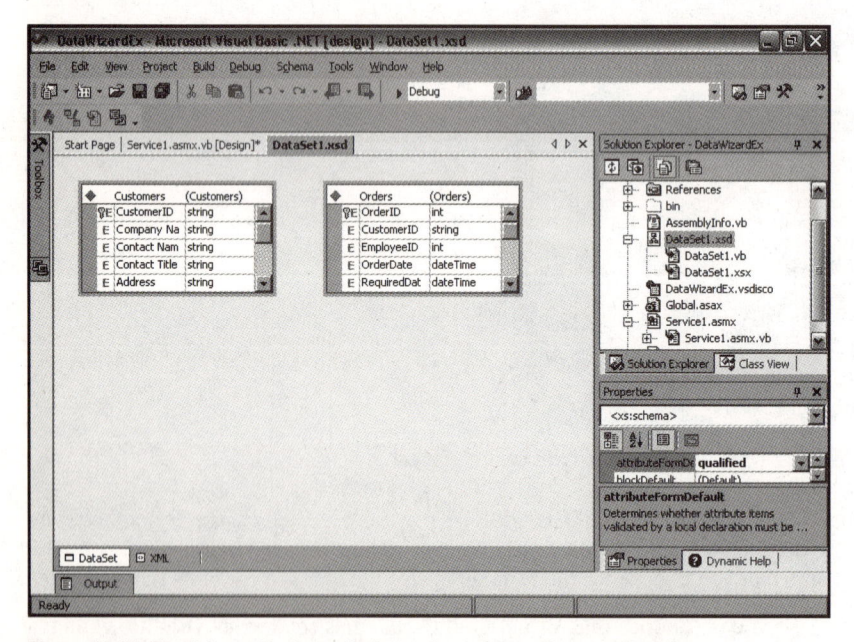

Figure 19-15: The Schema Designer displaying the contents of a typed DataSet.

Chapter 19: XML Web Services and ADO.NET   445

Included on the XSD design surface are the elements from the typed DataSet, the Customers element and the Orders element. Included in the element definitions are a number of subelement definitions. You also find any attribute definitions here.

You have not yet established a relationship between the Customers and the Orders tables. You need this relationship in place if you want to pass in a CustomerID and return all the customer information along with that customer's order history. As easy as it is to create the typed DataSet, it is that easy to create relationships in your typed DataSet.

To create the relationship between these two tables, right-click the Customers element and select Add ⇨ New Relation. This will give you the Edit Relation dialog (Figure 19-16).

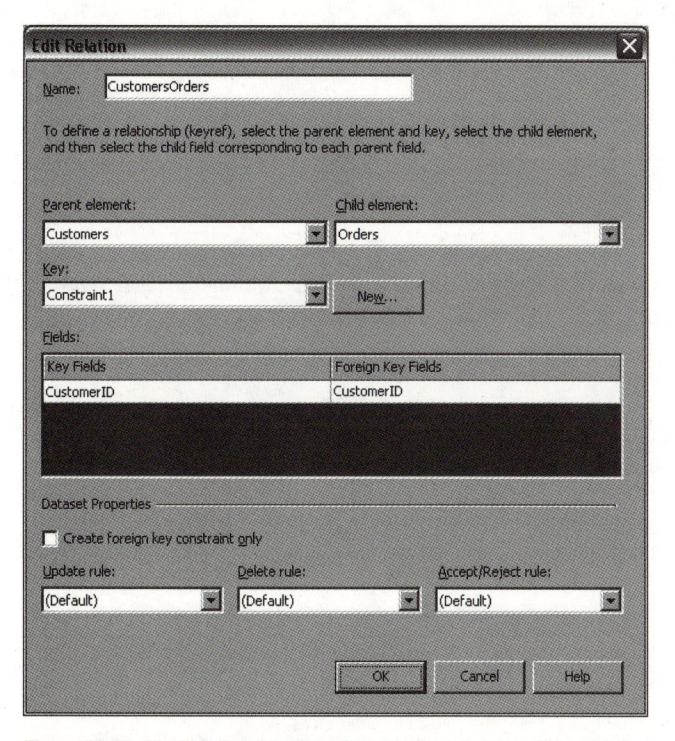

Figure 19-16: The Edit Relation dialog being used to build a relationship between the Customers table and the Orders table.

The Edit Relation dialog enables you to name the relationship. In this case, it is renamed `CustomersOrders` because there is going to be a relationship between these two tables. It is important to establish the relationship between the two tables by choosing one of the tables to be the parent element and the other to be the child element. Because you want to choose a single customer and all his related orders, you force the `Customers` table to be the parent element and the `Orders` table to be the child element. Within the Fields text box, notice that the two tables are tied together by the `CustomerID` field. This means that both of these tables will contain this field, and the data in each of these tables can be associated by this ID.

Clicking OK takes you back to the Schema Designer. On the Schema Designer, you now see the relationship visually represented (Figure 19-17).

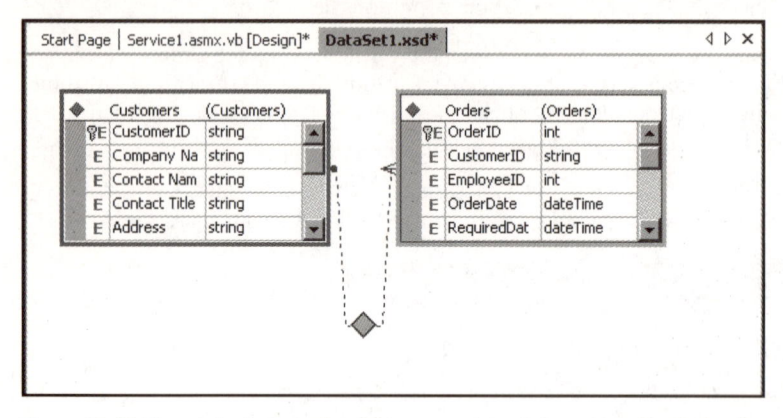

Figure 19-17: The relation between the Customers and the Orders tables visually represented in the Schema Designer.

After you have saved everything, you are ready to start coding and building the XML Web service that will use the two SqlDataAdapters, SqlConnection object, and the typed DataSet that you have just created.

Building the XML Web Service

Now comes the fun part, building the XML Web service that will use all the items that were just created! The goal is to allow the end user to send in a SOAP request that contains just the CustomerID. In return he gets back a complete DataSet containing not only the customer information and all the relevant order information, but an XSD definition of the XML data that is being sent. Listing 19-1 shows you the code to build all this functionality. You need only a single WebMethod, the `GetCustomerOrders()` method.

Listing 19-1: The GetCustomerOrders() WebMethod

VB

```
<WebMethod()> Public Function GetCustomerOrders(ByVal Custid As String) _
        As DataSet
  Dim myDataSet As New DataSet1()

  SqlDataAdapter1.SelectCommand.Parameters("@Customer").Value = custid
  SqlDataAdapter2.SelectCommand.Parameters("@Customer").Value = custid

  SqlDataAdapter1.Fill(myDataSet)
  SqlDataAdapter2.Fill(myDataSet)

  myDataSet.Customers(0).Phone = "NOT AVAILABLE"
  myDataSet.Customers(0).Fax = "NOT AVAILABLE"
```

```
    myDataSet.AcceptChanges()

    Return myDataSet
End Function
```

C#

```csharp
[WebMethod]
public DataSet GetCustomerOrders(string custid)
{
  DataSet1 myDataSet = new DataSet1();

  sqlDataAdapter1.SelectCommand.Parameters["@Customer"].Value = custid;
  sqlDataAdapter2.SelectCommand.Parameters["@Customer"].Value = custid;

  sqlDataAdapter1.Fill(myDataSet);
  sqlDataAdapter2.Fill(myDataSet);

  myDataSet.Customers[0].Phone = "NOT AVAILABLE";
  myDataSet.Customers[0].Fax = "NOT AVAILABLE";

  return myDataSet;
}
```

Now there isn't much code here, and all the data code that is contained within the hidden portion of the file is not being shown. This is the code that you generate to interact with the data code that has been generated for you by Visual Studio .NET.

Notice that the return type is a DataSet. This is a complex type. One of the first things done in the method is to create an instance of the typed DataSet. In the next two lines of code, the `SqlDataAdapter1` and the `SqlDataAdapter2` objects are used. In this case, the only accepted parameter, `Customer`, is being set for both the DataAdapters. After this parameter is passed to the SqlDataAdapter, this DataAdapter queries the database based upon the select query that you programmed into it earlier using the DataAdapter wizard.

After the query, the DataAdapter is instructed to fill the instance of the DataSet. Before the DataSet is returned to the consumer of this XML Web service, you can change how the XML is output to the client. If you are passing customer information, you may want to exclude some of the information. Because the DataSet is a typed DataSet, you have programmatic access to the tables. In this example, the code specifies that in the DataSet, in the Customers table, in the first row (remember it is zero-based), make the value of the Phone and Fax fields equal to `NOT AVAILABLE`. Next, you force the DataSet to accept the changes that were made through the code by using the `AcceptChanges()` method.

By compiling and running the XML Web service, you are able to test it from the test page using the CustomerID of ALFKI (the first record of the Customers table in the Northwind database). The results are returned to you in the browser (Figure 19-18).

[Figure 19-18 screenshot of Internet Explorer displaying XML output of the GetCustomerOrders WebMethod for ALFKI]

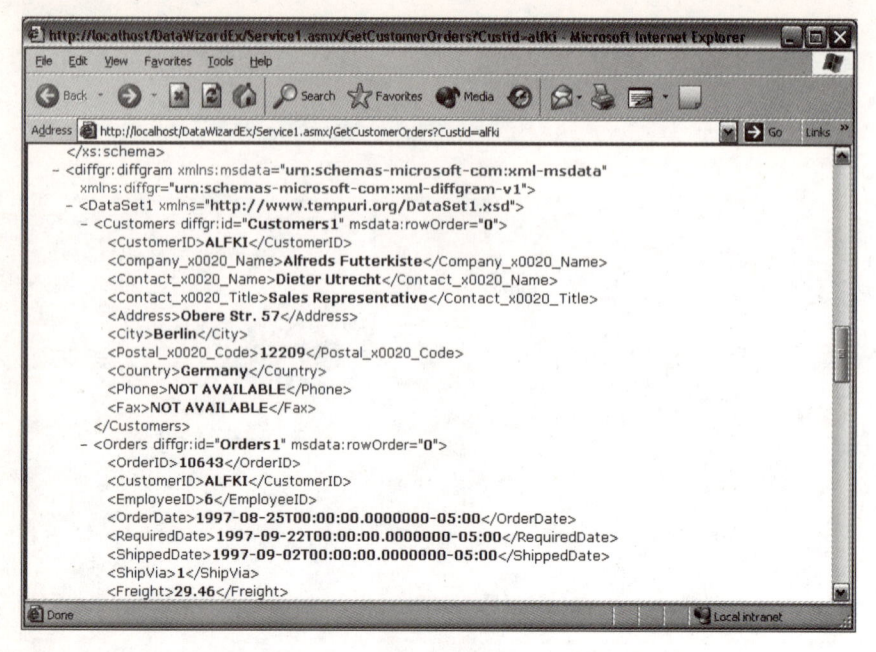

Figure 19-18: The ALFKI DataSet returned from the GetCustomerOrders WebMethod.

The returned DataSet contains a wealth of information, including

- An XSD definition of the XML that is contained in the DataSet
- The ALFKI customer information with the `<Phone>` and `<Fax>` elements not showing the phone numbers that are in the database, but instead showing NOT AVAILABLE.
- Six sets of order information directly related to the Alfreds Futterkiste company.

On the return side, consumers of this XML Web service can easily use the XSD definition and the XML that is contained within this DataSet in their own applications. If consumers are consuming this DataSet into .NET applications, they can easily bind this data to a DataGrid and use it in their applications with minimal lines of code.

Summary

In summary, ADO.NET is a powerful tool to incorporate within your XML Web services. ADO.NET, with its use of XML as data representation, has a number of new technologies that provide you with data solutions that you could only dream of in the past.

Visual Studio .NET also makes ADO.NET programming quick and easy when you use the wizards that are available. In this chapter, you got to see a number of the wizards that are there for your use. You don't have to use these wizards in order to work with ADO.NET. On the contrary, you can use some of the wizards and create the rest of the code yourself, or you can use none of the wizards. In any case, you have complete and full access to everything that ADO.NET provides.

The most important thing to take from this chapter is an understanding of the DataSet. The DataSet is the most revolutionary thing from ADO.NET, and one of the best solutions to many of the problems that limited applications in the past. The DataSet is a herald of brand new types of applications that will have increased functionality. It's a new world out there.

Part VIII

Advanced XML Web Services

Chapter 20: Error and Exception Handling

Chapter 21: Configuration and Optimization

Chapter 22: Advanced Issues in XML Web Services

Chapter 23: Screen Scraping

Chapter 20

Error and Exception Handling

*Intelligence is not to make no mistakes,
but quickly to see how to make them good.*
Bertolt Brecht, *The Measures Taken* (1930).

No matter how good the programmer, code is never built with the guarantee of being error free. Most programmers know this. If you don't, it is important to remember one point — *errors happen*! For this reason, it is best to approach programming with plans for the worst-case scenario. What is the worst-case scenario? Well, besides your server melting or detonating, you need to plan for connections not being made, values being null when they shouldn't be, and other upsetting occurrences. If you use error and exception handling properly, you can anticipate and trap these events and, thereby, prevent your XML Web services from coming to a screeching halt.

This chapter takes a look at some of the basics of error and exception handling and how you can use these handling techniques properly in order to produce better code and better applications.

More specifically, this chapter covers

- The types of errors that you might encounter
- Using `Try..Catch...Finally`
- Working with the `web.config` file for handling errors
- Using the `global.asax` file
- ASP.NET Tracing
- Utilizing SOAP extensions

Types of Errors

If errors happen, where and how should developers look for errors as they work through their applications? The first thing to understand about errors is that there are two kinds: development errors and runtime errors. Take a brief look at each of these types of errors.

Development errors

Development errors are the types of errors that a programmer can prevent. These errors include syntax and logic errors.

Syntax errors include misspelled words, misuse of keywords, misspelled variables, or improper use of a specific programming language. For instance, if you don't put the `End Select` at the end of a `Select` statement in Visual Basic .NET, this is a syntax error.

Visual Studio .NET is a great help in finding syntax errors and notifying you of these errors the moment that they occur. Development errors prevent the applications that you build in .NET from compiling correctly. In fact, you are notified about build errors in the compilation, and you are given the option of continuing the compilation or viewing a list of the compilation errors that occurred.

Figure 20-1 shows how Visual Studio .NET notifies you of syntactical errors as you are typing the code.

```
 1  Public Class WebForm1
 2      Inherits System.Web.UI.Page
 3      Protected WithEvents Image1 As System.Web.UI.WebControls.Image
 4      Protected WithEvents Label1 As System.Web.UI.WebControls.Label
 5
 6      Web Form Designer Generated Code
20
21      Private Sub Page_Load(ByVal sender As System.Object, ByVal e As Sys
22          Dim ws As New localhost.Service1()
23
24          Dim strLabelTxt As String
25          strLabelText = ws.Add(5, 5)
26      End Sub    Name 'strLabelText' is not declared.
27
28  End Class
29
```

Figure 20-1: Error notification is done as you type within Visual Studio .NET.

In this example, `strLabelText` was spelled incorrectly when it was initialized, and Visual Studio .NET is aware of the conflict because it cannot find where `strLabelText` is declared.

The other type of development error is a logical error. Logical errors are the worst because Visual Studio .NET does not give you any notification of logical errors in your code and, therefore, they may be quite difficult to find. Some examples of these errors include miscalculating functions or applying variables through processes in incorrect order or at incorrect times. I have no specific instructions on how to avoid logical errors; but to avoid this type of error, it is vital to have a good understanding of some of the basic principles of mathematics. The better you understand the basic principles of mathematics, the fewer logical errors you will make in your code. This understanding will help with logical divisions of your code and also help in working with any loops.

Runtime errors

Runtime errors are errors that occur while the application is running. For instance, you may experience a runtime error if a null value is passed to a function that doesn't know how to handle it. In another case, a server on which an application is running may not have enough hard-drive space to perform a file operation that is required. This is a type of error that can be handled through the process known, not surprisingly, as *error handling*. In this chapter, you learn how to handle errors and how to use wrappers to encase error-prone code to protect your application from stopping dead in its tracks.

Try ... Catch ... Finally

Whenever ASP.NET encounters an error, either on the system or within the application itself, this error is reported to the application or to the `Catch` blocks which encapsulates the code.

The `Try` command and the `Catch` keyword should be important parts of your application in order to catch any exceptions thrown in the application.

Exceptions

Before jumping straight into the `Try` command, here's a quick look at an exception. For this example, use the code from Listing 20-1 in the `Page_Load` event of your ASP.NET application.

Listing 20-1: Forcing an exception to occur

VB

```
Imports System.IO

Private Sub Page_Load(ByVal sender As System.Object, ByVal e As _
          System.EventArgs) Handles MyBase.Load
   Dim fs As New FileStream("Z:\myFile.txt", FileMode.Open)
End Sub
```

C#

```
using System.IO;

private void Page_Load(object sender, System.EventArgs e)
{
   FileStream fs = new FileStream("Z:\\myFile.txt", FileMode.Open);
}
```

This code should cause an exception to be thrown, unless you just happen to have a `Z` drive with a file in the root called `myFile.txt`. If this is not the case, you have an exception thrown, and this exception is propagated to the browser (Figure 20-2).

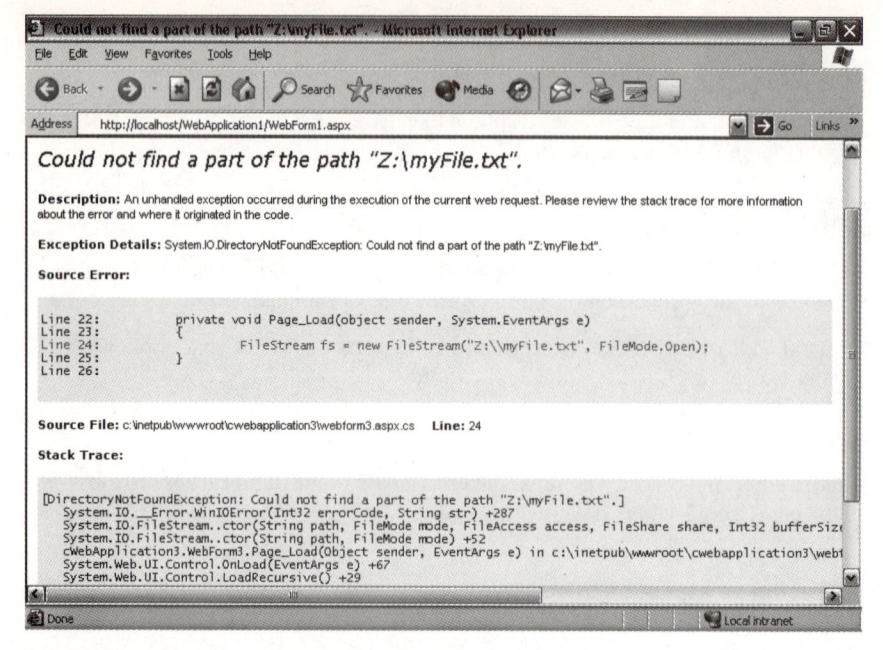

Figure 20-2: An exception has been thrown because the path could not be found

These errors happen. They may occur not because your code is in error or because you are not paying attention to the details, but for reasons outside of your control. For instance, your file in the Z drive, `myFile.txt`, may have been moved. This inadvertently breaks your application. The way around this is to use the `Try` command to encapsulate code where an error might occur and to prevent this error from bringing the application to a halt.

Using Try ... Catch

The basic construct of using the `Try` command and the `Catch` keyword is shown in Listing 20-2:

Listing 20-2: The basic construct of Try-Catch

VB

```
Try
    ' Try some code here
Catch ex As Exception
    ' Catch any exceptions here
End Try
```

Chapter 20: **Error and Exception Handling**

C#

```csharp
try
{
   // Try some code here
}
catch (Exception ex)
{
   // Catch any exceptions here
}
```

In this example, a piece of code is executed (the code is *tried*). If an exception is raised, it is caught by one or more exception handlers that are programmed into the `try-catch` encapsulation. For instance, try to open the file again at the path that doesn't exist using a `Try` command (Listing 20-3). Place this code with the `Page_Load` event of a Web application that contains a simple Label control.

Listing 20-3: Using a Try-Catch on the file search

VB

```vb
Try
   Dim fs As New FileStream("Z:\myFile.txt", FileMode.Open)
Catch ex As Exception
   Label1.Text = "There was an error accessing your file!<br>" & _
      "Actual error: " & e.ToString()
End Try
```

C#

```csharp
try
{
   FileStream fs = new FileStream("Z:\\myFile.txt", FileMode.Open);
}
catch (Exception ex)
{
   Label1.Text = "There was an error accessing your file!<br>" +
      "Actual error: " + ex.ToString();
}
```

In this sample code, the path and file are tried and, when the attempt is unsuccessful, an exception is thrown. Within the `catch` section, you can insert code to do any clean up or error reporting that may be required.

It is possible not only to look for specific types of errors, but also to have multiple `Catch` statements that catch different exception types. Listing 20-4 shows an example of a `Try` command that contains two `catch` statements.

Listing 20-4: Using the Try command with multiple Catch statements

VB

```
Try
   Dim fs As New FileStream("Z:\myFile.txt", FileMode.Open)
Catch e1 As FileNotFoundException
   Label1.Text = "The file was not found."
Catch e2 As DirectoryNotFoundException
   Label1.Text = "The directory was not found."
Catch e3 As Exception
   Label1.Text = "ERROR"
End Try
```

C#

```
try
{
   FileStream fs = new FileStream("Z:\\myFile.txt", FileMode.Open);
}
catch (FileNotFoundException)
{
   Label1.Text = "The file was not found.";
}
catch (DirectoryNotFoundException)
{
   Label1.Text = "The directory was not found.";
}
catch (Exception)
{
   Label1.Text = "ERROR";
}
```

In this example, you attempt to open the file and, when the file is not found, the `FileNotFoundException` is thrown and you can code specifically for that type of exception. The other `catch` statement used is the `DirectoryNotFoundException`. If the directory doesn't exist, the code for that particular type of exception is executed. Finally, if an exception is thrown, but this exception had nothing to do with either the file or the directory not being found, there is a catchall exception statement at the bottom of the entire collection of exception handlers.

Try ... Catch ... and *Finally!*

There is an additional piece to the `Try` command: the use of the `Finally` statement. The syntax required for the `Finally` statement is shown in Listing 20-5:

Chapter 20: **Error and Exception Handling**

Listing 20-5: The basic construct of Try-Catch-Finally

VB

```
Try
   ' Try some code here
Catch ex As Exception
   ' Catch any exceptions here
Finally
   ' This is always executed.
End Try
```

C#

```
try
{
   // Try some code here
}
catch (Exception ex)
{
   // Catch any exceptions here
}
finally
{
   // This is always executed
}
```

The `Finally` statement is always going to be executed whether there is an exception thrown or not. Certain coding commands must be given in any case, and this is the statement to use for that purpose. For instance, you might want to close a database connection, send an e-mail, or do something else that must be executed regardless of the success of the code in the `Try` statement.

Throwing Exceptions

You are not limited to working only with the errors that might be raised within your system or applications. It is also possible to throw your own exceptions based upon any situation that you program into your code, such as a user inputting an invalid value. For instance, because you are looking for a specific set of names, you throw an exception back at the user if the value of a certain variable isn't included in that specific set (see Listing 20-6).

Listing 20-6: Throwing an exception based upon a value

VB

```
If UserName = "Bill Evjen" Then
   ' Add two weeks to vacation time.
Else
   Throw New Exception("You are not entitled to extra vacation!")
End If
```

C#

```
if (UserName == "Bill Evjen")
{
    // Add two weeks to vacation.
}
else
{
    throw new Exception("You are not entitled to extra vacation!");
}
```

If an exception is thrown (such as the one shown in the preceding example), the following error is generated (see Figure 20-3):

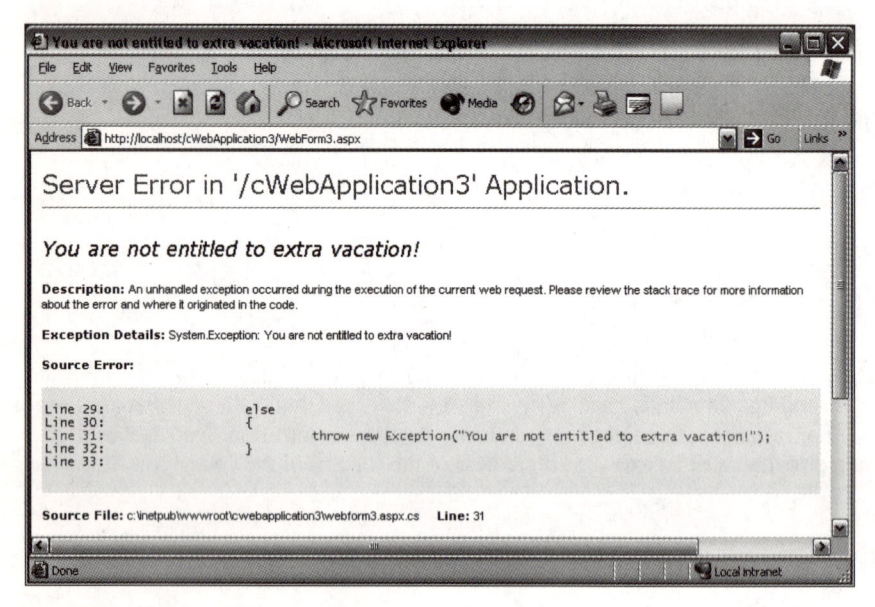

Figure 20-3: Throwing your own exception.

Web.Config Settings

Because XML Web services are part of ASP.NET, you are able to use all the tools and technologies that are provided by ASP.NET. One of the tools for your XML Web services is the `web.config` file. This file is covered in more detail in Chapter 21, but it is introduced now in the context of error handling. The `web.config` file contains a collection of XML nodes that you can modify to customize the settings of your ASP.NET applications. The node used for error handling is the `<customErrors>` node.

The `<customErrors>` node enables you to place instructions directly into your application about how to deal with errors that it encounters. The following example shows the structure of the `<customErrors>` node:

```
<customErrors
   defaultRedirect="url"
   mode="On|Off|RemoteOnly">
   <error statusCode="statuscode"
      redirect="url"/>
</customErrors>
```

Instead of allowing the application to just display errors to users, the `<customErrors>` node of the `web.config` file forwards the client to another page. The `<customErrors>` node allows you to specify the page where users are redirected in case of any errors. The mode can be set to `On`, which causes the `<customErrors>` rules to be applied to all users, even local users. The second value of the mode attribute is `Off`, which turns off this feature entirely. The final possible value is `RemoteOnly`, which applies the rules of the `<customErrors>` settings to all users except for those using the local server.

The `<customErrors>` node can take subnodes as well. The error node within the `<customErrors>` node can specify certain errors for which you want to make a special case in your application. This node takes two attributes. The first is `statusCode`. With this attribute, you can specify the particular error by its error code:

```
<error statusCode="500" redirect="ErrorInPage.aspx?er=500" />
```

The `redirect` attribute of the error node points to the page where users are redirected when the specified error occurs.

Before .NET, you were always forced to make these kinds of changes within the Internet Information Services metabase. Now you can make these changes within the `web.config` file. After the file is saved, the changes take effect.

Using the Global.asax

Another means of handling errors is by using the `global.asax` file. This file is used by the application to hold application-level events, objects, and variables. It's the next version of the `global.asa` file that was used in classic ASP 3.0; so if you are comfortable with that, you'll feel quite at home with `global.asax`.

There can only be one `global.asax` file for an application. However, it's possible for a `global.asax` file to reside next to a `global.asa` file. Just realize that running them side-by-side won't allow you to share sessions or events between the two. In this situation, your `.asp` pages within the application use the `global.asa` file, and the `.aspx` pages use the application file, `global.asax`.

You should pay special attention to a particular event within the `global.asax` file. The `Application_Error` event is used to work with exceptions. This is a good spot in the application to do any event logging, or any other notifications or processing that that might be necessary if an error occurs within the application.

VB

```
Sub Application_Error(ByVal sender As Object, ByVal e As EventArgs)
   Dim ex As Exception = Server.GetLastError()

   ' Perform error-logging or anything else here.
End Sub
```

C#

```
protected void Application_Error(Object sender, EventArgs e)
{
   Exception ex = Server.GetLastError();

   // Perform error-logging or anything else here.
}
```

Using ASP.NET Tracing with Your XML Web Services

As in classic ASP, finding errors within your applications can prove difficult. The only way to trace the information that flows from one page to the next within classic ASP is to output values of variables to the screen using `Response.write`. ASP.NET combats this by providing a simple way to output all the information that is occurring on the page at a particular moment directly to the screen when the page is generated.

You can also use ASP.NET Tracing for your XML Web services. Because XML Web services don't deal with actual pages (but instead with SOAP requests and responses), you are a little more limited in using this tool, but the capability is still there for some aspects of the tracing mechanics.

In order to initiate tracing, turn on tracing in the `web.config` file from the `<trace>` node.

`<trace>` node

The `<trace>` node enables you to work with debugging an ASP.NET application. The following code structure shows how to configure an application with tracing:

```
<trace
   enabled="true|false"
   requestLimit="integer"
   pageOutput="true|false" />
```

The `<trace>` node enables you to specify tracing settings for your application. You can turn tracing on or off by setting the enabled attribute to `true` or `false`, respectively. You can also output the tracing document to each page in an ASP.NET Web application by setting the `pageOutput` attribute to either `true` or `false`. Because XML Web services don't deal with pages, this setting doesn't have any meaning for them. Take a look at the meaning of each of these attributes in Table 20-1.

Table 20-1: Attributes in the <trace> Node

Attribute	Description
`Enabled`	This attribute turns the tracing on or off. The default is `false`.
`RequestLimit`	This is the number of HTTP requests recorded. The default setting is `10`. As the requests build up, ASP.NET tracing keeps track of the last specified number of requests.
`PageOutput`	A setting of `true` means that the tracing information is shown on each page as it's rendered, in addition to being recorded in the `trace.axd` file. The default is `false`. This setting is not important for XML Web services except that, when it is turned on (a setting of `true`), you see the tracing output on your ASP.NET test pages.
`TraceMode`	This attribute specifies the display order of the tracing information. Options include `SortByTime` or `SortByCategory`. `SortByTime` is the default setting.
`LocalOnly`	This attribute indicates whether the trace information is shown only on the local server or is shown to remote clients also.

Viewing tracing output

After you enable tracing on the application level in your `web.config` file, ASP.NET starts keeping track of all HTTP requests that are made. It logs all the tracing information automatically for you and only stores the ten most recent HTTP requests made to the application. You can change the number of requests that are stored by changing the `requestLimit` attribute to the desired number of requests.

These requests aren't shown on the page themselves unless the `pageOutput` attribute is set to `true`. In any case, tracing is still stored in a tracing log that is accessible through the browser.

To view the tracing log using your browser, navigate to your application and to the file `trace.axd`. This file is located in the root directory. Type in the following URL to see the application-tracing page:

```
http://localhost/webservice1/trace.axd
```

NOTE: If you use Windows Explorer to view the file in the root directory, you will not find it there. The file is only viewable through the browser.

The `trace.axd` file lists all the requests that have been made to the application and gives you some basic information about the requests, such as the time of the request and the file requested (see Figure 20-4).

464 Part VIII: **Advanced XML Web Services**

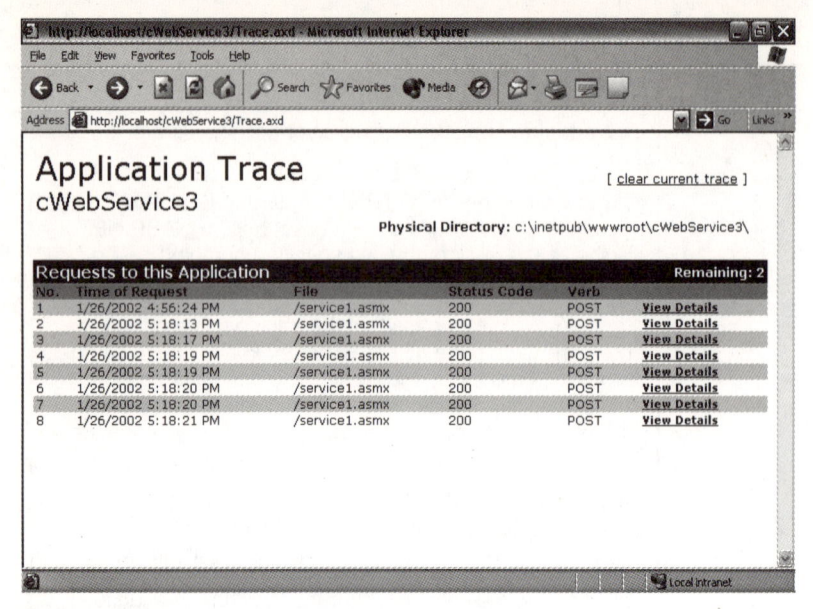

Figure 20-4: Viewing all the available trace logs at `Trace.axd`.

In the upper-left corner of the `trace.axd` file, you can clear the trace log by clicking the Clear Current Trace link. It's possible to view the details of the each HTTP request made by clicking the View Details link. This displays a new page that contains all the tracing information for that request (see Figure 20-5).

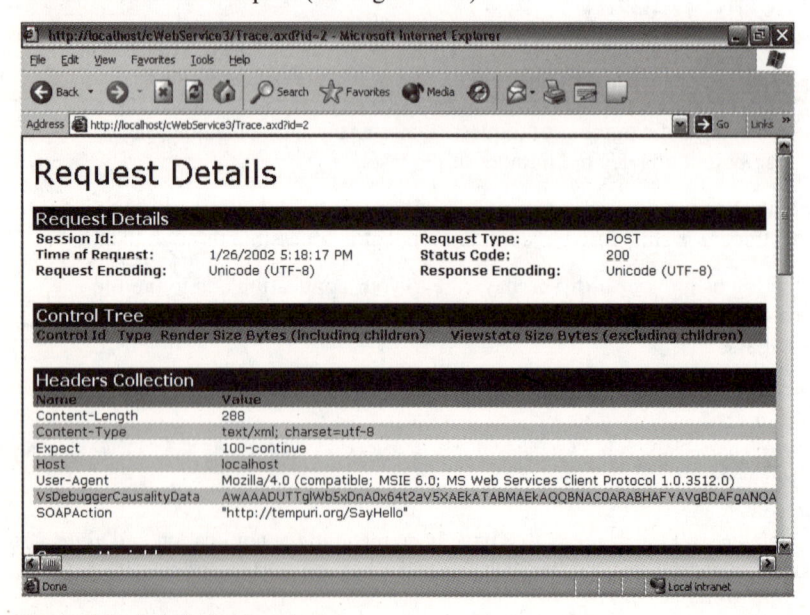

Figure 20-5: An individual trace log.

The information that ASP.NET gives you when you have tracing enabled is called the trace log. This log provides very detailed information about each HTTP request. Table 20-2 lists the sections that can be displayed in the trace log. This is not a complete list of all the items that are available in the trace log, just the ones that are shown for your XML Web services.

Table 20-2: Trace Log

Section	Description
Request Detail	Displays the generic information about the request, such as the session ID of the request, the time the request was made, the character encoding of the request, the request type (GET or POST), the status code value associated with the response, and the character encoding for the response.
Trace Information	Displays the execution order of the request and response. Information provided. Includes the category of the event, the message to display for the event, and the time in seconds from when the first message or event took place to when the last message or event took place.
Session State	Displays the sessions that are available to the page. The specifics of the sessions include the session key, the session type (such as System.String), and the value of the session.
Application State	Similar to the session state, but keeps track of all application variables.
Cookies Collection	Displays information about the page's cookies, including the name of the cookie, the keys and values of the cookie, and the byte size of the cookie.
Headers Collection	Displays the HTTP header information, such as the name and value of each header item.
Forms Collection	Displays the form variable data that is passed to the page, such as the name of the variable and its value.
QueryString Collection	Displays the querystring variable data that is passed to the page, such as the name of the querystring and its value.
Server Variables	Displays any available server variables.

Customizing the trace log

You can customize the trace log so that you can place your own messages within the log itself. For instance, if you want to record a specific event that's taking place in the page, you can place a trace message within the event and it appears in the trace log after the page is requested.

You can use the `TraceContext` object to trace certain pieces of information within your pages or applications. Simply place some code in the WebMethod you want to trace, as shown here in Listing 20-7:

Listing 20-7: Customizing the trace log

VB

```vb
Sub TraceTest(Sender As Object, E As EventArgs)
  HttpContext.Current.Trace.Write("Sub TraceTest", _
     "The subroutine has started!")

  Dim a As Integer = 2
  Dim b As Integer = 20

  a = a + b

  If a = 22 Then
     HttpContext.Current.Trace.Write("A", "A is True")
  Else
     HttpContext.Current.Trace.Write("A", "A is False")
  End If
End Sub
```

C#

```csharp
public void TraceTest(Object sender, EventArgs e)
{
   HttpContext.Current.Trace.Write("Sub TraceTest",
      "The subroutine has started!");

   int a = 2;
   int b = 20;

   a = (a + b);

   if (a == 22)
   {
      HttpContext.Current.Trace.Write("A", "A is True");
   }
   else
   {
      HttpContext.Current.Trace.Write("A", "A is False");
   }
}
```

When this page is loaded, you're writing two items to the trace log (see Figure 20-6). First, you're writing that the WebMethod took place, and second, you're writing whether your statement is either true or false. The structure of the `Trace.Write` statement requires that the values be contained within parentheses. The first value in the parentheses is the category, and the second is the message. They are separated by a comma.

You can even change `Trace.Write` statements to `Trace.Warn`. This makes custom traces appear in red so that they stand out on the page. This is quite useful if there are a lot of events taking place.

> **NOTE:** In order to use this functionality, you import the `System.Web` namespace into your XML Web service.

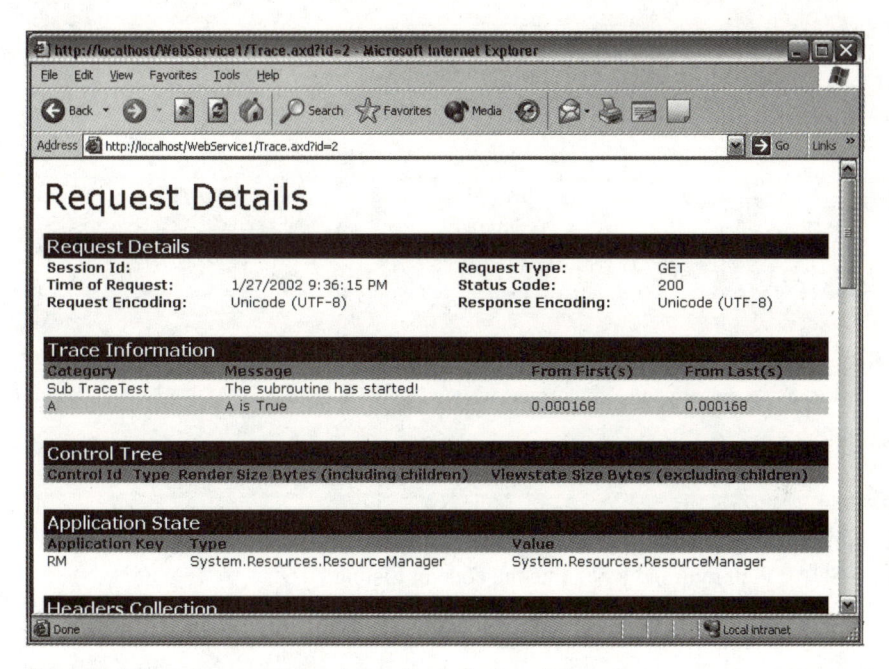

Figure 20-6: Recording custom trace information to the trace log.

SOAP Exceptions

Probably the most important way to deal with exceptions in your XML Web services is with SOAP exceptions. Exceptions can be thrown when an XML Web service is processing a request SOAP message or building a response SOAP message.

You may recall from reading Chapter 14 on Advanced SOAP that you can force your XML Web service to throw a SOAP exception by setting the `DidUnderstand` property to `false`. This action, in turn, sends a SOAP `<fault>` to the consumer of your XML Web service.

> **NOTE:** This type of exception, where you must specify the `DidUnderstand` property based upon information that is in the SOAP Headers, is actually called a SOAP Header Exception.

When an exception is thrown in an XML Web service, the error message is sent back inside the SOAP `<fault>` message according to SOAP specifications. The SOAP `<Fault>` XML element contains details such as the exception string and the source of the exception.

To see an example of throwing a SOAP exception from a WebMethod, look at the following example (Listing 20-8).

Listing 20-8: Throwing an exception within a WebMethod

VB

```vb
If UserName <> "Bill Evjen" Then
    Throw New SoapException("You are not validated", _
         SoapException.ClientFaultCode)
End If
```

C#

```csharp
if (UserName != "Bill Evjen")
{
    throw new SoapException("You are not validated",
        SoapException.ClientFaultCode);
}
```

Throwing this kind of exception from an XML Web service will result in the following announcement in the browser of the consumer of your XML Web service:

```
System.Web.Services.Protocols.SoapException: You are not validated
   at WebService1.SoapExceptionWS.HelloWorld() in
   c:\inetpub\wwwroot\WebService1\SoapExceptionWS.asmx.vb:line 46
```

The actual SOAP message that is sent to the consumer is a SOAP fault message. For this example, the SOAP fault returned looks like the code in Listing 20-9:

Listing 20-9: The SOAP fault message returned from the SOAP exception

```xml
<?xml version="1.0" encoding="utf-8" ?>
  <soap:Envelope xmlns:soap="http://schemas.xmlsoap.org/soap/envelope/">
    <soap:Body>
      <soap:Fault>
        <faultcode>soap:Client</faultcode>
        <faultstring>System.Web.Services.Protocols.SoapException: You
          are not validated at WebService1.SoapExceptionWS.HelloWorld()
          in c:\inetpub\wwwroot\WebService1\SoapExceptionWS.asmx.vb:line
          46</faultstring>
        <detail />
      </soap:Fault>
    </soap:Body>
</soap:Envelope>
```

In order to throw a SOAP exception in your XML Web service WebMethod, you first import the `System.Web.Services.Protocols` namespace. In your code, you must use the following structure and include at least some of the enclosed attributes.

VB

```
Throw New SoapException([message], [code], [actor], [detail])
```

C#

```
throw new SoapException([message], [code], [actor], [detail]);
```

Take a quick look at each of the available attributes that throw a SOAP exception.

Message

The message is the text-based message that you want to include with the exception details. This should be either a string variable or a text-based message enclosed within quotes. You should make an effort to make the message very specific and thorough to describe to the end client the actions that he must take in order to avoid this exception.

Code

The code attribute specifies the SOAP fault code that occurred with the exception. The possible values include `VersionMismatchFaultCode`, `MustUnderstandFaultCode`, `ClientFaultCode`, and `ServerFaultCode`.

Actor

The actor is the URL of the XML Web service WebMethod that caused the exception to be thrown. A possible value to use is `Context.Request.Url.AbsoluteUri`.

Detail

The detail is application-specific error information.

Summary

Error and exception handling is an important aspect of any application that you build, including XML Web services. You need to plan for different types of errors that your XML Web service might encounter. These errors may not come from your own system or code but from input parameters that come from the consumer of your XML Web service.

Using the `Try` command along with the `Catch` statement is a must for any code that performs an operation that has a possibility of failing. This chapter also examined additional means of handling errors using the `web.config` file and the `global.asax` file.

Finally, this chapter ended with a look at tracing within ASP.NET and how to use SOAP exceptions to your advantage.

Chapter 21

Configuration and Optimization

*Form and function are a unity,
two sides of one coin. In order to enhance function,
appropriate form must exist or be created.*
Ida P. Rolf (1896–1979), U.S. biochemist.

Just as you can configure and optimize any .NET application, you can also configure and optimize XML Web services in order to get the best performance. Because this new technology is part of ASP.NET, you have at your fingertips all the tools from ASP.NET, and you can use the web.config file for configuration. Within .NET, your life is made even easier because this is an XML-based configuration file.

This chapter also looks at one particular tool that you can use to optimize your XML Web services. You will learn to use the Application Center Testing tool that is provided with Visual Studio .NET to get the best possible performance from your XML Web services.

In this chapter, you learn the following:

- Using the web.config file to configure your XML Web services exactly as you want them
- Including caching with your XML Web services
- Working with Microsoft Application Center Test

Web.config

web.config is an application file that enables you to set application-wide settings from one convenient file. This file is created for you when you create an application. If you want to change any of the application settings in classic ASP, you have to do so in the IIS Microsoft Management Console (MMC), and the administrator has to stop and start your application for the settings to take effect. With ASP.NET, you just open the web.config file in any text editor, change the settings, and resave the file. ASP.NET can detect when there are new configuration settings for your application; it doesn't need to stop and start the application. Instead, ASP.NET lets current users finish with the application under the old settings, but any new users are directed to the application with the new settings applied.

> **NOTE:** The web.config file is an XML file, which makes it quite readable and understandable. Feel free to open it and change the settings.

The `web.config` file is created when you start an application. After doing so, you are presented with the code shown in Listing 21-1.

Listing 21-1: The web.config file

```xml
<?xml version="1.0" encoding="utf-8" ?>
<configuration>

  <system.web>

    <!-- DYNAMIC DEBUG COMPILATION
         Set compilation debug="true" to insert debugging symbols
         (.pdb information) into the compiled page. Because this
         creates a larger file that executes more slowly, you should
         set this value to true only when debugging and to
         false at all other times. For more information, refer to the
         documentation about debugging ASP.NET files.
    -->
    <compilation defaultLanguage="vb" debug="true" />

    <!-- CUSTOM ERROR MESSAGES
         Set customErrors mode="On" or "RemoteOnly" to enable custom
         error messages, "Off" to disable.
         Add <error> tags for each of the errors you want to handle.
    -->
    <customErrors mode="RemoteOnly" />

    <!-- AUTHENTICATION
         This section sets the authentication policies of the
         application. Possible modes are "Windows",
         "Forms", "Passport" and "None"
    -->
    <authentication mode="Windows" />


    <!-- AUTHORIZATION
         This section sets the authorization policies of the
         application. You can allow or deny access
         to application resources by user or role. Wildcards: "*" mean
         everyone, "?" means anonymous
         (unauthenticated) users.
    -->
    <authorization>
        <allow users="*" /> <!-- Allow all users -->

            <!-- <allow     users="[comma separated list of users]"
                            roles="[comma separated list of roles]"/>
                 <deny      users="[comma separated list of users]"
                            roles="[comma separated list of roles]"/>
```

Chapter 21: Configuration and Optimization 473

```
            -->
        </authorization>

        <!-- APPLICATION-LEVEL TRACE LOGGING
            Application-level tracing enables trace log output for every
            page within an application.
            Set trace enabled="true" to enable application trace logging.
            If pageOutput="true", the
            trace information will be displayed at the bottom of each
            page.  Otherwise, you can view the
            application trace log by browsing the "trace.axd" page from
            your web application root.
        -->
        <trace enabled="false" requestLimit="10" pageOutput="false"
         traceMode="SortByTime" localOnly="true" />


        <!-- SESSION STATE SETTINGS
            By default ASP.NET uses cookies to identify which requests
            belong to a particular session.
            If cookies are not available, a session can be tracked by
            adding a session identifier to the URL.
            To disable cookies, set sessionState cookieless="true".
        -->
        <sessionState
                mode="InProc"
                stateConnectionString="tcpip=127.0.0.1:42424"
                sqlConnectionString="data source=127.0.0.1;
                user id=sa;password="
                cookieless="false"
                timeout="20"
        />

        <!-- GLOBALIZATION
            This section sets the globalization settings of the
            application.
        -->
        <globalization requestEncoding="utf-8" responseEncoding="utf-8" />

    </system.web>

</configuration>
```

Because this is an XML file, you don't have to go through a wizard to change application-wide settings. Instead, you just make the appropriate changes to this file and save it in the root directory of your application. The changes take effect for all new requests immediately.

\<configuration> node

The following lines from the first part of the `web.config` file inform you that this is an XML file and open up the main node of the file:

```
<?xml version="1.0" encoding="utf-8" ?>
<configuration>
  <system.web>
            ... SETTINGS HERE ...
  </system.web>
</configuration>
```

You need to open and close the `web.config` file with `<configuration>` tags. Within these `<configuration>` tags are your `<system.web>` tags. Forgetting one of these tags causes an exception.

\<compilation> node

The `<compilation>` node enables you to directly affect how your ASP.NET application compiles. The following code shows the structure of the `<compilation>` node:

```
<compilation debug="true|false"
      batch="true|false"
      batchTimeout="number of seconds"
      defaultLanguage="language"
      explicit="true|false"
      maxBatchSize="maximim number of pages per batched compilation"
      maxBatchGeneratedFileSize="maximum combined size (in KB)
            of the generated source file per batched compilation"
      numRecompilesBeforeAppRestart="number"
      strict="true|false"
      tempDirectory="directory under which the ASP.NET temporary
            files are created" >

  <compilers>
     <compiler language="language"
        extension="ext"
        type=".NET Type"
        warningLevel="number"
        compilerOptions="options" />
  </compilers>

  <assemblies>
     <add assembly="assembly" />
     <remove assembly="assembly"  />
     <clear />
  </assemblies>

</compilation>
```

The compilation section of the `web.config` file enables you to configure how the ASP.NET application compiles, as shown here:

```
<compilation defaultLanguage="vb" debug="true" />
```

> **NOTE:** As you work through all these examples, remember that these settings are applied application-wide unless you override them directly within your page code.

The `<compilation>` tag takes a number of attributes, but there are two important ones. The first is the `defaultLanguage` attribute, which specifies the default compiler you use to compile all server-side code. In this case it's `"vb"`, so you don't need to specify the `language=vb` in your scripts. The second attribute is the `debug` attribute. Setting this to `true` turns on the debug compilers. This results in slower performance, but it's necessary in development. When your application is released, change this setting to `false`.

The compilation node can contain three subnodes: `<compilers>`, `<assemblies>`, and `<namespaces>`.

`<customErrors>` node

The `<customErrors>` node enables you to place instructions directly in your application regarding how it deals with errors that it encounters. The following example shows the structure of the `<customErrors>` node:

```
<customErrors
   defaultRedirect="url"
   mode="On|Off|RemoteOnly">
   <error statusCode="statuscode"
      redirect="url"/>
</customErrors>
```

> **CROSS-REFERENCE:** The `<customErrors>` node is covered in detail in Chapter 20.

`<authentication>` node

The `<authentication>` node enables you to control directly all the authentication aspects of your application. The following code shows the structure of the `<authentication>` node:

```
<authentication mode="Windows|Forms|Passport|None">

   <forms name="name" loginUrl="url"
      protection="All|None|Encryption|Validation"
      timeout="30" path="/" >

      <credentials passwordFormat="Clear|SHA1|MD5">
         <user name="username" password="password" />
      </credentials>
```

```
    </forms>

    <passport redirectUrl="internal"/>

</authentication>
```

CROSS-REFERENCE: The <authentication> node is covered in detail in Chapter 16.

<authorization> node

The `<authorization>` node works with the `<authentication>` node in the `web.config` file to apply an authorization model to your ASP.NET applications. The following code shows the structure of the `<authorization>` node:

```
<authorization>

    <allow users="comma-separated list of users"
        roles="comma-separated list of roles"
        verb="comma-separated list of verbs" />

    <deny users="comma-separated list of users"
        roles="comma-separated list of roles"
        verb="comma-separated list of verbs" />

</authorization>
```

CROSS-REFERENCE: The <authorization> node is covered in detail in Chapter 16.

<sessionState> node

The `<sessionState>` node enables you to configure how your ASP.NET application handles sessions. The following code snippet shows how to structure this node within the `web.config` file:

```
<sessionState
    mode="Off|Inproc|StateServer|SqlServer"
    cookieless="true|false"
    timeout="number of minutes"
    connectionString="server name:port number"
    sqlConnectionString="sql connection string" />
```

The `<sessionState>` node is a great new way to manage your sessions in ASP.NET. It's now possible to manage sessions in a process that is separate from the ASP.NET worker process. This wasn't possible in classic ASP.

Now you can store a user's sessions in an out-of-process mode that's separate from the ASP.NET worker process, even if the session is on a server different from that of the application. For maximum reliability, it's now possible to store sessions in SQL Server.

With these options, you can maintain a Web farm, and users can switch between servers and still maintain their sessions.

Table 21-1 lists the four modes for session management in ASP.NET.

Table 21-1: Session State Modes

Mode	Description
`InProc`	Session state is in-process with the ASP.NET worker process. Running sessions `InProc` is the default setting.
`Off`	Session state is not available.
`StateServer`	Session state is using an out-of-process server to store state.
`SQLServer`	Session state is using an out-of-process SQL Server to store state.

If you use the `cookieless` attribute, the user maintains his sessions within a cookie that's placed within the URL itself. The timeout attribute is the value in minutes that the sessions should be maintained.

> **CROSS-REFERENCE:** For more information on sessions and state management, review Chapter 8.

`<globalization>` node

The `<globalization>` node enables you to directly control how your application configures culture settings. The following code shows how to structure the `<globalization>` node:

```
<globalization
    requestEncoding="any valid encoding string"
    responseEncoding="any valid encoding string"
    fileEncoding="any valid encoding string"
    culture="any valid culture string"
    uiCulture="any valid culture string" />
```

Because the Internet is global, it's important to code applications that are internationally aware. For instance, when an application prints the date to the screen, the date should be formatted in the fashion that's expected by the viewing user, no matter which country she's in.

By using the `<globalization>` node in the `web.config` file, you can establish how the server should treat certain elements, such as dates. The following code sample shows how to format a date in a Label control using Visual Basic .NET.

```
Label1.Text = DateTime.Now.ToString("D")
```

By default, the date is printed out in the United States date format (Sunday, August 4, 2002). By using the `<globalization>` node of the `web.config` file, however, you can change the output format of the date in your applications as follows:

```
<globalization requestEncoding="utf-8"
responseEncoding="utf-8" culture="fi-FI" uiCulture="fi-FI" />
```

This sets the `web.config` file to print server-side outputs in the Finnish language:

```
4. elokuuta 2002
```

<appSettings> node

The `<appSettings>` node enables you to store key/value pairs within the `web.config` file to use anywhere within your ASP.NET application. The following code shows the structure of the `<appSettings>` node to use within the `web.config` file:

```
<appSettings>
      <add key="key" value="value"/>
</appSettings>
```

The `<appSettings>` node enables you to define custom application settings that can be used throughout your application. This node allows for one type of subnode, `<add>`, which specifies a key/value pair. You can have as many `<add>` nodes as you want.

One good example is storing your database connections and commonly used SQL strings within the `<appSettings>` node, as shown here:

```
<appSettings>
  <add key="DSN"
   value="server=localhost;uid=sa;pwd=;database=customers" />
  <add key="SQL1" value="Select * From CustomerOrders" />
</appsettings>
```

This allows you to change the connection easily because the change is in one spot and not scattered throughout the application. You can use the following code to retrieve these settings within your pages later:

VB

```
Imports System.Configuration

Dim DSN As String
Dim SqlString As String

DSN = ConfigurationSettings.AppSettings("DSN")
SqlString = ConfigurationSettings.AppSettings("SqlString")
```

C#

```
using System.Configuration;

string DSN;
string SqlString;

DSN = ConfigurationSettings.AppSettings["DSN"];
SqlString = ConfigurationSettings.AppSettings["SqlString"];
```

It's quite simple now to include these key/value pairs and refer to them throughout your pages. After it's changed, the application resets itself and immediately starts using the new key/value pairs.

<httpRuntime>

The `<httpRuntime>` node within the `web.config` file enables you to establish a data buffer for any SOAP requests that come to your XML Web service. The following code shows how to structure the `<httpRuntime>` node:

```
<httpRuntime useFullyQualifiedRedirectUrl="true|false"
        maxRequestLength="size in kbytes"
        executionTimeout="seconds"
        minFreeThreads="number of threads"
        minFreeLocalRequestFreeThreads="number of threads"
        appRequestQueueLimit="number of requests" />
```

Two of the more important attributes here for your XML Web services are `maxRequestLength` and `executionTimeout`.

The `maxRequestLength` attribute is used to specify the maximum size of the SOAP request message that is sent to XML Web service. Presently, by default, there is a 4mb maximum limit on the size of a SOAP message. In most cases, this size limit won't be much of a problem, but if you are dealing with binary SOAP messages that include files and images, you have to think about the size limits that you want to place on your XML Web service.

The `executionTimeout` attribute specifies the maximum number of seconds that the request is allowed to execute before it is shut down automatically by ASP.NET. If requests are using too many of your server's resources because of connectivity issues, you might want to adjust this number.

Caching

The first question you might ask is "What is a Cache?" A cache is an in-memory store where data, objects, and various items are stored for reuse. Many applications and Web sites use caching today in order to increase performance.

How is this done? Take a look at the browser as a prime example of a device that uses caching to greatly increase its performance.

When you pull up a page in your browser for the first time, the browser takes the items from the page (most notably the images) and stores these objects in memory. The next time you return to that same page, the browser will use the in-memory images and data to generate the page (if no changes were made to the original page). Using the in-memory version of the objects to generate the page greatly enhances performance.

Using this in-memory store is an easy way to greatly increase the performance of your XML Web services with little work on your end.

ASP.NET provides two different models for using caching in your XML Web services:

- *Output Caching*: The capability to store responses that are generated from your XML Web service to reuse on subsequent requests.
- *Data Caching*: The capability to cache entire objects, such as a DataSet.

In ASP.NET, when you build an `.aspx` page, you can cache the entire page. It doesn't make sense to do this when working with XML Web services. Output caching can be controlled in dealing with XML Web services on the WebMethod level by using the `CacheDuration` property (Listing 21-2).

Listing 21-2: Caching using the CacheDuration property

VB

```
<WebMethod(CacheDuration:=45)> Public Function ServerTime() As String
    Return DateTime.Now.ToLongTimeString()
End Function
```

C#

```
[WebMethod(CacheDuration=45)]
public string ServerTime()
{
    return DateTime.Now.ToLongTimeString();
}
```

The value of the `CacheDuration` property is a number that represents the number of seconds that ASP.NET stores the response from the XML Web service in memory. In this example, the WebMethod `ServerTime()` is returning the time on the server and caches itself for 45 seconds. After 45 seconds, the cache will be destroyed and the response will be generated again.

If you require input parameters for your WebMethod, the caching occurs for each unique set of parameters. If a consumer of the WebMethod uses a single parameter of A to get a response, this response is cached. If a second consumer of the WebMethod uses a parameter of B, this response is also cached along with the result from the A parameter. At this point, there are two cached results in the memory: one with the result set from the parameter A and another with the result set from the parameter B. If a third consumer uses either A or B and the cache has not expired for either of these result sets, the cached copy of the response is used.

The benefits of caching

As you can probably tell, there are plenty of benefits from caching the responses from your XML Web services. If you have a request that is basically recreated over and over again without much change, caching the response is quite beneficial. Caching these responses causes fewer stresses on the servers hosting the XML Web services because the servers fully process fewer requests. Working with cached information is faster than recreating the information time and time again. Therefore, you will find performance increases the more you fine-tune the cache settings in your application.

Why not cache?

To cache or not to cache, that is the question. You have already seen some of the benefits of caching and how it increases the performance of your XML Web services. It is important to understand, however, that not all WebMethods are created equal and, therefore, not all WebMethods need to be cached.

You do not want to cache if you have a set of parameters that the WebMethod can accept and the values of these parameters are either unrestricted or there is a vast selection of input parameters available. The chances of a user entering the same parameter set in order to get a cached version of the response is remote and, therefore, you are just wasting precious server memory by caching.

For instance, if you are using the Calculator XML Web service that has been used throughout this book, you would not set it up to cache its responses. There would be no need because the possibility of two users entering the same input parameters while the cache is still stored in memory is remote.

Application Center Test (ACT)

Within Microsoft's Application Center is a testing tool called Application Center Test (ACT). It is a powerful tool that is used for testing the performance of applications. Included within Visual Studio .NET is a lite version of this application.

Within Visual Studio .NET, ACT enables you to perform functional tests against your .NET applications. In addition to performing the tests, there is a complete set of graphical and informational reports for each of the tests that you initiate against your applications. This chapter focuses on using ACT with XML Web services.

Do you have ACT?

Not all versions of Visual Studio .NET have ACT available. There are three versions of Visual Studio .NET: Enterprise Architect, Enterprise Developer, and Professional. Both of the enterprise versions have this lite version of ACT integrated into Visual Studio .NET. If you are running the Professional version of Visual Studio .NET, you cannot work along with the examples in this chapter.

In order to find ACT, select Start ⇨ All Programs ⇨ Visual Studio .NET ⇨ Visual Studio .NET Enterprise Features ⇨ Microsoft Application Center Test. Figure 21-1 shows you the start page for ACT.

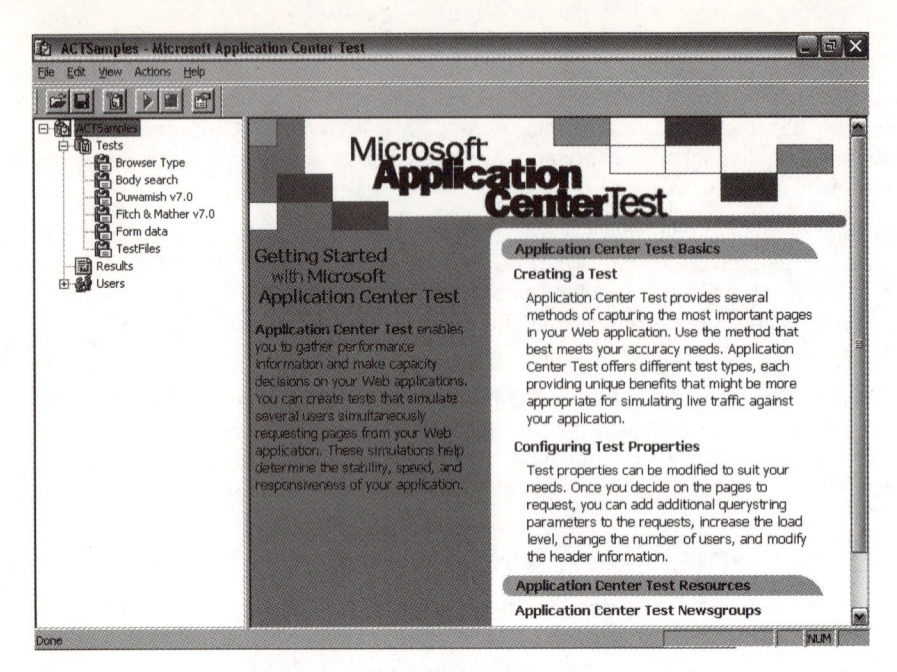

Figure 21-1: Application Center Test in Visual Studio .NET.

What ACT does to your XML Web service

If you put your XML Web service out for the public to consume within their own applications, you want to ensure that the product you are publishing can handle the load of traffic that the XML Web service will receive. In the past, testing your application was usually done with the Microsoft Web Stress Tool. This tool was a little difficult to understand and cumbersome to use.

Visual Studio .NET makes this entire process easy to understand and use. You work with ACT by constructing tests against your XML Web service. In the construction of these tests, you show ACT how to interact and work with your XML Web service. After this process is set up, you start the testing process.

The testing process basically consists of allowing ACT to pound your XML Web service with a number of simulated users. You can specify the number of consecutive users and how long this entire process should take.

After the test is complete, you are able to view a complete report on the test. Not only are there exceptional statistical results, but there are also visual graphs that go along with the stats. You can easily compare these test results with similar tests done in the past. This lets you see if your changes to the application have resulted in performance increases or decreases.

These test statistics and results are saved as an XML file that can be shared with others.

Developers find that ACT is a valuable tool. They commonly use this tool to run tests against their XML Web services, make changes, and modify the XML Web service. They then run the test again to see if the changes result in any dramatic performance improvement. You can easily tell if the changes or modifications made to the XML Web service have an impact on performance. If they do, you can also exactly measure the extent of the performance gains or losses made.

After a developer creates a test, it is easily transported and can be used by others who implement the application or the XML Web service. The people who implement the XML Web service may know absolutely nothing about programming or how to create these tests. A constructed test that is sent along with the XML Web service files, however, allows these folks to install the Web service, run the same test that the developer created, and even compare their results to the results that the developer generated in earlier tests.

Testing with ACT

To see a good example of using ACT, run a test against the GetCustomerOrders XML Web service that was built in Chapter 19 (Listing 19-1). The C# code for the WebMethod that you run ACT against looks like the following (Listing 21-3):

Listing 21-3: The GetCustomerOrders XML Web service for testing

C#

```
[WebMethod]
public DataSet GetCustomerOrders(string custid)
{
  DataSet1 myDataSet = new DataSet1();

  sqlDataAdapter1.SelectCommand.Parameters["@Customer"].Value = custid;
  sqlDataAdapter2.SelectCommand.Parameters["@Customer"].Value = custid;

  sqlDataAdapter1.Fill(myDataSet);
  sqlDataAdapter2.Fill(myDataSet);

  myDataSet.Customers[0].Phone = "NOT AVAILABLE";
  myDataSet.Customers[0].Fax = "NOT AVAILABLE";

  return myDataSet;
}
```

After you run the first test, you can make changes to this WebMethod. You can then rerun the tests in order to compare the difference in performance. This simple WebMethod returns a complete DataSet that contains customer information for a particular customer as well as all that customer's order information stored in SQL Server in the Customers table in the Northwind database.

The first step is to open ACT, right-click on Tests folder, and select New Test. You get the New Test Wizard. When you run this wizard, you create a custom test that runs ACT against

484   Part VIII: **Advanced XML Web Services**

whatever steps you choose in an application. When testing against an XML Web service, there is only a single step — invoking the WebMethod.

Clicking through the wizard, you are asked for a test source. Select Record New Test. This is shown in Figure 21-2.

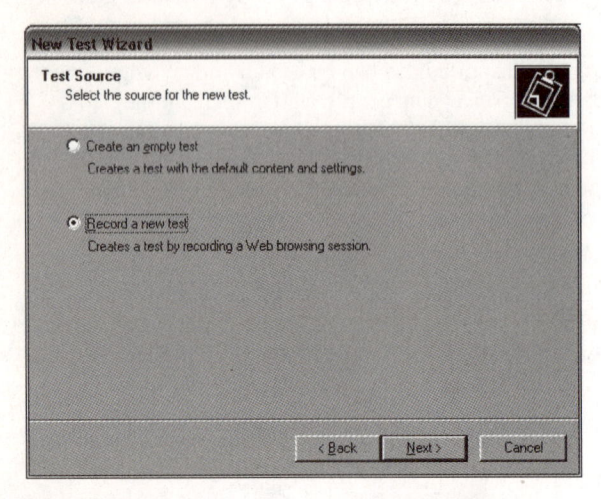

Figure 21-2: Working through the wizard to create a new test.

After selecting to record a new test, you are asked to select the language in which you will build the test object. Presently, you are limited to using VBScript or JScript. C# may be another possible language in the future. Select VBScript for this example and click Next.

After you have selected the scripting language to use for the test, you are given the Browser Record pane. Using this option, you record a set of actions that you take in the browser. The test replicates these actions numerous times over a set period. To start recording these actions, click the Start Recording button. After this button is clicked, a new browser instance opens. Within the browser's address bar, type the path to your XML Web service and include the parameter that the Web service requires in order to invoke the WebMethod.

```
http://localhost/WService1/Service1.asmx/GetCustomerOrders?custid=alfki
```

This XML Web service is calling the `GetCustomerOrders` WebMethod and passing in the value of `alfki` for the customer ID. Invoking this, WebMethod returns a complete DataSet that can be viewed in the browser. For an XML Web service, this is the only browser action that you need to take in the recording process. After this is complete, return to ACT and click the Stop Recording button (Figure 21-3).

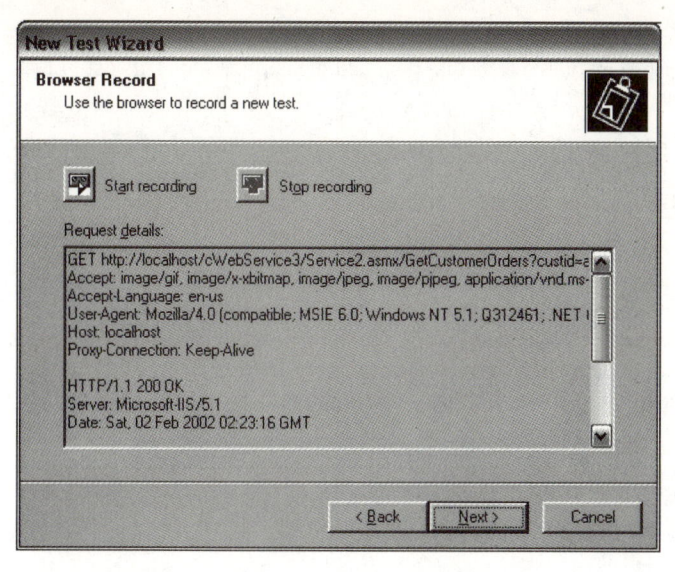

Chapter 21: **Configuration and Optimization** 485

Figure 21-3: The New Test Wizard for recording your tests.

You have now completely recorded the process that the testing application must follow in order to test your XML Web service. In the next step, you are asked to give the test a name (Figure 21-4).

Figure 21-4: Giving the created test a name.

After entering the name of the test, simply click Next and you are finished creating the test. The test then appears in the list of available tests that reside in the application. This list of tests is available in the left-hand pane of ACT.

If you highlight the test, two panes display that contain the details of the test. In the upper pane is an area where you are able to add notes about the test that you created. This is a good spot to enter in as much detailed information as possible, including information on the purpose of the test, what the test does, who created the test, and contact information.

The lower pane contains the test script (Figure 21-5). This is written in VBScript. This script has only one subroutine, the main routine. It is possible to have numerous subroutines in the test script depending upon the type of test created. Feel free to work within the code of the test script to change how things are done by revising the code. If there are numerous subroutines, feel free to comment out the calling of these routines in the Main routine.

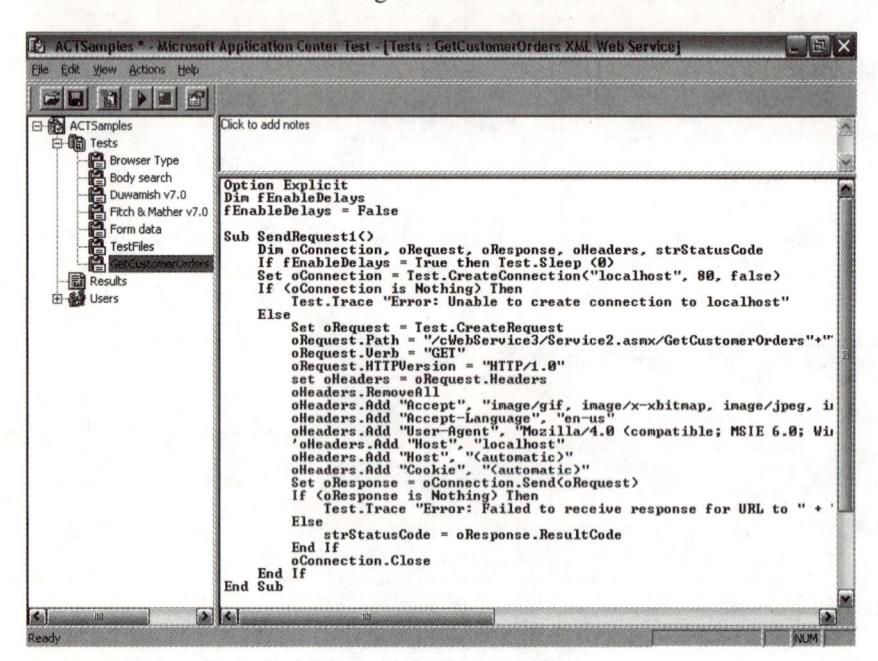

Figure 21-5: The VBScript result that is created from the wizard.

With the test highlighted in the left pane, you can click the Properties button at the top, or right-click on the test and select Properties. You are given three tabs that enable you to modify how the test is performed.

The first tab (Figure 21-6) is a General tab that enables you to configure some of the basic test functions. The first setting allows you to specify how many clients you want to emulate in the test by specifying the number of simultaneous connections to the XML Web service. For the test duration, you can specify a warm-up time. This is the amount of time that the test will run before ACT will start recording test results. This is important for proper testing. When you start an application, items must be placed in the cache, and objects are instantiated in the first few seconds of the application's life. Giving a warm-up period allows things to get started before the results are recorded. Leave this blank for now so that you can monitor this start-up period and what it does to your results.

The third important setting on the General tab is the Run time. This setting specifies the length of time that the test should run. You can actually set this for seconds, minutes, hours, or even by the number of days. You also have the option of running the test a set number of times.

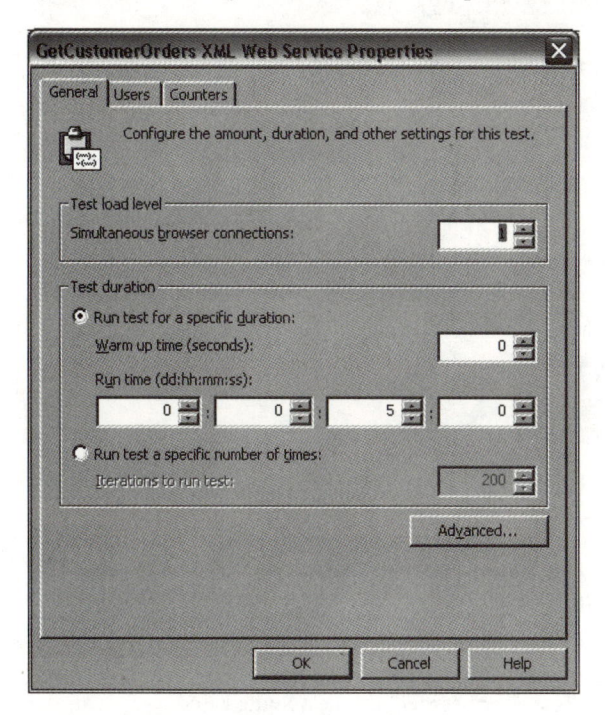

Figure 21-6: The test properties.

The Users tab enables you to specify that the testing application should dynamically create the users that are needed to access the application. You can manually create groups and add users to those groups.

The Counters tab allows you to add performance counters to the testing process (Figure 21-7). The data for these performance counters is stored along with the rest of the test data. You can also compare the performance counter data from one test to another. To add a performance counter, simply click the Add button and work through the wizard to add one of the many performance counters at your disposal.

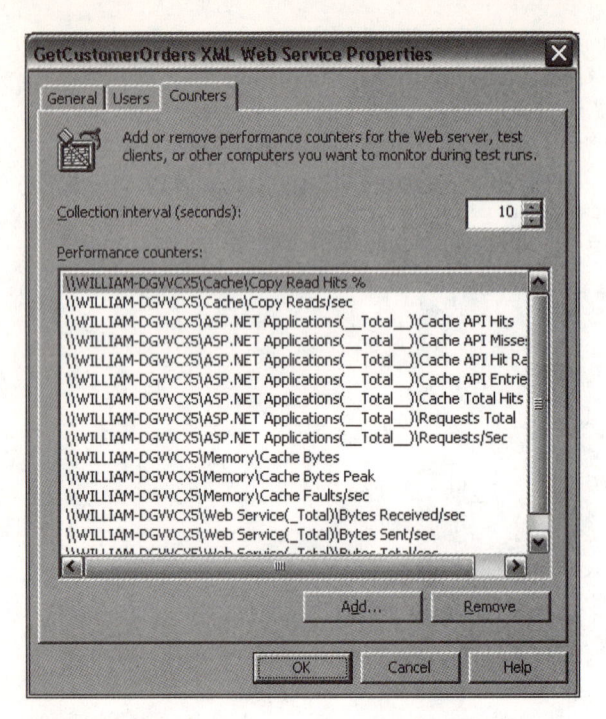

Figure 21-7: Adding performance counters to the test.

After clicking OK for the properties of this test, you are ready to start testing. You run the test through once and then make some changes to the XML Web service. After you have made the changes and recompiled the application, you can run the test again to see how the performance has changed.

To run the first test, select the green arrow at the top of the ACT application or right-click on the test in the left pane and select Start Test. Once started, the Test Status window appears and shows you the status of your test (Figure 21-8). Included in the Test Status window is a timer that shows you how far you are in the test. This is also a way to look at the details of the test as it is being performed. In the detailed mode, a graph shows the number of requests made to the XML Web service for each second.

NOTE: RPS stands for Requests Per Second.

You can also see how many requests have been made so far in the test and any errors that the test might have encountered with its requests. As mentioned earlier, you can see the warm-up period that was required for the application to cache itself and to get some of its internal objects instantiated.

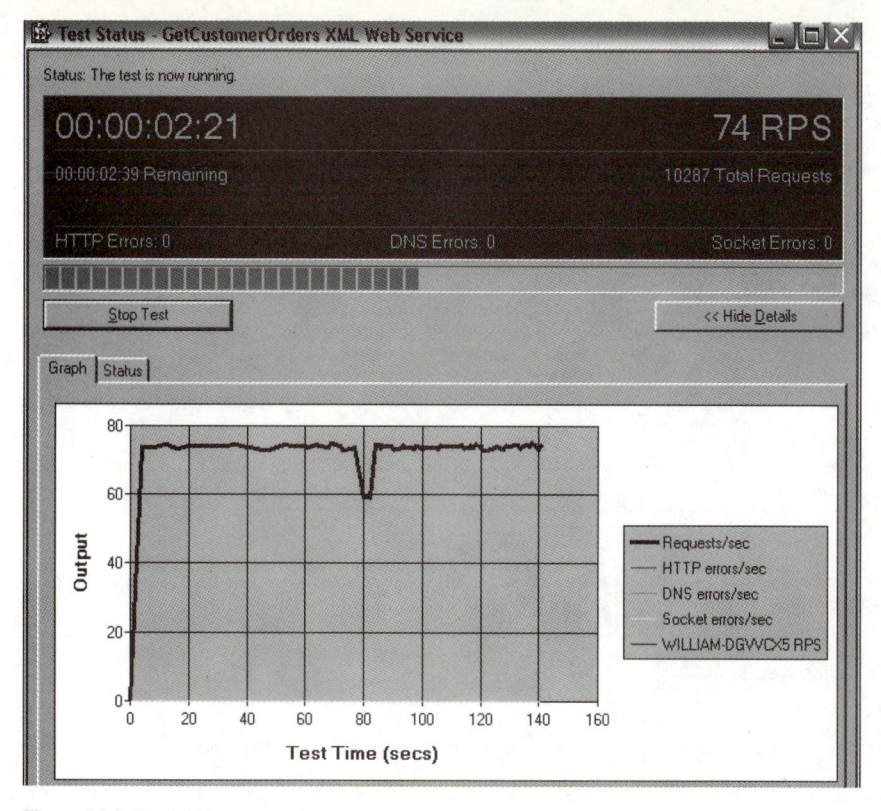

Figure 21-8: The test in progress.

After the test is complete, you can review the results of the test by clicking on the Results node within the left pane of ACT. In the Test Runs pane in the middle of the application, you see a list of tests that you have created or that are there for you to work with. Expanding the test that you created, you will see the single test run that you just performed. Next to the test is an empty check box. Click on the check box to review the test in the Summary pane (Figure 21-9). The ACT summary is a detailed list of the test results. Here you can see a graph that shows the results from the number of requests per second (RPS) that the XML Web service handled. You are able to view information about the test, including

- Date and time of the test
- Length of the test
- The number of iterations performed
- Average number of requests per second
- Total number of requests
- HTTP, DNS, and socket errors
- A list of the types of responses

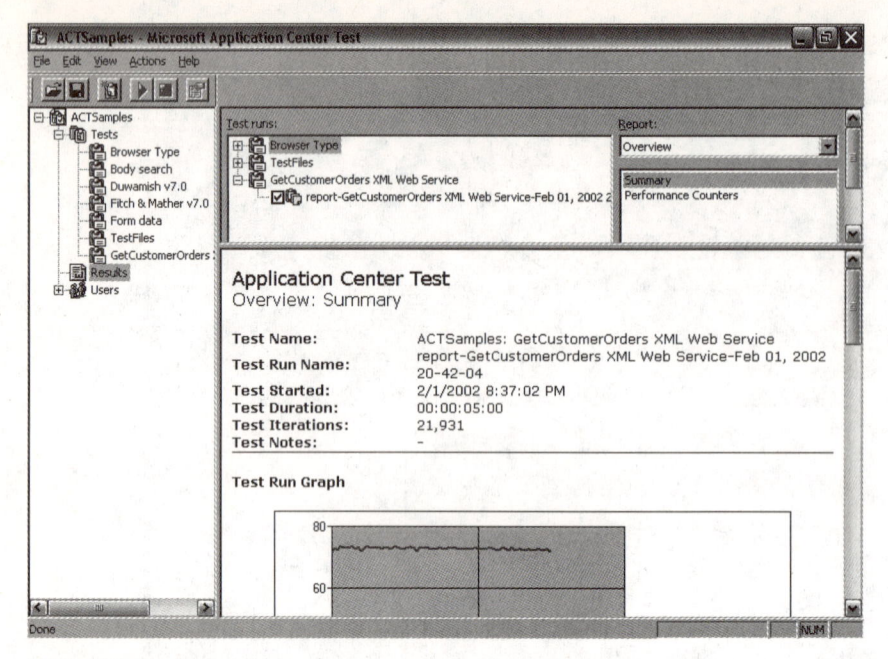

Figure 21-9: The test results.

Changing the XML Web service and retesting

In this section, you learn the power of using ACT for optimization of your XML Web services. After you have run through a single instance of the test that was created, you have some hard data on how the XML Web service performed.

The trick is to make optimal changes to the Web service and then retest the XML Web service to see if the changes you made were for the better. For the purposes of this example, you use the code from Listing 21-3. In order to make a dramatic change, change the first line of the WebMethod to allow the SOAP packets that are returned to be cached for 60 seconds using the `CacheDuration` property (see Listing 21-4).

Listing 21-4: Changing the WebMethod so that is now caches the data that is returned

C# (partial code)

```
[WebMethod(CacheDuration=60)]
public DataSet GetCustomerOrders(string custid)
```

After this change is in place, recompile the application and run the test again by simply starting the test. It is important to keep all the test properties the same as in the first test. This is a simple and logical change to the XML Web service, but the test shows you the results of the change to the Web service (Figure 21-10). To review both tests side-by-side so that you can make comparisons between the two tests, click the Results node and put a check in each of the two tests that appear. When you come to a point when you have numerous tests listed here, you can select just the ones that you want to compare.

Test Run Graph

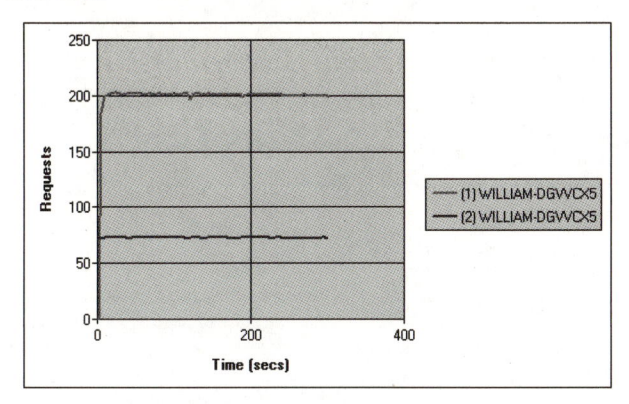

Figure 21-10: Comparing two test runs.

By simply caching the XML Web service, the requests per second went from being around 75 RPS to around 200 RPS. This is a dramatic change that is quite apparent when you view the test results side-by-side.

Summary

This chapter covered two separate points: configuration and optimization — both quite important in the development of powerful XML Web services. The web.config file is an XML-based file that enables you to make quick and easy changes to customize the XML Web service so that it performs exactly the way you want it to perform.

Included with Visual Studio .NET is a lightweight testing tool called Application Center Test that enables you not only to test your .NET applications, but also your XML Web services. After you build your XML Web services, it is important that you test them with this tool. It enables you to learn what kinds of customization and modifications you can make to your WebMethods in order to get more power from your XML Web services.

Chapter 22

Advanced Issues in XML Web Services

Don't wait until you are thirsty to dig a well.
Chinese Proverb

This chapter takes you through a collection of items and capabilities that you can use in your XML Web services. Some of these elements are a little more advanced, but you are sure to encounter them as you start demanding more and more from your XML Web services.

This chapter looks at

- Passing images through your XML Web services
- Overloading your WebMethods
- Working with XML Web services asynchronously

Passing Images in the SOAP Envelope

So far, this book has emphasized how to pass textual data, formulated into XML, through an XML Web service from one point to another.

This type of data, pressed into XML, is easily understood by receiving applications. But how do you put an image into an XML format? Invariably, you will want to use this great means of passing information to send items such as Word documents, PDF files, and images.

In this section, you take a look at passing images in the SOAP envelope from an XML Web service to a consuming application. You do this by converting the image to a binary format. Once converted, the binary text of the image can be encased in the SOAP envelope and then can be passed from the XML Web service's WebMethod.

For an example of this, look at a simple XML Web service that returns an image from a specified file path (Listing 22-1). You might need to make a reference to the `System.Drawing` DLL within the Solution Explorer window.

Listing 22-1: The ImageSend.asmx Web service

VB

```vb
Imports System.Web.Services
Imports System.Drawing
Imports System.IO

<WebService(Namespace := "http://tempuri.org/")> _
Public Class ImageSend
    Inherits System.Web.Services.WebService

    <WebMethod()> Public Function GetImage(ByVal FilePath As String) _
        As Byte()
        Dim myBitmap As Bitmap
        Dim myMemoryStream As MemoryStream

        myMemoryStream = New MemoryStream()

        Try
            myBitmap = New Bitmap(FilePath)
            myBitmap.Save(myMemoryStream, _
                System.Drawing.Imaging.ImageFormat.Jpeg)

            Return myMemoryStream.ToArray()
        Catch
            Return Nothing
        End Try
    End Function

End Class
```

C#

```csharp
using System;
using System.Collections;
using System.ComponentModel;
using System.Data;
using System.Diagnostics;
using System.Web;
using System.Web.Services;
using System.Drawing;
using System.IO;

namespace WebService1
{
  public class ImageSend : System.Web.Services.WebService
  {
    [WebMethod]
    public Byte[] GetImage(string FilePath)
```

```
{
  Bitmap myBitmap;
  MemoryStream myMemoryStream;

  myMemoryStream = new MemoryStream();

  try
  {
   myBitmap = new Bitmap(FilePath);
   myBitmap.Save(myMemoryStream,
        System.Drawing.Imaging.ImageFormat.Jpeg);

   return myMemoryStream.ToArray();
  }
  catch
  {
   return null;
  }
 }
}
```

This XML Web service returns a byte array and stuffs the image into this byte array using the Bitmap class that loads the image into a memory stream. Using the `Try` command, it first tries to serialize the image into a memory stream to the format of a jpg image using the `System.Drawing` namespace. If the try is unsuccessful, it returns a null value. The other namespace to be imported into this XML Web service in order to gain access to the memory stream is the `System.IO` namespace.

When this XML Web service is invoked, there isn't an actual image in the SOAP envelope, but a binary representation of the image. This is shown in Figure 22-1.

All in all, this is pretty simple and straightforward. This XML Web service can easily return an image without requiring much code. On the other end, the user must consume this XML Web service and display the image that is sent to it as a byte array.

For examples of how to convert this byte array back to an image for use within a .NET application, take a look at Listing 22-2 and Listing 22-3. These listings show how to consume this XML Web service in both a Windows Form and a Web Form (respectively). The steps are a little different in each case.

Part VIII: Advanced XML Web Services

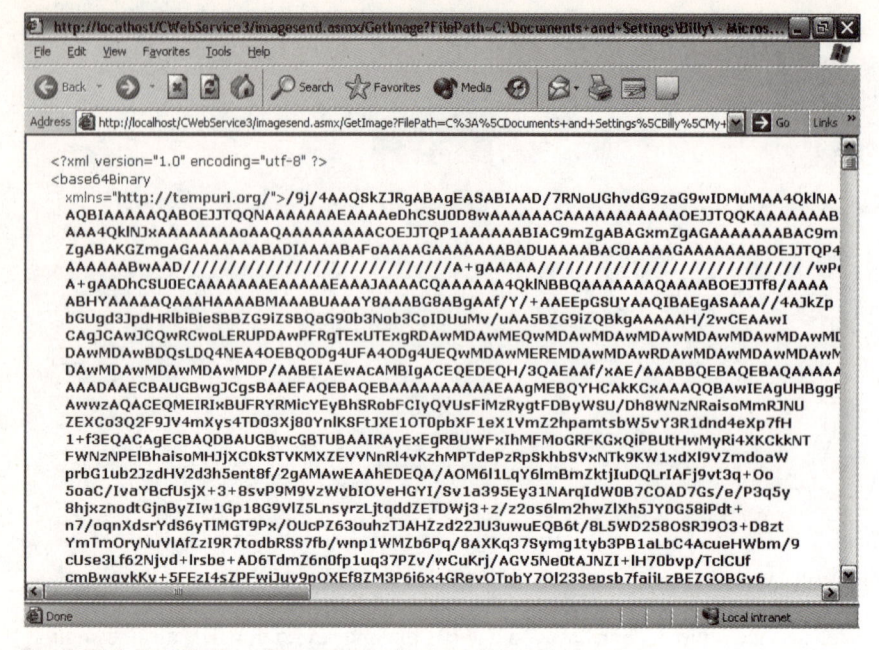

Figure 22-1: The SOAP envelope sends the image in a binary format.

For the Windows Application, there are three items on the form (Figure 22-2). The first is a text box that allows the end user to type in the full path of the image that he wants to receive from the XML Web service. There is also a button to invoke the Web service and, finally, an image placeholder, the picturebox, which displays the image from the memory stream. Listing 22-2 shows the code needed for the code-behind page of the form.

Listing 22-2: The Windows Form that consumes the GetImage XML Web service

VB

```
Imports System.IO

Public Class Form1
    Inherits System.Windows.Forms.Form

    Private Sub Button1_Click(ByVal sender As System.Object, _
            ByVal e As System.EventArgs) Handles Button1.Click
        Dim myByte As Byte()
        Dim myImage As Bitmap
        Dim myMS As MemoryStream

        Dim ws As New localhost.ImageSend()
        myByte = ws.GetImage(TextBox1.Text)

        myMS = New MemoryStream(myByte)
```

```vbnet
            myImage = New Bitmap(myMS)

        PictureBox1.Image = myImage
    End Sub

End Class
```

C#

```csharp
using System;
using System.Drawing;
using System.Collections;
using System.ComponentModel;
using System.Windows.Forms;
using System.Data;
using System.IO;

namespace WindowsApplication1
{
 public class Form1 : System.Windows.Forms.Form
 {
    private System.Windows.Forms.TextBox textBox1;
    private System.Windows.Forms.Button button1;
    private System.Windows.Forms.PictureBox pictureBox1;

    private System.ComponentModel.Container components = null;

   private void button1_Click(object sender, System.EventArgs e)
   {
     Byte[] myByte;
     Bitmap myImage;
     MemoryStream myMS;

     localhost.ImageSend ws = new localhost.ImageSend();

     myByte = ws.GetImage(textBox1.Text);
     myMS = new MemoryStream(myByte);
     myImage = new Bitmap(myMS);

     pictureBox1.Image = myImage;
   }
 }
}
```

This consuming application does a lot of the same work that the XML Web service is required to perform in order to send the image through the Web service. The end result is shown in Figure 22-2.

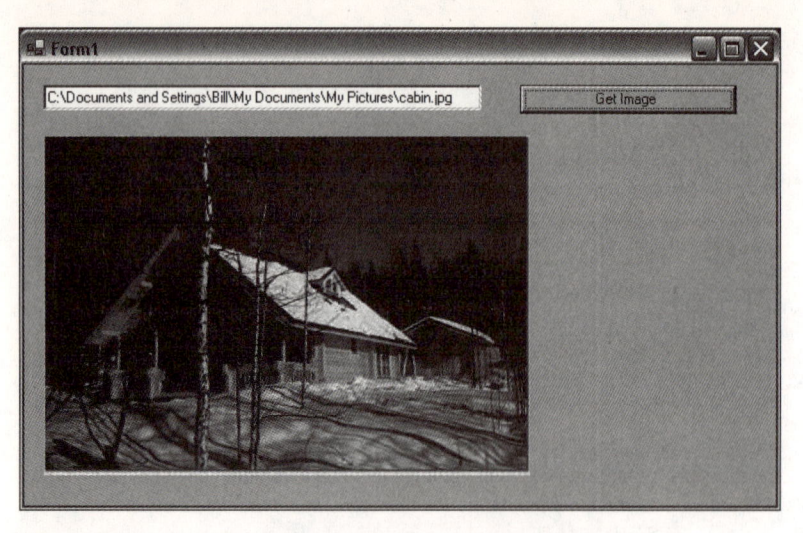

Figure 22-2: Passing an image from an XML Web service to a Windows Form.

In order to get this result, you once again import the `System.IO` namespace into your application to gain access to the memory stream that you need to grab the image. The result of the invocation of the XML Web service's `GetImage()` WebMethod is stuffed into a local byte array, passed into a memory stream, and then converted to an image using the Bitmap class. After this is done, the image associated with the picturebox is then assigned with the bitmap image from the XML Web service.

> **NOTE:** An important thing to remember when sending an image across the wire through an XML Web service is that images are large and take time. If you send large images, you may want consumers of your Web service to look at asynchronous programming. This is explained later in this chapter.
>
> One way to get around sending an image through an XML Web service is to send the link to the image instead.

This is an acceptable approach if you are trying to consume this type of XML Web service in a Windows application, but this process doesn't work if you are trying to consume this Web service from a Web application. There is no such control as a picturebox in a Web application, so you can't just assign the image as you can with a Windows application.

The best approach when you are working with a Web application is to place a blank image from the Toolbox on your page and turn the image's visibility property to `False`. This means that the image is not shown. This is a good thing because you are not assigning a URL location of that image.

The purpose in consuming this XML Web service in a Web application is to grab the image and save it locally. After the image is saved, the user can set the image URL to that local copy of the image. Listing 22-3 shows an example of this.

Listing 22-3: The Web Form that consumes the GetImage XML Web service

VB
```vb
Imports System.IO

Public Class WebForm1
    Inherits System.Web.UI.Page
    Protected WithEvents TextBox1 As System.Web.UI.WebControls.TextBox
    Protected WithEvents Button1 As System.Web.UI.WebControls.Button
    Protected WithEvents Image1 As System.Web.UI.WebControls.Image

    Private Sub Button1_Click(ByVal sender As System.Object, ByVal e As _
            System.EventArgs) Handles Button1.Click
        Dim bytes As Byte()
        Dim stream As MemoryStream
        Dim image As Bitmap
        Dim ws As New localhost.ImageSend()

        bytes = ws.GetImage(TextBox1.Text)
        stream = New MemoryStream(bytes)
        image = New Bitmap(stream)

        image.Save("C:\Documents and Settings\Bill\My Documents\My _
            Pictures\cabinCOPY.jpg")

        Image1.ImageUrl = "C:\Documents and Settings\Bill\My _
            Documents\My Pictures\cabinCOPY.jpg"
        Image1.Visible = True
    End Sub
End Class
```

C#
```csharp
using System;
using System.Collections;
using System.ComponentModel;
using System.Data;
using System.Drawing;
using System.Web;
using System.Web.SessionState;
using System.Web.UI;
using System.Web.UI.WebControls;
using System.Web.UI.HtmlControls;
using System.IO;

namespace WebApplication1
{
 public class WebForm1 : System.Web.UI.Page
 {
   protected System.Web.UI.WebControls.TextBox TextBox1;
```

```
   protected System.Web.UI.WebControls.Image Image1;
   protected System.Web.UI.WebControls.Button Button1;

   private void Button1_Click(object sender, System.EventArgs e)
   {
    Byte[] bytes;
    MemoryStream stream;
    Bitmap image;
    localhost.ImageSend ws = new localhost.ImageSend();

    bytes = ws.GetImage(TextBox1.Text);
    stream = new MemoryStream(bytes);
    image = new Bitmap(stream);

    image.Save("C:\\Documents and Settings\\Bill\\My Documents\\My
        Pictures\\cabinCOPY.jpg");

    Image1.ImageUrl = "C:\\Documents and Settings\\Bill\\My
        Documents\\My Pictures\\cabinCOPY.jpg";
    Image1.Visible = true;
   }
  }
}
```

On the button click event, the image is pulled from the memory stream and saved locally as `cabinCOPY.jpg`. After the image is saved, the image URL can be pointed to this local copy. Then the image is made visible by setting the value of the `Visible` attribute to `True`. Figure 22-3 shows what this looks like in the browser.

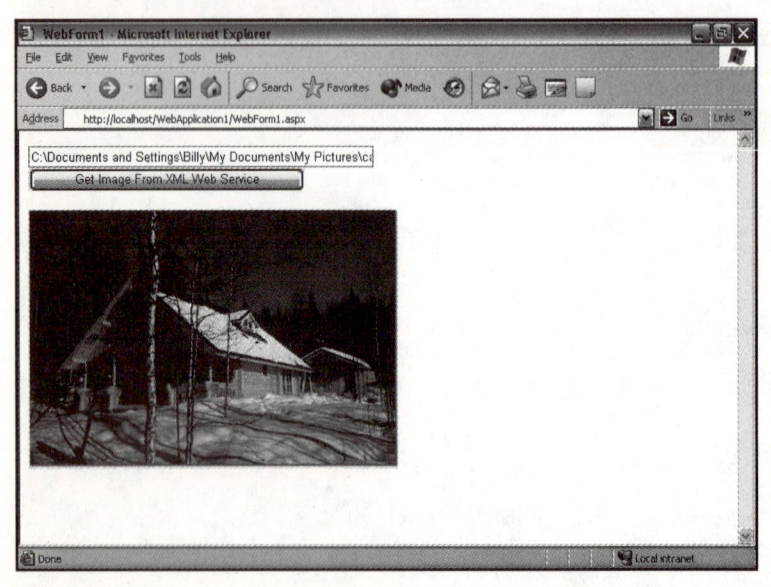

Figure 22-3: Calling an image from an XML Web service to use in a Web Form.

Chapter 22: Advanced Issues in XML Web Services

The lesson learned from this is that you can use XML Web services to expose not only data islands, but also image libraries and other files.

Overloading WebMethods

Another technique you will find useful as your XML Web services become more advanced is overloading WebMethods. .NET-compliant languages must abide by certain rules. One of the specified rules for a .NET-compliant language is that it must be an object-oriented language. Both Visual Basic .NET and C# are object-oriented (OO) languages and, because they are true OO languages, they support *polymorphism*. One of the forms of polymorphism that both these languages support is *method overloading*.

The process of overloading methods means that you create multiple methods that have the same name, but take unique parameters or sets of parameters that differentiate the methods from one another. Just as you can overload your methods in regular .NET applications, you can overload WebMethods in XML Web services. To do this, you have to take an additional step.

For an example of this, you can create an XML Web service that contains three overloaded WebMethods. Listing 22-4 demonstrates this process.

Listing 22-4: Overloading WebMethods

VB

```
<WebMethod(MessageName:="HelloWorld")>
Public Function HelloWorld() As String
    Return "HelloWorld"
End Function

<WebMethod(MessageName:="HelloWorldWithFirstName")>
Public Function HelloWorld(ByVal Fname As String) As String
    Return "HelloWorld " & Fname
End Function

<WebMethod(MessageName:="HelloWorldWithFirstAndLastName")>
Public Function HelloWorld(ByVal Fname As String, ByVal Lname As String) _
        As String
    Return "HelloWorld " & Fname & " " & Lname
End Function
```

C#

```
[WebMethod(MessageName="HelloWorld")]
public string HelloWorld()
{
    return "Hello World";
}

[WebMethod(MessageName="HelloWorldWithFirstName")]
```

```
public string HelloWorld(string Fname)
{
    return "Hello World " + Fname;
}

[WebMethod(MessageName="HelloWorldWithFirstAndLastName")]
public string HelloWorld(string Fname, string Lname)
{
    return "Hello World " + Fname + " " + Lname;
}
```

As you can tell from the code, each of the three methods has the same name — `HelloWorld`. These identical names wouldn't normally be a problem. These overloaded methods, however, are within an XML Web service; they must have a unique name, or an exception is raised when the XML Web service is run.

The way around this little problem is to use the `MessageName` property within the WebMethod attribute. Each of the overloaded WebMethods of the XML Web service must use this property, and each has a unique name contained as its value. For this example, even though each of the WebMethods is called `HelloWorld`, each uses a unique name to differentiate itself.

- `HelloWorld`
- `HelloWorldWithFirstName`
- `HelloWorldWithFirstAndLastName`

As you can see from the ASP.NET test page, the WebMethods are all labeled by the value given to them using the `MessageName` property as shown in Figure 22-4.

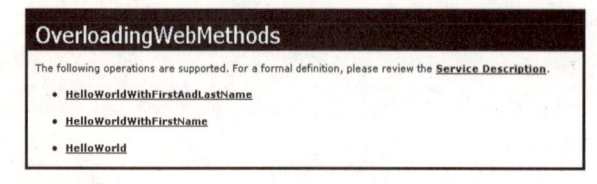

Figure 22-4: Three overloaded WebMethods.

On the client end, if you make a Web reference to this XML Web service, Visual Studio .NET will use IntelliSense to inform you that there are three different options on the types of numbers of parameters that can be input into the `HelloWorld()` WebMethod.

Asynchronous XML Web Services

Here's one more trick for you as you become more advanced at working with XML Web services. So far, this book has concentrated on *synchronous* invocations of XML Web services. A synchronous call to an XML Web service means that when the call is made to the WebMethod, everything in the calling application stops until a result is returned.

Chapter 22: Advanced Issues in XML Web Services

As you can tell, the process of invoking a WebMethod and getting back something in return takes time. Sometimes this process takes a number of seconds, and in some cases, you won't want to force an end user in the consuming application to sit and wait for the response. He could spend this time doing other things while the call is working.

An *asynchronous* call is the opposite of a synchronous call. Invoking an XML Web service asynchronously enables the consuming application to work on other items while it is making the call to the WebMethod. After working on other items, the client application can return to the WebMethod call to see what was returned.

To enable consumers of your Web service to work with it asynchronously, you don't have to change a thing. In fact, looking at the WSDL document that is generated from your XML Web service, you may notice that the capability to invoke the Web service asynchronously is already built in.

The choice to invoke a Web service asynchronously is made by the client and not in the XML Web service. Listing 22-5 shows a client application that is consuming the same XML Web service used earlier in this chapter (the one that returns an image). While the call to the ImageSend XML Web service is invoked, the program works on something else.

Listing 22-5: Invoking an XML Web service asynchronously

VB

```vb
Imports System.IO
Imports System.Runtime.Remoting.Messaging

Public Class Form1
    Inherits System.Windows.Forms.Form

    Private Sub Button1_Click(ByVal sender As System.Object, ByVal e As _
            System.EventArgs) Handles Button1.Click
        Dim myByte As Byte()
        Dim myImage As Bitmap
        Dim myMS As MemoryStream

        Dim ws As New localhost.ImageSend()

        Dim IAR As IAsyncResult = ws.BeginGetImage(TextBox1.Text, _
            Nothing, Nothing)

        If IAR.IsCompleted = False Then
            Label1.Text = "The request is off and while it was ... I
                        worked on this!"
        End If

        myByte = ws.EndGetImage(IAR)

        myMS = New MemoryStream(myByte)
        myImage = New Bitmap(myMS)
```

```vb
            PictureBox1.Image = myImage
    End Sub

End Class
```

C#

```csharp
using System;
using System.Drawing;
using System.Collections;
using System.ComponentModel;
using System.Windows.Forms;
using System.Data;
using System.IO;
using System.Runtime.Remoting.Messaging;

namespace WindowsApplication1
{
 public class Form1 : System.Windows.Forms.Form
 {
    private System.Windows.Forms.TextBox textBox1;
    private System.Windows.Forms.Button button1;
    private System.Windows.Forms.PictureBox pictureBox1;

    private System.ComponentModel.Container components = null;


   private void button1_Click(object sender, System.EventArgs e)
   {
    Byte[] myByte;
    Bitmap myImage;
    MemoryStream myMS;

    localhost.ImageSend ws = new localhost.ImageSend();

    IAsyncResult IAR = ws.BeginGetImage(textBox1.Text, null, null);

    if (IAR.IsCompleted == false)
    {
       Label1.Text = "The request is off and while it was ... I
                       worked on this!";
    }

    myByte = ws.EndGetImage(IAR);

    myMS = new MemoryStream(myByte);
    myImage = new Bitmap(myMS);
```

```
    pictureBox1.Image = myImage;
  }
 }
}
```

The first step in this code is to import both the `System.IO` and the `System.Runtime.Remoting.Messaging` namespaces. Many steps taken here are similar to the steps for invoking this XML Web service synchronously. However, to invoke the Web service asynchronously, the client must use the `BeginGetImage` and the `EndGetImage` methods.

The next step is to call the `BeginGetImage` method. This method always starts with the word *Begin* followed by the WebMethod's name (in this case `GetImage`). After this asynchronous method is called, instead of returning the result of the WebMethod, `IAsyncResult` is used so that the client can check whether the method call has been completed. At this point, the XML Web service has been invoked, but control at the client end of the application has been returned. The client is free to do whatever it wants before it goes back to check the return value of the XML Web service WebMethod call.

In this case, it checks whether the method call has been completed by using `IAR.IsCompleted` and by assigning a value to the Label control. After this is done, the client simply returns to the WebMethod and calls the `EndGetImage` method. This call returns the value of the WebMethod just as if the client called the WebMethod synchronously. The result is shown in Figure 22-5.

As you can tell, this is a powerful tool. It is important, however, to weigh all the pros and cons of using synchronous or asynchronous method calls in client applications that consume XML Web services.

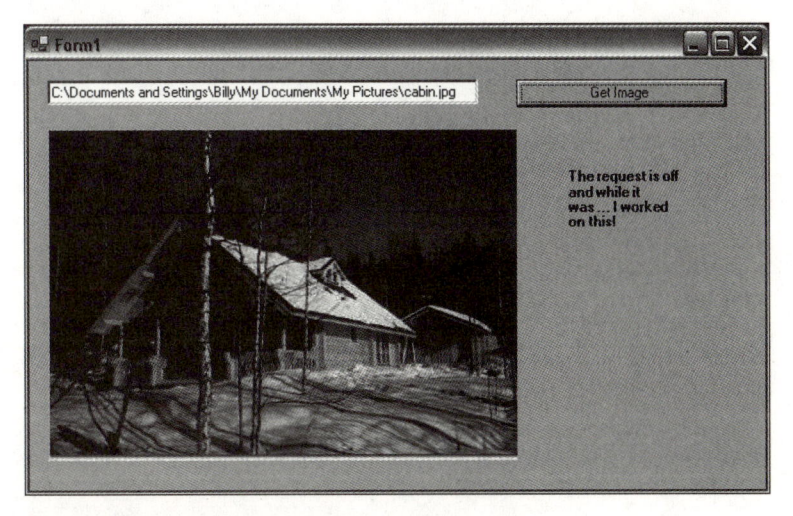

Figure 22-5: An asynchronous XML Web service call.

If you're thinking about calling the WebMethod asynchronously, be sure that you do not use the value returned from the WebMethod call anywhere in your code before the actual value is returned. If you have to call multiple XML Web services within the same application, it is beneficial to call each of these Web services asynchronously. You will end up saving the end user quite a bit of time. Just remember that there are advantages to using both synchronous and asynchronous calls, and you need to weigh each one before making your decision.

Summary

This chapter presented three different capabilities: working with images in your XML Web services, overloading WebMethods, and calling your XML Web services asynchronously. It is important to understand these capabilities because you are sure to need these operations in your XML Web services in the future.

You must be able to send not only data, but also files and images through your XML Web services. XML Web services have opened the door. You can now share application logic with and expose data islands to other systems in a way that you would have never dreamed of in the past. The power of this technology creates an environment where you want to expand even more, to share images and files as well. This is possible, but there is a cost to sharing such large packets across the wire.

One solution to this is to use an asynchronous programming model in your applications. Using asynchronous programming enables you to send a request to an XML Web service and then to return to your application and run through additional logic before returning to the call to get at the result. This can be a timesaving operation that the end users of your applications will appreciate.

Chapter 23
Screen Scraping

It's immoral to steal, but you can take things.
Anton Pavlovich Chekhov (1860–1904)

If you find some specific data on a Web site that you would love to consume for your own application, but (after an exhaustive search) you can't find an XML Web service that exposes this data in some manner, what are you to do?

There is a solution to this problem. Using the tools that have been described in this book, you can easily use screen scraping to invoke the page from your own application and strip it of the data that you want.

This chapter examines how to scrape exactly what you need for your application. Most notably, this chapter will review

- Using WSDL documents to build proxies
- Working with proxies to scrape Web pages
- Using the stripped data within your .NET applications

The Screen Scraping Process

You might not always be able to get at an XML Web service to obtain the data that you want. Some companies or organizations only expose limited data on their Web pages, making it difficult for you to get the complete data you want or need for use within your application. By using the tools and technologies described in this book, you can access the Web page that holds the data you want to consume. You can build the means of reading the Web page and taking from it the data that you need.

You can do this by using a WSDL document, along with regular expressions, to create a document that contains all the instructions about the specific data that you want from a certain Web page. No actual XML Web service exists behind this WSDL document and, therefore, you must build it from scratch. After this WSDL document is built, you can then create a proxy class that will enable your custom .NET application to consume the data from the Web page just as if it were consuming the data from an XML Web service.

It is an easy and quick process that greatly increases the capabilities of your .NET applications.

Stock Quote Example

You have probably seen a ton of examples of how to build an XML Web service that provides stock quotes. These examples always have the stock quotes hard-coded because getting an actual feed for stock quotes costs money. There is no point in purchasing such a service for a simple example. To give you an example of screen scraping, this chapter shows you all the steps for getting actual stock quotes from MSN.

Find your data source

The first step in the process is to find the actual page from which you want to strip data. Because you want to consume stock quotes and the stock's related data, turn to MSN at `http://moneycentral.msn.com`. You can then simply enter any stock symbol in the GET QUOTE text box to get to the page that displays a stock quote (Figure 23-1).

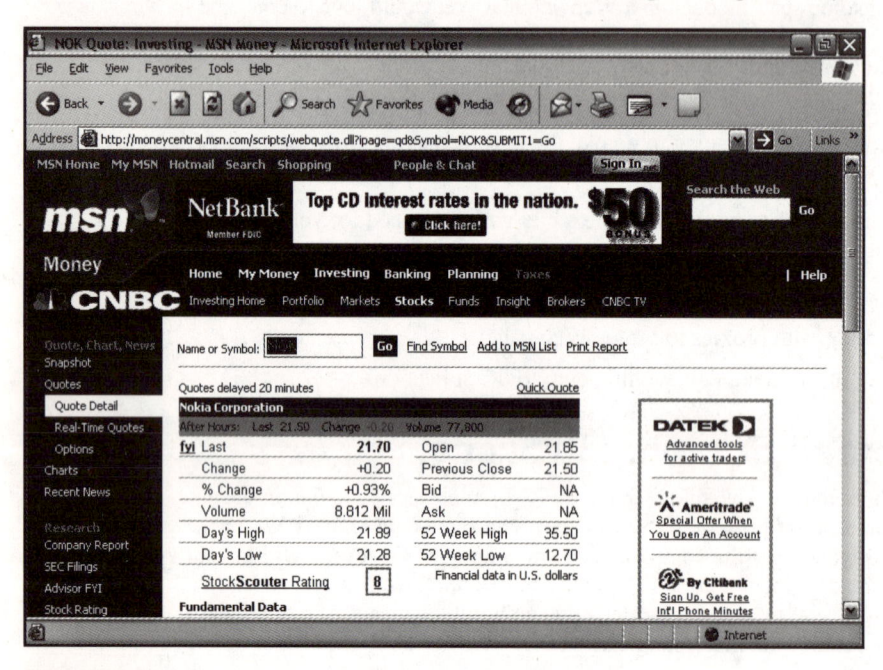

Figure 23-1: The MSN page showing the Nokia stock quote (Symbol- NOK).

This page shows all the details that you want to get at for your stock-quote screen scraper. The data on this page is company-specific (for Nokia). You are going to build your WSDL document and the related proxy class, however, so that you can simply enter in any stock symbol to get that particular company's stock data back as XML.

In order to build your WSDL document and its related proxy class properly, you must understand the structure of the URL. The root of the URL is

`http://moneycentral.msn.com`

Everything that comes after this is the folder and querystring data of the URL.

```
/scripts/webquote.dll?ipage=qd&Symbol=NOK&SUBMIT1=Go
```

There are quite a few variables in the querystring, and if you strip them all out except for the `Symbol=NOK` and click Enter, you still get this page and all the data. So in the end, you are interested in building a service that goes to the following URL to collect the page data:

```
http://moneycentral.msn.com/scripts/webquote.dll?Symbol=NOK
```

Building the WSDL document

You don't have to build the WSDL document in order to build a service that performs screen scraping. You can also start directly with the creation of a proxy class. Some people, however, find it easier to start with building a WSDL document and then creating a proxy class from this using `wsdl.exe`.

Listing 23-1 is the WSDL document that addresses all the data you want to strip from the MSN page.

Listing 23-1: The WSDL document, StockQuote.wsdl

```xml
<?xml version="1.0" encoding="utf-8" ?>
<definitions xmlns:s="http://www.w3.org/2000/10/XMLSchema"
 xmlns:http="http://schemas.xmlsoap.org/wsdl/http/"
 xmlns:mime="http://schemas.xmlsoap.org/wsdl/mime/"
 xmlns:soapenc="http://schemas.xmlsoap.org/wsdl/encoding/"
 xmlns:soap="http://schemas.xmlsoap.org/wsdl/soap/"
 xmlns:s0="http://tempuri.org/"
 targetNamespace="http://tempuri.org/"
 xmlns="http://schemas.xmlsoap.org/wsdl/"
 xmlns:msType="http://microsoft.com/wsdl/mime/textMatching/">
  <types />
  <message name="GetStockDetailsHttpGetIn">
    <part name="Symbol" type="s:string" />
  </message>
  <message name="GetStockDetailsHttpGetOut" />
  <portType name="StockHttpGet">
  <operation name="GetStockDetails">
    <input message="s0:GetStockDetailsHttpGetIn" />
    <output message="s0:GetStockDetailsHttpGetOut" />
  </operation>
  </portType>
  <binding name="StockHttpGet" type="s0:StockHttpGet">
  <http:binding verb="GET" />
  <operation name="GetStockDetails">
  <http:operation location="/scripts/webquote.dll" />
  <input>
    <http:urlEncoded />
  </input>
  <output>
```

```xml
    <msType:text>
      <msType:match name="CompanyName" pattern="HEIGHT=18
        NOWRAP&gt;&lt;B&gt;(.*?)&lt;/B&gt;&lt;/TH&gt;&lt;/TR&gt;"
        ignorecase="true" />
      <msType:match name="LastPrice"
        pattern="&lt;TD&gt;Last&lt;/TD&gt;&lt;TD ALIGN=RIGHT
        NOWRAP&gt;&lt;B&gt; (.*?)&lt;/B&gt;&lt;/TD&gt;"
        ignorecare="true" />
      <msType:match name="Change" pattern="Change&lt;/TD&gt;&lt;TD
        ALIGN=RIGHT NOWRAP&gt; (.*?)&lt;/TD&gt;" ignorecare="true"
        />
      <msType:match name="PercentChange" pattern="%
        Change&lt;/TD&gt;&lt;TD ALIGN=RIGHT
        NOWRAP&gt; (.*?)&lt;/TD&gt;&lt;TD" ignorecase="true" />
      <msType:match name="Volume" pattern="Volume&lt;/TD&gt;&lt;TD
        ALIGN=RIGHT NOWRAP&gt; (.*?)&lt;/TD&gt;&lt;TD"
        ignorecase="true" />
      <msType:match name="DaysHigh" pattern="Day's High&lt;/TD&gt;&lt;TD
        ALIGN=RIGHT NOWRAP&gt; (.*?)&lt;/TD&gt;&lt;TD"
        ignorecase="true" />
      <msType:match name="DaysLow" pattern="Day's Low&lt;/TD&gt;&lt;TD
        ALIGN=RIGHT NOWRAP&gt; (.*?)&lt;/TD&gt;&lt;TD"
        ignorecase="true" />
    </msType:text>
  </output>
 </operation>
</binding>
<service name="StockQuote">
  <port name="StockHttpGet" binding="s0:StockHttpGet">
    <http:address location="http://moneycentral.msn.com" />
  </port>
</service>
</definitions>
```

The great thing about using WSDL and this document built for screen scraping is that you can specify everything that is needed in this one document including the end location, parameters, and the regular expressions that are needed to scrape the page.

As you can see from the document, screen scraping doesn't involve sending SOAP packets back and forth as is the default with XML Web services. Instead, it uses HTTP-GET to perform all the operations needed.

The end user of the application that you build is going to consume this just as if it were an XML Web service. At the end of the document, the `<services>` node specifies the name of the service. This section of the document specifies the location where the scraping is going to occur.

The `<message>` node specifies the parameters that are sent into the page, if there are any. In this case, you want to send in a single parameter, a value for the `Symbol` parameter.

```
<message name="GetStockDetailsHttpGetIn">
    <part name="Symbol" type="s:string" />
</message>
```

Doing this enables you to build a consuming application used to send in a different stock symbol for each request and to get back data based upon that particular symbol.

The `<binding>` node specifies more explicitly the end point of the Web page that is going to be scraped, using the operation `GetStockDetails`.

```
<operation name="GetStockDetails">
   <http:operation location="/scripts/webquote.dll" />
```

This part of the document also specifies the data that is going to be scraped from the Web page using the `<msType:match>` nodes. You should have a least one of these nodes. In this case, seven pieces of information are to be scraped from the screen based upon the single parameter that is being passed in.

As you look at the value of the pattern attribute in the `<msType:match>` node, you might be wondering what this big mess of characters means. Each one of these characters has a specific meaning, and you must get them right if you are going to make a proper match.

For example, the first item that is being matched in this document is the company's name. If you study the outputted HTML, you find a string of code that you want to match. To get the company's name, examine the following HTML:

```
<TH ALIGN=LEFT CLASS=smallfontreverse COLSPAN=7 HEIGHT=18 NOWRAP><B>
Reuters Group PLC</B></TH></TR>
```

It isn't necessary to match the entire string, just the parts of the string that make the pattern search unique in the document. The pattern search is done in two parts: the piece before the item that you are looking for and the piece of the string that immediately follows this same item. For instance, the first part of the string prior the company's name that you can directly match is

```
HEIGHT=18 NOWRAP><B>
```

Mapped out as a regular expression, this reads as

```
HEIGHT=18 NOWRAP&gt;&lt;B&gt;
```

To match a company name of any size, you use a wildcard:

```
(.*?)
```

Finally, using a regular expression, you specify the part of the string that immediately follows the company's name:

```
&lt;/B&gt;&lt;/TH&gt;&lt;/TR&gt;
```

To help you understand the differences between the actual text and the text as it is explained in the regular expression view, here are some quick pointers:

<   is represented as   <

>   is represented as   >

"   is represented as   .

By using regular expressions, you can pretty much specify whatever data you want to scrape. Table 23-1 lists some of the regular expressions that you can use in your WSDL document to match the exact string you are looking for.

Table 23-1 Regular Expressions

Regular Expression	Description
ordinary characters	Characters other than . $ ^ { [(|) * + ? \ match themselves.
\a	Matches a bell (alarm) \u0007.
\b	Matches a backspace \u0008 if in a [ ] character class; otherwise, see the note following this table.
\t	Matches a tab \u0009.
\r	Matches a carriage return \u000D.
\v	Matches a vertical tab \u000B.
\f	Matches a form feed \u000C.
\n	Matches a new line \u000A.
\e	Matches an escape \u001B.
\040	Matches an ASCII character as octal (up to three digits); numbers with no leading zero are backreferences if they have only one digit or if they correspond to a capturing group number. The character \040 represents a space.
\x20	Matches an ASCII character using hexadecimal representation (exactly two digits).
\cC	Matches an ASCII control character; for example, \cC is control-C.
\u0020	Matches a Unicode character using hexadecimal representation (exactly four digits).
\	When followed by a character that is not recognized as an escaped character, matches that character. For example, * is the same as \x2A.
.	Matches any character except \n. If modified by the Singleline option, a period character matches any character.

Regular Expression	Description
`[aeiou]`	Matches any single character included in the specified set of characters.
`[^aeiou]`	Matches any single character not in the specified set of characters.
`[0-9a-fA-F]`	Use of a hyphen (-) allows specification of contiguous character ranges.
`\p{name}`	Matches any character in the named character class specified by name. Supported names are Unicode groups and block ranges. For example (`Ll`, `Nd`, `Z`, `IsGreek`, `IsBoxDrawing`).
`\P{name}`	Matches text not included in groups and block ranges specified in `{name}`.
`\w`	Matches any word character. Equivalent to the Unicode character categories

After you have built the WSDL document, you are ready to create the proxy class.

Building the proxy class

Creating a proxy class from a WSDL document is fairly simple and has already been explained fully in Chapter 9. Using the `wsdl.exe` tool, you can easily create this class.

VB

```
wsdl.exe /language:VB StockQuote.wsdl
```

C#

```
wsdl.exe /language:CS StockQuote.wsdl
```

After the proxy class is created, you get the following class files (Listing 23-2):

Listing 23-2: StockQuote.vb and StockQuote.cs

VB

```
'------------------------------------------------------------
' <autogenerated>
'    This code was generated by a tool.
'    Runtime Version: 1.0.3512.0
'
'    Changes to this file may cause incorrect behavior and will be lost if
'    the code is regenerated.
' </autogenerated>
'------------------------------------------------------------

Option Strict Off
```

```
Option Explicit On

Imports System
Imports System.ComponentModel
Imports System.Diagnostics
Imports System.Web.Services
Imports System.Web.Services.Protocols
Imports System.Xml.Serialization

'
'This source code was auto-generated by wsdl, Version=1.0.3512.0.
'

'<remarks/>
<System.Diagnostics.DebuggerStepThroughAttribute(),  _
 System.ComponentModel.DesignerCategoryAttribute("code")>  _
Public Class StockQuote
    Inherits System.Web.Services.Protocols.HttpGetClientProtocol

    '<remarks/>
    Public Sub New()
        MyBase.New
        Me.Url = "http://moneycentral.msn.com"
    End Sub

    '<remarks/>
<System.Web.Services.Protocols.HttpMethodAttribute(GetType(System.Web.
 Services.Protocols.TextReturnReader),
 GetType(System.Web.Services.Protocols.UrlParameterWriter))>  _
    Public Function GetStockDetails(ByVal Symbol As String) As
            GetStockDetailsMatches
        Return CType(Me.Invoke("GetStockDetails", (Me.Url +
            "/scripts/webquote.dll"), New Object()
            {Symbol}),GetStockDetailsMatches)
    End Function

    '<remarks/>
    Public Function BeginGetStockDetails(ByVal Symbol As String, ByVal
            callback As System.AsyncCallback, ByVal asyncState As
            Object) As System.IAsyncResult
        Return Me.BeginInvoke("GetStockDetails", (Me.Url +
            "/scripts/webquote.dll"), New Object() {Symbol}, callback,
            asyncState)
    End Function

    '<remarks/>
    Public Function EndGetStockDetails(ByVal asyncResult As
            System.IAsyncResult) As GetStockDetailsMatches
```

Chapter 23: Screen Scraping 515

```
            Return CType(Me.EndInvoke(asyncResult),GetStockDetailsMatches)
    End Function
End Class

Public Class GetStockDetailsMatches

    <System.Web.Services.Protocols.MatchAttribute("HEIGHT=18
            NOWRAP><B>(.*?)</B></TH></TR>")>  _
    Public CompanyName As String

    <System.Web.Services.Protocols.MatchAttribute("<TD>Last</TD><TD
            ALIGN=RIGHT NOWRAP><B> (.*?)</B></TD>")>  _
    Public LastPrice As String

    <System.Web.Services.Protocols.MatchAttribute("Change</TD><TD
            ALIGN=RIGHT NOWRAP> (.*?)</TD>")>  _
    Public Change As String

    <System.Web.Services.Protocols.MatchAttribute("% Change</TD><TD
            ALIGN=RIGHT NOWRAP> (.*?)</TD><TD")>  _
    Public PercentChange As String

    <System.Web.Services.Protocols.MatchAttribute("Volume</TD><TD
            ALIGN=RIGHT NOWRAP> (.*?)</TD><TD")>  _
    Public Volume As String

    <System.Web.Services.Protocols.MatchAttribute("Day's High</TD><TD
            ALIGN=RIGHT NOWRAP> (.*?)</TD><TD")>  _
    Public DaysHigh As String

    <System.Web.Services.Protocols.MatchAttribute("Day's Low</TD><TD
            ALIGN=RIGHT NOWRAP> (.*?)</TD><TD")>  _
    Public DaysLow As String
End Class
```

C#

```
//------------------------------------------------------------------------
// <autogenerated>
// This code was generated by a tool.
// Runtime Version: 1.0.3512.0
//
// Changes to this file may cause incorrect behavior and will be lost if
// the code is regenerated.
// </autogenerated>
//------------------------------------------------------------------------


//
// This source code was auto-generated by wsdl, Version=1.0.3512.0.
```

```csharp
//
using System.Diagnostics;
using System.Xml.Serialization;
using System;
using System.Web.Services.Protocols;
using System.ComponentModel;
using System.Web.Services;


/// <remarks/>
[System.Diagnostics.DebuggerStepThroughAttribute()]
[System.ComponentModel.DesignerCategoryAttribute("code")]
public class StockQuote :
System.Web.Services.Protocols.HttpGetClientProtocol {

    /// <remarks/>
    public StockQuote() {
        this.Url = "http://moneycentral.msn.com";
    }

    /// <remarks/>
[System.Web.Services.Protocols.HttpMethodAttribute(typeof(System.Web.
 Services.Protocols.TextReturnReader),
 typeof(System.Web.Services.Protocols.UrlParameterWriter))]
    public GetStockDetailsMatches GetStockDetails(string Symbol) {
        return ((GetStockDetailsMatches)(this.Invoke("GetStockDetails",
          (this.Url + "/scripts/webquote.dll"), new object[] {
                Symbol})));
    }

    /// <remarks/>
    public System.IAsyncResult BeginGetStockDetails(string Symbol,
          System.AsyncCallback callback, object asyncState) {
        return this.BeginInvoke("GetStockDetails", (this.Url +
          "/scripts/webquote.dll"), new object[] {
                Symbol}, callback, asyncState);
    }

    /// <remarks/>
    public GetStockDetailsMatches EndGetStockDetails(System.IAsyncResult
          asyncResult) {
        return ((GetStockDetailsMatches)(this.EndInvoke(asyncResult)));
    }
}

public class GetStockDetailsMatches {

    [System.Web.Services.Protocols.MatchAttribute("HEIGHT=18
```

```
            NOWRAP><B>(.*?)</B></TH></TR>")]
    public string CompanyName;

    [System.Web.Services.Protocols.MatchAttribute("<TD>Last</TD><TD
     ALIGN=RIGHT NOWRAP><B> (.*?)</B></TD>")]
    public string LastPrice;

    [System.Web.Services.Protocols.MatchAttribute("Change</TD><TD
     ALIGN=RIGHT NOWRAP> (.*?)</TD>")]
    public string Change;

    [System.Web.Services.Protocols.MatchAttribute("% Change</TD><TD
     ALIGN=RIGHT NOWRAP> (.*?)</TD><TD")]
    public string PercentChange;

    [System.Web.Services.Protocols.MatchAttribute("Volume</TD><TD
     ALIGN=RIGHT NOWRAP> (.*?)</TD><TD")]
    public string Volume;

    [System.Web.Services.Protocols.MatchAttribute("Day\'s High</TD><TD
     ALIGN=RIGHT NOWRAP> (.*?)</TD><TD")]
    public string DaysHigh;

    [System.Web.Services.Protocols.MatchAttribute("Day\'s Low</TD><TD
     ALIGN=RIGHT NOWRAP> (.*?)</TD><TD")]
    public string DaysLow;
}
```

This proxy class is pretty representative of what was in the WSDL document. There is a description of the parameters and the end location of the Web site where the scraping is going to take place. Most interestingly, the regular expressions that were in the WSDL document have been converted to regular text.

The proxy class is set up for synchronous or asynchronous programming. You can easily invoke the request and then continue onto some additional programming before returning to get the result scraped from the final destination. This is an ideal situation in a lot of cases because screen scraping is just as time-consuming as working with an XML Web service (even more so in some cases).

It is possible to actually start this entire process from the proxy class and completely avoid building a WSDL document from scratch. It can be a little trickier, however, to begin by building the proxy class. That's why I recommend starting with the WSDL document and using `wsdl.exe` to generate the proxy classes.

The delicate nature of screen scraping

Screen scraping is a tough business. Don't ever build any mission-critical applications that require information from screen scraping in order to continue functioning.

Screen scraping is a delicate operation because it is completely based upon matching specific HTML that is generated by a page that is not under your control. Developers change pages over time. The pages are re-engineered to perform better, to provide new functionality, or just to undergo a layout change.

If changes are made, the outputted HTML changes, and then your regular expressions can't find the particular pattern match that they are looking for. If your regular expressions don't find a match, nothing will be returned. In fact, by the time you try out the code from these examples, the HTML outputted by MSN may have changed and you won't get the same results.

For this reason, do not rely too heavily on screen scraping and check results quite regularly. If the HTML does change, you simply redo your regular expressions in the WSDL document and then re-create the proxy class to use within your application.

Building a consuming application

Now comes the fun part! To build your screen-scraping client, start by building an ASP.NET Web Form (Listing 23-3).

Listing 23-3: GetStockQuote.aspx

```
<%@ Page Language="vb" AutoEventWireup="false"
    Codebehind="GetStockQuote.aspx.vb"
    Inherits="ScreenScrapVB.GetStockQuote"%>
<!DOCTYPE HTML PUBLIC "-//W3C//DTD HTML 4.0 Transitional//EN">
<HTML>
 <HEAD>
  <title>GetStockQuote</title>
  <meta name="GENERATOR" content="Microsoft Visual Studio.NET 7.0">
  <meta name="CODE_LANGUAGE" content="Visual Basic 7.0">
  <meta name="vs_defaultClientScript" content="JavaScript">
  <meta name="vs_targetSchema"
   content="http://schemas.microsoft.com/intellisense/ie5">
 </HEAD>
 <body>
  <form id="Form1" method="post" runat="server">
   <P>
    <asp:TextBox id="TextBox1" runat="server"></asp:TextBox></P>
   <P>
    <asp:Button id="Button1" runat="server" Text="Get
     Quote"></asp:Button></P>
   <P>
    <asp:Literal id="Literal1" runat="server"></asp:Literal></P>
  </form>
 </body>
</HTML>
```

This form simply has a text box, a button, and a literal control to output the response. The idea is that the end user can enter the stock symbol into the text box and then get back a stock quote after clicking the button to initiate the button-click event. The code-behind page should be constructed in the following manner (Listing 23-4):

Listing 23-4: GetStockQuote.aspx.vb and GetStockQuote.cs

VB

```
Public Class GetStockQuote
    Inherits System.Web.UI.Page
    Protected WithEvents TextBox1 As System.Web.UI.WebControls.TextBox
    Protected WithEvents Button1 As System.Web.UI.WebControls.Button
    Protected WithEvents Literal1 As System.Web.UI.WebControls.Literal

    Private Sub Page_Load(ByVal sender As System.Object, ByVal e As _
      System.EventArgs) Handles MyBase.Load

    End Sub

    Private Sub Button1_Click(ByVal sender As System.Object, ByVal e As _
      System.EventArgs) Handles Button1.Click
        Dim sq As New StockQuote()
        Dim match As GetStockDetailsMatches

        match = sq.GetStockDetails(TextBox1.Text)

        Literal1.Text = "<b>" & match.CompanyName & "</b><P>" & _
            "Last Price: " & match.LastPrice & _
            "<br>Change: " & match.Change & _
            "<br>Percent Change: " & match.PercentChange & _
            "<br>Volume: " & match.Volume & _
            "<br>Day's High: " & match.DaysHigh & _
            "<br>Day's Low: " & match.DaysLow
    End Sub
End Class
```

C#

```
using System;
using System.Collections;
using System.ComponentModel;
using System.Data;
using System.Drawing;
using System.Web;
using System.Web.SessionState;
using System.Web.UI;
```

```csharp
using System.Web.UI.WebControls;
using System.Web.UI.HtmlControls;

namespace WebApplication1
{
 public class GetStockQuote : System.Web.UI.Page
 {
  protected System.Web.UI.WebControls.TextBox TextBox1;
  protected System.Web.UI.WebControls.Button Button1;
  protected System.Web.UI.WebControls.Literal Literal1;

  private void Button1_Click(object sender, System.EventArgs e)
  {
   StockQuote sq = new StockQuote();
   GetStockDetailsMatches match;

   match = sq.GetStockDetails(TextBox1.Text);

   Literal1.Text = "<b>" + match.CompanyName + "</b><P>" +
           "Last Price: " + match.LastPrice +
           "<br>Change: " + match.Change +
           "<br>Percent Change: " + match.PercentChange +
           "<br>Volume: " + match.Volume +
           "<br>Day's High: " + match.DaysHigh +
           "<br>Day's Low: " + match.DaysLow;
  }
 }
}
```

The first thing to do in the button-click event is to create an instance of the `StockQuote` class that enables you to have programmatic access to the screen-scraping method `GetStockDetails()`. The parameter passed into this method is the value that is passed into the TextBox1 control.

The great thing now is that you also have IntelliSense available, and you can see all the available items that can be returned from the HTTP-GET call. In this example, you simply return all the available information items from the screen scraping, including the company's name, that are related to the stock: the stock's last price, the change in price, percentage change, volume, the day's high price, and the day's low price. All this information is passed into the Literal control along with some formatting HTML. The end result is displayed in Figure 23-2.

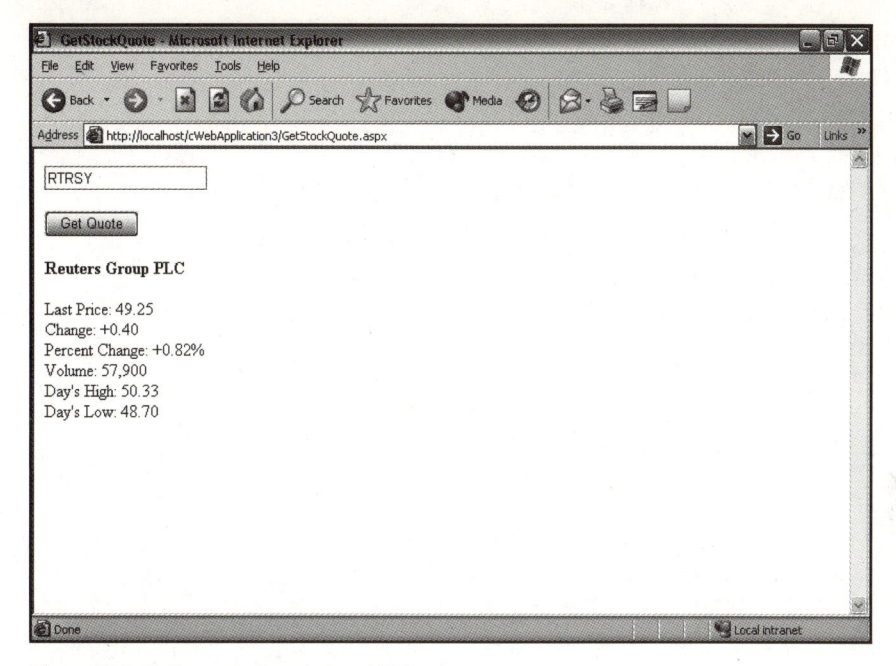

Figure 23-2: Getting a stock quote from MSN.

Summary

As you can tell, after going through a few steps and using some of the tools and technologies that are provided with XML Web services, you have the ability to use Web pages that are on the Internet as data sources. After you are tied into these data sources, you can use their data within your own applications.

This chapter showed you how to consume data from a screen scrape that required you to pass in a parameter in order to get back a result. It is quite possible, however, to build screen-scraping classes that do not require any parameters or that require multiple parameters.

Now that you have this knowledge, you need to think about how to use it. It is not the best practice to simply go out there and grab all the data that you need from Web pages whether the owners of this data want you to have it or not. It would be nice if you first got permission to harvest the data to use within your applications. So, ask first. Read copyright pages. And stay out of trouble.

Part IX

.NET My Services and .NET Remoting

Chapter 24: .NET My Services

Chapter 25: .NET Remoting: An Alternative to XML Web Services

Chapter 26: In Conclusion

Chapter 24
.NET My Services

The difficult and risky task of meeting and mastering the new — whether it be the settlement of new lands or the initiation of new ways of life — is not undertaken by the vanguard of society but by its rear. It is the misfits, failures, fugitives, outcasts and their like who are among the first to grapple with the new.
Eric Hoffer, U.S. philosopher. *The Passionate State of Mind* (1955).

XML Web services is a fairly new technology, and many of the things described in this book will change over the next few years as this technology matures. To get an understanding of where XML Web services can lead you, this chapter glimpses into its future — .NET My Services.

.NET My Services was originally introduced to everyone as HailStorm. Yes, it's true that HailStorm is a better name, but Microsoft was forced to change it for legal reasons. The new name is so dazzling, it could have been created by the U.S. Government.

.NET My Services is a collection of XML Web services that are meant to make it easier for developers to build user-oriented applications. .NET My Services are really XML Web services and, therefore, use the same standards as XML Web services such as XML, SOAP, and HTTP.

This chapter gives you a bird's-eye view of what .NET My Services are and what you can expect from them after they have been introduced.

What Exactly Is .NET My Services?

Not only did Microsoft build the means to construct XML Web services with ease, it also introduced a complete line of these services that will be offered to the public. The .NET My Services initiative was announced by Microsoft on March 19, 2001.

You, as a developer or IT Manager, might use these services and incorporate their functionality in some of your applications. This chapter is only an overview of .NET My Services because this technology is literally in the beginning stages, and changes are occurring constantly as this tool set evolves.

Each of these XML Web services is a service that Microsoft will provide and that will make the life of the end user easier as he finds more and more devices and applications that can be connected to the Internet.

Specific .NET My Services

Take a look at a list of the planned .NET My Services. Some of these services are already available for use in your applications, and some are still in development. These .NET My Services comprise Version 1 of the .NET My Services offerings, although as the business plan and the development of this new product line evolves, some of the services might not be offered in the end.

Table 24-1 .NET My Services

.NET My Service	*Description*
.NET Passport	This service is available today and provides authentication and authorization capabilities.
.NET Profile	This service enables users to store personal information such as birthdays, addresses, special dates, and pictures.
.NET Contacts	This service stores a user's personal and professional contacts and allows the user to share all or part of the contact list.
.NET Locations	This service enables the end user to specify his location. For instance, a user could assign his location to be home, work, or somewhere else. These location assignments could then be shared with other applications or individuals.
.NET Alerts	This is one of the more exciting .NET My Services. This service provides alert subscription, management, and routing.
.NET Presence	This services works with .NET Alerts in the sense that .NET Presence holds the end user's presence information: where the user want to receive his alerts. Some sample options include Online/Offline/Busy/Away/On-Phone/Off-Phone.
.NET Inbox	This allows the user to check his e-mail and voice mail from any device.
.NET Calendar	This service stores the user's calendar information and shows if the user is free or busy at particular moments. The user has the ability to open up his calendar to others.
.NET Documents	This service enables users to store documents so that the documents are accessible from any device at any time.
.NET ApplicationSettings	This service enables a user who logs onto any system to have access to his toolbars, icons, and screensavers that have been saved to the service. It allows for customization and personalization of a system regardless of location.
.NET FavoriteWebSites	This allows a user to store his Web site favorites (a collection of favorite URLs) so that he can access these links from a separate device.

.NET My Service	Description
.NET Wallet	This service allows the end user to store credit card and shipping information so that he doesn't need to re-enter this information into a commerce site each time that a purchase is made.
.NET Devices	This service enables a user to specify the devices that will be used with the other .NET My Services, including the capabilities of the device.
.NET Services	This service acts as an administrative tool, giving users the ability to turn on or off access to particular .NET My Services.
.NET Lists	This service enables the user to store lists of any kind including TO DO lists, shopping lists, member lists, and more.
.NET Categories	This service allows for a standard list of categories to be available across all the user services.

As you can tell from the services and their descriptions, these .NET My Services are meant to be user-centric services as opposed to application-centric services. These .NET My Services are there for users to store information in a secure environment where each user is the controller of the keys to unlock his information. Users can appoint access to these storage boxes of information to other individuals, groups, companies, or applications. Once given access, these appointed entities can use these services to better serve their customers by providing authentication, notifications, and alerts.

To get a glimpse of the power of these services and how they will affect application development, look at .NET Passport. This service provides end users the means of storing their login credentials to a central data store that can be used in multiple applications throughout the Internet as a means of authenticating and authorizing users. Presently .NET Passport has over 165 million users and is used in a number of different places throughout the Internet today. .NET Passport will be used in conjunction with the other .NET My Services to provide access to the control of the other services.

Before .NET My Services

This section shows you a time before .NET My Services (which is basically now) and then shows you where .NET My Services is going to take us. Figure 24-1 shows an example of how an end user deals with different devices in the Internet world of today.

In this model, the end user deals with multiple devices during his day. His cell phone, his PDA, and his laptop are each connected to a data store for various sorts of information. He might have his contact information stored in the cell phone, his calendar information in a PDA, and both contact and calendar information stored in a laptop. The problem is that this data is often replicated in multiple data stores across the Internet and when he wants to make changes, these changes must be made to each data store.

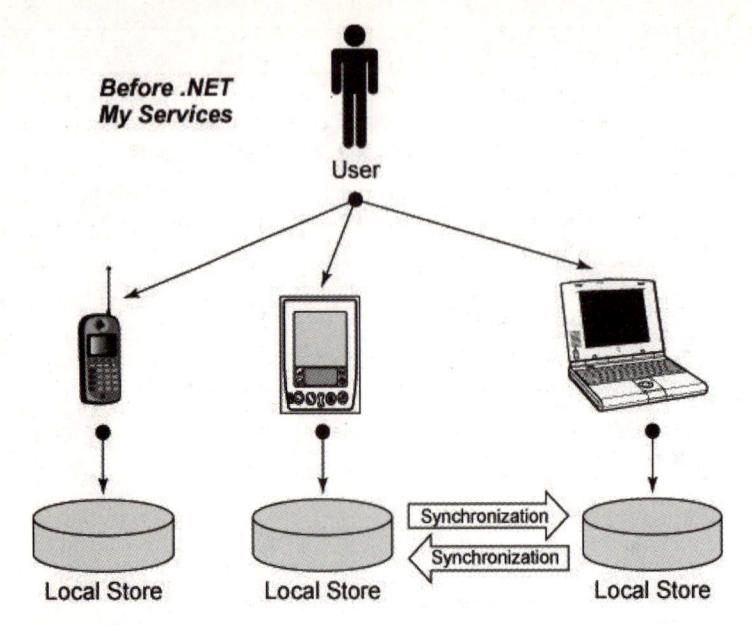

Figure 24-1: Before .NET My Services: All device data stores were kept separate or were difficult to synchronize.

Sharing information between these disparate data stores can be quite difficult and sometimes impossible. Sometimes there is a capability to synchronize data stores, but this has to be initiated by the end user. Therefore, the end user must always remember and take the time to perform the synchronization. Beyond the synchronization of larger devices, many new smaller devices will require reprogramming for new replicated data stores. These actions take time.

With .NET My Services

Now take a look at where .NET My Services can take you. Figure 24-2 shows an example of the same end user with multiple devices that have the capability to use a shared data store.

With .NET My Services, the end user has a single shared data store where all his information can be stored. This means that his cell phone's contact list will now be the same contact list that is used by the PDA or by Outlook on his laptop. The information stored will always be up-to-date and completely in sync. These different devices all share the same data store, and this data store is available from any of the devices at any time.

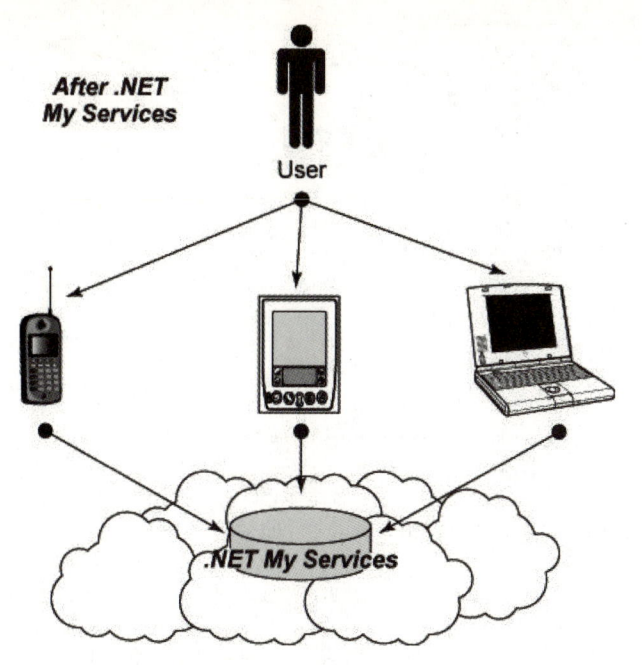

Figure 24-2: After .NET My Services: All devices will be able to share a single data store.

Along with this increased capability is the option of opening this data store to others, including individuals, groups, companies, or even other applications. .NET My Services offers the capability to fine-tune the level of access; so you are not required to completely open up the entire data store, but you have the option of opening specific parts.

You can see the power of this concept and how it will make programming an application easier. Your ability, as a developer, to tie in to these services will greatly increase your application's functionality and speed the development process. In addition to this, Microsoft will incorporate the capability to program .NET My Services directly from Visual Studio .NET. It will be just as easy to work with .NET My Services in Visual Studio .NET as it is to work with XML Web services.

These services are not meant to be used only by individuals. Groups and companies can use these services (see Figure 24-3). For instance, a company can use .NET Contacts to store all its contact information and then assign access to specific parts of the contact system to selected individuals or groups. The company can open up all the business leads to every member of its sales force.

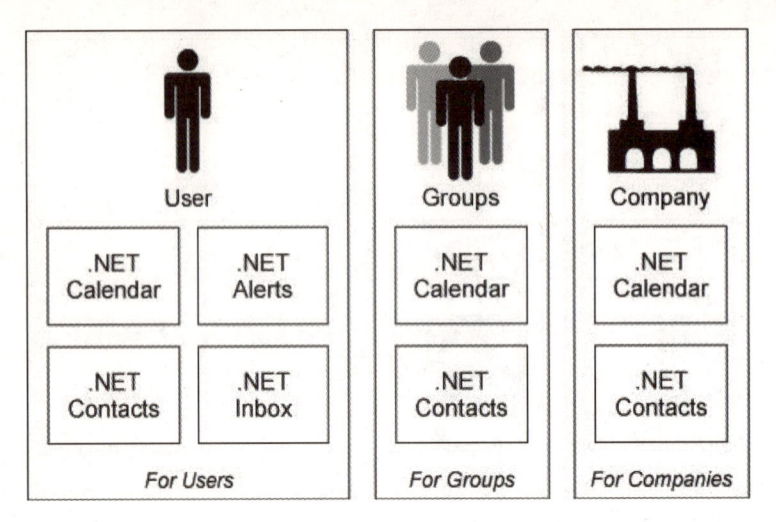

Figure 24-3: .NET My Services is not just for individual users, but also for groups and companies.

.NET Alerts

To give you an idea of some of the power behind .NET My Services, take a look at .NET Alerts, one of the .NET My Services available in Version 1. You probably have already dealt with .NET Alerts in one way or another as you work day-to-day on your computer. If you are running one of the latest versions of Microsoft's Instant Messenger, you might have noticed that when someone sends you a message through this tool, a square box slides open in the lower-right-hand corner of your desktop. This is affectionately called *toast* (Figure 24-4).

Figure 24-4: Toast showing a message arriving using .NET Alerts.

.NET Alerts works with .NET Passport, .NET Presence, and .NET Locations to cause this toast to pop up on your screen. You are logged into the Instant Messenger using .NET Passport. Using .NET Presence and .NET Locations, the message can be displayed in the appropriate place.

Think of the power behind just this one .NET My Service. For instance, suppose that an overnight delivery company is tied into using .NET Alerts. After the company has delivered a package to its final destination, .NET Alerts sends an alert to the end recipient of the package, informing him that the package has arrived and is with the receptionist on the first floor. This information comes across as a toast alert that pops up on the user's screen.

Other examples of using this alert system are meeting notices, auction notifications, traffic announcements, weather bulletins, and more. These alerts also don't have to go only to your operating system on your desktop computer, but can also be sent to other devices, including cell phones, PDAs, and pagers.

What's Next?

The services that I have described thus far are the first planned .NET My Services to come out the door from Microsoft. Plans are already underway for the next set of .NET My Services to head out the door. Possible future .NET My Services include the following:

- .NET Portfolio
- .NET Photos
- .NET Travel
- .NET Music
- .NET Movies
- .NET TV
- .NET Wishlist
- .NET School
- .NET Groceries
- .NET News
- .NET Sports
- .NET TopScores

As you can tell, there will plenty to choose from and to use within your applications if desired. The power of these services is incredible, and it isn't only Microsoft that is headed in this direction. AOL/Time Warner is in the process of creating its own services that will directly compete with Microsoft's .NET My Services. I suspect it will not be the last company to do so.

Now Wait a Minute ...

You might be wondering about the security implications of this model. Does this idea mean that Microsoft has the intention of storing everyone's private and personal information? You might be questioning whether a company should hold everyone's data, including contact information, location, calendars, and documents.

No, this is not a means for Microsoft to control the world. It has been developed and structured so that the information you store in these services is locked down, and you are the only individual who can access it. This means that no one at Microsoft and no one outside of Microsoft (except the people that you appoint) will have any sort of access to the information that is stored.

You can think of .NET My Services as a safe deposit box inside of a bank. If you obtain a safe deposit box in the bank, you are the only one who can access the box. Even the bank, the holder of the box and the company keeping the box secure, will not be able to access it.

In addition to storing this information, Microsoft will be looking to trusted third-party companies to store additional .NET My Services data stores so that you, as an end user, can make a decision about where you want your data stored.

Summary

This chapter examined where XML Web services is leading not only the end user, but also the application developers who build the applications that will integrate with .NET My Services.

The power of XML Web services is strong and the most aggressive change so far to technology that works over the Internet. .NET My Services is a part of this change because it is based upon XML Web services and the technologies and tools that make up XML Web services.

Chapter 25
.NET Remoting: An Alternative to XML Web Services

The difficulty in life is the choice.
George Moore, *The Bending of the Bough* (1900)

This chapter reviews another possibility for working with remote objects in .NET. Besides using XML Web services for working with remote objects in .NET, you can also use .NET Remoting. This technology is quite different from working with XML Web services; and in this chapter, you will learn the basic concepts of this technology.

More specifically, this chapter will cover

- Reviewing the .NET Remoting architecture
- Understanding the terminology
- Working with server and client objects
- Configuring remotable objects
- Hosting remotable objects

.NET Remoting Basics

.NET Remoting enables applications running on separate application domains to communicate using objects. These applications can reside on separate servers or even on the same server – just as long as they are in separate application domains. Like XML Web services, the objects are not concerned with the operating system of the consuming application. As long as the consuming application can consume either binary or SOAP messages that are SOAP 1.1-compliant, it is able to work with .NET Remoting.

XML Web Services versus .NET Remoting

As you have seen throughout this book, XML Web services is a powerful technology with the outstanding capability to call remote methods across the wire. .NET Remoting is also a great technology in this arena, but it works with the entire object and not just particular methods of the object. It's brought to you by the same folks that brought you XML Web services — Microsoft.

The main difference between these two technologies is that .NET Remoting allows for a lower level of programming that enables you to code directly to the APIs. With .NET Remoting you can control the means of communication and choose the protocol and the format that is used in the message transport. .NET Remoting, therefore, is not quite as easy to work with as XML Web services. You simply put a WebMethod attribute in front of any of your methods to easily create an XML Web service. Working with .NET Remoting is not as simple, but that shouldn't stop you from using this technology. XML Web services is not the answer to every client/server remote object call. There are situations where .NET Remoting will work better to meet your needs.

Another difference between XML Web services and .NET Remoting is that XML Web services can only be hosted on IIS, whereas .NET Remoting can be hosted on IIS, a Windows Form, a Windows Console application, a Windows Service, or any other type of application. This is one of the great features of .NET Remoting, and why you might choose .NET Remoting over XML Web services. Because .NET Remoting enables you to host in locations other than IIS, you are not limited to using HTTP protocol. You are also able to use protocols such as TCP or another custom protocol that you might develop.

A third difference between the two technologies is that with XML Web services you use HTTP-GET, HTTP-POST, or SOAP in the transmission of your messages across the wire. With .NET Remoting, you also have the option of using binary encoding in the formation of your objects.

.NET Remoting Architecture

.NET Remoting is a communication model between two application domains or isolated processes. You can think of .NET Remoting as a replacement for DCOM. Working with DCOM was often quite difficult. DCOM only worked on specific ports, and often encountered problems with firewalls in the call and consumption of the remote objects it offered. DCOM also used a ping in order to keep objects alive, and this was quite expensive in terms of a server's resources. .NET has eliminated this.

.NET Remoting allows you, as the client that is consuming the remote object, to create an instance of the object client-side by simply using the new keyword. After this object is instantiated on the client, you have programmatic access to the object just as if it were in the same process as your client application, even though it actually resides in a completely separate process — even on a completely separate machine. Just as in XML Web services, this is done by creating a proxy class that fools the client process into thinking that the object is local when it is actually in a remote process.

Channels

In order for two separate application processes to communicate with each other, a *transport channel* is opened between the processes. A transport channel is a combination of underlying technologies required to open a network connection and use a particular protocol to send the bytes to the receiving application. .NET Remoting uses two possible default channels as the transport channels, HttpChannel and TcpChannel. A channel works with a stream of data and creates an object based upon the transport protocol. Some available protocols can only work in a single direction, but the HTTP and TCP channels can work in either direction.

The HttpChannel uses HTTP as its means of transport. HTTP is a firewall-friendly transport because HTTP traffic generally flows directly through firewalls. Because it uses HTTP, HttpChannel uses SOAP as a means of moving objects across an open channel.

The TcpChannel uses TCP as the means of moving objects across an open channel. This type of protocol is more suited for an intranet environment because an intranet sits behind a firewall, and TCP does not cross firewalls. Using TCP also means that a binary formatter is used by default, and this actually reduces the size of the object that is being transported. Having smaller packages to transport allows for better and faster network communication.

Ports

When dealing with ports, .NET Remoting does not impose the same stringent requirements as XML Web services. XML Web services always use the port that is assigned to the server's HTTP traffic. .NET Remoting, however, allows you to assign a channel to any available port. This can play quite well with an increased demand for security.

Formatters

After a channel is established through a specific port, a formatter object is needed to initiate the serialization or deserialization of the object. There are two available formatters in .NET Remoting. The first is the SoapFormatter, and the other is the BinaryFormatter.

In order for an object to move through the channel from one application process to another, the formatter must take the object that you are sending and serialize it into the network stream.

SoapFormatter

The `SoapFormatter` class is the default formatter when using an HttpChannel with .NET Remoting and serializes any objects that it receives into a SOAP 1.1-compliant text format. The HttpChannel uses the `SoapFormatter` to serialize the objects that it sends through the channel. After the object is received and serialized into XML, this formatter also adds any appropriate SOAP Headers to the message before it is sent through the channel.

After the message that is sent through the channel is received in the client application, the client uses the `SoapFormatter` to deserialize the object.

BinaryFormatter

The `BinaryFormatter` class is typically used when sending an object through a TCP network protocol. As stated earlier, when objects are sent using the `BinaryFormatter`, these objects are more compact and, therefore, are less resource intensive for the server that is sending the object.

Figure 25-1 shows the process of sending objects through channels using .NET Remoting.

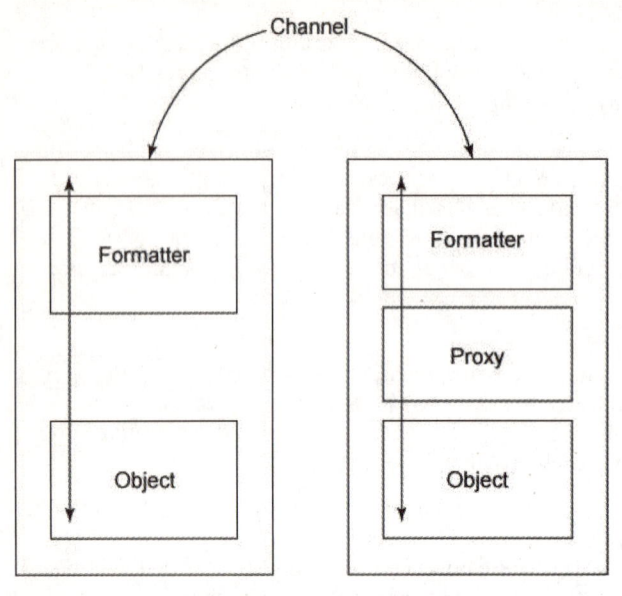

Figure 25-1: Moving an object across a channel using .NET Remoting.

In this diagram, there are two main boxes, each of which represents a separate application process. In order to have an object jump from one process to another, you must establish a channel across the processes. This channel can be either an HttpChannel or a TcpChannel.

In order to get the object from the process to the channel and on its way, the object is serialized into the network stream, and this is done using a formatter. The formatter on the server side of the process takes the object and serializes it using either the `SoapFormatter` or the `BinaryFormatter`. The formatter on the receiving end of the process takes this serialized object and deserializes it back into the object it was when the process started. The proxy class is the class that makes the initial request and delivers the response to its final destination.

.NET Remoting Example

The best way to show you how .NET Remoting really works is to have you work through an example. For this example, you create a simple remote object that just says a short hello to the user. This remote object will then be hosted by a separate console application, and finally you create a Windows Form to consume this remote object.

This will be a multistep process. The first step is to create the remote object. The second step is to create a host for the remote object. The third step is to create a client that will consume the remote object through the host. Creating a host and a client for the remoting includes the additional steps of building them with configuration files, as opposed to setting these details programmatically.

Creating the remote object

Start by creating the remote object. To accomplish this, create a brand new Class Library project called `myRemoteService`. Rename the `Class1` class file to `HelloUserClass.vb` or `HelloUserClass.cs`. Then use the code in Listing 25-1 to complete the class file.

Listing 25-1: HelloUserClass.vb / HelloUserClass.cs

VB

```vb
Namespace RemotingSample

    Public Class HelloUserClass
        Inherits MarshalByRefObject
        Public Function HelloUser(ByVal UName As String)
            Console.WriteLine("Hello user: " + UName + " called at " + _
                DateTime.Now.ToString())
            Return "Hello " + UName
        End Function
    End Class

End Namespace
```

C#

```csharp
using System;

namespace RemotingSample
{
 public class HelloUserClass : MarshalByRefObject
 {
  public string HelloUser(string UName)
  {
    Console.WriteLine("Hello user: " + UName + " called at " +
        DateTime.Now.ToString());
    return "Hello " + UName;
  }
 }
}
```

It is important to create a namespace with your class. In this case, you create a class that uses the namespace `RemotingSample`. The `HelloUserClass` must inherit from the `MarshalByRefObject` class because this class is called remotely.

The `HelloUserClass` class only contains one function, `HelloUser`. The `HelloUser` function takes a single parameter, `UName`. Using this parameter, you simply return a statement that includes the value entered:

```
Return "Hello " + UName
```

Before this, however, you write a line directly to the console stating the username that you entered, along with the date and time that the object was instantiated. Note that the console application that will host this remote object has not been built yet; that's the next step.

Creating the host for the remote object

One of the great things about .NET Remoting is that you can host the service in numerous types of applications. Unlike XML Web services that can only be hosted in IIS, .NET Remoting can be hosted in IIS, console applications, Windows Forms, and more. As an example of this, you host the `HelloUserClass` as a remote object in a console application. This is why the remote object has some lines of text to be output to the console window. Whenever the user calls this remote object, it will register in the hosting service by a textual registration output to the screen.

In order to create this host, create a new project and select Console Application. You can name this console application whatever you choose; it won't matter in your code.

In addition to this code, you must make a reference to the remote object. To do this, right-click on the References folder in the Solution Explorer window and select Add Reference. You are presented with the Add Reference dialog window. Select the Projects tab and add your remote object's DLL as a reference in this server application.

Listing 25-2 shows the code to use for this console application. After you have created this file, you will then create a configuration file for this server application as well as make a reference to the remote object.

Listing 25-2: Module1.vb / Class1.cs

VB

```
Imports System.Runtime.Remoting
Module Module1

    Sub Main()
        RemotingConfiguration.Configure("RemoteService.config")
        Console.WriteLine("Service running ...")
        Console.WriteLine("Hit Enter to end service")
        Console.ReadLine()
    End Sub

End Module
```

C#

```
using System;
using System.Runtime.Remoting;

namespace ConsoleApplication1
{
```

```
class Class1
{
 [STAThread]
 static void Main(string[] args)
 {
  RemotingConfiguration.Configure("RemoteService.config");
  Console.WriteLine("Service running ...");
  Console.WriteLine("Hit Enter to end service");
  Console.ReadLine();
 }
}
```

This file has a single routine that is started when the application starts. First, the server configuration file is loaded into the server application that will host the remote object using `RemoteConfiguration.Configure()`. After this, you simply write a few lines to the console window, and then the application waits for you to hit the Enter button. Until you do, the server is running, and it is hosting the remote object.

How is this console application hosting the remote object? It is getting all the information that it needs from the server configuration file.

Creating the server configuration file

In addition to the hosting application for the remote object, this console application also requires a configuration file in order to set the properties of the remote object. It is possible to avoid using a configuration file completely and instead program the configuration details directly into the object itself, but using a configuration file has some advantages. The main advantage in using a configuration file is that the settings for the remote object are kept separate from the code; and therefore, if there are future changes to the settings, you are not forced to recompile.

To create the configuration file follow these steps:

1. In the project of the console application that acts as a server to the remote object, right-click on the project in the Solution Explorer window.
2. Select Add ⇨ Add New Item.
3. Select XML File from the available templates.
4. Change the name of the file to `RemoteService.config`.
5. Use the code in Listing 25-3 to complete the file:

Listing 25-3: RemoteService.config

```
<?xml version="1.0" encoding="utf-8" ?>
<configuration>
 <system.runtime.remoting>
  <application>
   <service>
    <wellknown mode="SingleCall" type="RemotingSample.HelloUserClass,
```

```
            myRemoteService" objectUri="Hello" />
    </service>
    <channels>
      <channel ref="tcp" port="6789" />
      <channel ref="http" port="9100" />
    </channels>
  </application>
 </system.runtime.remoting>
</configuration>
```

Like most configuration files in .NET, this configuration file for the server application that is going to host the remote object is made up of XML. This makes the file easily human-readable.

This configuration file states that this remoting object will be "wellknown" and that the mode of the object will be `SingleCall` mode. This means that the server will create a single instance of the object for each call to the object. After the call to the object is complete, the instance is destroyed. When a second call is made to the remote object, another instance of that object is created. As an alternative to `SingleCall` mode, you can use `Singleton` mode. Using `Singleton` creates only one instance of the object that will be used for each call made to the remote object.

The `type` attribute specifies the namespace, class, and assembly names that are used. The value of the `type` attribute should be constructed in the following manner:

```
Namespace.Class, Assembly
```

In this example, it is written as

```
RemotingSample.HelloUserClass, myRemoteService
```

Within the `<channels>` nodes, you specify the available channels that the consumer of this remote object can use. In this configuration file, there are two possibilities: They can use either TCP port 6789 or HTTP port 9100.

Next, create a client application that will consume this remote object. After the client application loads, the configuration file is read and the remoting channels are registered. After this happens, the remote object's end points are determined and called.

Creating the client application

In the third step of this process, you create a client application that will consume this remote object. Your consuming application can be almost anything, but for the purposes of this example, create a Windows Form application.

Follow these steps to create your Windows Form:

1. Create a new project.
2. Select Windows Application from the available templates.

3. You will be presented with a form. Place a text box, button and label control on the form. This enables the end user of this application to enter his name in the text box with a button click. This triggers a call to the remote object, which will display a greeting message to the user.
4. After all these elements are in place on the form, double-click the button. Doing will take you to the code-behind page. Use the code from Listing 25-4 for your code-behind page.

Listing 25-4: Remoting client

VB

```
Imports System.Runtime.Remoting

Public Class Form1
    Inherits System.Windows.Forms.Form

    Private Sub Button1_Click(ByVal sender As System.Object, ByVal e As _
            System.EventArgs) Handles Button1.Click
        Dim myRemoteObj As New RemotingSample.HelloUserClass()
        Label1.Text = myRemoteObj.HelloUser(TextBox1.Text)
    End Sub

    Private Sub Form1_Load(ByVal sender As System.Object, ByVal e As _
            System.EventArgs) Handles MyBase.Load
        RemotingConfiguration.Configure("../client.config")
    End Sub
End Class
```

C#

```
using System;
using System.Drawing;
using System.Collections;
using System.ComponentModel;
using System.Windows.Forms;
using System.Runtime.Remoting;

namespace Client
{
 public class Form1 : System.Windows.Forms.Form
  {
   private System.Windows.Forms.TextBox textBox1;
   private System.Windows.Forms.Button button1;
   private System.Windows.Forms.Label label1;

   private void button1_Click(object sender, System.EventArgs e)
   {
     RemotingSample.HelloUserClass myRemoteObj = new
         RemotingSample.HelloUserClass();
     Label1.Text = myRemoteObj.HelloUser(TextBox1.Text.ToString());
```

```
    }

    private void Form1_Load(object sender, System.EventArgs e)
    {
      RemotingConfiguration.Configure("../client.config");
    }
  }
}
```

This client application initially loads the client configuration file. Just like the server application, the client application also uses a configuration file. This will be discussed shortly.

In the client application, when the button is clicked, a new instance of the remote object is created. You simply pass in the value that is entered into the text box as a parameter of the remote call.

The only other difference between a regular form and the form that makes a remote object call is the use of the `System.Runtime.Remoting` namespace. This namespace must be imported into the application in order to be able to load the configuration file.

In addition to this code, you must make a reference to the remote object just as you did in the server application. To do this, right-click on the References folder in the Solution Explorer window and select Add Reference. You are presented with the Add Reference dialog window. Select the Projects tab and add your remote object's DLL as a reference in this client application.

Creating the client configuration file

Just like the server application that hosts the remote object, the client application that is making the call to the remote object needs to have an associated configuration file in order to instruct the client application on how to make the call. In order to make a client configuration file, follow these instructions:

1. In the project of the Windows Form, right-click on the project in the Solution Explorer window.
2. Select Add ⇨ Add New Item.
3. Select XML File from the choice of available templates.
4. Change the name of the file to `Client.config`.
5. Use the following code (Listing 25-5) to complete the file.

Listing 25-5: Client.config

```xml
<?xml version="1.0" encoding="utf-8" ?>
<configuration>
 <system.runtime.remoting>
   <application name="Hello">
     <client>
       <!-- You can only use one URL at a time
            therefore the HTTP option is commented out -->
```

```xml
    <!-- TCP -->
    <wellknown type="RemotingSample.HelloUserClass, myRemoteService"
     url="tcp://localhost:6789/Hello" />

    <!-- HTTP -->
    <!-- wellknown type="RemotingSample.HelloUserClass,
myRemoteService"
          url="http://localhost:9100/Hello" / -->

   </client>
   <channels>
      <channel ref="TCP" />
      <channel ref="HTTP" />
   </channels>
  </application>
 </system.runtime.remoting>
</configuration>
```

This configuration file is quite similar to the configuration file for the server application. This XML file is used by the client application to make a connection to the remote object. The `<wellknown>` node is similar to that used by the configuration file for the server application, but there is a new attribute. The `url` attribute is used to show the end point of the remote object. The first example of this in this configuration file uses TCP to make the connection. This is one of the available options specified by the server application's configuration file. The other option is to connect to the remote object using HTTP as the protocol. This option is commented out in the code, but it is there so you can see how that would be accomplished.

Now you have created a remote object, a server application that will host the remote object, and a client application that will call and consume the remote object. Now it's time to test the applications.

Testing the remote call

After the remote object is ready to go, the first step in making this all work is to start the server application. Because the remote object is going to be hosted in a console application, it is important that the console application is started.

To start the console application, pull up an instance of Visual Studio .NET and press F5. This causes the application to be compiled and run. Note that the server application has started (Figure 25-2).

Hitting the Enter key will cause the console application to stop and shut down the service. So leave it running while you test it with your client application.

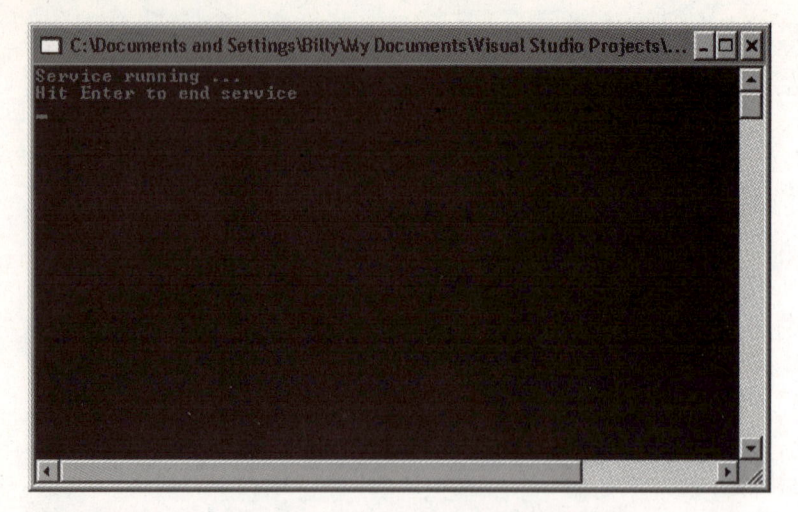

Figure 25-2: The .NET Remoting service is running a console application.

Next, start up a new instance of Visual Studio .NET and compile and run your client application. Enter a name and click the Submit button. Notice that you get a result from the remote object in the form's label control (Figure 25-3).

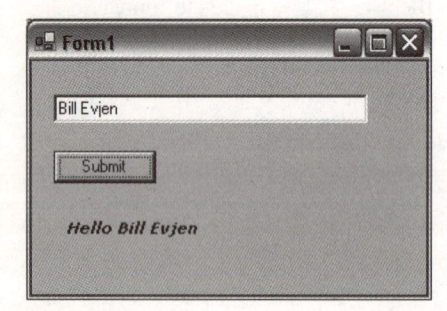

Figure 25-3: The client application calling the hosted remote object.

If you click the Submit button a few times, entering some new names, you cause new instances of the remote object to be called. If you go back to the server application, you see each of these calls is recorded in the console application (Figure 25-4). In reality, you might want to write these calls to a log rather than displaying them in the console application itself.

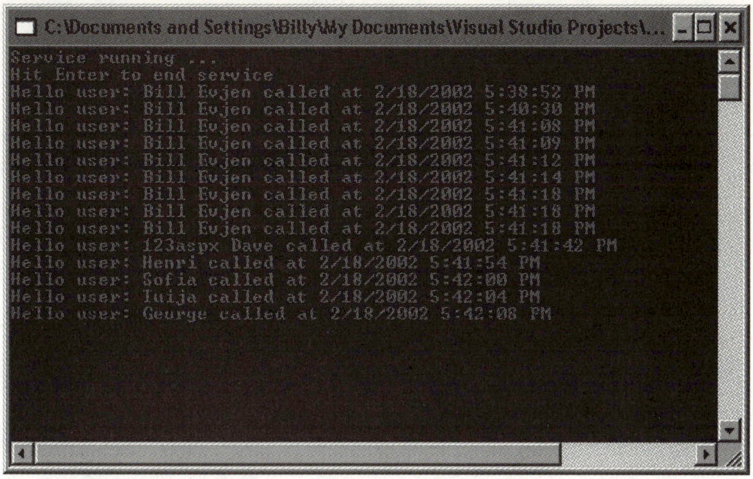

Figure 25-4: The console application keeping track of each of the calls to the remote object.

You have now seen all the steps needed to create and host a remote object and the procedures for consuming this remote object.

Summary

This chapter shows you an additional method to enable end users to call a remote object that is sitting on your server. XML Web services is not the only method to accomplish this. You can also use .NET Remoting.

.NET Remoting is better for working with remote objects that need to be callable over network protocols other than HTTP. If you are hosting the remote object on IIS and are going to use HTTP as the network protocol, XML Web services is definitely the way to go. The ease with which you can build and consume XML Web services outweighs the reasons for using .NET Remoting in this case.

If you are going to expand beyond this, however, or if you are looking for a more fine-grained control over your objects, .NET Remoting may be your answer. There are no hard and fast rules. Your best bet is to look closely at what you are trying to accomplish and then decide which technology works best for you.

Chapter 26
In Conclusion

Welcome to a new world. This is a new dawn in application development. As I mentioned earlier in the book, the introduction of Web services is as dramatic a change as when the client/server model was first introduced, maybe even bigger.

Now that we have the means of communicating across open spaces where once walls stood, we will see a wave of new products and new functionality in existing products that once we only wished for. In addition, this new technology gets us even closer to the holy grail of development — *code reuse!*

As the Web services model grows and matures, my hope is that all the major vendors see the goal of this technology and continue to cooperate with each other. This is absolutely essential if we are going to have seamless interoperability between platforms.

This book has focused on building Web services on the Microsoft .NET platform, but of course it is quite possible to build Web services on other platforms as well. In fact, the goal is to get every platform Web service-enabled so that everyone is able to communicate and share data with one another without any problems.

What I have explained in this book marks only the first steps of this model. This beginning is so exciting to me that I am already anxiously awaiting what comes next.

Happy Coding!

Bill Evjen
St. Charles, Missouri
March, 2002

Appendix A
XML Web Services Classes

System.Web.Services

The `System.Web.Services` namespace is a collection of classes that enables you to create XML Web services in the ASP.NET environment. It is important to understand these classes when building even the most basic XML Web services.

WebMethodAttribute

Applying a `WebMethod` attribute to a function causes that particular function to be callable as a remote object. This is a required attribute if you want to turn your methods into WebMethods. The `WebMethodAttribute` class includes the `BufferResponse`, `CacheDuration`, `Description`, `EnableSession`, `MessageName`, and `TransactionOption` properties.

> **NOTE:** Although the class name of an attribute ends with *attribute*, the usage of the class is without this ending.

VB

```
<WebMethod()> Public Function SayHello() As String
```

C#

```
[WebMethod()] public string SayHello()
```

BufferResponse property

When the `BufferResponse` property is set to `true`, the response from the XML Web service is held in memory and sent as a complete package. If it is set to `false`, which is the default setting, the response is sent to the client as it is constructed on the server.

VB

```
<WebMethod(BufferResponse:=True)> Public Function SayHello() As String
```

C#

```
[WebMethod(BufferResponse=True)] public string SayHello()
```

It is usually best to keep this property set at its default setting of `false` unless you are sending relatively small responses. Sending small responses with the `BufferResponse` property set to `true` can increase performance.

CacheDuration property

The `CacheDuration` property specifies the number of seconds that the response should be held in the system's cache. The default setting is 0. A setting of zero means that caching is disabled. Putting an XML Web service's response in the cache will increase the Web service's performance.

VB

```
<WebMethod(CacheDuration:=60)> Public Function SayHello() As String
```

C#

```
[WebMethod(CacheDuration=60)] public string SayHello()
```

Description property

The `Description` property applies a textual description to the WebMethod that appears on the .aspx test page of the XML Web service.

VB

```
<WebMethod(Description:="Description Goes Here")> _
Public Function SayHello() As String
```

C#

```
[WebMethod(Description="Description Goes Here")]
public string SayHello()
```

EnableSession property

Setting the `EnableSession` property to `true` enables session state for a particular WebMethod. The default setting is `false`.

VB

```
<WebMethod(EnableSession:=True)> Public Function SayHello() As String
```

C#

```
[WebMethod(EnableSession=True)] public string SayHello()
```

MessageName property

The `MessageName` property applies a unique name to a given WebMethod. This is a required step if you are working with overloaded WebMethods.

VB

```
<WebMethod(MessageName:="Add1")> Public Function Add() As String
```

C#

```
[WebMethod(MessageName="Add1")] public string Add()
```

TransactionOption property

The `TransactionOption` property specifies the transactional support for a particular WebMethod. The default setting of this property is `Disabled`. If the WebMethod is the root object that initiated the transaction, the Web service can participate in a transaction with another WebMethod that requires a transaction. Table A-1 describes each of the available settings for the `TransactionOption` property.

Table A-1: TransactionOption Property Values

Item	Description
`Disabled`	This is the default setting. When a WebMethod's `TransactionOption` property is set to `Disabled`, the capability to work with transactions is turned off.
`NotSupported`	This setting is basically the same as the `Disabled` setting. A setting of `NotSupported` indicates that transactions are not supported by the WebMethod.
`Supported`	Because sharing in transactions is not supported in the present version of XML Web services, this setting is the same as `Disabled`. This will most likely change in future versions.
`Required`	This setting indicates that the WebMethod requires a transaction. Because WebMethods can only participate in transactions as the root object of a transaction, a new transaction will be created.
`RequiresNew`	This setting indicates that the WebMethod requires a new transaction. This is effectively the same as the `Required` setting.

An example of using the `TransactionOption` property is as follows:

VB

```
<WebMethod(TransactionOption:=TransactionOption.Required)> _
Public Function SayHello() As String
```

C#

```
[WebMethod(TransactionOption=TransactionOption.Required)]
public string SayHello()
```

WebService

Although not required, the `WebService` class enables you to programmatically access certain properties of the Web service. Using this attribute gives you access to ASP.NET objects.

Application property

The `Application` property gets an application object from the current HTTP request. This enables you to work with application and session objects within your XML Web services much as you worked with these same objects in classic ASP.

Context property

The `Context` property gets the `HttpContext` property from the current request to the XML Web service.

Server property

The `Server` property gives you programmatic access to the server object that is used within ASP.NET.

Session property

The `Session` property is quite similar to the `Application` property. It enables you to work with sessions within your XML Web services.

User property

The `User` property gets the user object from the current request. This object can be used in the authentication process.

WebServiceAttribute

The `WebService` attribute is not a required element of publishing XML Web services, but it can help the end user understand the nature of the Web service that he is consuming. You set this attribute to the class of the Web service.

VB

```
<WebService()> Public Class SayHello
```

C#

```
[WebService()] public class SayHello
```

Description property

The `Description` property applies a textual description to the Web service. The description appears on the XML Web service's `.aspx` text page.

VB

```
<WebService(Description:="Description Goes Here")> _
Public Class SayHello
```

C#

```
[WebService(Description="Description Goes Here")]
public class SayHello
```

Name property

The `Name` property applies a textual title to the Web service. The name appears on the `.aspx` text page of the XML Web service.

VB

```
<WebService(Name:="Name Title Goes Here")> _
Public Class SayHello
```

C#

```
[WebService(Name="Name Title Goes Here")]
public class SayHello
```

By default, the value of the `name` property is the name of the class.

Namespace property

The `Namespace` property applies an XML namespace to the Web service that is used throughout the returned response to the consumer. If this property is not set, the Web service is given a temporary URI of `http://tempuri.org`. You should always use the root URL of your company's or organization's Web site as the URI of your Web service so that the consumer of your XML Web service knows who produced the service.

VB

```
<WebService(Namespace:="http://www.xmlws101.com")> _
Public Class SayHello
```

C#

```
[WebService(Namespace="http://www.xmlws101.com")]
public class SayHello
```

WebServiceBindingAttribute

Although the binding is specified within the WSDL document, you can specify other bindings by using the `WebServiceBinding` attribute in conjunction with your Web service.

Location property

The `Location` property sets the location where the binding is defined. The default is the URL of the XML Web service to which the attribute is applied.

Name property

The `Name` property sets the name of the binding that can be referenced by the WebMethod. The default is the name of the XML Web service with SOAP appended.

Namespace property

The `Namespace` property sets the namespace used for the binding. The default is `http://tempuri.org`.

WebServiceBindingAttribute example

The following listing shows an example of using the `WebServiceBinding` attribute.

VB

```
<WebServiceBinding(Name:="OtherBinding", _
   Namespace:="http://www.xmlws101.com/MyBinding", _
   Location:="http://www.xmlws101.com/Service1.asmx?wsdl")> _
Public Class MyClass

   <SoapDocumentMethod(Binding:="OtherBinding"), WebMethod()> _
     Public Function SayHello() As String
```

C#

```
[WebServiceBinding(Name="OtherBinding",
   Namespace="http://www.xmlws101.com/MyBinding",
   Location="http://www.xmlws101.com/Service1.asmx?wsdl")]
public class MyClass

   [SoapDocumentMethod(Binding="OtherBinding"), WebMethod()]
     public string SayHello()
```

After you have specified the binding by using the `WebServiceBinding` attribute, you can point to this binding declaration using the `SoapDocumentMethod` attribute

System.Web.Services.Description

The `System.Web.Services.Description` namespace contains classes that publicly describe your XML Web service. Each of the classes in this namespace directly corresponds with an element in the WSDL document. You can view the related WSDL document for your Web service by appending the text `?wsdl` at the end of the Web service's address.

```
http://www.xmlws101.com/service1.asmx?wsdl
```

It is possible to read from and write to your Web service's WSDL document at runtime. To do this, you import the `System.Web.Services.Description` namespace into your XML Web service.

VB

```
Imports System.Web.Services.Description
```

C#

```
using System.Web.Services.Description;
```

After this you can easily make a connection to your WSDL information.

VB

```
Dim myWSDL As ServiceDescription
myWSDL = ServiceDescription.Read("C:\service1\service1.wsdl")

' Read or set WSDL document properties
myWSDL.TargetNamespace = "http://www.xmlws101.com/"

' If you are setting properties, then you need to return the changes
myWSDL.Write("C:\service1\service1.wsdl")
```

C#

```
ServiceDescription myWSDL;
myWSDL = ServiceDescription.Read("C:\service1\service1.wsdl");

// Read or set WSDL document properties
myWSDL.TargetNamespace = "http://www.xmlws101.com/";

// If you are setting properties, then you need to return the changes
myWSDL.Write("C:\service1\service1.wsdl");
```

Binding

The `Binding` class directly corresponds to the `<binding>` element in the WSDL document. This element specifies the data format and the protocols that are used within the XML Web service. The properties of the `binding` class include: `Documentation`, `Extensions`, `Name`, `Operations`, `Service Description`, and `Type`.

BindingCollection

The `BindingCollection` class represents a collection of instances from the `binding` class that are represented in the XML Web service. The properties of the `BindingCollection` class include `Count` and `Item`.

DocumentableItem

You use the `DocumentableItem` class as an abstract class that can represent a number of other classes. The only property for this class is the `Documentation` property.

FaultBinding

When using the `FaultBinding` class, you can specify the format of the fault (error) messages that are output from the XML Web service. The properties of the `FaultBinding` class include `Documentation`, `Extensions`, `Name`, and `OperationBinding`.

FaultBindingCollection
The `FaultBindingCollection` class represents a collection of instances from the `faultbinding` class that are represented in the XML Web service. The properties of the `FaultBindingCollection` class include `Count` and `Item`.

HttpAddressBinding
This class specifies the base URI of a particular XML Web service. You can use the `Location` property to assign an address for the location of the port. The properties of this class include `Handled`, `Location`, `Parent`, and `Required`.

HttpBinding
The `HttpBinding` class is used to extend the information that is passed from the XML Web service via HTTP. The properties of this class include `Handled`, `Parent`, `Required`, and `Verb`. The property `Verb` enables you to get or set the value of the HTTP request as to whether it will be via HTTP-GET or HTTP-POST.

HttpOperationBinding
The `HttpOperationBinding` class is used to extend the information that is passed from the XML Web service via HTTP specifically. The properties of this class include `Handled`, `Location`, `Parent`, and `Required`.

HttpUrlEncodedBinding
The `HttpUrlEncodedBinding` class enables you to specify that the parameters passed into an XML Web service must use standard URL encoding (for example, `name1=value&name2=value`). It doesn't matter whether the method used is GET or POST. The properties of this class include `Handled`, `Location`, `Parent`, and `Required`.

HttpUrlReplacementBinding
The `HttpUrlReplacementBinding` class allows you to specify the format in which your XML Web services receive parameters and their values. For instance, instead of `name1=value&name2=value`, you may choose to receive this as `name1*value/name2*value`. The properties of this class include `Handled`, `Parent`, and `Required`.

Import
The `Import` class is associated with the `<import>` element in the WSDL document. This element enables you to separate the WSDL document into pieces and call these pieces as needed. The properties of this class include `Location`, `Namespace`, and `Service Description`.

ImportCollection

The `ImportCollection` class represents a collection of instances from the `Import` class that are represented in the XML Web service's WSDL document. The properties of the `ImportCollection` class include `Count` and `Item`.

InputBinding

This class specifies the data format and the message protocols used for messages that are inputted into the XML Web service. The `InputBinding` class is associated with the `<input>` element of the WSDL document. The properties of this class include `Documentation`, `Extensions`, `Name`, and `OperationBinding`.

Message

The `Message` class allows you to specify the message format for the messages that are outputted by the XML Web service. A message can either be made up of name/value pairs, or it can be in the form of a document that is sent to the consumer. The `message` class is associated with the `<message>` element in the WSDL document. The properties of the `Message` class include `Documentation`, `Name`, `Parts`, and `ServiceDescription`.

MessageBinding

The `MessageBinding` class is an abstract class that can be associated with the `FaultBinding`, `InputBinding`, and `OutputBinding` classes. The properties of this class include `Documentation`, `Extensions`, `Name`, and `OperationBinding`.

MessageCollection

The `MessageCollection` class represents a collection of instances from the `Message` class that are included in the XML Web service's WSDL document. The properties of the `MessageCollection` class include `Count` and `Item`.

MessagePart

The `MessagePart` class allows messages to be broken up into logical parts. It directly corresponds to the `<message>` element in the WSDL document. The properties of this class include `Documentation`, `Element`, `Message`, `Name`, and `Type`.

MessagePartCollection

The `MessagePartCollection` class represents a collection of instances from the `MessagePart` class that are represented in the XML Web service's WSDL document. The properties of the `MessagePartCollection` class include `Count` and `Item`.

MimeContentBinding

The `MimeContentBinding` class specifies the MIME format for the body of the message. The properties of this class include `Handled`, `Parent`, `Part`, `Required`, and `Type`.

MimeMultipartRelatedBinding

The `MimeMultipartRelatedBinding` class specifies the MIME format for parts of the message. The properties of this class include: `Handled`, `Parent`, `Parts`, and `Required`.

MimePart

The `MimePart` class specifies the extensibility element for each of the parts related to the `MimeMultipartRelatedBinding` classes. The properties of this class include `Extensions`, `Handled`, `Parent`, and `Required`.

MimePartCollection

The `MimePartCollection` class represents a collection of instances from the `MimePart` class that are represented in the XML Web service's WSDL document. The properties of the `MimePartCollection` class include `Count` and `Item`.

MimeTextBinding

The `MimeTextBinding` class specifies the extensibility element for each of the parts related to the `InputBinding`, `OutputBinding`, and `MimePart` classes. Using this class, you can specify the text patterns to search for in the HTTP transmission. The properties of this class include `Handled`, `Matches`, `Parent`, and `Required`.

MimeTextMatch

The `MimeTextMatch` class allows you to specify the text search patterns to look for in an HTTP transmission. The properties of this class include `Capture`, `Group`, `IgnoreCase`, `Matches`, `Name`, `Pattern`, `Repeats`, `RepeatsString`, and `Type`.

MimeTextMatchCollection

The `MimeTextMatchCollection` class represents a collection of instances from the `MimeTextMatch` class that are represented in the XML Web service's WSDL document. The properties of the `MimeTextMatchCollection` class include `Count` and `Item`.

MimeXmlBinding

The `MimeXmlBinding` class specifies the schema for XML messages that are not SOAP-compliant. The properties of this class include `Handled`, `Parent`, `Part`, and `Required`.

Operation

The Operation class describes an action that is permissible with an XML Web service. The `Operation` class corresponds with the `<operation>` element in the WSDL document. The properties of this class include `Documentation`, `Faults`, `Messages`, `Name`, `ParameterOrder`, `ParameterOrderString`, and `PortType`.

OperationBinding

The `OperationBinding` class provides the specifications for the data formats and the message protocols that are used in the action of the message being sent. The properties of this class include `Binding`, `Documentation`, `Extensions`, `Faults`, `Input`, `Name`, and `Output`.

OperationBindingCollection

The `OperationBindingCollection` class represents a collection of instances from the `OperationBinding` class that are represented in the XML Web service's WSDL document. The properties of the `OperationBindingCollection` class include `Count` and `Item`.

OperationCollection

The `OperationCollection` class represents a collection of instances from the `Operation` class that are represented in the XML Web service's WSDL document. The properties of the `OperationCollection` class include `Count` and `Item`.

OperationFault

The `OperationFault` class defines the specifications for the error messages that are output by the XML Web service. The properties of this class include `Documentation`, `Message`, `Name`, and `Operation`.

OperationFaultCollection

The `OperationFaultCollection` class represents a collection of instances from the `OperationFault` class that are represented in the XML Web service's WSDL document. The properties of the `OperationFaultCollection` class include `Count` and `Item`.

OperationInput

The `OperationInput` class defines the specifications for the input message, an XML Web service request. The properties of this class include `Documentation`, `Message`, `Name`, and `Operation`.

OperationMessage

The `OperationMessage` class serves as a base class for the `OperationFault`, `OperationInput`, and `OperationOutput` classes. The properties of this class include `Documentation`, `Message`, `Name`, and `Operation`.

OperationMessageCollection

The `OperationMessageCollection` class represents a collection of instances from the `OperationMessage` class that are represented in the XML Web service's WSDL document. The properties of the `OperationMessageCollection` class include `Count` and `Item`.

OperationOutput

The `OperationOutput` class defines the specifications for messages that are output by the XML Web service. The properties of this class include `Documentation`, `Message`, `Name`, and `Operation`.

OutputBinding

The `OutputBinding` class establishes a set of specifications for data formats and message formats for messages that are output by the XML Web service. The properties of this class include `Documentation`, `Extensions`, `Name`, and `OperationBinding`.

Port

The `Port` class defines the specific endpoint for the calling WebMethods. The properties of this class include `Binding`, `Documentation`, `Extensions`, `Name`, and `Service`.

PortCollection

The `PortCollection` class represents a collection of instances from the `Port` class that are represented in the XML Web service's WSDL document. The properties of the `PortCollection` class include `Count` and `Item`.

PortType

The `PortType` class represents a set of abstract operations and messages. The properties of this class include `Documentation`, `Name`, `Operations`, and `ServiceDescription`.

PortTypeCollection

The `PortTypeCollection` class represents instances from the `PortType` class that are represented in the XML Web service's WSDL document. The properties of the `PortTypeCollection` class include `Count` and `Item`.

Service

The `Service` class groups together a set of related instances of the `Port` class that are associated with a Web service. The properties of this class include `Documentation`, `Extensions`, `Name`, `Ports`, and `ServiceDescription`.

ServiceCollection

The `ServiceCollection` class represents instances from the `Service` class that are represented in the XML Web service's WSDL document. The properties of the `ServiceCollection` class include `Count` and `Item`.

ServiceDescription

The `ServiceDescription` class allows you to create and format a valid WSDL document. This is one of the more powerful classes that enables you to work with the WSDL document.

The properties of this class include: `Bindings`, `Documentation`, `Extensions`, `Imports`, `Messages`, `Name`, `PortTypes`, `RetrievalUrl`, `ServiceDescriptions`, `Services`, `TargetNamespaces`, and `Types`.

ServiceDescriptionBaseCollection

The `ServiceDescriptionBaseCollection` class represents a collection of instances from the `ServiceDescriptionBase` class that are represented in the XML Web service's WSDL document. The properties of the `ServiceDescriptionBaseCollection` class include `Count` and `Item`.

ServiceDescriptionCollection

The `ServiceDescriptionCollection` class represents instances from the `ServiceDescription` class that are represented in the XML Web service's WSDL document. The properties of the `ServiceDescriptionCollection` class include `Count` and `Item`.

ServiceDescriptionFormatExtension

The `ServiceDescriptionFormatExtension` class represents an extensibility element added to an XML Web service. The properties of this class include `Handled`, `Parent`, and `Required`.

ServiceDescriptionFormatExtensionCollection

The `ServiceDescriptionFormatExtensionCollection` class represents a collection of instances from the `ServiceDescriptionFormatExtension` class that are represented in the XML Web service's WSDL document. The properties of this class include `Count` and `Item`.

ServiceDescriptionImporter

The `ServiceDescriptionImporter` class exposes a means of generating client proxy classes for XML Web services. The properties of this class include `ProtocolName`, `Schemas`, `ServiceDescriptions`, and `Style`.

ServiceDescriptionReflector

The `ServiceDescriptionReflector` class provides a managed way of dynamically viewing, creating, or invoking types supported by an XML Web service. The properties of this class include `Schemas` and `ServiceDescriptions`.

SoapAddressBinding

The `SoapAddressBinding` class assigns an address to a port. The properties of this class include `Handled`, `Location`, `Parent`, and `Required`.

SoapBinding

The `SoapBinding` class represents an extension added to a specific Binding within an XML Web service. The properties of this class include `Handled`, `Parent`, `Required`, `Style`, and `Transport`.

SoapBodyBinding

The `SoapBodyBinding` class specifies how transmitted messages appear in the SOAP body. The properties of this class include `Encoding`, `Handled`, `Namespace`, `Parent`, `Parts`, `PartsString`, `Required`, and `Use`.

SoapFaultBinding

The `SoapFaultBinding` class specifies how the SOAP Fault message is returned to the client. The properties of this class include `Encoding`, `Handled`, `Namespace`, `Parent`, `Required`, and `Use`.

SoapHeaderBinding

The `SoapHeaderBinding` class specifies how the SOAP Header message is returned to the client. The properties of this class include `Encoding`, `Handled`, `MapToProperty`, `Message`, `Namespace`, `Parent`, `Part`, `Required`, and `Use`.

SoapHeaderFaultBinding

The `SoapHeaderFaultBinding` class specifies the message types that are used to transmit error messages in the SOAP Header. The properties of this class include `Encoding`, `Handled`, `Message`, `Namespace`, `Parent`, `Parts`, `Required`, and `Use`.

SoapOperationBinding

The `SoapOperationBinding` class specifies how the SOAP message will be formatted for the XML Web service. The properties of this class include `Handled`, `Parent`, `Required`, `SoapAction`, and `Style`.

SoapTransportImporter

The `SoapTransportImporter` class serves as a base class for derived classes that import SOAP transmission protocols into XML Web services. The only property for this class is the `ImportContext` property.

Types

The `Types` class specifies the user-defined data types for a particular message. The properties of this class include `Documentation`, `Extensions`, and `Schemas`.

System.Web.Services.Discovery

The `System.Web.Services.Discovery` namespace is a collection of classes that allows you to work with the process of discovering XML Web services on a particular Web server. Each of the following classes is part of this namespace and relate to the discovery document. You can view the related discovery document for your own Web service by appending the text `?disco` at the end of the Web service's address.

```
http://www.xmlws101.com/service1.asmx?disco
```

It is possible to read from and write to your Web service's discovery or disco document at runtime. To do this, you import the `System.Web.Services.Discovery` namespace into your XML Web service.

VB

```
Imports System.Web.Services.Discovery
```

C#

```
using System.Web.Services.Discovery;
```

After doing this, you can easily make a connection to your discovery information.

> **NOTE:** For this example, you also need to import the `System.XML` namespace.

VB

```vb
Dim myDisco As New DiscoveryDocument()
Dim myXmlTextReader As New
    XmlTextReader("http://localhost/myDiscoFile.disco")

' Read the given XmlTextReader.
myDisco = DiscoveryDocument.Read(myXmlTextReader)
```

C#

```csharp
DiscoveryDocument myDisco = new DiscoveryDocument();
XmlTextReader myXmlTextReader = new
        XmlTextReader("http://localhost/myDiscoFile.disco");

// Read the given XmlTextReader.
myDiscoveryDocument = DiscoveryDocument.Read(myXmlTextReader);
```

ContractReference

The `ContractReference` class represents a reference in a discovery document to a service description. The properties of this class include `ClientProtocol`, `Contract`, `DefaultFilename`, `DocRef`, `Ref`, and `Url`.

DiscoveryClientDocumentCollection

The `DiscoveryClientDocumentCollection` class allows you to have a representative list of documents that were downloaded to the client in the discovery process. The properties of this class include `Count`, `Item`, `Keys`, and `Values`.

DiscoveryClientProtocol

The `DiscoveryClientProtocol` class enables you to programmatically invoke the discovery process. The properties of this class include: `AdditionInformation`, `AllowAutoRedirect`, `ClientCertificates`, `ConnectionGroupName`, `Container`, `CookieContainer`, `Credentials`, `Documents`, `Errors`, `PreAuthenticate`, `Proxy`, `References`, `RequestEncoding`, `Site`, `Timeout`, `Url`, and `UserAgent`.

DiscoveryClientReferenceCollection

The `DiscoveryClientReferenceCollection` class represents instances from the `DiscoveryReference` class. The properties of this class include `Count`, `Item`, `Keys`, and `Value`.

DiscoveryClientResult

The `DiscoveryClientResult` class allows you to work with the details of a discovery reference without the contents of the referenced document. The properties of this class include `Filename`, `ReferenceTypeName`, and `Url`.

DiscoveryClientResultCollection

The `DiscoveryClientResultCollection` class represents instances from the `DiscoveryClientResult` class. The properties of this class include `Count` and `Item`.

DiscoveryDocument

The `DiscoveryDocument` class is an important class that can be used to represent the entire discovery document. The only property for this class is the `References` property.

DiscoveryDocumentReference

The `DiscoveryDocumentReference` class represents a reference to the discovery document. The properties of this class include `ClientProtocol`, `Contract`, `DefaultFilename`, `DocRef`, `Ref`, and `Url`.

DiscoveryExceptionDictionary

The `DiscoveryExceptionDictionary` class is a collection of errors that occur during the discovery process. The properties of this class include `Count`, `Item`, `Keys`, and `Values`.

DiscoveryReference

The `DiscoveryReference` class serves as a base class for the `ContractReference`, `SchemaReference`, and `DiscoveryDocumentReference` classes. The properties of this class include `ClientProtocol`, `DefaultFilename`, and `Url`.

DiscoveryReferenceCollection

The `DiscoveryReferenceCollection` class represents a collection of discovery references. The properties of this class include `Count` and `Item`.

SchemaReference

The `SchemaReference` class represents any references to an XML Schema Definition (XSD) language schema that are contained in a discovery document. The properties of this class include `ClientProtocol`, `DefaultFilename`, `Ref`, `Schema`, `TargetNamespace`, and `Url`.

SoapBinding

The `SoapBinding` class represents the SOAP binding in the discovery document. The properties of this class include `Address` and `Binding`.

System.Web.Services.Protocols

The `System.Web.Services.Protocols` namespace is a collection of classes that allows you to manipulate how XML Web services communicate with clients and how they transmit their data over the wire. Each of the following classes is part of this namespace and relates to this process.

HttpGetClientProtocol

This class derives from the `HttpSimpleClientProtocol` and represents any client proxies that use HTTP-GET. The properties of this class include: `AllowAutoRedirect`, `ClientCertificates`, `ConnectionGroupName`, `Container`, `CookieContainer`, `Credentials`, `PreAuthenticate`, `Proxy`, `RequestEncoding`, `Site`, `Timeout`, `Url`, and `UserAgent`.

HttpMethodAttribute

The `HttpMethodAttribute` class works with the client by serializing the parameters sent to an XML Web service. The properties of this class include `ParameterFormatter`, `ReturnFormatter`, and `TypeId`.

HttpPostClientProtocol

The `HttpPostClientProtocol` class works with messages from a proxy that are sent via HTTP-POST. The properties of this class include: `AllowAutoRedirect`, `ClientCertificates`, `ConnectionGroupName`, `Container`, `CookieContainer`,

`Credentials`, `PreAuthenticate`, `Proxy`, `RequestEncoding`, `Site`, `Timeout`, `Url`, and `UserAgent`.

HttpSimpleClientProtocol
This class serves as a base class for the `HttpGetClientProtocol`, `HttpPostClientProtcol`, and `SoapHttpClientProtocol` classes. The properties of this class include: `AllowAutoRedirect`, `ClientCertificates`, `ConnectionGroupName`, `Container`, `CookieContainer`, `Credentials`, `PreAuthenticate`, `Proxy`, `RequestEncoding`, `Site`, `Timeout`, `Url`, and `UserAgent`.

HttpWebClientProtocol
This class serves as a base class for all XML Web service client proxies that use the HTTP transport protocol. The properties of this class include: `AllowAutoRedirect`, `ClientCertificates`, `ConnectionGroupName`, `Container`, `CookieContainer`, `Credentials`, `PreAuthenticate`, `Proxy`, `RequestEncoding`, `Site`, `Timeout`, `Url`, and `UserAgent`.

LogicalMethodInfo
This class represents the attributes and metadata for an XML Web service method. The properties of this class include: `AsyncCallbackParameter`, `AsyncResultParameter`, `AsyncStateParameter`, `BeginMethodInfo`, `CustomAttributeProvider`, `DeclaringType`, `EndMethodInfo`, `InParameters`, `IsAsync`, `IsVoid`, `MethodInfo`, `Name`, `OutParameters`, `Parameters`, `ReturnType`, `ReturnTypeCustomAttributeProvider`

MatchAttribute
The `MatchAttribute` class works with the match that is made when using text-pattern matching. The properties of this class include: `Capture`, `Group`, `IgnoreCase`, `MaxRepeats`, `Pattern`, and `TypeId`.

SoapClientMessage
This class works with the SOAP response that is sent or the SOAP message that is received by the client application that is consuming the XML Web service. The properties of this class include: `Action`, `Client`, `ContentType`, `Exception`, `Headers`, `MethodInfo`, `OneWay`, `Stage`, `Stream`, and `Url`.

SoapDocumentMethodAttribute
Using this class on an XML Web service enables the Web service to use document formatting. The properties of this class include: `Action`, `Binding`, `OneWay`, `ParameterStyle`, `RequestElementName`, `RequestNamespace`, `ResponseElementName`, `ResponseNamespace`, `TypeId`, and `Use`.

SoapDocumentServiceAttribute

This class sets the default format used for SOAP requests and SOAP responses from an XML Web service. The properties of this class include `ParameterStyle`, `RoutingStyle`, `TypeId`, and `Use`.

SoapException

The `SoapException` class works with an exception that is thrown when a request is made to an XML Web service. The properties of this class include: `Actor`, `Code`, `Detail`, `HelpLink`, `InnerException`, `Message`, `Source`, `StackTrace`, and `TargetSite`.

SoapExtension

This is the base class that you use to create your own SOAP extensions. The SoapExtension class enables you to interact with the XML Web service at specific points during the response or request of an object.

SoapExtensionAttribute

The `SoapExtensionAttribute` class allows you to assign the fact that a particular WebMethod should work with a SOAP extension. The properties of this class include `ExtensionType`, `Priority`, and `TypeId`.

SoapHeader

This class represents the contents of the SOAP header. The properties of this class include `Actor`, `DidUnderstand`, `EncodedMustUnderstand`, and `MustUnderstand`.

SoapHeaderAttribute

This class specifies the SOAP header for a particular WebMethod. The properties of this class include `Direction`, `MemberName`, `Required`, and `TypeId`.

SoapHeaderCollection

The `SoapHeaderCollection` class represents a collection of instances from the `SoapHeader` class. The properties of the `SoapHeaderCollection` class include `Count` and `Item`.

SoapHeaderException

This class deals with the exception that is thrown from a SOAP header. The properties of this class include: `Actor`, `Code`, `Detail`, `HelpLink`, `InnerException`, `Message`, `Source`, `StackTrace`, and `TargetSite`.

SoapHttpClientProtocol

This class represents the client proxy when it is dealing with SOAP. The properties of this class include: `AllowAutoRedirect`, `ClientCertificates`, `ConnectionGroupName`,

`Container`, `CookieContainer`, `Credentials`, `PreAuthenticate`, `Proxy`, `RequestEncoding`, `Site`, `Timeout`, `Url`, and `UserAgent`.

SoapMessage

This class represents the SOAP message at specific points in the request for a response to the message. The properties of this class include: `Action`, `ContentType`, `Exception`, `Headers`, `MethodInfo`, `OneWay`, `Stage`, `Stream`, and `Url`.

SoapRpcMethodAttribute

Using this class forces the WebMethod to use RPC formatting in all messages that are sent to and from a WebMethod. The properties of this class include: `Action`, `Binding`, `OneWay`, `RequestElementName`, `RequestNamespace`, `ResponseElementName`, `ResponseNamespace`, and `TypeId`.

SoapRpcServiceAttribute

Using this class with a particular XML Web service forces all the methods in the Web service to use RPC formatting. The properties of this class include `RoutingStyle` and `TypeId`.

SoapServerMessage

This class represents the data that is contained in a SOAP request or response that is sent to or received from an XML Web service. The properties of this class include `Action`, `ContentType`, `Exception`, `Headers`, `MethodInfo`, `OneWay`, `Server`, `Stage`, `Stream`, and `Url`.

SoapUnknownHeader

This class represents the data that is sent in a SOAP header but not understood by the XML Web service. The properties of this class include `Actor`, `DidUnderstand`, `EncodedMustUnderstand`, and `MustUnderstand`.

WebClientAsyncResult

This class offers an implementation of IAsyncResult for use by XML Web service proxies to implement the standard asynchronous method pattern. The properties of this class include `AsyncState`, `AsyncWaitHandle`, `CompletedSynchronously`, and `IsCompleted`.

WebClientProtocol

The class represents all the base classes that work with client proxies. The properties of this class include `ConnectionGroupName`, `Container`, `CookieContainer`, `Credentials`, `PreAuthenticate`, `RequestEncoding`, `Site`, `Timeout`, and `Url`.

Appendix B
XML Primer

As you may have noticed, XML is everywhere in this book. It is mentioned on the cover, and almost every chapter uses these three letters. The reason for this is plain and simple — XML is an important part of Microsoft's Web services platform. Not only is XML important for Web services, but it is baked into almost everything in .NET. In this new platform, XML is a key component. That is why it is vital that you have a general understanding of XML. Not understanding this markup language will seriously limit you as a programmer in the new world of .NET.

This appendix is meant to be what its title says — simply a primer. For those of you who are brand new to the world of XML, this appendix will get you up to speed quickly. It covers only the major points of XML, a topic quite deserving of its own book; so you will need to look elsewhere to become an expert on the fine-grained details of this language. This appendix is meant to help you understand what is going on in the Web services model.

What is XML?

XML — e**X**tendable **M**arkup **L**anguage — is used to markup data. That is why this markup language has become one of the most talked about things in the programming world today.

Data is what makes the Internet world go around, and XML is the best way to represent that data. Just as HTML is used to markup the presentation layer, XML is used to markup data. This makes it easier for one company to send data to another company. Without XML, you can send data in a tab-, comma-, or pipe- delimited fashion. Here's an example of comma-delimited data:

```
23.99, 44.76, 36.00, 68.40
```

Actually, you divide the individual pieces of data in any fashion that you want. On the receiving end of the data, the consumer must pay attention to how the data is divided (in this case with a comma) to understand what the data means. In the preceding example, it is actually quite difficult to apply any meaning to these numbers. They could mean almost anything. But what happens when that company begins using XML and marking up its data with a pre-arranged XML structure? You can see the result in Listing B-1.

Listing B-1: A sample XML file

```
<?xml version="1.0" encoding="UTF-8" ?>
<Products>
   <Prices>
      <Item1>23.99</Item1>
      <Item2>44.76</Item2>
      <Item3>36.00</Item3>
      <Item4>68.40</Item4>
   </Prices>
</Products>
```

Now the data is a lot easier to understand. First of all, you can easily put a value to the numbers and what they represent. In this case, you can tell that the numbers represent a price for selected products. Although XML may be a little more verbose, it makes a lot more sense to use XML to represent your data.

XML Structure

XML is made up of tags or elements. In the preceding example, there is a single element `<Prices>` that is made up of two tags – an opening tag, `<Prices>`, and a closing tag, `</Prices>`.

These tags are completely defined by you. There is no list of available tags to use in XML (except for the `<xml>` element). You can make the tags whatever you choose; my only suggestion is to make them truly explain the data that they are representing.

In XML, a particular piece of data is encased between an element's opening tag and its closing tag. A backslash at the start of a tag signifies a closing tag.

```
<Item1>23.99</Item1>
```

An XML file

Now create a simple XML file. Using the preceding example, save the code in a file. To accomplish this, you can use almost any editing tool you want. It might be simplest to use Notepad. Type the preceding code in Notepad and save it as `"myXMLfile.xml"`. You need to encase the filename in quotes in order to get Notepad to save the file correctly (Figure B-1). Save this file in the root of your `Inetpub/wwwroot` directory.

After you have saved your file, you can use any browser that supports XML to view the file. Microsoft's Internet Explorer 5.0 and 6.0 both support viewing XML documents directly in the browser's window, just as you would view any HTML file.

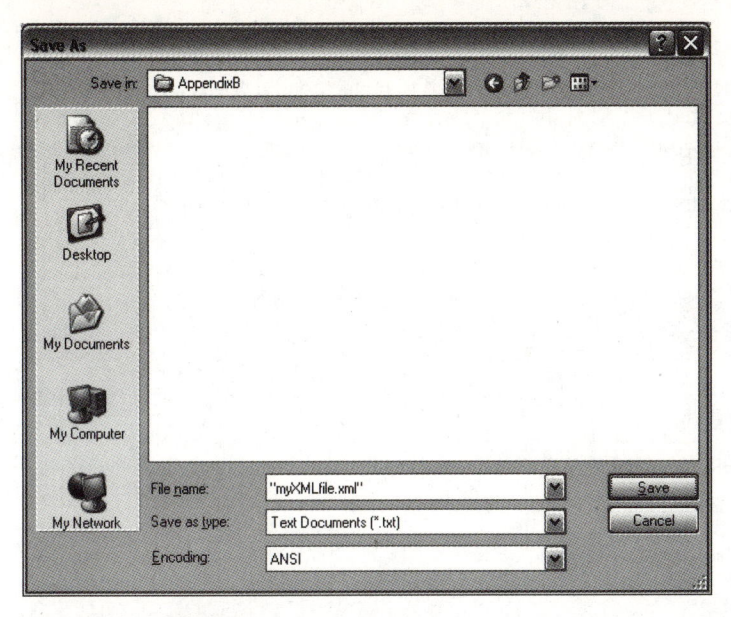

Figure B-1: Saving your XML file using Notepad.

Different browsers, such as Netscape and Opera, may show your XML file differently. Figure B-2 shows you how this XML file appears in IE 6.0.

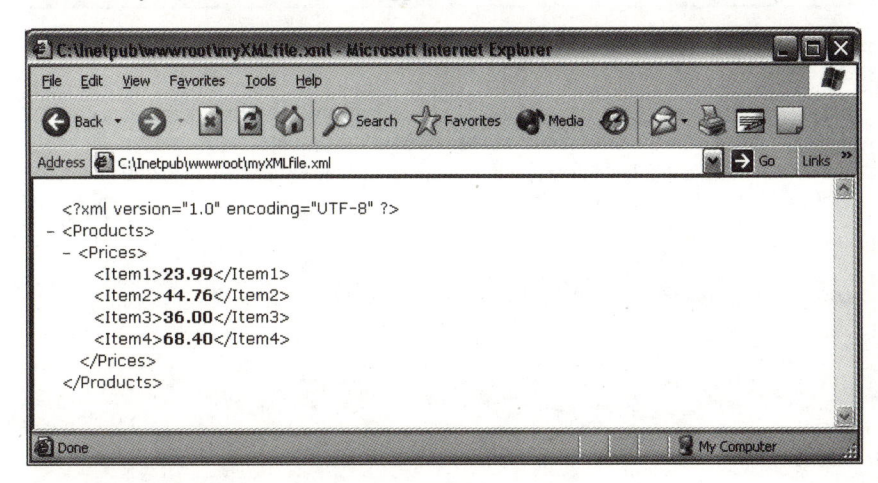

Figure B-2: The XML file in Internet Explorer 6.0.

As you can tell, the XML document is shown directly in the browser. (It appears in a nicely color-formatted view.) Microsoft's Internet Explorer even lets you click on the minus sign next to certain elements to collapse that particular node for better readability.

Properly nesting elements

Just like HTML, XML needs to be properly formatted to create a valid XML document. In order to be properly formatted, the XML has to be correctly nested. The nesting of elements has to do with the order in which elements are opened and closed. Therefore, if you open tag A and then you open tag B, you will not be able to close tag A until you close tag B. Let's take a look at an example of how to correctly nest elements in your XML documents.

Correct Nesting

```
<tagA>
   <tagB>
     ...
   </tagB>
<tagA>
```

Now take a look at a similar XML file that is improperly nested.

Incorrect Nesting

```
<tagA>
   <tagB>
     ...
   </tagA>
</tagB>
```

NOTE: The indenting of the XML file is done for readability and is not required.

Whitespace

HTML is good at ignoring whitespace, but XML is not. Whitespace is considered any part of the document that is between an opening and closing XML tag that has no character representation (such as a space). Therefore, in the following code samples, Listing B-2 is not the same as Listing B-3.

Listing B-2

```
<Movie>Office Space</Movie>
```

Listing B-3

```
<Movie>
 Office
 Space
</Movie>
```

Attributes

XML tags can also have attributes. An attribute's value must be contained within quotes.

```
<Weather City="Helsinki">COLD</Weather>
```

It is also possible to have multiple attributes.

```
<Weather City="Helsinki" Country="Finland">COLD</Weather>
```

Empty elements

Empty elements can be represented in one of two ways. The first way is as a single tag.

```
<ISBN />
```

The other way to represent an empty element is with an opening and a closing tag.

```
<ISBN></ISBN>
```

Comments

Just like HTML, XML allows comments in the following format:

```
<?xml version="1.0" encoding="UTF-8" ?>
<Products>
   <Prices>
      <!-- Prices good till this summer -->
      <Item1>23.99</Item1>
      <Item2>44.76</Item2>
      <Item3>36.00</Item3>
      <Item4>68.40</Item4>
   </Prices>
</Products>
```

Therefore, anything that is in between the `<!--` and the `-->` is considered a comment and is ignored.

Case sensitivity

XML is case sensitive. Therefore, the `<Movie>` tag is not the same as `<movie>`. This means that the following code sample is an invalid document.

```
<Book>Visual Basic .NET Bible</book>
```

> **NOTE:** Other rules for elements specify that the element's name cannot start with any numbers, underscores, or with the word XML. Also, element names cannot contain any spaces.

The root element

Your XML document can have only a single root element. Therefore, the following code sample is invalid.

Invalid

```
<Customer>
   <Name>Bill Evjen</Name>
   <Address>123 Main Street</Address>
</Customer>
<Order>
   <Item>One ticket to Las Vegas</Item>
</Order>
```

If you construct your XML in this manner, you have to encase it all in a root element because you are only allowed one root element per XML document.

Valid

```
<Document>
   <Customer>
      <Name>Bill Evjen</Name>
      <Address>123 Main Street</Address>
   </Customer>
   <Order>
      <Item>One ticket to Las Vegas</Item>
   </Order>
</Document>
```

The XML declaration

It is recommended, but not required, to use an XML declaration at the top of your XML file. The XML declaration should be written in the following format:

```
<?xml version="1.0" ?>
```

This declaration isn't very important now, because the only version of XML presently available is Version 1. When future versions of XML come out, however, this declaration will play a greater role.

Namespaces

Because everyone is allowed to construct and develop his own elements for his XML documents, there are bound to be conflicts where two parties have some elements that are in conflict with one another. The conflict comes into play when two elements have the same name, but their meanings are altogether different. To get around this, use XML namespaces. XML namespaces are an important way of differentiating between tags that are identical, but have different meanings.

> **CROSS-REFERENCE:** XML namespaces are discussed in detail in Chapter 3.

Entity References

There are some characters that cannot be contained as a value between two XML tags. Take a look at the following code and see if you can tell where the problem might occur.

Incorrect

```
<Value>Do if 5 > 3</Value>
```

Right away you should be able to tell that a processing error will occur with the character directly after the 5. The *greater than* sign is used to close a tag, but as a value it will just confuse the XML parser.

The trick is to encode this character so the parser will treat it in the appropriate manner. There are five characters for which you cannot use the actual character, but instead have to encode the character. Table B-1 displays a list of the characters that need to be encoded and their encoded values.

Table B-1: Entity Substitutions

Character	Entity
<	&lt;
>	&gt;
"	&quot;
'	&apos;
&	&amp;

The semicolon following each entity is required. With the entity substitution, the previous example would be written as follows:

Correct

```
<Value>Do if 5 &gt; 3</Value>
```

Summary

These are just some of the basics to get you up and running with XML in a hurry. Of course, as I stated earlier, reading just a couple of pages on XML will not make you a grand master. There are a lot of good books and Web sites out there that have more detailed explanations of this markup language.

Appendix C
XSD Primer

XML Schemas, or XSD documents, are an important part of working with XML. XSD documents support an XML document by specifying the structure of the XML document. Without an XSD document, applications have a hard time understanding XML documents.

The Purpose of an XSD Document

XSD documents are a replacement for Document Type Definition (DTD) documents. In the past, DTDs were used to fully describe an XML document; but their use is falling out of favor because DTDs are not based upon XML. Now everyone is turning to XML Schemas. DTDs use a separate language that is tougher to learn than XML and that is really meant for computer-to-human transfer of data. The increasing number of computer-to-computer data transfers requires a definition language that can easily describe XML. XSD documents are the solution, and they require no separate language. In fact, XSD documents use XML itself to describe the structure of the XML document.

NOTE: For more information on XML Schemas, visit www.w3.org.

Elements and Attributes

Just like XML documents, XML Schemas are made up of elements and attributes. Elements are the items that contain the data, and attributes are used to further define elements.

Elements

The main purpose of using elements in your XML Schema is to define the data types that are used in the XML document itself. The following example shows how you define an element and the data type of the value that is contained in the element.

```
<xsd:element name="age" type="xs:integer" />
```

The definition specifies the element age and that this particular element has to be an integer data type. Therefore, the following XML is valid if validated against this XSD Schema.

```
<age>31</age>
```

However, this also means that the following XML is invalid and would produce an error, because the element is not in integer form:

```
<age>Thirty-one</age>
```

The minOccurs and maxOccurs elements

There may be certain elements that you allow to appear only a limited number of times within an XML document. There also may be elements that are allowed to occur only once. For instance, if you have an XML document that provides customer details, you might want only one instance of the `<customerName>` element. The way in which you can enforce this is by using the `minOccurs` and the `maxOccurs` attributes within your element declarations.

```
<?xml version="1.0" ?>
<xsd:schema xmlns:xsd="http://www.w3.org/2001/XMLSchema">
    <xsd:element name="CustomerDetails" type="CustomerType" />
    <xsd:complexType name="CustomerType">
        <xsd:sequence>
            <xsd:element name="customerName" type="xsd:string"
                        minOccurs="1" maxOccurs="1" />
            <xsd:element name="customerID" type="xsd:integer"
                        minOccurs="1" maxOccurs="1" />
            <xsd:element name="customerAddress" type="xsd:string"
                        minOccurs="1" maxOccurs="2" />
            <xsd:element name="favoriteFoods" type=xsd:string"
                        minOccurs="0" maxOccurs="unbounded" />
        </xsd:sequence>
    </xsd:complexType>
</xsd:schema>
```

In this schema, there are four elements declared. There is also a set of rules in place stating the number of times each element may occur in the XML document. The `<customerName>` and the `<customerID>` elements are required to appear exactly once. Therefore, if these two elements are used within the `<CustomerDetails>` element more than once, the document won't be valid. The `<customerAddress>` element is allowed to appear twice in this sequence, so that the customer can have two addresses. The `maxOccurs="unbounded"` enables the `<favoriteFoods>` element to appear as many times as needed.

Attributes

Attributes are there to further define an element. Any element can contain as many attributes as it needs. Take a look at how to declare an attribute in an XML Schema document.

```
<xsd:element name="Customer">
    <xsd:complexType>
        <xsd:attribute name="Sex" type="xs:string" />
    </xsd:complexType>
<xsd:element>
```

This construction would allow you to have an element such as the following:

```
<Customer Sex="M">Bill Evjen</Customer>
```

Now the `<Customer>` element becomes even more defined with an attribute definition in place. Just as with the element definition, you can specify the type. In this case, the type is defined as a string, so that it can contain an "M" or an "F".

An attribute is declared within the `schema`, `complexType`, or `attributeGroup` elements. If there are other declarations within this complex type, such as other elements, the attribute declarations appear at the bottom of the element declaration.

If you are declaring multiple attributes, they do not need to appear in any specific order. Look at the following element declarations in your XML Schema file.

Default

The attribute tag within an XML Schema document can contain the attribute default. This specifies the initial value of the attribute as it is created. If the end user doesn't override the initial value, the default value is used.

```
<xsd:element name="Customer">
   <xsd:complexType>
      <xsd:attribute name="Member" type="xs:string" default="No" />
   </xsd:complexType>
<xsd:element>
```

Use

The `use` attribute allows you to specify whether the attribute for the element is required. This is an optional attribute and can take one of three values: `optional`, `prohibited`, or `required`.

```
<xsd:element name="Customer">
   <xsd:complexType>
      <xsd:attribute name="Sex" type="xs:string" use="required" />
   </xsd:complexType>
<xsd:element>
```

The default setting is `optional`, and this element is best used when you want to require an attribute to be used with an element.

Putting restrictions on attribute values

There will be times when you don't want to let the end user put in certain values for an attribute, but instead you choose to put a limit on the attribute's value.

```
<xsd:attribute name="age">
  <xsd:simpleType>
   <xsd:restriction base="xs:integer">
    <xsd:minInclusive value="12"/>
    <xsd:maxInclusive value="95"/>
   </xsd:restriction>
```

```
        </xsd:simpleType>
</xsd:attribute>
```

This is done is by using `minInclusive` and `maxInclusive`. The preceding example specifies an attribute age where the minimum value is 12 and the maximum value is 95. Therefore, if the end user inputs a value that is not within this range, the XML document is invalid.

Attribute groups

If you have a set of attributes that is used across a wide variety of elements, it is easier to create an attribute group in order to manage these attributes. This function allows you to create a group of attributes that you can assign to different elements without having to declare the same attributes over and over again for each element.

```
<xsd:attributeGroup name="myAttributes">
  <xsd:attribute name="x" type="xs:integer"/>
  <xsd:attribute name="y" type="xs:integer"/>
</xsd:attributeGroup>

<xsd:complexType name="myElementType">
  <xsd:attributeGroup ref="myAttributes"/>
</xsd:complexType>
```

The idea is to declare a group of attributes within the `<xsd:attributeGroup>` element. When you are ready to declare a set of attributes within an element, you simply make a reference to the attribute group using the `<xsd:attributeGroup>` element. Within this tag, you simply point to the attribute group using the `ref` attribute.

Even when using the attribute groups to define attributes for your elements, you can still provide an element with attributes other than those that the attribute group specifies.

```
<xsd:attributeGroup name="myAttributes">
  <xsd:attribute name="x" type="xs:integer"/>
  <xsd:attribute name="y" type="xs:integer"/>
</xsd:attributeGroup>

<xsd:complexType name="myElementType">
  <xsd:attribute name="z" type="xs:integer"/>
  <xsd:attributeGroup ref="myAttributes"/>
</xsd:complexType>
```

With this declaration, you assign the attributes that are represented in the attribute group `myAttributes` as well as a new attribute z.

There also may be situations where you don't want to use every attribute that is defined within the attribute group. In these cases, you simply use the `prohibited` keyword to turn off the capability for the end user to employ that particular attribute within the element.

```
<xsd:attributeGroup name="myAttributes">
  <xsd:attribute name="x" type="xs:integer"/>
```

```xml
    <xsd:attribute name="y" type="xs:integer"/>
</xsd:attributeGroup>

<xsd:complexType name="myElementType">
  <xsd:complexContent>
   <xsd:restriction base="xsd:myAttributes">
    <xsd:attribute name="x" use="required" />
    <xsd:attribute name="y" use="prohibited"/>
   </xsd:restriction>
  </xsd:complexContent>
</xsd:complexType>
```

Summary

This appendix gave you a quick overview of some of the basics of XML Schemas and told you what to look for when working with the schemas that are sent from your XML Web services. You will notice that, in most cases, all the work needed to create XML Schemas is done for you automatically, either by Visual Studio .NET or when you output a dataset from your XML Web service.

Appendix D
Bill Evjen's .NET Resources

Table D-1   Public Sites

Site Name	Description	Web Address
XML Web Services for ASP.NET	Web site for the book. Here you will find code from the book and any errata.	www.xmlws101.com
123aspx.com	The largest and best directory of .NET articles and tutorials on the Internet.	www.123aspx.com
ASPNG	Listservers galore.	www.aspng.com
DotNet Junkies	News and tutorial site.	www.dotnetjunkies.com
Learn XML WS	Learn all about XML Web services with Visual Basic .NET. This site also includes a book on Web services.	www.vbws.com
KB Alertz – Knowledge Base Alerts	Be alerted by e-mail whenever there is a new knowledge base article put out by Microsoft.	www.kbalertz.com
SOAP Web Services	News on Web services.	www.soapwebservices.com
Sal Central	Web services directory.	www.salcentral.com
X Methods	Web services directory.	www.xmethods.com
ASP Alliance	Article and tutorial site.	www.aspalliance.com
4 Guys From Rolla	Article and tutorial site.	www.4guysfromrolla.com
W3C	Where some of the standards used in Web services are managed.	www.w3.org

Site Name	Description	Web Address
AspFree	Article and tutorial site.	www.aspfree.com
XML Web Services	Article and tutorial site.	www.xmlwebservices.cc

Table D-2   Microsoft Sites

Site name	Web Address
MSDN	http://msdn.microsoft.com
XML Web Services	http://msdn.microsoft.com/webservices
GotDotNet	www.gotdotnet.com
ASP.NET	www.asp.net
IBuySpy	www.ibuyspy.com

Index

?
? (help) (wsdl.exe option), 208

<
<% (page directive) tags, 85

A
element (WSDL documents), 358
ACT (Application Center Test), 481
    locating, 481
    principles of operation, 482-483
    retesting Web services, 490-491
    running, 483-489
actor attribute (SOAP), 303-304
    exceptions, 469
Add Table dialog (Data Adapter Configuration Wizard), 439
Add Web Reference dialog, 105
    Disco files, 279, 284
    proxy classes and, 197
ADO .NET, 45-46
    architecture, 420-421
    DataAdapter, 424-425
    DataSet
        accessing fields, 423
        DataColumn, 423
        DataConstraint, 423
        DataRelation, 423
        DataRow, 423
        DataTable, 422
        overview, 421-422
        populating, 431-432
        typed, 424

namespaces, 425
.NET Framework Base Classes, 4
typed DataSets, creating, 443-446
XML and, 419-420
angle brackets (tags), 57
API (application programming interface)
    UDDI
        Inquiry, 263-264
        Publishing, 261-263
Application object
    compared to Session object, 184
    managing state, 181-183
Application property (WebService class), 552
Application State section (trace log), 465
applications
    Active Server Pages, consuming Web services from, 129-135
    assemblies
        components, 11-12
        overview, 11
    browser-based, advantages of, 112-113
    consuming Web services, compatibility, 101
    sample (UDDI SKD), 266
    security, 393
        authorization, 370
    VB 6, consuming Web services from, 124-128
    Web services concept, 49-51
appsettingbaseurl (wsdl.exe option), 207
appSettings node (web.config file), 478-479

586 Index

appsettingurlkey (wsdl.exe option), 207
architecture
  ADO .NET, 420-421
  .NET Remoting
    channels, 534
    formatters, 535-536
    overview, 534
    ports, 535
arguments, Open method, 130
arrays, sending images, 495
.asmx files, 141
ASP .NET, 4
  authentication models, 384
  error tracing, 462
    customizing log, 465-467
    trace node, 462-463
    viewing output, 463-465
  overview, 40
  Web Forms
    HTML controls, 41-42
    overview, 40
    Server controls, 40
    Web controls, 42-44
  web.config file, 371
    authentication element, 371
    authentication modes, 371
    authorization element, 372-373
  XML Web Services, 44
ASP applications, consuming Web services from, 129-130
  returning XML documents, 131-135
ASPState (Windows service), running, 175
.aspx files, test pages, 168
assemblies
  components, 11-12
  location of, 11
  overview, 11
assembly manifest, 12
asynchronous Web services, 502-506
attributes
  AttributeUsage, 333
  Class, 141-142
  Debug, 143
  docRef, 280
  <FORM> tag, 149
  Language, 141
  name, 149, 227, 232
  page, 85
  ref, 280
  SOAP
    actor, 303-304
    mustUnderstand, 304
  SOAP exceptions, 469
  targetNamespace, 228
  WebMethod
    Description property, 167
    EnableSession property, 172
    MessageName property, 168
    overview, 166
  WebService, 162
    Description property, 163-165
    Name property, 165-166
    Namespace property, 162-163
XML, 572
XML serialization, 345
XML syntax, 58
xmlns, 60
XmlRoot, 350
XSD, 578-579
  default, 579
  groups, 580-581

Index   587

restrictions on, 579
use, 579
XSD files, 62
AttributeUsage attribute, 333
authentication, 370
  ASP .NET, 384
  groups
    creating, 380
    IIS, 381
  IIS
    Basic authentication, 374-375
    Digest authentication, 375
    Integrated Windows
      authentication, 373
    overview, 373
  models, 373
  SOAP Headers, 393-396
    consuming Web services
      requiring, 397-399
  specific files, 383-384
  users
    creating, 376-378
    gathering information about,
      390-392
    IIS, 378
  users and groups, 376
  validating credentials, XML files
    and, 400-403
  Web services, consuming, 381-383
authentication node (web.config file),
  475
AuthenticationHeader class, 395
authorization, 370
  Context property, 385
  groups, IIS, 381
  Identity property, 385-387
  IsInRole method, 387-388

overview, 384
SOAP Headers, 393-396
users, IIS, 378-380
authorization node (web.config file),
  476
autogenerated Disco files, compared
  to manually created, 283

B

Base Class Libraries (BCL), 15-18
base classes, 4
Basic authentication, 374-375
BCL (Base Class Libraries), 15-18
BeginGetImage method, 505
BinaryFormatter class (.NET
  Remoting), 535-536
Binding class, 555
binding description (WSDL document
  structure), 226
binding node, screen scraping, 511
<binding> element (WSDL
  documents), 234
BindingCollection class, 555
bindingTemplate (UDDI data
  structure type), 257-258
Bitmap class, 495
body (SOAP), 151
Body element (SOAP), 304
  requests, 304-305
  response, 305
browser-based applications,
  advantages of, 112-113
BufferResponse property,
  WebMethodAttribute class,
  549

business classification section (UDDI Business Registry), 251
Business Detail section (UDDI Business Registry), 247
business layer, 158
business models, XML Web services, 78-79
businessEntity (UDDI data structure type), 255-256
businessService (UDDI data structure type), 256-257
byte arrays, sending images, 495

C

C#
   Application object, 181
   Application object compared to Session object, 182
   ASP .NET, customizing trace log, 466
   authentication, 385
      consuming Web services requiring, 382
      identifying user roles, 388
      verifying, 387
   CacheDuration property, 480
   calculator button functionality, code-behind page, 109
   calculator Web service source code, 84
   classes, 142
      creating, 27-28
   cookies, 187
   CurrencyConverter Web service source code, 95
   DataReader class, 427
   DataSets
      accessing fields, 423
      populating, 432
   descriptions, adding to test pages, 165
   descriptoin property (WebMethod attribute), 167
   EnableSession property, 172
   EncryptionExtension class, 413
   exceptions
      forcing, 455
      throwing, 460
   GetCustomerOrders WebMethod, 447
   Hello World program, 30-32
   images, displaying, 497
   ImageSend Web service, 494-495
   methods, defining, 145
   name property, 165
   namespaces
      declaring, 163
      importing, 13-14, 426
   .NET Remoting
      client application, 541
      creating host for remote objects, 538
      creating remote objects, 537
   overview, 26-27
   Page_Load event, 320
   procedures, 28-30
   random image Web service source code, 155
   Reference.cs file, 201-203
   sessions, creating, 174
   SOAP, throwing exceptions, 468
   SOAP extension for encrypting responses, 405, 410

SOAP Headers
   consuming Web services requiring, 398
   controlling transmission direction, 324
   not requiring, 322
   requiring for authentication, 394
   validating, 327
SoapHeader class, 316
SQL Server
   deleting data, 431
   inserting data, 429
SqlConnection class, 426
TraceExtension class, 335-337
TraceExtensionAttribute class, 333
Try-Catch code, 457-458
Try-Catch-Finally code, 459
typed DataSets, accessing fields, 424
validating login credentials, 402
variables, declaring, 27
ViewState, extending, 190
Web Forms, retrieving images, 499-500
Web service references, 199
Web services, invoking asynchronously, 504-505
WebMethods
   overloading, 501
   SOAP Headers, 317
XmlSerializer class
   automatic generation, 347
   modifying output, 349
CacheDuration property, 480
   WebMethodAttribute class, 550
caching, 479-480
   benefits, 480

   limitations, 481
calculator Web service, creating, 84-86
Calculator Web service
   button functionality, code-behind page, 108-109
   consuming, Windows Forms, 103-111
   cookies, 185-188
   Windows Forms, creating, 111-112
calendars, 53
case sensitivity
   C#, 27
   XML, 58, 578
certificates, WS-License protocol, 364
channels, .NET Remoting, 534
Class View window (Visual Studio .NET), 36-37
classes
   AuthenticationHeader, 395
   BCL (Base Class Libraries), 15-18
   BinaryFormatter, 535-536
   Binding, 555
   BindingCollection, 555
   Bitmap, 495
   ContractReference, 563
   creating
      C#, 27-28
      Visual Basic .NET, 21-22
   DataReader, 427-428
   declaring, 141-142
   defining, 86
   DiscoveryClientDocument-Collection, 564
   DiscoveryClientProtocol, 564
   DiscoveryClientReference-Collection, 564

DiscoveryClientResult, 564
DiscoveryClientResultCollection, 564
DiscoveryDocument, 564
DiscoveryDocumentReference, 564
DiscoveryExceptionDictionary, 564
DiscoveryReference, 565
DiscoveryReferenceCollection, 565
DocumentableItem, 555
ExtensionEngine, 411
FaultBinding, 555
FaultBindingCollection, 556
HttpAddressBinding, 556
HttpBinding, 556
HttpGetClientProtocol, 565
HttpMethodAttribute, 565
HttpOperationBinding, 556
HttpPostClientProtocol, 565
HttpSimpleClientProtocol, 566
HttpUrlEncodedBinding, 556
HttpUrlReplacementBinding, 556
HttpWebClientProtocol, 566
Import, 556
ImportBinding, 557
ImportCollection, 557
inheritance, Visual Basic .NET, 22
locating, Windows Forms Class Viewer, 17-18
LogicalMethodInfo, 566
MatchAttribute, 566
Message, 557
MessageBinding, 557
MessageCollection, 557
MessagePart, 557
MessagePartCollection, 557
MimeContentBinding, 557
MimeMultipartRelatedBinding, 558

MimePart, 558
MimePartCollection, 558
MimeTextBinding, 558
MimeTextMatch, 558
MimeTextMatchCollection, 558
MimeXmlBinding, 558
modifiers
   C#, 27-28
   Visual Basic .NET, 22
namespaces, 13
   importing, 13-15
.NET Framework Base Classes, 4
number of in .NET Framework, 425
Operation, 558
OperationBinding, 559
OperationBindingCollection, 559
OperationCollection, 559
OperationFault, 559
OperationFaultCollection, 559
OperationInput, 559
OperationMessage, 559
OperationMessageCollection, 559
OperationOutput, 560
OutputBinding, 560
Port, 560
PortCollection, 560
PortType, 560
PortTypeCollection, 560
proxy
   compiling, 210, 211
   creating, 107, 195
   creating with wsdl.exe, 205-210
   examining, 214
   overview, 194
   timeout property, 215
   URL property, 214-215

viewing in Solution Explorer, 199
Visual Studio .NET, 195-198
SchemaReference, 565
Service, 560
ServiceCollection, 560
ServiceDescription, 560
ServiceDescriptionBaseCollection, 561
ServiceDescriptionCollection, 561
ServiceDescriptionFormatExtension, 561
ServiceDescriptionFormatExtensionCollection, 561
ServiceDescriptionImporter, 561
ServiceDescriptionReflector, 561
SoapAddressBinding, 561
SoapBinding, 562, 565
SoapBodyBinding, 562
SoapClientMessage, 566
SoapDocumentMethodAttribute, 566
SoapDocumentServiceAttribute, 567
SoapException, 567
SoapExtension, 567
SoapExtensionAttribute, 567
SoapFaultBinding, 562
SoapFormatter, 535
SoapHeader, 316, 567
SoapHeaderAttribute, 567
SoapHeaderBinding, 562
SoapHeaderCollection, 567
SoapHeaderException, 567
SoapHeaderFaultBinding, 562
SoapHttpClientProtocol, 567
SoapMessage, 568
SoapOperationBinding, 562
SoapRpcMethodAttribute, 568
SoapRpcServiceAttribute, 568
SoapServerMessage, 568
SoapTransportImporter, 562
SoapUnknownHeader, 568
SQLConnection, 426-427
TraceExtension, 334-337
TraceExtensionAttribute, 332-333
Types, 562
UDDI SKD, 267-269
WebClientAsyncResult, 568
WebClientProtocol, 568
WebMethodAttribute, 549-551
WebService, 552
WebServiceAttribute, 552-553
WebServiceBindingAttribute, 553-554
XmlSerialization
   automatic XML generation, 346-347
   modifying XML output, 348-349
client configuration file (.NET Remoting), 542-543
client/server model, compared to Web services, 49
clients
   .NET Remoting, creating, 540-542
   RPC SOAP message generation, 345
   screen scraping, creating, 518-520
CLR (Common Language Runtime), 4
   CTS and, 20
   overview, 9
code attribute (SOAP exceptions), 469
code reuse, advantages of, 113-114

code window (Visual Studio .NET), 39, 93
code. *See* source code
code-behind pages, 108, 142
   Visual Basic .NET, cookies, 186
COM (Component Object Model), 3
comments, XML, 573
commerce (XML Web services), overview, 77-79
Common Language Runtime. *See* CLR
Common Type System. *See* CTS
compatibility
   compilers, 9
   Disco files, 279
   enterprise servers, 8
   importance of, 139
   programming languages, 8
   UDDI, NET Servers, 274
   Web services, applications for consumption of, 101
compilation node (web.config file), 474-475
compiling
   compatible compilers, 9
   JIT compilers, 10-11
   process description, 10-11
   proxy classes, 210
      command line options, 210-211
complex-type definitions, 62
Component Designer, 433-434
Component Object Model (COM), 3
configuration
   web.config file, 371
      appSettings node, 478-479
      authentication element, 371
      authentication node, 475
      authorization element, 372-373
      authorization node, 476
      compilation node, 474-475
      configuration node, 474
      customErrors node, 475
      globalization node, 477
      httpRuntime node, 479
      overview, 471-473
      sessionState node, 476
   wsdl.exe, 213-214
configuration node (web.config file), 474
connections
   creating, Visual Studio .NET, 435-437
   data sources, 426-427
consuming Web services
   application compatibility, 101
   authentication and, 381-383
   from Active Server Pages applications, 129-130
      returning XML documents, 131-135
   from VB 6 applications, 124-128
   overview, 102-103
   Web Forms, 112
      browser-based applications, 112-113
      EnglishGermanEnglish Dictionary Web service, 114-121
   Windows Forms
      Calculator Web Service, 103-111
      creating, 111-112
   within other Web services, 121-124
consuming Web services, 193

Contacts section (UDDI Business Registry), 247
Context property
    authorization, 385
    WebService class, 552
<contractRef> element (Disco files), 280-281
ContractReference class, 563
controls
    HTML, 41-42
    Server, 40
    Web, 42-44
cookieless sessions, 179-181
cookies
    disadvantages, 185
    overview, 185
Cookies Collection section (trace log), 465
CTS (Common Type System), 20
CurrencyConverter Web service
    creating, 91-97
    testing, 97-99
customErrors node (web.config file), 460-461, 475

D

Data Adapter Configuration Wizard, 437
    adding queries, 440
    Use SQL Statements option, 438-439
Data Encryption Standard. *See* DES
data layer, 158-160
Data Link Properties dialog (Visual Studio .NET), 435
data sources, connecting to, 426-427

data types
    defining, 228
    mapping XML to .NET, 143-145
    SOAP encoding, 307-309
    XSD compared to .NET, 229-231
DataAdapter, 424-425
    changing field mappings, 441-442
    Web Services Designer Generated Code, 442
databases, SQL Server, 178
DataColumn, 423
DataConstraint, 423
DataReader class, 427-428
DataRelation, 423
DataRow, 423
DataSet
    accessing fields, 423
    creating, 433
        changing field mappings, 441-442
        Data Adapter Configuration Wizard, 437-440
    DataColumn, 423
    DataConstraint, 423
    DataRelation, 423
    DataRow, 423
    DataTable, 422
    overview, 421-422
    populating, 431-432
    returning, creating Web service for, 446-448
    typed, 424
        creating, 443-446
DataTables, 422
DCOM, protocols, 146
Debug attribute, 143
declarations

594   Index

classes, 141-142
methods, 145-146
variables
  C#, 27
  Visual Basic .NET, 21
Web services, 141-143
XML, 57, 574
Decrypt property, 411
default attribute, XSD, 579
default namespaces, 60
definitions
  classes, 86
  data types, 228
  XSD files, 61
<definitions> element (WSDL documents), 226-228
deleting data into SQL Server, 430-431
DES (Data Encryption Standard), 404-414
Description property
  WebMethod attribute, 167
  WebMethodAttribute class, 550
  WebService attribute, 163-165
  WebServiceAttribute class, 552
<description> element (WSIL documents), 358
descriptions (XML Web services), WSDL, 71-74
deserialization, 331
Design mode (Visual Studio .NET)
  creating Web Forms, 116
  compared to HTML mode, 39
detail attribute (SOAP exceptions), 469
detail element (SOAP), 307
development

business environments, presentation layer, 158
multitiered environments, 153-154
  data layer, 158-160
  presentation layer, 154-158
development type errors, 453-454
DidUnderstand property (SoapHeader class), 328
Digest authentication, 375
Direction property (SoapHeader class), 322
directories. *See* folders
Disco file, 74-75
  Add Web Reference dialog, 284
  autogenerated compared to manually created, 283
  <contractRef> element, 280-281
  creating, 282-284
  Disco.exe, 288
    options, 289-290
  <discovery> element, 280
  <discoveryRef> element, 281
  overview, 278-279
  <schemaRef> element, 281
  <soap> element, 281
  structure, 279
Disco.exe, 288
  options, 289-290
discovering Web services, 140
discovery
  Disco file
    Add Web Reference dialog, 284
    autogenerated compared to manually created, 283
    <contractRef> element, 280-281
    creating, 282-284
    <discovery> element, 280

<discoveryRef> element, 281
overview, 278-279
<schemaRef> element, 281
<soap> element, 281
structure, 279
Disco.exe, 288
options, 289-290
overview, 277
vsdisco files, 285
creating, 286
<dynamicDiscovery> element, 287
enabling, 285
<exclude> element, 287
WS-Inspection protocol, 356
WSIL document structure, 357-359
WSIL documents, 356-357
WS-License protocol, 364-365
WS-Referral protocol, 361-363
WS-Routing protocol, 359-361
WS-Security protocol, 363
Discovery URLs section (UDDI Business Registry), 251-252
<discovery> element (Disco files), 280
DiscoveryClientDocumentCollection class, 564
DiscoveryClientProtocol class, 564
DiscoveryClientReferenceCollection class, 564
DiscoveryClientResult class, 564
DiscoveryClientResultCollection class, 564
DiscoveryDocument class, 564
DiscoveryDocumentReference class, 564

DiscoveryExceptionDictionary class, 564
<discoveryRef> element (Disco files), 281
DiscoveryReference class, 565
DiscoveryReferenceCollection class, 565
DNA (Distributed interNet Applications Architecture), 3
docRef attribute, <contractRef> element, 280
document encoding (SOAP), 341
using with RPC encoding, 343-345
DocumentableItem class, 555
<documentation> element (WSDL documents), 237-238
documents
WSDL, viewing, 88
WSIL, 356-357
structure, 357-359
domain (wsdl.exe option), 207
dynamic discovery, 285
Dynamic Help window (Visual Studio .NET), 38-39
<dynamicDiscovery> element (vsdisco file), 287

E

early-binding, 195
Edit Relation dialog (Visual Studio .NET), 445
elements
element (WSDL documents), 358
<binding> element (WSDL documents), 234

596 Index

<contractRef> element (Disco files), 280-281
    docRef attribute, 280
<definitions> element (WSDL documents), 226-228
<description> element (WSIL documents), 358
<discovery> element (Disco files), 280
<discoveryRef> element (Disco files), 281
<documentation> element (WSDL documents), 237-238
<dynamicDiscovery> element (vsdisco files), 287
<exclude> element (vsdisco files), 287
<fault> element (WSDL documents), 233
<imports> element (WSDL documents), 236-237
<input> element (WSDL documents), 233
<inspection> element (WSIL documents), 358
<message> element (WSDL documents), 231-232
<operation> element (WSDL documents), 235
<output> element (WSDL documents), 233
<part> element (WSDL documents), 232
<path> element (WS-Routing protocol), 361
<portType> element (WSDL documents), 232-233
    renaming, 350
<schemaRef> element (Disco files), 281
<service> element (WSDL documents), 235-236
<service> element (WSIL documents), 358
<soap> element (Disco files), 281
<types> element (WSDL documents), 228-231
<wssec:credentials> element (WS-License protocol), 364
<x:action> element (WS-Routing protocol), 361
<x:from> element (WS-Routing protocol), 361
<x:fwd> element (WS-Referral protocol), 363
<x:id> element (WS-Routing protocol), 361
<x:prefix> element (WS-Referral protocol), 362
<x:to> element (WS-Routing protocol), 361
EnableSession property, 172
    WebMethodAttribute class, 550
encoding types (SOAP), 307-309
    document, 341
    overview, 340-341
    RPC, 341-343
        client-side generation, 345
    using both in same service, 343-345
Encrypt property, 411
encryption
    DES, 404-414
    SOAP extensions, 403
        creating, 404-411

EncryptionEngine, 411-414
    Web services, consuming, 414-416
EncryptionEngine extension, 411-414
EnglishGermanEnglish Dictionary
    Web service, consuming with
    Web Forms, 114-121
enterprise servers, compatibility, 8
entity references, XML, 575
envelope (SOAP), 151, 302
error handling. *See also* exceptions
    global.asax file, 461-462
    web.config file, customErrors node,
        460-461
errors
    SOAP
        detail element, 307
        fault element, 305-306
        faultcode element, 306
        faultfactor element, 306
        faultstring element, 306
    types
        development, 453-454
        runtime, 454
events, Page_Load, 319-320
exceptions. *See also* error handling
    error tracing (ASP .NET), 462
        customizing log, 465-467
        trace node, 462-463
        viewing output, 463-465
    overview, 455-456
    SOAP, 467-469
        attributes, 469
    SOAP Headers, 330
    throwing, 459-460
    Try-Catch construct, 456-458
    Try-Catch-Finally construct, 458-459

<exclude> element (vsdisco file), 287
ExtensionEngine class, encryption
    keys and, 411
extensions, SOAP, 331-340

F

fault element (SOAP), 305-306
    exceptions, 468
<fault> element (WSDL documents), 233
FaultBinding class, 555
FaultBindingCollection class, 556
faultcode element (SOAP), 306
faultfactor element (SOAP), 306
faultstring element (SOAP), 306
files
    .asmx (Web service extension), 141
    Disco, 74-75
        Add Web Reference dialog, 284
        autogenerated compared to
            manually created, 283
        <contractRef> element, 280-281
        creating, 282-284
        Disco.exe, 288-290
        <discovery> element, 280
        <discoveryRef> element, 281
        overview, 278-279
        <schemaRef> element, 281
        <soap> element, 281
        structure, 279
    pipe-delimited, 55
    saving, 86
    vsdisco, 285
        creating, 286
        <dynamicDiscovery> element, 287

598 Index

enabling, 285
<exclude> element, 287
web.config, sessionState node, 174
folders
    assembly locations, 11
    IIS, wwwroot, 83
<FORM> tag, attributes, 149
formatters, .NET Remoting, 535-536
Forms Collection section (trace log), 465
Function procedures (Visual Basic .NET), 23-25
functions
    GetData, 427
    UDDI Inquiry APIs, 263-264
    UDDI Publisher APIs, 261

G

GAC (Global Assembly Cache), 11
garbage collection, overview, 12-13
Generate Dataset dialog (Visual Studio .NET), 443
GetData function, 427
GetImage method, 498
Global Assembly Cache. *See* GAC
global.asax file, error handling, 461-462
globalization node (web.config file), 477
Green Pages (UDDI Business Registry), 244
GridLayout (Visual Studio .NET), 116
groups
    authentication, 376
        creating, 380
        IIS, 381

authorization, IIS, 381
XSD attributes, 580-581
GXA (Global XML Web Services Architecture)
overview, 354-355
WS-Inspection protocol, 356
    WSIL document structure, 357-359
    WSIL documents, 356-357
WS-License protocol, 364-365
WS-Referral protocol, 361-363
WS-Routing protocol, 359-361
WS-Security protocol, 363

H

hardware requirements, 81
Headers (SOAP), 151, 302-303
    accepting, 316-319
    collecting names and e-mail addresses, 315
    controlling direction of transmission, 322-325
    exceptions, 330
    not requiring, 321
    overview, 315-316
    passing, from clients, 319-321
    requiring, 321
    validating, 325
        MustUnderstand property, 325-330
Headers Collection section (trace log), 465
Hello World source code
    C#, 30, 31-32
    Visual Basic .NET, 25-26

Index 599

HTML (Hypertext Markup Language), compared to XML, 57
HTML controls, 41-42
HTML mode (Visual Studio .NET), compared to Design mode, 39
HTTP (Hypertext Transfer Protocol)
  SOAP and, 295-296
  Web services and, 49
HttpAddressBinding class, 556
HttpBinding class, 556
HttpChannel (.NET Remoting), 535
HTTP-GET, 67-69
  methods, calling, 147-149
  overview, 147
  QueryStrings, 147
HttpGetClientProtocol class, 565
HttpMethodAttribute class, 565
HTTP-POST, 67-69, 149-150
HttpPostClientProtocol class, 565
httpRuntime node (web.config file), 479
HTTPS (security), 404
HTTPSessionState object, 172
HttpSimpleClientProtocol class, 566
HttpUrlEncodedBinding class, 556
HttpUrlReplacementBinding class, 556
HttpWebClientProtocol class, 566

I

IDE (Integrated Development Environment), 8
  Visual Studio .NET
    Class View window, 36-37
    Code window, 39
    Design mode compared to HTML mode, 39
    Dynamic Help window, 38-39
    overview, 33-34
    Properties window, 38
    Server Explorer, 35
    Solution Explorer, 35-36
    Start Page, 34-35
    Toolbox, 37
identifiers section (UDDI Business Registry), 251
Identity property, authorization, 385-387
IIS (Internet Information Server)
  authentication
    Basic authentication, 374-375
    Digest authentication, 375
    groups, 381
    Integrated Windows authentication, 373
    overview, 373
    users, 378
  authorization
    groups, 381
    users, 378-380
  checking installation, 82
  installing, 83
IL (Microsoft Intermediate Language), 10
images, returning, 493-501
ImageSend Web service source code, 494-495
Implements keyword (Visual Basic .NET), 22
Import class, 556
ImportBinding class, 557
ImportCollection class, 557

importing namespaces, 13-15, 85, 425
<imports> element (WSDL documents), 236-237
inheritance (Visual Basic .NET), 22
Inherits keyword (Visual Basic .NET), 22
in-process sessions, 175
<input> element (WSDL documents), 233
Inquiry APIs (UDDI), 263-264
inserting data into SQL Server, 428-429
<inspection> element (WSIL documents), 358
installation
   IIS (Internet Information Server), 83
   SQL Server, 178
   Web services compared to traditional applications, 51
Integrated Windows authentication, 373
interfaces, XML Web services, 88
intermediaries (SOAP), 303-304
Internet, state and, 171
IsInRole method, authorization, 387-388

J

JIT compilers, 10-11
JScript .NET, 32

K

keywords
   C#, procedures, 29-30
   Visual Basic .NET
      Implements, 22
      Inherits, 22
      Sub and Function procedures, 23-24

L

language (wsdl.exe option), 207
Language attribute, 141
late-binding, 196
libraries, BCL (Base Class Libraries), 15-18
links, sending images, 498
location element, authentication and, 384
Location property (WebServiceBindingAttribute class), 553
Lock method (Application object), 181, 184
logical errors, 454
LogicalMethodInfo class, 566
login element, validating credentials, 401
logins, authentication and, 370

M

machine.config file, enabling dynamic discovery, 285
managed code, 9
Managed Extensions for C++, 33
MatchAttribute class, 566
mathematics, importance of, 454
maxOccurs element (XSD), 578
memory
   caching, 479-480
      benefits, 480

limitations, 481
garbage collection, 12-13
message attribute (SOAP exceptions), 469
Message class, 557
message description (WSDL document structure), 226
message node, screen scraping, 510
<message> element (WSDL documents), 231-232
MessageBinding class, 557
MessageCollection class, 557
MessageName property, 502
   WebMethod attribute, 168
   WebMethodAttribute class, 550
MessagePart class, 557
MessagePartCollection class, 557
messages, SOAP, 301-302
   interaction points, 330-331
   Trace Utility, 310-313
   viewing, 309-310
   writing input/output to text files, 339-340
metadata, 9
methods
   adding, 86
   BeginGetImage, 505
   defining, 145-146
   GetImage, 498
   IsInRole, 387-388
   Lock, 181-184
   ProcessMessage, 337, 411
   SessionCounter, 173
   SOAP, 151
   UnLock, 181, 184
   USDConvert, 229
   Web, testing, 89-91

WebMethods
   overloading, 501-502
   SOAP Headers and, 317
microwaves, 52-53
MimeContentBinding class, 557
MimeMultipartRelatedBinding class, 558
MimePart class, 558
MimePartCollection class, 558
MimeTextBinding class, 558
MimeTextMatch class, 558
MimeTextMatchCollection class, 558
MimeXmlBinding class, 558
minOccurs element (XSD), 578
models
   authentication, 373
      Basic authentication, 374-375
      Digest authentication, 375
      Integrated Windows authentication, 373
MSIL (Microsoft Intermediate Language). *See* IL
msType:match node, screen scraping, 511
multitiered environments, 153-154
   business layer, 158
   data layer, 158-160
   presentation layer, 154-158
mustUnderstand attribute (SOAP), 304
MustUnderstand property (SoapHeader class), 325-330

N

name attribute, 149

<definitions> element (WSDL documents), 227
<message> element (WSDL documents), 232
Name property, 165-166
    WebServiceAttribute class, 553
    WebServiceBindingAttribute class, 553
namespace (wsdl.exe option), 207
Namespace property, 162-163
    WebServiceAttribute class, 553
    WebServiceBindingAttribute class, 554
namespaces, 13
    ADO .NET, 425
    default, 162
    <definitions> element (WSDL document), 226-228
    Envelope, 302
    importing, 13-15, 85, 425
    SOAP Headers, accepting, 316
    System, classes, 15-18
    System.Security.Cryptography, 404
    System.Security.Principal, 389
    System.Web.Services, classes, 549-554
    System.Web.Services.Description, classes, 554-562
    System.Web.Services.Discovery, classes, 563-565
    System.Web.Services.Protocol, security and, 395
    System.Web.Services.Protocols, classes, 565-568
    System.Security.Principal, 389
    XML, 58-61, 574
naming elements, 350

NASSL (Network Accessibility Service Specification Language), 219
nesting, XML elements, 58, 572
.NET Alerts, 530-531
.NET Framework
    classes, number of, 425
    data types
        compared to XSD data types, 229-231
        XML mappings, 143-145
    development environment, 7-8
    enterprise servers, compatibility, 8
    IDE, 8
    Microsoft product development philosophy and, 5-7
    overview, 3-5
    programming languages, 8
    state, 172-173
.NET My Services
    history, information sharing, 527-528
    information sharing model, 528-529
    .NET Alerts, 530-531
    overview, 525
    possible future services, 531
    security considerations, 531-532
    services included, 526-527
.NET Remoting
    architecture
        channels, 534
        formatters, 535-536
        overview, 534
        ports, 535
    client application, 540-542
    client configuration file, 542-543

compared to Web services, 533-534
overview, 533
remote objects
   creating, 537-538
   creating host for, 538-539
server configuration file, 539-540
testing remote call, 543-545
.NET Servers, UDDI support, 274
Network Accessibility Service Specification Language (NASSL), 219
New Project dialog box (Visual Studio .NET), 91
New Test Wizard (Application Center Test), 483-485
nologo (wsdl.exe option), 207
Notepad, creating XML Web services, 84-86

O

object-oriented programming languages, characteristics of, 21
objects
   Application
      compared to Session object, 184
      managing state, 181-183
   garbage collection, 12-13
   HTTPSessionState, 172
   .NET Remoting
      creating, 537-538
      creating host for, 538-539
   WindowsIdentity, 390
Ole DB DataAdapter, 424
Open method, arguments, 130

operating systems, .NET Framework support, 4
Operation class, 558
operation description (WSDL document structure), 226
OperationBinding class, 559
OperationBindingCollection class, 559
OperationCollection class, 559
OperationFault class, 559
OperationFaultCollection class, 559
OperationInput class, 559
OperationMessage class, 559
OperationMessageCollection class, 559
OperationOutput class, 560
operator nodes (UDDI Business Registry), 242
out (wsdl.exe option), 207
out-of-process sessions, 175-177
   SQL Server, 178-179
<output> element (WSDL documents), 233
OutputBinding class, 560
overloading WebMethods, 501-502

P

page attributes, 85
page directive, 85
Page_Load event, 319-320
part description (WSDL document structure), 226
<part> element (WSDL documents), 232
password (wsdl.exe option), 207
passwords, authentication and, 370

604 Index

<path> element (WS-Routing protocol), 361
performance
  Application Center Test, 481
    locating, 481
    principles of operation, 482-483
    retesting Web services, 490-491
    running, 483-489
  caching, 479-480
    benefits, 480
    limitations, 481
  security and, 370
persisting information, cookies and
  disadvantages, 185
  overview, 185
pipe-delimited text files, 55
populating DataSets, 431-432
PorcessMessage method, 411
port 80, 146
Port class, 560
port description (WSDL document structure), 226
PortCollection class, 560
ports, NET Remoting, 535
PortType class, 560
portType description (WSDL document structure), 226
<portType> element (WSDL documents), 232-233
PortTypeCollection class, 560
presentation layer, 154-158
private assemblies, 11
procedures
  C#, 28-30
  Visual Basic .NET, 23-25
ProcessMessage method (TraceExtension class), 337

products
  digital calendars, 53
  microwaves, 52, 53
  refrigerators, 53
programming languages, 8
  C#
    creating classes, 27-28
    declaring variables, 27
    overview, 26-27
    procedures, 28-30
  compatibility, 19-20
  JScript .NET, 32
  object-oriented, 21
  platform independence, 20
  selecting, 20
  Visual Basic .NET
    creating classes, 21-22
    declaring variables, 21
    overview, 21
    Sub and Function procedures, 23-25
  Visual C++ .NET, 33
  Visual J# .NET, 33
programming code reuse, Web services and, 113-114
properties
  Application, 552
  BufferResponse, 549
  CacheDuration, 480, 550
  Context, 385, 552
  Description, 550, 552
  DidUnderstand, 328
  Direction, 322
  EnableSession,, 550
  Identity, 385-387
  Location, 553
  MessageName, 502, 550

MustUnderstand, 325-328, 330
Name, 165-166, 553
Namespace, 162-163, 553-554
proxy classes
    timeout, 215
    URL, 214-215
Required, 321
Server, 552
Session, 552
SOAP response encryption, 411
timeout, sessions, 174
TransactionOption, 551
User, 552
WebMethod attribute
    Description, 167
    MessageName, 168
WebService attribute, Description, 163-165
Properties window, 93
Properties window (Visual Studio .NET), 38
protocol (wsdl.exe option), 208
protocols, 50
    DCOM, 146
    HTTP-GET
        calling methods, 147, 149
        overview, 147
        QueryStrings, 147
    HTTP-POST, 149-150
    overview, 146
    proxy classes and, 208-209
    SOAP, 69-70, 150-153
        Body element, 304-305
        data type encoding, 307-309
        detail element, 307
        fault element, 305-306
        faultcode element, 306

faultfactor element, 306
faultstring element, 306
SOAP (Simple Object Access Protocol)
    actor attribute, 303-304
    advantages of, 294
    complex response, 297-300
    envelope, 302
    header, 302-303
    HTTP and, 295-296
    message, 301-302
    mustUnderstand attribute, 304
    overview, 295
    requests, 296
    response, 296
    specification, 300-301
    Web services and, 293
    XML and, 295
WS-Inspection, 356
    WSIL document structure, 357-359
    WSIL documents, 356-357
WS-License, 364-365
WS-Referral, 361-363
WS-Routing, 359-361
WS-Security, 363
XML Web services, 67-69
proxy (wsdl.exe option), 208
proxy classes
    alternative protocols, generating for, 208-209
    compiling, 210
        command line options, 210-211
    creating, 107, 195
        screen scraping and, 513-517
        Visual Studio .NET, 195-198
        wsdl.exe, 205-210

examining, overview, 214
overview, 194
timeout property, 215
URL property, 214-215
viewing in Solution Explorer, 199
proxydomain (wsdl.exe option), 208
proxypassword (wsdl.exe option), 208
proxyusername (wsdl.exe option), 208
publisherAssertion (UDDI data structure type), 260-261
Publishing APIs (UDDI), 261-263
publishing services (UDDI Business Registry), 244
   categories, 244, 246
   test registry, 246

Q

Query Builder dialog (Data Adapter Configuration Wizard), 440
QueryString Collection section (trace log), 465
QueryStrings, 147

R

random image Web service source code, 154-155
reading data, 427-428
ref attribute (<contractRef> element), 280
Reference.cs file, 201-203
Reference.vb file, 200-201
references
   code, making in, 199
   renaming, 199
   Web services, updating, 204-205
referencing

early-binding, 195
   UDDI DLL, 267
   Web services, 106
   WebMethods, 331
refrigerators, 53
registration
   UDDI Business Registry, 246
      authentication and authorization, 269
      business classification section, 251
      Business Detail section, 247
      Contacts section, 247
      Discovery URLs section, 251-252
      identifiers section, 251
      limitations, 252
      publishing data structures, 271-273
      publishing tModels, 269-271
      Services section, 248, 250
      SKD, 269
regular expressions, screen scraping and, 510-513
relationships, editing (Schema Designer), 445
Request Detail section (trace log), 465
requests, SOAP, 152, 296
   Body element, 304-305
Required property (SoapHeader class), 321
resources, 583-584
response, SOAP, 153, 296
   Body element, 305
   complex data, 297-300
root elements
   renaming, 350

XML, 573-574
root tags, 57
routing
   WS-Referral protocol, 361-363
   WS-Routing protocol, 359-361
RPC encoding (SOAP), 341-343
   client-side generation, 345
   using with document encoding, 343-345
runtime type errors, 454

S

saving source code files, 86
Schema Designer, 444
<schemaRef> element (Disco files), 281
SchemaReference class, 565
schemas
   XML, creating in Visual Studio .NET, 64
   XSD files, 61-63
SCL (Service Contract Language), 220
screen scraping
   clients, creating, 518-520
   disadvantages of, 517
   overview, 507
   stock quote example, 508
      locating data, 508-509
      proxy class, creating, 513-517
      WSDL document, creating, 509-513
searching, UDDI Business Registry, 253
security
   application security, 393

authentication, 370
   ASP .NET, 384
   consuming Web services requiring, 381-383
   creating groups, 380
   creating users, 376, 378
   gathering information about users, 390-392
   IIS, 373-375, 378, 381
   models, 373
   specific files, 383-384
   users and groups, 376
authorization, 370
   Context property, 385
   Identity property, 385-387
   IIS, 378-381
   IsInRole method, 387-388
   overview, 384
encryption
   consuming Web services, 414-416
   DES, 404-414
   EncryptionEngine extension, 411-414
   SOAP extensions, 403
   SOAP extensions, creating, 404-411
HTTPS, 404
logged-on users, System.Security.Principal namespace, 389
NET My Services, 531-532
overview, 369
performance considerations, 370
SOAP Headers, 393-396
   consuming Web services requiring, 397-399

608   Index

validating credentials, 400-403
Web services compared to Web sites, 369
web.config file, 371
   authentication element, 371
   authorization element, 372-373
serialization, 331
   data types, 307
   SOAP, changing output, 345-351
server (wsdl.exe option), 208
server configuration file (.NET Remoting), 539-540
Server controls, 40
Server Explorer (Visual Studio .NET), 35
   data sources, accessing, 436
Server property (WebService class), 552
Server Variables section (trace log), 465
Service class, 560
Service Contract Language (SCL), 220
service descriptions. *See also* WSDL alternatives, 220
service providers, locating, 75-77
<service> element (WSDL documents), 235-236
<service> element (WSIL documents), 358
ServiceCollection class, 560
ServiceDescription class, 560
ServiceDescriptionBaseCollection class, 561
ServiceDescriptionCollection class, 561
ServiceDescriptionFormatExtension class, 561
ServiceDescriptionFormatExtensionCollection class, 561
ServiceDescriptionImporter class, 561
ServiceDescriptionReflector class, 561
services description (WSDL document structure), 226
services node, screen scraping, 510
Services section (UDDI Business Registry), 248-250
Session object, compared to Application object, 184
Session property (WebService class), 552
Session State section (trace log), 465
SessionCounter method, 173
sessions
   cookieless, 179-181
   overview, 173-175
   running in-process, 175
   running out-of-process, 175-177
      SQL Server and, 178-179
   selecting modes, 179
sessionState node (web.config file), 174, 476
simple-type definitions, 61
SKD (Software Development Kit), UDDI, 265-266
   authentication and authorization, 269
   classes, 267-269
   publishing, 269
   publishing data structures, 271-273
   publishing tModels, 269-271
   sample application, 266

SOAP (Simple Object Access
    Protocol), 69-70, 150-153
  advantages of, 294
  <binding> element (WSDL
      documents), 234
  <body> element (WSDL
      documents), 235
  Body element, 304
    requests, 304-305
    response, 305
  complex response, 297-300
  data type encoding, 307-309
  detail element, 307
  encoding types
    document, 341
    overview, 340-341
    RPC, 341, 342-343
    RPC client-side generation, 345
    using both in same service, 343-345
  envelope, 302
  Envelope element, 302
  Header element, 302-303
  exceptions, 467-469
    attributes, 469
  extensions, 331-340
    creating, 404-411
    DES, 404
    encryption and, 403
    EncryptionEngine, 411-414
  fault element, 305-306
  faultcode element, 306
  faultfactor element, 306
  faultstring element, 306
  header, 302-303
  Headers
    accepting, 316-319
    authentication and authorization, 393-396
    consuming Web services requiring, 397-399
    controlling direction of transmission, 322-325
    exceptions, 330
    MustUnderstand property, 325-330
    not requiring, 321
    overview, 315-316
    passing from clients, 319-321
    requiring, 321
    validating, 325
  HTTP and, 295-296
  images, sending, 493-501
  intermediaries, actor attribute, 303-304
  message, 301-302
  messages
    interaction points, 330-331
    viewing, 309-310
    writing input/output to text files, 339-340
  mustUnderstand attribute, 304
  <operation> element (WSDL
      documents), 235
  overview, 295
  proxy classes and, 194
  requests, 296
  response, 296
  serialization, changing output, 345-351
  specification, 300-301
  Web services and, 293
  WS-Referral protocol, 361-363
  WS-Routing protocol, 359-361

XML and, 295
<soap> element (Disco files), 281
SOAP Toolkit, 310
    Trace Utility, 310-313
SoapAddressBinding class, 561
SoapBinding class, 562, 565
SoapBodyBinding class, 562
SoapClientMessage class, 566
SoapDocumentMethodAttribute class, 566
SoapDocumentServiceAttribute class, 567
SoapException class, 567
SoapExtension class, 567
SoapExtensionAttribute class, 567
SoapFaultBinding class, 562
SoapFormatter class (.NET Remoting), 535
SoapHeader class, 316, 567
SoapHeaderAttribute class, 567
SoapHeaderBinding class, 562
SoapHeaderCollection class, 567
SoapHeaderException class, 567
SoapHeaderFaultBinding class, 562
SoapHttpClientProtocol class, 567
SoapMessage class, 568
SoapMessageStage enumerations, 337
SoapOperationBinding class, 562
SoapRpcMethodAttribute class, 568
SoapRpcServiceAttribute class, 568
SoapServerMessage class, 568
SoapTransportImporter class, 562
SoapUnknownHeader class, 568
software requirements, 81
Solution Explorer (Visual Studio .NET), 35-36, 93
    viewing proxy classes, 199

source code
  C#
    authentication, 385
    automatic XML generation, 347
    CacheDuration property, 480
    calculator Web service, 84
    consuming Web services requiring SOAP Headers, 398
    consuming Web services, authentication and, 382
    controlling SOAP Header transmission direction, 324
    creating host for remote objects, 538
    creating remote objects, 537
    CurrencyConverter Web service, 95
    customizing ASP .NET trace log, 466
    displaying images, 497
    EncryptionEngine class, 413
    extending ViewState, 190
    forcing exceptions, 455
    GetCustomerOrders WebMethod, 447
    Hello World, 30-32
    identifying user roles, 388
    ImageSend Web service, 494-495
    invoking Web services asynchronously, 504-505
    modifying XML output, 349
    NET Remoting client application, 541
    not requiring SOAP Headers, 322
    overloading WebMethods, 501

Index 611

Page_Laod event, 320
random image Web service, 155
Reference.cs file, 201-203
requiring SOAP Headers for
   authentication, 394
retrieving images, 499-500
SOAP extension for encrypting
   responses, 405-410
SoapHeader class, 316
throwing exceptions, 460
throwing SOAP exceptions, 468
TraceExtension class, 335-337
TraceExtensionAttribute class,
   333
Try-Catch code, 457-458
Try-Catch-Finally code, 459
validating login credentials, 402
validating SOAP Headers, 327
verifying authentication, 387
WebMethods for SOAP Headers,
   317
calculator button functionality,
   code-behind page, 108-109
data type definitions, 228
DataReader class, 427
DataSets, populating, 431
<definitions> element (WSDL
   documents), 226
Disco files, 74
  creating, 283
  XML declaration, 279
imported type definitions, 237
<message> element (WSDL
   documents), 231
<portType> element (WSDL
   documents), 232-236

<service> element (WSDL
   documents), 235
SOAP envelope, 302
SOAP header, 303
SOAP request, 296
SOAP response, 296
  complex data, 297-300
SQL Server
  deleting data, 430
  inserting data, 428
  updating data, 429
using cookies, 185-188
Visual Basic .NET
  authentication, 385
  automatic XML generation, 346
  CacheDuration property, 480
  calculator Web service, 84
  consuming encrypted Web
    services, 414-415
  consuming Web services
    requiring SOAP Headers, 397
  consuming Web services,
    authentication and, 382
  controlling SOAP Header
    transmission direction, 323
  creating host for remote objects,
    538
  creating remote objects, 537
  CurrencyConverter Web service,
    95
  customizing ASP .NET trace log,
    466
  displaying images, 496-497
  EncryptionEngine class, 413
  extending ViewState, 190
  forcing exceptions, 455

612 Index

GetCustomerOrders WebMethod, 446
Hello World, 25-26
identifying user roles, 387
ImageSend Web service, 494
invoking Web services asynchronously, 503-504
modifying XML output, 348
NET Remoting client application, 541
not requiring SOAP Headers, 321
overloading WebMethods, 501
Page_Laod event, 319
random image Web service, 154
Reference.vb file, 200-201
requiring SOAP Headers for authentication, 394
retrieving images, 499
SoapHeader class, 316
throwing exceptions, 459
throwing SOAP exceptions, 468
TraceExtension class, 334-335
TraceExtensionAttribute class, 332
Try-Catch code, 457-458
Try-Catch-Finally code, 459
validating login credentials, 401
validating SOAP Headers, 326
verifying authentication, 386
WebMethods for SOAP Headers, 317
vsdisco file, 286
web.conf file
　appSettings node, 478
　authentication node, 475
　authorization node, 476
　compilation node, 474
　configuration node, 474
　customErrors node, 475
　globalization node, 477
　httpRuntime node, 479
　sessionState node, 476
web.config file, 472-473
WSDL document
　example, 221-224
　SOAP Headers, accepting, 318
WSDL file, 71-74
WSIL documents, 357
WS-Referral protocol, 362
WS-Routing protocol, 360
XML example file, 56
XML file example, 55
XSD file, 64
specifications, SOAP Header, 315
SQL Server
　data sources, creating connections, 435-437
　DataAdapter for, 424
　deleting data, 430-431
　inserting data, 428-429
　out-of-process sessions, 178-179
　updating data, 429-430
SQLConnection class, 426-427
standards, usefulness of, 239
Start Page (Visual Studio .NET), 34-35
state
　Application object, 181-183
　　compared to Session object, 184
　Internet and, 171
　NET Framework and, 172-173
　sessions
　　cookieless, 179-181

overview, 173-175
running in-process, 175
running out-of-process, 175-177
running out-of-process on SQL Server, 178-179
selecting modes, 179
ViewState
extending, 190-191
overview, 188-189
toggling on and off, 189
State Service (ASP .NET), running, 176
StateServer mode (sessionState node), 177
static discovery, 278
stock quote screen scraping example, 508
locating data, 508-509
WSDL document
creating, 509-513
proxy class, creating, 513-517
Sub procedures
Visual Basic .NET, 23-25
syntax
Disco files, viewing, 278
proxy classes, creating, 206
XML, 56
rules, 57
syntax errors, 454
System namespace, classes, 15-18
system requirements, creating Web Services, 81
System.Security.Cryptography namespace, 404
System.Security.Principal namespace, 389

System.Web.Services namespace, classes, 549-554
System.Web.Services.Description namespace, classes, 554-562
System.Web.Services.Discovery namespace, classes, 563-565
System.Web.Services.Protocol namespace, security and, 395
System.Web.Services.Protocols namespace, classes, 565-568

T

Table Mappings dialog (Visual Studio .NET), 441-442
table relationships, editing in Schema Designer, 445
tags, 57
page directives, 85
Target property, 411
targetNamespace attribute, <definitions> element (WSDL documents), 228
TcpChannel (.NET Remoting), 535
tempuri.org namespace, changing, 162
test pages, 162
Description property, 163-165
disabling, 169
Name property, 165-166
Namespace property, 162-163
overview, 168
testing
Application Center Test, 481
locating, 481
principles of operation, 482-483
retesting Web services, 490-491
running, 483-489

614 Index

CurrencyConverter Web service, 97-99
    remote call (.NET Remoting), 543-545
    Web methods, 89-91
    XML Web services, 87-88
throwing exceptions, 459-460
    SOAP, 467-469
        attributes, 469
timeout property
    proxy classes, 215
    sessions, 174
titles, XML Web services, 88
tModels
    publishing, UDDI SKD, 269-271
    specification (UDDI data structure type), 259-260
Toolbox (Component Designer), Data tab, 434
Toolbox (Visual Studio .NET), 37
Trace Information section (trace log), 465
trace log (ASP .NET error tracing), 463-465
    customizing, 465-467
trace node (ASP .NET), 462-463
Trace Utility, 310-313
TraceExtension class, 334-337
TraceExtensionAttribute class, 332-333
tracing errors (ASP .NET), 462
    customizing log, 465-467
    trace node, 462-463
    viewing output, 463-465
TransactionOption property (WebMethodAttribute class), 551

Try command, images and, 495
Try-Catch construct, 456-458
Try-Catch-Finally construct, 458-459
typed DataSets, 424
Types class, 562
<types> element (WSDL documents), 228-231

U

UDDI (Universal Description, Discovery, and Integration)
    Disco files, 279
    Inquiry APIs, 263-264
    NET Servers support, 274
    overview, 240-241
    Publishing APIs, 261-263
    SKD, 265-266
        classes, 267-269
        sample application, 266
    UDDI Business Registry, 241-242
        authentication and authorization, 269
        business classification section, 251
        Business Detail section, 247
        Contacts section, 247
        Discovery URLs section, 251-252
        identifiers section, 251
        information categories, 243
        locating services, 252-253
        publishing, 269
        publishing data structures, 271-273
        publishing services, 244-246
        publishing tModels, 269-271

registering, 246
    registration limitations, 252
    replicating information, 242-243
    Services section, 248-250
  usefulness of, 239-240
  XML Schema document, 254
    bindingTemplate, 257-258
    businessEntity, 255-256
    businessService, 256-257
    publisherAssertion, 260-261
    tModel specification, 259-260
UDDI Business Registry, 241, 242
  information categories, 243
  locating services, 252-253
  publishing services, 244-246
  registering, 246
    authentication and authorization, 269
    business classification section, 251
    Business Detail section, 247
    Contacts section, 247
    Discovery URLs section, 251-252
    identifiers section, 251
    publishing data structures, 271-273
    publishing tModels, 269-271
    registration limitations, 252
    Services section, 248-250
    SKD, 269
  replicating information, 242-243
UDDI DLL, referencing, 267
UDDI Web site, 76
Universal Resource Identifiers. *See* URIs
Universally Unique IDs (UUIDs), 254

UnLock method, Application object, 181-184
updating
  data into SQL Server, 429-430
  Web service references, 204-205
URIs (Universal Resource Identifiers), 60
URL property, proxy classes, 214-215
URLs (Uniform Resource Locators), URIs and, 60
USDConvert method, required data types, 229
use attribute, XSD, 579
Use SQL Statements option (Data Adapter Configuration Wizard, 438-439
User property, WebService class, 552
username (wsdl.exe option), 208
users
  authentication, 376
    creating, 376-378
    gathering information about, 390-392
    IIS, 378
  authorization, IIS, 378-380
UUIDs (Universally Unique IDs), 254

V

validation
  security credentials, XML files and, 400-403
  SOAP Headers, 325
    MustUnderstand property, 325-330
variables
  declaring

616 Index

C#, 27
    Visual Basic .NET, 21
    SOAP Headers and, 317
VB 6 applications, consuming Web services from, 124-128
versions, assemblies and, 12
viewing
    Disco files, 278
    error tracing output (ASP .NET), 463-465
    proxy classes, Solution Explorer, 199
    SOAP messages, 309-310
    WSDL documents, 88
    XML Web services, 87-88
ViewState
    extending, 190-191
    overview, 188-189
    toggling on and off, 189
Visual Basic .NET
    Application object, 181
    Application object compared to Session object, 182
    ASP .NET, customizing trace log, 466
    authentication, 385
        consuming Web services requiring, 382
        identifying user roles, 387
        verifying, 386
    CacheDuration property, 480
    calculator button functionality, code-behind page, 108
    calculator Web service source code, 84
    classes, 141
        creating, 21-22

cookies, 185
CurrencyConverter Web service source code, 95
DataReader class, 427
DataSets
    accessing fields, 423
    populating, 431
descriptions, adding to test pages, 164
descriptoin property (WebMethod attribute), 167
EnableSession property, 172
encryption, consuming Web services, 414-415
EncryptionExtension class, 413
exceptions
    forcing, 455
    throwing, 459
GetCustomerOrders WebMethod, 446
Hello World program, 25-26
images
    displaying, 496-497
ImageSend Web service, 494
inheritance, 22
methods, defining, 145
name property, 165
namespaces
    declaring, 163
    importing, 13-14, 426
NET Remoting
    client application, 541
    creating host for remote objects, 538
    creating remote objects, 537
overview, 21
Page_Load event, 319

Index 617

random image Web service source
    code, 154
Reference.vb file, 200-201
sessions, creating, 174
SOAP, throwing exceptions, 468
SOAP Headers
    consuming Web services
        requiring, 397
    controlling transmission
        direction, 323
    not requiring, 321
    requiring for authentication, 394
    validating, 326
SoapHeader class, 316
SQL Server
    deleting data, 430
    inserting data, 428
    updating data, 429-430
SqlConnection class, 426
Sub and Function procedures, 23-25
TraceExtension class, 334-335
TraceExtensionAttribute class, 332
Try-Catch code, 457-458
Try-Catch-Finally code, 459
typed DataSets, accessing fields, 424
validating login credentials, 401
variables, declaring, 21
ViewState, extending, 190
Web Forms, retrieving images, 499
Web service references, 199
Web services, invoking
    asynchronously, 503-504
WebMethods
    overloading, 501
    SOAP Headers, 317

XmlSerializer class
    automatic generation, 346
    modifying output, 348
Visual C++ .NET, 33
Visual J# .NET, 33
visual pages, 142
Visual Studio .NET
    Class View window, 36-37
    code window, 93
    Code window, 39
    Component Designer, 433-434
    data sources, creating connections, 435-437
    DataSets, creating, 443
    Design mode, creating Web Forms, 116
    Design mode compared to HTML mode, 39
    Disco files, creating, 282-283
    Dynamic Help window, 38-39
    GridLayout, 116
    language independence, 20
    New Project dialog box, 91
    overview, 33-34
    Properties window, 38, 93
    proxy classes, creating, 107, 195-198
    Server Explorer, 35
    Shema Designer, 444
    Solution Explorer, 35-36, 93
    Start Page, 34-35
    syntax errors, notification of, 454
    Toolbox, 37
    Web Forms, consuming Web services, 114-121
    Web References, creating, 105
Web services

creating, 91-97
testing, 97-99
Windows Forms, creating, 103-104
XML files, creating, 63-66
vsdisco files, 285
creating, 286
<dynamicDiscovery> element, 287
enabling, 285
<exclude> element, 287

W

Web applications, images, 498
Web controls, 42-44
Web Forms
consuming
EnglishGermanEnglish Dictionary Web service, 114-121
within other Web services, 121-124
consuming Web services, 112
browser-based applications, 112-113
HTML controls, 41-42
overview, 40
screen scraping clients, 518
Server controls, 40
source code, retrieving images, 499-500
Web controls, 42-44
Web methods, testing, 89-91
Web References, creating, 105
Web Services Designer Generated Code, 442
Web services. *See* XML Web services
Web sites

resources, 583-584
security, compared to Web services, 369
SOAP Toolkit, 310
UDDI, 241
UDDI SKD, 265
Web service search engines, 75
XML Web services, usefulness of, 53-54
web.config file, 371
appSettings node, 478-479
authentication element, 371
authentication node, 475
authorization element, 372-373
authorization node, 476
compilation node, 474-475
configuration node, 474
customErrors node, 475
error handling, customErrors node, 460-461
globalization node, 477
httpRuntime node, 479
overview, 471-473
sessionState node, 174, 476
WebClientAsyncResult class, 568
WebClientProtocol class, 568
WebMethod attribute
Description property, 167
EnableSession property, 172
MessageName property, 168
overview, 166
WebMethodAttribute class, 549-551
WebMethods
overloading, 501-502
referencing, 331
SOAP Headers and, 317
WebService attribute, 162

Description property, 163-165
Name property, 165-166
Namespace property, 162-163
WebService class, 552
WebServiceAttribute class, 552-553
WebServiceBindingAttribute class, 553-554
White Pages (UDDI Business Registry), 243
whitespace (XML), 572
WinCV tool, 17-18
Windows Forms, 5, 44
   Class Viewer, 17-18
   creating, 103-104
System.Security.Principal namespace, 389
WindowsBuiltInRole enumeration, 389
WindowsForms
   consuming Web services, Calculator Web service, 103-111
   creating, Calculator Web service, 111-112
WindowsIdentity object, 390
WSDL (Web Services Description Language), 71-74. *See also* service descriptions
   Disco files, 74-75
   documents
      usefulness of, 161
      viewing, 88
   overview, 219-220
WSDL documents
   creating, screen scraping and, 509-513

proxy classes, screen scraping and, 513-517
reasons to use, 224
screen scraping, overview, 507
SOAP Headers, requiring, 397
SOAP Headers, accepting, 318
source code example, 221-224
structure
   <binding> element, 234
   <body> element, 235
   <definitions> element, 226-228
   <documentation> element, 237-238
   <fault> element, 233
   <imports> element, 236-237
   <input> element, 233
   <message> element, 231-232
   <operation> element, 235
   <output> element, 233
   overview, 225-226
   <part> element, 232
   <portType> element, 232-233
   <service> element, 235-236
   <types> element, 228-231
UDDI and, 240
wsdl.exe
   command line options, 206
   configuring, 213-214
   proxy classes, creating, 205-210
WSIL documents, 356-357
   structure, 357-359
WS-Inspection protocol, 356
   WSIL document structure, 357-359
   WSIL documents, 356-57
WS-License protocol, 364-365
WS-Referral protocol, 361-363
WS-Routing protocol, 359-361

<wssec:credentials> element (WS-License protocol), 364
WS-Security protocol, 363
wwwroot folder (IIS), 83

X

<x:action> element (WS-Routing protocol), 361
<x:from> element (WS-Routing protocol), 361
<x:fwd> element (WS-Referral protocol), 363
<x:id> element (WS-Routing protocol), 361
<x:prefix> element (WS-Referral protocol), 362
<x:to> element (WS-Routing protocol), 361
XML (Extensible Markup Language)
    ADO .NET and, 419-420
    attributes, 572
    case sensitivity, 573
    comments, 573
    compared to HTML, 57
    creating and viewing files, 570-571
    data representation, advantages, 56
    data types, .NET mappings, 143-145
    declaration, 574
    elements
        empty, 573
        nesting, 572
        root, 573-574
    entity references, 575
    example file, 56
    exposing files for public consumption, 159
    files
        creating in Visual Studio .NET, 63-66
        example source code, 55
    namespaces, 58-61, 574
    overview, 55-56, 569-570
    porting data from one system to another, 66-67
    schemas, 61-63
        creating in Visual Studio .NET, 64
    serialization, attributes, 345
    SOAP and, 295
    structure, 570
    syntax, 56
        rules, 57
    tags, 57
    whitespace, 572
XML Schema document
    bindingTemplate, 257-258
    businessEntity, 255-256
    businessService, 256-257
    publisherAssertion, 260-261
    tModel specification, 259-260
    UDDI and, 254
XML Web services
    advantages of, 51-52
    as a business, 77-79
    asynchronous, 502-506
    Calculator Web service, cookies, 185-188
    capabilities, 353
    code-reuse and, 113-114
    compared to .NET Remoting, 533-534

components, 239-240
consuming, 193
creating
   system requirements, 81
   Visual Studio .NET, 91-97
data representation, 55
   XML, overview, 55-56
declaring, 141-143
discovery, 140
discovery mechanisms, providing, 74-75
exposing for public consumption, 159
future of, 365
GXA, 354-355
interface, 88
locating, 140
Microsoft product development philosophy and, 5
operational principles, 140-141
overview, 49-51, 354
protocols, 67-69
references, updating, 204-205
service providers, locating, 75-77
SOAP, 69-70, 293
SOAP Headers
   accepting, 316-319
   passing from clients, 319-321
testing, 87-88
   Visual Studio .NET, 97-99
uses for
   digital calendars, 53
   microwaves, 52-53
   refrigerators, 53
   Web sites and, 53-54
WSDL, 71-74
XML Web Services, 44

xmlns attribute, 60
XmlRoot attribute, 350
XmlSerialization class
   automatic XML generation, 346-347
   modifying XML output, 348-349
XSD (XML Schema Definition Language)
   attributes, 578-579
      default, 579
      groups, 580-581
      restrictions on, 579
      use, 579
   data types
      compared to .NET data types, 229-231
      defining, 228
   documents
      elements, 577
      minOccurs and maxOccurs elements, 578
      purpose, 577
XSD (XML Schema definition language) files, 61-63

Y

Yellow Pages (UDDI Business Registry), 243